"This is not just another MOOC book providing the 'openness philosophy.' Instead, it is a well-balanced realistic overview of projects, ideas, and evaluations throughout the world. A valuable addition to a too often dominant western world view and approach."
– Theo J. Bastiaens, Rector Magnificus, Open University, the Netherlands

"I have been so looking forward to this edited volume from Zhang, Bonk, Reeves, and Reynolds. It is yet another extraordinary book by a set of proven authors on topics that are highly current and extremely relevant to educators in the Global South and beyond."
– Zoraini Wati Abas, Deputy Vice-Chancellor (Academic and Educational Technology), Wawasan Open University, Malaysia

"This book offers an insightful and rare perspective on the evolution of MOOCs in the Global South. An illustrious group of authors address issues ranging from historical perspectives, current practices, designs, multi-country collaborations, policies, and organizational innovations that impact the implementation of MOOCs in specific contexts. The diverse perspectives from several countries make this unique offering a must read for those who want to design online learning environments to enable more people from more places to learn with and from each other."
– Charlotte Nirmalani (Lani) Gunawardena, Distinguished Professor, Organization, Information, & Learning Sciences Program, University of New Mexico, USA

Contributions from 25 emerging economies make this book a unique compendium of innovative ideas and valuable insights. The chapters highlight the 'open' dimension of MOOCs and the potential impact on promoting lifelong learning and sustainable development. The range and diversity of contributions is a fulfilling read for both policy makers and practitioners and demonstrates the vision and commitment of the editors to inclusion, innovation, and collaboration.
Asha Kanwar, President and CEO, Commonwealth of Learning, Vancouver, Canada

MOOCs have reached a plateau. This book helps to understand how different type of economies have made use of this innovative delivery mechanism and are preparing to overcome the current plateau to take advantage of as well as expand upon the potentiality of MOOCS.
Prof. Miguel Nussbaum, Co-Editor Computers & Education, School of Engineering, Universidad Católica de Chile

Since its introduction a dozen years ago the MOOC has become a global phenomenon. The editors do an excellent job capturing a diversity of applications and perspectives. We see the MOOC not merely as an online course, but a vehicle for improving access, advancing pedagogy, and fostering progress for good around the world. This reflects the original purpose of the MOOC and I am delighted to see it carried forward in this volume.
Stephen Downes, Senior Researcher, National Research Council of Canada and the originator of the MOOC

Following a common pattern for innovations in educational technology, Open Educational Resources—MOOCs in particular—were grossly over-hyped in the early 2010s. This book takes a global perspective in providing a reality check for the 2020s. While only a few emerging economies (e.g., India) are deploying home-produced MOOCs at scale, fears that they would be a vehicle for a neo-colonialist agenda have proved over-blown. Encouragingly, the book reports burgeoning research activity on open education, boding well for the future.

Sir John Daniel, Chancellor, Acsenda School of
Management, Vancouver, BC

Informative and inspiring! This edited collection of studies, research, reports, and experiences on specific countries and regions across the global setting provides invaluable information on the current situation, trends, and challenges of MOOCs and OERs. We will apply the enhanced understanding and insight to keep innovating and expanding the impact of these knowledge tools to improve social and economic development in Latin America and the Caribbean.

Juan Cristóbal Bonnefoy, Chief, Inter-American Institute for Economic and
Social Development (INDES), Inter-American Development Bank (IDB)

Not often do so many famous names get together to share such relevant information. At a time when MOOCs have become mainstream it is necessary for us to re-think their position in emerging economies. The authors provide a comprehensive look at the past, present, and future of MOOCs and give valuable insights into international policy and practice. This book is a must-have for open education practitioners world-wide.

Johannes Cronje, Dean of Informatics and Design,
Cape Peninsula University of Technology
(CPUT), South Africa

Informative and inspiring! This edited collection of studies, research, reports, and experiences on specific countries and regions across the global setting provides invaluable information on the current situation, trends, and challenges of MOOCs and OERs. We will apply the enhanced understanding and insight to keep innovating and expanding the impact of these knowledge tools to improve social and economic development in Latin America and the Caribbean.

Juan Cristóbal Bonnefoy, Chief, Inter-American Institute for
Economic and Social Development (INDES)
Inter-American Development Bank (IDB), Washington, DC, USA

MOOCs have been a game changer in the higher education world for over a decade now. What is clear from this fascinating book is that the trend toward MOOCs and open education is not only impacting in affluent countries, but today they play a huge role throughout the developing world. In fact, late starter countries benefit from the success and limits of various trials in advanced countries as well as their own innovations and in-roads. This book delineates myriad exciting MOOC approaches, open education perspectives, and real world lessons as well as the associated social and political issues and ramifications in the Global South. As such, it provides diverse points of view for educators who need to practice MOOC approaches in developing countries.

Okhwa Lee, Professor, Chungbuk National University, Korea

MOOCs and Open Education in the Global South brings together the multi-country issues on MOOCs and OERs which are 21st century innovations. The authors have explored a variety of interesting data across the regions of the world. This insightful new guide helps the readers to make smart decisions while designing and creating MOOCs and OERs, respectively.

Prof. Madhu Parhar, Director STRIDE, Indira Gandhi
National Open University, New Delhi India

MOOCS AND OPEN EDUCATION IN THE GLOBAL SOUTH

With e-learning technologies evolving and expanding at high rates, organizations and institutions around the world are integrating massive open online courses (MOOCs) and other open educational resources (OERs). *MOOCs and Open Education in the Global South* explores the initiatives that are leveraging these flexible systems to educate, train, and empower populations previously denied access to such opportunities.

Featuring contributors leading efforts in rapidly changing nations and regions, this wide-ranging collection grapples with accreditation, credentialing, quality standards, innovative assessment, learner motivation and attrition, and numerous other issues. The provocative narratives curated in this volume demonstrate how MOOCs and OER can be effectively designed and implemented in vastly different ways in particular settings, as detailed by experts from Asia, Latin America, the Middle East, Africa, the Pacific/Oceania, and the Caribbean.

This comprehensive text is an essential resource for policy makers, instructional designers, practitioners, administrators, and other MOOC and OER community stakeholders.

Ke Zhang is Professor of Learning Design and Technology at Wayne State University, USA.

Curtis J. Bonk is Professor of Instructional Systems Technology at Indiana University, USA, and President of CourseShare.

Thomas C. Reeves is Professor Emeritus of Learning, Design, and Technology at The University of Georgia, USA.

Thomas H. Reynolds is Professor of Teacher Education at National University, USA.

MOOCS AND OPEN EDUCATION IN THE GLOBAL SOUTH

Challenges, Successes, and Opportunities

Edited by
Ke Zhang, Curtis J. Bonk, Thomas C. Reeves,
and Thomas H. Reynolds

First published 2020
by Routledge
52 Vanderbilt Avenue, New York, NY 10017

and by Routledge
2 Park Square, Milton Park, Abingdon, Oxon, OX14 4RN

Routledge is an imprint of the Taylor & Francis Group, an informa business

© 2020 Taylor & Francis

The right of Ke Zhang, Curtis J. Bonk, Thomas C. Reeves, and Thomas H. Reynolds to be identified as the authors of the editorial material, and of the authors for their individual chapters, has been asserted in accordance with sections 77 and 78 of the Copyright, Designs and Patents Act 1988.

All rights reserved. No part of this book may be reprinted or reproduced or utilised in any form or by any electronic, mechanical, or other means, now known or hereafter invented, including photocopying and recording, or in any information storage or retrieval system, without permission in writing from the publishers.

Trademark notice: Product or corporate names may be trademarks or registered trademarks, and are used only for identification and explanation without intent to infringe.

Library of Congress Cataloging-in-Publication Data
A catalog record for this book has been requested

ISBN: 978-0-367-02576-2 (hbk)
ISBN: 978-0-367-02577-9 (pbk)
ISBN: 978-0-429-39891-9 (ebk)

Typeset in Bembo
by Apex CoVantage, LLC

Visit the eResource: www.routledge.com/9780367025779

This book is dedicated to Fred Mulder, Emeritus Professor and Rector of the Open University of the Netherlands as well as the first UNESCO chair on Open Educational Resources. Fred was a visionary pioneer whose legacy in the Open Education field will continue to have impact for many years to come.

CONTENTS

Foreword   xiii
Mimi Miyoung Lee

Preface: MOOCs and Open Education—Wandering and Winding Our Way to Today   xvi
Curtis J. Bonk, Ke Zhang, Thomas C. Reeves, and Thomas H. Reynolds

1   MOOCs and Open Education in the Global South: Successes and Challenges   1
    Ke Zhang, Curtis J. Bonk, Thomas C. Reeves, and Thomas H. Reynolds

SECTION 1
Historical Perspectives   15

2   A Historical Journey Into K-MOOCs Leading to Possible Collaborations With North Korea   17
    Yong Kim, Ock Tae Kim, and Jin Gon Shon

3   Current State of Practice and Research on MOOCs in Mainland China: A Critical Review   28
    Jianli Jiao and Yibo Fan

SECTION 2
Current Practices and Designs   41

4   The Different Faces of Open in Egypt   45
    Maha Bali and Nadine Aboulmagd

5   Delivering on the Promise of Open Educational Resources: Pitfalls and Strategies   56
    Rajiv S. Jhangiani

6 Massive Open Online Courses: The State of Practice in
   Indonesia   63
   Tian Belawati

7 Orchestrating Shifts in Perspectives and Practices About the Design
   of MOOCs   72
   Som Naidu and Shironica P. Karunanayaka

8 A Different Kind of MOOC Architecture for Emerging Economies in
   Oceania and the Pacific   81
   Deepak Bhartu and Som Naidu

9 Nepali High School Students in Massive Open Online Courses
   (MOOCs): Impressive Results and a Promising Future   90
   Baman Kumar Ghimire and Bishwa Raj Gautam

10 MOOCs in Latin America: Trends and Issues   99
   Jaime Sánchez and José Reyes-Rojas

11 The Emotional Benefits of Diversity in MOOCs: Reshaping Views of
   Online Education Through Exposure to Global Learners   113
   Trang Phan

   Appendix 11.A: Interview Protocol   124

SECTION 3
MOOCs and Open Education for Professional Development   127

12 Insights Into a Nationwide pdMOOC Portal: Bilgeis.net
   of Turkey   130
   Kursat Cagiltay, Sezin Esfer, and Berkan Celik

13 Promoting Open Education and MOOCs in Thailand: A Research-Based
   Design Approach   140
   Thapanee Thammetar and Jintavee Khlaisang

14 Capacity Building of Teachers: A Case Study of the Technology-Enabled
   Learning (TEL) Massive Open Online Courses   156
   Sanjaya Mishra, Martha Cleveland-Innes, and Nathaniel Ostashewski

15 The Development of MOOCs as Incubation Space for Professional and
   Institutional Learning: A View From South Africa   169
   Antoinette van der Merwe, J.P. Bosman, and Miné de Klerk

SECTION 4
Multi-Country Collaborations and Collections 179

16 Courses for a Cause: MOOC Contributions to a "Better Place for All" 181
Marianne E. Krasny, Zahra Golshani, Brittney López Hampton Coleman, Juan Felipe Restrepo Mesa, Michael Schrenk, Masango Roderick Warakula, Gail Woon, and Yueyang Yu

17 MOOCs in Six Emerging APEC Member Economies: Trends, Research, and Recommendations 199
Insung Jung, Gibran A. Garcia Mendoza, Jennifer Christine Fajardo, Roberto B. Figueroa Jr., and Siaw Eng Tan

18 A Glimpse on How MOOCs From IDB Are Impacting Learners in Latin America and the Caribbean 212
Edgar González, Antonio García, Carlos Macher, and Dou Zhang

SECTION 5
Government Policies and Strategies 227

19 Advancing Open Education Policy in Brazilian Higher Education 229
Tel Amiel and Tiago C. Soares

20 Global Trends and Policy Strategies and their Implications for the Sustainable Development of MOOCs in Malaysia 236
Purushothaman Ravichandran

21 OERs for Development (OERs4D) Framework as Designed and Implemented in the Philippines 245
Melinda dela Peña Bandalaria

22 Disruptive Learning: Inspiring the Advancement of MOOCs in the Middle East 256
Abtar Darshan Singh, Sumayyah Abuhamdeih, and Shriram Raghunathan

SECTION 6
Organizational Innovations 271

23 Open Education in the World Bank: A Significant Dividend for Development 273
Sheila Jagannathan

24 From OER to OEP: The Case of an OER-Integrated Teacher Education eLearning Program in Africa 286
Atieno Adala

25 Responsive Innovations in MOOCs for Development: A Case Study of
    AgMOOCs in India   300
    Balaji Venkataraman and Tadinada V. Prabhakar

26 Implementing a Skills Accelerator to Prepare Students in Kenya for
    Online-Only Bachelor's and MBA Programs That Require MOOCs
    and OER: A Case Study   310
    *Michael C. Mayrath, Craig Brimhall, Graham Doxey, Scott Doxey, and
    Joshua Stroup*

    Appendix 26.A: Accelerator Learning Objectives   322

SECTION 7
The Future of MOOCs and Open Education   **327**

27 Evolution of Online Learning Environments and the Emergence of
    Intelligent MOOCs   329
    Paul Kim and Jieun Lee

28 MOOCs and Open Education in the Global South: Future Opportunities   342
    Thomas H. Reynolds, Thomas C. Reeves, Curtis J. Bonk, and Ke Zhang

Acknowledgments   *351*
Index   *353*

FOREWORD

Mimi Miyoung Lee

The rapid rise and continuous proliferation of massive open online courses (MOOCs) and open education during the last decade have been documented in many forms of media, academic journals, and professional meetings. A cadre of high-profile trailblazers and early adopters have enthusiastically embraced MOOCs and open education for their potential to foster greater educational equity. In his 2013 keynote speech for the International E-Learn Conference in Las Vegas, one such MOOC pioneer, George Siemens, emphasized the power of MOOCs "as a keystone concept in reformulating education models and creating new ecosystems." Others, more cautiously, have looked for firm evidence of learning success, in part, through a critical examination of attrition and completion rates.

While the impact of MOOCs and open education is global, there has always been a need and a demand for more local stories of applications and implementations from different parts of the world, especially those from emerging and less developed economic regions. Such local stories are important for several reasons. For instance, understanding the regionally specific implementation and subsequent outcomes of various MOOC or open education initiatives have huge implications for adoption and implementation policies at multiple levels of practice. Second, as the connections between formal and informal learning are becoming more seamless, MOOCs can play a vital role bridging the formal to the informal and vice versa. Third, localized cases can help policymakers and practitioners find better ways to design, implement, and evaluate new initiatives related to MOOCs and open education in their communities.

The localized examples also serve to challenge possible assumptions and beliefs behind the production and dissemination of MOOCs and open educational resources. For champions and skeptics alike, the promises and challenges of MOOCs and open education have largely been discussed within the social and cultural values based on North American and European educational systems. Locating the predominance of the MOOC and open education conversation in parts of what some now refer to as "the Global North" is not surprising as these regions continue to be the top producers of MOOCs as well as the prime investigators engaged in MOOC research. Equally important and more urgently needed are investigations into the ways these MOOCs get socially and culturally translated and interpreted in different parts of the world, especially areas with limited educational access and resources.

In response, this book makes salient all of these important issues related to MOOCs and open education in "the Global South" via powerful narratives of local and regional applications and implementations. The editors of this book, Ke Zhang, Curt Bonk, Tom Reeves, and Tom Reynolds, brought their many years of experience and recognized expertise both in research and practice to assemble and curate this much-needed platform of provocative dialogues and reflections. As you will discover in the Preface, these four renowned scholars have been at the forefront of MOOCs and open education as well as online learning in general from the early days, serving as designers, instructors, researchers, and evaluators of many types of educational innovations.

One could not hope for a better team of experts than these four editors to address the various pivotal issues related to open education in the Global South. As this volume shows, their long record of individual and collective successes as champions of MOOCs and OER is extended in multiple novel and exciting directions with the publication of this timely and eye-opening book. Each chapter will transport you to a different part of the world where MOOCs and/or open educational resources (OER) are being deployed.

The idea for this volume was conceived during the 2017 E-Learn Pre-conference in Vancouver whose goal was to draw attention to how developing countries of the world are taking advantage of these exciting and impactful innovations known as MOOCs and open education. Interestingly, this pre-conference traces its origin back to the 2013 E-Learn Pre-conference resulting in an earlier parallel volume, *MOOCs and Open Education Around the World*, published by Routledge in 2015, of which I was personally fortunate to play a part. These two pre-conference symposia served as working sessions aimed at defining a robust research agenda around open education and MOOCs. In the process, they responded to the increasing need to better understand how people in different regions of the world are implementing and using these innovations. In both symposia, many important issues related to OER and MOOCs were identified and discussed with participants from around the world; among them, accreditation, credentialing, quality standards, instructor roles, participant motivation, assessment, and attrition. The excitement during those symposia can be experienced in many of the pages of this particular volume as well as the first.

The possibilities for transformational changes in education through MOOCS and open education, especially for learners in developing regions of the world, have been widely debated and, for many, generally accepted. However, cases from the direct narratives of local educators, researchers, and administrators have rarely been reported and shared in a common platform with such depth until this volume. Readers will find this timely edition full of valuable case studies, critical perspectives, powerful lessons, and thoughtful answers that will prompt deeper questions as well as capture the continuing evolution and growth of MOOCs and open education. As indicated, the following 28 chapters with cases from Asia, Latin America, the Middle East, Africa, the Pacific/Oceania, and the Caribbean were all masterfully curated by Zhang, Bonk, Reeves, and Reynolds. Each chapter speaks for itself but also engages in a dialogue with other chapters in ways that are sure to challenge the readers' previous assumptions and stimulate future creative initiatives.

Mimi Miyoung Lee

Mimi Miyoung Lee is Professor in the Department of Curriculum and Instruction at the University of Houston (UH). She received her Ph.D. in Instructional Systems Technology from Indiana University at Bloomington in 2004. She is an expert in critical ethnography and design-based research as well as online, flexible, and open forms of learning. Mimi has published research on STEM-related professional development programs, global and multicultural education, cross-cultural training research, interactive videoconferencing, woman leaders in Asia, self-directed learning from MOOCs and OpenCourseWare (OCW), and emerging learning technologies such as wikis. Dr. Lee was co-editor of *MOOCs and Open Education Around the World* published by Routledge in 2015 which was awarded the 2016 AECT DDL Distance Education Book Award. At the same time, Mimi led a special issue of the *International Journal on E-Learning* on MOOCs and Open Education which simultaneously was published as a book by AACE. She may be contacted at mlee7@uh.edu.

PREFACE

MOOCs and Open Education—Wandering and Winding Our Way to Today

Curtis J. Bonk, Ke Zhang, Thomas C. Reeves, and Thomas H. Reynolds

Wandering in the Global South

More than a century ago, the Spanish poet, Antonio Machado (Wikipedia Contributors, 2019a), with his immortalized lines, *caminante no hay camino* (i.e., wanderer there is no path [or road]), *se hace camino al andar* (i.e., you make the path by walking [or wandering]) (Machado, 1912), affirmed the idea that much of life's direction is derived through the process of making one's way in the world. As the editors of this book, we took this idea to heart and moved forward with this project with no clear blueprint as to its final form in mind. At times, of course, we did glance behind as the poem suggests to get a glimpse of the path we had taken that most likely would never be trod again. Whereas others might call this an organic process, we think of it as in Machado's (1912) poem—we made our way by making our way.

Although we had a general idea for some of what you will find contained herein, the book was actually formulated, edited, and reformulated as we foraged through different steps in the process. In fact, even the book title was changed a couple of weeks prior to going to production. In effect, our path to completion was altered many times based on the people we encountered, the news we read, and the research we analyzed. We learned much along the way, especially through reading and editing all the chapters of the wonderful contributors, most of whom we met for the first time and many others with whom we had traveled before.

Making our way based on the experiences and events that we encountered led to our insight that this is an apt metaphor for how MOOCs and open educational resources (OER) have evolved, especially for the current generation of individuals, organizations, institutions, and consortia involved in designing, implementing, using, and evaluating them. Naturally, we were cognizant of the fact that much progress had been made since our previous book on MOOCs and Open Education in 2015 (Bonk, Lee, Reeves, & Reynolds, 2015). As the project evolved, however, we began to seriously reflect on the diverse stories, goals, and outcomes that had been shared with us. We quickly realized that different paths were being forged by all the wanderers found in this book, including those who strategically planned for MOOCs and open education in a particular country, region, organization, or institution as well as those individuals who designed and delivered them. So, too, the various MOOC researchers and evaluators contributing to this book. Each had a different purpose. Each recounted unique outcomes of that experience.

We can now attest to the fact that there is no one path for MOOCs and OER or for the creation of such an edited volume as this—rather, for all the wanderers we encountered while drafting this book, the path has been a winding road with pivotal setbacks and momentous achievements. As such, it has taken each of us to places that we had no idea we were going to go but we are much better off for having gone there.

The Long and Winding Open Ed Journey

Fast forward 84 years from when those beautiful lines about wandering were first penned by Machado (1912). The year was 1996 and Grammy award–winning artist, Sheryl Crow, put out a self-titled album with a similar enchanting invitation to find one's way or path in the world by walking. The second release from that album was, in fact, "Everyday Is a Winding Road." In it, Crow recommended that everyone just jump in and enjoy the show called life. She cautioned that there may be high days and low days and days when pretty much anything will go. Nevertheless, as Machado had argued long before, every day would be a type of winding road and the journey would be even more difficult since there would likely be faded signs of what to do and where to go along the way. Simply put, life's pathways will never be totally clear.

One might juxtapose those lyrics with the events occurring in open and online education around that time. A few years prior to the release of "Everyday Is a Winding Road," the road led all the way "down under" to Western Australia for the third author, Tom Reeves. A noted pioneer and scholar in the field of educational technology, Reeves, and his wonderful colleague Ron Oliver from Edith Cowan University, spent several months in 1993 evaluating an early form of online learning called telematics, being used at that time to teach English as a Second Language (ESL) to Aboriginal youth living in outback settlements as well as Japanese to children in schools located in remote mining towns (Oliver & Reeves, 1994). They traveled by small planes, rugged Land Rovers, and other vehicles to carry out their extensive evaluation studies. At each stopping point of this expedition, from Port Hedland, Karratha, and Newman in the Pilbara region to Beagle Bay and Broome in the Kimberley region, it became increasingly clear to Oliver and Reeves that online learning could provide previously unavailable language development opportunities to remote learners. At the same time, they fully realized that much research would need to be conducted before the potential of telematics and other emerging online learning systems would begin to reach their potential. This evaluation adventure for Oliver and Reeves enabled them to learn much about the cultures, norms, and geographies of the Australian outback as well as to develop a lifelong friendship. Every day truly was a winding road.

During the rest of the decade, we four editors began pondering the exciting pedagogical possibilities of Web-based instruction. We were designing online courses and programs and writing some of the first papers on how to make Web-based learning more interactive (e.g., Bonk & Reynolds, 1997; Reeves & Reeves, 1997; Zhang & Harkness, 2002). And we were conducting research on unique forms of blended and fully online learning, including designing online interaction tools that would later be embedded in standard learning management systems (Bonk, Fischler, & Graham, 2000) and investigating innovative strategies for assessing student learning online in higher education (Reeves, 2000).

Curt Bonk (the first author of this Preface), in fact, has been teaching blended learning courses since the early 1990s and his first fully online course was an undergraduate educational psychology offering from 1997 to 2000 called the "Smartweb." Preservice teachers in the Smartweb utilized online technology from a sociocultural point of view. For instance, they were crafting and sharing cases detailing problems that they had observed in schools during their early field experiences with students of Tom Reynolds (the fourth author) who was at Texas A&M at the time. Also participating were students from universities in Finland, the UK, Peru, South Korea, and the University of South Carolina, while extensions of the project to preservice teachers working in Native American reservation schools turned out to be more difficult due to access and training issues. These students were using a free tool called "Conferencing on the Web" or COW to draft problematic case situations and then offer solutions on each other's cases (Bonk, Daytner, Daytner, Dennen, & Malikowski, 2001). This project would evolve and eventually become known as "The Intraplanetary Learning Exchange" or TITLE project (Bonk, Hara, Dennen, Malikowski, & Supplee, 2000) which revealed interesting cross-cultural differences in terms of learner interactions and exchanges (Kim & Bonk, 2002).

As Bonk's research showed, ideas related to how the Web could be used for global collaboration and exchange, including critical thinking and in-depth analysis of contextually rich and localized online cases, were on full display in this project (Kim & Bonk, 2002). Students in Indiana could quickly get feedback and ideas for addressing or solving their case problems from peers in East Asia, Europe, and South America. While not yet fully open, the COW, and later, TITLE, cases were available for anyone with the website URL and proper passcodes to contribute. The next step toward openness, however, was a set of best practice cases that were soon made open to the world community in the "Caseweb." As a prime example of a rich open educational resource, cases on the Caseweb were widely used by educational psychology instructors and students across the planet.

The fourth author, Tom Reynolds, also understood the cross-continent collaborative potential of the Web; however, he soon felt the power of the Internet as a platform for online educational delivery of contents and resources for upskilling local communities. The year was 1998 when Reynolds was on a lecture tour of around ten Peruvian universities as a Fulbright scholar. Ironically, he gave the very first lecture at the Universidad Nacional De San Cristobal in Ayacucho since the armed military guards had been removed from the university entrance earlier that same day. The guards had been a long-standing and welcome sight during the tumultuous and violent years of the Shining Path terrorism in the region.

Exiting that well-attended event, Reynolds observed the lack of lighting in the city streets so the taxi ride to the hotel was more than welcomed. Arriving at the hotel, he noticed a light-filled storefront in the darkness about a block from his hotel; so, he very cautiously walked up the narrow street to gain a better view. To Reynolds's surprise, there, in the middle of an otherwise darkened and quiet city, was the glowing presence of an Internet café full to overflowing with students taking an MSWindows class. In the poverty that characterized Ayacucho in the late 1990s, throngs of young learners were willing to stake their last Sole (Peruvian currency) and invest in technological literacy and the potential it held to transport their lives to better surroundings.

It was clear from that experience and across the year that Tom Reynolds spent in Peru, as well as a more recent Fulbright year in Colombia, that the Internet offered vital educational opportunities to those in the Global South. But what if they could access those same sorts of online educational contents and courses for free? Would they no longer need to part with their Soles to advance their educational skill-base and professional growth?

Also in the mid-1990s, Ke Zhang (the second author) was heavily involved in designing e-training modules in China that were highly interactive and rich in multimedia for clients like Siemens and PepsiCo. However, instead of learning a language in the Australian outback via telematics, discussing and debating globally shared OER in the form of problematic cases and other forms of collaboration with distant peers one would likely never physically meet, or immersing oneself in on-demand instruction from Internet cafes, as detailed by the previous anecdotes from Reeves, Bonk, and Reynolds, such efforts were limited to company intranets. As was perhaps inevitable, just a few short years later, Zhang was creating interactive e-books for undergraduate classes, while revising large statistics classes with online collaborative activities that fully embraced and exploited the Web (Zhang & Harkness, 2002; Zhang & Peck, 2003). Clearly, the pace of change on the Internet was astounding in those early years of Web-based instruction.

More recently, Ke Zhang has collaborated with educators, researchers, and public health professionals to create mobile training systems on HIV prevention and patient communications for barefoot doctors (World Health Organization, 2008) in remote China. In this groundbreaking mobile project, she and her colleagues utilized authentic case scenarios collected from the diverse populations in those remote areas. Later Zhang was consulted on a major international initiative by the World Bank to address the global food crisis. The significance of knowledge sharing was stressed throughout the projects, and e-learning was strategically leveraged in the Eurasian region (World Bank, 2015).

Of vast importance to those reading this book, in these various projects, Zhang and her team discovered that mobile learning research is much more pervasive in the Global South than the Global North (Hung & Zhang, 2012). Not too surprisingly, they also found that issues of culture and language were among the most important factors for successful designs of learning technologies, programs, and experiences. Such findings beg the question about whether the pervasiveness of mobile technology in the Global South has impacted the design or delivery of MOOCs and open education in such regions of the world. In addition, it is crucial to start asking to what extent MOOC and OER designers are creating culturally sensitive and appropriate courses and contents (Zhu et al., 2019).

What the various vignettes disclose is that each of us has had different open and online learning experiences with people and places considered part of the Global South; some were direct physical experiences, whereas others were part of global collaborative exchanges. But just what is the Global South? And what does it represent? Per Wikipedia (2019b), "The **Global South** is an emerging term which refers to countries seen as low and middle income in Asia, Africa, Latin America and the Caribbean by the World Bank. These nations are often described as newly industrialized or in the process of industrializing." Some definitions also include most of the Middle East and other parts of the world (Wikimedia, 2019).

While the term is somewhat controversial (Toshkov, 2018), we feel that it best suits the assembly of chapters found in the present book. In providing an historical overview of the evolution of MOOCs and open education, the next section is more focused on the Global North than the Global South; a central reason for that focus is that pedagogical experiments in the United States were a key factor in the history of the open education movement.

The Emergence of Open Educational Resources

During the next decade, our respective online and blended learning projects continued to meander and evolve. As Sheryl Crow stated, every day was indeed a winding road in terms of Web-based learning in the 1990s. Back in the early days of the Web, we would get excited about any new education-related website, whether it was the World Lecture Hall for sharing faculty syllabi from the University of Texas at Austin in April 1995 or the Lesson Plans Page from the University of Missouri launched in October 1996 to help K–12 educators with their instructional ideas and plans.

The following year something even more exciting was brewing called MERLOT. Designed by Dr. James Spohrer, Distinguished Scientist in Learning Research at Apple Computer, MERLOT was purposefully created by the California State University Center for Distributed Learning to help share valued educational content over the Web (Bonk, 2009). MERLOT dramatically extended beyond portals of online educational resources like the World Lecture Hall and the Lessons Plans Page as it allowed for the formation of communities around shared knowledge bases of learning materials, primarily focused on the higher education sector. These communities could rate, discuss, and share contents. Even at this early stage of Web development, MERLOT stuck out as an interesting trend in education. In fact, Bonk engaged in several research studies related to why higher education instructors and others would freely share their creative designs and innovative course content online (Bonk, 2002).

The 1990s were also a time of content sharing experiments via online portals of educational resources whether it was course syllabi, lesson plans, practice tests, or rich multimedia about complex concepts. Such openly shared course items were early versions of what would later be known as open educational resources (OER). The MERLOT and TITLE projects offered a unique lens on what the Web offered, especially because the materials were reviewed and vetted by peers and thus could be trusted.

Such tools and projects pushed the educational world to think about the Web as a space for dialogue, community building, idea generation, learning object exchanges, and curation and repositories. And when early learning management systems of the mid-1990s like Nicenet were coupled with asynchronous conferencing tools like FirstClass and experimental video conferencing systems like CU-SeeMe, education on the Web would no longer be limited to simple knowledge portals. Instead, significant learning activities could transpire virtually anytime and anywhere as long as one had Internet access and sufficient time.

For savvy and novice educators alike, whether in the Global North or Global South, the 1990s was the age of the learning portal. While the specific websites might be different for each country or region of the world, the Lesson Plans Page and the World Lecture Hall exemplified it for those of us in the Global North. At the time, a teacher could go online and learn how to design an assessment rubric, record grades in an online gradebook, or take attendance online.

But would that be it? Was the excitement about the Web simply relegated to the land of online forms and teaching efficiencies? What about the learner? Where, if anywhere, was active learning in this equation? The Smartweb and COW offered some hints of what was becoming possible for supporting active, engaging, and effective learning online. Fortunately, what happened next was much more than a faded sign or subtle hint of the learning possibilities for the masses. While initially centered squarely within the Global North, the OER movement was a stunning eye opener as to the power of the Web to offer open education to the masses, from the North, South, East, and West.

The Emergence of OpenCourseWare

Within a few years, the world moved to the next stage. In 2001, not only was Wikipedia launched, but Charles Vest, then President of MIT, announced the OpenCourseWare (OCW) initiative which would place key parts of all MIT courses on the Web for anyone to freely access (MIT News, 2001). As he put it,

> I have to tell you that we went into this expecting that something creative, cutting-edge and challenging would emerge. . . . OpenCourseWare is not exactly what I had expected. It is not what many people may have expected. But it is typical of our faculty to come up with something as bold and innovative as this. . . . It expresses our belief in the way education can be advanced—by constantly widening access to information and by inspiring others to participate. . . . OpenCourseWare combines two things: the traditional openness and outreach and democratizing influence of American education and the ability of the Web to make vast amounts of information instantly available.
>
> *(MIT News, 2001)*

While that speech from Vest was momentous, OCW was actually an idea that had popped into the head of MIT Professor Richard (Dick) Yue while on his exercise machine. Not necessarily a eureka moment, however, Yue admitted that the idea came to him after many years, and perhaps even decades, of contemplation about his educational experiences both in Hong Kong as a child and later on as an adult in the United States (Bonk, 2009). An Internet-related planning committee Yue led at MIT debated the idea and eventually gave it the green light. With that, course syllabi, readings, assignments, lecture slides, images, course calendars, instructor insights, and so on from some of the most brilliant minds on the planet were made available for free to masses of people who previously never contemplated learning from award-winning MIT professors.

Importantly, most MIT faculty members and staff embraced this idea. In fact, in less than seven years, content from all 2,000+ MIT courses (MIT, 2007) was open to anyone in the world with an Internet connection (or access to one) to explore and learn from. Astoundingly, since inception, there have been over 1.4 trillion page views from 166 million unique visitors of MIT OCW and 158 million views of MIT OCW videos in YouTube (MIT, 2018).

While impressive numbers to be sure, this was a much bigger deal than a solitary initiative from MIT. As Vest stated in his OCW proclamation signaling that educational contents should be free and open:

> This is about something bigger than MIT. I hope other universities will see us as educational leaders in this arena, and we very much hope that OpenCourseWare will draw other universities to do the same. We would be delighted if—over time—we have a world wide web of knowledge that raises the quality of learning—and ultimately, the quality of life—around the globe.
>
> *(MIT News, 2001)*

That far-reaching vision from Vest is exactly what happened. Universities in the United States such as Tufts University, Utah State University, the University of Notre Dame, and Johns Hopkins University quickly joined in the OCW movement, as did numerous other institutions of higher learning from throughout the world including the UK Open University, Beijing Normal University, and the Japan OpenCourseWare consortium (Carson, 2009; Caswell, Henson, Jensen, & Wiley, 2008). In addition, in early 2008, seven Indian Institutes of Technology (IITs) began uploading a wealth of free lecture content to YouTube without much fanfare but with national as well as global intentions to increase the quality of engineering education (Bonk, 2009). Suffice to say, there was much momentum for notions of openness! Charles Vest, Dick Yue, and others at MIT simply opened the spigot.

As an example, our friend, Lucifer Chu, translator of *The Lord of the Rings* (to traditional Chinese) and the founder of Fantasy Foundation, began to use personal funds acquired from sales of his bestselling books as well as a grant from the Hewlett Foundation to translate MIT and other university OCW contents to simplified and traditional Chinese. Chu led an all-volunteer organization called the Opensource Opencourseware Prototype System (OOPS), headquartered in Taiwan (Bonk, 2009). This project brought up many issues and questions as to the purpose and goals for online global education communities to localize resources such as the OOPS (Lee, Lin, & Bonk, 2007).

As such translation projects began receiving attention, critics began raising legitimate questions and issues related to how Western culture from these top-tier research universities would be significantly influencing, and potentially dominating, educational practices in developing parts of the world community. In effect, for each deemed success in this open educational world, there were many challenges and issues that needed addressing.

Despite the criticisms, there was much intended and unintended success and impact (Bonk, 2009; Iiyoshi & Kumar, 2008); so much so, that one must ask whether these open education pioneers fully realized what they were doing. The gold-plated entry gates, obscure passcodes, and secret handshakes that had locked out billions of potential learners from higher education for centuries were now unlocked, revealed, and permanently left open for anyone to enter at any time and from any place. Fortunately, assorted OCW and other open education efforts soon resulted in millions of people browsing or downloading content from MIT OCW and other OCW sites each month (MIT, 2012). Surprisingly, the goals of these OCW users were not necessarily degrees or credentials (Bonk & Lee, 2017; Bonk, Lee, Kou, Xu, & Sheu, 2015). Actually, what most people desired, and still do to this day, is the freedom to learn when, how, where, and what they wish.

In today's landscape, OCW is only part of the open education movement; there are numerous other kinds of learning portals and forms of OER for teaching and learning. For example, the complete works of significant literary, musical, scientific, cultural, and historical figures are now easily accessed, rapidly searched, and freely available to listen to or interact with online (Bonk, 2009; Iiyoshi & Kumar, 2008). When surveyed and appreciated in sum, these learning portals decisively disrupt the balance of power from those who previously controlled access to knowledge—to those seeking to learn from such open online resources. Arguably, we had entered a new era of learner-directed or learner-selected learning, which was made possible, at least in part, by the sharing age.

The Sharing Age

As MIT was completing the initial version of its OCW project, something fundamentally remarkable arrived on the scene; specifically, MOOCs or "massive open online courses" sprung up. While stating exactly who to credit for offering the first MOOC is somewhat contentious, according to most sources, the MOOC trend started in 2008 in Canada with a massively open online course offered by George Siemens and Stephen Downes (Downes, 2012). Once the word got out, the notion of MOOCs swiftly spread to the United States and many other parts of the world. In addition to MIT, universities in the Global North such as Harvard University, Stanford University, Duke University, the University of Pennsylvania, the University of Michigan, Georgia Tech, and the University of Edinburgh, were among the prominent early MOOC adapters; many of which conducted research on the design and implementation of their early MOOC offerings (Bonk, Lee, Reeves, & Reynolds, 2015; Bonk, Lee, Reynolds, & Reeves, 2015; edX, 2014).

MOOC-related technology platforms, companies, programs, and governmental initiatives arose during these same years as this new form of educational delivery was widely and critically examined, discussed, promoted, and implemented. Entities to deliver MOOC courses such as Udacity, Udemy, edX, NovoEd, FutureLearn, XuetangX, and Coursera were the focus of considerable attention, classification (e.g., see Liyanagunawardena, Lundqvist, Mitchell, Warburton, & Williams, 2019), speculation, and in some cases, alarm (Finkle & Masters, 2014).

What may come as a surprise for some, however, is that MOOCs were not the only educational headline at the time. By the mid to late 2000s, there were numerous people in and out of academia playing around with different forms of openness with their courses and programs. Many of us had already been teaching online for over a decade and wanted to extend our classes even more. We noticed that friends and colleagues of ours such as David Wiley at Utah State University and later BYU were offering certificates of completion from their university to anyone who wanted to complete their coursework (Wiley, 2008). Other colleagues like Ron Owston at York University in Toronto were experimenting with putting their course syllabi in a wiki and allowing students to structure and negotiate it. Correspondingly, during the decade of the 2000s, Curt Bonk was building a suite of nine "sharing" sites including CourseShare, ResourceShare, PublicationShare, LibraryShare, SurveyShare, Quizshare, BookstoreShare, InstructorShare, and TrainingShare as a means to experiment with the sharing of educational content or links to such content. What was beginning to become clear to folks like Wiley, Owston, and Bonk was that, at a very minimum, courses in higher education were increasingly reliant on OER. With OER, OCW, and other forms of openness, online learning innovation and sharing of such pedagogical and technological innovations was occurring on an unprecedented pace and scale.

There was a growing awakening and eventual embrace of OER in higher education, corporate, and military settings and later in K–12 ones as well (Bonk, 2009). Nonetheless, few people fully realized that the course being offered by our friends George Siemens and Stephen Downes in Canada, mentioned earlier, in which anyone could enroll, was the initial seed of what was soon to germinate and take root around the world; namely, Massive Open Online Courses or MOOCs.

Although we heard the excited voices of our own students when we mentioned this free and open course to them, we did not foresee how quickly collegial conversations about our respective teaching loads would go from teaching a dozen or two students to having thousands, if not tens of thousands, of enrollees in our courses. In fact, by the summer of 2012, Bonk had 3,800 people enrolled in his MOOC, the first one ever offered by Blackboard, related to how to teach online. At the time, that was actually a modest-sized MOOC (Jordan, 2014).

Those were exciting times. Not only was 2012 the celebrated "Year of the MOOC" (Pappano, 2012), it was the dawn of the age of rapid course experimentation and course content sharing for the masses. Although only a few courses at that time were truly free and open ones, those that were drew thousands, and, in some cases, more than 100,000 participants. There were no strings attached. And open truly meant open. MOOCs quickly emerged that focused on a wide range of topics, some of which had never before been imagined. With the resulting explosion of open access courses and contents, many of us were acting like little kids in open education candy stores. We wanted to take this one and that one and a few other courses just for luck. There were typically no fee payments required if you wanted a certificate of completion or to complete a specialization. Not surprisingly, various constraints and limitations were soon introduced (Schaffhauser, 2018). As Wiley (2015) noted, what was once totally "free" and "open" was no longer the case.

Stepping Into and Out of This Book

Can the world return to the day when all MOOC content was free and open? Or will some other technology or educational innovation be fashioned that allows learners worldwide to access educational contents to reskill and upskill themselves? The many contributors to this book have penned their chapters from vastly different geographical, economic, social, and educational situations and perspectives. What they all have in common is an increasing reliance on projects, initiatives, and policies related to MOOCs and other forms of open education.

As you will see in the respective 28 chapters of this edited book as well as in the foreword and this preface, MOOCs and open education are having marked impacts across regions of what was once labeled as the "developing world" and is now more commonly termed "the Global South." For example, government officials and other stakeholders are attempting to improve the quality of OER and MOOC-based certification programs at the tertiary education level in the Philippines (see Chapter 21 from Melinda dela Peña Bandalaria). Of course, in this fast-changing economic age, such quality enhancements are particularly important for continuing professional education. Other innovative educators are providing high school students with a sense of accomplishment and identity as successful learners in Nepal (see Chapter 9 from Baman Kumar Ghimire and Bishwa Raj Gautam). MOOCs are also being deployed to address serious societal problems such as better preparing the local citizenry for climate change in Fiji (see Chapter 8 from Deepak Bhartu and Som Naidu) as well as to teach about global environmental education and civic ecology in the Bahamas (see Chapter 16 from Marianne Krasny and her colleagues). Still other initiatives aim to extend access to university education, as in the islands of Indonesia (see Chapter 6 from Tian Belawati) or meet specific societal goals, such as training farmers in India about emerging agricultural production, protection, and processing techniques (see Chapter 25 from Balaji Venkataraman and Tadinada V. Prabhakar). Each of these situations and experiences as well as many other highly impactful undertakings are chronicled in the chapters of this book.

The various passageways through this book encompass a wide range of applications and innovations. For instance, one moment you will be in Brazil where you will learn about open access policies and issues encouraging OER developments and inroads across more than 100 higher education institutions (see Chapter 19 from Tel Amiel and Tiago Chagas Soares). Or, you could find yourself in Egypt where many different faces and formats of openness will present themselves (see Chapter 4 from Maha Bali and Nadine Aboulmagd). Journey on and learn about government policies and efforts related to advancing MOOCs and open education throughout the Middle East (see Chapter 22 from Abtar Darshan Singh, Sumayyah Abuhamdeih, and Shriram Raghunathan). You will soon discover that there are an interesting mix of countries in the Middle East representing stunning extremes in technological connectivity that range from fully modern to scarce availability. Keep moving and you might also find yourself in Turkey—a country that appears to be on the cusp of an explosion of MOOC-related professional development efforts (see Chapter 12 from Kursat Cagiltay, Sezin Esfer, and Berkan Celik).

In effect, you can open most any page of this book and you will learn about many exciting projects, potential opportunities, and pitfalls and problems of the OER movement. Despite the problems and delays in open access, the underlying fiber of this book is one of accomplishment and hope. What has been accomplished gives rise to hope. Hope for openness. Hope for expanding one's place in the world. Hope for accessing a goldmine of valuable educational materials that can bring one a step closer to admission, graduation, employment, or promotion. Hope for a sense of self-worth and personal growth. And a sincere hope that the minimum requirements to enroll in a MOOC will be the same for one's children and grandchildren.

MOOC'ing an Impact

People become fairly glassy-eyed when they read about MOOC enrollments. What they too often fail to realize is that whether it is a median size MOOC of 40,000 participants (Jordan, 2014) or much lower figures (e.g., 8,000, see Chuang & Ho, 2016), the fact is that MOOCs offer access to top-tier institutions and well-known experts from places that MOOC participants will likely never visit, let alone study and live. As Trang Phan alludes to in Chapter 11, MOOCs offer wondrous connections to international peers; each MOOC has an extraordinary variety of fellow learners with highly diverse backgrounds, skills, and interests. Such a situation can contribute to a deeply valued and enriched learning environment that is beneficial to all participants and observers (Hew & Cheung, 2014). There are no lengthy application processes or logistical restrictions (Kop, 2011). Do you have access to the Internet or know someone who does? If so, come on in.

Before you enter the land of MOOCs, it is important to ask in what massively open courses might you enroll. In 2014, the most popular MOOCs included those on statistics, learning how to learn, computer science, strategic management, finance, and R programing (Shah, 2014). The following year, when our previous book on MOOCs and open education was released (Bonk, Lee, Reeves, & Reynolds, 2015), the top-rated MOOC courses had switched entirely to such gems as "A Life of Happiness and Fulfillment," "The Great Poems Series," "What Is Mind," "Fractals and Scaling," "Mindfulness for Wellbeing and Peak Performance," "Algorithms for DNA Sequencing," and "Programming for Everybody" by Chuck Severance (Shah, 2015) who wrote a chapter in our previous book (Severance, 2015).

Clearly the reason people signed up for MOOCs had undergone a significant change in a short time. Whether a function of an expanding curriculum or personal needs and preferences, the road quickly shifted from computer science and business courses to MOOCs for personal growth and development. As the contents of this book head to press in May 2019, the most popular MOOCs include ones on weight management, mathematical game theory, computer networking for teachers, innovation management, and the role of nurses around the world (Shah, 2019b). What a diverse array of courses for personal selection and consumption! If you recheck that list every year or six months, you will see that MOOCs might be deemed a reflection of life in the 21st century.

According to recent data from Class Central, the number of people engaging in MOOC activities is growing at a mind-boggling rate. The year in which we were completing our previous book *MOOCs and Open Education Around the World* (Bonk, Lee, Reeves, & Reynolds, 2015), some 400 universities around the globe offered 2,400 assorted MOOCs to around 17 million participants (Shah, 2014). At the time of this writing, just four years later, such numbers had widened to 900 universities offering over 11,000 MOOCs to more than 100 million learners (Shah, 2019a). Extrapolate such data for a decade and it is relatively easy to envision MOOC enrollments numbering near a billion. As this occurs, MOOCs will surely play a significant role in 21st-century literacy development and skill upgrades with up to one out of every ten humans on the planet participating. As with other mass adoptions, we may quickly lose count of the total courses offered or learners participating. However, as that happens, the questions will hopefully shift to more momentous ones such as to what extent MOOCs have helped sustain a planet undergoing a series of crises including climate change, sustainable food production, marine plastic pollution, species extinction, depopulation as well as overpopulation, massive waves of immigration, and a prevailing lack of human decency and compassion.

Outside the higher educational context, MOOCs are being used as an alternative to traditional corporate and governmental training. Statistics show that Coursera, one of the fastest-growing MOOC providers, is working with over 1,400 companies globally to fulfill the training needs of 34 million working professionals (Schaffhauser, 2018). As these numbers continue to escalate, MOOCs are transforming both formal and informal educational practices with more viable, scalable, and sustainable opportunities (Selwyn, Bulfin, & Pangrazio, 2015). With at least 35 master's degrees currently available via the MOOC (Pickard, 2019) at significantly reduced pricing levels (McKenzie, 2018), and perhaps hundreds of possible MOOC-related specializations, nanodegrees, and micro-credentials (Coursera, 2019; Ravipati, 2017), MOOCs are increasing the professional credentials and work-related skills and competencies of many individuals.

Of no surprise given the rapid expansion and variety of content noted previously, MOOCs have come to mean different things to different people. For some, MOOCs are allowing instructors unique opportunities to diversify one's student base. For others, the emphasis is on the creation of global learning communities that share ideas, resources, and best practices. Still others view MOOCs as a tool for expanding access to education and perhaps stacking an online credential received from taking a series of MOOCs into an application for an on-campus or online master's program (DeVaney & Rascoff, 2019). According to DeVaney and Rascoff, it is in such stackability options wherein MOOCs, at present, seem to be the most disruptive to the status quo in higher education. As shown in this particular book, such disruptiveness may be even more vital and pronounced in economically emerging parts of the world.

New acronyms are proliferating along with the divergent visions that drive MOOC development and use. For example, there are cMOOCs (testing the theoretical and practical viability of connectivist-styled learning), xMOOCS (highlighting massive quantity of throughput with thousands of students in some cases), pMOOC (experimenting with problem- or project-based forms of learning), and, most recently, PD-MOOCs (related to the professional development of teachers and other professionals). Still other types of MOOCs are targeting remedial education, advanced placement, and many other niche areas.

Globally, organizations and institutions are engaged in fascinating experiments to take advantage of advances in digital technologies and e-learning design to educate, train, or otherwise empower people around the world. For example, the World Bank, UNESCO, the Commonwealth of Learning (COL), and the Inter-American Development Bank all have exciting initiatives and regional as well as international projects to provide education, training, and professional development opportunities to people across many populations who previously could not partake of these educational openings and innovations. Even though MOOCs and various MOOC-like derivatives as well as OER are proliferating and benefitting millions of people around the globe each week, enormous potential for expansion and improvement remains.

What about specific MOOC vendors? Well, in 2017, Coursera alone had over 30 million registered users, signaling an increase of 7 million users from 2016. By the end of 2018, Coursera's enrollments spiked again to 37 million participants (Shah, 2019b). Not too surprisingly, interest in certification and micro-credentials from MOOC completion has exploded during the past few years. Today, sequences of MOOCs can lead a learner to one of over 250 different specializations and credentials. In terms of MOOC vendors and platforms, Coursera has created more than 160 such specializations including popular ones in data science, robotics, creative writing, game design and development, inspired leadership, Python programming, virtual teaching, Spanish, music production, investment management, and cybersecurity, among many other topics (Coursera, 2019). Similarly, edX offers MicroMaster's degrees in big data, cybersecurity, solar energy engineering, human rights, instructional design and technology, supply chain management, artificial intelligence, international hospitality management, and much more (Gordon, 2018; McKenzie, 2018).

It is clear from such data that learning opportunities and outcomes are being transformed. Unfortunately, limited attention has thus far been placed on how specific regions of the world are taking advantage of these new forms of technology-enabled learning—even though many exciting and impactful innovations are currently occurring. As digital forms of informal and formal learning proliferate, there is an increasing need to better understand how people in fast-changing regions of the world are implementing MOOCs and OER. Clearly, a better understanding of the outcomes of different projects and initiatives could aid researchers as well as government managers, trainers, MOOC instructors, and instructional designers.

As detailed in this book, organizations like the Commonwealth of Learning (COL) have worked diligently to find unique ways to deliver open content to educators and learners, especially in parts of the world with the most rapidly emerging or changing economies (Commonwealth of Learning, 2019). COL efforts have benefitted farmers in Jamaica, Antigua, and rural India, K–12 teachers and university instructors in Pakistan, St. Lucia, and Uganda, and other traditionally underserved learners in Sri Lanka, Samoa, and Nigeria. COL is also providing support for instructional innovations such as flipped classrooms, MOOCs for development, blended online teacher training models, and many other distance learning innovations and models. Clearly, the COL is among the organizations leading the way toward a more equitable, sustainable, and empowering educational future. Accordingly, COL members have authored two chapters of this book (see Chapter 14 by Sanjaya Mishra and his colleagues and Chapter 25 from Venkataraman and Prabhakar).

Assembling This Book

Although e-learning continues to proliferate globally, minimal attention has been placed on how emergent economic countries and regions, especially across the Global South, are taking advantage of technology-enabled learning. The possibilities for transformational change in these regions are widely accepted as is the notion that e-learning is impacting young as well as older learners around the planet. The emergence of new forms of blended learning as well as variations and inroads in MOOCs and OER have made these developments front-page news across all continents and societies. Nonetheless, there is scant knowledge related to the inroads actually being made in emerging economies; especially scholarship focusing across countries in the Global South. To that end, this book offers dozens of candid looks at many of the challenges, successes, and opportunities that exist right now in the Global South.

As new digital forms of informal and formal learning proliferate, there is an urgent need to better understand how people in different regions of the world are implementing and evaluating MOOCs and assorted OER. Even more importantly, educators, researchers, educational change agents, politicians, and countless others want to better understand the outcomes of these initiatives and how they can be improved. So, along with the current tidal wave of changes in educational practices and participants enabled by blended and fully online e-learning, those fostered by MOOCs and open education have caused institutions and organizations to grapple with issues of accreditation, credentialing, quality standards, and learner motivation and attrition, among numerous other areas of concern.

There are many other challenges affiliated with understanding MOOCs and OER. For instance, institutions and organizations continue to struggle with notions of plagiarism, copyright, and innovative assessment—to name but a few. Alignment among eight essential learning dimensions (i.e., objectives, content, instructional design, learning tasks, learner roles, instructor roles, technological affordances, and assessment) is another vital issue (Reeves, 2006), as is finding effective ways to use technology to empower women and girls to shape their own futures. At the same time, researchers are exploring critical issues such as openness, ethics, privacy and security, fiscal responsibility, and different business models of success. Many educators are looking for answers and ideas in fields such as learning analytics, adaptive learning, and alternative assessment. In addition, there are impact and outcome studies that are geared to address what the designers and implementation teams had envisioned when fashioning and later piloting their MOOCs or OER projects.

In response to these issues, this book project explores and probes unique implementations of MOOCs and open education across several rapidly changing and economically emergent regions of the world from Egypt to India to the Philippines to Fiji to Chile to Brazil to South Africa and onward. We also focus on the various opportunities as well as the dilemmas presented in this new age of technology-enabled learning.

By now it should be clear that there are numerous goals underpinning this book. First, we intend to help the reader better understand the wide array of MOOC initiatives and open education projects in rapidly changing, highly diverse, and economically emergent Global South countries and regions. At the same time, we hope to help others learn how MOOCs and open educational resources are impacting learners in different ways. A better grasp of the potential global impact of these open educational contents is also a key goal. Third, we expect that those perusing this volume will be better equipped to identify emerging trends, projects, and innovations in e-learning as well as new possibilities for professional development at a distance. The casual reader will also have an enhanced understanding of the educational, cultural, political, and economic challenges and issues facing various stakeholders in open education environments. Different chapters will highlight pressing issues and controversies where there presently is impassioned debate and controversy.

Readers of this volume will have their own intended goals. Whatever the premise for leafing through different pages of this book, we hope that readers become inspired to contribute to the prevailing research and discussion related to MOOCs and open education. Some chapters may answer the concerns of critics, whereas several others may add fuel to their talking points. Still other chapters might be embraced by both MOOC advocates and critics, but for vastly different reasons.

While the editors of this book have been involved in online learning, including MOOCs and open education, since inception, no one person or small group of people can know the entire story. Fortunately, this edited volume has 68 contributors who describe what is occurring in this realm in around 47 different countries, primarily in the Global South. Our contributors were purposely selected to tell individual stories from the viewpoint of their initiative(s), institution(s) or organization(s), and region(s) of the world. When reading across the different sections of this book, you will discover many wondrous stories being told. As such, the chapter contributors will effectively offer insights into the role of MOOCs and open education for individual learners as well as for policy makers intending to use such new forms of educational delivery to address some of the learning needs and gaps found in their own situation.

This book also offers varied historical perspectives in terms of open education movements in different countries and regions of the world. The opening chapters from China and Korea discuss the evolution of distance learning in addressing the educational needs of its citizenry (see Chapter 2 from Yong Kim, Ock Tae Kim, and Jin Gon Shon and Chapter 3 from Jianli Jiao and Yibo (Jeremy) Fan). Several chapters attempt to lay out many new initiatives and their actualized impact to date as well as their sustainability and envisioned growth or unreached potential. In addition, insights will be offered in terms of current design practices and delivery mechanisms for such massive courses and the results to date.

In the end, we are most fortunate to have been able to assemble so many world-renowned scholars who contributed to this edited volume. Some of them presented with us at the pre-conference symposium on "MOOCs and Open Education in the Developing World" that was held in Vancouver, Canada, in October 2017. We also invited other researchers, educators, and world leaders of the movement toward open education and MOOCs; most of whom are involved in advancing or researching different learning technologies. They may have designed and taught a MOOC, tested a unique MOOC platform or system, authored strategic plans on MOOCs and open education for their institution or organization, written or advocated for needed open education policies, or conducted research and evaluation of MOOCs and open education contents. Their stories and reflections should lend insight into the present state of open education around the world. They might also inspire others to do the same.

Final Thoughts

We hope this book can shine a light on the path toward globally transformative educational change. However, the changes required will not be easy; in part, since the road toward such change will never be clearly marked or smoothly paved. Nevertheless, each person reading this book may make distinctive contributions in some aspect of the world of MOOCs and open education; they might be targeted for parts of the world most in need of development such as in countries across the Global South. These contributions might also be on behalf of the entire planet and beyond. For the billions of learners in the Global South yearning for access to high-quality and respected educational opportunities, this is our Sputnik moment, moonshot, Panama Canal, and Great Pyramid of Giza all rolled into one. Learners in the Global South as well as the Global North can no longer wait a decade or two for things to change. They need wide and pervasive access to education today. Accordingly, we hope that this book adds to the world of open possibilities and potentialities for those in the Global South and all over the planet.

Our intended goal is to take you on a journey through an expansive array of MOOC-related developments and initiatives in Global South regions of the world. As you "wander" through the pages of this book, as Machado's (1912) lines of poetry at the start recommended, you will be exposed to dozens of key innovators, educators, and stakeholders in this wonderful world of MOOCs and open education. Your journey will also bring to light myriad challenges, successes, and opportunities as seen through the eyes of those in the Global South. As singer-songwriter Sheryl Crow suggested, let's all take a moment to step back and enjoy the show, both as found in the 28 chapters of this book as well as in everyday news, research reports, video documentaries, and various open and online resources, tools, courses, and programs. On whatever learning path you wander, we four editors wish each of you a most pleasant journey down this winding road. Keep wandering!

Curtis J. Bonk, Ke Zhang, Thomas C. Reeves,
and Thomas H. Reynolds

Curtis J. Bonk is Professor at Indiana University teaching psychology and technology courses. He can be contacted at cjbonk@indiana.edu and his homepage is at http://curtbonk.com/.

Ke Zhang is Professor in the Learning Design and Technology Program at Wayne State University. Inquiries are welcome by email to ke.zhang@wayne.edu.

Thomas C. Reeves is Professor Emeritus of Learning, Design, and Technology at the University of Georgia. He can be reached at treeves@uga.edu and his homepage can be found at www.evaluateitnow.com/.

Thomas H. Reynolds is Professor of Teacher Education at National University in La Jolla, California. He can be contacted at treynold@nu.edu.

References

Bonk, C. J. (2002, January). Executive summary of "Online teaching in an online world". *United States Distance Learning Association (USDLA)*, *16*(1). Retrieved from http://64.92.209.134/~usdla/usdla.org/public_html/cms/html/journal/JAN02_Issue/article02.html

Bonk, C. J. (2009, July). *The world is open: How Web technology is revolutionizing education*. San Francisco, CA: Jossey-Bass, a Wiley imprint.

Bonk, C. J., Daytner, K., Daytner, G., Dennen, V., & Malikowski, S. (2001). Using web-based cases to enhance, extend, and transform preservice teacher training: Two years in review. *Computers in the Schools*, *18*(1), 189–211.

Bonk, C. J., Fischler, R. B., & Graham, C. R. (2000). Getting smarter on the Smartweb. In D. G. Brown (Ed.), *Teaching with technology: Seventy-five professors from eight universities tell their stories* (pp. 200–205). Boston, MA: Anker Publishing.

Bonk, C. J., Hara, H., Dennen, V., Malikowski, S., & Supplee, L. (2000). We're in TITLE to dream: Envisioning a community of practice, "The intraplanetary teacher learning exchange." *CyberPsychology and Behavior*, *3*(1), 25–39.

Bonk, C. J., & Lee, M. M. (2017). Motivations, achievements, and challenges of self-directed informal learners in open educational environments and MOOCs. *Journal of Learning for Development*, *4*(1), 36–57. Retrieved from http://jl4d.org/index.php/ejl4d/article/view/195/188

Bonk, C. J., Lee, M. M., Kou, X., Xu, S., & Sheu, F-R. (2015). Understanding the self-directed online learning preferences, goals, achievements, and challenges of MIT opencourseware subscribers. *Educational Technology and Society*, *18*(2), 349–368. Retrieved from www.ifets.info/journals/18_2/26.pdf

Bonk, C. J., Lee, M. M., Reeves, T. C., & Reynolds, T. H. (Eds.). (2015). *MOOCs and open education around the world*. New York: Routledge.

Bonk, C. J., Lee, M. M., Reynolds, T. H., & Reeves, T. C. (2015). Preface to MOOCs and open education special issue: The power of four. *International Journal on E-Learning*, *14*(3), 265–277.

Bonk, C. J., & Reynolds, T. H. (1997). Learner-centered web instruction for higher-order thinking, teamwork, and apprenticeship. In B. H. Khan (Ed.), *Web-based instruction* (pp. 167–178). Englewood Cliffs: Educational Technology Publications.

Carson, S. (2009). The unwalled garden: Growth of the opencourseware consortium, 2001–2008. *Open Learning*, *24*(1), 23–29. Retrieved from http://tofp.org/resume/Unwalled_Garden.pdf

Caswell, T., Henson, S., Jensen, M., & Wiley, D. (2008, February). Open educational resources: Enabling universal education. *International Review of Research in Open and Distance Learning*, *9*(1). Retrieved from www.irrodl.org/index.php/irrodl/article/viewFile/469/1009

Chuang, I., & Ho, A. D. (2016). *HarvardX and MITx: Four years of open online courses—Fall 2012-Summer 2016*. Retrieved from https://papers.ssrn.com/sol3/papers.cfm?abstract_id=2889436

Commonwealth of Learning. (2019). *Member countries*. Retrieved from www.col.org/member-countries

Coursera. (2019). *Top specializations*. Retrieved from www.coursera.org/featured/top_specializations_locale_en_os_web

DeVaney, J., & Rascoff, M. (2019, January 20). Stackability as a learning strategy. *Inside Higher Ed*. Retrieved from www.insidehighered.com/blogs/technology-and-learning/guest-post-stackability-learning-strategy

Downes, S. (2012, May). *Connectivism and connected knowledge: Essays on meaning and learning networks*. Retrieved from www.downes.ca/files/Connective_Knowledge-19May2012.pdf

edX. (2014, January 21). Harvard and MIT release working papers on open online courses. *edX Blog*. Retrieved from www.edx.org/blog/harvard-mit-release-working-papers-open#.VOEnbo1TFjs

Finkle, T. A., & Masters, E. (2014). Do MOOCs pose a threat to higher education? *Research in Higher Education Journal*, *26*, 1–10.

Gordon, A. (2018, February 13). "MicroMasters" surge as MOOCs go from education to qualification. *Forbes*. Retrieved from www.forbes.com/sites/adamgordon/2018/02/13/voice-of-employers-rings-out-as-moocs-go-from-education-to-qualification/#288cd8ad564b

Hew, K. F., & Cheung, W. S. (2014). Students' and instructors' use of massive open online courses (MOOCs): Motivations and challenges. *Educational Research Review*, *12*, 45–58. doi:10.1016/j.edurev.2014.05.001

Hung, J. L., & Zhang, K. (2012). Examining mobile learning trends 2003–2008: A categorical meta-trend analysis using text mining techniques. *Journal of Computing in Higher Education*, *24*(1), 1–17.

Iiyoshi, T., & Kumar, M. (Eds.). (2008). *Opening up education: The collective advancement of education through open technology, open content, and open knowledge*. Cambridge, MA: MIT Press.

Jordan, K. (2014). Initial trends in enrolment and completion of massive open online courses. *The International Review of Research in Open and Distributed Learning*, *15*(1). doi:10.19173/irrodl.v15i1.1651

Kim, K. J., & Bonk, C. J. (2002). Cross-cultural comparisons of online collaboration among pre-service teachers in Finland, Korea, and the United States. *Journal of Computer-Mediated Communication*, *8*(1). Retrieved from http://onlinelibrary.wiley.com/enhanced/doi/10.1111/j.1083-6101.2002.tb00163.x/

Kop, R. (2011). The challenges to connectivist learning on open online networks: Learning experiences during a massive open online course. *The International Review of Research in Open and Distributed Learning*, *12*(3), 19–38. doi:http://dx.doi.org/10.19173/irrodl.v12i3.882

Lee, M., Lin, M-F., & Bonk, C. J. (2007, November). OOPS, turning MIT opencourseware into Chinese: An analysis of a community of practice of global translators. *International Review of Research in Open and Distributed Learning*, *8*(3), 1–21. https://doi.org/10.19173/irrodl.v8i3.463

Liyanagunawardena, T. R., Lundqvist, K., Mitchell, R., Warburton, S., & Williams, S. A. (2019). A MOOC taxonomy based on classification schemes of MOOCs. *European Journal of Open, Distance and e-Learning, 22*(1), Retrieved from www.eurodl.org/?p=current&sp=full&article=798

Machado, A. (1912). Proverbios y cantares XXIX [Proverbs and Songs 29]. In G. Ribbans (Ed.), *Campos de Castilla* (pp. 222–223). Madrid: Catedra, Mil Letras, 2008.

McKenzie, L. (2018, October 12). EdX: From micromasters to online master's degrees. *Inside Higher Ed.* Retrieved from www.insidehighered.com/news/2018/10/12/edx-launches-nine-low-cost-online-degrees

MIT. (2007, November 28). MIT marks opencourseware milestone. *November 2007 Newsletter.* Retrieved from https://ocw.mit.edu/about/media-coverage/press-releases/milestone/

MIT. (2018, September). *OpenCourseWare: Dashboard report.* Retrieved from https://ocw.mit.edu/about/site-statistics/monthly-reports/MITOCW_DB_2018_09_v1.pdf

MIT News. (2001, April 4). *MIT to make nearly all course materials available free on the world wide web.* Cambridge, MA: MIT Press. Retrieved from http://web.mit.edu/newsoffice/2001/ocw.html

MIT Open Course Ware. (2012). *Site statistics.* Retrieved from http://ocw.mit.edu/about/site-statistics/

Oliver, R., & Reeves, T. C. (1994). *Telematics in rural education.* Perth, Western Australia: InTech Innovations.

Pappano, L. (2012, November 2). The year of the MOOC. *The New York Times.* Retrieved from www.nytimes.com/2012/11/04/education/edlife/massive-open-online-courses-are-multiplying-at-a-rapid-pace.html?pagewanted=all&_r=0

Pickard, L. (2019, March 4). 35+ legit master's degrees you can now earn completely online. *Class Central.* Retrieved from www.classcentral.com/report/mooc-based-masters-degree/

Ravipati, S. (2017, March 1). edX expands micromasters programs with data science, digital leadership and more. *Campus Technology.* Retrieved from https://campustechnology.com/articles/2017/03/01/edx-expands-micromasters-programs-with-data-science-digital-leadership-and-more.aspx

Reeves, T. C. (2000). Alternative assessment approaches for online learning environments in higher education. *Journal of Educational Computing Research, 23*(1), 101–111.

Reeves, T. C. (2006). How do you know they are learning? The importance of alignment in higher education. *International Journal of Learning Technology, 2*(4), 294–309.

Reeves, T. C., & Reeves, P. M. (1997). The effective dimensions of interactive learning on the WWW. In B. H. Khan (Ed.), *Web-based instruction* (pp. 59–66). Englewood Cliffs, NJ: Educational Technology Publications.

Schaffhauser, D. (2018). Coursera's CEO on the evolving meaning of "MOOC". *Campus Technology.* Retrieved from https://campustechnology.com/articles/2018/09/12/courseras-ceo-on-the-evolving-meaning-of-mooc.aspx

Selwyn, N., Bulfin, S., & Pangrazio, L. (2015). Massive open online change? Exploring the discursive construction of the "MOOC" in newspapers. *Higher Education Quarterly, 69*(2), 175–192. doi:http://dx.doi.org/10.1111/hequ.12061

Severance, C. (2015). Learning about MOOC by talking to students. In C. J. Bonk, M. M. Lee, T. C. Reeves, & T. H. Reynolds (Eds.), *MOOCs and open education around the world* (pp. 169–179). New York: Routledge.

Shah, D. (2014, December 27). *Online courses raise their game: A review of MOOC stats and trends in 2014.* Retrieved from www.classcentral.com/report/moocs-stats-and-trends-2014/

Shah, D. (2015, December 30). Less experimentation, more iteration: A review of MOOC stats and trends in 2015. *Class Central.* Retrieved from www.classcentral.com/report/moocs-stats-and-trends-2015/

Shah, D. (2019a, March 20). Ten most popular MOOCs starting in April 2019. *Class Central.* Retrieved from www.classcentral.com/report/moocs-stats-and-trends-2014/

Shah, D. (2019b). Year of MOOC-based degrees: A review of MOOC stats and trends in 2018. *Class Central.* Retrieved from www.class-central.com/report/moocs-stats-and-trends-2018/

Toshkov, D. (2018, November 6). The "Global South" is a terrible term: Don't use it! *Research Design Matters.* Retrieved from http://re-design.dimiter.eu/?p=969

Wikimedia. (2019). List of countries of regional classification. *Wikimedia Meta-Wiki from the Wikimedia Foundation.* Retrieved from https://meta.wikimedia.org/wiki/List_of_countries_by_regional_classification

Wikipedia Contributors. (2019a). Antonio Machado. *Wikipedia, the Free Encyclopedia.* Retrieved from https://en.wikipedia.org/wiki/Antonio_Machado

Wikipedia Contributors. (2019b). Global South. *Wikipedia, the Free Encyclopedia.* Retrieved from https://en.wikipedia.org/wiki/Global_South

Wiley, D. (2008, September 30). On open accreditation. *Iterating Toward Openness Blog.* Retrieved from https://opencontent.org/blog/archives/585

Wiley, D. (2015). The MOOC misstep and open education. In C. J. Bonk, M. M. Lee, T. C. Reeves, & T. H. Reynolds (Eds.), *MOOCs and open education around the world* (pp. 3–11). New York: Routledge.

World Bank. (2015). *Increasing food security in Eurasia and beyond through shared knowledge and expertise*. Retrieved from www.worldbank.org/en/news/feature/2015/04/30/increasing-food-security-in-eurasia-and-beyond-through-shared-knowledge-and-expertise

World Health Organization. (2008). China's village doctors take great strides. *Bulletin of the World Health Organization, 86*(12). Retrieved from www.who.int/bulletin/volumes/86/12/08-021208/en/

Zhang, K., & Harkness, W. (2002). Small online groups in a large class: Critical reflections. *Journal of Interactive Instruction Development, 14*(3), 14–18.

Zhang, K., & Peck, K. (2003). The effects of peer-controlled or moderated online collaboration on group problem solving and related attitudes. *Canadian Journal of Learning and Technology/La revue canadienne de l'apprentissage et de la technologie, 29*(3). Retrieved from www.learntechlib.org/p/43193/

Zhu, M., Sabir, N., Bonk, C. J., Sari, A., Xu., S., & Kim, M. (2019). *Addressing learner cultural diversity in MOOC design and delivery: Strategies and practices of instructors and experts*. Bloomington, IN: Indiana University.

1
MOOCs AND OPEN EDUCATION IN THE GLOBAL SOUTH

Successes and Challenges

Ke Zhang, Curtis J. Bonk, Thomas C. Reeves, and Thomas H. Reynolds

The United Nations (2015) announced ambitious goals for sustainable development, including Goal 4, to "ensure inclusive and equitable quality education and promote lifelong learning opportunities for all" by 2030. Further, in the *Education 2030* (UNESCO, 2015) framework for actions, UNESCO expressly suggested that massive open online courses (MOOC) (p. 40) and open educational resources (OER) (p. 31 and p. 41) should be promoted as powerful strategies to increase access to education and to improve the quality of learning as well. During the past decade, many other scholars have also consistently confirmed the potential of MOOCs and OER for development and to perhaps even transform education in fundamental ways (e.g., Anderson, 2013; Hodgkinson-Williams & Arinto, 2017; King, Pegrum, & Forsey, 2018; Koller, 2012). As people become familiar with these and other forms of open and distance learning, the advocacy base continues to expand.

Yet, not enough is known about the landscape of MOOCs and OER in the Global South. In fact, the Global South is a relatively new designation for countries that are emerging economically, mostly, but not exclusively located in Asia, Africa, the Caribbean, the Middle East, and Latin America, in comparison to wealthier countries (Hollington, Salverda, Schwarz, & Tappe, 2015). Gunawardena (2014) wisely argues, even if they are free and open, MOOCs will be of scant value to those in the Global South if they do not fit their specific context. The resources and examples connected with a particular MOOC must be relevant to the local community. In fact, a recent systematic review of publications on MOOCs and OER (King et al., 2018) revealed that more research is necessary to investigate how learners in countries or regions of the Global South manage to negotiate with the various challenges in MOOCs. Clearly, their stories and research findings should be integrated into the foundations of the design, delivery, and evaluation of MOOCs and OER in the Global South as well as in the rest of the world.

Despite the growing number of publications on MOOCs and OER, over 82% of published empirical MOOC research through 2015 has been from North America and Europe (Veletsianos & Shepherdson, 2016) and those trends have continued (Zhu, Sari, & Lee, 2018). Perhaps more interesting, findings from the developed economies and those from the Global South are often inconsistent, and, in some cases, even contradictory. In a recent study by Reich and Ruipérez-Valiente (2019), for example, a large data set of 5.63 million MOOC learners in edX courses was analyzed. The study examined data across six years (2013 to 2018) from courses developed at MIT and Harvard University and provided through the edX platform. The trends in MOOC participation clearly indicated that the growth of MOOC learners was mostly from some of the richest countries. Among the more than 5 million MOOC participants in this study, less than 1.5% were from the Global South. Worse still, as is often criticized in the MOOC research literature and prevailing press, MOOC completion rates continued to be very low with less than 4% of participants completing the MOOCs in which they had enrolled. Unfortunately, trend analyses did not project likely increases in completion rates in the near future.

Surprisingly, another study, focusing on MOOC usage in Colombia, the Philippines, and South Africa (Garrido et al., 2016) found that 80% of the participants in professional development MOOCs completed at least one course. More impressively, roughly half of the participants (i.e., 49%) earned certifications. The divergent results of these two studies signal that much additional research and experimentation is needed for better understanding and appreciation of MOOCs and other forms of open education in the Global South.

Despite the limitations of each of these studies, the dramatic differences in their findings naturally raise some striking questions including the following:

- Why are MOOC- and OER-related phenomena so different in the North and the South?
- What are the challenges and opportunities in the Global South?
- How does the Global South negotiate with various challenges inherent in MOOCs and OER developed elsewhere?
- What may have contributed to much higher rates of MOOC participation and completion in the Global South?
- In what ways does the Global South benefit from MOOCs and OER?
- What can we learn from the Global South to leverage MOOCs and OER for sustainable development?

The collection of chapters in this book attempts to answer critical questions, such as these, with first-hand accounts of MOOC and OER research, projects, programs, initiatives, evaluations, and policy development in the Global South. The 28 chapters cover a total of 47 countries, including 8 in Africa, 11 in Asia, 3 in the Caribbean, 16 in Latin America, 8 in the Middle East, and 1 in the Pacific. The following tables summarize the various countries that are directly addressed or reported on in the book.

What is clear from Table 1.1 is that a huge swath of the Global South is represented in the chapters of this book. They include both top 20 economies like China, India, Brazil, Mexico, Indonesia, Saudi Arabia, and Turkey as well as much poorer ones like Zimbabwe, Zambia, Uganda, the Bahamas, Somalia, and Fiji. Clearly, the educational resource base for the Global South is quite varied and differentiated. As shown by Atieno Adala in Chapter 24, research on OER in teacher education in six countries in Africa indicates that the creation, repurposing, use, and sharing of OER dramatically vary by country as well as by institution within each country. Issues of accessibility, awareness, and policy have considerable impact on ultimate use and extendibility of OER.

While we highlight the unique chapter from Adala here, we hope that the reader will find critical perspectives on the landscape of MOOCs and OER in the Global South across the 28 chapters of this book as well as the preceding Preface by us editors and Foreword by Mimi Lee. The chapters describe an assembly of national initiatives, international design and development projects, systematic literature reviews, empirical studies, and institutional policies. Of course, it also includes various design and development frameworks, applications, and evaluation criteria. To help you more quickly locate needed information, Table 1.2 summarizes the chapter topics, foci, and organizations found in this book.

TABLE 1.1 List of Countries Discussed in the Book

Region	Countries and Chapters
Africa	1. Egypt (Chapters 4, 22) 2. Kenya (Chapters 24, 26) 3. Somalia (Chapter 24) 4. South Africa (Chapters 15, 16) 5. Tanzania (Chapter 24) 6. Uganda (Chapter 24) 7. Zambia (Chapter 24) 8. Zimbabwe (Chapters 16, 24)
Asia	1. China (Chapters 3, 16) 2. India (Chapter 25) 3. Indonesia (Chapters 6, 17) 4. Malaysia (Chapters 17, 20) 5. Nepal (Chapter 9) 6. North Korea (Chapter 2) 7. Philippines (Chapters 17, 21) 8. Sri Lanka (Chapter 7) 9. South Korea (Chapter 2) 10. Thailand (Chapters 13, 17) 11. Vietnam (Chapter 17)
Latin America	1. Argentina (Chapters 10, 18) 2. Belize (Chapter 18) 3. Bolivia (Chapter 18) 4. Brazil (Chapters 10, 18, 19) 5. Chile (Chapters 10, 18) 6. Colombia (Chapters 10, 16, 18) 7. Costa Rica (Chapters 10, 18) 8. El Salvador (Chapter 10) 9. Ecuador (Chapter 18) 10. Guatemala (Chapter 10) 11. Honduras (Chapter 10) 12. Mexico (Chapters 10, 16, 17, 18) 13. Paraguay (Chapter 10) 14. Peru (Chapters 10, 18) 15. Uruguay (Chapter 10) 16. Venezuela (Chapter 18)
The Caribbean	1. Bahamas (Chapter 16) 2. Barbados (Chapter 18) 3. Dominican Republic (Chapter 10)
The Middle East	1. Israel (Chapter 22) 2. Jordan (Chapter 22) 3. Kuwait (Chapter 22) 4. Lebanon (Chapter 22) 5. Qatar (Chapter 22) 6. Saudi Arabia (Chapter 22) 7. Turkey (Chapter 11) 8. UAE (Chapter 22)
The Pacific/Oceania	1. Fiji (Chapter 8)
Total Countries	47

TABLE 1.2 Chapter Foci, Topics, and Organization

Section 1: Historical Perspectives

Chapter	Region of Focus	Countries covered	Main Topics
2	Asia	South Korea North Korea	• Evolution and innovative roles of K-MOOC • Unique opportunities to bridge two countries via K-MOOC • Cultural sensitivities • National initiatives • International collaborations in MOOC and OER
3	Asia	China	• Landscape of MOOC in China: Trends and issues • Systematic analysis of MOOC research in China: A critical review • National initiatives by the Ministry of Education in China

Section 2: Current Practices and Designs

Chapter	Region	Country	Main Topics
4	Africa	Egypt	• Localized designs of MOOCs for the Global South • Contextualization and globalization • Cultural sensitivities and diversifications • Access • Localization and translation of content
5	Global	n/a	• OER challenges and solutions: The critical perspectives • Contextualization and globalization • Cultural sensitivities and diversifications
6	Asia	Indonesia	• MOOCs and MOOC-inspired courses and initiatives • A critical review of MOOCs in Indonesia
7	Asia	Sri Lanka	• Contextualized MOOC design and development
8	Oceania and the South Pacific	Fiji	• Culturally sensitive design of MOOC architecture • Contextualization and globalization
9	Asia	Nepal	• High school students in MOOC • Younger generations of learners • Innovations in teaching and learning
10	Latin America	Argentina Brazil Chile Colombia Costa Rica Cuba Equador Guatemala Mexico Peru	• Systematic review of publications on MOOCs in Latin America • Trends and issues as evident in research publications
11	n/a	n/a	• Emotional benefits of diversity in MOOCs • Design MOOCs for diverse learners

Section 3: MOOCs and Open Education for Professional Development

12	Middle East	Turkey	• pdMOOC: Transforming professional development via MOOCs
13	Asia	Thailand	• Thai MOOC for lifelong learning and open education • Continued education • Lifelong learning
14	International organization initiatives	Commonwealth of Learning (COL)	• Technology-enabled MOOC • Faculty professional development
15	Africa	South Africa	• Institutional learning • Incubation of meaningful and innovative learning processes at different levels of the university

Section 4: Multi-Country Collaborations and Collections

16	Multi-national: Africa, Asia, Latin America, North America, The Caribbean	Bahamas China Colombia Iran Mexico Zimbabwe South Africa	• MOOC for a course of change • Contextualization • Cultural sensitivities and diversifications • MOOCs as a transformational approach to sustainable changes and development
17	Asia and South America	Asia-Pacific Economic Cooperation (APEC) Indonesia Malaysia Mexico Philippines Thailand Vietnam	• MOOC development in APEC countries • Contextualization and globalization • Cultural sensitivities and diversifications • Trends, research, and recommendations
18	International organization initiatives Latin America and the Caribbean	Inter-American Development Bank (IDB)	• Landscape of IDBx MOOCs • Impacts of MOOCs on the academic, professional, and social life of learners in Latin America and the Caribbean

Section 5: Government Policies and Strategies

19	Latin America	Brazil	• Development of open education in Brazilian higher education • National and international policies advancing open education
20	Asia	Malaysia	• Policies and implications for sustainable development of MOOCs • National and institutional policies
21	Asia	The Philippines	• OER for development • Design and implementation of OER
22	Middle East	Jordan Saudi Arabia UAE	• Arab MOOCs • Disruptive learning

(Continued)

TABLE 1.2 (Continued)

Section 6: Organizational Innovations			
23	International organization initiatives Multi-national	The World Bank	• World Bank initiatives • Dividend for development • Sustainable development
24	Multi-national	6 African countries: Kenya, Somalia, Tanzania, Uganda, Zambia, and Zimbabwe	• Does adoption of open educational resources (OER) lead to open education practices (OEPs)? • Faculty use of OER as a resource for course development, training new faculty, lesson preparation, and student readings • OER uses lead to practices of repurposing, creation, and sharing of open education
25	Asia	India	• 16 MOOCs on agriculture in India • MOOCs for sustainable development
26	Africa	Kenya	• Instructional design framework for online degree programs using MOOC and OER • Instructional design

Section 7: The Future of MOOCs and Open Education			
27	n/a	n/a	• Intelligent MOOCs • Future of MOOCs and OER
28	n/a	n/a	• Future of MOOCs and OER • Predictions

Challenges Facing the Global South

Various scholars have examined the countless challenges to fully realize the potentials of MOOCs and OER in the Global South (e.g., Hodgkinson-Williams & Arinto, 2017; James & Bossu, 2014; Khan et al., 2018; King et al., 2018; Nkuyubwatsi, 2014). The most prevailing challenges include: (a) limited access to the Internet or bandwidth; (b) significant technological barriers; (c) the lack of prerequisites in terms of knowledge, skills, and language and digital literacy; and, perhaps most critically, (d) mis-alignments between MOOCs and OER developed in the Global North and the cultures, languages, pedagogies, and local contexts of the Global South. It appears to be clear that, despite all the promising potential, MOOCs and OER originating in the Global North have rather limited capacities to provide localized or contextualized learning opportunities for the diverse populations in the Global South (e.g., Bidaisee, 2017; Castillo, Lee, Zahra, & Wagner, 2015; Ichou, 2018).

Success in the Global South

In the few years since the Incheon Declaration (UNESCO, 2015), MOOCs and OER have been scaled up across the Global South through a wide range of local, national, and international initiatives as well as individual and organizational efforts. Chapters in this book showcase some of the most influential and impactful projects, frameworks, policies, research, programs, and evaluations, which are enjoying notable success in overcoming the varied challenges in the Global South. By featuring them in one book, there is a greater opportunity for insightful and creative applications and replications. The chances that they can be further refined and extended is also elevated.

The Global South has a long history in distance education (DE). For decades, DE has been tactically leveraged and engineered at the national level as a powerful strategy to address the ever-growing demands for education (e.g., Bonk, Lee, Reeves, & Reynolds, 2015; Carr-Chellman, 2005;

Carr-Chellman & Zhang, 2000; Garrido et al., 2016; Hodgkinson-Williams & Arinto, 2017; King et al., 2018; Zhang & Hung, 2006, 2009; Zhang, Liang, & Sang, 2013). The MOOC phenomenon has spurred new initiatives in those countries with a long record in DE. For example, during the past few years, China has proactively responded to the MOOC explosion started in the Western world. In 2015, the Chinese Ministry of Education (MoE) published an aggressive national plan "to strengthen the construction, use and management of MOOCs" (MoE, 2015). Less than three years later in January 2018, the MoE in China introduced 490 National Elite Online Courses, which were selected and recognized as the best open online courses in China. With the goal to offer approximately 3,000 national elite online courses free to the general public by 2030, the Chinese government provides generous funding and resources for the creation and delivery of online open courses.

Likewise, as Yong Kim, Ock Tae Kim, and Jin Gon Shon examine in detail in Chapter 2, the South Korean Ministry of Education has also been pressing the development and promotion of MOOCs in Korea, known as K-MOOC. Further, Kim and colleagues have proposed innovative and promising applications of K-MOOC to connect the two countries, North Korea and South Korea, through national initiative and developments. Similarly, nationwide, government-driven MOOC movements are widespread in the Global South. For instance, our authors critically review Thai MOOCs (Chapter 13), the MOOC portal in Turkey (Chapter 12), MOOC-like or MOOC-inspired OER in Indonesia (Chapter 6), and MOOCs and OER integrated as open education practices in Africa (Chapter 24), to name a few. These national initiatives and government-supported structures and programs have generated a rapid, massive growth of MOOCs and OER in the Global South.

Consequently, the Western-born MOOC hype has taken various new forms and perspectives (e.g., Weiland, 2015; Zheng, Chen, & Burgos, 2018; Zawacki-Richter, Bozkurt, Alturki, & Aldraiweesh, 2018) in the Global South to serve the different needs in countries and regions, where the demands for education are ever growing, while resources and access are quite limited. The Global South has generated an enormous amount of newly created MOOCs for the specific populations and needs there. For instance, they must be offered in their languages (e.g., Arabic, Chinese, Korean, Portuguese, Spanish, etc.), and with culturally sensitive customizations. More remarkably, with strong government support and national initiatives, the South has created many culturally contextualized, country-specific, or language-specific MOOC platforms and OER portals. Proactively through such MOOC platforms, the Global South has been contributing to the global community with new knowledge, ample resources, and innovative opportunities for continuing lifelong learning, and much more. Table 1.3 summarizes some of the most popular country-specific MOOC platforms developed by countries or organizations in the Global South.

TABLE 1.3 A Partial List of Country-Specific MOOCs in the South

Country-Specific MOOC Platforms in the South (in alphabetical order)	Country of Origin
Edraak	Jordan
K-MOOC	South Korea
IndonesiaX	Indonesia
Mena Versity	Lebanon
MexicoX	Mexico
National Programme on Technology Enhanced Learning (NPTEL)	India
Rwaq	Saudi Arabia
SkillAcademy	Egypt
Study Webs of Active-Learning for Young Aspiring Minds (SWAYAM)	India
ThaiMOOC	Thailand
XuetangX	China

These various MOOC platforms serve a great number of people in the Global South. In fact, many of them have millions of registered users. Several of these MOOC platforms have been integrated into formal educational systems, again with governmental support and guiding policies at the national level. For example, in India, students may earn up to 20% of their degree program from SWAYAM, the Indian MOOC platform. SWAYAM also enables schools to reach remote, rural areas in India. With SWAYAM, India is able to increase its Gross Enrollment Ratio (GER) in higher education from 24.5% in 2015–2016 to 25.8% in 2017–2018; the Indian government further aims to reach 30% of GER by 2021 (Press Information Bureau, 2018a). Additionally, in December 2018, the Indian government signed a memorandum with Afghanistan, another country in the Global South, for Afghanistan educational institutions and students to offer MOOCs and take courses on SWAYAM (Press Information Bureau, 2018b).

In addition to leveraging MOOCs to supplement and transform traditional higher education or degree programs, MOOCs and OER are also widely applied in the Global South to provide non-traditional opportunities for informal, lifelong learning, professional development initiatives, and micro-credentials (e.g., Commonwealth of Learning, n.d.; Dodson, Kitburi, & Berge, 2015; Garrido et al., 2016; IBL News, 2019; Shah, 2019; Wagner, 2018; XuetangX, n.d.; Zhang, 2015; Zhang & Gao, 2014). It is noteworthy that XuetangX, a MOOC platform developed by China, for instance, has reached 16.3 million users in January 2019 (IBL News, 2019) with over 200 corporate partners and MOOC offerings in multiple languages (XuetangX, n.d.). It is now the world's third-largest MOOC platform in terms of users, only after Coursera (37 million) and edX (18 million) (IBL News, 2019). Many chapters in this book discuss in detail the design, development, implementation, research, and evaluation mechanisms of these Global South–oriented MOOCs.

MOOCs and OER in the South also boast creative ways of integration and application by employing diverse learning modalities (e.g., IBL News, 2019; XuetangX, n.d.). For example, Rain Classroom, a mobile app featured on XuetangX, empowers over 7 million users with interactive learning activities and instant assessments for blended learning or in flipped classrooms via smartphones. Paired with XuetangX Cloud, a teaching platform for faculty to use on campus, instructors can easily integrate Rain Classroom into their daily teaching practices. Another novel product by XuetangX is AI Xuetang. Backed by the Online Research Center of China's Ministry of Education, AI Xuetang specializes in K–12 education where it provides personalized learning and enables dynamic assessments for K–12 students. XuetangX even offers a virtual teacher using AI technology, named Xiaomu, for learners. Xiaomu monitors learners' progress, while guiding them with prompts as well as questions and answers. It also engages learners with constant encouragement and suggestions at different stages of the learning process. Such innovative technologies and new ways of teaching are gradually transforming education in the Global South.

As evident in the stories of success from the 47 countries highlighted in this book, MOOCs and OER have provided a wide variety of participants in the Global South with much needed opportunities for education, especially for adult learners. In particular, they can offer unique opportunities for professional development, and skill-focused or job-critical training and learning. For example, chapters in Section 3 of this book share details of MOOCs for professional development in Turkey, Thailand, South Africa, and various countries of the Commonwealth.

Open Education: Open Educational Resources to Open Education Practices

Intense research studies as well as the everyday press have articulated numerous challenges in the Global South as related to OER, and more broadly to open education (e.g., Arinto, Hodgkinson-Williams, King, Cartmill, & Willmers, 2017; Commonwealth of Learning, n.d.; de Oliveira Neto, Pete, Daryono, & Cartmill, 2017). Nevertheless, open practices in the Global South continue to grow and remain emergent and responsive, as consistently confirmed in several studies from researchers in South Africa (e.g., Czerniewicz, Deacon, Glover, & Walji, 2017; Czerniewicz & Goodier, 2014; Hodgkinson-Williams & Arinto, 2017). In fact, in a comparative international study, the reported uses of OER in the Global South were remarkedly higher than those reported in more developed countries (de Oliveira et al., 2017). What may have contributed to the differences in OER uses and open education practices between the North and the South? The collection of chapters in this book provide rich, contextualized, and culturally diverse insights that will help readers consider different perspectives on these complex issues.

Different frameworks are proposed to help understand the difficulties and issues in open education. For example, Hodgkinson-Williams (2014) identifies technical, cultural, legal, pedagogical, and financial dimensions of openness. Next, she explains the ease or difficulty of adopting open education from the five dimensions or perspectives. A couple of years prior, Beetham and colleagues (Beetham, Falconer, McGill, & Littlejohn, 2012) proposed six main features of open education practices and encouraged educators to: (a) allow non-registered students to access learning materials, (b) re-use course materials, (c) engage practitioners in the creation of course documents, (d) share knowledge with the public, (e) encourage others in open education practices, and (f) use open networks for teaching. While such frameworks will continue to be fine-tuned in the coming decade, they already serve a vital role in understanding issues related to the design, adoption, and use of open education.

The many Global South scholars found in this book share concrete examples, projects, strategies, and institutional and national policies associated with OER and OEP in countries and regions like Africa (Chapter 24), APEC (Chapter 17), Brazil (Chapter 19), Egypt (Chapter 4), Indonesia (Chapter 6), Kenya (Chapter 26), Malaysia (Chapter 20), and the Philippines (Chapter 21). At the same time, some of these lenses extend more globally via critical perspectives (Chapter 5) whereas others offer international perspectives with organizations like the World Bank (Chapter 23), the Commonwealth of Learning (Chapter 14), the Inter-American Development Bank (Chapter 18), and much more.

In Conclusion

This book is a compilation of the experience and wisdom of many different scholars and education leaders. None of them warrant that they have all the answers, or all the questions, for that matter. In fact, they would probably all agree that there are many serious issues and concerns that must be confronted as MOOCs and open education evolve around the world. For example, if someone in the Global South completes a MOOC offered by a prestigious university in the North such as Harvard, MIT, or Stanford, and even has earned a certificate of completion, what is its ultimate value or worth?

While the knowledge and skills gained will certainly have intrinsic value, it is important to ponder whether employers will place any faith in certificates, nanodegrees, digital badges, microcredentials, or other forms of certification emanating from MOOCs and OER. Although in the North this acceptance may seem to be up to individual employers, strong national policies in many Global South countries have been promoting awareness and acceptance of such varied forms of open education, including the implementation of MOOCs and OER. As MOOCs and open forms of education evolve, will the elite institutions continue to stand behind and support these products; and if so, how? If government support or incentives fade, how would the practice of open education be sustained? Similar issues arise when considering home-grown forms of open education.

The editors of this volume have vastly different experiences in the Global South. The first author has extended roots in the Global South, together with substantial experiences in educational research and development at the national, international, and organizational levels in Asia and Eurasia. The third and fourth authors have been Fulbright scholars in Peru and Columbia, and have been involved in research in several other Global South countries; in fact, the fourth author conducted OER research when in Columbia a decade ago. And the second author has made dozens of visits to parts of the Global South in higher education settings related to online and blended learning, including MOOCs and open education. We have learned much from each journey there; in fact, we met many contributors to this particular book during our professional experiences in the Global South. While each of us had a unique set of personal experiences and stories on which we drew upon when drafting and editing this book, we structured this book in the hopes of sharing a widely diverse range of views and perspectives that may stimulate important new conversations flowing South and North as well as East and West.

If successful, some of the ideas and perspectives presented in the ensuing chapters will spark new collaborations in research and development at the national, international, regional, local, organizational, or individual levels. They may also attract new and continuing investments from government agencies, educational institutions, not-for-profit organizations, and corporate interests. These are among the key goals that have driven our efforts to curate this book. We trust that you share some of them and welcome you to add many of your own goals, targets, and purposes.

It is now time to journey ahead to the next 27 chapters. We hope that you glance back to this introductory chapter from time to time, and compare and contrast the insights that may gently, or more forcefully, emerge in your own interpretations and conclusions with what we, the team of editors, have attempted to highlight for you. Nevertheless, each of you should have personally meaningful and professionally relevant themes and takeaways that are solely your own. As you generate such personal insights and conclusions, we welcome you to share them with us or forward any reviews of this book that you may produce or oversee. Let's work together to realize the sustainable development goal for "inclusive and equitable quality education" (United Nations, 2015) across the world, North, South, East, and West!

Ke Zhang is Professor in Learning Design and Technology at Wayne State University in Detroit, Michigan, USA. As a multilingual, international educator and researcher, her work focuses on e-learning, innovative technologies, and emerging methods for research and development. Her collaborative research is supported by the federal government and agencies, like the US Department of Health and Human Services and National Institute of Health, as well as private foundations, with multimillion-dollar grants to design, develop, and research emerging technologies for education, professional development, and health information management. Dr. Zhang is also a popular speaker and consultant in Asia, Eurasia, the Middle East, Latin America, and North America. She has consulted for large-scale projects and initiatives by international organizations, national governments and agencies, corporations, educational institutions, and healthcare systems in the USA and overseas. Inquiries are welcome by email to: ke.zhang@wayne.edu.

Curtis J. Bonk is Professor at Indiana University teaching psychology and technology courses. He is a passionate and energetic speaker, writer, educational psychologist, instructional technologist, and entrepreneur as well as a former certified public accountant and corporate controller. He has published more than 340 manuscripts and spoken in dozens of countries around the world. Among his numerous research and teaching awards are the Cyberstar Award, the Charles Wedemeyer Award for Outstanding Practitioner in Distance Education, the AACE Fellowship Award, and the Online Learning Journal Outstanding Research Achievement Award in Online Education. Bonk has been annually named among the top 100 contributors to the public debate about education from more than 20,000 university-based academics. He has authored a dozen books, including *The World Is Open*, *Empowering Online Learning*, *The Handbook of Blended Learning*, *Electronic Collaborators*, *Adding Some TEC-VARIETY*, which is free (http://tec-variety.com/), and *MOOCs and Open Education Around the World* (www.moocsbook.com/). He can be contacted at cjbonk@indiana.edu and his homepage is at http://curtbonk.com/.

Thomas C. Reeves is Professor Emeritus of Learning, Design, and Technology at the University of Georgia. Professor Reeves has designed and evaluated numerous interactive learning programs and projects. In recognition of these efforts, in 2003 he received the AACE Fellowship Award, in 2010 he was made an ASCILITE Fellow, and in 2013 he received the AECT David H. Jonassen Excellence in Research Award. His books include *Interactive Learning Systems Evaluation* (with John Hedberg), *Guide to Authentic E-Learning* (with Jan Herrington and Ron Oliver), and *Conducting Educational Design Research* (with Susan McKenney). His research interests include evaluation, authentic tasks for learning, educational design research, and educational technology in developing countries. He can be reached at treeves@uga.edu and his homepage can be found at www.evaluateitnow.com/.

Thomas H. Reynolds is Professor of Teacher Education at National University in La Jolla, California, where he researches design of online learning, standards-based online assessment, and innovations in e-learning. Among his awards and honors are two Fulbright Scholar awards (2010 in Colombia where he researched open educational resources, and 1998 in Peru where he lectured on Web-based learning and technology-enhanced instruction), a Texas A&M University honored faculty recognition, director and co-principal investigator of a multimillion-dollar center for professional development and technology, and, in 2016, the First Place Book Award from the AECT Division of Distance Education (DDL) for *MOOCs and Open Education Around the World* that was co-edited with Mimi Lee, Curt Bonk, and Tom Reeves and published by Routledge. Present activities and responsibilities include research on the status of e-learning in Latin America and academic program direction of an e-teaching master's degree at National University. He can be contacted at treynold@nu.edu.

References

Anderson, T. (2013). Promise and/or peril: MOOCs and open and distance education. *Commonwealth of Learning*, *3*, 1–9.

Arinto, P. B., Hodgkinson-Williams, C., King, T., Cartmill, T., & Willmers, M. (2017). *Research on open educational resources for development in the global South: Project landscape*. Retrieved from https://open.uct.ac.za/bitstream/handle/11427/26435/ROER4D-ch1-final.pdf?sequence=7

Beetham, H., Falconer, I., McGill, L., & Littlejohn, A. (2012). *Open practices: Briefing paper*. Retrieved from https://oersynth.pbworks.com/w/page/51668352/OpenPractices

Bidaisee, S. (2017, May 8). Creating MOOCs for students in developing countries. *Educational Review*. Retrieved from https://er.educause.edu/articles/2017/5/creating-moocs-for-students-in-developing-countries

Bonk, C. J., Lee, M. M., Reeves, T. C., & Reynolds, T. H. (2015). *MOOCs and open education around the world*. New York: Routledge.

Carr-Chellman, A. A. (2005). *Global perspectives on e-learning: Rhetoric and reality*. Thousand Oaks, CA: Sage.

Carr-Chellman, A. A., & Zhang, K. (2000). China's future with distance education: Rhetoric and realities. *Information, Communication & Society*, *3*(3), 303–312.

Castillo, N. M., Lee, J., Zahra, F. T., & Wagner, D. A. (2015). MOOCs for development: Trends, challenges, and opportunities. *Journal Articles (Literacy.org)*, *6*. Retrieved from https://repository.upenn.edu/literacyorg_articles/6

Commonwealth of Learning. (n.d.). *Open educational resources: Global report 2017*. Retrieved from http://oasis.col.org/bitstream/handle/11599/2788/2017_COL_OER-Global-Report.pdf?sequence=1&isAllowed=y

Czerniewicz, L., Deacon, A., Glover, M., & Walji, S. (2017). MOOC—making and open educational practices. *Journal of Computing in Higher Education, 29*(1), 81–97.

Czerniewicz, L., & Goodier, S. (2014). Open access in South Africa: A case study and reflections. *South African Journal of Science, 110*(9–10), 1–9.

de Oliveira Neto, J. D., Pete, J., Daryono, & Cartmill, T. (2017). OER use in the global South: A baseline survey of higher education instructors. In C. Hodgkinson-Williams & P. B. Arinto (Eds.), *Adoption and impact of OER in the global South*. Chapter 3 advance publication. Retrieved from http://dx.doi.org/10.5281/zenodo.154559

Dodson, M. N., Kitburi, K., & Berge, Z. L. (2015). Possibilities for MOOCs in corporate training and development. *Performance Improvement, 54*(10), 14–21. doi:10.1002/pfi.21532

Garrido, M., Koepke, L., Anderson, S., Felipe Mena, A., Macapagal, M., & Dalvit, L. (2016). *The advancing MOOCs for development initiative: An examination of MOOC usage for professional workforce development outcomes in Colombia, the Philippines, & South Africa*. Seattle: Technology & Social Change Group, University of Washington Information School. Retrieved from https://digital.lib.washington.edu/researchworks/bitstream/handle/1773/35647/Advancing_MOOCs_for_Development_Final_Report_2016_Final.pdf?sequence=4&isAllowed=y

Gunawardena, C. (2014, March). MOOCs: Students in the global south are wary of a "sage on the stage". *The Guardian*. Retrieved from www.theguardian.com/education/2014/mar/19/cost-barrier-students-global-south

Hodgkinson-Williams, C. (2014). Degrees of ease: Adoption of OER, open textbooks and MOOCs in the Global South. In *2nd regional symposium on open educational resources: beyond advocacy, research and policy*. Penang, Malaysia. Retrieved from https://open.uct.ac.za/handle/11427/1188

Hodgkinson-Williams, C. A., & Arinto, P. B. (2017). *Adoption and impact of OER in the global South*. Cape Town and Ottawa: African Minds, International Development Research Centre & Research on Open Educational Resources. doi:10.5281/zenodo.1005330

Hollington, A., Salverda, T., Schwarz, T., & Tappe, O. (2015). *Concepts of the global South* (vol. 2015). Global South Studies Center Cologne. Retrieved from https://kups.ub.uni-koeln.de/6399/1/voices012015_concepts_of_the_global_south.pdf

IBL News. (2019, January 3). XuetangX, China's open edX platform, reaches 16M learners. *IBL News*. Retrieved from https://iblnews.org/2019/01/03/xuetangx-open-edx-chinas-platform-reaches-16m-learners-2/

Ichou, R. P. (2018). Can MOOCs reduce global inequality in education? *Australasian Marketing Journal, 26*(2), 116–120.

James, R., & Bossu, C. (2014). Conversations from south of the equator: Challenges and Opportunities in OER across broader Oceania. *International Journal of Educational Technology in Higher Education, 11*(3), 78–90.

Khan, I. U., Hameed, Z., Yu, Y., Islam, T., Sheikh, Z., & Khan, S. (2018). Predicting the acceptance of MOOCs in a developing country: Application of task-technology fit model, social motivation, and self-determination theory. *Telematics and Informatics, 35*, 964–978. doi:10.1016/j.tele.2017.09.009

King, M., Pegrum, M., & Forsey, M. (2018). MOOCs and OER in the global South: Problems and potential. *The International Review of Research in Open and Distributed Learning, 19*(5). https://doi.org/10.19173/irrodl.v19i5.3742

Koller, D. (2012). *What we're learning from online education*. Retrieved from www.ted.com/talks/daphne_koller_what_we_re_learning_from_online_education.html

Ministry of Education of the People's Republic of China. (2015, February 12). *The key work of the ministry of education in 2015*. Retrieved from www.moe.gov.cn/srcsite/A02/s7049/201502/t20150212_189347.html (in Chinese)

Nkuyubwatsi, B. (2014, March). Cultural translation in massive open online courses (MOOCs). *eLearning Papers, 37*, 1–10. Retrieved from https://lra.le.ac.uk/bitstream/2381/28554/4/In_depth_37_3.pdf

Press Information Bureau (PIB), Ministry of Human Resource Development, India. (2018a, August 2). *Gross enrolment ratio target in higher education has been achieved*. Retrieved from www.pib.nic.in/Pressreleaseshare.aspx?PRID=1541358

Press Information Bureau (PIB), Ministry of Human Resource Development, India. (2018b, December 17). *Cabinet approves memorandum of understanding between India and Afghanistan in the field of human resource development*. Retrieved from http://pib.nic.in/newsite/PrintRelease.aspx?relid=186523

Reich, J., & Ruipérez-Valiente, J. A. (2019). The MOOC pivot. *Science, 363*, 130–131. doi:10.1126/science.aav7958

Shah, D. (2019). *Year of MOOC-based degrees: A review of MOOC stats and trends in 2018*. Retrieved from www.class-central.com/report/moocs-stats-and-trends-2018/

UNESCO. (2015). *Education 2030: Incheon declaration and framework for action for the implementation of sustainable development goal 4: Ensure inclusive and equitable quality education and promote lifelong learning*. Retrieved from https://unesdoc.unesco.org/ark:/48223/pf0000245656

United Nation. (2015). *About the sustainable development goals*. Retrieved from www.un.org/sustainabledevelopment/sustainable-development-goals/

Veletsianos, G., & Shepherdson, P. (2016). A systematic analysis and synthesis of the empirical MOOC literature published in 2013–2015. *The International Review of Research in Open and Distributed Learning*, 17(2), 198–221. doi:10.19173/irrodl.v17i2.2448

Wagner, D. A. (Ed.). (2018). *Learning as development: Rethinking international education in a changing world*. New York: Routledge.

Weiland, S. (2015). Open educational resources: American ideals, global questions. *Global Education Review*, 2(3), 4–22. Retrieved from https://files.eric.ed.gov/fulltext/EJ1074097.pdf

XuetangX. (n.d.). *About us*. Retrieved from www.xuetangx.com/global

Zawacki-Richter, O., Bozkurt, A., Alturki, U., & Aldraiweesh, A. (2018). What research says about MOOCs—an explorative content analysis. *The International Review of Research in Open and Distributed Learning*, 19(1), 242–259. Retrieved from www.irrodl.org/index.php/irrodl/article/view/3356/4490

Zhang, K. (2015). Mining data from Weibo to WeChat: A comparative case study of MOOC communities on social media in China. *International Journal on E-Learning*, 14(3), 305–329.

Zhang, K., & Gao, F. (2014). Social media for informal science learning in China: A case study. *Knowledge Management & E-Learning: An International Journal*, 6(3), 262–280.

Zhang, K., & Hung, J. L. (2006). E-learning in Taiwan's higher education: Policies, practices, and problems. *International Journal of Information and Communication Technology Education*, 2(1), 37–52.

Zhang, K., & Hung, J. L. (2009). E-learning in supplemental educational systems in Taiwan: Present status and future challenges. *International Journal on e-Learning*, 8(4), 479–494.

Zhang, K., Liang, L., & Sang, X. (2013). Educational technology in China: Past & present. In X. Li (Ed.), *Education in China: Cultural influences, global perspectives and social challenges* (pp. 271–288). Hauppauge, NY: Nova Science Publishers.

Zheng, Q., Chen, L., & Burgos, D. (2018). Emergence and development of MOOCs. In Q. Zheng, L. Chen, & D. Burgos (Eds.), *The development of MOOCs in China* (pp. 11–24). Singapore: Springer.

Zhu, M., Sari, A., & Lee, M. M. (2018). A systematic review of research methods and topics of the empirical MOOC literature (2014–2016). *The Internet and Higher Education*, 37, 31–39. https://doi.org/10.1016/j.iheduc.2018.01.002

SECTION 1
Historical Perspectives

At first glance, it may seem odd to have a "Historical Perspectives" section about a phenomenon as new as MOOCs and Open Education. But things move fast online especially with respect to the rise and fall of Internet enterprises. Just think about the "Dotcom Bubble" that saw the Nasdaq stock index rise five-fold between 1995 and 2000, and then crash from a peak of over 5,000 in March 2000 down to close to 1,000 in October 2002, a decline of nearly 80%!

Considering how often pundits and journalists have declared the imminent demise of MOOCs despite their continuing expansion, such naysayers may see them as the zombies of the online learning world which keep dying and coming back to life despite their many flaws and imperfections, while, at the same time, myriad MOOCs advocates may view them as some sort of superhero which can teach millions of people in a single bound. Whether zombie or superhero, MOOCs are still quite young for such worldwide fandom. The roots of MOOCs go back to just 2008 when the innovative "Connectivism and Connectivity Knowledge" online course was first offered by Stephen Downes from the Canadian Research Council and George Siemens of the University of Manitoba in Canada. While the course had around 20 tuition-paying folks, another 2,300 signed up for the free and open version of this online course. Fellow Canadian, Dave Cormier, would quickly label it a "massive open online course" or MOOC. He and Alec Couros, also from Canada, would assist Siemens and Downes in later iterations of their innovative connectivist MOOCs. Needless to say, much has transpired in the dozen or so years since MOOCs first emerged in the distance and open education scene.

The history of "Open Education" as a recognizable field of study, however, is much older than MOOCs; some trace it back to 1998 when David Wiley coined the term "open content," whereas others push it back further still to the emergence of open universities in the late 1960s. It was exactly 50 years prior to the drafting of this book on MOOCs and open education that the UK Open University was established back in 1969. Interestingly, the Open Education Working Group in the United Kingdom has developed an "Open Education Timeline" (Guy, 2013) that extends the development of open education all the way back to the Oxford Extension Movement in 1878! Who knows how far back it might lead? There may be those who would extend the credit for open education all the way back to Plato's *Akedemos*.

History, of course, is not about the "facts of the past," but rather an interpretation of the past. With that in mind, this initial section of the *MOOCs and Open Education in the Global South* book includes two chapters that provide interesting historical perspectives from Korea and China. In Chapter 2, Yong Kim, Ock Tae Kim, and Jin Gon Shon from Korea National Open University (KNOU) in South Korea describe the fascinating development of K-MOOCs. These authors explain when, why, and how K-MOOCs have been opened and report the general usages of MOOCs in Korea, quality management of K-MOOCs, and several contributions of K-MOOCs to Korean learners.

In addition, this chapter details the history and evolution of distance learning in North Korea, which has recently attempted to become involved as a member of the international community with possible nuclear disarmament in order to achieve rapid economic development. This interesting chapter describes the current situation of South and North Korea as well as the historical transition of North Korean distance higher education. Importantly, the chapter concludes with the prospects for an open education détente between South and North Korea that may include educational exchanges between the two Koreas via MOOCs! If such a bold plan were to transpire, K-MOOCs would assume a prominent role in international diplomacy.

In Chapter 3, Jianli Jiao and Yibo (Jeremy) Fan explain the past, present, and future of MOOCs in China, including an overview of MOOC learners and the ambitious MOOC research agenda underway there. First, the mainstream MOOC platforms in China are introduced in chronological order. Second, in an attempt to depict a general picture of Chinese MOOC learners, the data generated in a MOOC titled, "English Teaching and Internet," which was developed by Dr Jianli Jiao and his team, are presented. This analysis indicated that the majority of MOOC learners are well educated. With regard to this MOOC research, the authors analyzed 147 peer-reviewed journal papers published between 2012 and 2017 from five dimensions; namely: (1) the research aim, (2) research paradigm, (3) data collection, (4) data analysis method, and (4) research types. Next, the challenges and best practices facing MOOCs in China are presented. Finally, the authors discuss the future directions of MOOC practice and research, suggesting that more attention should be paid to MOOC pedagogy and the influence of MOOCs on the status quo of higher education.

Some readers might contend that Korea and China should not be considered as part of the Global South, but we believe that the development of MOOCs in these two countries has important implications for most of the other countries represented in this book. In addition, western regions of China are still very much in a state of development and increasingly reliant on open and online education experiments and initiatives, including MOOCs, to prepare teachers and students there. The mobilization of the Chinese workforce and rapid education and training of its citizenry through a variety of educational delivery mechanisms is something the entire world has been intensively watching for the past few decades; fortunately, much of it is documented in the chapter from Jiao and Fan.

Additionally, as noted in the chapter from our Korean colleagues at KNOU, there is much to learn about open and distance education in what some consider the Hermit Kingdom to the north as well as from the economic miracle in the south. We editors were surprised by the impact of distance forms of learning in North Korea since the Korean War armistice in 1953; we think you will be too. Intensive focus on education helped to transform South Korea from an underdeveloped agrarian economy which depended heavily on foreign aid from the United States and others in the 1950s to the 11th largest economy in the world. In effect, when reading this chapter, one can simultaneously envision the possibilities of MOOCs and other forms of open education in a closed country that one day may open up to outside influences as well as how MOOCs and open education might impact much more highly developed countries and regions.

So, while one region of a country is highly developed and significantly impacting the world community, another part might clearly be underdeveloped or emerging as seen in Korea north and south and China east and west. Additional historical perspectives can also be found in several of the other chapters of this book from countries more clearly identified with the Global South. We start with China and Korea because we hope that the world community can learn from aspects of their educational policies and practices as well as from their overall transition and transformation over time.

Reference

Guy, M. (2013, October 25). *Open education timeline building*. Open Education Working Group. Retrieved from http://education.okfn.org/timeline/

2
A HISTORICAL JOURNEY INTO K-MOOCs LEADING TO POSSIBLE COLLABORATIONS WITH NORTH KOREA

Yong Kim, Ock Tae Kim, and Jin Gon Shon

Introduction to K-MOOC

Even before the establishment of K-MOOC (Korean Massive Open Online Courses), Korea was providing video lectures developed by domestic universities and specialized institutions open to the public through the Korea Open Course Ware (KOCW) service. In December 2007, KOCW launched its service providing 200 video lectures from 40 universities to the public through the Internet. KOCW service has since grown to more than 20,500 lectures provided by 218 Korean and foreign institutions and schools within 10 years (Ministry of Education, Korea Education & Research Information Service, 2017). However, KOCW simply provides free video lectures to the general public without any necessary learning services or support, such as a learning management system (LMS) that can offer academic management and academic courses for learners who are interested.

On the other hand, MOOC-type academic programs have the capacity to provide not only lectures and other learning materials on a designated platform, but also active teaching and learning. And, more importantly, MOOC programs may provide a variety of academic services, such as grade transfer, credit acquisition, and even the conferral of diplomas. Considering the advantages of MOOC-type programs, the Korean government launched a Korean version of a MOOC in 2014, which is now officially known as K-MOOC (K-MOOC, n.d.).

Before 2014, foreign MOOC platforms, like Coursera, were introduced in Korea, and as a result, public awareness of the MOOC movement grew. Korea sought to promptly participate in the MOOC movement that started in the US and had been expanding quickly throughout the world, including much of the EU and Asia (including China, India, and Japan). Interestingly, a key difference is that the MOOC movement in the US developed in a bottom-up manner from the private sector in collaboration with major universities, both public and private, whereas the K-MOOC started in a top-down manner with strong initiatives from the national government like the Korean Ministry of Education (MOE).

More specifically, the Korean MOE proposed the background plan of K-MOOC with the following key action items:

- We must actively respond to the international expansion of MOOCs and paradigm changes.
  - The Open Educational Resources (OER) movement that has been carried forward in Korea has expanded and developed in a form of MOOCs since 2012.

- We need to adopt K-MOOCs as a method to enhance the quality of higher education and innovation.
  - We carry forward educational innovations by adopting up-to-date teaching and learning methods, such as blended learning and flipped classrooms.
  - We improve lecture quality by making professors' lectures open to the public.
- By making top lectures public and jointly utilizing those lectures from different universities, we increase their social impacts.
  - We establish a base for acceptance of credit and credit transfer for MOOCs between universities.
  - We expand the role of universities as a major base of the lifelong learning era.

For successful establishment and operation of K-MOOC, the MOE prioritized the development of university-based MOOCs and strategized to expand MOOCs into an "online lifelong education support system". Moreover, for successful brand establishment, it chose Korea's most prestigious universities as leading schools to be the first to participate in the creation of K-MOOCs. Those top universities included Seoul National University, Korea University, Yonsei University, and more, and they were expected to lead other schools to join the K-MOOC initiatives progressively.

For the operation of K-MOOCs, the MOE created a basic implementation and operation model, using direct government investment from the beginning. After 2020, the operation will be stabilized by implementing a revenue model that includes for-profit services. As a strategy for K-MOOC utilization and content procurement, the MOE promoted institutionalization to enable various types of services, such as credit recognition, training of incumbents at companies, and lifelong education for the general public. The MOE has also pushed ahead with the development of learning resources and re-processing of video lectures that had already been developed (e.g., KOCW, etc.) to secure numerous high-quality learning resources for K-MOOC. The platform that the K-MOOC operation is based on is the open source Open edX system. Open edX was chosen as the system due to its fast implementation time, reduced trial and error, and the interoperability of its content with foreign institutions. The layout of the K-MOOC operational system is shown in Figure 2.1.

As detailed in Figure 2.1, the K-MOOC project is operated by the MOE, which is in charge of the overall planning and management of the project. The MOE also oversees institutions related to elementary, middle school, high school, and lifelong education, such as the Korea Education and Research Information Service (KERIS), National Institute for Lifelong Education (NILE), the Korean Council for University Education (KCUE), and Education Broadcasting System (EBS). Additionally, K-MOOC participating universities take the role as the content provider, while college students as well as all general public can be K-MOOC users or consumers. Table 2.1 summarizes MOE's core promotional directions and roadmap of K-MOOC.

According to Table 2.1, K-MOOC's mid- to long-term development strategy is mainly divided into two steps. Step 1 is primarily concerned with launching K-MOOCs, while Step 2 is concerned with self-support so that operations can proceed without government support. After launching the service in 2015, establishment of the base for K-MOOC activation continued until 2017 with stable service of K-MOOC expected to continue until 2019. In Step 2, a self-supporting foundation of K-MOOC services will be established. At the same time, the revenues generated via the profit-based model, mentioned earlier, will be expanded starting in 2020. The goal is that after 2024, K-MOOCs can operate privately without government support. Currently, the K-MOOC project is focusing on service activation and settlement. The main projects are shown in Table 2.2.

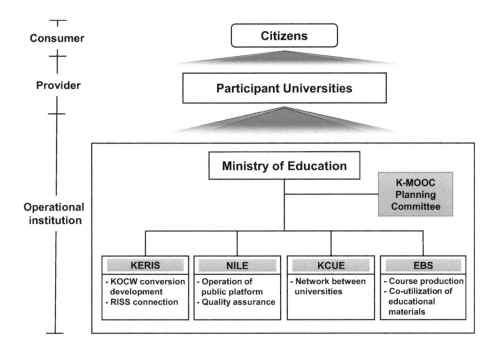

FIGURE 2.1 The Layout of the K-MOOC Operational System

TABLE 2.1 Medium-Term Strategy of K-MOOC

Division	Step 1 [Start and Settlement]			Step 2 [Financial Independence]		
	Y2015	Y2016~Y2017	Y2018~Y2019	Y2020~Y2021	Y2022~Y2023	Y2024~
Major directions	Service opening	Establish activation base	Service settlement	Establish self-supporting base	Expand profit model	Operate private autonomous development
Number of lectures	27	300	600	Approximately 1,000	Approximately 1,500	Approximately 2,000
Main projects	Pilot operation of university-level accreditation of lecture development	Excavation of application, such as credit recognition and incumbent training	Expand consortium of participant universities	Operate trial paid service	Diversification of profit, i.e., B2C, B2B	Self-support of lecture development and operation

TABLE 2.2 Top Priority Projects of K-MOOC in 2018

Division	Contents
Expansion of excellent lectures	• Development of new lectures through universities • Sharing of university financial support utilizing developed lectures
Strengthening of lecture quality and operation management	• Strengthening of content quality management • Improvement of lecture operation quality
Improvement of lecture utilization	• Development of English service and statistical functions through learning style analysis • Improvement of platform functionalities to optimize the environment for learners
Service settlement and self-support base establishment	• Expansion of course completion result utilization • Improvement of universities' autonomous participation competency

Outcomes of K-MOOC

The State of K-MOOC Usage

Since launching its services in 2015, K-MOOCs have been used by 32 participant universities offering 181 online lectures. Equally impressive, K-MOOCs have had about 4.74 million visitors, and claimed about 228,000 registered members as of 2017 (MOE·KERIS, 2017). K-MOOC provides lectures in seven academic fields, including the humanities, social sciences, education, engineering, natural sciences, medical science and pharmacology, and arts and physical education. The number of courses for each field as of July 2018 is shown in Table 2.3. The field with the greatest number of lectures is the humanities, followed by social sciences and engineering. If we take a look at the most popular MOOCs during the past three years, the humanities and social sciences, such as economics and Analects of Confucius were popular in 2015, but in 2017, MOOCs related to computer and data science such as "big data" and "artificial intelligence and machine learning" appeared to be more popular. The average number of students per course was 887 and the average number of students completing a course was 97, indicating an average completion rate of 10.9%, which is quite similar to other MOOC services (Bennett & Kent, 2017). One conclusion is that plans are needed to increase the average completion rate (NILE, 2018).

Table 2.4 illustrates K-MOOC users by age. K-MOOC was based on university involvement, which led to an increase in the demand of college students. Therefore, the age group of 20- to 29-year-olds accounted for the highest percentage of K-MOOC participants, which was over 40%. In the future, we plan to expand K-MOOC services so that participants across all age groups will be better represented.

A recent survey of K-MOOC users' satisfactions (NILE, 2018) showed that learners were generally satisfied with K-MOOC services. Comments from participants included the following, "Have an intention to continue taking the lecture in the future" (97.9%), "Helpful in reaching the purpose" (84.4%), and "Satisfied with the contents of the lecture and method" (87.8%). The user survey results indicated that the main K-MOOC users were high school and college graduates in their 20s and 30s. In particular, users with high loyalty regarding MOOCs appeared to be females in their 20s graduated from high school and colleges. Such data begs for additional research such as why female populations find MOOCs more beneficial than males and whether there are certain types of MOOCs that Korean females in their 20s find particularly valuable and perhaps even life-changing.

At the present time, K-MOOC courses can be taken and applied in basically three ways. First is the flipped learning track that induces student-led learning outside of class while the class is overseen by a professor who focuses on student participation, problem solving, and group discussions.

TABLE 2.3 K-MOOC Courses Classified by Academic Field

Humanities	*Social Sciences*	*Education*	*Engineering*	*Natural Sciences*	*Medical Science and Pharmacy*	*Arts and Physical Education*	*Sum*
92	83	14	64	45	19	21	338

TABLE 2.4 K-MOOC Users Classified by Age

Ages	*~20*	*20~29*	*30~39*	*40~49*	*50~59*	*60~*	*Total (%)*
Users	34,638 (15.20)	91,525 (40.17)	35,019 (15.37)	35,823 (15.72)	22,558 (9.90)	8,281 (3.64)	227,844 (100.00)

Source: (NILE, 2018)

Out of 70 K-MOCC participant universities, 24 appeared to use K-MOOC via flipped learning. Second is the transference of credit among the universities. When a student completes a K-MOOC-provided course, the university that provided the course as well as other universities recognize and accept the credit. An investigation revealed that 33 universities recognize the credit of 101 selected K-MOOC courses, and 11 universities recognize K-MOOC courses provided by other schools. Third is the continual learning track. By using K-MOOC courses for training of college students as well as job seekers, those currently employed, and people trying to change their job situation or obtain a promotion, K-MOOCs are used not only for higher education credentials, but for lifelong education and personal improvement as well. It is the third option that is perhaps the most common form of MOOC worldwide (Bonk, Lee, Reeves, & Reynolds, 2015).

For 2018, the MOE in Korea established a K-MOOC utilization plan as part of its online lifelong education ecosystem buildout. Until now, the K-MOOCs initiative has generated course content based on courses developed and offered by Korean universities, but it now plans to extend its goals to both higher education pursuits as well as lifelong education. Therefore, the K-MOOC initiative plans to create high-quality content for universities as well as government, public institutions, and the general public. As part of these efforts, it will expand a service that develops and provides K-MOOC lectures related to the fourth industrial revolution; an effort that can help equip the Korean people with skills needed for the 21st century.

K-MOOC Quality Management

The K-MOOC system provides content development guidelines that educational institutions can use for the content quality management of their MOOC lectures and resources. These guidelines are intended to secure good quality lectures by managing the course quality from the very beginning of lecture development. The plan is to divide lecture content into four stages, which are design, development, review, and operation, and additionally provide a checklist of items that need to be considered in each stage.

The design stage provides review items related to learning content, teaching design, interchange, learning support, and evaluation. Out of the review items, the guidelines compel accuracy of the lecture content (e.g., "Does the learning content contain accurate information?"), "ethics", and "concreteness of learning purpose" as items that must be checked for (MOE·NILE, 2016).

In the development stage, considerations related to production standards concerning videos, images, and documents used in lectures are provided as well as ways to verify their accuracy. The guidelines especially emphasize Web accessibility as well as respect for copyrights so that everyone can access all of the content in an ethical manner.

The review stage guidelines require that content be inspected for errors. In addition, the review stage is designed so that the opinions of experts and their feedback are heeded regarding the developed lecture contents through pilot operation of the lecture contents.

Lastly, the operation stage guidelines stipulate that for successful course completion procedures are in place that support prompt problem solving in case a problem occurs with any of the lectures. These guidelines also present matters related to objective academic evaluation of learners who can reach the completion standard.

Contributions of K-MOOC to Korean Learners

MOOCs are educational services that use the advantages of e-Learning, which can provide educational opportunities to everyone with an Internet connection. Korea expects that K-MOOCs provide opportunities for higher education as well as lifelong education to Korean citizens and eventually contribute to the improvement of the overall quality of life and national competitiveness of the Korean people.

In the higher education field, K-MOOCs are expected to share the high-value educational content that universities offer and expand the credit transfer scheme, which will lead to the overall improvement of university-level education. Moreover, by co-utilizing the educational content, this policy can prevent unnecessary redundant investment and increase public utility. K-MOOCs are expected to have universities provide educational content for higher education purposes as well as to contribute to lifelong educational opportunities.

In the field of lifelong education, K-MOOCs are expected to provide learners who need re-education and reskilling after graduating from college with more opportunities to succeed. By utilizing the diverse K-MOOC educational content, learners are able to select the educational content that fit the purposes and appropriate levels of their needs. Eventually, they will be able to have a fully customizable learning environment based on e-Learning such as offered by MOOCs and other forms of open education.

Furthermore, K-MOOCs will not only be used by the citizens of South Korea but it is possible that they can also provide educational services for educational exchange with North Korea. Some possibilities of educational collaboration between South and North Korea will be discussed in the following section.

Educational Collaboration With North Korea

The Situation of South Korea and North Korea

After the Korean War, the relationship between South Korea and North Korea has endured a series of conflicts and has continued to exist in a state of tension. Especially after North Korea's first nuclear test in 2006, the nuclear crisis has not only threatened South Korea but also world peace. In 2018, however, efforts were made to overcome the crisis and establish a peace settlement through exchange and cooperation between South and North Korea (Choi, 2018). There are even prospects for re-unification, although it will be extremely complex economically and socially (Macdonald, 2018).

It is difficult to predict when or how Korean re-unification will be enacted but we can easily predict that when it does happen, there will be high demand for the re-education of North Korean adults. Various solutions can help minimize the inevitable social problems that will surely arise between South and North Korean citizens, such as petty conflicts, by helping people understand the differences in social and economic systems. It will be especially helpful to produce programs with North Korea for production and broadcasting of educational programs to help overcome South and North Korea's heterogeneous cultural systems before re-unification with a focus on resolving the many differences. Without a doubt, education, especially cross-border education, will become a vital component of any such re-unification efforts. Fortunately, the technology tools and resources for freely and openly sharing educational contents have accelerated during the past decade to offer hopeful opportunities for virtual cultural exchanges and reskilling. Now is the perfect time to plan and establish goals and benchmarks for such an event.

There are many reasons why education for North Koreans, especially adults, will be necessary before and after re-unification. First, the number of people needing education on all the pressing issues will rise dramatically immediately after re-unification. In particular, participating in a more technologically robust economy will require new skill sets. The sheer size of such efforts will be monumental. Second, at the same time, educational demand will also rise with the increase of learner groups different from those that the MOE in South Korea traditionally targets. New curricula will need to be approved, developed, piloted, and refined for a diverse population. Third, an educational system for groups with substantive differences in prerequisite learning will be needed. Fourth, it is obvious that there will be needs for various types of educational contents and materials following the rapid social changes that will likely occur. Lastly, educational guidelines and equipment for learning activities will be needed as solutions to bridge the gaps and imbalances existing between regions (Kim, 2014).

Eventually, during the re-unification process, traditional school-based education with time and location limits will be difficult to apply to North Korean adults; instead, open and online educational methods using various educational media will be most suitable. Online tutorials and demonstrations, synchronous training sessions, and self-paced learning modules in the form of MOOCs and open educational contents can all play a role. In this respect, while purposely not attempting to impose South Korean values and cultural norms on those in North Korea, K-MOOCs are expected to play a vital role in addressing many of these issues. Clearly, now is the time to predict and plan for such needs. The Korean National Open University (KNOU) where we work is one such entity that has the mission, personnel, resources, and rich history of distance learning experiences to potentially lead such thinking and planning efforts.

Transition and Situation of North Korean Distance Higher Education

To forecast South and North Korean educational exchange through the K-MOOC initiative, we must understand some basics of North Korean distance education. North Korean distance higher education, after South and North Korea divided in 1945, is detailed in the following sections (Kim, 2009).

The Quickening Period (1945~1950)

During this period, North Korea's higher distance education for adults was mainly in charge of training and re-education of incumbents through the department of correspondence education, which was established at educator training institutions such as colleges and universities. At the time, schools in North Korea were rapidly expanding and there were needs for mass training of educators in a short period of time.

The basic framework of North Korean higher distance education based on correspondence courses and broadcast communication was established at that time, and the department of distance education was made a part of the existing higher education institutions. In addition, the school year and graduation requirements were made the same as regular educational institutions. Regarding educational methods, lessons with Q&As were delivered via postal correspondence during this time.

Expansion and Development Period (1951~1960)

In 1950, North Korea's correspondence education for adults went beyond educator training and expanded to various industrial fields. At that time, the national level support system for management of correspondence education was strengthened. Such systems were naturally impacted by the breakout of the Korean War, which lasted from June 25, 1950, to July 27, 1953. After the Korean War ended, in order to mass produce professionals for industrial restoration, the department of correspondence education was also established at technology and engineering universities.

During these years the method of distance education was more systematic. In fact, by organizing job-based learning classes and combined classes, North Korea operated face-to-face supplementary education under the supervision of city instructors and advanced school teachers. Lessons with Q&A exchanges and reviews of assignments were handled through postal correspondence.

Adjustment Transformation Period (1961~1970)

A transformation in North Korean distance education occurred in the 1960s. During this time, managers and executives from each field started using correspondence education for re-education purposes. As part of the re-education process for executives without high school diplomas, correspondence courses for executives began to be designed.

While prior to 1960 the correspondence education process utilized the same school year as regular universities, it was during this time that a rising problem of the quality of the correspondence education was observed and the school year was extended one year longer than regular universities. Also, new departments in charge of correspondence education were established at institutions for higher education. Concurrent with other changes, in addition to conventional courses, correspondence education departments were established for North Korean factory workers.

Broadcasting Media Conjunction Period (1970s~early 1990s)

In 1973, North Korea opened Kim Il-Sung Broadcasting University, which broadcast lessons via Pyongyang broadcasting radio towers for three hours a day. The main educational contents were about the "Juche" ("joo-chay", i.e., self-reliance) ideology. Considering that personal possession of radios is prohibited in North Korea, it was thought that Kim Il-Sung Broadcasting University targeted only a small number of ruling class people or South Korea. However, the fact that Kim Il-Sung Broadcasting University switched to Internet broadcasting in 2004 disproves this hypothesis.

In 1982, Television Broadcasting University opened and provided ideology, culture, and foreign-language courses three times a week through the Korean Central Broadcasting Station. However, this also was not a regular university but an educational institution that broadcast courses that nationwide correspondence education students commonly took.

At that time, the original correspondence learning method was maintained while the broadcasting courses were added. Another major change occurred at that time when night classes were introduced in which professors started to conduct face-to-face lectures for blended learning.

e-Learning Introduction Period (mid-1990s~)

Computer-based education was introduced in the 1990s and 2000s. At that time, a distance education center was established at Kim Chaek University of Technology that provided distance learning courses using a local network serving universities all over the country. By 2007, about 1,200 lecture plans were offered to both regular and correspondence education university students.

If we summarize the characteristics of North Korean distance education, there is no open university that confers an independent degree (Han, 2014; Kim, 2014). Distance education and degrees are given through correspondence education departments attached to regular universities. Regular university courses and correspondence education department courses are all regulated by the state, and there is no discrimination towards any degree. As a method of education, the more conventional and established postal distance education has recently been combined with media-focused e-Learning.

Plan of Distance Education for North Korean Adults: A Role of K-MOOC

If South and North Korea gradually re-unite, it looks feasible to use a strategy of maintaining North Korean higher educational institutions, while gradually expanding distance education that includes K-MOOCs and other relevant forms of open and distance learning. It must be noted that the North Korean people and government may prove a bit recalcitrant towards rapid entrance of outside educational institutions. Therefore, a careful and high-level strategic approach seems to be necessary. For this, we first need to analyze the situation of North Korea's ICT (information and communication technology) in detail.

For the past seven decades, North Korea has been operating in an unprecedented fashion as a highly secluded society. As a direct result, critical information regarding the equipment and resources used for distance education is lacking. If North Korea's technological infrastructure for distance education falls short, this must be solved first. Afterwards, there should be strategic attempts to provide the fields and subjects that they want and need. If they show any resistance to existing curricular content, then it will surely be better to cooperatively develop educational courses and jointly create and refine lecture materials. Through this process, we will lead the interaction in a direction whereby their ability to develop and produce the subjects they need is strengthened.

Conclusion

Since 2014, K-MOOCs has been providing education services to the Korean people and now they have about 22.8 million registered members, which is about 44% of the whole population. While KOCW, its predecessor, emerged in a bottom-up way, K-MOOCs opened up in a top-down way with a strategic plan by the Korean government, which has been driving K-MOOCs as an "online lifelong education support system" for the Korean people. It is reported that K-MOOCs learners are generally satisfied with its education services, so far. The Ministry of Education has pushed K-MOOCs to operate autonomously after 2024 without government support, emphasizing not only the quantity and diversity but also the quality of K-MOOCs. It can be expected that K-MOOCs and other forms of open education will continue to evolve and become a greater part of the education and training of the citizens of South Korea.

In the meantime, K-MOOCs will not only be used by the citizens of South Korea but it is possible that they can also provide educational services for educational exchange with North Korea. Recently, the Korean Peninsula has been dramatically moving into a peaceful atmosphere followed by inter-Korean summit meetings and the North Korea–US summit meetings. An official declaration to end the Korean War will definitely give not only the permanent peace but also extraordinary opportunities for both sides of Korea. There will be a lot of exchanges (such as human exchange, economic exchange, cultural exchange, and so on) between them. Even though it is easy for both peoples to understand each other because they use the same Korean language, they still need to know each other better. It means learning about each other will be essential. That is why K-MOOCs can be considered as one of great bridges linking the two parts of Korea.

In South Korea alone, the coming decade of open education initiatives and experiences will undoubtedly be quite exciting to witness. KNOU will be among the organizations which continues to experiment in this space and share the results of those experiments with others. Hopefully, someday soon we will be among those sharing educational contents, ideas, and other forms of support with those involved in the North Korean open and online educational systems. We also expect that MOOCs and open education can be a key peg in the transformational processes that will unfold when re-unification between South and North Korea eventually occurs. As such, we fully look forward to interesting days ahead.

Yong Kim received a BS degree in education and an MS in computer education from Korea National University of Education and his PhD degree in computer education from Korea University. He had worked for KERIS since 1997. Dr Kim has over 20 years of research experience in e-Learning and computer education. Since 2010, he has been with the Department of e-Learning, graduate school, Korea National Open University. His research interests are not limited to e-Learning such as LMS/LCMS, educational contents and mobile computing, but also computer education such as educational programming languages.

Ock Tae Kim is an assistant professor in the Department of Media Art and Science at Korea National Open University. He has a PhD in Telecommunications from Indiana University at Bloomington. His scholarship focuses on the intersections among media effects on individuals and society, communication technology, and educational psychology. His work has appeared in a number of conferences and journals in Korea and abroad.

Jin Gon Shon received a BSc degree in mathematics and MS and PhD degrees in computer science from Korea University in Seoul, Korea. Since 1991, he has been with the Department of Computer Science at Korea National Open University (KNOU). He was a visiting scholar at the State University of New York (SUNY) at Stony Brook (1997), Melbourne University (2004), and Indiana University at Bloomington (2013). Professor Shon established the Department of e-Learning in KNOU providing the first master's degree program on e-Learning in Korea. He has published over 40 scholarly articles in noted journals and has written several books on computer science and e-Learning.

References

Bennett, R., & Kent, M. (2017). *Massive open online courses and higher education: What went right, what went wrong and where to next?* New York: Routledge.
Bonk, C. J., Lee, M., Reeves, T. C., & Reynolds, T. (Eds.). (2015). *MOOCs and open education around the world.* New York: Routledge.
Choi, K. (2018). From anxiety to impression. *Kwanhun Journal*, 60(1), 55–63.
Han, M. (2014). *The direction and tasks of education for realizing unification of North and South Korea.* Korea Unification Education for Unification of the Korean Peninsula]. Paper presented at the 4th Creative Talent Education Forum and the 62nd KEDI Education Policy Forum, Seoul, Korea.
Kim, J. (2009). A study on distance education for adult in North Korea. *Journal of Lifelong Learning Society*, 5(2), 183–206.
Kim, J. (2014). *Characteristics of the acts related to North Korean education and exchange and integration of education in North and South Korea.* Paper presented at the 66th KEDI Education Policy Forum, Seoul, Korea.
K-MOOC. (n.d.). Retrieved from www.kmooc.kr
Macdonald, D. S. (2018). *The Koreans: Contemporary politics and society.* New York: Routledge.
Ministry of Education, Korea Education & Research Information Service. (2017). *White paper on ICT education Korea.* Korea Education & Research Information Service. Retrieved from http://lib.keris.or.kr/download/bbs/6_1176
MOE·NILE. (2016). *Guideline for K-MOOC lecture development and management.* National Institute for Lifelong Education.
NILE. (2018). *K-MOOC introduction.* Presentation paper for the Dept. of e-Learning, KNOU, Seoul, Korea. Retrieved from www.selearning.org/?module=file&act=procFileDownload&file_srl=1753&sid=0bcecb5aa9396dff72cdad7d8e528480&module_srl=159

3

CURRENT STATE OF PRACTICE AND RESEARCH ON MOOCs IN MAINLAND CHINA

A Critical Review

Jianli Jiao and Yibo Fan

Introduction

From its humble beginnings nearly a decade ago, massive open online courses or MOOCs (Bonk, Lee, Reeves, & Reynolds, 2015) have been popular around the world with its widespread influence on stakeholders in the field of higher education. Let us take mainland China (hereinafter referred to as China unless otherwise indicated) as an example. In a recent search, more than 6,000 MOOC-related academic articles were discovered, including journal papers, theses, and dissertations, that were published in China from 2012 to 2017 (Fan & Jiao, 2017). A wide range of topics are covered in the MOOC literature, including the high drop-out rate in MOOCs (Breslow et al., 2013; Jordan, 2014), the reasons learners drop out from MOOCs (Gillani & Eynon, 2014; Gütl, Rizzardini, Chang, & Morales, 2014; Hew, 2016), the impact of MOOCs on higher education (Dennis, 2012; Liyanagunawardena, Williams, & Adams, 2014; Yuan & Powell, 2014), learning and teaching in MOOCs (Breslow et al., 2013; de Freitas, Morgan, & Gibson, 2015), peer assessment (del Mar Sánchez-Vera & Prendes-Espinosa, 2015; Suen, 2014), and more. In addition, workshops, symposiums, and conferences on MOOCs have also been quite popular across China and around the world for the past several years.

Admittedly, MOOCs in China have seen a rapid development since 2012. And this should be largely attributed to the encouragement of policy preference and financial support from the government and a large number of colleges, universities, and industries. For instance, in an official report issued by the Ministry of Education (MoE) in 2015, a work plan was clearly proposed "to strengthen the construction, use and management of MOOCs" (MoE, 2015). MoE in China introduced 490 "National Elaborate Online Courses" (NEOC) in January 2018, which represents the highest level of open online courses in China. In 2020, roughly 3,000 NEOCs will be offered to the public, with the government facilitating development of these local MOOCs. Of course, this large-scale development of MOOCs is not only a way to educate people throughout China, but, perhaps equally important, Chinese MOOCs are now exerting influence globally and increasing the reputation of Chinese institutions.

Given its soaring development and success in China, MOOCs also experience some challenges that should not be overlooked. In this chapter, the development, challenges, successes, and best practices related to MOOC design and implementation will be described and discussed. The goal is to provide a clear picture on MOOCs in China. Along the way, its possible future development will also be forecasted.

MOOCs in China: Where Are We Now?

In this section, a general picture on the development of MOOCs in China is presented. In particular, the state of MOOC platforms and courses, learner profile, and MOOC research will be reported.

MOOC Platforms and Courses

Speaking of MOOC platforms in China, XuetangX always plays the most important and pivotal role. As the earliest founded MOOC platform in China, XuetangX was initiated by Tsinghua University under the auspices of the MoE Research Center for Online Education in October 2013. It was built upon edX open-source code repository and its establishment was symbolic by opening a window for more later-founded platforms. Through the years, the platform has been cooperating with top-level higher education institutions both domestically and abroad to offer high-quality courses, and now it tops all the major Chinese MOOC platforms (Shah, 2017), and is the third-largest MOOC platform around the world in terms of registered users (9.3 million in 2017) (Shah, 2018). As of November 2018, more than 1,900 courses covering 13 major disciplines (e.g., science, engineering, and literature) were available on this platform (XuetangX, 2018), and the participating institutions include Tsinghua University, Beijing University, MIT, Stanford University, and many others around the world (XuetangX, 2018).

The second major Chinese MOOC platform is CNMOOC, which was launched in April 2014. As of November 2018, a total of 817 courses covering a wide range of disciplines were offered on this platform, with 327 of them ongoing (CNMOOC, 2018). In partnership with 93 universities and institutions, CNMOOC aims to offer many more high-quality courses to benefit increasing numbers of MOOC learners around the globe in the near future.

icourse163 is another major Chinese MOOC platform built by Higher Education Press and an Internet technology company named NetEase, which was launched in May 2014. In collaboration with 270 universities and institutions, icourse163 is now offering 2,204 courses covering a wide range of disciplines (e.g., philosophy, science, and education). Learners who successfully finish courses are eligible to be awarded a completion certificate that possibly could be useful for their career development. More important, icourse163 even offers China Advanced Placement (CAP) courses (e.g., calculus, linear algebra, literature writing, and micro-economics), and by taking those courses students could experience the college-level courses in advance which will prepare them for their future university life. icourse163 not only cooperates with higher education institutions, it also partners up with major vocational colleges (e.g., Guangzhou Panyu Polytechnic, Zhejiang Financial Professional College, and Shandong Transport Vocational College) to offer vocational training courses. The offering of these courses echoes the central government's call for improving the quality of further education (MoE, 2018a). What is more, icourse163 offers a series of teaching education MOOCs which has attracted a huge number of pre-service and in-service teachers from different disciplines.

With the aim to provide high-quality educational resources for Chinese MOOC learners, including both matriculated and non-matriculated students, and better represent the characteristics of local universities, the UOOC Alliance, initiated by Shenzhen University, was founded on May 12, 2014, by an initial group of 76 member colleges and universities (Chen & Yan, 2017). This alliance has been developing rapidly since its launch. In fact, as of August 2018, there were 125 participating colleges and universities covering 63 cities from 28 provinces, and 2.5 million students have benefited from the alliance accumulatively (UOOC, 2018). To some extent, the UOOC Alliance cannot be regarded simply as a MOOC platform; instead, it operates more like an association in which the partnering local colleges and universities mutually acknowledge credits within the association. However, due to

TABLE 3.1 MOOC Platforms and Course Numbers

Platform	Founded date	Course number	Website
XuetangX	October 2013	More than 1,900	www.xuetangx.com/
CNMOOC	April 2014	943	www.cnmooc.org/
icourse163	May 2014	2,204	www.icourse163.org/
UOOC Alliance	May 2014	309	www.uooc.net.cn/

Note. The number of courses listed in the table are known as of November 2018.

its significance in offering Chinese students high-quality educational resources and narrowing the education gap between developed and developing areas, we believe it is fair to introduce the Alliance as a MOOC platform. More details on the UOOC Alliance can be found in the "best practices" section.

Table 3.1 presents the mainstream MOOC platforms in China. As is clear, there is much momentum in China at present related to MOOC design and delivery.

MOOC Learner Profile: An Example

Due to the free and open access nature of MOOCs, they have attracted many motivated learners around the world. Although exact numbers are unavailable, the figure is easily in the millions. Unfortunately, at present, there is no known national survey or statistics on the demographics of these learners (e.g., age, gender, and education). Therefore, in this brief introduction, the authors will try to depict a general picture of the learners using data generated in one MOOC course titled, "English Teaching and Internet (ETI)" offered by the Future Education Research Center at South China Normal University. To be noted, the "ETI" MOOC course belongs to the series of MOOCs offered by the icourse163 platform introduced previously. The "ETI" MOOC course has been offered six times since 2016 with a seventh iteration ongoing at the time of writing. This course mainly targets pre- and in-service English teachers to help them design more effective and interesting instruction by integrating technologies into their daily teaching.

This course has enrolled 48,273 learners all over China since first being offered in March 2016. In the first session of this course, the MOOC instruction team posted a survey in which the learners reported their demographic information. However, the survey was not mandatory and the participation in the survey did not affect whether the learners would pass or fail the course. In this course, 805 learners participated in the survey, among them 719 (89.3%) were female learners. In addition, the majority of the respondents (538 of 805 participants or 66.8%) had a bachelor's degree. With regard to their current position, 210 of them were college students, 132 were primary school teachers, and 126 were middle school teachers. More than half of the learners (432 of 805 participants or 53.7%) were under 30 years old, indicating that the young generation was the main audience for MOOC learning in this particular course. Generally, the data suggested that the majority of these learners were well educated and the same result could also be found in Breslow et al. (2013). By communicating with learners via different channels (e.g., discussion forum, personal face-to-face conversations), the authors found that the main reasons these learners registered in the course was to receive further education and develop skills necessary for their career.

MOOC Research

As alluded to in the introduction, to better understand the status of MOOC research in China, the authors performed a comprehensive search in the largest academic database—China National

TABLE 3.2 Analysis Framework

Dimension	Category
Research aim	Contribution of MOOC to educational theory, technological tools for MOOC, MOOC pedagogy, MOOC for institutional development, literature review, learning process in MOOC, teaching process in MOOC, design for learning
Research paradigm	Qualitative research, quantitative research, mixed research, design-based research, theoretical-conceptual research, not clear
Data collection	Survey, interview, observation, documents collection, literature collection, data tracking, not clear
Data analysis	Qualitative documents analysis, factor analysis, inferential statistics, social network analysis, descriptive statistics, scientific metrics, not clear
Research types	Desk research, descriptive research, intervention research

Source: The analysis framework in this study was adapted from Raffaghelli et al. (2015).

Knowledge Infrastructure (CNKI) with the terms "MOOC," "MOOCs," or "MUKE" (in Chinese Pinyin) in the title, abstract, and keywords with a time-span from 2012 to 2017. The search initially generated more than 6,000 related results, including journal papers, theses, dissertation, and news reports. Since only peer-reviewed studies were in the scope of analysis, the following filtering criteria were employed: (1) results that were not published in peer-reviewed journals were cleaned out; (2) duplicated items were eliminated; (3) papers translated from other languages into Chinese were deleted; (4) general background or introductory studies with "under the background of MOOCs" or similar description in the title were ruled out. After the screening, 147 MOOC-related research studies were identified and entered the analysis pool. The framework used to analyze these studies was adopted from Raffaghelli, Cucchiara, and Persico (2015) which can be found in Table 3.2.

After the analysis framework was determined, one researcher first analyzed these studies independently. Then the second researcher performed another independent analysis. An initial 80.5% ratio of agreement was reached. Disagreements were resolved through face-to-face discussions between the two authors. The analysis results in detail are presented in the following sections.

Dimension One: Research Aim

The studies in the dimension of "Design for Learning" (DL, 4 of 147 studies or 2.7%) mainly focus on the "design of personalized learning ecosystem," "design of personalized learning environment," "factors that impact the success of MOOC design," and "design of learning activities from the perspective of activity theory." Compared with DL, the studies in "Learning Process in MOOCs" (LPM, 23 of 147 studies or 15.6%) examine learners from micro-perspectives and include the analysis of learning behavior and learning assessment.

It is worth noting that "Literature Review" studies (LR, 46 of 147 studies or 31.3%) make up almost one-third of all the studies; Li, Chen, and Gong (2017) have similar findings in their study. It is worth noting that the large number of theoretical studies like literature review reflects the fact that the MOOC research in China is still in its infancy stage and researchers are still on the way to harness the massive data generated in MOOCs. The dimension, "MOOCs for Institutional Development" (MID, 32 of 147 studies or 21.8%), is on the value of MOOC for universities, the effects of MOOCs, quality assurance of MOOCs, and business models of MOOC, and so on.

Another dimension, the "Teaching Process in MOOCs" (TPM, 14 of 147 studies or 9.5%), relates to the role of the MOOC instructors and MOOC instructional design (Watson et al., 2016; Yousef, Chatti, Schroeder, & Wosnitza, 2014), which has been studied thoroughly. The success of

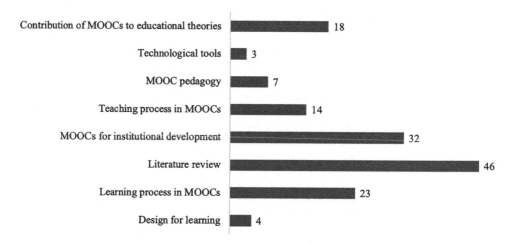

FIGURE 3.1 The Number of Studies in Each Category of Research Aim

MOOC learning does not only depend on learners, but also on the quality of instructors and instructional design. However, most of the current studies tackle the issue of high attrition rate from the perspective of learners (Rai & Chunrao, 2016; Veletsianos, Collier, & Schneider, 2015), rather than instructors or instructional design (Watson et al., 2016; Yousef et al., 2014). Figure 3.1 shows the number of studies in each category.

Dimension Two: Research Paradigm

Figure 3.2 reveals that the descriptive and theoretical-conceptual studies make up the majority of publications, which is similar to the MOOC research in the Western world (Raffaghelli et al., 2015). As an emerging field, it is quite normal to produce descriptive and theoretical studies in the early stages, yet what should be acknowledged is that the number of these studies is worrisomely excessive (85 of 147 studies or 57.8%). Therefore, more studies that employ sound evidence and rigid research design should be conducted to better promote and understand MOOCs in China.

The majority of quantitative studies (Depp & Jeste, 2006) focus on learning process in MOOCs that analyze survey data as well as learning behavior data generated and stored in MOOC platforms. What should be noted is that those literature reviews that implemented scientific metrics were categorized as quantitative studies for the use of clustering analysis and co-word analysis (i.e., the analysis of co-occurrences of key words to reveal patterns and trends in one research field, see also [Ding, Chowdhury, & Foo, 2001]). Except for the previously mentioned quantitative research and theoretical studies, there were 23 studies in the category of "not clear," which exceeded the combined number of mixed-method research (4 of 147 studies in this sample) (Johnson & Onwuegbuzie, 2004) and qualitative research (Just one study) (Lewis, 2015; Taylor, Bogdan, & DeVault, 2015).

It was somewhat surprising that none of these studies in the analysis pool employed a design-based research (DBR) approach (Amiel & Reeves, 2008; Wang & Hannafin, 2005), while the same finding could also be found in Raffaghelli et al. (2015). DBR requires iterations in the research process to develop theories as well as products, which is hard to implement in MOOCs due to the immense amount of human labor and financial resources needed for the mere development of a MOOC course as shown in a study (Hollands & Tirthali, 2014),

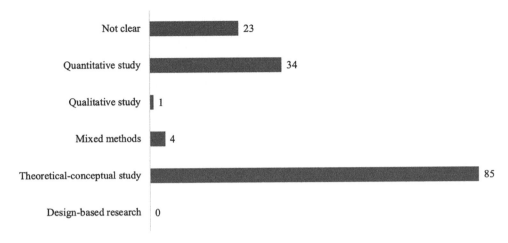

FIGURE 3.2 The Number of Studies in Each Category of Research Paradigm

let alone the constant revision and improvement of it. Perhaps this huge financial investment is a key reason why there are few MOOC studies employing this research approach.

Dimension Three: Data Collection Method

Through the analysis, it was obvious that most of the studies were published without clearly describing specific data collection methods, as shown in the category of "not clear" (73 of 147 studies or 49.7%) in Figure 3.3. Admittedly, studies that focused on the MOOC concept, the construction of specific MOOC models, and the effects that MOOCs exert on universities are valuable to some extent. However, when the majority of studies analyzed lack basic research methods or fail to describe them, as a researcher, you feel the urgency to conduct more empirical studies that employ rigorous research design and collect sound data. What some Chinese researchers need is to get rid of the eagerness for quick publication and instant benefit; instead, it would be more beneficial not only for them but for the whole academic community to conduct studies for the sake of producing new knowledge and improving academy.

The most commonly used data collection method is "literature collection" (44 of 147 studies or 29.9%). Most of the studies in this category are literature reviews, which corresponds to the findings in the dimension of "Research Aim." A small number of studies employed surveys (13 of 147 studies) as the primary data collection method. It is important to point out that the topics studied using survey methods included learner attitudes toward MOOCs, the quality of MOOC design, factors that affect learners behavior, and learning assessment in MOOCs.

Dimension Four: Data Analysis Method

In terms of the methods adopted for data analysis (Figure 3.4), surprisingly, 104 of 147 (70.7%) studies in this sample did not employ specific data analysis methods. The rapid development of visualization analysis software contributes to the use of scientific metrics (e.g., co-word analysis, clustering analysis) as a way to identify research trends in MOOCs. It was found that 14 of the 147 studies utilized descriptive statistics to describe the MOOC platforms, learning behavior, learners' attitudes toward MOOCs, and so on. Studies using inferential statistics (12

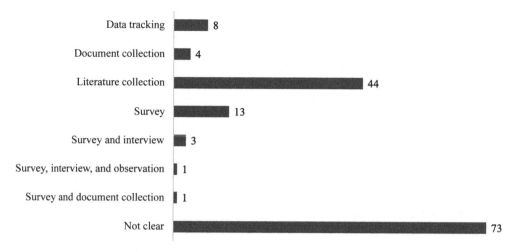

FIGURE 3.3 The Number of Studies in Each Category of Data Collection Method

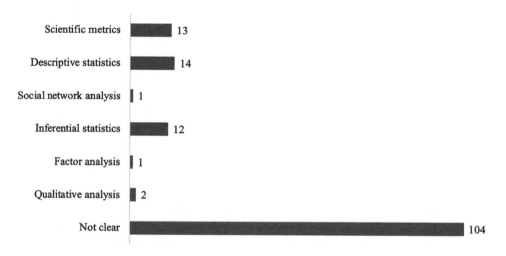

FIGURE 3.4 The Number of Studies in Each Category of Data analysis Method

of the 147 studies) focused on factors affecting learners' continuous learning in MOOCs, the acceptance of learners and universities towards MOOCs, the design of MOOCs, and so on.

Dimension Five: Research Types

Using the framework proposed by Raffaghelli et al. (2015), we employed the following three categories to describe the types of research:

- Desk research which included theoretical and conceptual studies as well as literature reviews;
- Descriptive research which was further divided into "descriptive-exploratory" and "descriptive-observational" research. Both categories involved studies exploring phenomena related to intervening in an existing situation, with the former focusing on more than one case study and the latter concentrating on a single case;
- Interventionist research was further divided into "interventionist-case study," "interventionist-design experiment," and "interventionist-random experiment" forms of research.

TABLE 3.3 Number of Studies in Each Type of Research

Research types	Number of studies
Desk research	118
Descriptive	29
Descriptive-observational	19
Descriptive-exploratory	10
Interventionist	0
Interventionist-case study	0
Interventionist-design experiment	0
Interventionist-random experiment	0

It can be concluded that the majority of studies analyzed are literature reviews. By contrast, the number of the same type of studies published in English is much smaller (Ebben & Murphy, 2014; Liyanagunawardena et al., 2014). As shown in the results, many studies lack a theoretical framework, specific data collection methods, or analysis methods. As of 2017, MOOC research in China mainly focused on MOOCs for institutional development, the exploration of the value of MOOCs for universities, the effects of MOOCs on higher education, quality assurance of MOOCs, and business models. The use of qualitative methods (e.g., literature collection) for MOOC research largely outnumbered the use of quantitative methods (e.g., survey research) and mixed methods. A large proportion of studies were based on desk-based forms of research like literature reviews and conceptual thought studies, rather than on interventionist research.

Challenges Remain

As to the development of MOOCs in China, the best description may be "much progress made but challenges remain," for instance, the passive pedagogy reflected in the Chinese MOOCs. Almost all of the existing MOOC platforms focus on content delivery instead of collaboration among learners and content generation. Most of the traditional classrooms in China have a heavy reliance on the teacher-centered approach, in which the teachers are the all-knowing "sage on the stage." And inevitably, the learners are affected by such a passive teaching and learning culture. In fact, these teacher-centric approaches are deeply ingrained in the learning culture, which makes it hard for MOOC learners to actively engage in the discussion forum. And to a large extent, most of the current MOOCs in China are the replicas of traditional teacher-centered courses in nature.

Most MOOC learners are likely accustomed to watching videos on demand just like they did in traditional classrooms. Instructional designers, instructors, and learners design, teach, and learn MOOCs using old habits of knowledge transmission from an expert instructor to awaiting learners which does not fulfill the original intention of MOOCs to transform higher education design and delivery. There are far too few research studies focusing on the pedagogy of MOOCs in which the culture of user-generated content (UGC) is encouraged and realized, and instructors are no longer teaching; instead, they are co-learning with learners with different backgrounds. In this way, the instructor's role will be redefined and they are not only tutors but also moderators of a community of practice and co-learners. The second challenge relates to the continuing development of MOOCs, namely, what design mechanisms the MOOCs should follow, how to keep universities and companies investing in the development of MOOCs, and how to provide needed learning support to MOOC learners. There are many other challenges that Chinese MOOCs face, for example, (1) the MOOCs quality assurance and criteria; (2) the way to motivate learners to take and complete MOOC courses; and (3) the development and (re-)use of MOOCs. Only by solving these problems can the continuous development of MOOCs become possible.

MOOCs Empower Instructional Experimentation

The high-profile six-month experimentation between San Jose State University and Udacity showed that students who learned from online Udacity courses did not perform as well as their counterparts in traditional classes, which put a pause on the project in July 2013 (Rivard, 2013). The possible failure of this project offered a warning that pure online learning via MOOCs may not be the best option in improving students' performance; however, blended learning based on MOOCs may be a better solution.

As highlighted earlier, there are a large number of MOOC courses now available in various Chinese MOOC platforms for potential learners. Among these courses, one of the most famous and influential courses is the "Principles of Electric Circuits" (PoEI) offered by Tsinghua University via XuetangX. Impressively, this course enrolled more than 60,000 learners by April 2015. To experiment with the blended learning pedagogy and promote a student-centered learning culture in this MOOC, Tsinghua University authorized several other universities (e.g., Qinghai University) to freely use all the teaching materials in the PoEI course. These participating universities utilized the materials to conduct instructional experimentations based on their specific goals. The results revealed that students in the blended learning model based on the MOOCs outperformed their peers in the traditional learning model in terms of learning performance and learning will (Center for Faculty Development, 2015).

UOOC Alliance Narrows the Education Gap

Given their extensive resources and large investments in MOOCs, elite universities around the world have become the backbone of the rapid development of MOOCs. But compared to those elite universities, smaller local universities as well as community colleges lack adequate resources to support the development of MOOCs. With the implementation of a resource-sharing mechanism, the member institutes in UOOC Alliance are striving to avoid developing duplicative resources, thereby, saving huge amounts of time and effort.

More importantly, their students have the opportunity to select courses not offered by their home institutions from other member institutes, and for which they can obtain course credit. In this way, it becomes more flexible for colleges and universities in the set-up and development of their programs and curriculum. In addition, the UOOC Alliance is a viable supplement to other MOOC platforms (e.g., XuetangX) in which the elite universities are the main force. On the one hand, the courses selected from other universities could be acknowledged and highlighted by the home institutions which would add a degree of flexibility in terms of course offerings to their students. On the other hand, their students can now freely learn using other MOOC platforms in a way of individual learning without worrying about course accreditation issues.

With its noble intentions, the UOOC Alliance is a bold and solid endeavor aimed at narrowing down the education gap among different areas by creating an atmosphere in which the membership universities can share high-quality educational resources within the alliance. Given it has accomplished much in just four years of existence, it will be interesting to watch it hopefully realize these initial goals and much more in the coming decade.

Future Directions

As of the end of December 2017, the Internet population in China has topped the globe and reached 772 million (CINIC, 2018). In fact, a record-breaking number of 8 million students graduated from universities in China in 2017 which is more than two times the number of students who graduated the same year from universities in the US (Stapleton, 2017). Given its largest student population, it is fair to believe that MOOCs could offer even more potential in China. Stakeholders such as higher education institutions, corporations, and governmental organizations are investing large amounts of financial support and issuing specific favorable policies for MOOCs to boost their rapid development in China since 2013. More specifically, MoE plans to certify another 800 high-quality online courses in 2018 (MoE, 2018b).

As noted previously, MoE encourages the rapid development of MOOCs in China by issuing policies and certifying high-quality online courses. The number of Chinese students learning online has increased by double digits for seven consecutive years which brings the total online learners in China to 100.1 million (Crace, 2018). Since online learning has become increasingly widespread in people's lives, it is fair to expect that more colleges, universities, and other institutes will get involved in the development of MOOCs. As this occurs, the influence of MOOCs on the status quo of higher education will become more evident (Kaplan & Haenlein, 2016; Sandeen, 2013; Yuan & Powell, 2014).

With regards to MOOC research in China, more empirical studies that harness the large amount of learning behavior data generated in MOOC platforms rather than theoretical studies (e.g., overviews of the possible influences of MOOCs on higher education) should be conducted. Several studies on the reasons learners drop out from MOOCs have been carried out in the Western world (Gillani & Eynon, 2014; Gütl et al., 2014; Hew, 2016); however, it may be as interesting to explore the reasons why Chinese MOOC learners drop out from the perspective of culture. Then studies could be conducted in terms of the ways to motivate learners—especially those with low levels of self-directed learning readiness—through the design and optimization of MOOCs.

As noted in the "MOOC Research" section, studies on instruction and instructional design have not paid enough attention to pedagogy. Therefore, future studies should focus on better understanding the teaching and learning process and strategies related to MOOCs. Such research should also target ways to prepare instructors for this new teaching environment so that they have the necessary information literacy skills and competencies to effectively implement instruction in a MOOC. No matter which way the issue of high attrition rate is addressed, either from the teaching or the learning perspective, a key focus is to decrease the drop-out or attrition rates. If successful, it could largely affect whether higher education institutions, industries, and governmental entities will continue to invest into MOOCs.

If such critical problems, issues, and challenges cannot be thoroughly addressed, then it is likely that MOOCs will have a much shorter life than we hope. Clearly, the expectations are great. The audience in China is indeed quite massive. The resources are abundantly open, while the learners in China as well as elsewhere in the world are increasingly found online. Thousands of MOOCs and other forms of open courses are waiting for these tens of millions of online Chinese learners. Without a doubt, the opportunities are seemingly endless in China today. Let's hope that tomorrow even more such mechanisms for massively open forms of learning will appear that can offer high-quality online contents and experiences that enhance, expand, and transform the educational prospects of all Chinese learners.

Jianli Jiao is Professor of Educational Technology and Director of the Future Education Research Center at the School of Information Technology in Education, South China Normal University in Guangzhou, China. He is a pioneer in teaching and learning with the Web in mainland China. His research interests span educational technology, blended and online learning, technology-enhanced learning in K–12, higher education, and continuing professional education. He has spoken at numerous local, national, and international conferences about educational technology, MOOCs, blended and online learning. He has published over 10 books, more than 110 articles in refereed journals, and more than 2,100 posts covering an expansive list of important educational technology topics and trends that has been a highly popular and valued resource throughout China for nearly two decades (www.jiaojianli.com). Currently, Dr. Jiao is researching on MOOCs, technology-enhanced learning, and blended learning in K–12 and higher education settings.

Yibo Fan is now a doctoral student in the program of Curriculum and Education with a cognate in Educational Technology at Boise State University. Before joining Boise State, he received his MS in Educational Technology at South China Normal University in 2017, and his BS from Henan University in 2014. His research interests include STEM education, learning science, MOOCs, and online education.

References

Amiel, T., & Reeves, T. C. (2008). Design-based research and educational technology: Rethinking technology and the research agenda. *Educational Technology & Society, 11*(4), 29–40. Retrieved from www.j-ets.net/ETS/journals/11_4/3.pdf

Bonk, C. J., Lee, M. M., Reeves, T. C., & Reynolds, T. H. (2015). *MOOCs and open education around the world*. New York: Routledge.

Breslow, L., Pritchard, D. E., DeBoer, J., Stump, G. S., Ho, A. D., & Seaton, D. T. (2013). Studying learning in the worldwide classroom research into edX's first MOOC. *Research & Practice in Assessment, 8*, 13–25.

Center for Faculty Development. (2015, April 12). *Dr. Xinjie Yu from Tsinghua university lectured the fifth term teachers' professional development training program on blended instruction*. Retrieved from http://cfd.fudan.edu.cn/news/xwbd/1148.html (in Chinese)

Chen, D-S., & Yan, G-P. (2017). MPOC experiential learning model of engineering education based on distributed flip in local engineering colleges and universities in "Post MOOC" era. *Journal of Discrete Mathematical Sciences and Cryptography, 20*(6–7), 1375–1379.

China Internet Network Information Center. (2018). *The 41st statistical report on internet development in China*. Retrieved from https://cnnic.com.cn/IDR/ReportDownloads/201807/P020180711391069195909.pdf

CNMOOC. (2018). *Courses*. Retrieved from www.cnmooc.org/portal/frontCourseIndex/course.mooc (in Chinese)

Crace, A. (2018, Febuary 6). *Chinese online learners increase 20%*. Retrieved from https://thepienews.com/news/chinese-online-learners-increase-20/

de Freitas, S. I., Morgan, J., & Gibson, D. (2015). Will MOOCs transform learning and teaching in higher education? Engagement and course retention in online learning provision. *British Journal of Educational Technology, 46*(3), 455–471.

del Mar Sánchez-Vera, M., & Prendes-Espinosa, M. P. (2015). Beyond objective testing and peer assessment: Alternative ways of assessment in MOOCs. *International Journal of Educational Technology in Higher Education, 12*(1), 119–130.

Dennis, M. (2012). The impact of MOOCs on higher education. *College & University, 88*(2), 24–30. Retrieved from http://libproxy.boisestate.edu/login?url=http://search.ebscohost.com/login.aspx?direct=true&db=ehh&AN=85363271&site=ehost-live

Depp, C. A., & Jeste, D. V. (2006). Definitions and predictors of successful aging: A comprehensive review of larger quantitative studies. *The American Journal of Geriatric Psychiatry, 14*(1), 6–20.

Ding, Y., Chowdhury, G. G., & Foo, S. (2001). Bibliometric cartography of information retrieval research by using co-word analysis. *Information Processing & Management, 37*(6), 817–842.

Ebben, M., & Murphy, J. S. (2014). Unpacking MOOC scholarly discourse: A review of nascent MOOC scholarship. *Learning, Media and Technology, 39*(3), 328–345.

Fan, Y., & Jiao, J. (2017). *The research on the relationship between adult learners' self-directed learning readiness and the percentage of MOOC completion*. Unpublished manuscript.

Gillani, N., & Eynon, R. (2014). Communication patterns in massively open online courses. *The Internet and Higher Education, 23*, 18–26.

Gütl, C., Rizzardini, R. H., Chang, V., & Morales, M. (2014). *Attrition in MOOC: Lessons learned from drop-out students*. International workshop on learning technology for education in cloud (pp. 37–48). Springer, Cham.

Hew, K. F. (2016). Promoting engagement in online courses: What strategies can we learn from three highly rated MOOCS. *British Journal of Educational Technology, 47*(2), 320–341.

Hollands, F., & Tirthali, D. (2014). *MOOCs: Expectations and reality*. Retrieved from https://files.eric.ed.gov/fulltext/ED547237.pdf

Johnson, R. B., & Onwuegbuzie, A. J. (2004). Mixed methods research: A research paradigm whose time has come. *Educational Researcher, 33*(7), 14–26.

Jordan, K. (2014). Initial trends in enrolment and completion of massive open online courses. *The International Review of Research in Open and Distributed Learning, 15*(1), 133–160. Retrieved from www.irrodl.org/index.php/irrodl/article/view/1651

Kaplan, A. M., & Haenlein, M. (2016). Higher education and the digital revolution: About MOOCs, SPOCs, social media, and the Cookie Monster. *Business Horizons, 59*(4), 441–450.

Lewis, S. (2015). Qualitative inquiry and research design: Choosing among five approaches. *Health Promotion Practice, 16*(4), 473–475.

Li, X., Chen, Y., & Gong, X. (2017). MOOCs in China: A review of literature, 2012–2016. In *New ecology for education—communication X learning* (pp. 21–32). Singapore: Springer.

Liyanagunawardena, T. R., Williams, S., & Adams, A. (2014). The impact and reach of MOOCs: A developing countries' perspective. *ELearning Papers*, 38–46. http://doi.org/10.1016/j.jbusres.2007.11.013

Ministry of Education of the People's Republic of China. (2018a, February 26). *The key work on vocational education and continuing education in 2018*. Retrieved from www.moe.gov.cn/s78/A07/A07_gggs/A07_sjhj/201802/W020180227502160533334.docx (in Chinese)

Ministry of Education of the People's Republic of China. (2018b, July 24). *Notice from the general office of the ministry of education on carrying out the certification of national quality open online course in 2018*. Retrieved from www.moe.gov.cn/srcsite/A08/s5664/s7209/s6872/201807/t20180725_343681.html (in Chinese)

Ministry of Education of the People's Republic of China. (2015, February 12). *The key work of the ministry of education in 2015*. Retrieved from www.moe.gov.cn/srcsite/A02/s7049/201502/t20150212_189347.html (in Chinese)

Raffaghelli, J. E., Cucchiara, S., & Persico, D. (2015). Methodological approaches in MOOC research: Retracing the myth of proteus. *British Journal of Educational Technology*, 46(3), 488–509. http://doi.org/10.1111/bjet.12279

Rai, L., & Chunrao, D. (2016). Influencing factors of success and failure in MOOC and general analysis of learner behavior. *International Journal of Information and Education Technology*, 6(4), 262–268.

Rivard, R. (2013). *Udacity project on "Pause"*. Retrieved from www.insidehighered.com/news/2013/07/18/citing-disappointing-student-outcomes-san-jose-state-pauses-work-udacity

Sandeen, C. (2013). Integrating MOOCs into traditional higher education: The emerging "MOOC 3.0" era. *Change: The Magazine of Higher Learning*, 45(6), 34–39.

Shah, D. (2017, June 5). *Massive list of MOOC providers around the world*. Retrieved from www.class-central.com/report/mooc-providers-list/

Shah, D. (2018, January 22). *A product at every price: A review of MOOC stats and trends in 2017*. Retrieved from www.class-central.com/report/moocs-stats-and-trends-2017/

Stapleton, K. (2017, April 13). *China now produces twice as many graduates a year as the US*. Retrieved from www.weforum.org/agenda/2017/04/higher-education-in-china-has-boomed-in-the-last-decade

Suen, H. K. (2014). Peer assessment for massive open online courses (MOOCs). *The International Review of Research in Open and Distributed Learning*, 15(3), 312–327. Retrieved from www.irrodl.org/index.php/irrodl/article/view/1680

Taylor, S. J., Bogdan, R., & DeVault, M. (2015). *Introduction to qualitative research methods: A guidebook and resource*. Hoboken, NJ: John Wiley & Sons.

University Open Online Courses. (2018). *UOOC introduction*. Retrieved from www.uooc.net.cn/league/union/intro (in Chinese)

Veletsianos, G., Collier, A., & Schneider, E. (2015). Digging deeper into learners' experiences in MOOCs: Participation in social networks outside of MOOC s, notetaking and contexts surrounding content consumption. *British Journal of Educational Technology*, 46(3), 570–587.

Wang, F., & Hannafin, M. J. (2005). Design-based research and technology-enhanced learning environments. *Educational Technology Research and Development*, 53(4), 5–23.

Watson, S. L., Loizzo, J., Watson, W. R., Mueller, C., Lim, J., & Ertmer, P. A. (2016). Instructional design, facilitation, and perceived learning outcomes: an exploratory case study of a human trafficking MOOC for attitudinal change. *Educational Technology Research and Development*, 64(6), 1273–1300.

XuetangX. (2018). *About us*. Retrieved from www.xuetangx.com/about#about_us (in Chinese)

Yousef, A. M. F., Chatti, M. A., Schroeder, U., & Wosnitza, M. (2014). *What drives a successful MOOC? An empirical examination of criteria to assure design quality of MOOCs*. 2014 IEEE 14th International Conference on Advanced Learning Technologies (ICALT) (pp. 44–48). IEEE, Athens.

Yuan, L., & Powell, S. (2014). MOOCs and open education: Implications for higher education. *JISC Cetis*. Retrieved from http://publications.cetis.ac.uk/2013/667

SECTION 2
Current Practices and Designs

Chapter 4 is the first of eight chapters in this section. In it, Maha Bali and Nadine Aboulmagd from the American University in Cairo highlight the importance of describing the potential and reality of open education in the context of specific and complex cultural environments. In this chapter, they contextualize "open" from an Egyptian perspective and refer to different open educational practices that they have been involved in, including the creation of Arabic content based on Western models (e.g., Edraak MOOCs, Wikipedia Arabic, and Tahrir Academy). In addition, Bali and Aboulmagd discuss the creation of local OERs using local models, the reuse of existing English-language Global North content (e.g., MITx with AUC/AUB, translating edX content in Edraak, etc.), and participation in existing connectivist MOOCs as facilitators. These authors also describe an open project co-founded by one of the authors called "Virtually Connecting". Importantly, this project challenges the marginalization of Global South scholars and others in education such as contingent academics, graduate students, and others. In doing so, they highlight how openness, when contextualized to different regions, can look vastly different and have multiple faces.

Chapter 5 takes us into a critical discussion of OER and issues to ponder taking the plunge into open textbooks and other forms of open content. In this chapter, Rajiv S. Jhangiani from Kwantlen Polytechnic University in British Columbia, Canada, describes five critical pitfalls that may thwart the efforts of academics and commercial interests to widen equitable access to education via OERs. These problems and pitfalls include the assumption that all students have access to digital technologies. Another issue relates to the overreliance on under-compensated or voluntary academic labor to create OER. A third pitfall is the ignorance of critical accessibility requirements while developing OER. The fourth issue relates to the disregard for data privacy when utilizing educational technologies. Finally, there is the mounting problem of the undermining of the spirit and practice of "open" education with the entry of commercial publishers into the OER space. Each of these challenges and issues is addressed in this chapter.

Chapter 6 was written by Tian Belawati from Universitas Terbuka (UT) (i.e., the Indonesia Open University). Belawati describes how MOOCs are being designed and implemented to increase access to quality educational opportunities in the fourth most populated nation on earth. As she notes, the first MOOC in Indonesia was offered by a private university known as the Ciputra University in 2013, followed by UT in 2014. Even though several universities and organizations such as SEAMEO-SEAMOLEC (South East Asian Ministry of Education Organization Regional Center for Open Learning), IndonesiaX, and SPADA have followed the initiative, the ability for Indonesia to fully take advantage of ample MOOC resources is still a long way off. According to

Belawati, Indonesia needs a systematic campaign and an awareness-raising effort to make MOOCs beneficial to the greater part of Indonesian society. As someone who initially started working at the UT in 1985 just after its inception and has twice been its rector, Dr. Belawati has a highly unique lens in which to view the emergence of MOOCs and open education in her country.

Chapter 7 comes from Som Naidu from the University of the South Pacific, Fiji Islands, and Shironica P. Karunanayaka from the Open University of Sri Lanka. Importantly, Naidu and Karunanayaka demonstrate how MOOCs are being shifted from being overly content- and teaching-centric to a more learner- and learning-oriented focus in order to better mesh with local educational needs. As these authors argue, there is a better way to design MOOCs, and this alternative approach is about starting with the learning *context* and asking what is it that we want the learners to be able to do, and what are their possible learning outcomes. Next, there is a need to design a learning experience that will be able to offer MOOC participants an internship in solving real-world problems. Such an approach entails a radical paradigm shift in the design of MOOCs. Admittedly, this kind of shift in perceptions and perspectives about teaching and learning will not readily occur without careful redesign of conventional choreographies. In response, this chapter describes the development of a redesign process that is based on thinking around general systems theory.

In Chapter 8, Deepak Bhartu and Som Naidu from the University of the South Pacific, Fiji Islands explain the importance of designing MOOCs that are appropriate to the technological infrastructures that are accessible by learners in emerging economies such as Fiji where the high-tech affordances of more developed countries are not yet possible. As they put it, in developing contexts, where direct access to learning opportunities is either lacking or restricted for various reasons, a different kind of MOOC architecture is required. Contemporary MOOCs emanating from developed educational contexts tend to include learning resources that require large bandwidth to access, thereby moving them beyond the reach of the majority of learners in developing educational contexts. To be able to serve the needs of learners in resource-limited educational contexts, it is imperative that MOOCs are designed with a different perspective including innovative architecture and educational resources. In response, this chapter describes early efforts in the development of MOOCs at the University of the South Pacific, and especially their focus on climate change which is an area of enormous local and regional concern, as well as very deserving of global attention.

The sixth chapter in this section is from Baman Kumar Ghimire and Bishwa Raj Gautam in Nepal. In Chapter 9, Ghimire and Gautam offer an intriguing look at how MOOCs are being used by high school teachers to spark learner interests and increase the level of educational engagement of young Nepali students. As they describe, lively, interactive pedagogical practices played a key role in their MOOC initiative, effectively demonstrating how MOOCs can broaden and brighten the current and future educational possibilities of learners in countries with limited or inadequate resources such as Nepal. Importantly, the chapter explains how MOOCs in one of the least developed countries became a highly successful learning tool. It also attempts to delineate the formula that led to this success. By reading this chapter about educational innovation in Nepal, teachers, instructional developers, and other professionals may obtain insights into designing successful online and open education courses through effective involvement of committed educators and advocates.

In the next chapter in this section (i.e., Chapter 10), Jaime Sánchez and José Reyes-Rojas from Chile provide an important overview of the state of MOOCs in Latin America. As they point out, the majority of existing MOOCs offerings, as well as related publications, are from North America and Europe. Latin American institutions, in contrast, have been late entries to the MOOC world. To make matters worse, scientific information on the state of MOOCs in Latin America, while slowly evolving, is still scattered, incomplete, and often confusing in terms of the actual developments, implementations, and research. To address this concern, Sánchez and Reyes-Rojas extensively researched the scientific production around MOOCs in Latin America (2014–2019), including publications in two languages, English and Spanish.

This Chilean research team conducted a systematic review of the research literature concerning the studies, research, reports, and experiences informed in the indexed scientific literature concerning MOOCs in Latin America. Sánchez and Reyes-Rojas characterized the phenomenon to draw some main trends and issues. In particular, they address research questions concerning the distribution of the scientific productivity throughout the scientific data bases chosen, and the types of documents/publications. They also explore the study areas, impact of this productivity of MOOCs in Latin America on the scientific community, the profiles of the most productive MOOC researchers, and the places, institutions, nuclei, and programs from where that scientific production emanates. In the end, Sánchez and Reyes-Rojas offer a comprehensive picture and characterization of the MOOC phenomenon in Latin America via what may be the first attempt to perform a systematic literature research study of it.

Finally, in Chapter 11, Trang Phan from California State University at Fresno discusses the emotional benefits of diversity in MOOCs as seen in her groundbreaking dissertation study. The purpose of her qualitative study was to describe the emotional benefits of teaching and learning resulting from exposure to highly diverse global audiences and expectations in MOOCs. Participants were 15 instructors and instructional designers in American higher educational institutions who were involved in designing and delivering MOOC courses on the Coursera platform to learners in hundreds of countries throughout the world. Phan explains how these MOOC course designers and instructors adapted their courses to a wide range of learners, whether from the Global North or Global South. Multiple roles of participants in their MOOC design, development, and delivery are described. Also detailed are their perceptions of diversity, including some of the key merits as well as several marked challenges. Phan also describes how exposure to global learners has enabled these MOOC instructors and instructional designers to be more culturally sensitive and compassionate in their thoughts and acts towards engaging global learners with the course content and associated learning activities. Those teaching or developing MOOCs for the Global South should find high value and personal meaning in her scholarship.

4
THE DIFFERENT FACES OF OPEN IN EGYPT

Maha Bali and Nadine Aboulmagd

MOOC Hype and Open Education Realities in the Global South

The sudden hype about MOOCs from 2012 has slowed down, but MOOCs live on. Although most MOOCs are in English and from the Global North (cf. Bali, 2014), there are now numerous MOOCs from different parts of the world in different languages (Bali & Sharma, 2017; Adham & Lundqvist, 2015). MOOC pedagogies and epistemologies vary across the spectrum of xMOOCs, cMOOCs, and pMOOCs (cf. Bali, 2014; Bali, Crawford, Jensen, Signorelli, & Zamora, 2015; Bonk, Lee, Reeves, & Reynolds, 2017).

Advances in educational technologies, including open education and MOOCs, mostly tend to reproduce the balance of power between Global North and Global South, with geopolitical power dynamics tending to "interfere with the quality and effectiveness of teaching and learning" (Bali & Sharma, 2017, p. 27). For example, Africans are portrayed almost exclusively as the recipients rather than producers of knowledge (Asino, 2018) even when that knowledge is not relevant to local contexts (Mboa Nkoudou, 2016).

Openness in access to information has not challenged the power and hegemony of who determines which information becomes accessible: including/excluding particular content can reproduce inequalities and perpetuate dominant ideologies which further disadvantage oppressed and colonized populations (Knox, 2013). Although openness "can become a source of epistemic alienation and neocolonialism in the South" (Piron et al., 2017, quoted, translated, in Nobes, 2017, n.p.), the creation of OERs can become an opportunity for historically marginalized populations to use the Internet to amplify their voices and share their knowledge and stories, to become part of the global conversation (Arinto, Hodgkinson-Williams, King, Cartmill, & Willmers, 2017). According to Anant Agrawal, the Chief Executive of edX, many participants in their MOOCs are from the Arab world so there is, in a general sense, an awareness growing in the region about MOOCs as a concept and educational innovation, and in specific that content of these courses need to be translated and offered in Arabic (Adham & Lundqvist, 2015) and many of those developing Arabic platforms do just that; offer MOOCs by Arabs for Arabs.

While OERs are free to use, they are not free to produce (Bali & Sharma, 2017). Global South participation in the open movement requires resources such as stable electricity, strong infrastructure, affordable high bandwidth Internet, and digital literacy—and these require governments or external funding agencies to develop (Hodgkinson-Williams, 2018). Research on OER for Development (ROER4D, reported in Arinto et al., 2017), shows that many in the Global South use online materials regardless of the licenses on them, and that the majority of OERs are in English and require translation to be used in local contexts. Moreover, few educators have the time, resources, or technical knowhow to adapt OERs: most use them as is, and as such, cannot counter the colonial and hegemonic dimension of the knowledge in them.

Openness can be viewed as multidimensional, including technical, legal, cultural, pedagogical, and financial dimensions (Hodgkinson-Williams, 2018), including MOOCs, OERs, and Open Educational Practices. MOOCs include xMOOCs which run on platforms such as Coursera, edX, Rwaq, and Edraak, and which have defined start and end points, and are offered by an institution; and their predecessors, cMOOCs, which are more participatory and run on connectivist principles where knowledge is distributed and networked amongst participants (see Aboulmagd, 2018; Bali, 2014; Conole, 2016). These two MOOC types are on a spectrum and not mutually exclusive, or descriptive of all MOOCs: dual pathway MOOCs (Crosslin, 2018) and pMOOCs (ref) exist, and MOOCs differ on many dimensions including pedagogical design (Bali, 2014), degree of openness, use of multimedia, learner interaction and collaboration, and degree of instructor versus learner centeredness (Conole, 2016).

UNESCO (2012) defines OERs as "teaching, learning and research materials in any medium, digital or otherwise, that reside in the public domain or have been released under an open license that permits no-cost access, use, adaptation and redistribution by others with no or limited restrictions".

Cronin and MacLaren (2018) critique those in the field who wish to restrict definitions of open education to the creation, reuse, and adaptation of OER, and instead suggest the more expansive definition used by The Cape Town Open Education Declaration (2007, para. 4):

> open education is not limited to just open educational resources. It also draws upon open technologies that facilitate collaborative, flexible learning and the open sharing of teaching practices that empower educators to benefit from the best ideas of their colleagues. It may also grow to include new approaches to assessment, accreditation and collaborative learning.

Contextualizing Open for Egypt and the Region

It is important to note that K–16 public education in Egypt is officially free, though there are hidden costs and problems with quality (e.g., literacy rates in the 70% range versus school enrollments in the 80s and 90s—see Egypt Independent, 2017; UNESCO, undated). Among literate Egyptians, a small percentage are able to learn in English. The Internet penetration in Egypt is around 44% (MCIT, 2018), whereas mobile penetration exceeds 100% (MCIT, 2018). Therefore, for many Egyptians, MOOCs are irrelevant. The Arab League Educational, Cultural, and Scientific Organization (ALECSO), which consists of 22 Arab countries, is developing projects to promote open and online learning and increase the accessibility of education in the region (Jemni & Khribi, 2017).

The American University in Cairo (AUC), where the authors currently work, is a private English-language liberal arts institution, with a majority Egyptian and Arab student population. Within Egypt and the MENA region, this institution has mostly elite students. AUC features in some way in all three examples we focus on.

Open Educational Practices in Egypt: Inclusions and Exclusions

Rizk and Shaver assert that "the demand for access is . . . also the **right to participate as producers** in . . . creation, manipulation and extension" (2010, p. 6, emphasis added), but ROER4D findings suggest that:

> *educators and students in the Global South can be deprived of participatory parity due to the current domination of Western oriented epistemic perspectives and hegemonic English-language OER unless the*

opportunity to create or, at least, localise and redistribute OER in preferred languages and from alternative epistemic stances, is grasped and recognised.

(Hodgkinson-Williams, 2018, para. 3)

The OEPs (Open Educational Practices) we discuss are only a sample of practices that address at least one of the ways openness is being practiced in Egypt. We focus particularly on initiatives both co-authors have personally been involved in which OEPs were developed to reduce challenges by:

a. **Reusing or repurposing existing** open educational materials into local courses. The example we offer here is the integration of MITx materials at AUC.
b. **Remixing or translating existing** *content* into Arabic—which Edraak has done by translating some edX MOOCs and contextualizing them for the Arab world.
c. **Replicating or adapting existing** *models* into local languages and adapt them for context. Examples of this include Wikipedia Arabic. The example which we expand on here is original content on Edraak, the Arabic MOOC platform.
d. **Achieving parity of** *participation:* where Global South educators are facilitators, designers, creators, or leaders of open educational experiences such as cMOOCs and Virtually Connecting.
e. Creating local approaches to openness using local models (e.g., OpenMed project, A2K4D) which are attempts to encourage alternative epistemic stances. However, there is no space in this chapter to delve into all these worthwhile projects.

In what follows, we focus on MITx at AUC, Edraak Arabic MOOCs, and Virtually Connecting.

Reusing Open Content From Global North: Integration of MITx materials

This project was a collaboration between the Al-Ghurair Foundation for Education (AGFE), MIT's Office of Digital Learning (ODL), and two universities, AUC and the American University of Beirut (AUB). The program, entitled "Transforming Teaching and Learning in the Arab Region Through Online Learning", included several online meetings and a three-day Design Camp MIT offered in Cairo involving face-to-face training for AUC and AUB faculty (and faculty developers) on pedagogy to support integration of MITx materials into their credit-bearing courses (Ellozy, 2017). The choice of courses to redesign was guided by AGFE's interest in STEM undergraduate education, and by finding AUC/AUB credit-bearing courses whose content and outcomes overlapped with existing MITx courses.

We (the authors) were involved in the redesign of a mathematics course at AUC, and our experience does not necessarily apply to other courses at AUC or AUB. This information is based on unpublished research reported in Bali, Awwad, and Aboulmagd (2018) on the integration of MITx materials into an AUC mathematics course. We do not delve here into details of student feedback on the course, but highlight some general points that are transferable to other contexts of North–South collaboration.

In any collaboration, who makes decisions on how the collaboration will proceed? In this case, AGFE restricted the participating universities to undergraduate STEM courses which had an MITx equivalent, but other aspects of collaboration were participatory, and both MIT and AGFE were open to different opportunities for future collaboration. While undergraduate STEM courses were not AUC's strategic priority for digital education at the time, AUC welcomed this opportunity to learn via MIT, and both faculty and faculty developers were enthusiastic about the experience. The design camp was perceived to be useful by faculty participants. For example, mathematics professor Wafik Lotfallah said "we learned how to make things more interactive in class, correct our mistakes, [and] get reasonable expectations from the students' side" (Ellozy, 2017, p. 2). Faculty found MIT's approach, content, and process to teaching useful and a good model upon which to redesign their own courses, not only reusing the content into the existing course, but rethinking how they teach their own course.

One way to examine the effects and benefits of the MITx project is to view it from the lens of the 5 Rs of Openness, and question whether or not this project really does fulfill these aspirations. The 5 Rs are Retain, Reuse, Revise, Remix, and Redistribute (Wiley, 2014).

Retention, the right for users to make, own, and control copies of the content, was restricted by MITx; AUC faculty were not allowed to own the content or make copies, as all the content was uploaded on the edX platform, giving access to the faculty only to download their students' grades, rather than the material itself. Granted, that material is readily available in the edX MOOCs; however, there wasn't a way for faculty to add to the content in order to share ownership or autonomy, and faculty had no perpetual rights to continue using the content beyond the end date of the project. With regards to Reusing, which is the right to use the content in a wide range of ways, this was partially the case because AUC faculty were given a choice of whether to assign this content to students as an at-home online activity, or to go over them in class; however, AUC faculty could not download this content in order to reuse it in other ways. The third is Revise, which is the right to adapt, adjust, modify, or alter the content itself. This was slightly applicable as AUC faculty were allowed to remove parts of the content from the course; however, they were neither allowed to add anything to the content (technically did not have the permissions on the platform) nor change or alter parts of what was included in the course. Removal of parts was restricted to removing entire units, rather than only parts of the units. This was explained as a platform limitation; although edX is an open source platform, this rigidity seemingly imposed by the platform takes away from its potential openness. The AUC support staff were also not given administrator access on the platform in order to solve technical issues that surfaced during the semester, which were also not solved in a timely manner when reported to MITx administrators. The faculty were able to change deadlines for their student assessments, but not to modify the number of attempts allowed on quizzes, which were apparently hard-coded on the platform for each quiz. This rigidity created anxiety for AUC students. This brings us to the fourth element: Remix, which is the right to combine the original or revised content with other (open) content to create something new. The faculty's inability to add their own content to the course in order to remix it with the MITx content further shows the rather closed nature of the resource—students had to check Blackboard for regular course content and edX Edge for MIT content, and found the MIT content less organized to navigate. The fifth and final element is Redistribute, which is the right to share copies of the original content, your revisions, or your remixes with others. This was not possible as AUC did not have any rights to the material beyond using it in class.

If open implies to give autonomy and share ownership, the way this project was framed and implemented still reinforced the idea of North to South educational borrowing, rather than an open collaborative project with both parties equally participating in the overarching goal. As Bali and Sharma (2017) posit, even though MOOC providers like Edraak are advancing in the production of knowledge in the South, there still is an imbalance of power because the MOOC models and the universities that provide these MOOCs are very Westernized and in some cases are in fact American or European universities, rather than local ones. Analyzing the previous project using the 5 Rs, we could say that the project only partially fulfilled these, and the result was not as empowering as it had potential to be, despite good intentions of all involved.

In some instances, open practices are two-faced in the sense that some aspects are indeed open, but others are quite closed. This project was about using OERs in a closed environment and without much control from the instructors on the AUC side. Many of the limitations relate to the edX platform rather than the intentions of AGFE or MITx.

Arabic Content, Western Models: Focus on Edraak

According to Anant Agrawal, the Chief Executive of edX, many participants in their MOOCs are from the Arab world so there is, in a general sense, an awareness growing in the region about MOOCs as a concept and educational innovation, an opportunity to reach more Arab learners by translating and offering MOOCs in Arabic (Adham & Lundqvist, 2015). Edraak has translated many Western MOOCs, and both Rwaq and Edraak produce MOOCs by Arabs for Arabs.

Other Western open models that have been adapted into Arabic and other languages include Wikipedia, which is available in Arabic. Content is sometimes a translation of the English version, and sometimes, importantly, differently written content from an Arab epistemic perspective (e.g., the story of the 1973 war between Egypt and Israel is told completely differently in the English Wikipedia than the Arabic Wikipedia—both versions use the same set of facts to come up with different conclusions on the interpretation of that history and who won that war). In the past, Tahrir Academy aimed to go beyond Khan Academy's broadcasting pedagogy and offer interaction between learners besides instructional video; however, this project has shut down due to legislative restrictions on funding for NGOs in Egypt (Shams El-Din & Abd El-Galil, 2015). One of the initiatives that continues to this day is MOOCs offered in Arabic, offered via several platforms.

The prominent Arabic MOOC platform we will focus on is Edraak, which was established in 2014 by the Queen Rania Foundation in Jordan. Edraak aims to put the Arab world at the forefront of educational innovation through presenting important opportunities that could play an integral role in the revolution of education and learning (Edraak, 2019). We focus on the MOOCs by Arabs for Arabs, where material is fully developed and taught in the Arabic language. Edraak is based on the open-source edX platform, and most MOOCs on the platform follow the model of brief, instructor-centric instructional videos and multiple choice quizzes for assessment. While Edraak has adapted the platform to work better with Arabic, the platform itself has limited options for assessment, making it difficult to conduct creative assessments that do not have clear-cut correct answers. The inflexibility of edX restricts developers, instructors, and designers from adapting the technology to fit diverse pedagogical values, and does not quite embody openness. One aspect Edraak has done well is to encourage instructors to use social media outside the platform for social interaction (although at first, they discouraged it) and this also has the advantage of allowing learners to continue in a learning community beyond the dates of a course and outside edX's rigid discussion forum format.

Clinnin (2014) critiques some xMOOCs for not following good pedagogical practice: "[I]f MOOCs remain 'nonsocial media environment[s]' then ultimately MOOCs are a massive form of educational malpractice by perpetuating teacher-focused, knowledge disseminating according to the banking model as evidenced by quizzes and instructor-produced video lectures" (p. 158). Edraak MOOCs have largely followed this banking model approach, with occasional learner interaction. Even though Edraak is giving access to education to people who don't already have access, according to their mission, they are still requiring the learners to both have high speed Internet to watch the instructional videos, solve quizzes without Internet outages, and the necessary digital literacy to learn and interact with the platform. Also, even though the aim is to provide education to learners to help with their professional development, most of the courses on Edraak are practice- and skills-oriented rather than academic so it may not offer the necessary content knowledge, or at least an insufficient diversity of choices for learners. At launch, some of Edraak's content was original Arabic content, and some was translated from edX into Arabic and adapted, but more recently, they have been relying more on original content. While doing more practice-based MOOCs (such as interviewing skills or entrepreneurship skills) may be a way for Edraak to address the need for employability in the Arab world, this may feed into a neoliberal agenda of only addressing needs of the job market, rather than potentially expanding knowledge in a more liberating manner.

If employability were a goal of Edraak's, then one important missing dimension is that Edraak does not offer credentialing beyond free certificates of attendance. Many other MOOC platforms offer opportunities to take an exam at an exam center and receive a low-cost certificate that has more weight than the free one. As Czerniewicz (2015) points out, in Global South countries, learning without credentials is often not valued by employers. It is possible that Edraak is unable to implement a feasible financial model for this kind of certification to work, or that there are logistical hurdles.

Moreover, when choosing universities to partner with, Edraak chose the elite Westernized universities and their professors (Bali & Sharma, 2017), namely the American Universities in Beirut and Cairo.

Another important angle to consider is Edraak's implementation of learning analytics in order to develop and enhance the MOOCs provided on their platform by collecting data to try and address some of the learner issues that surface. Most learning analytics data however provide little insight about matters such as engagement and actual learning (Aboulmagd, 2018). Research done about learning analytics and learner engagement about a MOOC taught on Edraak showed that for that MOOC, analytics for the instructional videos, for example, are not indicative of whether the learners watched the videos or not, since the analytics record as instances of video watching simply when a video is *visited*, rather than whether it is *watched* in part or in whole. Another issue that surfaced from this research is that the platform does not collect learning analytics from learners who engage with the videos through the Edraak mobile app (Aboulmagd, 2018), and since many in the Arab world access their learning via mobile devices, the resulting analytics are grossly inaccurate representations.

Parity of Participation in Open Educational Experiences

Most cMOOCs focus more on the process of learning than any particular hegemonic content imparted by instructor(s), where learners interact and participate to drive the direction of the MOOC—facilitator(s) have strong roles in the cMOOCs, but their roles are usually more as guides than instructors (Bali, Crawford, Jessen, Signorelli, & Zamora, 2015). Parity of participation can occur when Global South voices are heard when they participate in cMOOCs (Bali & Sharma, 2014), but even more so if they are (co)-designers or creators (e.g., see the inclusive nature of Digital Writing Month described in Bali, 2019).

Challenging Academic Gatekeeping: Virtually Connecting

Virtually Connecting is an example of an OEP that arose out of needs and interests of the Global South, but has benefitted (particularly marginal) academics elsewhere. Conferences are important sites for academic knowledge sharing yet they reproduce inequality of access (Nicolson, 2018): the costs of travel and registration are prohibitive for Global South scholars, contingent faculty, and graduate students, and others cannot travel for health, social, financial, or logistical reasons—and recently, border restrictions directed most prominently against individuals from Muslim states (Nicolson, 2018).

Virtually Connecting was co-founded by an Egyptian academic (Maha) and a Canadian Ph.D. student (Rebecca J. Hogue). VC affords marginalized and often excluded communities a voice and opportunity to "participate in a global conversation" (Arinto et al., 2017) at conferences in an equitable manner. VC invites virtual participants into hallway conversations with onsite participants and speakers via web-based video conferencing. These are not conference presentations and broadcasts—but rather informal, reciprocal hallway-type conversations. These conversations are livestreamed and recorded for those who are unable to participate live.

VC is neither OER nor MOOC, but a connected and connectivist open online volunteer movement (Bali, Caines, DeWaard, & Hogue, 2016) which fulfills DeRosa and Jhangiani's (2017) understanding of open pedagogy as learner-centered, democratic, and facilitating human communication and collaboration among diverse people from around the globe—and being motivated by a desire to promote social justice. Koseoglu and Bozkurt (2019) mention VC as an informal hybrid space for "enhancing pedagogic and narrative capacities . . . as it opens up a space of dialogue that is independent, inclusive, and organically developed" (p. 169).

Beckingham (2018) refers to how VC founders eventually became an "interconnected community and developed a team of volunteers across the globe" (p. 164) and how the variety of modes of participation (from being in the conversation onsite or virtually, to watching live, to watching the recording) makes it an inclusive space for people who are still unsure how deeply they are willing to participate. We would add that this also enables people of varying time zones and bandwidth to benefit.

Although English-language fluency is still needed for such a global community, we have recently been clarifying languages our volunteers speak and have spontaneously conducted some sessions in multiple languages, and also planned sessions in German and Portuguese. There is potential to grow beyond English—but of course, most international conferences are in English, especially those related to educational technology. A notable exception is eLearning Africa, which offers simultaneous translations across English, French, and Arabic, addressing the majority languages of the region.

Also, even though reasonably good bandwidth and digital literacies are needed, we insist on using technologies that work on low bandwidth (Google hangouts work well on 4G in Egypt, for example) and mobile (the mobile app works really well) and our volunteers work closely with participants to help them figure out the (relatively simple, once you get used to it) technology. We use Hangouts on Air (YouTube live) because it automatically livestreams and records to YouTube, without requiring the facilitator of the session to upload video later (something that takes hours on a typical Egyptian DSL home connection). However, the use of Google comes with all the risks of using Google products that collect data on users and change their mode of operation often without notifying users. Moreover, YouTube remains banned in certain countries altogether.

VC has room for improvement in becoming a more inclusive space as its volunteers aspire to, and ensuring that marginalized voices are centered and not overshadowed by powerful voices in conversations (see Bali et al., 2016; Bali et al., 2017). Nonetheless, VC is still regarded as a useful open educational practice by participants. For example (see Bali, 2018 for several), one participant whose Visa got refused three times to a conference eventually was able to participate in the event via Virtually Connecting, and later became a volunteer in the team. Graduate students have said that it helps them speak directly and informally with keynote speakers and known scholars previously inaccessible to them (Bali et al., 2016).

Discussion

The majority of existing MOOCs and OERs benefit what Andreotti (2006, p. 45) calls the "elite global professional class", i.e., those who have English-language and digital fluency, those who have access to Internet and well-connected devices (Adham & Lundqvist, 2015). In this chapter, three examples of initiatives to make learning more open, some more successful than others, have been described.

The MITx project initially targeted an already privileged class via the American institutions in Egypt and Lebanon. Even with good intentions to support good pedagogical use of their material, the project implementation did not challenge global power dynamics. In the end, we consider it an incomplete approach to openness.

Models like Edraak overcome the English-language fluency barrier, but continue to benefit the mostly educated, digitally literate class who have access to well-connected devices (because their content is video-centric), and are therefore already privileged in some way. They may be able to reach learners who are less mobile, whether due to physical disabilities or women with family responsibilities or restrictions, but they do not offer those learners credentials. Nor do these models adapt substantially in ways that better address the Arab learner or provide a more locally or contextually relevant education. However, it still fills an important gap of offering Arabic-language educational content.

Virtually Connecting still requires, for the most part, English-language fluency, reasonably high bandwidth, and digital literacy; however, its main target are academics, and within that already elite class, academics who are otherwise marginalized are able to benefit: those from emerging economies, contingent faculty, graduate students, parents with young children, people with health issues and disabilities, and those who come up against visa restrictions. Also, the main advantage here is in the two-way reciprocal exchange of knowledge between those privileged enough to be at conferences and those who are perpetually excluded from such experiences—there is parity of participation. Virtually Connecting's main benefit here is in the dialogical nature of the connection and flow of knowledge in both directions in an equitable manner.

Conclusion

If we were to understand open education from the metaphor of seats at tables, then the typical model of inviting others to use what has been created and openly available or openly licensed is simply to ask someone to join an existing table with rules already set and inflexible. It is therefore not truly open or inclusive as it does not take into account the difference in that new member's context and resources that would require changes in order to have equitable experiences and outcomes. It also does not account for whether one's table meets the needs of that new member at all.

Inviting a person to replicate and adapt a table in their own way is one step better in that they have an opportunity to recreate it differently and not just to translate its language. However, if the tools available remain those initially created, their constraints and their model may make it difficult for the adapters to innovate in ways that better benefit their local context. This is the case for Edraak that provides Arabic-language MOOCs, but reproduces many of the disadvantages of xMOOCs, partly due to the rigidity of the edX platform that promotes teacher-centered learning and assessment.

What is needed is parity of participation in creating the table and setting its rules. At first glance, VC may appear as offering an inferior seat at an existing table. However, on closer inspection, it is the creation of a completely new hybrid table and forcing it into a previously exclusively face-to-face space. It creates reciprocal conversations that not only allow marginalized remote participants to learn from conference attendees, but also vice versa: attendees listen to and learn from virtual participants, and their voices then get heard in a space from which they were previously entirely excluded. While Virtually Connecting cannot solve all problems for all people, its creators were marginal in some way (a Global South mother partnering with a graduate student) and many volunteers are marginal in other ways that limit their conference participation—and VC is a process developed by those who will benefit from it, not by a dominant group gifting it to them.

For MOOCs and open education to be truly empowering for people in countries like Egypt, they need to be reimagined in a participatory manner, where those from local contexts are able to define what they consider to be pressing challenges and imagine their own solutions, using their own epistemologies and content and processes, explicitly remaining aware of existing models from the North, but also striving not to allow hegemony of Western knowledge and technologies. Such solutions may not be straightforward, they may indeed not be technological . . . and they may or may not be open.

Maha Bali is Associate Professor of Practice at the Center for Learning and Teaching at the American University in Cairo where she has been a faculty developer since 2003. She holds a PhD in Education from the University of Sheffield and teaches digital literacies and intercultural learning to undergraduate students. She is on the editorial boards of *Teaching in Higher Education*; *Learning Media, and Technology*; the Online Learning Journal; *Hybrid Pedagogy*, and the *Journal of Pedagogic Development*. Dr Bali is the co-founder of Virtually Connecting. She writes regularly for Prof Hacker and her own blog at http://blog.mahabali.me.

Nadine Aboulmagd is Senior Instructional Designer at the Center for Learning and Teaching at the American University in Cairo, where she supports faculty in designing their courses (i.e., online, face-to-face, blended, and MOOCs), designing engaging learning experiences, integrating technology in their classrooms, and developing course content. Aboulmagd has a Master of Arts degree in Educational Leadership with a concentration in higher education from the Graduate School of Education (GSE) at AUC and is a member of Virtually Connecting, holding the role of Middle East and Africa Lead Buddy. Her main areas of research include massive open online courses (MOOCs), online and blended learning, learner engagement, adult learning, instructional design, educational technology, and faculty development.

References

Aboulmagd, N. (2018). *Learner engagement in a MOOC in the Arab world: A case study analysis using the community of inquiry framework* (Master's thesis). The American University in Cairo, Cairo, Egypt.

Adham, R. S., & Lundqvist, K. O. (2015). MOOCS as A method of distance education in the Arab world—a review paper. *European Journal of Open, Distance and E-Learning, 18*(1), 123–138. doi:10.1515/eurodl-2015-0009

Andreotti, V. (2006). Soft versus critical global citizenship education. *Policy & Practice: A Development Education Review*, 3 (Autumn), pp. 40–51.

Arinto, P., Hodgkinson-Williams, C., King, T., Cartmill, T., & Willmers, M. (2017). Research on open educational resources for development in the global South: Project landscape. In Hodgkinson-Williams, C., & Arinto, P. B. (Eds.), *Adoption and impact of OER in the Global South* (pp. 3–26). Retrieved from https://doi.org/10.5281/zenodo.1038980

Asino, T. (2018, July). *Bridging Afrikan and global perspectives about technology in education*. Keynote at Festival of eLearning, University of Capetown, Online.

Bali, M. (2014). MOOC pedagogy: gleaning good practice from existing MOOCs. *Journal of Online Learning and Teaching, 10*(1), 44–56. Retrieved from: http://jolt.merlot.org/vol10no1/bali_0314.pdf

Bali, M. (2018). Challenging academic gatekeeping: Open scholarship and virtually connecting. *E/merge Africa Festival of e-Learning*. Keynote address; online conference organized by University of Cape Town, South Africa.

Bali, M. (2018). The unbearable whiteness of the digital. In Kim, D., & Stommel, J. (eds). *Disrupting the digital humanities*. Punctum books.

Bali, M., Awwad, A., & Aboulmagd, N. (2018). *MITx-AUC Report—Calculus Pilot Spring 2018*. Unpublished internal report.

Bali, M., Beckingham, S., Zamora, M., Caines, A., Hogue, R. J., & Weller, M. (2017, April 5). Breaking the physical presence barrier: Virtually Connecting as an approach to open, inclusive conferences. *Open Educational Resources (#OER17)*. London, UK.

Bali, M., Caines, A., DeWaard, H., & Hogue, R. (2016). Ethos and practice of a connected learning movement: interpreting virtually connecting through alignment with theory and survey results. *Online Learning, 20*(4). DOI: http://dx.doi.org/10.24059/olj.v20i4.965

Bali, M., Crawford, M., Jessen, R., Signorelli, P., & Zamora, M. (2015). What makes a cMOOC community endure? Multiple participant perspectives from diverse cMOOCs. *Educational Media International, 52*(2), 100–115. DOI: https://doi.org/10.1080/09523987.2015.1053290

Bali, M., & Sharma, S. (2014, April 11). Bonds of difference: Participation as inclusion. *Hybrid Pedagogy*. Retrieved from www.hybridpedagogy.com/journal/bonds-difference-participation-inclusion/

Bali, M., & Sharma, S. (2017). 3 Envisioning post-colonial MOOCs. *Massive Open Online Courses and Higher Education: What Went Right, What Went Wrong and Where to Next?* 26–44.

Beckingham, S. (2018). Using social media to learn from conferences. In C. Popovic (Ed.), *Learning from academic conferences*. Leiden: Brill | Sense.

Bonk, C., Lee, M., Reeves, T., & Reynolds, T. (2017). The emergence and design of massive open online courses (MOOCs). In R. A. Reiser & J. V. Demsey (Eds.), *Trends and issues in instructional design and technology* (4th ed., pp. 250–258). Boston, MA: Pearson.

Clinnin, K. (2014). Redefining the MOOC: Examining the multilingual and community potential of massive online courses. *Journal of Global Literacies, Technologies, and Emerging Pedagogies, 2*(3), 140–62.

Conole, G. (2016). MOOCs as disruptive technologies: Strategies for enhancing the learner experience and quality of MOOCs. *Revista De Educación a Distancia, 50*(2). doi:10.6018/red/50/2

Cronin, C., & MacLaren, I. (2018). Conceptualising OEP: A review of theoretical and empirical literature in open educational practices. *Open Praxis, 10*(2). doi:https://doi.org/10.5944/openpraxis.10.2.825

Crosslin, M. (2018). Exploring self-regulated learning choices in a customisable learning pathway MOOC. *Australasian Journal of Educational Technology, 34*(1), 131–144.

Czerniewicz, L. (2015, September 10). Inequality in higher education (keynote). *Association for Learning Technology Conference*, Manchester, UK.

DeRosa, R., & Jhangiani, R. (2017). Open pedagogy. In E. Mays (Ed.), *A guide to making open textbooks with students*. Rebus Community for Open Textbook Creation (PressBooks). Retrieved from https://press.rebus.community/makingopentextbookswithstudents/

Edraak. (2019). *About us*. Retrieved from www.edraak.org/en/about-us/

Egypt Independent. (2017, September 7). Egypt illiteracy rates stand at 14.4% for males, 26% for females: CAPMAS. *Egypt Independent*. Retrieved from www.egyptindependent.com/egypt-illiteracy-rates-stand-14-4-males-26-females-capmas/

Ellozy, A. R. (2017, November 14). Issue Three: MIT Office of Digital Learning conducts design camp for AUC and AUB faculty. *New Chalk Talk*, *16*(3). Retrieved from https://documents.aucegypt.edu/Docs/llt_clt/Chalk%20Talk/Vol%2016/MITx%20New%20Chalk%20Talk_volume%2016.issue%203.pdf

Hodgkinson-Williams, C. (2018, April 17). Guest post: Provocation for #breakopen by Cheryl Hodgkinson-Williams. *Towards Openness (blog)*. Retrieved from https://towards-openness.org/guest-post/provocation-for-breakopen-by-cheryl-hodgkinson-williams/

Jemni, M., & Khribi, M. K. (2017). Toward empowering open and online education in the Arab world through OER and MOOCs. In M. Jemni & K. M. Kinshuk (Eds.), *Open education: from OER to MOOCs* (p. 73). Berlin and Heidelberg: Springer. Lecture Notes in Educational Technology. Retrieved from https://link.springer.com/chapter/10.1007/978-3-662-52925-6_4

Knox, J. (2013). The limitations of access alone: Moving towards open processes in education technology. *Open Praxis*, *5*(1), 21–29.

Koseoglu, S., & Bozkurt, A. (2018). # DigPed Narratives in Education: Critical Perspectives on Power and Pedagogy. *Online Learning Journal*, *22*(3), 157–174.

MCIT. (2018, April). ICT indicators in brief. *Ministry of Communication and Information Technology*. Retrieved from www.mcit.gov.eg/Upcont/Documents/Publications_362018000_ICT%20Indicators_inbrief_%20April_2018_EN.pdf

Mboa Nkoudou, T. H. (2016). Les injustices cognitives en Afrique subsaharienne: réflexions sur les causes et les moyens de lutte'. In Piron, F., Madiba, D., & Regulus, S. (eds.), *Justice cognitive, libre accès et savoirs locaux*. Pressbooks. Retrieved from https://scienceetbiencommun.pressbooks.pub/justicecognitive1/

Nicolson, D. (2018, August 28). For some, borders are now an insurmountable barrier to attending international academic conferences. *Impact of Social Sciences LSE Blog*. Retrieved from http://blogs.lse.ac.uk/impactofsocialsciences/2018/08/28/for-some-borders-are-now-an-insurmountable-barrier-to-attending-international-academic-conferences/

Nobes, A. (2017, December 8). Must we decolonize open access? Perspectives from Francophone Africa. *Journalologik*. Retrieved from http://journalologik.uk/?p=149

Piron, F., Dibounje Madiba, M. S., & Regulus, S. (2016). *Justice cognitive, libre accès et savoirs locaux*. Pressbooks. Retrieved from https://scienceetbiencommun.pressbooks.pub/justicecognitive1/

Rizk, N., & Shaver, L. (2010). *Access to knowledge in Egypt*. London: Bloomsbury Academic.

Shams El-Din, M., & Abd El-Galil, T. (2015, August 25). Tahrir academy's shutdown casts a shadow over educational NGOs. *Al-Fanar Media*. Retrieved from www.al-fanarmedia.org/2015/08/tahrir-academys-shutdown-casts-a-shadow-over-educational-ngos/

UNESCO (2012). *2012 Paris OER Declaration*. Retrieved from https://unesdoc.unesco.org/ark:/48223/pf0000246687

UNESCO. (n.d.). UIS: Egypt. *UNESCO*. Retrieved from https://en.unesco.org/countries/egypt

Wiley, D. (2014). The access compromise and 5th R [blog post]. *Open Content*. Retrieved from https://opencontent.org/blog/archives/3221

5

DELIVERING ON THE PROMISE OF OPEN EDUCATIONAL RESOURCES

Pitfalls and Strategies

Rajiv S. Jhangiani

"Higher education shall be equally accessible to all on the basis of merit," or at least so proclaims Article 26 of the United Nations' Universal Declaration of Human Rights (1948). However, whether due to a shortage of seats, deficient infrastructure, or geographic or economic barriers, access to higher education remains an elusive dream for millions. This access dilemma is true in the Global South as well as the Global North, where education continues to shift in many countries from being considered a public good worthy of societal investment to an individual choice available only to those who enjoy significant privilege. For example, according to a study commissioned by the U.S. Department of Education, in just the first decade of this century, an estimated 2.4 million students in that country could not attend or complete college because of the cost barrier (Advisory Committee on Student Financial Assistance, 2006). Indeed, higher education is structured to reinforce and replicate existing power structures in ways that are sometimes blatant (e.g., legacy admissions) and sometimes subtle (e.g., exorbitant textbook costs).

While there are numerous institutional innovations and international initiatives that are being developed and deployed to address this problem (e.g., MOOCs, OERu, Commonwealth of Learning, etc.), in this chapter I will discuss the potential of open educational resources (OER) to help widen equitable access to higher education, including within traditional post-secondary institutions. In addition, given increasing government and institutional support of the creation, adaptation, and adoption of OER through both funding and policy, I will briefly outline a few pitfalls that OER advocates and practitioners and policy makers must attend to if they wish to deliver on the great promise of OER.

The Problem of Unaffordable Textbooks

The cost of commercial textbooks in North America rose by over 1,000% between 1977 and 2016, and by 204% between 1997 and 2018 (Perry, 2018). For context, this was between three and four times the rate of inflation and, incredibly, at a higher rate than any other consumer good. These data often surprise faculty who select and assign these expensive textbooks to their students. But faculty ignorance of the price of commercial textbooks is facilitated by what is a good example principal-agent problem, wherein one person (an agent) makes decisions that impacts another (the principal; Eisenhardt, 1989). What these faculty members might want to remind themselves when selecting textbooks is that the true cost of expensive textbooks is measured in terms of educational outcomes. For example, a survey of over 22,000 students in Florida showed that two-thirds of undergraduate students in that state do not purchase at least some of their required textbooks because of their high cost, while nearly half tend to choose or drop courses on the basis of textbook costs (Florida Virtual Campus, 2016). These findings have been echoed by recent research in British Columbia, where students who make these same choices were found to be more likely to hold a student loan, work more hours during the week, or identify as members of a visible minority group (Jhangiani & Jhangiani, 2017).

The problem of unaffordable textbooks, while certainly not the most significant contributing factor to inequitable access to higher education, is a tangible issue that the open education movement has great potential to tackle. Indeed, the creation, adaptation, and adoption of open textbooks and other OER is rapidly becoming normative practice in North America. For example, OpenStax, an open textbook project based at Rice University, reports that its 29 textbooks have been adopted by 48% of all U.S. post-secondary institutions (Ruth, 2018). In British Columbia, open textbooks from the curated BCcampus repository have been adopted by more than 450 faculty at 40 institutions (BCcampus, 2018). The UK Open Textbook project was launched in 2017 (UKOpenTextbooks, n.d.). And the University of Minnesota–based Open Textbook Network continues to grow rapidly, exceeding 600 campus members at the time of writing, including expansion into Australia.

Although the use of open textbooks is a burgeoning phenomenon in the Global North, despite significant challenges (cf. Hodgkinson-Williams, 2014, 2015), it is also beginning to gain traction in pockets across the Global South for reasons that range from a preference for localized content to reducing textbook costs. For example, approximately 10 million Siyavula open textbooks were printed and distributed to government schools across South Africa between 2012 and 2014 (Pitt & Beckett, 2014). In addition, OER have been integrated into the teacher education program at the Open University of Sri Lanka (Karunanayaka & Naidu, 2017). These are not singular initiatives. In fact, projects to support OER creation and use by teachers have been launched in India (Kasinathan & Ranganathan, 2017), Afghanistan (Oates, Goger, Hashimi, & Farahmand, 2017), Colombia (Sáenz, Hernandez, & Hernández, 2017), and Mauritius, Tanzania, Uganda (Wolfenden, Auckloo, Buckler, & Cullen, 2017). In a survey of 295 randomly selected instructors from 29 higher education institutions in Brazil, Chile, Colombia, Ghana, Kenya, South Africa, India, Indonesia, and Malaysia, 51% reported having used OER (de Oliveira Neto, Pete, Daryono, & Cartmill, 2017).

With a view to sustainability, many post-secondary institutions have been taking steps to embed support for open textbooks in several key ways including within their policies (e.g., tenure and promotion criteria), procedures (e.g., course development workflow), practices (e.g., course registration timetables that indicate courses that are using OER), roles (e.g., the creation of OER librarian positions), and budgets (e.g., allocations for OER grants). Open textbook initiatives themselves have grown more intentional and programmatic such that a number of institutions across North America now offer entire academic programs with zero required textbook costs, known as Z Degrees or Zed Creds in the U.S. and Canada, respectively (Bliss, 2015).

On the surface, the argument for OER as a force for equity is straightforward and powerful: Ensure free, immediate, and permanent access to educational resources and marginalized students who disproportionately suffer as a result of high textbook costs will disproportionately benefit, in both economic and educational terms (see Colvard, Watson, & Park, 2018 for evidence of this disproportionate impact). However, alongside this transformational potential lies several pitfalls, including inequitable access to the technology and platforms necessary to deliver OER, an over-reliance on voluntary academic labor to create OER, a neglect of accessibility requirements when developing OER, disregard for data privacy, and the practices of commercial publishers of "open washing" (explained later in this chapter).

Digital Redlining

A term derived from racist housing loan practices in the United States known as "redlining," digital redlining examines the causes of the digital divide, including "a set of education policies, investment decisions, and IT practices that actively create and maintain class boundaries through strictures that discriminate against specific groups" (Gilliard & Culik, 2016). In the context of OER, considering digital redlining might interrogate the assumption that all students own or have access to internet-enabled devices or that they enjoy Internet access of sufficient quality, including when off campus. More broadly, considering digital redlining requires investigating whether initiatives that center on free digital textbooks are addressing or in fact exacerbating present inequities in the classroom. Strategies that may be deployed to tackle this issue include ensuring after-hours access to computing facilities on campus, establishing a no-cost student laptop/tablet loan program, delivering digital content offline (e.g., using CDs, USB drives, or other innovations such as the Commonwealth of Learning's Classroom-Without-Walls system), and exploring low-cost print (including print on demand) options for open textbooks.

Over-Relying on Voluntary Academic Labor

Although advocates of OER often articulate the importance of social justice and equity, this thinking is usually limited to students and not extended to the educators and subject matter experts who create or adapt OER. It is a fair appraisal to say that the OER movement is guilty of an overreliance on voluntary academic labor (or at least severely under-compensated academic labor) to create, peer-review, and contextualize OER. This practice perpetuates an implicit form of creative redlining, one that reserves the capacity to create or adapt OER for those who already enjoy positions of privilege, such as the tenured or those who do not need the income (Jhangiani, 2018). Unfortunately, problems that stem from a lack of diversity in design teams have long been witnessed in products that range from automatic soap dispensers (that have been known to fail to recognize hands with darker skin tones) to voice recognition applications (that fail to correctly interpret women's voices). If the OER movement values not just diversity but also inclusion, it must ensure equitable access not just to knowledge but also to knowledge creation. Providing incentives for OER creation and adaptation, whether during the tenure and promotion process, time releases, or other forms of institutional recognition is an effective strategy. However, institutions should ensure that these incentives and opportunities are also available to contingent and non-tenure-track faculty.

Overlooking Accessibility

Consider the following: Open textbooks that are published in only PDF format; images that are embedded without including alternative text; videos that are uploaded without captioning; and charts that cannot be interpreted by those with color blindness. These are just four of the many ways in which the issue of accessibility is often overlooked when trying to address access via open educational resources. Although resources such as BCcampus' Open Textbook Accessibility Toolkit (Coolidge, Doner, Robertson, & Gray, 2018) and projects such as the Inclusive Design Research Centre's Flexible Learning for Open Education provide guidance and support to the OER movement, inclusive design practices have not yet been universally adopted. A simple but effective strategy to address this issue is for institutions and granting agencies to embed accessibility requirements among the criteria for OER projects that receive funding while ensuring that the necessary training and support is made available (e.g., from the institution's Office for Services for Students with Disabilities).

Disregarding Data Privacy

Educators are too often unwitting brokers for surveillance capitalism. Whether it is the use of platforms like Turnitin, where students are required to submit their academic work for automated plagiarism detection or the use of the platforms of commercial publishers that monitor students' online activity, student data is often commodified and monetized by ed tech companies (Morris & Stommel, 2017). These concerns apply equally within open education, given both the number of commercial players entering this space and the number of groups using proprietary tools and platforms to achieve open ends. As Amy Collier reminds us:

> we have to realize that there is no such thing as harmless collection of data. Or benevolent collection of data. Much of what we collect could be used in ways we do not want it to be used, to harm or imperil our students. This disproportionately affects our most vulnerable students. Low-income students, students of color, LGTBQ+ students, students who are immigrants ... their data are most at risk to surveillance, discrimination. And many of our vulnerable students are less likely to have experience with digital literacy skills.
>
> *(2017, para 33)*

Two tools that are helpful when critically evaluating digital tools and platforms are Audrey Watters's "Audrey Test" for education (2012) and Jesse Stommel's (2016) critical evaluation activity from his Digital Studies 101 course.

Open Washing

Following the initial strategies of denial (e.g., "OER are not a threat to commercial publishing") and discrediting (e.g., "OER are low quality"), commercial textbook companies have lost enough market share to open textbooks to turn to a third strategy: co-option. At the present time most of the large traditional textbook publishers have launched their own "open" platforms. However, as with the environmentalism movement and the phenomenon of greenwashing, we are increasingly witnessing something that has been referred to as "open washing" (Openwashing, n.d.) or sometimes "*faux*-pen" (Searls, 2009). In simple terms, open washing involves a company using the language of open education to dress up what is otherwise a traditional, proprietary practice. For example, such a practice may involve hosting open textbooks on a platform that requires registration and password protection, which, in turn, enables data tracking, surveillance, and monetization. Another instance of this less-than-honest approach is the use of the term "open" to describe resources that are not openly licensed or that may not be revised or remixed (Wiley, 2015). Still another widely deployed tactic is to impose restrictions on uses of content such as copying and pasting or printing. Institutions of higher education are, thus, increasingly wading through waters that are being deliberately muddied, often in a way that focuses solely on alleged cost savings to students at the expense of faculty choice, student agency, and data privacy. Although excellent efforts are being made to articulate the values and practices of "open" (see the CARE framework; Petrides, Levin, & Watson, 2018), it is important to be aware that the battle for open is not occurring on neutral territory (Weller, 2014).

Cable Green from Creative Commons has articulated a number of questions that serve as an effective starting list when interrogating the use of the term "open" in marketing materials or vendor pitches. These include:

- What will your company be contributing to the Commons?
- What content, software, [and] services will you share freely [without having to register and without tracking] and under open licenses [in editable and downloadable format]?
- How will your work increase equitable access to quality OER?
- Will you give more than you take? Are you contributing back useful OER to the Commons ... in addition to taking and reusing existing OER? Please give some examples of what you will contribute.
- How will you develop the trust with educators and the open education community?

(2018)

Closing Thoughts

The goals of the open education movement are noble, lofty, and utterly worthy. However, like all educators, open educators are capable of perpetrating harm even with the very best of intentions. As the movement continues to mature and grow more diverse, more attention is being paid to voices at the margins. However, as the pitfalls briefly described in this chapter illustrate, it is not until the marginalized are truly welcomed, and not suppressed, tolerated, or perceived as inconvenient, that the open education movement will be able to fulfill its true potential. Therein lies the gap between diversity and inclusivity. As Maha Bali reminds us:

> In open online spaces, opening doors is not enough.
> In open online spaces, an open door means easy exit just as it means easy entry.
> In open online spaces, we are not there on equal footing.
> In open online spaces, we are not equally fragile.
> It is everyone's responsibility to listen and care and support marginal voices. Whether or not they wish to speak. Whether or not they wish to be present. Whether or not they like what we do.
> It is everyone's responsibility to recognize their own privilege and to use it with purpose.
>
> *(2016, para. 19)*

Rajiv Jhangiani is the Associate Vice Provost, Open Education, at Kwantlen Polytechnic University in British Columbia. His research and practice currently focus on open education, student-centered pedagogies, and the scholarship of teaching and learning. A recipient of the award for Excellence in Open Education from BCcampus, Rajiv is a co-founder of the Open Pedagogy Notebook and an Ambassador for the Center for Open Science. A co-author of three open textbooks in psychology, his most recent book is *Open: The Philosophy and Practices That Are Revolutionizing Education and Science* (2017) which is an open access resource from Ubiquity Press. You can find him online at @thatpsychprof or thatpsychprof. com. He can be contacted at rajiv.jhangiani@kpu.ca.

References

Advisory Committee on Student Financial Assistance. (2006). *Mortgaging our future: How financial barriers to college undercut America's global competitiveness.* Washington, DC. Retrieved from http://files.eric.ed.gov/fulltext/ED529499.pdf

Bali, M. (2016, September 4). *Reproducing marginality?* [Blog post]. Retrieved from https://blog.mahabali.me/pedagogy/critical-pedagogy/reproducing-marginality/

BCcampus. (2018). *Open textbook stats.* Retrieved from https://open.bccampus.ca/open-textbook-stats/

Bliss, T. J. (2015, January 16). *Z as in zero: Increasing college access and success through zero-textbook-cost degrees.* Retrieved from https://hewlett.org/z-as-in-zero-increasing-college-access-and-success-through-zero-textbook-cost-degrees/

Collier, A. (2017, September 13). *Platforms in education: A need for criticality and hope* [Blog post]. Retrieved from http://redpincushion.us/blog/technology-2/platforms/

Colvard, N. B., Watson, C. E., & Park, H. (2018). The impact of open educational resources on various student success metrics. *International Journal of Teaching and Learning in Higher Education, 30*(2), 262–276.

Coolidge, A., Doner, S., Robertson, T., & Gray, J. (2018). *Accessibility toolkit* (2nd ed.). BCcampus Open Education. Retrieved from https://opentextbc.ca/accessibilitytoolkit/

de Oliveira Neto, J. D., Pete, J., Daryono, & Cartmill, T. (2017). OER use in the global South: A baseline survey of higher education instructors. In C. Hodgkinson-Williams & P. B. Arinto (Eds.), *Adoption and impact of OER in the global South.* Chapter 3 advance publication. Retrieved from http://dx.doi.org/10.5281/zenodo.154559

Eisenhardt, K. M. (1989). Agency theory: An assessment and review. *The Academy of Management Review, 14*(1), 57–74. doi:10.2307/258191

Florida Virtual Campus. (2016). *2016 Florida student textbook survey.* Tallahassee, FL: Author. Retrieved from https://florida.theorangegrove.org/og/file/3a65c507-2510-42d7-814c-ffdefd394b6c/1/2016%20Student%20Textbook%20Survey.pdf

Gilliard, C., & Culik, H. (2016, May 24). *Digital redlining, access, and privacy* [Blog post]. Retrieved from www.commonsense.org/education/privacy/blog/digital-redlining-access-privacy

Green, C. (2018, April 14). For-profit companies working with OER [Session notes]. *Hot topic panel at the 2018 creative commons global summit.* Toronto, ON. Retrieved from https://docs.google.com/document/d/1A061d6zEbHcDxYYLhDorR9bDwlJMjZVEfHO87yfGkeA/edit?usp=sharing

Hodgkinson-Williams, C. (2014). *Degrees of ease: Adoption of OER, open textbooks and MOOCs in the global South.* Retrieved from https://open.uct.ac.za/handle/11427/1188

Hodgkinson-Williams, C. (2015, November 10). *OER and open textbooks part of the solution to the current higher education crisis* [Blog post]. Retrieved from http://roer4d.org/1944

Jhangiani, R. S. (2018, April 6). *OER, equity, and implicit creative redlining* [Blog post]. Retrieved from https://thatpsychprof.com/oer-equity-and-implicit-creative-redlining/

Jhangiani, R. S., & Jhangiani, S. (2017). Investigating the perceptions, use, and impact of open textbooks: A survey of post-secondary students in British Columbia. *International Review of Research in Open and Distributed Learning, 18*(4). http://dx.doi.org/10.19173/irrodl.v18i4.3012

Karunanayaka, S. P., & Naidu, S. (2017). Impact of integrating OER in teacher education at the Open University of Sri Lanka. In C. Hodgkinson-Williams & P. B. Arinto (Eds.), *Adoption and impact of OER in the global South.* Chapter 13 advance publication. http://dx.doi.org/10.5281/zenodo.161293

Kasinathan, G., & Ranganathan, S. (2017). Teacher professional learning communities: A collaborative OER adoption approach in Karnataka, India. In C. Hodgkinson-Williams & P. B. Arinto (Eds.), *Adoption and impact of OER in the global South.* Chapter 14 advance publication. Retrieved from http://dx.doi.org/10.5281/zenodo.160680

Morris, S. M., & Stommel, J. (2017). A guide for resisting edtech: The case against Turnitin. *Hybrid Pedagogy.* Retrieved from http://hybridpedagogy.org/resisting-edtech/

Oates, L., Goger, L. K., Hashimi, J., & Farahmand, M. (2017). An early stage impact study of localised OER in Afghanistan. In C. Hodgkinson-Williams & P. B. Arinto (Eds.), *Adoption and impact of OER in the global South.* Chapter 15 advance publication. doi:10.5281/zenodo.161288

Openwashing. (n.d.). Retrieved from http://openwashing.org/

Perry, M. (2018, July 13). *The CD "chart of the century" makes the rounds at the federal reserve* [Blog post]. Retrieved from www.aei.org/publication/the-chart-of-the-century-makes-the-rounds-at-the-federal-reserve/

Petrides, L., Levin, D., & Watson, C. E. (2018, March 4). *Toward a sustainable OER ecosystem: The case for OER stewardship.* Retrieved from https://careframework.org/

Pitt, B., & Beckett, M. (2014, June 30). *Siyavula educator survey results: Educational contexts (Part I)* [Blog post]. Retrieved from http://oerhub.net/college/siyavula-educator-survey-results-sample-part-i/

Ruth, D. (2018, August 1). *48 percent of colleges, 2.2 million students using free OpenStax textbooks this year* [Press release]. Retrieved from http://news.rice.edu/2018/08/01/48-percent-of-colleges-2-2-million-students-using-free-openstax-textbooks-this-year-2/

Sáenz, M. P., Hernandez, U., & Hernández, Y. M. (2017). Collaborative co-creation of OER by teachers and teacher educators in Colombia. In C. Hodgkinson-Williams & P. B. Arinto (Eds.), *Adoption and impact of OER in the global South*. Chapter 5 advance publication. http://dx.doi.org/10.5281/zenodo.161271

Searls, D. (2009, August 26). Open vs. fauxpen. *Linux Journal*. Retrieved from www.linuxjournal.com/content/open-vs-fauxpen

Stommel, J. (2016, January 21). *Critically evaluating digital tools*. Retrieved from https://dgst101.com/activity-critically-evaluating-digital-tools-3f60d468ce74

UKOpenTextbooks. (n.d.). Retrieved from http://ukopentextbooks.org/

United Nations. (1948). *The universal declaration of human rights*. Retrieved from www.un.org/en/universal-declaration-human-rights/

Watters, A. (2012, March 17). *"The Audrey Test": Or, what should every techie know about education?* [Blog post] Retrieved from http://hackeducation.com/2012/03/17/what-every-techie-should-know-about-education

Weller, M. (2014). *The battle for open: How openness won and why it doesn't feel like victory*. London: Ubiquity Press. https://doi.org/10.5334/bam

Wiley, D. (2015). The MOOC misstep and the open education infrastructure. In C. J. Bonk, M. M. Lee, T. C. Reeves, & T. H. Reynolds (Eds.), *MOOCs and open education around the world* (pp. 3–11). New York: Routledge.

Wolfenden, F., Auckloo, P., Buckler, A., & Cullen, J. (2017). Teacher educators and OER in East Africa: Interrogating pedagogic change. In C. Hodgkinson-Williams & P. B. Arinto (Eds.), *Adoption and impact of OER in the global South*. Chapter 8 advance publication. Retrieved from http://dx.doi.org/10.5281/zenodo.161285

6
MASSIVE OPEN ONLINE COURSES
The State of Practice in Indonesia

Tian Belawati

Background

Myriad discussions in the press, at conferences, and even in the literature concerning MOOCs and related forms of open education (OE) have focused on finding sustainable business models for MOOCs (cf. Belleflamme & Jacqmin, 2016). If the tuition is free, certification of some type has often been used as one income source. For instance, some MOOC providers have offered certificates indicating a specialization for a moderate fee upon the completion of courses (McKenzie, 2018; Ravipati, 2017; Schaffhauser, 2019). As an example, Coursera charges around US$50 for students who want to receive certificates acknowledging their successful completion of MOOCs. In some cases, they also offer fee waivers for students who lack the means to afford these certificates.

Despite the many concerns regarding the business model, MOOCs continue to grow and are being adopted worldwide, including in the Global South (King, Pegrum, & Forsey, 2018). New providers and university affiliates continue to appear; in fact, in 2017, there were more than 9,400 MOOCs offered by more than 800 universities worldwide (Shah, 2018). The following year, this jumped to 11,400 MOOCs from over 900 universities (Shah, 2019). In terms of individuals that MOOCs address, Class Central (Shah, 2018) also reports that more than 81 million people participated in one or more MOOCs in 2017; an increase of 23 million people over the prior year (Class Central, 2017). In 2018, MOOC enrollments jumped again to over 100 million MOOC participants worldwide (Shah, 2019). Of these data, the biggest provider was Coursera MOOCs with around 37 million participants followed by edX with 18 million, XuetangX (14 million), Udacity (10 million), and FutureLearn (8.7 million). Together, these four providers accounted for approximately 88% of all MOOCs participants in the world as well as a majority of MOOCs being offered.

Such data beg the question about the specific countries that are embracing MOOCs. For instance, XuetangX is a consortium of leading universities in China, and it is the only top MOOC provider located in an emerging economy. The other top five MOOC providers are all located in either the US or Europe. Nevertheless, MOOCs and MOOC-like or MOOC-inspired online courses are also being developed and offered by many educational institutions and organizations in other parts of the world, including in Indonesia (Belawati, 2014; Berliyanto & Santoso, 2018).

About Indonesia

Indonesia is an archipelago in the South-East Asia region with over 17,000 islands and a population of about 255 million. It is now the fourth-largest population in the world after China, India, and the USA. While Indonesia possesses abundant natural resources, its human development index is still classified as medium and ranks at 115 in the 2014 Human Development Index, with a Gross National Income per capita of US$10,846 (UNDP, 2018). The McKinsey Global Institute (2012) forecasted Indonesia to become the seventh-largest economy in the world by 2030, assuming that it can accelerate the number of skilled workers from about 55 million to 135 million (Padmo & Belawati, 2017). This projection is based on the demographic benefit of having a higher percentage of productive-age group members within the population. Hence, education has been considered the top priority by the government, as shown by a commitment of 20% of the national budget allocated to the educational sector (Padmo & Belawati, 2017).

The formal education system in Indonesia consists of four main levels: (1) primary, (2) junior secondary, (3) senior secondary, and (4) tertiary level. Participation rates at the three lower education levels are approximately 96% for primary, 74% for junior secondary, and 54% for senior secondary, respectively (Padmo & Belawati, 2017). At the tertiary level, although Indonesia has a large number of higher education institutions, about 4,200 in total, the participation rate is much lower, only 32%. The low participation rate at the tertiary level is mostly related to the geographical situation and the unequal spread of higher education institutions within the country (Padmo & Belawati, 2017). More specifically, those looking for higher education institutions in Indonesia will find them primarily in Java and Sumatera, which are located in the southwestern part of the country. To address this challenge, the Government of Indonesia founded an open university, Universitas Terbuka (UT), in 1984 with the mandate to fill the geographical gaps of higher education provision. Now some 35 years later, new forms of open and online learning like MOOCs have also become part of the educational solution within Indonesia (Abas, 2015; Sari, Bonk, & Zhu, 2019).

Before describing MOOC trends in Indonesia, it is useful to understand the technological infrastructure in Indonesia, including the degree of Internet penetration. Generally speaking, the advancement of information and communication technologies (ICT) and the development of an IT infrastructure within the country have opened up many opportunities for Indonesia to increase access to quality tertiary education. Most notably, the establishment of UT has helped the country to educate many people through its open system and policies. No less than 2 million graduates have been produced by Universitas Terbuka since inception, and about 300,000 students are enrolling every semester. Notably, of this huge population accessing open education, roughly 95% are working adults (Open Education Consortium, 2019). And with nearly 650,000 enrolled, Universitas Terbuka is considered a "Top Ten Mega University" (Wikipedia Contributors, 2019; World Atlas, 2019).

The existence of UT also signals Indonesia's commitment towards open education. Through UT, the Government of Indonesia is able to offer more people access to flexible lifelong learning opportunities, regardless of their domicile, age, and ethnicity. It is through UT's pathway of flexible education that Indonesian society has come to understand that learning beyond walls can be as effective as the traditional face-to-face mode of learning. It is also UT's learning system that has helped introduce online and mobile learning to the general public.

Regarding Internet access, although Indonesia is among the top three countries with Internet users in Asia, after China and India, the overall penetration rate is only about 53.7% (InternetWorldStats, 2018). In particular, as with the location of higher education institutions, mentioned previously, Indonesia faces an unequal distribution of IT infrastructure throughout the country. Nevertheless, the increasing utilization of smartphones is slowly but surely accelerating the degree of Internet penetration in Indonesia. In fact, the current 27% penetration of mobile phone Internet users in Indonesia in 2017 is projected to rise to 36% by 2023 (Statista, 2019).

As reported by Growth For Knowledge or GFK (2016), more than 93% of Internet users in Indonesia regularly search online with their smartphones, spending an average of 5.5 hours per day accessing an average of 46 apps and Web domains with their mobile devices. GFK reported that

TABLE 6.1 Internet Users and Penetration

Country	Internet Users 31-Dec-17	Penetration (% Population)	Users % Asia
China★	772,000,000	54.60%	38.10%
India	462,124,989	34.10%	22.80%
Indonesia	143,260,000	53.70%	7.10%
Japan	118,626,672	93.30%	5.90%
Bangladesh	80,483,000	48.40%	3.80%
Philippines	67,000,000	62.90%	3.30%
Vietnam	64,000,000	66.30%	3.20%
Thailand	57,000,000	82.40%	2.80%
Korea, South	47,353,649	92.60%	2.30%
Pakistan	44,608,065	22.20%	2.20%

★Does not include SAR Hong Kong.

Source: InternetWorldStats, 2018

while the majority of Internet users in Indonesia (93%) access the Internet via their smartphones, the other platforms used to go online, albeit to a lower level, were desktops (11%) and tablets (5%). Similarly, Gusti (cited in Padmo, Belawati, Idrus, & Ardiasih, 2017) reported that in 2013, there were 270 million mobile phone users in Indonesia, which resulted in a 108% penetration rate for a population of 250 million. It is further reported that about 24% of those mobile phone users owned a smartphone (Statista, 2018).

In line with the increase in Internet penetration, online learning has been steadily increasing at Universitas Terbuka. As an open university, UT immediately embraced online learning as soon as the Internet came to Indonesia in the mid-1990s. The first online learning services offered to students were online tutorials that were provided using mailing-list systems for each course. The system was eventually upgraded in line with the availability of Web-based learning management systems. The lack of Internet access at the time was evidenced by the low participation rate of UT online system users, which was only about 1% of the entire student body. Internet access since then has accelerated at a rapid pace and illustrates how fast people adopt online learning modes when access has been secured. At the time of this writing, no less than 28% of UT students are actively learning online, resulting in almost 460,000 student-course enrollments per semester (Universitas Terbuka, 2017).

MOOCs in Indonesia

Given the thousands of islands in Indonesia and the relatively low enrollments in higher education, it is a country that is ideally suited to take advantage of MOOCs and other open forms of education (Firmansyah & Timmis, 2016; Sari et al., 2019). The nomenclature of MOOCs was not known in Indonesia until 2013, when the first MOOC was offered by an Indonesian private university, Ciputra University (Hewindati & Belawati, 2017). A well-known private university, Ciputera University is located in Surabaya, East Java. Even though several universities and organizations have followed Ciputra University's initiative, MOOCs in Indonesia are still in the infancy stage. Most universities that offer MOOCs are big universities, and they are developing or deploying MOOCs either independently or collaboratively.

Three institutions have developed and offered MOOCs through their own platforms and websites, specifically Ciputera University, Universitas Terbuka, and the South East Asian

Ministry of Education Organization Regional Center for Open Learning (SEAMEO-SEAMOLEC) (Abas, 2015). In addition, other universities and organizations are offering MOOCs through a common platform, such as IndonesiaX and SPADA. These are the top five MOOC providers in Indonesia. In that MOOCs are not centrally controlled by one or two entities in the country, as of March 2019, there were at least 10 active MOOC providers in Indonesia including IndonesiaX, iMOOC, MOOCs Universitas Terbuka, FOCUS Fisipol UGM, Akademi CIPS, XL FutureLearn, Sibejoo, UCEO Universitas Ciputra, Dicoding, and SekolahPintar (Sari et al., 2019).

Ciputra University offers its free courses, which are not explicitly labeled as MOOCs through the Ciputra Entrepreneurship Online (CE-O). The mission of CE-O is to provide free entrepreneurship educational content to Indonesians. The CE-O was initially launched on August 24, 2013, as a MOOC platform offering free courses on entrepreneurship. At present, it has 15 free courses on basic entrepreneurship, with lecturers coming from various backgrounds, including entrepreneurs, university lecturers, government officers, and professional trainers. The language of instruction is Bahasa Indonesia. Since its inception, some 122,000 participants from more than 1,000 cities in over 100 countries have registered, but attrition data indicate that less than 3% of those participants completed the courses for which they registered (A. Tanan, personal e-mail communication, April 2, 2018). Though free courses (e.g., Project Management, Supply Chain Management, Beyond Silicon Valley, etc.) are still available through the CE-O website (https://ciputrauceo.com/), the university, unfortunately, has decided that there would be no new courses developed until further notice due to financial constraints.

In 2014, Universitas Terbuka (UT) started offering MOOCs as part of its community services (https://moocs.ut.ac.id/). In the first term, UT offered 14 MOOCs but later reduced the number of offerings to only eight MOOCs. UT's MOOCs are designed as free online courses accessible to the public without any requirements so that all levels of society can obtain high-quality knowledge without payment. In addition, through the provision of MOOCs, UT intends to encourage members of the community to become lifelong learners by utilizing ICT and online learning. UT's data shows that 16% of over 6,000 participants completed the MOOCs in which they registered, a completion rate that is much higher than MOOC completion rates reported elsewhere (Jordan, 2015; Reich, 2014). Part of the reason for the higher completion rates may be due to MOOCs enrollments in Indonesia being smaller (i.e., generally under 1,000 participants) and being offered in a hybrid or blended format with virtual as well as face-to-face meet-ups (Firmansyah & Timmis, 2016; Sari et al., 2019) which can enhance community building and perhaps completion rates.

SEAMEO-SEAMOLEC is an intergovernmental organization that is part of the ASEAN Ministry of Education and it is responsible for enhancing the practice of open learning within the ASEAN region. SEAMEO-SEAMOLEC started offering MOOCs in 2016 with 27 free courses on various topics related to information and communication technologies, such as programming, animation, and educational game development. Given that the target audience is people from different countries in the South East Asian region, the courses are conducted in English. Pascua-Valenzuela and Sujak reported (2018) that more than 30,000 learners have participated in its MOOCs.

IndonesiaX is a MOOC platform provided by a private organization that was established in 2015. The MOOCs within IndonesiaX are developed and offered by partner institutions such as universities and private corporations. Its vision is to be the most preferred independent online MOOC/SPOC hosting platform for enriching the lives of Indonesians. This platform currently offers 26 free courses from 17 partner institutions, with an accumulated total participation number of 154,751 learners. Aside from the free courses, IndonesiaX also offers a certification track for a small fee (i.e., IDR 50 thousand or slightly more than US $3).

SPADA (Sistem Pembelarajan Daring Indonesia or Indonesia Online Learning System) is a project initiated by the Ministry of Research, Technology, and Higher Education that facilitates the development and deployment of shared courses via an online system among seven universities. In 2015, the Ministry expanded the project and started to provide grants to lecturers of both the initial seven universities and others to develop and offer free and open courses. From 2015 to 2018, at least 143 courses were developed and deployed; however, at the time of this writing, only 32 free courses remained active on its website (http://spada.ristekdikti.go.id/).

In addition to the previously mentioned MOOCs providers, there are other organizations that offer online but not entirely free types of courses that are akin to MOOCs. Among them are the following examples:

- CodeSaya (https://codesaya.com/) started in 2013. It focuses on providing free online courses on coding.
- SekolahPintar (https://sekolahpintar.com/) was established by a private consulting company specializing in Web design, animation, and an online business called BabaStudio. It currently has approximately 57 free courses in various disciplines. In addition to the free ones, Sekolah-Pintar also offers premium track courses for a fee.
- FOCUS (http://focus.fisipol.ugm.ac.id/) offers open online courses provided by the Faculty of Social and Political Sciences of Gajah Mada University (FISIPOL UGM). FOCUS is sponsored by a private bank and it has offered 12 free online courses in social and political science fields through its website since 2016.

As detailed by Table 6.2, in terms of number of MOOC participants, IndonesiaX is the most popular MOOC provider followed by Ciputra University, SEAMOLEC, and UT, respectively. Such participant data likely correlate with the promotion that the programs receive. As with many new products, exposure through marketing resources and public initiatives do matter. KampusUNJ.com reported that Ciputra University and IndonesiaX promote their MOOCs through various social media such as Facebook, Twitter, Instagram, and YouTube (KampusUNJ, 2016). With regards to the age of MOOC participants, data from IndonesiaX and UT indicate that they range from teenagers as young as 15 to participants over 65 years old. However, over 88% of IndonesiaX participants fall into the age group of 18 to 44 years old, whereas about 51% of UT participants are between 19 to 39 years old.

The data in Table 6.2 depict the limited state of practice of MOOCs in Indonesia. Many of the providers of free online courses do not even explicitly label their courses as MOOCs. Such oversight shows that Indonesia is still in its initial stage in the implementation of MOOCs. For example, in a study conducted by DailySocial (2017), it was reported that even though 56% of its 11,023 respondents claimed to have heard the term "MOOC", nearly 80% indicated that they had never attempted to learn through a MOOC. Among those who have participated in a MOOC, 57% stated that they participated in a MOOC related to learning a foreign language. The other popular fields among MOOC participants in that 2017 study were computer programming and IT (39%) and business-related subjects (34%). Nevertheless, most respondents (91%) agreed that MOOCs have the potential to help students study their school work

TABLE 6.2 A Summary of MOOCs in Indonesia

Provider	Establishment	Current # of MOOCs	# of Participants	% of Completers
Ciputra University	2013	15	122,000	< 3
Universitas Terbuka	2014	8	6,726	16
SEAMOLEC	2016	27	31,043	–
IndonesiaX	2015	26	154,751	–
SPADA	2015	32	–	–

Source: Data provided by the Management of the Providers

effectively, and, therefore, suggested that MOOCs providers consider school and university students as their main target audiences.

To further understand the characteristics of MOOC participants and expectations in Indonesia, survey data from Hewindati and Belawati (2017) indicated that 74% of 283 participants of UT MOOCs in the first batch of 2015 lived in districts considered to be rural areas. In addition, the survey also found that most participants (66%) accessed MOOCs from home followed by accessing from their offices (18%) or Internet kiosks (14%). Regarding survey participant backgrounds, more than half of participants (63%) worked full time in either the private sector or in government offices, 25% were entrepreneurs, and 12% of them claimed to be unemployed. In addition, 74% of the participants were high school graduates, while the other 24% held either a bachelor's or master's degree. Such data are pertinent to the goals of this particular book related to how MOOCs and open education can help those in developing parts of the world. It is clear from this data that, at least in Indonesia, there are new avenues to education across the lifespan for those who previously were unable to obtain it. Such findings are particularly important given much previous MOOC research bemoans the fact that MOOC participants typically already have college degrees (Ho et al., 2015 and McKenzie, 2014 as cited in Hewindati & Belawati, 2017). UT's survey also revealed that 65% of the participants stated that the reason they took the course was to upgrade their knowledge, whereas 35% of them aimed to obtain certification.

There is also a need to better understand MOOC instructor goals and needs in Indonesia. A recent study of 46 Indonesian and Malaysian MOOC instructors found that half of the MOOC courses in Indonesia were a hybrid or blended type of course (Sari et al., 2019). In addition, in that study nearly 80% of these MOOC instructors had under 1,000 participants enrolled and all had under 5,000 people enrolled, which represents a much lower size than MOOCs offered by Western universities and institutions of higher learning (Dillahunt, Wang, & Teasley, 2014; Jordan, 2014). In addition, Sari et al. (2019) found that the key reasons for offering MOOCs were personal and altruistic such as intending to increase access to higher education and hoping to contribute to human development in general as well as in response to institutional encouragement. Many instructional design challenges and issues were also revealed in that study including difficulties in designing videos, assessments, and offering feedback to large learner populations as well as ways to encourage learner collaboration and engagement (Sari, Bonk, & Zhu, 2018). Not surprisingly, various time constraints were also mentioned by these MOOC instructors.

These are just a few initial studies. Much more research needs to be conducted on MOOCs in Indonesia. With the rapid increase in Internet users in Indonesia during the past decade, there is potential that MOOCs might serve as a cost-effective supplement to existing higher education practices (Firmansyah & Timmis, 2016; Sari et al., 2019). As such, the different MOOC initiatives as well as MOOC-like derivatives deserve serious attention. To what degree do they reduce or eliminate tuition costs for learners in different parts of the country? To what extent will these MOOC experiences encourage learners to pursue other opportunities for tertiary education or technical training? MOOC inroads are still fairly limited in Indonesia; however, the coming decade will be filled with open and online learning experimentations that attempt to address the fact that just "30 percent of school leavers" enroll in the approximately "5,000 higher education institutions" in Indonesia (Abas, 2015, p. 239). Suffice to say, while there is much room to grow, Indonesia seems ideally situated to capitalize on innovations related to MOOCs and open forms of education (Sari et al., 2019).

Concluding Remarks

MOOCs have become the most recent means of opening access to quality education; other educational delivery mechanisms will arise in the coming decades. But, for now, however, the focus is on the potential of MOOCs and MOOC-like offerings. Every day there are new MOOCs being developed and offered by various institutions around the world. Many countries have even embraced MOOC-based education as a national strategy for equalizing access to education. Indonesia is no different. Many initiatives, typically begun by individual institutions, have become endorsed regionally or across the entire country. As this occurs, many such organizations and institutions are continuing to jump onto the MOOC bandwagon. Such initiatives have elevated the status of MOOCs to the public discourse about education. Nevertheless, the date in which Indonesia fully takes advantage of the ample MOOC resources and associated certification possibilities is still a long way off. Indonesia needs a systematic campaign and an awareness-raising effort to make MOOCs beneficial to the greater part of the Indonesian society. Research is also needed to investigate the quality of the learning that results from MOOCs in Indonesia, especially as these courses are intended to foster a more qualified workforce.

As detailed elsewhere in this book, Indonesia is not atypical of what is transpiring related to MOOCs and open forms of education delivery around the planet. Access to the Internet is exploding in the midst of much experimentation with MOOCs and open educational resources (OER) (Abas, 2015). While much more needs to be learned about the impact of MOOCs, they will definitely play a significant role across educational settings in Indonesia and globally in the coming decade. Although the specifics of that role in Indonesia will evolve and unfold in the coming years, my colleagues and I at the Universitas Terbuka and other institutions of higher learning in Indonesia intend to help shape this next evolution in MOOCs and open education—not just in Southeast Asia, but around the planet. These are exciting times indeed!

Professor Tian Belawati has been working in the field of open and distance education (ODE) for over 30 years. She has had extensive experiences in research, teaching, and administration of a large-scale open university system. She has also been involved in many international ODE movements that has led to her appointments as President of the Asian Association of Open Universities or AAOU (2009–2010) and of the International Council for Open and Distance Education or ICDE (2012–2015). She is also a member of the ICDE Board of Trustees (2017–present), and a member of the Board of Directors of the Open Education Consortium (2017–present). Notably, Professor Belawati also served as Rector of Universitas Terbuka in Indonesia from 2009–2017 where she mobilized unique partnerships and introduced innovations and sound practices in the use of new technology for the delivery of ODL.

References

Abas, Z. W. (2015). The glocalization of MOOCs in Southeast Asia. In C. J. Bonk, M. M. Lee, T. C. Reeves, & T. H. Reynolds (Eds.), *MOOCs and open education: Around the world* (pp. 232–242). New York: Routledge.

Belawati, T. (2014). Open education, open educational resources and massive open online courses. *Journal of Continuing Education and Lifelong Learning, 7*(1). Retrieved from https://oerknowledgecloud.org/sites/oerknowledgecloud.org/files/tian02eng.pdf

Belleflamme, P., & Jacqmin, J. (2016). An economic appraisal of MOOC platforms: Business models and impacts on higher education. *CESifo Economic Studies, 62*(1), 148–169.

Berliyanto, & Santoso, H. B. (2018). Indonesian perspective on massive open online courses: Opportunities and challenges. *Journal of Educators Online, 15*(1). Retrieved from www.thejeo.com/archive/archive/2018_151/berliyanto_santosopdf

Class Central. (2017). *By the number: MOOCs in 2017*. Retrieved from www.class-central.com/report/mooc-stats-2017/

DailySocial. (2017). *MOOC in Indonesia Survey 2017*. Retrieved from https://dailysocial.id/post/survei-mooc-di-indonesia

Dillahunt, T. R., Wang, B. Z., & Teasley, S. (2014). Democratizing higher education: Exploring MOOC use among those who cannot afford a formal education. *International Review of Research in Open and Distance Learning, 15*(5), 177–196.

Firmansyah, M., & Timmis, S. (2016). Making MOOCs meaningful and locally relevant? Investigating IDCourserians—an independent, collaborative, community hub in Indonesia. *Research and Practice in Technology Enhanced Learning, 11*(11), 1–23. Retrieved from https://link.springer.com/article/10.1186/s41039-016-0032-6

Growth for Knowledge (GFK). (2016, March 23). *Over 9 in 10 online users in Indonesia access the internet via their smartphone* [Press Released]. Retrieved from www.gfk.com/nl/

Hewindati, Y. T., & Belawati, T. (2017). Massive open online courses as a community programme. *ASEAN Journal of Open and Distance Learning, 9*(1), 1–11.

Ho, A., Chuang, I., Reich, J., Coleman, C., Whitehill, J., Northcutt, C., Williams, J., Hansen, J., Lopez, G., and Petersen, R. (2015). *HarvardX and MITx: Two Years of Open Online Courses Fall 2012-Summer 2014*. Retrieved from https://papers.ssrn.com/sol3/papers.cfm?abstract_id=2586847

Jordan, K. (2014). Initial trends in enrolment and completion of massive open online courses. *The International Review of Research in Open and Distributed Learning, 15*(1), 133–160. Retrieved from www.irrodl.org/index.php/irrodl/article/view/1651/2813

Jordan, K. (2015). Massive open online course completion rates revisited: Assessment, length, and attrition. *International Review of Research in Open and Distributed Learning, 16*(3), 341–358. Retrieved from www.irrodl.org/index.php/irrodl/article/view/2112/3394

KampusUNJ. (2016). *Inikah situs kuliah online (MOOC) terbaik Indonesia?* Retrieved from https://kampusunj.com/situs-kuliah-online/

King, M., Pegrum, M., & Forsey, M. (2018). MOOCs and OER in the global South: Problems and potential. *The International Review of Research in Open and Distributed Learning, 19*(5), 1–20. Retrieved from www.irrodl.org/index.php/irrodl/article/download/3742/4825/

McKenzie, J. (2014). More evidence that MOOCs are not great equalizers. *Techpresident*. Retrieved from http://techpresident.com/news/wegov/24830/more-evidence-moocs-are-not-great-equalizers

McKenzie, L. (2018, October 18). EdX: From micromasters to online master's degrees. *Inside Higher Ed*. Retrieved from www.insidehighered.com/news/2018/10/12/edx-launches-nine-low-cost-online-degrees

McKinsey Global Institute. (2012). *The archipelago economy: Unleashing Indonesia's potentials*. Retrieved from https://www.mckinsey.com/~/media/mckinsey/featured%20insights/asia%20pacific/the%20archipelago%20economy/mgi_unleashing_indonesia_potential_executive_summary.ashx

Open Education Consortium. (2019). *Universitas Terbuka (Indonesian Open University)*. Retrieved from www.oeconsortium.org/members/view/568/

Padmo, D., & Belawati, T. (2017). Implementing sustainable ICT-supported innovation policies: Case of Universitas Terbuka—Indonesia. In I. A. Lubin (Ed.), *ICT-supported innovations in small countries and developing regions: Perspectives and recommendations for international education*. New York: AECT, Springer.

Padmo, D., Belawati, T., Idrus, O., & Ardiasih, L. S. (2017). The state of practice of mobile learning in Indonesia. In A. Murphy, H. Farley, L. Dyson, & H. Jones (Eds.), *Mobile learning in higher education in the Asia Pacific: Harnessing trends and challenging orthodoxies* (pp. 173–190). Singapore: Springer.

Pascua-Valenzuela, E. A., & Sujak, A. (2018, March 26–30). *Integrating the digital literacies in South East Asia: Success stories from SEAMEO*. Unpublished presentation file presented at the UNESCO Mobile Learning Week, Paris.

Ravipati, S. (2017, March 1). edX expands micromasters programs with data science, digital leadership and more. *Campus Technology*. Retrieved from https://campustechnology.com/articles/2017/03/01/edx-expands-micromasters-programs-with-data-science-digital-leadership-and-more.aspx

Reich, J. (2014, December 8). MOOC completion and retention in the context of student intent. *Educause Review*. Retrieved from https://er.educause.edu/articles/2014/12/mooc-completion-and-retention-in-the-context-of-student-intent

Sari, A. R., Bonk, C. J., & Zhu, M. (2018, October 25). *The design challenges of MOOCs: A case study of Indonesian and Malaysian MOOCs*. Paper presented at the 2018 Association for Educational Communications and Technology (AECT) Annual Meeting, Kansas, MO.

Sari, A. R., Bonk, C. J., & Zhu, M. (2019). MOOC Instructor Designs and Challenges: What can be Learned from Existing MOOCs in Indonesia and Malaysia? *Asia Pacific Education Review*. https://doi.org/10.1007/s12564-019-09618-9

Schaffhauser, D. (2019, March 20). How MOOCs make money. *Campus Technology*. Retrieved from https://campustechnology.com/articles/2019/03/20/how-moocs-make-money

Shah, D. (2018, January 22). A product at every price: A review of MOOC stats and trends in 2017. *Class Central*. Retrieved from www.class-central.com/report/moocs-stats-and-trends-2017/

Shah, D. (2019, January 6). Year of MOOC-based degrees: A review of MOOC stats and trends in 2018. *Class Central*. Retrieved from www.classcentral.com/report/moocs-stats-and-trends-2018/

Statista. (2018). *Smartphone user penetration in Indonesia as share of mobile phone users from 2014 to 2019*★. Retrieved from www.statista.com/statistics/257046/ smartphone-user-penetration-in-indonesia/

Statista. (2019). *Mobile phone internet user penetration from 2017 to 2023*★. Retrieved from www.statista.com/statistics/309017/indonesia-mobile-phone-internet-user-penetration/

United Nation Development Programme (UNDP). (2018). *Human development index*. Retrieved from http://hdr.undp.org/en/2018-update

Universitas Terbuka. (2017). *Laporan kerja tahunan Rektor Universitas Terbuka 2016 [Universitas Terbuka Rector's Report of 2016]*. Jakarta: Universitas Terbuka.

Wikipedia Contributors. (2019, March 21). List of largest universities and university networks by enrollment. *In Wikipedia, the Free Encyclopedia*. Retrieved from https://en.wikipedia.org/w/index.php?title=Slavery&oldid=857306597

World Atlas. (2019). *The largest universities in the world by enrollment*. Retrieved from www.worldatlas.com/articles/universities-with-the-largest-enrollments-in-the-world.html

7
ORCHESTRATING SHIFTS IN PERSPECTIVES AND PRACTICES ABOUT THE DESIGN OF MOOCs

Som Naidu and Shironica P. Karunanayaka

Introduction

Generally, when asked to teach something, instructors begin with the subject matter content that needs to be taught. They start to research the topic, how others have approached its teaching, and plan to teach it from simple to complex concepts. This constitutes a *content-centric* approach designed to teach learners the subject matter content. When that is done, and even if their performance on assessments indicate that students know all the content, they are often left asking—so now what? Sure they might know many facts, principles and procedures, but given a situation or specific problem to solve, they are unable to apply their content knowledge to solve the problem in that setting, because they have not learned how to do so. In effect their knowledge is inert (see Brown, Collins, & Duguid, 1989). As a result, many students are left to muddle through their work and learn by direct experience how to apply their knowledge only after they have entered the work force.

The first generation of MOOCs that came out of the developed world, many from Ivy League institutions, replicated this content-centric approach to learning and teaching (Romiszowski, 2013). So, despite their widely vaunted promises, MOOCs, including those purported to be based on constructivist principles, have so far failed to live up to their expectations of opening up and democratizing learning (Naidu, 2013). In fact most of them fail to meet the minimalist expectations of good teaching and learning practices. Most of them demonstrate models of conventional lecture-based practices with limited or no interaction between students and staff, and among students, disregarding existing good principles of learning and teaching (Romiszowski, 2013. They continue to be developed with a highly content-centric focus, mostly using video-based lectures, promoting an outdated model of content and teacher-centered learning.

There is a better way to design MOOCs. This much better approach promises to teach the learner the subject matter, but also how to apply that subject matter in authentic settings, such that at the end of this learning experience, the student has both subject matter knowledge and the capacity to apply that knowledge in real-world settings. This is not the same as workplace-based learning or work-integrated learning which requires learners to be placed in the workplace for periods of internship. This alternative approach is about starting with the *context* and not the content, and asking what is it that we want our learners to be able to do, what are our commitments to them, and what are their learning outcomes. And from there, designing a learning experience that will be able to offer that internship in solving real-world problems as part of their learning process, and not after it.

These are the same questions that we would, and should, ask in the design and development of any effective, efficient and engaging learning and teaching experience (see Merrill, 2002; Naidu, 2010). We have known that this works, and that learning and teaching is most effective, efficient and engaging when:

1. Teachers and learners are clear about the learning outcomes;
2. Learning is situated within a meaningful context and within the culture and the community in which learners live and work;
3. Learners are engaged in pursuing and solving meaningful and real-world challenges and problems, and where they have opportunities to work on a variety of problems and tasks of increasing complexity with timely and useful feedback;
4. The learning activities in these learning situations are clearly articulated and explicitly linked to knowledge and skills already mastered;
5. Learners, while working on learning situations, are required to think for themselves by reflecting in, and upon their actions and regulating their own performance;
6. The development of understanding is promoted as a social process with learners acting upon authentic situations in groups and with dialogue, discussion and debate;
7. The assessment of learning outcomes is closely aligned with the learning context;
8. The assessment of learning outcomes is linked to meaningful problems and tasks, and aimed at helping students further develop their knowledge, skills and problem-solving abilities; and
9. The assessment of learning outcomes is designed to develop self-regulatory and meta-cognitive skills.

Orchestrating Shifts in Perspectives About MOOC Design

This approach comprises a radical shift in thinking about the design of MOOCs and it involves a fundamental rethink of our approach to the design of learning and teaching experiences. But this kind of shift in perceptions and perspectives about teaching and learning generally, and MOOCs in particular, does not and will not happen easily without careful rethinking. It requires a great deal of structure and guidance and orchestration of that process.

The orchestration of such shifts in mindsets of MOOC developers is a creative process. It is also a process that is based on well-established principles of learning and teaching (Naidu & Karunanayaka, 2014). This chapter describes a model for the application of this process that is based on thinking around viable systems and general systems theory (see Figure 7.1). This process draws on thinking around how viable systems work to propose an engine for the design of the learning and teaching experience, guiding teachers and designers to start where the learner is, and not where the content is at. In this chapter, we describe this framework and its application to shift the perceptions and practices of MOOC developers. We do this with reference to the design and development of a suite of MOOCs for continuing professional development (CPD) on the adoption of open educational resources (OER) and open educational practices (OEP) by practitioners in the South Asian region foremost, but internationally as well.

Design of CPD MOOCs on OER and OEP

This suite of CPD MOOCs has been developed at the Open University of Sri Lanka (OUSL) with the sponsorship of the Commonwealth Educational Media Center for Asia (CEMCA) in New Delhi. The goal of this initiative is to raise awareness on the potentials of OER and OEP among practitioners, from any field of study.

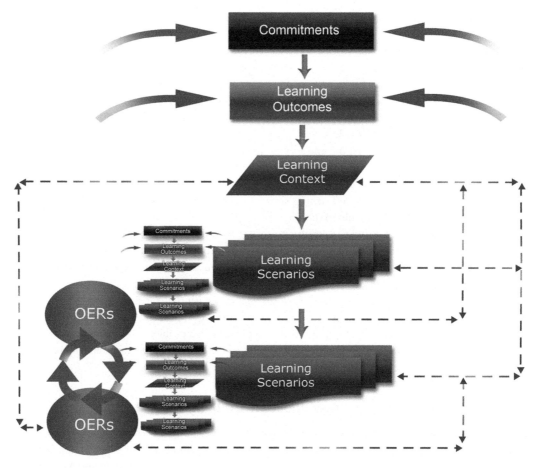

FIGURE 7.1 The "Learning Engine"

Source: Naidu & Karunanayaka, 2014, p. 8

This whole initiative comprises four CPD MOOCs that enable participants to solve authentic and real-world problems and issues that they are likely to be facing in their workplace, in relation to adopting OER and OEP. A defining characteristic of these MOOCs is their unique scenario-based design. Learning scenarios have been carefully crafted to reflect the kinds of questions, issues and challenges that practitioners are likely to be facing in their environments with the adoption and integration of OER. We begin with making clear our commitments to students, as we should, in the design of any learning and teaching transaction.

Our Commitments

We commit to making clear to our learners their learning outcomes, the learning context and learning activities, assessment tasks and resources to which they will require access to support them to achieve the learning outcomes. In order to accomplish this, we place learners in real-life-like situations where they are confronted with real-world issues, and ask them to resolve these issues, and not simply define concepts or principles. To be able to address the challenges with which they are confronted, they will need access to subject matter knowledge and we will provide them access to this content.

The following sections of this chapter serve as a window to our design of the learning experiences to meet our commitments to the learners. For a more detailed look at our design architecture, it's best that you look at the MOOCs themselves at www.ou.ac.lk/apps/mooc/ which are housed at the Open University of Sri Lanka.

Learning scenario

'Smart HR Institute' is an organization that conducts staff development programs to assist a variety of organizations in enhancing the skills of their staff. The costs of purchasing or developing resource materials for these programs are becoming an increasing concern to the management and the staff. The program is about to begin next month so there is limited time to update the existing material. The feedback received from participants of the previous training program reveal issues in relation to the quality of some of the materials, including unrelated and outdated information and copyright violations. The program team is confronted with the problem of how these issues could be addressed within the stipulated time period and the limited budget available, and a meeting has been convened to discuss this real-world challenge.

The video shows a meeting in progress in which various options are proffered along with the exploration of the potentials of OER. However, since few participants are likely to be familiar with this concept, as is currently the case more generally, they decide to explore the potential of OER for their purpose. The challenge for the learner then is to explore options and propose a robust solution for a way forward at the next program committee meeting. This task involves learning about OER, and not just learning it for oneself, but representing the key and related concepts and helping others to understand it as well by engaging them in a discussion of it. This then also serves as an assessment activity for this segment of the MOOC.

What is different about this MOOC is that it avoids using video primarily as a presentation tool to present subject matter content to learners. Instead our design uses video to situate learners in the learning context and requires them to engage with the content and see the point of doing so.

The second MOOC adopts the same strategy, and takes the learner on to the next logical step. Now that they have some understanding of OER, the natural follow-on question is, where I can find these kinds of resources and how I will be able to ascertain their quality and suitability for my purpose. A short video segment is used to highlight the challenges faced in searching OER and evaluating its fitness for purpose. Various suggestions are proffered including working with librarians. The lesson here is for learners to be able to learn how to figure out solutions for themselves as opposed to being told what a solution might look like. The task requires proposing strategies for searching OER and how to evaluate their quality.

Now that the learners have an understanding of OER, where and how to find them and ascertain their quality and fitness for purpose, the next logical question is how one can adapt these if there is a need to do so, as well as how one can create their own OERs and share with others. The third MOOC in this suite of MOOCs helps participants with these issues.

Learning scenario

The National Teacher Training College (NTTC) has recently taken a policy decision to use only OER as resource materials in the development of their training modules, and also to release those with the Open License—CC BY-SA. Instructors in NTTC are increasingly using OER in their day-to-day teaching practices, and are currently in the process of preparing new training modules integrating OER for their next intake. However, the Head/Academic Affairs is very concerned about the delay in getting this task completed by the staff within the scheduled time-frame. He noticed that even though the staff has been made aware of different open licensing types in OER permitting them to reuse, revise and remix, most of the time the tendency was only to reuse existing OER as is. He sends an email to the instructors advising them not only to consider reusing available OER, but also to adapt existing OER by revising and remixing, and/or to create new materials as OER to meet different purposes and specific needs.

In the video segment, instructors at NTTC are seen discussing their experience with the task in hand, and about the challenges in being able to find an OER that meets their needs. A common issue emerging is that even though they are able to find a number of relevant OER, many of these resources do not exactly suit their specific purposes and context. Can they revise and remix OER, and if so, then how? What will one need in order to be able to revise an open educational resource? The next task requires learners to engage with issues around revising and remixing of OER and the need for releasing it under similar conditions.

The final MOOC in this suite of four MOOCs addresses the question of the integration of OER in learning and teaching. This is a critical issue because we believe that how a learning resource is licensed cannot influence the learning outcomes one way or another. What does influence the achievement of learning outcomes is how a learning resource is integrated into a learning and teaching transaction (Naidu, 2017; Karunanayaka & Naidu, 2014, 2017). So, in this fourth MOOC, participants are required to demonstrate their competency in integrating OER in their professional practices.

Learning scenario

There is a growing interest in the Western University of Sri Lanka to progress with adopting innovative open practices in teaching and learning. It has recently established an institutional policy on OER. The Vice Chancellor of the University is very keen to take measures in facilitating this transition towards open educational practices (OEP) at the institutional level. The University has recently received an opportunity to get financial support from an international funding agency, to develop innovative teaching-learning practices with OER integration too. However, changing thinking and practices of the academic staff members is very challenging. A majority of staff members are happy to be in their comfort zone maintaining status quo, and reluctant to change from their conventional practices, while a few members are making individual efforts.

In a short video segment, the Vice Chancellor of the Western University of Sri Lanka in a meeting with the Deans of Faculties and Heads of the Departments is presenting the current measures being taken at the University to adopt OER and OEP, and underscoring the importance of promoting open educational practices at the institutional level. At the end of his presentation, he suggests that each Faculty put together a team to develop a plan for the adoption and integration of OER at the University, with strategies to facilitate this transition towards open educational practices. The learner in this MOOC is required to lead such a team to develop a plan to promote the integration of OER and adoption of OEP generally in teaching and learning at the University. The developed plan fulfills an assessment requirement as well.

Development and Implementation of the CPD MOOCs

We adopted a design-based research (DBR) approach in the design, development and implementation of these four MOOCs. The DBR process offers an ideal scaffold for improving educational practices through an iterative process of design, development and implementation of solutions, testing and refinement, and critical reflection to produce design solutions (Reeves, 2006). The approach enables researchers to work in partnership with practitioners to engage in systematic refinement of design strategies during different phases of the process. This work was achieved in series of interactive workshops with the course team.

Goals and Challenges

Our goal has been to design effective, efficient and engaging learning experiences in the four CPD MOOCs on OER and OEP, using a scenario-based approach to learning. This required developing meaningful and effective learning scenarios to place our learners in challenging situations, and supporting them to achieve the intended learning outcomes.

Our challenge was threefold. Firstly, we were faced with an existing participant mindset that was clouded by a content-centric focus of what teaching is and what MOOCs are like, especially their use of videos to present subject matter knowledge to learners. Secondly, very few members in the course team had any experience with a scenario-based approach to the design of productive learning experiences. Thirdly, most members of the course team were themselves not very conversant with OER and open educational practices.

For each learning scenario, first, it was essential to identify an educational issue or challenge, one that is not only topical, but meaningful and relevant, which we expected our learners to be able to solve. And in doing so, acquire knowledge of the facts and principles. Next, we had to think of authentic scenarios ('contexts') that will help to take the learners through the learning process. It was important to be very clear on the specific role of the learner in each scenario, and specific activities that they will actually do (which will serve as learning and assessment tasks), to meet the intended learning outcomes, with the support of OER (the 'content') provided.

The Development Process

A series of interactive face-to-face workshops were scheduled, combined with online interactions, to develop these MOOCs. This was a very interactive process involving a series of collaborative activities including:

- Developing understanding of key concepts—MOOC; CPD MOOC; OER and OEP; e3teaching; first principles of instruction; scenario-based learning (SBL), as many course team members were not very familiar with several of these constructs.
- Deciding on the focus and structure of the four CPD MOOCs. What and how much on the subject could be covered in four MOOCs.
- Identifying the key competencies and the learning outcomes expected from our target group of learners (practitioners).
- Constructive alignment of learning outcomes with the learning activities and assessment tasks within the SBL approach.
- Developing specific learning scenarios to be able to provide learners with a productive learning experience.
- Creating the scenario-based videos (SBVs) to provide the learning context and activate learning.
- Identifying and creating appropriate OER to integrate in the learning experience as learning resources.

Throughout this design and development process, the course team engaged in brainstorming, concept mapping, writing critical reflections, group discussions, and in analyzing the designed artifacts which enabled systematic refinement of the design strategies through constant review, reflection and discussion (see Karunanayaka, Naidu, Rajendra, & Ariadurai, 2018). The development of scenario-based videos (SBVs) and using these videos to provide the learning context as opposed to presenting the learning content was a unique feature of this whole exercise. And it comprised a significant shift away from a *content-driven* focus of MOOC design towards a more *context-driven* emphasis.

Concluding Remarks

MOOCs are online courses which provide learners free and open access to learning opportunities. In order to be able to take advantage of these opportunities, learners require access to the Internet. And this is where the major problem lies with MOOCs for emerging economies of the world. In these contexts, either there is no access to the Internet, or when there is access, it is intermittent, weak, unreliable and above all very expensive. But these are technical problems that are being addressed with solutions such as mobile network connectivity from local devices.

The more serious problem with the current crop of MOOCs is their pedagogical design. Ten years after their emergence, MOOCs have failed to live up to its promises as a mode of learning in which knowledge is gained through negotiation of meaning and understanding in a networked learning environment (Naidu, 2013). The majority of contemporary MOOCs replicate a tired and an ineffective model of teaching that is based on the presentation of subject matter content by a lecture (Morrison, 2013). That was not the intention of its protagonists. On the contrary, MOOCs were supposed to be learning environments in which knowledge was to be gained from connection and connectivity, afforded by the Internet and the Web (see Siemens, 2008–2012).

The current model of MOOCs, with their heavy reliance on the use of videos for presenting content, promotes a failed pedagogy (Reeves & Hedberg, 2014). More importantly, no sound pedagogical reason has ever been proffered for this kind of use of the video tool in MOOCs. MOOCs do not have to be like those we know now. In fact MOOCs do not have to have video lectures at all. MOOCs are based on the premise that knowledge and understanding is best developed through communication, collaboration and connection, and not just connection online.

MOOCs are also a form of OER. However, 15 years after the adoption of the term 'OER' by UNESCO (UNESCO, 2002), most educators and students are still unfamiliar with the concept of OER, and do not fully understand its meaning and potentials for teaching and learning (Kinskey, King, & Carrie, 2018; Senack, 2014).

This chapter describes the design and development of a suite of MOOCs to educate practitioners about OER and OEP. But more importantly, it is about orchestrating shifts in mindsets in the design of MOOCs on any other topic as well, because without such a shift, the uptake of any disruptive innovation is going to be challenging (Kinskey et al., 2018). Disruption requires more than simply explaining the concepts and its advantages. And in this case, it had to be about showing practitioners how the adoption of OER and OEP can help resolve real-world issues and challenges. For this shift in mindsets, a radically different approach to the design of MOOCs was necessary. And in this chapter, we explain the foundations of that alternative approach, and its implementation in the design and development of four MOOCs on the integration of OER and the adoption of OEP.

Acknowledgments

The work reported in this chapter has been supported with funding from the Commonwealth Educational Media Centre for Asia (CEMCA), New Delhi, India. The contribution of all members of the development team at the Open University of Sri Lanka (OUSL) is gratefully acknowledged.

Som Naidu is currently Pro-Vice Chancellor Flexible Learning and Director, Center for Flexible Learning, at the University of the South Pacific. Dr Naidu possesses undergraduate qualifications in Education from the University of Waikato in New Zealand, and graduate qualifications in Educational Technology from Concordia University in Montreal, Canada. A former president of the Open and Distance Learning Association of Australia, Dr Naidu has served as Executive Editor of its journal *Distance Education* since 1997. In May 2014 the Open University of Sri Lanka awarded Dr Naidu a D.Litt. *(Honoris Causa)*, in recognition of his extensive contribution to the field of open, flexible, distance and e-learning both regionally and internationally.

Shironica P. Karunanayaka is Professor in Educational Technology and the current Dean of the Faculty of Education at the Open University of Sri Lanka (OUSL) where she has been housed since 1993. Prof. Karunanayaka holds a first class in the Bachelor's degree in Science from the OUSL, the Post Graduate Diploma in Education from the University of Colombo, and the Degree of Doctor of Education from the University of Wollongong, Australia, specializing in Information Technology in Education and Training. Being an active researcher, Prof. Karunanayaka has many publications in both national and international fora. Her key research focus areas include ICT in education, instructional design for enhancing learning and teaching experiences, open educational resources, and open educational practices.

References

Brown, J. S., Collins, A., & Duguid, P. (1989). Situated cognition and the culture of learning. *Educational Researcher, 18*(1), 32–42.

Karunanayaka, S., & Naidu, S. (Eds.). (2014). *Integrating OER in educational practice: Practitioner stories* (ISBN 978-955-23-152-68). Nugegoda: The Open University of Sri Lanka. Retrieved from www.ou.ac.lk/home/images/OUSL/publications/intergratingOERinEducationalPractice.pdf

Karunanayaka, S., & Naidu, S. (2017). Impact of integrating OER in teacher education at the Open University of Sri Lanka. In C. Hodgkinson-Williams & P. B. Arinto (Eds.), *Adoption and impact of OER in the global South* (pp. 459–498). Cape Town & Ottawa: African Minds, International Development Research Centre & Research on Open Educational Resources. doi:https://doi.org/10.5281/zenodo.10005330

Karunanayaka, S., Naidu, S., Rajendra, J. C. N., & Ariadurai, S. A. (2018). Designing continuing professional development MOOCs to promote the adoption of OER and OEP. *Open Praxis, 10*(2), 179–190. doi:http://dx.doi.org/10.5944/openpraxis.10.2.826.

Kinskey, C., King, H., & Carrie, L. M. (2018). Open educational resources: An analysis of Minnesota state colleges and universities student preferences. *Open Learning: The Journal of Open, Distance and e-Learning.* doi:https://doi.org/10.1080/02680513.2018.1500887

Merrill, M. D. (2002). First principles of instruction. *Educational Technology Research and Development, 50*(3), 43–59.

Morrison, D. (2013, April 22). *The ultimate student guide to xMOOCs and cMOOCs* [Web log post]. Retrieved from http://bit.ly/ZDCQzW

Naidu, S. (2010). Using scenario-based learning to promote situated learning and develop professional knowledge. In E. P. Errington (Ed.), *Preparing graduates for the professions using scenario-based learning* (pp. 39–49). Brisbane, Australia: Post Pressed.

Naidu, S. (2013). Transforming MOOCs and MOORFAPs into MOOLOs. *Distance Education, 34*, 253–255. doi:10.1080/01587919.2013.842524

Naidu, S. (2017). Open educational practice: Caveat Emptor. In D. Singh & C. Stückelberger (Eds.), *Ethics in higher education: Values-driven leaders for the future* (pp. 287–305). Geneva: Globethics.net, ISBN 978-2-88931-164-4 (online version) ISBN 978-2-88931-165-1 (print version).

Naidu, S., & Karunanayaka, S. (2014). Engines of education: Integrating OER in learning and teaching. In S. Karunanayaka & S. Naidu (Eds.), *Integrating OER in educational practice: Practitioner stories* (pp. 3–22). The Open University of Sri Lanka. Retrieved from www.ou.ac.lk/home/images/OUSL/publications/intergratingOERinEducationalPractice.pdf

Rajendra, J. C. N., & Ariadurai, S. A. (2018). Designing continuing professional development MOOCs to promote the adoption of OER and OEP. *Open Praxis, 10*(2), 179–190. doi:http://dx.doi.org/10.5944/openpraxis.10.2.826

Reeves, T. C. (2006). Design research from a technology perspective. In J. van den Akker, K. Gravemeijer, S. McKenney, & N. Nieveen (Eds.), *Educational design research* (pp. 52–66). London: Routledge. Retrieved from www.fisme.science.uu.nl/publicaties/literatuur/EducationalDesignResearch.pdf#page=102

Reeves, T. C., & Hedberg, J. G. (2014). MOOCs: Let's get REAL. *Educational Technology, 54*(1), 3–8.

Romiszowski, A. J. (2013). What's really new about MOOCS? *Educational Technology, 53*(4), 48–51.

Senack, E. (2014). *Fixing the broken textbook market: How students respond to high textbook costs and demand alternatives (Report).* Washington, DC: PIRG Education Fund and the Student PRIGS. Retrieved from https://uspirg.org/reports/usp/fixing-broken-textbook-market

Siemens, G. (2008–2012). MOOCs [Series of blog posts]. *Connectivism.* Retrieved from www.connectivism.ca/?s=MOOC

UNESCO. (2002). *Forum on the impact of open courseware for higher education in developing countries.* Final report. Retrieved from www.unesco.org/iiep/eng/focus/opensrc/PDF/OERForumFinalReport.pdf

8
A DIFFERENT KIND OF MOOC ARCHITECTURE FOR EMERGING ECONOMIES IN OCEANIA AND THE PACIFIC

Deepak Bhartu and Som Naidu

While the notion of online education is not new, many Higher Education Institutions (HEI), policy makers and private companies from all over the world have started to explore, create and offer Massive Open Online Courses or MOOCs. MOOCs are large online courses that provide learners free and open access to learning opportunities via the Web. Due to growing interest in MOOCs from stakeholders, the MOOC movement has grown rapidly since Stanford University offered three of its courses free of charge to about 400,000 participants worldwide in 2011 (Rodriguez, 2012; Ng & Widom, 2014).

In developed countries, Internet services are relatively cheap or free; however, the same is not true for the emerging economies of the world (Kirkpatrick, 2018). In these contexts, there is often no access to the Internet; and when there is access, it is intermittent, weak, unreliable and, above all, very expensive. These challenges are certainly true of the South West Pacific region and the member countries of the University of the South Pacific (USP). The USP member countries are Cook Islands, Fiji, Kiribati, Nauru, Niue, Republic of Marshall Islands, Samoa, Solomon Islands, Tokelau, Tonga, Tuvalu and Vanuatu (see Figure 8.1). For these reasons, one could argue that popular models of MOOCs, with their reliance on rich multimedia content including videos and frequent interaction among student peers and course support personnel, often including the MOOC instructors, is an ineffective and unsustainable model across the USP region (Bates, 2015). Until connectivity improves or becomes cheaper, a different model of MOOCs will have to be imagined for the South Pacific Region and similar emerging economies.

USP has a very strong pedigree in open, flexible and distance learning with the use of a wide range of technologies and online resources. The university has been involved in distance education since its inception and has been providing high-quality education to the remotest parts of the region. Given the digital revolution and USP's leadership mandate in the region's ICT development, USP has seen a transition in its modes of learning and teaching from a reliance on print and face-to-face instruction to an increasing use of blended and online technologies to make learning more open and accessible. MOOCs align well with this trajectory and USP's leadership mandate and its current Strategic Plan 2019–2024.

MOOCs are based on the premise that knowledge and understanding is best developed through communication, collaboration and connection among participants (see Siemens, 2008–2012). However, a vast majority of the MOOCs offered to date replicate the structure of traditional university courses. These types of MOOCs, more commonly known as xMOOCs, offer structured learning experiences with an instructor providing guidance on the course via a course syllabus

82 Deepak Bhartu and Som Naidu

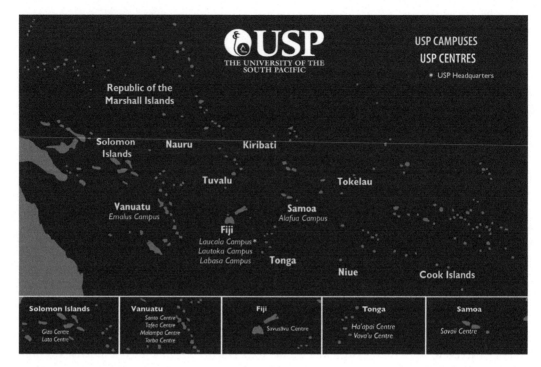

FIGURE 8.1 The USP Footprint

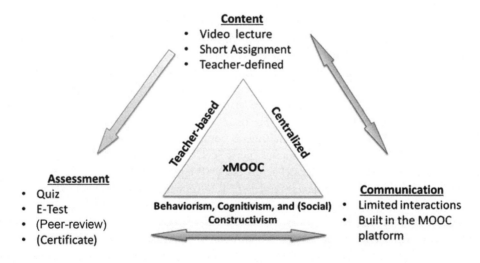

FIGURE 8.2 xMOOC Components

and guiding participants through their learning journey in the course (Sokolik, 2014). Yousef et al. (2014) represents the components of xMOOCs graphically as shown in Figure 8.2 (p. 13).

In this chapter, we describe our early efforts in the development of the first MOOC for USP in the area of climate change, which has relevance for the global audience as well. MOOCs offer the University of the South Pacific an opportunity to reach out to many more of its students in the region and at the same time reach out to those outside the region so that they too can benefit from the unique knowhow and expertise and experience of this region.

Structure of the Climate Change and Pacific Islands MOOC

The member countries of USP region and their people are heavily dependent on their environment for their livelihood, and most at risk when anything threatens it such as climate change. Climate change is one of the biggest challenges facing the region today. In fact, it has already led to significant rise of sea levels and changes in weather patterns.

The MOOC on Climate Change and Pacific Islands was a funded project of UNESCO's CONNECT ASIA programme. The project was implemented in 2015 by USP's Pacific Centre for Environment and Sustainable Development (PaCE-SD) and was the first MOOC that USP offered (www.usp.ac.fj/index.php?id=19481). The course was designed to target environmental professionals, existing tertiary students, and especially those working in governments or NGOs who wished to enhance their understanding of climate change and its impacts on Pacific Island Countries (PICs) and communities. Its main focus was to give an overview of the science of climate change, its effects across the Pacific, highlighting the particular challenges and vulnerabilities of PICs. In addition, it was intended to help build resilience for people involved with planning for natural resources, economic and social development, and protecting the natural environment. Since it was the first time that USP offered a MOOC, a MOOC development cycle was created (see Figure 8.3). The development cycle defined tasks which had to be achieved at each phase and served as a method of quality control.

The MOOC was divided into five core modules of one week each and each module focused on a specific theme. In addition to these five key modules, there was also an "Overview" module in the first week and a "Concluding" module in the last week. The Overview module introduced participants to the course guide that explained the course structure (including the weekly schedule), course learning outcomes and course certification criteria. It also included an introductory video to set the scene for the course and invited participants to introduce themselves to the online community. The concluding module entitled "*The Journey Ends . . .*" provided a summary of the course and focused on the course evaluation and the certification requirements for the participants.

The first module (*Climate Change Science and the Pacific Islands*) provided important insights into the rapidly developing realm of climate science to enhance understanding of the scientific basis of the threats of the impacts of climate change. The second module (*Disaster Risk Reduction and Ecosystem Services*) focused on the causes and impacts of disasters for PICs and provided an overview of disasters, disaster preparedness, mitigation and rehabilitation. It also looked at the causes and effects of climate change on ecosystems and the inter-linkages between climate change and ecology, ecosystem-based adaptation and the importance of incorporating traditional and cultural approaches. The third module (*Impact of Climate Change and Food Security*) looked at building resilience in PICs through understanding risks to food security, reducing vulnerability through optimal choices of crops and enhancing adaptive capacity by better anticipating natural variability and climate change impacts. This particular module also focused on key lessons learned from the use of weather information for food security at the community level and the impacts of tropical cyclones on food security. The fourth module (*Options for Pacific Islands to Mitigate GHG Emissions and Build Their Resilience*) focused on how the Pacific can both reduce its own carbon emissions and build the resilience of PICs in the face of increasing climate change impacts for two key sectors: energy and transport.

The fifth module (*Field Visits: Community Vulnerability and Adaptation Assessment*) provided participants the opportunity to undertake practical field work in a community of their choice using vulnerability and adaptation toolkits that had been developed by PaCE-SD staff and used in over 100 communities. A key incentive for this assessment was that assessments were showcased in the Pacific stand by PaCE-SD staff at the Conference of Parties (COP) 21; this was also known as the 2015 Paris Climate Conference which raised awareness of climate change in the Pacific considerably.

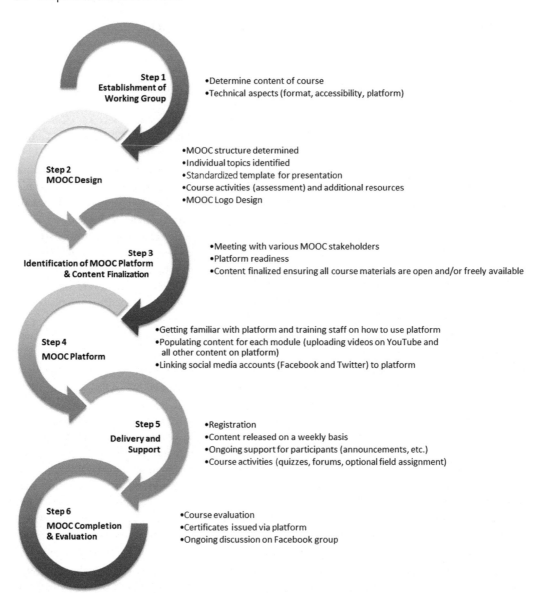

FIGURE 8.3 MOOC Development Cycle

During the re-run of the course in 2017, all the core modules were designed to have a similar structure to foster rich learning experiences and student success except for the fifth module, which was assessment-only. These learning experiences included two-core learning resources in the form of lectures (video lecture, PowerPoint slide with narration, lecture script and audio file of video lecture), additional learning resources, collaboration in discussion forums and social media integration (Facebook and Twitter) and quizzes (multiple choice type) for the two-core learning resources.

Strategies to Support MOOCs for Emerging Economies

To begin with, it was crucial to ensure that all learning resources in the course were either open or freely available on the public domain. This requirement was to make certain that participants did not need any special privileges or incur additional costs to access the resources (Omoeva, Moussa, &

Gale, 2018). In addition, all materials were vetted for copyright compliance and any new content created as part of the MOOC was released under an open license.

Considering the connectivity and technical limitations regarding Internet bandwidth in the South Pacific Region, several short video lectures (5–20 minutes) were developed to prevent wait time in accessing the material either while downloading or streaming. Furthermore, to reduce the size of the video files, only a brief introduction and conclusion was included within the video itself. However, most importantly all core learning resources (lecture notes) were made available in multiple formats to ensure that participants could access the resources with minimal connectivity. These included documents with transcripts and an audio file of the core video lecture. Additionally, participants themselves also took notes from each lecture and shared these with fellow participants.

During the first offer of the course in 2015, USP in collaboration with the Commonwealth of Learning (COL) used a platform called "*mooKIT*" to offer the course (www.col.org/news/connectionsedtech-news/connections-november-2015-vol20-no3). The mooKIT platform developed by the Indian Institute of Technology Kanpur has been specifically designed for Internet access challenged situations and is able to adjust to variable bandwidth (i.e., poor, unstable and expensive). The platform includes a feature utilized by about 8% of the total participants, whereby the course content could be delivered to participants over a phone (mobile phone or landline) without the need for Internet connectivity. Content was transmitted in audio format through a voice call at no cost to the participant.

Another important aspect of the MOOC was the integration of Facebook and Twitter within the platform. The platform would allow participants to use their social media accounts to track and post to discussions and not have to visit the course space to learn of new developments as they were alerted via social media (Prabhakar, Shukla, & Shukla, 2016).

Results and Success Stories

The Climate Change and Pacific Islands MOOC has run twice so far (i.e., in 2015 and 2017) with over 1,500 participants in each offering (see Table 8.1). Participants from over 60 countries around the globe registered for the course with the majority of the participants from Fiji and about 10% from outside the Pacific region. The course offered free certification of participation to all those who met the criteria of "*attempting and scoring at least 50% or more in 5 out of 8 quizzes.*" This particular MOOC has seen impressive completion rates at an average rate of 33.25% compared to the world average of less than 15% (Jordan, 2015).

In addition to the relatively high completion rate for a MOOC, learner engagement was significantly higher than a typical face-to-face university course for the same discipline. Such results could be attributed to the effective use of discussion forums and integration of social media in the course. From an instructor's perspective, the ability to view interaction between participants with many of the questions/queries being answered by fellow participants themselves was fascinating. In effect, peer-to-peer learning was a key aspect of this MOOC on Climate Change and the Pacific Islands. The level of excellent thought and discussions by participants provoked by the instructors, and the interaction between participants from different parts of the world was of high value (e.g., discussions on use of community-based participatory actions and traditional knowledge between Europeans, South Americans and Pacific Islanders). Instructors were also generally astounded by the level and scope of cross-cultural exchanges that transpired on social media. Stated another way,

TABLE 8.1 MOOC Enrollments and Completion Rates

Year of Offering	2015	2017
Number of Registered Participants	1,534	1,636
Number of Participants Completing	411	650
Completion Rate	26.8%	39.7%

it was immediately apparent that participants were quite familiar with social media and were able to assuage concerns about the course using them. The MOOC also encouraged more and free discussions of thoughts and ideas in comparison to traditional courses. The Social Network Graph detailed in Figure 8.4 illustrates how participants made use of social media during the course from the first week to the last week.

Importantly, 10 participants from the course in 2015 applied for a Post Graduate programme in Climate Change offered by USP. As such, the MOOC directly contributed to transfer rates. Table 8.2 shows the average pass rate for the quizzes.

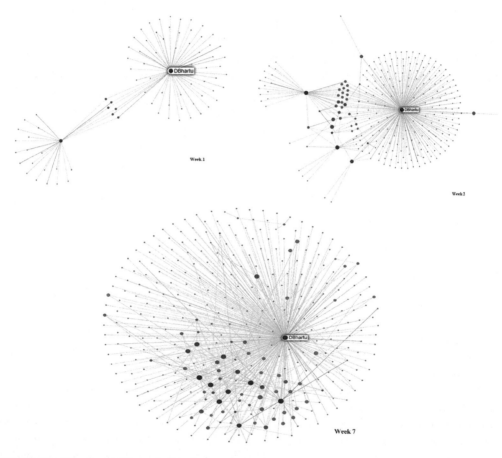

FIGURE 8.4 The Social Network Graph

TABLE 8.2 Summary of Quiz Responses for Certification

Quiz No.	No. of Responses		Pass Rate (50% or more)		Average Mark	
	2015	2017	2015	2017	2015	2017
1	590	808	90%	98%	76%	92%
2	529	779	89%	97%	68%	83%
3	485	731	78%	91%	62%	70%
4	454	697	89%	93%	74%	77%
5	439	680	96%	94%	85%	81%
6	430	665	98%	99%	83%	85%
7	413	658	92%	95%	84%	84%
8	400	646	79%	80%	65%	65%

Concluding Remarks

One of the 17 Sustainable Development Goals (SDG) of the United Nations is to have Quality Education (SDG 4). Its intention is to "Ensure inclusive and equitable quality education and promote lifelong learning opportunities for all" (SDG Compass, 2015). The MOOC on Climate Change and Pacific Islands displayed how island nations face a unique set of challenges to sustainable and prosperous development. It presented different aspects of the topic, from the scientific background to impacts on different sectors and the various options for the Pacific Islands to reduce their already minimal contribution to the global greenhouse gas emissions.

Furthermore, although MOOCs were initially seen as a means of raising the institutional profile and reputation, there were clearly other associated benefits for institutions and academics. Such benefits include encouraging engagement amongst staff and students, targeting alumni, conducting educational research and promoting interdisciplinary and international collaboration. Other unique opportunities that can be derived from MOOCs include enhancing the institutional brand and reputation from outreach activities, generating unique pathways for student recruitment, encouraging an atmosphere of open education and open licensing, piloting various pedagogical practices, enhancing digital literacies and fostering international experiences and new forms of institutional globalization and partnerships. Perhaps most importantly, and in tough budgetary times, MOOCs offer a potential source of alternative revenues when students pay for certification and/or instructional support. For USP, there seems to be three possibilities in the near future in relation to MOOCs. These are (1) MOOCs for revenue generation, (2) MOOCs for lifelong learning and (3) MOOCs for alternative pathways to learning.

One of the ways in which the USP can make its educational offerings accessible to a wider community is through targeted initiatives, which ensure that educational materials are available in a format that potential participants in emerging economies can access. The Climate Change and Pacific Islands MOOC and all its content was prepared in ways such that participants based anywhere in the world were able to download the learning resources in formats that best suited them and their learning context. It also provided the participants with the opportunity to reach out to instructors via discussion forums and social networks.

Deepak Bhartu is an open education design architect in the Centre for Flexible Learning at the University of the South Pacific. Mr. Bhartu possesses a master's degree in Computing Science and Information Systems from the University of the South Pacific. He has worked in the higher education sector as a teaching academic, and a learning experience designer. In the latter role he has developed and supported the development of courses for online and blended learning on various platforms including Open edX, mooKIT and Moodle. Mr. Bhartu is also a certified Higher Education Peer Reviewer with Quality Matters with research interests in open education practices; specifically, open educational resources and massive open online courses.

Som Naidu is currently Pro-Vice Chancellor Flexible Learning and Director, Center for Flexible Learning, at the University of the South Pacific. Dr Naidu possesses undergraduate qualifications in Education from the University of Waikato in New Zealand, and graduate qualifications in Educational Technology from Concordia University in Montreal, Canada. A former president of the Open and Distance Learning Association of Australia, Dr Naidu has served as Executive Editor of its journal *Distance Education* since 1997. In May 2014 the Open University of Sri Lanka awarded Dr Naidu a D.Litt. *(Honoris Causa)*, in recognition of his extensive contribution to the field of open, flexible, distance and e-learning both regionally and internationally.

References

Bates, A. W. (2015). *Teaching in a digital age*. Vancouver, BC: BCcampus. Retrieved from https://opentextbc.ca/teachinginadigitalage/

Jordan, K. (2015). *MOOC completion rates: The data*. Retrieved November 23, 2018, from www.katyjordan.com/MOOCproject.html

Kirkpatrick, K. (2018, June). Bringing the internet to the (developing) world. *Communications of the ACM, 61*(7), 20–21. doi:https://doi.org/10.1145/3213775

Ng, A., & Widom, J. (2014). *Origins of the modern MOOC (xMOOC)*. Retrieved November 23, 2018, from http://robotics.stanford.edu/~ang/papers/mooc14-OriginsOfModernMOOC.pdf

Omoeva, C., Moussa, W., & Gale, C. (2018). The economic costs of educational inequality in developing countries. In I. BenDavid-Hadar (Ed.), *Education finance, equality, and equity* (pp. 181–217). Cham: Springer International Publishing.

Prabhakar, T. V., Shukla, S., & Shukla, G. (2016). Mobi-MOOCs: A simple and effective way to deliver educational content. *Commonwealth of Learning (COL)*. Retrieved from https://oerknowledgecloud.org/sites/oerknowledgecloud.org/files/PDF%20(7).pdf

Rodriguez, C. O. (2012). MOOCs and the AI-Stanford like courses: Two successful and distinct course formats for massive open online courses (p. 1–13). *European Journal of Open, Distance and E-Learning*. Retrieved from http://www.eurodl.org/?article=516

SDG Compass. (2015). *The guide for business action on the SDGs*. Retrieved from https://sdgcompass.org/wp-content/uploads/2015/12/019104_SDG_Compass_Guide_2015.pdf

Siemens, G. (2008–2012). MOOCs [Series of blog posts]. *Connectivism*. Retrieved from www.connectivism.ca/?s=MOOC

Sokolik, M. (2014). What constitutes an effective language MOOC? *Language MOOCs: Providing Learning, Transcending Boundaries*, 16–32. https://doi.org/10.2478/9783110420067.2

Yousef, A. M. F., Chatti, M. A., Schoroeder, U., Wosnitza, M., & Jacobs, H, et al. (2014). *MOOCs: A review of the state-of-the-art*. Proceedings of 6th International Conference on Computer Supported Education—CSEDU 2014. Barcelona, Spain.

9

NEPALI HIGH SCHOOL STUDENTS IN MASSIVE OPEN ONLINE COURSES (MOOCs)

Impressive Results and a Promising Future

Baman Kumar Ghimire and Bishwa Raj Gautam

Introduction

Massive open online courses (MOOCs) are a relatively recent development with great potential to help people access better learning opportunities from higher education institutions around the world (Bonk, Lee, Reeves, & Reynolds, 2015). MOOCs may be especially beneficial for students from developing countries who would not otherwise have these opportunities because of geographic or time constraints. However, research is needed to demonstrate the realities of these benefits in specific contexts. This is especially important because MOOCs and indeed online learning in general often necessitate some substantial changes in traditional educational practices and policies, and these changes should be guided by sound scholarship.

With the onset of MOOCs, students from all levels potentially have exciting opportunities to "build new knowledge without necessarily having to move between countries" (Balula & Moreira, 2014, p. 6). Thankfully, as a result of the expansion of Internet accessibility, affordability and operational skills, e-learning is now seen as a viable alternative to complement the existing curricula in developing countries, including those designated as Least Developed Countries (LDCs) (Lambert & Hassan, 2018, p. 156). More specifically, richness of the content, massiveness in participation, and low-cost accessibility anywhere or anytime the Internet is available appears to make MOOCs good options for learners who lack access to more traditional forms of advanced education.

In the light of growing viability of MOOCs, this chapter presents the patterns of participation in MOOCs of high school students in Nepal. The chapter seeks to describe the factors responsible in vitalizing the efficacy of their MOOC engagement. To that end, the authors have conducted pre- and post-MOOC participation surveys with Nepalese high school students for urban areas of the country; we did not address learners in rural settings in this particular study. The students surveyed completed at least one course through a MOOC platform. The chapter concludes with the argument that engagement with MOOCs benefits young learners in different ways, but most notably with regard to the overall development of personality. The authors also offer insights into how to motivate students for enrollment and completion of online courses.

Dawning of MOOCs in Emerging Economies

Davidson (2013) posited that the first really large-scale MOOC was developed in 2011 by Sebastian Thrun and Peter Norvig, who attracted about 160,000 online registrants to an online course focused on artificial intelligence. In less than seven years, Shah (2018) asserted that the number of students using MOOC platforms like Coursera, edX, and Udacity rose to 81 million. As shown in the various chapters of this book, millions of these learners are likely from emerging economies. According to Palin (2014), out of edX's 1.9 million users back in 2014, 48 percent were from developing countries. Cheney (2017) noted that of the roughly 24 million Coursera users in April 2017, 45 percent were from developing countries. Interestingly, Coursera claimed to be committed to increasing the number of learners from emerging economies.

The unprecedented growth in the number of mobile phone users and the introduction of MOOC mobile phone apps have resulted in an increase in the student participation and performance in MOOCs among participants from underdeveloped nations. The number of Internet users is growing exponentially in the developing world. In terms of statistics, the International Telecommunication Union (ITU, 2017) reported that over 41 percent of the population in developing nations now have access to and use the Internet. Importantly, two thirds of these numbers are youths (aged 15–24). Mobile-broadband subscriptions increased by almost 55 percent in 2012–2017 in least developed countries (LDCs). The price of such subscriptions plunged in LDCs from 32.4 percent to 14.1 percent of GNI p.c. from 2013 to 2016, whereas it dropped to 6 percent from 11.6 percent in developing countries (International Telecommunication Union, 2017, pp. 1–5). Similarly, the availability of perhaps thousands of courses from major MOOC providers like Coursera, edX, and Udacity in mobile phones have also eased the barriers to accessing online educational opportunities.

Internet in Nepal: Records and Realities

Connectivity is a very powerful tool for success and fulfillment in the 21st century. Thus, the International Telecommunications Union (ITU, 2017) aimed to spread broadband to at least "half of the world population by 2017" (p. 1). Citing the Nepal Telecommunication Authority, the regulatory body for Internet penetration in Nepal, Neupane (2018) reported that about 63 percent of people have access to the Internet in that country of nearly 30 million people. This report indicated that Nepal adds roughly 256 new Internet users every hour. In the same vein, Dhungana (2018) revealed that the Government of Nepal plans to orchestrate a substantial decrease in the price of mobile-broadband to or below 5 percent of Gross National Income (GNI) by 2020. Though the surging price of Internet poses a threat to this target, almost 6.3 percent increase in per capita income in 2017 (The World Bank, 2018) shows that the nation can bear the price if per capita income gradually ascends. Such unprecedented extension of the possibilities of connectivity is a challenge and an opportunity for Nepal.

Research shows that a majority of the population in developing countries use the Internet for social connectivity. Undoubtedly, the Internet has much more to offer than merely social interactions; however, Poushter (2016) noticed that Internet users in developing nations are more likely to use social media than those in developed nations. We turn our attention now to a study that we oversaw in Nepal during the past couple of years.

To better understand the possibility and prospects of online learning among young learners in Nepal, the authors conducted a survey on 644 high school students from June 2016 to January 2017 before they introduced MOOCs. This study included 312 students from public schools and 322 from institutional schools from 10 different urban locations across Nepal. The survey questioned their Internet access, purpose and period of Internet use. It discovered that the majority of high school students in Nepal frequently use Internet for social networks. Only 26 among 644 participants noted that they did not have access to Internet. From among those with access, respondents indicated that 69.2 percent enjoyed engagement in social media, 14.4 percent played games, and the rest (12.4 percent) used it for assignment support. A report from Acharya (2016) supplements the finding of maximum use of social media among the teenagers. In a 2015 survey of 15- to 17-year-old students at three schools in Kathmandu, the capital city of Nepal, Acharya (2016) reported that the majority of the students used the Internet either for socialization or for entertainment purposes. At the same time, the use of the Internet for educational purposes was found to be extremely low. It is evident that high school students in Nepal are very attracted to social media, as are students from around the world. Unfortunately, most of these students fail to perceive the timely and pervasive support that the Internet can provide for academic advancement and life-skill enhancement.

Educational Technology: A Promising Choice for Nepal

The Government of Nepal (GoN) is committed to promoting and integrating educational technology to enhance learning outcomes for its students at every level. The GoN concedes that increased access to the Internet is a must to promote quality education in rural areas as well as in more urban settings. The Nepal Telecommunications Authority (2015) of the GoN demonstrated its interest, as the Policy aimed to reach at least 20 percent of public secondary schools with at least 1 Mbps broadband connection and use it for educational purposes as well as pedagogical tools by 2018.

In addition, Nepal's Information and Communication Technology Master Plan (2013–2017) aimed to create 1,000 model schools equipped with ICT learning centers (Ministry of Education, 2013). Moreover, the School Sector Development Plan 2016–2023 acknowledged that ICT skills were fundamental tools to improve both the quality and the relevance of education (Ministry of Education, 2016). These and other plans demonstrate the government's interest in providing ample ICT opportunities to the high schools to enable their students to cope with the rapidly changing technological world.

MOOCs have lately been a hot issue among academicians around the world interested in educational and instructional technology (Bonk, Lee, Kou, Xu, & Sheu, 2015). Regardless of the geographical location of learners, MOOCs offer an array of learning opportunities that can address the interests and needs of varied levels of participants. The increased access to technology has enabled the promotion of MOOCs in developing countries as well as LDCs. Referring to research carried out in Malaysia, Fadzil, Abdol, and Munira (2015) asserted that MOOCs can be implemented to complement "current educational delivery systems at the higher education level by leveraging on the use of web-technology" (p. 65). Similarly, Pushpanadham (2015) described MOOCs as a democratized form of advanced learning opportunity that is "creating a global education platform to make knowledge and educational resources accessible to all" (p. 23). Lauding the efforts made by a high school teacher in Nepal, a country that saw more than 35,000 schools devastated by earthquakes in 2015, Mason (2017) stressed that MOOCs have been an invaluable educational resource to foster "new champions of digital learning" in Nepal. Increased Internet accessibility and the growth of online course interest among Nepali learners show that MOOCs have abundant prospects in Nepal.

MOOC Usage Among the Young Learners in Nepal: Motivation and Completion

Most MOOC providers try to address the needs and the demands of its diverse factions of the learners. In effect, they tend to "appeal to a broader cross-section of students" (Kauza, 2014, p. 106). These providers offer their MOOC courses in different modes like archived, self-paced or switch-session, languages, and levels. Such options indicate that they are attempting to attract as many learners as possible by respecting their competencies, backgrounds, preferences, and technology availability. For example, edX caters courses in 16 different languages and Coursera boasts 2700+ courses with 250+ specializations (edX, 2018; Coursera, 2018). Such variation is a boom not only for the novice but also for more experienced MOOC learners. Undeniably, the popular MOOC platforms strive to contain both the high quality of information and effective instructional methods.

MOOCs bring diverse options "for genuinely curious learners" (Kauza, 2014, p. 112) who love to spare some time and energy to learn something new for free.

MOOCs dish abundant opportunities with multiple appropriate choices for young Nepali learners who seek to study both mandatory and elective subjects. Like elsewhere in the world, Nepalese students from different age groups and attitudes have different experiences with MOOCs. The stories of 10- to 18-year-old high school students in Nepal emerging from our research justify the benefits of MOOCs to young learners. After participating in a day long workshop given during October 2015 to June 2017 in 24 different locations across the country, Nepalese high school students enrolled in and successfully completed 64 different courses which were in some ways connected to their curriculum. The motivation for enrolling in these MOOCs appears to have been primarily self-determined. Milligan, Littlejohn, and Margaryan (2013) concluded that it is equally important that a participant must "self-motivate and self-direct their learning" (p. 157) in MOOCs. MOOC participants do not get individual feedback from the instructors, so they must keep abreast of the contents and assignment deadlines. Experience, enthusiasm, and education are essential for the successful completion of MOOCs. Besides enriching oneself within a particular subject matter area, MOOCs also provide opportunities for learners to enhance their multicultural understanding through the interactions with other course participants.

With "a complicated set of conditions—access, language, computer literacy among others" (Liyanagunawardena, Williams, & Adams, 2013, p. 3), until recently, MOOCs were a next-to-impossible means of learning for the majority of the people in developing countries. As a result, much educational potential went untapped. In 2013, when the Internet penetration was roughly 31 percent in developing countries, Trucano (2013) wrote that MOOCs were "still not a hot topic of consideration for educational policymakers in most middle and low income countries." Now with seemingly miraculous innovations in educational technology and the rapid growth in the number of Internet users coinciding with major decreases in the price of Internet access, educational entrepreneurs have been encouraged to rethink and redesign the teaching and learning practices in developing and least developed countries. The growth of the Internet penetration rate, the changes in government policies to integrate technology in education and the interest of the young learners to utilize the Internet for learning and living indicate that the prospects for MOOCs in high schools in Nepal are indeed quite promising.

There are numerous reasons that motivate a registrant to enroll in an online course. Some are very crucial in sticking the participant into a course that does not end simply in clicks, but instead results in genuine academic engagement. For Zheng, Rosson, Shih, and Carroll (2015), some reasons behind MOOC participation included "fulfilling current needs, preparing for the future, satisfying curiosity and connecting with the people" (p. 1886). Milligan et al. (2013) conceded that confidence, prior experience and motivation were important determinants of successful engagement in a MOOC. The studies among the students from developed or developing countries show that those whose reasons for registering for the course were earning a certificate, gaining skills, and improving professional practice had a greater chance of completing the course successfully (Phan, McNeil, & Robin, 2016). Horn (2014) observed that low-income high school students in an urban school district were beginning to take MOOCs in greater numbers than students from more privileged backgrounds (p. 83). What motivates the students from high schools particularly in LDCs is still intriguing since most of the prior findings were telescopic representations of the overall developing nations.

Until 2015, there was hardly any documented evidence about the MOOCs for high schools in Nepal. In early March 2015, 18 out of 27 students from the Motherland Secondary School in Pokhara, Nepal, registered for a MOOC on *English Grammar and Essay Writing* offered by University of California, Berkeley, and completed in five weeks. The school recognized the accomplishments of the students in the school assembly and through publications in local and national print media. The U.S. Embassy in Nepal also posted their achievements in its official social media pages on how the Internet can support students' regular studies (U.S. Embassy, Nepal, 2015). The posts were very popular and instrumental in motivating the MOOC learners.

A grant from the International Research & Exchanges Board (IREX) in October 2015 and Department of State's Award for Innovation for English Language Programs–2016 helped to further popularize MOOCs in Nepal. The grant aimed to provide MOOC orientation and workshops for 15 high schools in Pokhara, Nepal. It was further extended across the country through the Award under the title of *Mentoring in MOOC Magic*. From June 2016 to June 2017, almost 2,000 students and nearly 200 teachers from 18 urban locations participated in *Mentoring in MOOCMagic*. In addition, "about 1,400 high school students have completed at least one MOOC in Nepal" (Ghimire, 2018, p. 116). The media also continued favorable reporting about the initiation and accomplishments of MOOC camps across the country. Such coverage stimulated the curiosity and interest among the learners as well as the teachers, and, thereby, steered the exploration, participation, and completion of a number of MOOCs from different platforms.

A Journey in Crowds to a Self-Identification

Generally, MOOC participants do not belong to any fixed age group. Pappano (2012) reported that MOOC users range from teenagers to retirees. When you are in an online world of learning, "Education is a more significant factor in Internet use than age" (International Telecommunications Union, 2018, p. 83). A few months following their achievement, the first group of MOOC completers from Motherland High School turned out to be the facilitators leading sessions for their colleagues and guardians. They shared their perceived benefits and challenges of MOOCs in their community and also travelled for hours to co-facilitate workshops in neighboring districts.

The researchers believe that opportunities on democratization of learning through MOOCs for learners in developing countries are "real and achievable" (Patru & Balaji, 2016). The course completion rate of the high school MOOC learners from Nepal is very high as compared to those from other parts of the world that staggers between 10–15 percent. For instance, in March 2015, about 67 percent of the 27 students aged 12 to 17 from Motherland Secondary School, Pokhara, Nepal, completed an *English Grammar and Essay Writing* MOOC. Even more astoundingly, 88 percent of 75 participants completed a MOOC on *How to Write an Essay* in October 2015. The following year in July, the course completion rate dropped nominally to 78 percent when 54 students from the same school registered for *TOEFL® Test Preparation: The Insider's Guide*. All the five-week-long courses were offered and recognized by edX, with an Honor Code for the first two courses, and the third with the Verified Certificate on 100 percent scholarship, which was unfortunately the first and the last of its kind in edX. Such provisions were instrumental in bringing in the digitally and financially challenged learners to the MOOC world. Our survey reports reveal that the interconnection the participation develops between the existing curriculum and the online courses was a key source of motivation for continuous engagement of young learners in MOOCs in Nepal.

In June–July 2017, the authors conducted a Post-MOOC workshop survey among 206 school students aged 10–18 from 15 urban areas across Nepal who completed at least one MOOC. Findings reveal that 96 students chose *Computer Science* as their first MOOC subject area, whereas 76 opted for *English Language* and 15 took *Life Science and Math*. Such results show that the participants want to align the MOOC course with the knowledge and skills obtained in their regular school courses. In effect, these findings justify the claim that online courses targeting high school students are more popular because the courses help them prepare for and "succeed in STEM fields in college" (Mintz, 2015).

The participation in MOOCs has brought some impressive feedback from the students, guardians, and teachers. Sharing their varied learning experiences was another skill of young MOOC learners in Nepal. The Post-MOOC workshop survey indicated that 91 percent of the respondents facilitated others in the online course. The students were proud to inspire peers at school as well as earn prestige for their family since they were the first to receive a course completion certificate from a foreign university in their community (Poudel, 2017, p. 30). They seemed to feel that the engagement has elevated their self-confidence, competence, and public attention. The video records in Call Interest Section—2017 (2017) indicate that even reserved students transformed into impressive public speakers with logical expressions. Equally impressive, guardians shared stories of the positive effects of MOOCs on their children's academic progress—who before wasted time playing video games or any other social media. Their better performance in school examinations also garnered prestige after obtaining certificates from universities abroad.

Conclusion

Initially, some school students enrolled in MOOCs partly out of simple curiosity and perhaps the desire to be a celebrity in media and school assembly; however, most enrollees were enticed by the anticipation of their name on the certificates from renowned academic institutions abroad. By completing MOOCs the participants acquired extra value; namely, increased knowledge and skills as well as instant certificates. In terms of their academic career development, such competencies and certifications took place despite making just a small investment of time, money, and personal effort. Not too surprisingly, most students appreciated the provision of financial aid which made a big difference.

When MOOCs were completed, the students became role models among their peers; especially the female students who developed more confidence and started to perceive that their image was influential as a role model in an ideal society. Teachers and students in high schools in Nepal look forward to more facilitated MOOC camps since they can result in not just course completion, but can also extensively impact their life and the local community.

Baman Kumar Ghimire is a high school English language teacher from Nepal. He is a recipient of Endeavour Executive Fellowship–2014 from the Australian Government and Teaching Excellence and Achievement (TEA) Program–2014 Award by the Department of State. Mr. Ghimire completed an MA in English literature from Tribhuvan University, TESOL Core Certificate from TESOL International Association, and over two dozen of MOOCs. He was awarded with an Alumni Grant–2015 by IREX, Federal Assistance Award–2016, and the International Visitor Leadership Program (IVLP)–2017 Award by the Department of State to encourage his efforts in mentoring MOOCs to high school students and teachers in Nepal. He has penned some articles, run a number of workshops, and made presentations in national and international conferences on educational technology.

Bishwa Raj Gautam manages English language programs at the US Embassy in Nepal and provides teacher training on materials production and open learning. Mr. Gautam gave plenary addresses at international conferences of the Nepal English Language Teachers' Association (NELTA) on *Technology and Connectivism: ELTian's Future* in 2018 and *TESOL's Six Principles for Learning Centered Teaching* in 2019. He has authored two books, *Open Library* and a workbook, *Professional Spoken English: Take It Easy!* He completed a Master's of Philosophy in English Literature, Master's in English Education, and Library and Information Sciences from the Tribhuvan University, TESOL Core Certificate from TESOL International Association, and E-Teacher from the University of Maryland Baltimore County (UMBC).

References

Acharya, S. (2016). *Internet usage of teenagers in Nepal for educational purposes* (Austrian Matura). Retrieved from www.centrum3.at/fileadmin/downloads/VWA/Acharya_Internet_Nepal.pdf

Balula, A., & Moreira, A. (2014). *Evaluation of online higher education learning interaction and technology*. Retrieved from https://doi.org/10.1007/978-3-319-05425-4

Bonk, C. J., Lee, M. M., Kou, X., Xu, S., & Sheu, F. R. (2015). *Understanding the self-directed online learning preferences, goals, achievements, and challenges of MIT opencourseware subscribers*. Retrieved from http://publicationshare.com/J_Ed-Tech_Society_Bonk_Lee_et_al_MIT_OCW_MOOCs_Self_directed_Lrng_in_press.pdf

Bonk, C. J., Lee, M. M., Reeves, T. C., & Reynolds, T. (Eds.). (2015). *MOOCs and open education around the world*. New York: Routledge.

Call Interest Section—2017. (2017, March 24). *Hot topics: Digital literacy*. Retrieved from www.youtube.com/watch?v=1cKSCpsnj1U&feature=youtu.be

Cheney, C. (2017, April 3). The road to real results for online learning in developing countries. *Devex*. Retrieved from www.devex.com/news/the-road-to-real-results-for-online-learning-in-developing-countries-89884

Coursera. (2018, November 21). Retrieved from https://about.coursera.org/

Davidson, C. (2013, September 27). What was the first MOOC? *Hastac Blog*. Retrieved from www.hastac.org/blogs/cathy-davidson/2013/09/27/what-was-first-mooc

Dhungana, S. (2018, July 18). Surging internet cost to affect national broadband policy target. *The Himalayan Times*. Retrieved from https://thehimalayantimes.com/business/surging-internet-cost-to-affect-national-broadband-policy-target/

edX. (2018, November 21). Retrieved from www.edx.org/course

Fadzil, M., Abdol, L., & Munira, T. A. (2015). MOOCs in Malaysia: A preliminary case study. In B. Kim (Ed.), *MOOCs and educational challenges around Asia and Europe* (pp. 65–85). Seoul, South Korea: KNOU. Retrieved from http://asemlllhub.org/fileadmin/www.asem.au.dk/publications/MOOCs_and_Educational_Challenges_around_Asia_and_Europe_FINAL.pdf

Ghimire, B. K. (2018). Maximizing continuous professional and academic development through MOOC. In S. Shrestha (Ed.), *NELTA Forum* (pp. 114–123). Kathmandu, Nepal: Nepal English Language Teachers' Association (NELTA).

Horn, M. B. (2014). MOOCs for high school unlocking opportunities or substandard learning? *Education Next, 14*(3), 82–83. Retrieved from www.educationnext.org/moocs-high-school/

International Telecommunications Union. (2017). *ICT facts and figures 2017*. Retrieved from www.itu.int/en/ITU-D/Statistics/Documents/facts/ICTFactsFigures2017.pdf

International Telecommunications Union. (2018). *ICTs, LDCs and the SDGs: Achieving universal and affordable Internet in the least developed countries (Thematic report)*. Retrieved from www.itu.int/en/ITU-D/LDCs/Pages/Publications/LDCs/D-LDC-ICTLDC-2018-PDF-E.pdf

Kauza, J. (2014). More questions than answers: Scratching at the surface of MOOCs in higher education. In S.D. Krause & C. Lowe (Eds.), *Invasion of the MOOCs: The promises and perils of massive open online courses* (pp. 105–114). Anderson, SC: Parlor Press.

Lambert, L. A., & Hassan, H. (2018). MOOCs and international capacity building in a UN framework: Potential and challenges. In W. L. Filho, M. Mifsud, & P. Pace (Eds.), *Handbook of lifelong learning for sustainable development* (pp. 155–164). Cham, Switzerland: Springer.

Liyanagunawardena, T., Williams, S., & Adams, A. (2013). The impact and reach of MOOCs: A developing countries' perspective. *eLearning Papers, 33*, 1–8. Retrieved from http://centaur.reading.ac.uk/32452/1/In-depth_33_1.pdf

Mason, R. (2017, March 24). Using MOOCs to advance education in Nepal. *The Huffington Post*. Retrieved from www.huffingtonpost.com/entry/using-moocs-to-advance-education-in-nepal_us_58fde998e4b0f02c3870ec59

Milligan, C., Littlejohn, A., & Margaryan, A. (2013). Patterns of engagement in connectivist MOOCs. *MERLOT Journal of Online Learning and Teaching, 9*(2), 149–159.

Ministry of Education. (2013). *Information &communication technology (ICT) in education master plan (2013–2017)*. Retrieved from http://moe.gov.np/assets/uploads/files/ICT_MP_2013_(Final)_.pdf

Ministry of Education. (2016). *School sector development plan 2016–2023*. Retrieved from www.moe.gov.np/assets/uploads/files/MOE_SSDP_Final_Document_Oct_2016.pdf

Mintz, S. (2015, September 1). *MOOC providers* [Blog Post]. Retrieved from https://blog.edX.org/mooc-providers

Nepal Telecommunications Authority. (2015). *National broadband policy-2071*. Retrieved from www.nta.gov.np/old/ne/component/joomdoc/Broadband%20Policy . . . /download.html

Neupane, N. (2018, January 20). Nepal added over 250 internet users per hour. *The Kathmandu Post*. Retrieved from http://kathmandupost.ekantipur.com/news/2018-01-20/nepal-added-over-250-internet-users-per-hour.html

Palin, A. (2014, March 10). *MOOCs: Young students from developing countries are still in the minority*. Retrieved from www.ft.com/content/8a81f66e-9979-11e3-b3a2-00144feab7de

Pappano, L. (2012, November 2). The year of the MOOC. *The New York Times*. Retrieved from www.nytimes.com/2012/11/04/education/edlife/massive-open-online-courses-are-multiplying-at-a-rapid-pace.html

Patru, M., & Balaji, V. (Eds.). (2016). *Making sense of MOOCs: A guide for policy-makers in developing countries*. Paris, France: UNESCO and Commonwealth of Learning. Retrieved from http://unesdoc.unesco.org/images/0024/002451/245122E.pdf

Phan, T., McNeil, S. G., & Robin, B. R. (2016). Students' patterns of engagement and course performance in a massive open online course. *Computers & Education, 95*, 36–44.

Poudel, P. (2017, June). University certificate. In K. Gautam & P. Basukala (Eds.), *Access newsletter*(p. 30). Kathmandu, Nepal: English Access Microscholarship Program Nepal English Language Teachers' Association (NELTA). Retrieved from https://englishaccessnepal.files.wordpress.com/2016/12/access-newsletter-vol-11-june-2017.pdf

Poushter, J. (2016). *Smartphone ownership and internet usage continues to climb in emerging economies* (Research Discussion paper). Pew Research Center Website. Retrieved from http://s1.pulso.cl/wp-content/uploads/2016/02/2258581.pdf

Pushpanadham, K. (2015). Universalizing university education: MOOCs in the era of knowledge based society. In B. Kim (Ed.), *MOOCs and educational challenges around Asia and Europe* (pp. 21–33). Seoul, South Korea: KNOU. Retrieved from http://asemlllhub.org/fileadmin/www.asem.au.dk/publications/MOOCs_and_Educational_Challenges_around_Asia_and_Europe_FINAL.pdf

Shah, D. (2018). *By the numbers: MOOCs in 2018.* Retrieved from https://www.classcentral.com/report/mooc-stats-2018/

Trucano, M. (2013, November 12). *More about MOOCs and developing countries* [Blog post]. Retrieved from http://blogs.worldbank.org/edutech/moocs-developing-countries

U.S. Embassy, Nepal. (2015, March 23). *Did you know that the internet can be used in many ways to help you with your studies? . . . In conjunction with . . .* [Facebook Page]. Retrieved from www.facebook.com/nepal.usembassy/posts/did-you-know-that-the-internet-can-be-used-in-many-ways-to-help-you-with-your-st/807142249322836/

The World Bank. (2018). *GDP per capita growth (annual %).* Retrieved from https://data.worldbank.org/indicator/NY.GDP.PCAP.KD.ZG

Zheng, S., Rosson, M. B., Shih, P. C., & Carroll, J. M. (2015). *Understanding student motivation, behaviors, and perceptions in MOOCs.* Proceeding of 18th ACM Conference on Computer Supported Cooperative Work & Social Computing. Vancouver, Canada. Retrieved from https://doi.org/:10.1145/2675133.2675217

10
MOOCs IN LATIN AMERICA
Trends and Issues

Jaime Sánchez and José Reyes-Rojas

Introduction

This chapter intends to provide a comprehensive look at the scientific production around the MOOC movement in Latin America. Although there are other systematic reviews focused on MOOCs in the Latin American region, according to Veletsianos and Shepherdson (2016), this region has produced the least MOOC literature. As such, it is the exactly the area in dire need of the various analyses found in this chapter.

This study includes a review of the specialized literature on MOOCs in Latin America, published both outside and within the Latin American region. For replication purposes, we also include a brief methodological description of our study steps and search decisions including our interpretations and categorizations of emerging issues. Finally, we discuss the findings from a critical viewpoint based on the data collection processes undertaken throughout the entire research project.

In this study, we wanted to reveal the studies, investigations, reports, and experiences found in the scientific literature on MOOCs in Latin America. The objective of this research was to characterize and determine the trends and issues concerning MOOCs in Latin America based on indexed scientific documentation. It was expected that this study could serve as an empirical tool for researchers, professionals, practitioners, students, and anyone interested in better understanding the scientific literature around the MOOC phenomenon in Latin America.

MOOC Research Literature

In addition to the multiple reports on experiences and research associated with the MOOC phenomenon, there are several systematic reviews and bibliometric studies that provided vital findings for the scientific community. In particular, the work of Liyanagunawardena, Adams, and Williams (2013) is considered one of the pioneering systematic reviews with regard to the MOOC phenomenon. In their study, the authors analyzed documents published between 2008 and 2012, with a sample drawn from both academic databases and specialized journals. Liyanaguwardena et al. compiled a sample of 45 MOOC research documents including articles, conference papers, and scientific and professional reports which yielded important insights related to the scientific literature associated with the MOOC phenomenon. Specifically, the authors detected methodological limitations in the approach to the MOOC literature based mainly on the extracted quantitative data.

The work of Yousef, Chatti, Schroeder, Wosnitza, and Jakobs (2015) published two years later offers a sample spectrum of 93 documents; their study sample is approximately twice that of

Liyanagunawardena et al., 2013 and entails a longer study period from 2008 to 2014. Through qualitative and quantitative analysis, Yousef et al. (2015) found a contradiction between the innovative discourse characteristic of the beginnings of the MOOC phenomenon and the actual practices associated with the implementation of MOOCs, characterized by a more behavioral and teacher-centered approach than the early MOOC rhetoric had proclaimed.

Importantly, the works of Liyanagunawardena et al. (2013) and Yousef et al. (2015) address the MOOC phenomenon since the beginning of the MOOC movement in 2008. The systematic research review studies from these researchers detail a progressive increase in scientific production in the area as indicated in the specialized academic literature. Themes that they discussed included the conceptualization of MOOCs, the educational theories behind the proposals under study, the platforms associated with the delivery of the service, the types of technological resources associated with the MOOC experience, the forms of evaluation inserted into the experience, and various case studies related to MOOCs. As a consequence, an area of study has begun to form which attempts to characterize the MOOC movement in Latin America.

The seminal work of Veletsianos and Shepherdson (2016), which, although it only included one more year in the search spectrum beyond what we have reviewed thus far (2013–2015), encompassed a broader sample than the two works mentioned previously. It contained 183 MOOC documents including research articles, conference papers, reports, and book chapters thanks to the multiple search strategies developed in various sources and academic databases. More recently, in following on the lead of Liyanagunawardena et al. (2013) and Veletsianos and Shepherdson (2016), Zhu, Sari, and Lee (2018) conducted a systematic review of 146 empirical studies of MOOCs that were published between October 2014 and November 2016, which Zhu and her colleagues later expanded to include 2017 MOOC research (Zhu, Sari, & Bonk, 2018). Importantly, these newer studies revealed strikingly similar findings to the previous reported works.

A significant contribution of Veletsianos and Shepherdson's (2016) systematic review is that it clearly established the geographical distribution of the scientific production related to MOOC research. It also revealed the type of documents that were collected, the sources that originated them, the levels of impact and citations of the works under review, and the methods of data collection and analysis. In addition, they identified the specific themes of the phenomenon under study. One of the most salient findings of this study was that the region producing the lowest amount of scientific literature on the MOOC phenomenon was Latin America, representing 0.5% of the literature, whereas 82.2% of the total literature emerged from North America and Europe (Veletsianos & Shepherdson, 2016). It is important to note that similar findings were more recently reported by Zhu and her colleagues (e.g., Zhu, Sari, & Bonk, 2018; Zhu, Sari, & Lee, 2018).

Although the Veletsianos and Shepherdson (2016) research did not consider languages other than English to generate their corpus of documents, the data is relevant if we consider that the leading journals in learning technology and education typically publish in English. In addition, most of the countries in Europe and the entire Asian region (8.0% of the total production in the study) do not embrace the English language as their native language; nevertheless, they irrefutably surpass Latin America in terms of MOOC research. Another finding that stood out in this research was the prevalence of quantitative research methods throughout the publications analyzed; in particular, the use of descriptive statistics (93.4%), correlational studies (52.5%), and experimental and quasi-experimental (25.7%), over qualitative methods detected, such as basic qualitative inquiries (38.8%), grounded theory (7.6%), ethnography (4.4%), and discourse analysis (1.0%) (Veletsianos & Shepherdson, 2016). Thus, the trend detected by Yousef et al. (2015) is reaffirmed at the methodological level concerning the difference between the innovative discourses promoted at the beginning of the MOOC movement and the reality that most MOOCs are delivered from a more traditional educational approach.

For Veletsianos and Shepherdson (2016, p. 214), the lack of qualitative approaches to investigate MOOC educational experiences was revealed despite the fundamental focus of MOOC research on student learning. As such, they note that it excludes the voices of learners and urgently suggest the "expansion of methodological approaches applied to MOOC research."

In the Spanish language, we can also find systematic reviews and bibliometric studies that complement the findings already described, or, in other cases, reveal a different focus of attention according to the objectives deployed in each investigation. The study by López-Meneses, Vázquez-Cano, and Román-Graván (2015), for instance, on the impact of the MOOC movement in the scientific literature based on two academic databases between 2010 and 2013, exposed the low impact of research on MOOCs in the scientific community. That statement is supported by data extracted by various methods of bibliometric analysis on a corpus of 159 selected articles. At the same time, this research presents findings similar to the studies by Veletsianos and Shepherdson (2016) and Zhu, Sari, and Lee (2018) that the most research-producing countries in the area of MOOCs are the United States, Australia, Canada, the United Kingdom, and Spain; in addition, such countries are the most cited in terms of scientific impact of their findings (López-Meneses et al., 2015, p. 79).

On methodological approaches, the report by López-Meneses et al. (2015) also addressed the investigative perspective of the different studies analyzed. They argued that, in line with what was proposed by Veletsianos and Shepherdson (2016) on the prevalence of quantitative methods in the area, the most cited works would not be high-level qualitative or quantitative analyses of MOOC experiences, but mainly ascribed to theoretical approaches (López-Meneses et al., 2015, p. 79). Such theoretical publications are conceivably less susceptible to methodological criticism.

Another contribution by López-Meneses et al. (2015) to the reviews of scientific literature on MOOCs is its attempt to interpret the low impact detected in scientific production. The low impact counters the various blog postings and other writings of MOOC leaders like Stephen Downes and George Siemens (e.g., Siemens, 2012). Research publications from Siemens and Downes are noticeably absent from the main academic databases such as Web Of Science (WOS) and Scopus. This contradiction between daily social media influence of these MOOC pioneers and their limited presence in the databases consulted leads the authors to wonder about the role that scientific journals are having when it comes to identifying emerging fields of research. In effect, such trends position alternative media, such as blogs and social networks, as spaces that more effectively influence the academic community (López-Meneses et al. 2015, p. 80).

In the case of Duart, Roig-Vila, Mengual-Andrés, and Maseda Durán (2017), the systematic review proposed for the period from 2013–2015 through publications found in WOS and Scopus focused fundamentally on the issue of pedagogical quality of MOOCs (see also López-Meneses et al., 2015). As a specific topic, Duart et al.'s (2017) sample of 33 empirical study documents allowed the authors to make comparisons between the years of publication, in particular, highlighting the year 2015. They also explored the main categories of topics addressed in these 33 documents. Not too surprisingly, the study showed a major inclination for MOOC research to address student motivation in terms of the quality of MOOC experiences (Duart et al., 2017). Such data is consistent with the approach of Veletsianos and Shepherdson (2016) as well as Zhu, Sari, and Lee (2018), who also pointed out that most MOOC research approaches and methodologies centered on the student, not the MOOC instructor.

Finally, and almost exclusively, the state-of-the-art study related to MOOCs in higher education in Latin America and Europe appeared under the framework of the MOOC Maker Project (Sanagustín, Maldonado, & Morales, 2016), a review that specifically included the Latin American region. Supported by the Erasmus+ program of the European Union, the MOOC Maker Project proposed the creation of "an intercontinental network between Higher Education Institutions (HEIs) in Europe and Latin America to improve the quality, relevance, and access of teaching-learning programs through the implementation of quality MOOCs" (MOOC Maker, 2019). As a result, researchers in universities throughout the Europe and Latin America have prepared technical and scientific reports on MOOC initiatives carried out in Latin America. The ultimate goal was to "offer the different actors of the system of higher education institutions (IES), managers, academics, researchers, regulators, etc., a global vision" related to the development of MOOCs in Europe and Latin America (Sanagustín et al., 2016, p. 4).

Sanagustín and her colleagues consulted different portals looking for an empirical base mainly in universities and MOOC platforms. In the end, they found 418 MOOCs in the region (far from the 1,705 registered in Europe). Among their main findings included that the largest producer of MOOCs in Latin America was Colombia (24%) followed by Mexico (22%). In addition, they discovered that Costa Rica was the country that produced the most MOOCs per inhabitant. And third, the university that offered the most MOOCs in the region was the Tecnológico de Monterrey (Mexico) (Sanagustín et al., 2016, p. 12).

One aspect that draws attention in this study and that does not appear in the reviews is the type of MOOC-producing institution. Although universities appear as the main producers of MOOCs, national governments emerge as the second type of institution offering such massive courses, mainly in countries such as Colombia (Sanagustín et al., 2016, p. 16). Sanagustín and her colleagues highlighted the main issues addressed by MOOCs, finding the topic "Professional and/or applied sciences" in almost half of all production in the region (48.09%), as well as formal sciences (18.66%), humanities (12.20%), and social sciences (9.57%) (Sanagustín et al., 2016, p. 17). In general, the study confirmed a clear supremacy of Europe with regard to the creation of MOOCs when comparing the most productive universities on each continent, and when conducting the same analysis at the country level.

Research Methodology

As noted earlier, our study seeks to better understand MOOC trends and issues in Latin America. Our findings not only highlight the current status of MOOCs from the perspective of scientific production, they can also serve as a vehicle for future research. In this section, we present the methodology used to answer the different research questions, the process of data collection, and the classification and analysis of the information.

The following six main Research Questions (RQ) guided our study.

RQ1: How is scientific production related to MOOC research in Latin America distributed in the selected scientific databases?

RQ2: What are the main areas of study found in Latin American research documents related to MOOCs?

RQ3: What is the level of impact of scientific publications (papers, articles, reviews, conference papers, book chapters, etc.) related to MOOC research in Latin America in the scientific community?

RQ4: Who are the most productive MOOC researchers in Latin America? What units do they come from?

RQ5: What are the places from which the selected scientific production arises? Are there institutions or programs that sponsor scientific production on MOOCs in Latin America?

RQ6: In what type of documents is MOOC research in Latin America published in the selected academic databases?

Data Collection

For data collection, a review of the literature associated with the phenomenon under study was carried out by searching digital sources (Fink, 2013). These sources were academic databases of high impact: WOS, Scopus, JSTOR, PubMed, and Springer Link.

Selection Criteria

Of course, it was necessary to limit the search scope to the objectives of the research. The criteria that define the scope were the following:

1. Documents that address the MOOC and Latin America phenomenon.
2. Documents that address the MOOC phenomenon explicitly from Latin America through any of its countries or sub-regions.
3. Documents in English, Spanish, or Portuguese.
4. Documents of any type and of any date present in any of the selected databases.
5. Documents whose results, findings, or conclusions allow for characterizing the Latin American region or part of it around the MOOC phenomenon.

Search Procedure

The focus was the development of scientific literature related to MOOCs in Latin America. We conducted the first search in Scopus, whereas similar procedures were carried in the Web of Science (WOS), Springer Link, PubMed, and the JSTOR database.

The total volume was 34 documents. After the application of an input filter to find duplicate studies, the number of the sample was reduced to 24 documents. Within this sample of 24 documents, the first 17 were characterized by having more explicitly the concepts of "MOOC" and "Latin America." The other seven documents also identified MOOC projects located in the region as a base of their experiences and analysis. A summary of the results of the search process can be seen in Table 10.1.

The total sample of 24 documents includes different formats such as articles, book chapters, and conference papers, written in Spanish or English, published between 2014 and 2019. The following

TABLE 10.1 Data Collection Methods, Number of Documents, Filters, and Dates

Method	Subtotal	In the scope of the study	Date
Search: Scopus	38	16	3 January 2019
Search: Web of Science	18	9	3 January 2019
Search: Springer Link	79	4	3 January 2019
Search: PubMed	13	4	3 January 2019
Search: JSTOR	69	1	3 January 2019
Overall search	**217**	**34**	
Filter 1: Reduce repetitions		24	4 January 2019
Filter 2: Reading and refinement of the scope (Partial sample)		17	4–8 January 2019
Forward referencing search	29	22	12 January 2019
Application of forward filters		7	14 January 2019
Total sample		**24**	14 January 2019

Latin American countries emerged in this MOOC document sample: Argentina, Brazil, Chile, Columbia, Dominican Republic, El Salvador, Guatemala, Honduras, Mexico, Paraguay, Peru, and Uruguay.

Results

Characterization of MOOC Research Documents

After the application of the different filters, the JSTOR database was not represented because the only document selected from its platform was out of our scope. The documents were grouped according to the database (RQ1); naturally, some documents were present in more than one database (see Table 10.2):

Despite not restricting the search to a specific range of dates, the literature on MOOCs in Latin America started appearing in 2014, with three documents published each in 2014 and 2015, four in 2016, five in 2017, eight in 2018, and one in 2019 (as of January 2019).

Regarding the type of documents in which scientific production is disseminated around the MOOC phenomenon in Latin America (RQ1), our study did not restrict its search results to a particular document format. Conference papers made more than half of the entire sample selected, followed by journal articles and book chapters.

Impact of MOOC Research

In terms of the impact level of selected scientific production (RQ3), the data revealed similar findings to López-Meneses et al. (2015) who noted the low impact of the MOOC literature on the rest of the scientific community. When comparing the number of citations with the type of document, book chapters accounted for just 12% of the documents but were 24% of the total citations.

The most cited document in the sample was a book chapter (35 citations), while the most cited document type was the conference paper (51 citations), which is consistent with the literature. Although the documents were clearly included in the citation records of the different databases, the Google Scholar platform was used to unify the quantification and extend the range of influence. Such a technique helped grasp the number of documents in the sample, the databases to which they belonged, and the number of citations. Only one document exceeded 30 citations, one was between 20 and 29 appointments, and four documents had 10 or more citations. Unfortunately, 10 documents had just between one and five citations, and eight documents were not cited by anyone.

MOOC Authors in Latin America

Concerning the profile of the authors (RQ4), among the selected 24 MOOC documents, we counted 61 authors in total, some of whom appear in more than one text. Of these 61 authors,

TABLE 10.2 Presence of Documents According to Database (considering repeated documents)

Database	Total
Scopus	18
Web of Science	5
Springer Link	8
PubMed	2
JSTOR	0

TABLE 10.3 Main Authors According to Number of Selected Documents, Affiliation, and Country

Author	Documents	Filiation
Hernández, Rocael	9	Universidad Galileo, Guatemala
Morales, Miguel	7	Universidad Galileo, Guatemala
Gütl, Christian	7	Universidad Técnica de Graz, Austria
Amado-Salvatierra, Héctor	5	Universidad Galileo, Guatemala
Pérez-Sanagustín, Mar	4	Pontificia Universidad Católica de Chile, Chile
Hilliger, Isabel	3	Pontifica Universidad Católica de Chile, Chile
Delgado Kloos, Carlos	2	Universidad Carlos III de Madrid, España
Alario-Hoyos, Carlos	2	Universidad Carlos III de Madrid, España
Teixeira, Antonio	2	Universidade Aberta, Portugal
Hernández, Josefina	2	Pontifica Universidad Católica de Chile
Meléndez, Alejandra	2	Universidad Panamericana, Guatemala
Román, Mariela	2	Universidad Panamericana, Guatemala

those that have more presence throughout the documents are listed in Table 10.3. The most productive group is characterized by maintaining production networks in terms of the scientific literature.

Geographical Distribution of Authorships and Publications

Regarding the specific geographical presence of all the registered authors (RQ4–RQ5), a majority were from the Latin American region; in particular, Guatemala, Chile, and Mexico. The authorship and publication distribution resulted in three productive axes: 1. Guatemala-Austria-Australia; 2. Chile and Spain; and 3. Mexico, Colombia, and the United States appearing as smaller axes but with a considerable presence in the literature of the region. In the case of Colombia, however, much of it was due to the MOOC Maker Project.

Regarding the geographical distribution of MOOC research by university, the most prominent country in the Latin America MOOC literature was Guatemala, where there was more than one university active in the creation of scientific literature related to MOOCs. Most notably, Galileo University in Guatemala continues to be the main reference in terms of the volume and impact of scientific production on MOOCs in Latin America.

Overall, the place of work or research of the authors of these documents fails to characterize those places where their findings are published or disseminated. In other words, it seems that authors must look to other countries and regions for conferences and journals to disseminate their scientific production at a higher or more prestigious academic level than what is available in their own countries.

MOOC-Related Conferences, Reviews, and Books

Of the 13 documents that were "conference papers," it was possible to extract information related to the conferences in which they were presented as well as the countries in which they have been developed. By grouping the conference venues by continent, the largest percent were from Europe. Hence, as explained earlier, there appears to be a need for MOOC and open education scholars in the Latin American region to look for academic spaces suitable for the dissemination and indexing of their scientific production outside their continent.

Thus, in the case of journals and books the situation is more acute. Our research reveals that the European continent doubles the Latin American region in terms of the publication of scientific production considering conferences, journals, and books. Moreover, 25% of the total number of scientific documents selected in the study were published in Latin America, well below the 61% of authors that were from the Latin America region.

MOOC Sponsorship

Another aspect of the RQ5 is the presence of programs or institutions that specifically promote the MOOC initiative in the region. National and transnational programs and organizations are distinguished, since the former correspond to specific initiatives that are sponsored and financed by the latter.

At the level of programs that promote the development of MOOC initiatives in terms of specific experiences such as reports or related scientific research, there is a clear influence of the MOOC Maker Project in Chile, Colombia, and Guatemala in Latin America, and the TELESCOPE Project based mainly on Guatemala. Of the 24 documents that are part of our sample, about one-third were related to the MOOC Maker initiative (Alario-Hoyos et al., 2018, De la Roca, Morales, Teixeira, Hernández Rizzardini, & Amado-Salvatierra, 2018; Hernández, Rodríguez, Hilliger, & Pérez-Sanagustín, 2018; Meléndez, Román, & Barreno, 2018; Morales, Amado-Salvatierra, Hernández, Pirker, & Gütl, 2016; Pérez-Sanagustín et al., 2016, 2017; Vitiello, Gütl, Amado-Salvatierra, & Hernández Rizzardini, 2017), while almost one-fifth corresponded to documents framed in the TELESCOPE project (Hernández Rizzardini, Gütl, & Amado-Salvatierra, 2014; Hernández Rizzardini, Morales, & Gütl, 2016; Morales, Hernández Rizzardini, Barchino Plata, & Amelio Medina, 2015; Morales, Hernández Rizzardini, & Gütl, 2014; Vitiello et al., 2017).

In some cases, researchers from these two projects (TELESCOPE and the MOOC Maker Project) managed to come together to write and publish joint documents across both projects (Vitiello et al., 2017), thereby tightening the productive links of the main authors in the region. When visualized, in fact, the possible relationships among the authors involved in the two projects are striking. We provide an account of the networks of co-authorship and the identification of the two outstanding nuclei in the region in relation to the production of scientific literature on MOOCs and Latin America. Between these two projects, they represent 50% of all the documents selected for the present study, which sheds light on the undeniable relevance of the initiatives and the authors associated with them in terms of MOOCs in Latin America.

In addition to the TELESCOPE and MOOC Maker Project, it is possible to verify the presence of similar initiatives (Fueyo & Hevia, 2017; Jiménez-Castañeda, Cipri, Clavijo-Blanco, & Moreno-Ruiz, 2018) as well as those carried out in parallel by authors already identified with the projects mentioned above (De la Roca et al., 2018). Projects are also identified in areas such as health (Mena, Flores, Ramírez-Velarde, & Ramírez-Montoya, 2018) and other areas promoting employability and economic development (González, García, Macher, & Zhang, 2017).

Regarding the sponsorship of different programs in the region, there are active and direct impacts of the European Union as the main sponsor (Alario-Hoyos et al., 2018; De la Roca et al., 2018). To a lesser extent documents are linked to international organizations such as the Inter-American Development Bank (González et al., 2017), direct alliances between countries (Mena et al., 2018), national institutions such as the Ministry of Education in the case of Chile (Pérez-Sanagustín et al., 2016, 2017), or the direct intervention of the Ministry of Health of Mexico (Magaña-Valladares et al., 2018). In this way, a panorama of scientific production is consolidated that is largely supported by the intervention of international and national organizations.

Application Areas

Regarding the topics that characterize MOOC publications in the region (RQ2), we identified four large areas that manage to group the content of the documents studied, namely: 1. Methodologies of Learning and MOOCs; 2. Health and MOOCs; 3. Engineering and MOOCs; and 4. MOOCs as a meta-area. Also, there were other less frequent areas in terms of their presence throughout the documents, represented by only one text, namely: Languages (Charbonneau-Gowdy, 2016), Philosophy (Ramírez, 2018), Digital Competition (De la Roca et al., 2018), and Economic Development (González et al., 2017).

The Methodologies for Learning area refers to specific strategies that are associated with MOOC initiatives as educational proposals aimed at improving academic results (Pérez-Sanagustín et al., 2016) and increased motivation or commitment to educational activities (Morales et al., 2015). The increasing presence of "Gamification" as a recurring strategy was associated with the MOOC phenomenon (Hernández Rizzardini et al., 2016; Mena et al., 2018; Morales et al., 2016). In addition, the implementation of "Cloud-Based" tools is noteworthy (Hernández Rizzardini, Gütl, & Amado-Salvatierra, 2014, Morales et al., 2015) among various complementary methodologies to the implementation of MOOCs (Fueyo & Hevia, 2017; Hernández Rizzardini, Gütl, Chang, et al., 2014; Meléndez et al., 2018).

The Health area refers to those documents that have MOOCs as a strategy to directly or indirectly influence the health reality of a community. In this sense, MOOCs are considered as a tool such as the training of professionals in various health areas (Armentano & Chatterjee, 2015; Culquichicón et al., 2017, Saldanha Brites & Famer Rocha, 2019) or a direct action as in a health-related crisis (Magaña-Valladares et al., 2018).

In the literature on MOOCs in Latin America, the area of Engineering differs from the Health area since it does not appear as susceptible to intervention at a professional level. Instead, it is almost exclusively addressed at the level of higher education. As in the previous area, MOOCs appear as a learning strategy, but are directly linked to professional careers including as courses to be embedded in the formal curriculum (Aguilar & Suárez, 2015; Jiménez-Castañeda et al., 2018) or as remedial courses (Hernández et al., 2018; Pérez-Sanagustín et al., 2016).

Finally, the "MOOC" meta-area brings together all those documents whose content specifically focuses on the phenomenon in question, proposing analyses and actions aimed at the study or continuous development of different initiatives deployed throughout the Latin American region. Some of these documents recount experiences based on the aforementioned TELESCOPE project (Morales et al., 2014) and MOOC Maker project (Alario-Hoyos et al., 2018). Other publications address the documented problem of learner desertion or attrition in MOOCs (Hernández Rizzardini et al., 2016; Vitiello et al., 2017). And, finally, there are proposals for conceptualizations around the MOOC construct based on practical experiences in the region (Pérez-Sanagustín et al., 2017).

Discussion and Conclusions

We conclude this chapter by addressing each of the research questions (RQ) set out in this study. As hoped, the findings start to reveal the main trends and issues related to MOOCs in Latin America.

RQ1: How is scientific production related to MOOC research in Latin America distributed in the selected scientific databases? And RQ6: In what type of documents is MOOC research in Latin America published in the selected academic databases?

After the searching and filtering phases of the documents with our criteria, it was possible to compile a document sample whose presence was spread across almost all the chosen databases. However, this sample did not manage to be abundant in terms of the documents that had as key concepts or specific topics the development of MOOCs in Latin America. Although most of the texts were placed in the SCOPUS database (75%), the majority of those were conference papers.

RQ2: What are the main areas of study found in Latin American research documents related to MOOCs?

In light of the data, it is possible to affirm that MOOCs in the Latin American region are strongly associated with the educational experience both complementarily with other innovative methods and as formal courses or supports for academic training, mainly in higher education. Based on our data, among the key areas that we project for future academic research include gamification, cloud-based tools, the preparation of predictive profiles to lower the dropout rate in MOOCs, and learning analytics. At the same time, an interest in MOOCs in engineering and health was revealed. In the case of the latter, there are now MOOC experiences arranged as direct action in the face of health crises, while engineering MOOCs are still maintained in university professional training plans.

RQ3: What is the level of impact of publications related to MOOC research in Latin America in the scientific community?

The level of impact of the publications on MOOC and Latin America is very low. Many of the selected documents have 0 citations in some of the journals or conference proceedings in which they are published. Moreover, of those documents that do have a high level of citations (the highest-cited document has 31 citations), most of the citations are self-citation. In short, not only is the academic production of MOOC documents in Latin America extremely low (Veletsianos & Shepherdson, 2016), the impact of those articles is characterized by few citations other than self-citation.

RQ4: Who are the most productive MOOC researchers in Latin America? What units do they come from?

In the region, while we detected 61 active scholars publishing about MOOCs in the Latin America region, the six authors who published the most scientific literature accounted for 57% of the documents. These six individuals work in two centers: one located at the Galileo University of Guatemala, in common work with the Technique University of Graz of Austria and the Curtin University of Australia, and the other is located at the School of Engineering at Pontificia Universidad Católica de Chile. In our data analysis, both groups were affiliated in the nucleus of the Carlos III University of Madrid and the MOOC Maker project, financed by the European Union. In turn, the Guatemala-Austria nucleus is part of the TELESCOPE project on which a large part of the scientific production on MOOCs in the region has been developed.

RQ5: What are the places from which the selected scientific production arises? Are there institutions or programs that sponsor scientific production on MOOCs in Latin America?

There is a great distance between the regions of the authors of the MOOC documents considered in this study; while most are located in Latin America (i.e., 61%), the regions where the outlets of scientific production are located are mainly Europe (i.e., 50%) and to a less extent Latin America (i.e., 25%). Such findings project an image of the Latin America MOOC researcher as a kind of "academic migrant," who in the absence of high-quality journals or conferences of global reach, has to search other regions to disseminate the results of their research. Adding our results to the fact that Latin America is the region that tends to publish the least worldwide on MOOCs, the landscape becomes even more discouraging as authors are too often forced to develop and disseminate their knowledge outside their region, if at all.

At the same time, there are programs funded mainly by the European Union throughout the Latin American region. The MOOC Maker Project is an example of this sponsorship, which has generated multiple experiences, reports, and academic meetings. In so doing, it generates valuable knowledge about MOOCs throughout the region. Finding that almost half of the production selected in this study on MOOCs and Latin America is sponsored by the European Union, and the growing interest of governments or organizations such as the Inter-American Development Bank in the implementation of projects based on MOOCs, it is worth asking about the rationale and future direction of such initiatives.

Finally, it is necessary to amplify the production of scientific literature in the region with more autonomous relationships that can sustain the inquiry (Restrepo & Martinez, 2010). In effect, the resulting knowledge base needs to not just characterize the MOOC phenomenon from the Latin American region, but, more importantly, from the standpoint of Latin American thinking and perspectives. In the future, we intend to continue expanding and characterizing the Latin American regional reality related to MOOCs for which the results presented here constitute an important marker, but by no means the endpoint. During the coming decade, we will continue to be attentive to the challenges that currently constitute the key trends and issues concerning MOOCs in Latin America.

Acknowledgments

This work was partially funded by the Basal Funds for Centers of Excellence, Project FB0003, from the Associative Research Program of CONICYT—Chile.

Jaime Sánchez received the MA, MSc, and PhD degrees from Columbia University, New York, USA. He has also been a postdoctoral research fellow at MIT Media Lab (Computers, Learning and Cognition) and Cornell University (Metacognition). Since 2010, he is Professor of Human-Computer Interaction at the Department of Computer Science of the University of Chile. He is also Adjunct Full Professor at TC Columbia University, New York, USA. Since 1995, Dr. Sánchez has been the Director of the Center for Computing and Communication for the Construction of Knowledge C5, at the Department of Computer Science, University of Chile. He has been involved in research in the areas of human-computer interaction, computers and education, software usability, game-based learning and cognition. He published profusely on these topics and has also authored several books on learning with computers. He has been Visiting Professor in diverse worldwide universities in the Department of Mathematics, Science and Technology at TC Columbia University and the Center for Non-Invasive Brain Stimulation at Harvard University.

José Reyes-Rojas is a researcher at the University of Chile where he has received the EdM in Computers and Education. His professional and research work has been in both school education and research on the use of technology in education, inclusion, epistemological criticism of ICT, art education, and the practical application of theories of learning. He has participated in diverse research projects in education and authored conference and journal publications.

References

Aguilar, R., & Suárez, A. R. (2015). Los Cursos Masivos en Línea en Coursera y su Empleo Potencial en los Programas de Ingeniería en América Latina. *Lámpsakos*, (14), 61–70.

Alario-Hoyos, C., Pérez-Sanagustín, M., Morales, M., Delgado Kloos, C., Hernández Rizzardini, R., Román, M., Ramírez-González, G., Luna, T., Jeréz, O., Gütl, C., Moreira, A., Maldonado-Mahauad, J., Amado-Salvatierra, H., Meléndez, A, & Solarte, M. (2018). *MOOC-Maker: Tres Años Construyendo Capacidades de Gestión de MOOCs en Latinoamérica*. Proceedings of the II International Conference MOOC-Maker (MOOC-Maker 2018), pp. 4–14, Medellín, Colombia, http://ceur-ws.org/Vol-2224/1.

Armentano, R. L., & Chatterjee, P. (2015). *MOOC on biomedical engineering for Latin American students—Unleashing the potential of virtual learning*. Computational Intelligence and Communication Networks (CICN), 2015 International Conference on Computational Intelligence and Communication (pp. 405–410). IEEE.

Charbonneau-Gowdy, P. (2016). *Exploring the experiences of learners in a large scale distance language learning program offered in countries across Latin America*. International Conference on e-Learning (pp. 37–45). Academic Conferences International Limited.

Culquichicón, C., Helguero-Santin, L. M., Labán-Seminario, L. M., Cardona-Ospina, J. A., Aboshady, O. A., & Correa, R. (2017). Massive open online courses in health sciences from Latin American institutions: A need for improvement? *F1000Research*, *6*, 940. doi:10.12688/f1000research.11626.1

De la Roca, M., Morales, M., Teixeira, A., Hernández Rizzardini, R., & Amado-Salvatierra, H. (2018). *The experience of designing and developing an edX's micromasters program to develop or reinforce the digital competence on teachers*. 2018 Learning with MOOCS (LWMOOCS) (pp. 34–38). IEEE.

Duart, J. M., Roig-Vila, R., Mengual-Andrés, S., & Maseda Durán, M-Á. (2017). La calidad pedagógica de los MOOC a partir de la revisión sistemática de las publicaciones JCR y Scopus (2013–2015). *Revista Española de Pedagogía*, 75(1), 29–46. https://doi.org/10.22550/REP75-1-2017-02

Fink, A. (2013). *Conducting research literature reviews: From the Internet to paper*. Thousand Oaks, CA: Sage Publications.

Fueyo, A., & Hevia, I. (2017). Aprendizaje en red mediante comunidades de indagación en entornos de formación masiva online. *Digital Education Review*, (31), 116–130.

González, E., García, A., Macher, C., & Zhang, D. (2017, November 16–17). *A glimpse on how MOOCs from IDB are impacting learners in Latin America*. Proceedings of the International Conference MOOC-MAKER 2017. Antigua Guatemala, Guatemala.

Hernández, J., Rodríguez, M. F., Hilliger, I., & Pérez-Sanagustín, M. (2018). MOOCs as a remedial complement: Students' adoption and learning outcomes. *IEEE Transactions on Learning* Technologies, *12*(1), 133–141. Retrieved January–March 1, 2019. doi:10.1109/TLT.2018.2830373

Hernández Rizzardini, R., Gütl, C., & Amado-Salvatierra, H. (2014). *Cloud learning activities orchestration for MOOC environments*. International Workshop on Learning Technology for Education in Cloud (pp. 25–36). Springer, Netherlands.

Hernández Rizzardini, R., Gütl, C., Chang, V., & Morales, M. (2014). *MOOC in Latin America: Implementation and lessons learned*. The 2nd International Workshop on Learning Technology for Education in Cloud (pp. 147–158). Springer, Netherlands.

Hernández Rizzardini, R., Morales, M., & Gütl, C. (2016). An attrition model for MOOCs: Evaluating the learning strategies of gamification. In *Formative assessment, learning data analytics and gamification* (pp. 295–311). Elsevier, London.

Jiménez-Castañeda, R., Cipri, K., Clavijo-Blanco, J. A., & Moreno-Ruiz, J. (2018). *The support of European programmes in the internalization process of engineering courses: DIEGO project—Development of high quality courses on renewable technologies and energy efficiency*. Global Engineering Education Conference (EDUCON), 2018 IEEE (pp. 196–201). IEEE.

Liyanagunawardena, T. R., Adams, A. A., & Williams, S. A. (2013). MOOCs: A systematic study of the published literature 2008–2012. *The International Review of Research in Open and Distributed Learning*, *14*(3), 202–227. https://doi.org/10.19173/irrodl.v14i3.1455

López-Meneses, E., Vázquez-Cano, E., & Román-Graván, P. (2015). Analysis and implications of the impact of MOOC movement in the scientific community: JCR and scopus (2010–13). *Comunicar*, *22*(44), 73–80. https://doi.org/10.3916/C44-2015-08

Magaña-Valladares, L., Rosas-Magallanes, C., Montoya-Rodríguez, A., Calvillo-Jacobo, G., Alpuche-Arande, C. M., & García-Saisó, S. (2018). A MOOC as an immediate strategy to train health personnel in the cholera outbreak in Mexico. *BMC Medical Education*, *18*(1), 111.

Meléndez, A., Román, M., & Barreno, I. (2018). *Experiencias del MOOC: Aprendizaje Invertido para la Formación Docente*. Proceedings of the II International Conference MOOC-Maker (pp. 68–76) MOOC-Maker.

Mena, J., Flores, E. R., Ramírez-Velarde, R., & Ramírez-Montoya, M. S. (2018). *The use of gamification as a teaching methodology in a MOOC about the strategic energy reform in México*. International Conference in Methodologies and Intelligent Systems for Technology Enhanced Learning (pp. 29–36). Springer International Publishing.

MOOC Maker. (2019). *Objetivos—MOOC Maker*. Recuperado 8 de enero de 2019, de. Retrieved from www.mooc-maker.org/?page_id=153&lang=es

Morales, M., Amado-Salvatierra, H. R., Hernández, R., Pirker, J., & Gütl, C. (2016). *A practical experience on the use of gamification in MOOC courses as a strategy to increase motivation*. International Workshop on Learning Technology for Education in Cloud (pp. 139–149). Springer, Netherlands.

Morales, M., Hernández Rizzardini, R., Barchino Plata, R., & Amelio Medina, J. (2015). MOOC using cloud-based tools: A study of motivation and learning strategies in Latin America. *International Journal of Engineering Education*, *31*(3), 901–911.

Morales, M., Hernández Rizzardini, R., & Gütl, C. (2014). *Telescope, a MOOCs initiative in Latin America: Infrastructure, best practices, completion and dropout analysis*. Frontiers in Education Conference (FIE), 2014 IEEE (pp. 1–7). IEEE.

Pérez-Sanagustín, M., Hernández, J., Gelmi, C., Hilliger, I., & Rodríguez, M. F. (2016). *Does taking a MOOC as a complement for remedial courses have an effect on my learning outcomes? A pilot study on calculus*. European Conference on Technology Enhanced Learning (pp. 221–233). Springer International Publishing.

Pérez-Sanagustín, M., Hilliger, I., Alario-Hoyos, C., Delgado Kloos, C., & Rayyan, S. (2017). H-MOOC framework: Reusing MOOCs for hybrid education. *Journal of Computing in Higher Education*, *1*(29), 47–64.

Ramírez, D. (2018). Platón y la democratización digital saber: Una crítica al uso de MOOCs como estrategia de inclusión digital. *Revista San Gregorio*, *1*(22), 116–125.

Restrepo, E., & Martinez, A. A. R. (2010). *Inflexión decolonial: Fuentes, conceptos y cuestionamientos*. Colombia: Universidad del Cauca, Popayán.

Saldanha Brites, L., & Famer Rocha, C. (2019). Massive open online health courses (MOOCs): Brazilian initiatives. In Neto, A. P., & Flynn, M. B. (eds.), *The internet and health in Brazil* (pp. 297–311). Springer, Cham, Switzerland.

Sanagustín, M. P., Maldonado, J., & Morales, N. (2016). *Estado del arte de adopción de MOOCs en la Educación Superior en América Latina y Europa.* MOOC-Maker Construction of Management Capacities of MOOCs in Higher Education. MOOC-Maker.

Siemens, G. (2012, July 25). MOOCs are really a platform. *Elearningspace.* Retrieved from www.nmc.org/clipping/moocs-are-really-a-platform/

Veletsianos, G., & Shepherdson, P. (2016). A systematic analysis and synthesis of the empirical MOOC literature published in 2013–2015. *The International Review of Research in Open and Distributed Learning, 17*(2), 1–17. Retrieved from https://files.eric.ed.gov/fulltext/EJ1093662.pdf

Vitiello, M., Gütl, C., Amado-Salvatierra, H., & Hernández Rizzardini, R. (2017). *MOOC learner behaviour: Attrition and retention analysis and prediction based on 11 courses on the TELESCOPE platform.* International Workshop on Learning Technology for Education in Cloud (pp. 99–109). Springer.

Yousef, A. M. F., Chatti, M. A., Schroeder, U., Wosnitza, M., & Jakobs, H. (2015). The state of MOOCs from 2008 to 2014: A critical analysis and future visions. In S. Zvacek, M. T. Restivo, J. Uhomoibhi, & M. Helfert (Eds.), *Computer supported education* (vol. 510, pp. 305–327). Cham: Springer International Publishing. https://doi.org/10.1007/978-3-319-25768-6_20

Zhu, M., Sari, A., & Bonk, C. (2018, June). *A systematic review of MOOC research methods and topics: Comparing 2014–2016 and 2016–2017.* Proceedings of EdMedia 2018: World Conference on Educational Media and Technology (pp. 1676–1685). Association for the Advancement of Computing in Education (AACE), Amsterdam, Netherlands.

Zhu, M., Sari, A., & Lee, M. M. (2018). A systematic review of research methods and topics of the empirical MOOC literature (2014–2016). *The Internet and Higher Education, 37,* 31–39. https://doi.org/10.1016/j.iheduc.2018.01.002

11
THE EMOTIONAL BENEFITS OF DIVERSITY IN MOOCs

Reshaping Views of Online Education Through Exposure to Global Learners

Trang Phan

Purpose and Intent

Massive open online courses (MOOCs) are an evolving platform of online course structure used to deliver instruction to learners around the world regardless of their age, race, social, or educational status. This chapter reports an analysis of 15 interviews with MOOC instructors and instructional designers in the United States who were providing MOOCs on the Coursera platform to learners spanning the globe, both the Global South and Global North.

The purpose of this chapter includes describing the roles of the instructors in the design, development, and delivery of MOOCs. The chapter also intends to describe how these MOOCs were developed, while presenting the pedagogical concerns of these 15 instructors. In addition, the chapter highlights the thoughts and accommodating acts towards global learners. Finally, the author attempts to identify the emotional benefits for these instructors resulting from their interactions with global learners. Based upon an interpretive analysis, the chapter aims to highlight stories of hope and compassion, especially in terms of learners whom they normally would never meet. The author shows how MOOC learning opportunities created with deliberate care in design and delivery touched and changed lives of others; in particular, those in the emerging economies, where there is a lack of quality educational resources. In the process, there is a realization as well as a revelation of how instructors' views on teaching and learning are in turn impacted by their interaction with these learners.

Background

Cultural and language differences among learners can cause major barriers for the design and implementation of online communication (Dillon, Wang, & Tearle, 2007; Ke, Chavez, & Herrera, 2013). Different learning preferences, forms of communication, and personal expectations among different cultural groups of learners can make an impact on their learning effectiveness (Dillon et al., 2007). Those designing or delivering MOOCs and other forms of open education and hoping to appeal to those in the Global South need to make their content appropriate and relevant for their local needs and preferences (Gunawardena, 2014). Without such resource relevance and content accessibility, the enrollment and completion of MOOCs by those in the Global South will be highly limited.

Quality of instruction plays an important role in MOOC effectiveness (Margaryan, Bianco, & Littlejohn, 2015). Research shows that learner-instructor and learner-learner interaction are critical to increasing online learners' persistence (Croxton, 2014). Hence, individualizing and personalizing practices to enhance interaction with learners, especially those who were not exposed to Western educational culture before, should be encouraged. At present, learner-instructor interaction in MOOCs remains highly limited due to the massive enrollment. Also, applying best practices in MOOCs varies greatly among the instructors by the subjects they teach, their level of subject expertise, their level of comfort in using technology in teaching, and the group of learners that they are interacting with. Thus, matching the instructor's teaching skills and the learners' diverse needs is a complex negotiation.

In the meantime, the openness of MOOC content provides a learning environment with unique forms of connecting and reconnecting learning participants (Jacoby, 2014). Furthermore, the change of the instructor's role to that of facilitator and a fellow contributor, the recognition and utilization of the expertise of the learning participants, and the proactive engagement of these participants in an increasingly networked learning environment such as a MOOC (Stewart, 2013) are among the predominant opportunities and values of these new forms of educational delivery.

Methods

Data Collection

The researcher interviewed 15 MOOC instructors and designers at higher education institutions in the United States. All of these individuals had designed and/or taught at least one MOOC on the Coursera platform. As shown in Table 11.1, they represented a diverse set of institutions, and they worked either individually or in a collaboration team. Data were gathered using a semi-structured interview protocol (see Appendix 11.A), in which participants' perceptions of the multicultural learners' needs were addressed in depth. In addition to cultural issues, these interviews also addressed important instructional design topics, such as the course objectives, course duration, the measurement of learning outcomes, and other aspects of MOOC course design and delivery that emerged during the research process.

TABLE 11.1 Participant Profile

Participant	Highest Degree	Years of Exp.	Academic Rank	Research interest(s)	MOOC topic	MOOC category
1	Ph.D.	31	Professor of Astronomy	Extragalactic astronomy, cosmology, galaxy formation	Galaxies and Cosmology	Science/physics
2	Ph.D.	15	Assistant Research Professor	Cell biology	Introduction to Human Physiology	Life science/biology
3	Ph.D.	43	Associate Research Professor	Cell biology cell/systems physiology	Introduction to Human Physiology	Life science/biology
4	Ph.D.	34	Associate Professor	Neurobiology	Medical Neuroscience	Life science/medicine and healthcare

Participant	Highest Degree	Years of Exp.	Academic Rank	Research interest(s)	MOOC topic	MOOC category
5	Ph.D.	5	Adjunct Assistant Research Scientist	Web survey; visual design effects	Questionnaire Design for Social Surveys	Social science/ psychology
6	Ph.D.	8	Assistant Teaching Professor	Theory of computation, algorithms, and problem solving	Specialization in Intermediate Java Software Engineering*	Computer science/ software development
7	Ph.D.	11	Education Director Research Affiliate	Countering violent extremism Resilience	Understanding Terrorism and the Terrorist Threat	Social science
8	Ph.D.	23	Associate Professor	Genome Precision medicine	Genomic and Precision Medicine	Medicine/ biology and life sciences
9	Ph.D.	50	Professor Emeritus of History	Russian history, Eastern Europe, 20th-century Europe, Soviet film	The Holocaust: The Destruction of European Jewry	Arts and humanities/ history
10	Ph.D.	–	Faculty of Education	History and lore of Curanderismo	Curanderismo Part 1: Traditional Healing of the Body	Medicine/ humanities/ health and society/food and nutrition
11	Ph.D.	10	Clinical Assistant Professor	Comprehensive ophthalmology and cataract surgery	Introduction to Cataract Surgery	Life science/ medicine and healthcare
12	Ph.D.	23	Associate Professor	Teacher training Educational uses of digital storytelling	Powerful Tools for Teaching and Learning: Digital Storytelling	Teacher professional development
13	Ph.D., FNP-C	5	Assistant Clinical Professor	Nurse practition	Rural Health Nursing	Life science/ medicine and healthcare
14	Ph.D.	41	Professor of Economics	Economics, law, history, and philosophy Historical development of social institutions	Property and Liability: An Introduction to Law and Economics	Social science/ law
15	Ph.D.	43	Distinguished University Professor	How do people change, learn, and grow throughout their lives and careers?	Inspiring Leadership through Emotional Intelligence	Business/ leadership and management

* This specialization included five courses: 1. Object Oriented Programming in Java, 2. Advanced Data Structures in Java, 3. Mastering the Software Engineering Interview, 4. Data Structures Made Easy, and 5. Capstone: Analyzing (Social) Network Data.

Data Analysis

Qualitative research recommendations for recording and securing the records (e.g., see Stake, 2006; Yin, 2014) guided this study. For instance, a case database was generated for recording secondary research results as well as the interview transcripts and related documents such as analysis of course syllabus, types of assessment, and discussion forums. After transcribing the interviews, member checking was conducted to confirm their accuracy (Merriam, 2009).

Building Category List

After reviewing and sorting through the transcripts, a set of categories was created. Among these categories were those related to demographic information of MOOC participants, ideas related to developing a specific MOOC or topic area for MOOCs, institutional strategies related to the design and development of MOOCs, and the use of different instructional strategies to address different learner needs.

Building Themes and Testing Findings

During the coding process, the themes that emerged were matched to the key research questions. By aligning the data with the themes, additional insights about how the exposure to global participants in a MOOC alter instructor views about online learning and various pedagogical activities and designs were uncovered. Of course, as might be anticipated when following qualitative research design approaches (see Merriam, 2009; Stake, 2006), each of the 15 case interviews provided its own set of unique individual themes, ideas, and insights. As detailed below, interpreting the themes and assertions from the participants resulted in highly interesting findings that addressed the research issues described earlier.

Findings

Roles of MOOC Instructors

In most cases, MOOC instructors in this study were the subject matter experts of their courses and key personnel who were responsible for investigating and addressing student learning needs and outcomes. They played multiple individual and collaborative roles in the design and development of their MOOCs, depending on the way the campus-based courses were structured. They also considered the resources and pedagogical concerns that they had for their global audience. Some of the roles of those in this study are detailed below and illustrated in Figure 11.1.

A Course Designer

As the subject matter experts (SME), all participants were the primary course designers of their MOOCs responsible for making the design and delivery choices of the course content. A participant shared that the key to teaching was emotional, including relationship building and understanding of learning. As one of the participants argued, such findings raise questions of how to develop relationships online and how to get the learners emotionally involved when working/playing with the computer.

An Administrator and a Teacher

As the SME of their MOOC, most participants took on the role of administrator and/or teacher/facilitator during the course delivery.

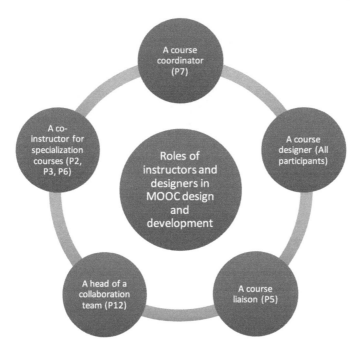

FIGURE 11.1 Roles of Instructors and Designers in MOOC Design and Development

A Head of the Collaboration Team That Involved Doctoral Students

Two instructors at the University of Houston used the "Webcapes" model (Robin & McNeil, 2015), a design-based research project model that focused on improving educational practices, promoting reflection, and encouraging collaboration between researchers and practitioners in real-world settings (Wang & Hannafin, 2005). The model allowed the design teams to work collaboratively to develop multimedia-rich content projects, used a range of technological tools and resources to create actual projects that would be used by teachers and students around the world. It is worth mentioning that each member of the design teams contributed uniquely to MOOC design and development with insights and experience combined with the educational background they brought from home. Some came from Southeast Asian countries such as Vietnam, the Philippines, and Indonesia, whereas others were from East Asia (i.e. China), and South-Central Asia (i.e., India). As one of these instructors stated:

> My role is to be the head of the team. I worked with the other faculty members and with some of our doctoral students who come from different countries to develop the MOOCs. We thought it would be a very good educational experience for the students to not only learn about MOOCs but also to design and deliver a MOOC. They are instrumental in helping us put a MOOC together and then putting them on Coursera, delivering them, participating in the discussion, and giving feedback to MOOC students.
>
> *(Participant 5)*

Coordinators to Develop a Specialization Series of Courses

As the following quote reveals, a team approach leading to a specialization or micro-credential of some type can be quite beneficial for motivating the instructors to get involved in a MOOC.

> It started with my two colleagues and I answered the call for proposals from Coursera to develop one of their specializations that involved courses taken in sequence and combined

> with a capstone project. My two colleagues and I put in the proposal and when it got accepted, the three of us have co-designed, co-taught and co-run the courses.
>
> *(Participant 6)*

Similarly, at Duke University, as co-instructors, the participants shared the workload among themselves with the support from the Coursera IT team to record the content videos. As one of the participants indicated, the team at Duke demonstrated deep knowledge of the features of the implemented platforms and could also offer suggestions on how to use online tools to achieve instructional goals.

A Course Liaison

As one of the study participants noted, there is a perpetual need to monitor the functioning of the MOOC after it is designed; in effect taking on the role of course liaison.

> I am working closely with both the instructors in our two MOOCs, which have been running for four times now. I am in charge of everything that has to do with fixing or making the MOOC better. When the MOOC was running I browsed the discussion forums daily to see what's going on there and what people were talking about and trying to fix any problems. After each round of the MOOC we got back together and reflected on what went well and what did not go that well and tried to fix things that didn't work.
>
> *(Participant 5)*

Merits and Challenges of Engaging Global Learners

Challenges to engage MOOC learners with the course content can be attributed to the topics that generated controversies and created heated conversations among the learners. That was the case of the "*Understanding Terrorism and the Terrorist Threat*" MOOC in which the topic drew in the two groups of learners whose levels of prior topical knowledge were strikingly different and revealed vast divergences in educational background. The instructor strategically calmed down the frequent heated discussions by allocating the learners into multiple regional discussion groups, deleting posts that did not sound appropriate, and reminding the students of the spirit of learning and discovery.

Likewise, in the "*Rural Health Nursing*" MOOC, the invitation of global, rural nurse learners to the discussion allowed for the gathering of substantial insights and sharing of personal experiences. At the same time, it revealed many learners struggling with limited or no solutions to the problems and issues being posed. According to the instructor, if the learners were struggling with how they could use nurses in a general philosophical sense, they would get help having their issue addressed. However, specifically understanding what nurses could do legally in respective countries, states, or regions of the world was an enormous challenge, since it varied wildly from one to the next on a global level. To illustrate this, the instructor gave an example of how nursing educators in Albuquerque could help somebody in North Korea to figure out the range of expertise or skill level that they could expect from a nurse and what they could do for independent practice. Furthermore, different cultural perspectives and prior experiences could sometimes consciously or unconsciously cause one student to stumble in some cases or be perceived in a manner that may be different from what the other was attempting to communicate.

> We had overcome some of those obstacles occasionally and sometimes that required a lot of discussion board comments back and forth where you get to the point that you felt like the

other person understood. One of the hard things about doing an online [course], particularly with different cultures and languages involved is that you are never really sure whether the other person got the gist of what you were trying to explain any more than you are sure you got the gist of what the person was trying to say to you.

(Participant 13)

On a different category, the "*Powerful Tools for Teaching and Learning: Digital Storytelling*" MOOC team struggled with the efficiency (whether it was done on time) of the peer assessment process and the subjectivity and quality of the feedback (i.e., whether it met all the goals or not) as the submissions of digital stories were products of peer review. The other challenges they raised included encouraging the learners to think about personally meaningful stories they would have to produce in the educational contexts, how to use digital stories to support and improve teaching or learning as this may mean different things to people from different parts of the world.

It is also important to reflect on what transpired in a more niche subject such as the "*Galaxies and Cosmology*" MOOC. While this MOOC was specifically intended for learners with specialized skills, more than half of the audience consisted of lay people. The instructor received multi-directional and diverse feedback and comments from the participants related to the extreme course difficulty from some viewpoints and that it was actually deemed too easy of a course by others.

Similarly, the "*Introduction to Cataract Surgery*" MOOC designed for residents in the ophthalmology residency program had more than 50% of the audience who were lay people. The instructor confessed it was very difficult to target the level of difficulty of the materials. Some learners wanted more in-depth materials while others struggled with their level of difficulties. The instructor was frustrated with this degree of mismatch. At the same time, this MOOC instructor realized her inability to respond to the massive group of learners in time despite her willingness to help. The instructor was also concerned about (1) her lack of experience doing cataract surgery in other countries and regions of the world as she was trained to do it only in the United States, and (2) the ability to perform cataract surgery in a particular place or situation based on available equipment and resources (Participant 11).

On connecting with the learners online, the instructor of the "*Property and Liability: An Introduction to Law and Economics*" MOOC expressed his struggle to completely engage with the learners due to the fact that he could not see them and attach names or faces to individual learners or when a group of learners were not very vocal on the discussion forum (Participant 11).

Emotional Benefits of Diversity: How Exposure to Global Learners Reshaped Views on (Online) Education

Most of the participants reported coming to MOOC design and development with some expectations of diversity among the audience. Yet, they became surprised with the volume of diversity among the student population who came from North America as well as different parts of Asia and Africa with their different language, cultural, ethnic, and educational backgrounds; and their patterns of engagement in the course. Table 11.2 describes the expectations and reality of the MOOC audience for these instructors.

A number of participants of this study reported experiencing giant cultural differences among learners' attitudes toward MOOCs. These MOOC instructors also argued that the merits of MOOCs lie in such appreciative attitudes of learners from the emerging parts of the world such as

TABLE 11.2 Expectations and Reality of MOOC Learners' Backgrounds

Participant	MOOCs	Learners' Expected Backgrounds	Reality
1	Galaxies and Cosmology	• Physics • Astronomy • Cosmology • Anyone interested	• 20% expected audience • 20% science education • 60% regular people • Age: 16–82 • Global audience
2 and 3	Introductory Human Physiology	• Biology • Anyone interested	• Social science: 13.9% • Health science: 30.6% • Professional: 11.6% • Technical: 11.1% Wide range of academic backgrounds (Engle, Mankoff, & Carbrey, 2015) • Humanities: 15.1% • Natural science: 17.8%
4	Medical Neuroscience	• Doctors—physicians • Those with neuroscience knowledge • Anyone interested	A lot of non-native speakers of English (who did or did not struggle with the language)
5	Questionnaire Design for Social Surveys	Students and professionals from all fields of social science	N/A
6	Specialization in Intermediate Java Software Engineering*	• Undergraduates around the world • Working professionals • Programming	Diverse programming skill levels
7	Understanding Terrorism and the Terrorist Threat	U.S. government officials (Homeland Security, Intelligence, Justice, etc.)	• 30% from developing economies • 30% from the U.S. • Subject expert (to seek network) vs. novice (to learn something new)
9	The Holocaust: The Destruction of European Jewry	Anyone interested	People who lived during the Holocaust
10	Curanderismo Part 1: Traditional Healing of the Body	Anyone interested	• Mexicans • Tex-Mex
11	Introduction to Cataract Surgery	• Residents in the ophthalmology residency program • Anyone interested	• < 50% expected audience • > 50% lay people
12	Powerful Tools for Teaching and Learning: Digital Storytelling	• Primarily Texas K–12 teachers • Anyone interested	• 1% Texas K–12 teachers • Everyone else
13	Rural Health Nursing	• Nurses • Other backgrounds	Global audience
14	Property and Liability: An Introduction to Law and Economics	Anyone interested	• 70% Americans • 30% internationals
15	Inspiring Leadership through Emotional Intelligence	Anyone interested	Global audience

* This specialization included five courses: 1. Object Oriented Programming in Java, 2. Advanced Data Structures in Java, 3. Mastering the Software Engineering Interview, 4. Data Structures Made Easy, and 5. Capstone: Analyzing (Social) Network.

Source: This table appears in the Online Learning journal (Phan, 2018) and is reprinted here with permission of the editor.

those in the Global South. As an example, one participant provided an anecdote of a student from Egypt expressing his appreciation of the MOOC that he took at (*name of the university*):

> At one point, I got an email from a fellow in Egypt, who said "I am emailing you on behalf of my brother who is taking your class, who could not email you himself. And here is the fax": "Professor, I love your class, I am so sorry I will not be able to finish it because I was arrested by military police in Egypt during the demonstration, and I don't know when I will get out, but I am so sorry." I am thinking, "Good God, if I were arrested by military police in Egypt, . . . class will be the last thing in my mind." This person was so grateful that they had the opportunity that they took trouble to send this message from jail.
>
> *(Participant 1)*

Even more evidence of the merits of MOOCs was attributed to the expertise and reputation of the instructor and the institution and the instructor's availability to have a live conversation with learners across the globe. Such a perspective is evident in the following quote with another participant from the Global South, this time India.

> I try to do a live chat, about once a month. When I do the live chat people call in for an hour and a half on a video chat and they can ask any questions. It was 4 o'clock in the afternoon my time in Cleveland at the university and I told this young man from India "What time is this there for you?" and he said "It's 2:30 in the morning," I said "Why aren't you in bed?" he said "Oh, professor, I've been waiting for so many weeks to be able to talk to you."
>
> *(Participant 15)*

As displayed in the following quote, MOOC instructors were highly concerned about their content reaching those in the Global South. For instance, this interview participant concurred that MOOCs were more appreciated by the learners from parts of the world who had limited access to quality learning resources and opportunities:

> The real value of the MOOC is not that some college sophomores are going to see it in America where the alternative is that the college sophomores could get it in a college class. It's going to be somebody in Vietnam or somebody in Peru or somebody in Africa for whom the alternative is not an American college course but nothing at all. Many of them wrote to me saying the discussion was the best part of the whole experience without which they wouldn't have any idea of the subject and there's no opportunity in their life to do anything remotely like this and that just cheerfully changed my attitude about online learning completely.
>
> *(Participant 14)*

Another major merit of MOOCs was created by the diverse student body; in effect, the widely diverse MOOC audiences enriched the learning outcomes with their diverse and authentic viewpoints, experiences, and personal stories. Here is an example:

> Another aspect of MOOCs, what I would call spontaneous self-crowdsourcing of education. . . . Students will post questions on the forums, and other students would answer them. In many cases, almost all cases, those would be excellent answers . . . sometimes it's a fairly trivial thing over such and such lecture, and sometimes it will be a person who actually has a real expertise in that particular aspect, and answered it better than I would.
>
> *(Participant 15)*

As the participant put it, a "spontaneous self-crowdsourcing of education" was created in which learners would support and encourage each other during the learning process.

In other cases, the instructors embrace global insights and diversity by gathering and showcasing students' postings from all over the world in the class discussion forum, as in the Rural Health Nursing MOOC:

> We addressed unconscious bias, which stimulated a lot of discussion. We did an assessment of resources (i.e.) geographic, economic, political and social aspects of healthcare that the students were provided to see how they're related to health. We even read the posts from participants around the world and got into an exchange with someone who was in India. He was struggling with some of the cultural diversity that involved the castes there. If you're in one particular caste level, you're provided with healthcare that's somehow different from the other caste level from the other areas of the country.
>
> *(Participant 13)*

Likewise, extended discussion forums were created to house learners' inspiring stories from across the globe:

> The other thing we have done is we have an extended discussion forum. Our learners are really active on the discussion forum and really supportive of one another. They share the stories about being stay-at-home parent for 10 years trying to get back into the workforce or moving from one aspect of industry to another and they share tips with one another about how to write their resume or how to prepare for interviews. It's just amazing to see this community form from around the world, people who are in the States, in Europe, in Russia and it's just amazing and they are working together, giving each other advice.
>
> *(Participant 6)*

Participant 6 also mentioned that instructors were well aware of the language barriers encountered by students coming from non-English-speaking countries. She stated that apart from providing content and language support such as captioning the video lectures, providing chapter notes, and translation services, non-native-speaker students were allowed to submit an assignment in their own language provided that there would be peers who spoke the same language to assess their work.

Scholarly Significance of the Work

Major contributions of this study include hearing the MOOC instructors and designers' voices when it comes to the global aspects of the MOOC participant community. This study also offered key insights and actions of support derived from the sophisticated professional experience of the 15 instructors and instructional designers who participated in this study. While they were all from the Global North, they were particularly concerned with how their content could be better accessed, used, and repurposed by those in the Global South. Among the findings was a strong commitment to democratize online education, which was strongly evidenced in the MOOC course designs and development as well as participant interactions with students. The compassionate thoughts and actions of caring towards the learners were at the heart of their impetus and dedication for teaching a MOOC. These authentic and organic thoughts and sharing from the participants reflected both merits and challenges of dealing with a global unknown audience.

At the same time, there was a pervasive tone and positive attitude about the possibilities within the participant MOOCs. Stated another way, there was some altruism in helping fellow humans on this planet who may be vastly different from the students who typically sign up for their residential courses. Each was engaged in a good deed to enhance the educational opportunities on this planet. Such stories of hope, despite the many constraints and barriers confronting that hope, are what many view as exactly what is needed today.

There are now opportunities and possibilities for other educators and researchers to tell a more complete story of how MOOC instructors and course designers perceive and respond to multicultural learners' needs; especially those with inferior technological and educational access such as those in the Global South. For instance, one opportunity would be for MOOC researchers to investigate the global issues and challenges on a MOOC platform besides Coursera to possibly identify, compare, and contrast pedagogical strengths and weakness available from different MOOC providers and their potential impact on learning outcomes. Given the importance of global education today, such studies might prove particularly welcome to those still not fully benefitting from MOOCs and open education because of the lack of cultural sensitivity or awareness.

APPENDIX 11.A

Interview Protocol

Researcher Name(s):
Mode of communication (Phone, Skype, face-to-face meeting and location):
Participant Name:
Job title:
Institution/department:
Date:
Start time:			End time:

---

1. What is your institution doing currently with respect to MOOCs?
2. What are the primary goals of your institution in pursuing MOOCs?
3. What is your role in this work and how did this role develop?
4. How do you and your institution define a MOOC?
5. For specific MOOCs:

    - What MOOC is your institution developing at the moment?
    - What are the educational objectives of the MOOC(s) you are offering?
    - Who is the target audience for your MOOC(s)?
    - What educational outcomes are being measured? (Rate of completion? Number of students receiving certificates? Or the degree of participation of the learners? (i.e. numbers of students participating in an activity? Number of views on the materials?)

6. Students attending your course come from different cultures and diverse background. In what way does your curriculum deal with diversity/diverse populations?
7. What data are you collecting for your MOOC(s)? (i.e. pre-, post- and during the course, enrollment, demographics of participants, reasons for taking course, participation, test scores, completion, post-course applications (networking, pursuit of further study, employer acceptance of any credentials).
8. Can you share with us some demographic information of the audience in the MOOC(s) you are offering?
9. How is data collected from MOOCs being used to improve pedagogy either online or on-campus?
10. How do you think the following factors will possibly affect student's learning behaviors and their participation in a MOOC?

    - Language and ethnicity background
    - Education level

- Employment status
- Gender
- Age

11. Which of the above issues did you address in designing your MOOC activities? Can you please give some examples?

Trang Phan is Assistant Professor and Director of Instructional Technology Resource Center (INTERESC) at Kremen School of Education and Human Development at California State University, Fresno. Phan's interest in massive open online courses (MOOCs) derived from her research work at the University of Houston where she earned her doctorate. Her other areas of focus include faculty uses of technology to enhance student-centered learning and human-centered design in education. As Director of INTERESC, she is in charge of training for the integration of technology in the classroom.

References

Croxton, R. A. (2014). The role of interactivity in student satisfaction and persistence in online learning. *MERLOT Journal of Online Learning and Teaching, 10*(2), 314–325. Retrieved from http://jolt.merlot.org/vol10no2/croxton_0614.pdf

Dillon, P., Wang, R., & Tearle, P. (2007). Cultural disconnection in virtual education. *Pedagogy, Culture & Society, 15*(2), 153–174. http://dx.doi.org/10.1080/14681360701403565

Engle, D., Mankoff, C., & Carbrey, J. (2015). Coursera's introductory human physiology course: Factors that characterize successful completion of a MOOC. *The International Review of Research in Open and Distributed Learning, 16*(2), 46–67. Retrieved from http://www.irrodl.org/index.php/irrodl/article/view/2010/3317

Gunawardena, C. (2014, March). Moocs: Students in the global South are wary of a "sage on the stage". *The Guardian*. Retrieved from www.theguardian.com/education/2014/mar/19/cost-barrier-students-global-south

Jacoby, J. (2014). The disruptive potential of the massive open online course: A literature review. *Journal of Open, Flexible, and Distance Learning, 18*(1), 73–85. Retrieved from www.jofdl.nz/index.php/JOFDL/article/view/214

Ke, F., Chávez, A. F., & Herrera, F. (2013). *Web-based teaching and learning across culture and age*. New York: Springer.

Margaryan, A., Bianco, M., & Littlejohn, A. (2015). Instructional quality of massive open online courses (MOOCs). *Computers & Education, 80*, 77–83.

Merriam, S. B. (2009). *Qualitative research: A guide to design and implementation*. San Francisco, CA: Jossey-Bass.

Phan, T. (2018). Instructional strategies that respond to global learners' needs in massive open online courses. *Online Learning, 22*(2), 95–118. doi:10.24059/olj.v22i2.1160

Robin, B., & McNeil, S. (2015). Webscapes: An academic vision for digital humanities projects on the web. *Book 2.0, 4*(1–2), 121–141. http://dx.doi.org/10.1386/btwo.4.1-2.121_1

Stake, R. E. (2006). *Multiple case study analysis*. New York: Guilford Press.

Stewart, B. (2013). Massiveness + openness = new literacies of participation? *MERLOT Journal of Online Learning and Teaching, 9*(2), 228–238. Retrieved from http://jolt.merlot.org/vol9no2/stewart_bonnie_0613.htm

Wang, F., & Hannafin, M. J. (2005). Design-based research and technology-enhanced learning environments. *Educational Technology Research and Development, 53*(4), 5–23. http://dx.doi.org/10.1007/bf02504682

Yin, R. K. (2014). *Case study research: Design and methods* (5th ed.). Los Angeles, CA: Sage.

SECTION 3
MOOCs and Open Education for Professional Development

MOOCs have perhaps enjoyed their greatest success as a means of professional development for teachers and other professionals. Recognizing this trend, in August 2017, the Open University of the UK and the European Union collaborated on the provision of a four-week MOOC focused on "Learning with MOOCs for Professional Development" (Kalafusová, 2017). In this section, authors from Turkey, Thailand, Canada, and South Africa describe important advances made in providing opportunities for professional development via MOOCs.

First, in Chapter 12, Kursat Cagiltay, Sezin Esfer, and Berkan Celik from Turkey describe the development of a unique pdMOOC portal (i.e., bilgeis.net) for Turkish professionals and students. As they readily admit, the number of MOOC portals in Turkey is relatively low when compared to its Western counterparts since MOOCs are still a new phenomenon for Turkey and the Middle East region. In this chapter, the authors reveal the insights of a Turkish pdMOOC (professional development MOOC) portal which offers 100 courses in order to support the development of soft and technical skills of individuals. In less than two years, registered users on bilgeis.net have reached to 100,000+. Bilgeİş pdMOOCs are increasingly used by different audiences, including employees, employers, university students, unemployed people, and even K–12 students. Bilgeİş pdMOOCs provide many benefits to these audiences. However, running such MOOCs also brings its own set of challenges and unexpected problems. In response, the authors of this chapter shed light on those complex issues as well as potential resolutions.

Of course, it is expected that this is just the opening act of a much longer play. Five or ten years from now, there may be thousands of niche pdMOOCs in Turkey. Accordingly, this chapter may provide hints for future MOOC developers in Turkey and beyond to help improve and perhaps transform traditional professional development policies and practices. What is clear is that despite the challenges inevitably involved in such an enterprise, the authors predict that professional development MOOCs will be a growth industry in Turkey.

In Chapter 13, Thapanee Thammetar and Jintavee Khlaisang from Thailand explain how systematic research methods are being used to develop MOOCs uniquely tailored to professional development needs as part of Thailand's ambitious plans for economic development. As the authors of this chapter explain, they live in a country that aspires to build toward Thailand 4.0; a hopeful economic model that will modernize the country and increase income equally across the country. In response to the role of education in the Thailand 4.0 era, there is increasing focus on the opportunities for Thai people to learn continuously throughout their lives by using ICT that improves access to educational services equally and efficiently in formal, non-formal, and informal contexts.

For instance, Thailand Cyber University Project (TCU) has developed a strategic plan related to open education that will lead to a learning society and promote lifelong learning via ICT. TCU's flagship project over the past three years has been Thai MOOC, a national MOOC platform of Thailand.

Using a research-based design approach, these two TCU leaders, Khlaisang and Thammetar, describe their analysis of the current conditions relating to open education in Thailand. They also discuss the results of a gap analysis and SWOT analysis of open educational operations in Thailand. In addition, they present the TCU 2018–2022 strategic plan on open education via ICT of higher education institutions. Finally, a Thai MOOC is presented as a case study for promoting open education and MOOCs in Thailand.

In the third chapter of this section, Chapter 14, Canadians Sanjaya Mishra, Martha Cleveland-Innes, and Nathaniel Ostashewski describe a collaborative effort between the Commonwealth of Learning and Athabasca University to test and refine the Technology-Enabled Learning (TEL) MOOC for global teacher professional development. Mishra, Ostashewski, and Cleveland-Innes argue that for education to be accessible and valuable, teachers must have the pedagogical and technological skill to engage learners in ways that lead to the development of appropriate knowledge, skills, and attitudes. Considering the huge number of trained teachers required to achieve UNESCO's Sustainable Development Goal 4, a massive open online course (MOOC) on Technology-Enabled Learning (TEL) was jointly developed by the Commonwealth of Learning (COL) and Athabasca University, Canada, to address the lack of adequately trained teachers globally, and, particularly, in the Commonwealth.

To begin, this chapter presents the design, development, and delivery of the TEL MOOC. Then, an analysis of the data collected from two offerings of the MOOC in 2017 is presented. Preliminary findings from TEL MOOC #1 and #2 revealed that the design adopted improved learner engagement and completion rates. Data also reveal that more than 30% of the participants joined this course for specific professional development reasons. Importantly, active participation of a large number of those registered shows the potential of MOOCs for professional development of the teachers in the Commonwealth and beyond.

Given that the chapter authors are from Canada, it is important to point out that there are more than 50 member countries of the COL which are primarily in the Global South. For example, COL member countries include those in Africa (e.g., Botswana, Malawi, Nigeria, Ghana, Uganda, Mozambique, Gambia, and Cameroon), Asia (e.g., Bangladesh, India, Pakistan, and Sri Lanka), the Caribbean and Americas (e.g., the Bahamas, Belize, Jamaica, Guyana, and Trinidad and Tobago), Europe (e.g., Malta, Cyprus, the UK), and the Pacific (e.g., Samoa, Papua New Guinea, Fiji, and Tonga). As such, the teacher educators and other participants in this MOOC came from a wide swath of the Global South.

In Chapter 15, the last chapter in this section, Antoinette van der Merwe, J.P. Bosman, and Miné de Klerk from South Africa describe how Stellenbosch University developed a "Teaching for Change" MOOC using a pedagogical approach that is grounded in an African Philosophy of Education. This unique MOOC served as a flexible incubation space for different dimensions of professional and institutional learning at Stellenbosch. The development process of the MOOC fostered experimentation in dimensions such as pedagogy, technology systems, and partnerships between professional academic support environments and teaching staff. Such experimentation resulted in better informed institutional strategy and decision making regarding the use of learning technologies for face-to-face, online, and hybrid modes of learning and teaching. Consequently, the return on investment of the MOOC in this South African, resource-constrained environment is not calculated in terms of short-term financial gains but rather in terms of longer-term gains that include organizational resilience and sustainability. This chapter describes how the development of a MOOC generated the incubation of meaningful and innovative learning processes at different levels of the university. The authors insightfully note that the iterative process that they describe sparked valuable dialogue, leading to the purposeful application of learning technologies for a range of learning and teaching modalities. Such applications, which operated in a complex, emerging (South) African context, that, importantly, were not limited to the MOOC format.

Reference

Kalafusová, A. (2017, August 25). Learning with MOOCs for professional development. *Biz MOOC*. Retrieved from www.open.edu/openlearncreate/course/view.php?id=2696

12
INSIGHTS INTO A NATIONWIDE pdMOOC PORTAL

Bilgeis.net of Turkey

Kursat Cagiltay, Sezin Esfer, and Berkan Celik

Introduction

MOOCs are a popular worldwide phenomenon, which effectively has resulted in a new research field with widespread attention in a short time period. In terms of raw data, while MOOC participants worldwide were 35 million people in 2015 (Shah, 2015), a year later, this jumped to about 58 million (Shah, 2016). As the number of global online learners rise rapidly (Morris, Hotchkiss, & Swinnerton, 2015), the aforementioned MOOC participant numbers are but one example of the similar expansion taking place in the world of MOOCs.

In the very early stages of MOOC research, Downes classified MOOCs into two main types: cMOOCs and xMOOCs (Downes, 2008). xMOOCs, which are more didactic, include video lectures, discussions, and quizzes (Bali, 2014; Kopp & Lackner, 2014), whereas cMOOCs foster connections among participants and learning resources while creating learning communities based on connectivist principles (Gerber, 2014; Fournier & Kop, 2015). Therefore, xMOOCs are somewhat more related to formal learning practices, whereas cMOOCs typically are more related to informal learning. Furthermore, in a best practice study of MOOCs, Cagiltay and Esfer (2016) noted that MOOCs can be described according to their different pedagogical models. In addition, MOOCs may also differ based on their served purposes (Daniel, 2012; Esfer & Cagiltay, 2018). Not too surprisingly, MOOC participants are generally a very heterogeneous group in terms of age, learning needs, education levels, work status, and prior online learning experience. In addition, each learner enrolled in MOOCs has various aims, motivations, and characteristics (Xiong et al., 2015). In part due to such a diverse pool of learners, MOOCs suffer from low completion rates, often between 5% and 12% in general (Perna et al., 2014). These factors lead designers to create more specific online courses that can be compatible with swiftly changing learner needs, as noted in many research studies (Chen, 2009; Egloffstein & Ifenthaler, 2017; Karnouskos, 2017; Milligan & Littlejohn, 2017).

Current Situation of MOOCs and OCW Portals in Turkey

MOOCs have begun to be offered in Turkey by universities and private enterprises; albeit at a slower rate than experienced in the United States. More specifically, some private Turkish universities have published a number of courses on popular MOOC portals, such as *edX* and *Coursera*. More detailed information about Turkish MOOC portals is provided in Table 12.1.

In addition to MOOC portals, there are OpenCourseWare (OCW) portals in Turkey that mostly provide video-based educational resources. Among them, *ODTU OCW* (ocw.metu.edu.tr/), *Khan Academy* (khanacademy.org), *Campus Online* (campusonline.com), *Turkcell Akademi*

TABLE 12.1 Turkish MOOC Portals

Name	University	Total # of Courses	Course Categories	Course Access	Cost
AtademiX	**Atatürk University** atademix.atauni.edu.tr	12	Technical and Soft Skills	MOOCs are accessible on specific dates	Totally free of charge
Akadema	**Anadolu University** ekampus.anadolu.edu.tr	56	Technical and Soft Skills	MOOCs are accessible on specific dates	Totally free of charge
Bilgeİş	**Middle East Technical University** bilgeis.net	100	Technical and Soft Skills	Self-paced	Totally free of charge
İstanbul İşletme Enstitüsü*	Not supported by a university www.iienstitu.com	61	Technical and Soft Skills	MOOCs are accessible on specific dates	Free in digital format, but requires payment for printed verified certificate
Coursera (Note: Turkey originated MOOCs in Turkish)	**Koç University** www.coursera.org/koc	6	Technical and Soft Skills	MOOCs are accessible on specific dates	Free, but requires payment for verified certificates
edX (Note: Turkey originated MOOCs in Turkish)	Not supported by a university, but sponsored by Turkcell Akademi www.edx.org/course?search_query=turkish	3	Soft skills	Self-paced (MOOCs are archived)	Free, but requires payment for verified certificates

* Also includes other paid courses in addition to free ones.

(www.turkcellakademi.com), *Çanakkale University OCW* (adm.comu.edu.tr), and *Yaşar University Lifelong Learning Portal* (hayatboyu.yasar.edu.tr) are examples of these OCW portals. For more OCW portals, see the *Turkish Academy of Sciences National OpenCourseWare* website (www.acikders.org.tr). In addition, there are some other platforms such as *UniversitePlus* (www.universiteplus.com) and *Netkent* (www.netkent.edu.tr) that provide e-certificates and online courses.

Bilgeİş pdMOOC Portal

The Bilgeİş Project was led by Middle East Technical University and supported by the European Union. The Bilgeİş Project was initially funded between 2015–2017 by the European Union and the Republic of Turkey. Both the researchers and Operation Coordination Unit Members of the project considered the MOOCs on the bilgeis.net portal as "pdMOOCs" since all of these courses were prepared specifically to support the professional development of its users. In particular, with the help of information and communication technologies (ICTs), the key goal in developing these large-scale courses was to help users with their daily lives or work environments in a relatively short time frame (i.e., completed in approximately three weeks).

Some elements of MOOCs differentiate pdMOOCs from other types of MOOCs. For instance, the course structure, users' motivations, course topics, and some instructional elements of pdMOOCs are slightly different from other known MOOCs. Given their wide-ranging goals and expectations, MOOC participant motivation may have a positive or negative effect on course retention and completion (Essex & Cagiltay, 2001; Hew & Cheung, 2014). Also, it is important to point out that the bilgeis.net system does not support any kind of direct communication with the other learners such as direct messaging. Moreover, peer evaluation is not used to grade required assignments or projects. Another difference, the initial pdMOOCs at bilgeis.net were produced in accordance with informal learning, procedural learning, and workplace learning principles. Naturally, the main idea behind this pdMOOC creation was to support the professional development of adults. In addition, about 80 of the bilgeis.net pdMOOCs addressed ICT-related topics like *Mobile Programming*, *Drone Operation*, *3D Modelling*, *Wearable Technology*, and *HTML5*, while the remaining 20 courses were related to soft skill topics like *Leadership*, *Mobbing*, and *Stress Management*. All of the course topics were selected based on the results of a need analysis survey combined with SWOT analysis results, expert opinions, and projections on possible user demands. When compared to traditional courses, the scope of the pdMOOCs are generally limited to basic skills so they could be completed in a short time frame. The initial pdMOOCs found at bilgeis.net had similar assessments in the form of online exams, assignments, and project work.

Having been one of the earliest MOOC portals in Turkey, Bilgeİş has now become one of the biggest Turkish MOOC portals. As of November 2017, Bilgeİş provided 100 courses for 30,000 users who had received over 12,800 certificates. Within a year, the Bilgeİş portal had more than 90,000 registered users and distributed approximately 60,000 certificates. Currently, bilgeis.net continues to grow rapidly.

Sustainability of the pdMOOC Portal

The pdMOOCs prepared within the scope of the aforementioned EU project were designed to be offered to users free of charge. However, the project had no official sustainability plan at that time. After the project finished, the pdMOOC portal lacked official funding. Fortunately, actions have been taken in regards to the sustainability of the pdMOOC portal, thereby allowing this important learning portal to survive for more than its initial year. More specifically, volunteers help maintain the portal's status. Middle East Technical University staff and Operation Coordination Unit Members work voluntarily for the portal. Moreover, five undergraduate students are responsible for the portal's help desk, and eight online tutors are responsible for evaluating the submitted assignments and projects to the portal.

Demographics of pdMOOC Users

The demographics of users were obtained from the system logs. The data cover the dates between August 8, 2017, and December 20, 2018. This study utilized descriptive statistical analyses, such as frequencies and percentages, focusing on the current status of the bilgeis.net pdMOOCs to reveal the user characteristics, trends, preferences, and tendencies regarding pdMOOC usage.

By December 20, 2018, there were 96,656 users registered on the bilgeis.net pdMOOC portal. Due to a technical problem, only the demographics data of 90,422 users were available and reported here. Of the users, 49,347 (55%) were students or unemployed people, 36,950 (41%) were employees, and 4,125 (4%) were employers. Also, 51,328 (56.8%) of the users are males and 38,026 (42.1%) of them are females. The age of the users ranges from 13 to 70 ($M = 26.98$, $SD = 9.85$). The majority of the users ($n = 61,296$, 67.8%) have no previous online learning experience, and 28,059 of them (31%) have a previous online learning experience. Only a few of the users reported that they have a disability ($n = 1,188$, 1.3%). When the education levels of the users were inspected, it was seen that almost 70% ($n = 61,794$) of the users are either university students or university graduates. Only very few users ($n = 345$, 0.4%) did not finish any school. Low number of users ($n = 1,068$, 1.2%) did not provide their background information.

While the majority of the users on the Bilgeİş pdMOOC portal are from Turkey ($n = 88,369$, 97.7%), a small number of the users ($n = 2,053$, 2.3%) are from other countries. Nearly 58% of the users ($n = 52,455$) live in the top five metropolitan cities in Turkey; namely, Istanbul, Ankara, Izmir, Bursa, and Antalya.

Registration Trends

While the number of users was 12,196 on August 19, 2017, the number of users reached 96,656 by December 20, 2018. This finding points out that the number of the users on the pdMOOC portal has increased by more than six times the initial registration in just 13 months after the launching of the pdMOOC platform. Figure 12.1 captures and illuminates the specific data on the registration trends.

In each course, the users are required to complete at least 70% of the pdMOOC successfully in order to receive a certificate. When the number of certificates earned is examined, the results showed that in total 59,044 certificates were earned by the users. The number of certificates obtained by the users ranges from 1 to 100, with a mean of 2.64 and a standard deviation of 3.60. On the pdMOOC portal, 21,689 users received at least one or more certificates, and 11,079 users received at least two or more certificates.

Average Duration of Course Completion

The users completed pdMOOCs in 17 days and 14 hours on average. The shortest completion duration average was 8 days and 21 hours for the "Food and Drink Services" course. In contrast, the longest completion duration average was 55 days and 10 hours for the "Developing IoT Applications with Raspberry Pi" course.

FIGURE 12.1 Registration Trends (August 2017–December 2018)

Most and Least Popular pdMOOCs

Impressively, 40,202 users enrolled in more than one course. When the most popular pdMOOCs were examined, it was seen that "Personal Stress Management" was the most preferred pdMOOC with 11,005 registered users. The "Photography Techniques" was the most preferred 10th pdMOOC with 5,544 registered users. Table 12.2 details the 10 most preferred pdMOOCs.

When the least popular pdMOOCs were examined, it was seen that "Database Management with OpenOffice Base" had been the least preferred pdMOOC with 472 registered users. "Intellectual Property Rights for Small Medium Enterprises" had been the least preferred 10th pdMOOC with 701 registered users. Table 12.3 shows the least preferred 10 pdMOOCs.

Completion Rates for the Most and Least Popular pdMOOCs

The completion rates were calculated using the traditional method of dividing the total enrollment numbers by the number completing each MOOC. When the completion rates for the most popular pdMOOCs were examined, it was found out that the completion rates were between 11.39% and 66.15%. While the "Work Health and Safety" pdMOOC had the highest completion rate (66.15%), the pdMOOC on "Basics of Project Management" had the lowest completion rate (11.39%). The completion rates figures including the enrolled users, completed users, and completion percentage for the most popular pdMOOCs are provided in Figure 12.2.

TABLE 12.2 The Most Preferred pdMOOCs in the Bilgeİş pdMOOC Portal

#	Most Preferred pdMOOCs	Enrolled Users
1	Personal Stress Management	11,005
2	Coping with Problematic People	10,170
3	Leadership	9,367
4	Python Programming I	8,463
5	Work Health and Safety	7,215
6	Innovation	6,661
7	Basics of Programming	5,827
8	Social Media for Your Job	5,584
9	Basics of Project Management	5,557
10	Photography Techniques	5,544

TABLE 12.3 The Least Preferred pdMOOCs in the Bilgeİş pdMOOC Portal

#	Least Preferred pdMOOCs	Enrolled Users
1	Database Management with OpenOffice Base	472
2	OpenOffice Writer	508
3	Accessible Workplace Design	557
4	Virtual Reality for Small Medium Enterprises	581
5	Information and Communication Technology Experiences of Small Medium Enterprises	589
6	Developing IoT Applications with Raspberry Pi	614
7	Integrated Business Management Application Odoo (OpenERP)	654
8	Basic Concepts and Major Advantages of Web Conferencing Tools	677
9	Advanced Raspberry Pi	677
10	Intellectual Property Rights for Small Medium Enterprises	701

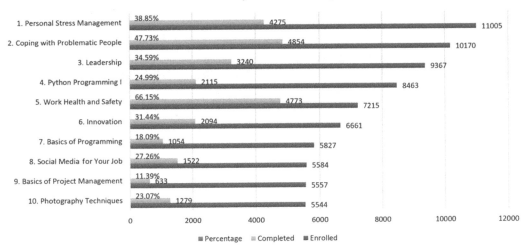

FIGURE 12.2 The Most Preferred pdMOOC Completion Rates on bilgeis.net (August 2017–December 2018)

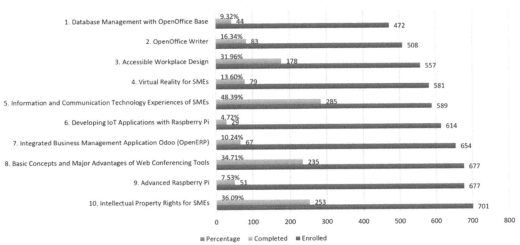

FIGURE 12.3 The Least Preferred pdMOOC Completion Rates on bilgeis.net (August 2017–December 2018)

When the completion rates for the least popular pdMOOCs were examined, it was found out that the completion rates were between 4.72% and 48.39%. While the pdMOOC on "Information and Communication Technology Experiences of Small Medium Enterprises" had the highest completion rate (48.39%), the "Developing IoT Applications with Raspberry Pi" pdMOOC experienced the lowest completion rate (4.72%). The completion rates figures including the enrolled users, completed users, and completion percentage for the least popular pdMOOCs are provided in Figure 12.3.

Discussion

The rate of user registration on bilgeis.net, while increasing, no longer shows a sharp increase when compared to the increasing number of global online learners (Morris et al.,

2015). Still, Turkish MOOC users' numbers have risen rapidly, and fortunately, pdMOOCs have received the attention of students, unemployed people, employees, and employers in Turkey. However, popular MOOC portals such as edX generally have a well-educated audience with a high percentage holding a bachelor's degree (Chuang & Ho, 2016). Such data was confirmed in our study as almost 70% ($n = 61,794$) of the users on the bilgeis. net pdMOOC portal were either university students or university graduates. Additionally, they are primarily located in the most developed cities of Turkey. Moreover, there are very few disabled users taking pdMOOCs. Clearly, pdMOOCs are more appealing to people who have better access to education. At the same time, the majority of the pdMOOC users ($n = 61,296$, 67.8%) in our study had no previous online learning experience. By taking a pdMOOC, the users gained at least some online learning experience. Accordingly, such pdMOOC experience can help Turkish citizens be familiar with the structure of online courses and hopefully this will lead them to further online courses, and hence, enhance their personal growth and development.

In sum, the users earned a total of 59,044 certificates. More specifically, 21,689 users received at least one or more certificates, and 11,079 users received at least two or more certificates. These numbers reflect the interest of the users towards pdMOOCs. In terms of time required to earn a certificate, the shortest pdMOOC completion duration average was 8 days and 21 hours, whereas the longest one took 55 days and 10 hours. The overall average duration of completion was 17 days and 14 hours. These results show that pdMOOC completion requires users to spare a considerable amount of time to learn regardless of the content. Since every MOOC participant has different learner characteristics, goals, needs, and expectations (Xiong et al., 2015), such results need to be analyzed in depth and interpreted from learners' perspectives in future studies.

Somewhat surprising in this study, while the majority of the pdMOOCs in the Bilgeİş pdMOOC portal are based on technology and programming, the users showed a strong preference towards pdMOOCs focusing on personal development and soft skills such as "Personal Stress Management," "Coping with Problematic People," and "Leadership". Another surprising finding concerned completion rates. In contrast to formal learners, typical MOOC participants behave like *tourists*, which significantly lowers MOOC completion rates (Xiong et al., 2015). In fact, a study from Perna et al. (2014) found the completion rates were between 5% and 12% in general. However, in the present study, the traditional completion rates of pdMOOCs were between 4.72% and 66.15%. Such results are dramatically different from the prevailing literature. One of the main reasons for this difference is that pdMOOCs in the Bilgeİş pdMOOC portal can be completed in a short time frame, approximately three weeks, due to their short and simplified course structure.

Conclusion

In conclusion, similar to the late adopters of MOOCs like countries in Africa (Rambe & Moeti, 2017), Turkish universities have also been attempting to keep up with the developments in the MOOC world. Although the number of users taking MOOCs currently is not that massive when compared to other MOOC portals outside of Turkey, MOOCs, in particular, pdMOOCs, maintain their popularity in Turkey. In fact, the number of MOOC users in Turkey is on the rise. At the same time, given that less educated people, disabled people, and people living in small cities are not the primary beneficiaries of pdMOOCs in Turkey, pdMOOCs and other forms of MOOCs have not yet been successful in democratizing education in this large country.

Perhaps the key finding of this study tells us that pdMOOCs are popular in Turkey. Many of them enrolled more than 4,000 people with one approaching 11,000 participants; even the least popular one had 472 participants. Further research might explore how the lives of specific individuals changed from this new form of educational delivery. Clearly, MOOCs for professional development are serving a need for the citizenry of Turkey. Whether the goal is to obtain a certificate or just a few new skills, they are serving a key need in rapidly changing economic and educational times. With pdMOOCs related to programming, leadership, project management, photography, instructional design, and many other areas available for free and on demand, people throughout Turkey have a vital avenue for personal and professional development. Thousands who perhaps once would have given up can now find opportunity, hope, and a sense of identity.

We expect that this is just the opening act of a much longer play. Five or ten years from now there may be thousands of niche pdMOOCs in Turkey and tens of thousands more globally that can literally change the spectrum of what it means to be human and how one can quickly retool to continue to make vital contributions to the evolving needs of this planet. What a wondrous time to be an educator. What a fortunate time to be alive!

Acknowledgments

This study is a part of *Europe Aid/136645/IH/SER/TR* with *TRH3.2METU/P-01 Contract Number—Capacity Development of Employees and Employers via Information and Communication Technologies* by its short name, Bilgeİş Project, led by Middle East Technical University and supported by the European Union. We are grateful to Bilgeİş Technical Assistance Team, Delegation of the European Union, EU Coordination Department of Ministry of Labor and Social Security and finally members of Operation Coordination Unit. The findings in this chapter were orally presented at the *E-Learn 2018* Conference.

Kursat Cagiltay is currently a professor in the Department of Computer Education and Instructional Technology at the Middle East Technical University (METU), Ankara, Turkey. He is the director of the Audio-Visual Systems Research and Development Center and coordinator of Instructional Technology Support Office at METU. He has been working as the coordinator of Bilgeİş MOOC Project since 2015. He earned his BS in Mathematics and MS in Computer Engineering from the METU and holds double PhDs in Cognitive Science and Instructional Systems Technology from Indiana University, USA. His research focuses on human-computer interaction, technology enhanced learning, social and cognitive aspects of electronic games, human performance technology, OER/OCW, and MOOCs. He can be contacted at kursat@metu.edu.tr.

Sezin Esfer is an expert researcher at the Audio-Visual Systems Research and Development Center and Instructional Technology Support Office at the Middle East Technical University (METU), Ankara, Turkey. She has been working as Operation Coordination Unit member in the BilgeİŞ MOOC Project since 2015. She is PhD candidate in the Department of Computer Education and Instructional Technology at METU and her PhD thesis is related to the dynamics of design and development of MOOCs. She earned her MS degree from the Computer Education and Instructional Technology program at Marmara University, İstanbul, in 2010 and BS degree in the same department at Uludag University, Bursa, in 2006. Her research interests include human-computer interaction, computer-aided language learning, e-learning, and MOOCs. She can be contacted at sesfer@gmail.com.

Berkan Celik is an experienced teaching assistant and PhD candidate in the Department of Computer Education and Instructional Technology at the Middle East Technical University (METU), Ankara, Turkey. He earned his BS and MS degrees in Computer Education and Instructional Technology from METU in 2011 and 2014, respectively. His research focuses on pre-service teacher education, technology integration, gamification, mobile learning, e-learning, MOOCs, adult education, and all phases of instructional design and development. He can be contacted at berkancx@gmail.com.

References

Bali, M. (2014). MOOC pedagogy: Gleaning good practice from existing MOOCs. *Journal of Online Learning and Teaching, 10*(1), 44.

Cagiltay, K., & Esfer, S. (2016). *Best practices analysis of MOOCs*. Proceedings of E-Learn. World Conference on E-Learning in Corporate, Government, Healthcare, and Higher Education 2016 (pp. 138–144). Association for the Advancement of Computing in Education (AACE), Chesapeake, VA.

Chen, C. (2009). Personalized e-learning system with self-regulated learning assisted mechanisms for promoting learning performance. *Expert Systems with Applications, 36*(5), 8816–8829.

Chuang, I., & Ho, A. (2016). *HarvardX and MITx: Four years of open online courses*. doi:10.2139/ssrn.2889436.

Daniel, J. (2012). Making sense of MOOCs: Musings in a maze of myth, paradox, and possibility. *Journal of Interactive Media in Education, 3*. Retrieved from http://www-jime.open.ac.uk/jime/article/viewArticle/2012-18/html.

Downes, S. (2008). Places to go: Connectivism & connective knowledge. *Innovate, 5*(1). Retrieved from https://nsuworks.nova.edu/cgi/viewcontent.cgi?article=1037&context=innovate.

Egloffstein, M., & Ifenthaler, D. (2017). Employee perspectives on MOOCs for workplace learning. *TechTrends, 61*(1), 65–70.

Esfer, S., & Cagiltay, K. (2018). Creating a MOOC Portal for Workplace Learning. In Ifenthaler, D. (Ed.), *Digital Workplace Learning*. Springer, Cham.

Essex, C., & Cagiltay, K. (2001). Evaluating an online course: Feedback from "distressed" students. *Quarterly Review of Distance Education, 2*(3), 233–239.

Fournier, H., & Kop, R. (2015). MOOC learning experience design: Issues and challenges. *International Journal on E-Learning, 14*(3), 289–304.

Gerber, J. (2014). MOOCs: Innovation, disruption and instructional leadership in higher education. *Journal of Educational Technology & Society, 15*(4), 380–389.

Hew, K. F., & Cheung, W. S. (2014). Students' and instructors' use of massive open online courses (MOOCs): Motivations and challenges. *Educational Research Review, 12*, 45–58.

Kopp, M., & Lackner, E. (2014). *Do MOOCs need a special instructional design?* Proceedings of EDULEARN14 Conference (pp. 7138–7147). Barcelona, Spain.

Morris, N. P., Hotchkiss, S., & Swinnerton, B. (2015). *Can demographic information predict MOOC learner outcomes?* Proceedings of the European MOOC Stakeholder Summit (pp. 199–207).

Milligan, C., & Littlejohn, A. (2017). Why study on a MOOC? The motives of students and professionals. *The International Review of Research in Open and Distributed Learning, 18*(2). doi:10.19173/irrodl.v18i2.3033.

Karnouskos, S. (2017). Massive open online courses (MOOCs) as an enabler for competent employees and innovation in the industry. *Computers in Industry, 91*, 1–10.

Perna, L. W., Ruby, A., Boruch, R. F., Wang, N., Scull, J., Ahmad, S., & Evans, C. (2014). Moving through MOOCs: Understanding the progression of users in massive open online courses. *Educational Researcher, 43*(9), 421–432.

Rambe, P., & Moeti, M. (2017). Disrupting and democratising higher education provision or entrenching academic elitism: Towards a model of MOOCs adoption at African universities. *Educational Technology Research and Development, 65*(3), 631–651.

Shah, D. (2015, December). By the numbers: MOOCs in 2015. *Class Central*. Retrieved from www.class-central.com/report/moocs-2015-stats.

Shah, D. (2016, December). By the numbers: MOOCs in 2016. *Class Central*. Retrieved from www.class-central.com/report/mooc-stats-2016.

Xiong, Y., Li, H., Kornhaber, M. L., Suen, H. K., Pursel, B., & Goins, D. D. (2015). Examining the relations among student motivation, engagement, and retention in a MOOC: A structural equation modeling approach. *Global Education Review, 2*(3), 23–33.

13
PROMOTING OPEN EDUCATION AND MOOCs IN THAILAND

A Research-Based Design Approach

Thapanee Thammetar and Jintavee Khlaisang

Introduction

Thailand 4.0 is an economic model that aims to take Thailand out of the trap of middle-income countries, inequality, and imbalances (Ministry of Industry, 2016; Jones & Pimdee, 2017). It will modernize the country and enhance peoples' income equality. Such economic prosperity will not appear magically. Clearly, new innovations in education must be created to provide the base for the development of the country. Fortunately, there is a path forward for the Thai public promoted alongside the emergence of the Thailand 4.0 Model in the Educational Development Plan of the Ministry of Education (2017–2021) regarding the promotion and development of digital technology for education. The aim of this plan is to provide new opportunities for the Thai people to learn continuously throughout their lives by using information technology that improves access to educational services equally and efficiently in formal, non-formal, and informal contexts (Office of the Permanent Secretary, Ministry of Education, 2016).

Additionally, the Information Technology Policy (2011–2020) of Thailand has set the strategy for ICT infrastructure development as well as the development of human capital to be able to create and use information efficiently, critically, and consciously. This policy also aims to develop ICT personnel with international expertise and mastery. It develops and applies ICT with the goal of reducing economic and social gaps by creating equal opportunities to access public resources and services for all people, especially, the basic services necessary for a healthy life including education and public health services. Such aspirations are in line with the aims of the Thailand 4.0 policy in elevating Thailand's education to be competitive at the international level.

Such a strategy will provide Thai people with the opportunity to have quality education at all ages, thereby fostering a sense of pride on the world stage. To prepare the Thai citizenry for the 21st century, there will be an emphasis on higher-order thinking skills, learning and innovation skills, and information, communication and technology skills, as well as life and career skills (Ministry of Commerce, 2016; Ministry of Information and Communication Technology, 2011; Khlaisang & Songkram, 2019; Khlaisang, 2013). While challenging, such goals offer many new opportunities within Thailand.

The Thailand Cyber University (TCU) Project was established in 2005. Its organizational structure is illustrated in Figure 13.1. This project is based on a strategy to create educational opportunities by increasing educational access. Its aim is to produce a lifelong learning society to enhance the expertise of public and private sector personnel. In response to the role of education in the Thailand 4.0 era, TCU has developed a strategic plan centered around open education that will lead to a

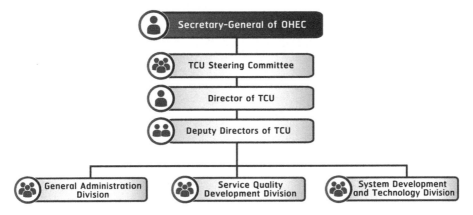

FIGURE 13.1 TCU's Organizational Structure

learning society and promote lifelong learning via a sophisticated digital learning platform. TCU's flagship project over the past three years has heavily focused on Thai MOOC, which is the national MOOC provider (Thammetar, Theeraroungchaisri & Khlaisang, 2018). At present, Thai MOOC has a total of 261 courses that have emerged from the cooperation of nine regional hubs. As of November 19, 2018, the Thai MOOC platform had 83,344 active students (http://thaimooc.org).

This bold initiative is driven by research designed to provide insights into the process of developing a strategic plan and implementation strategies for open education in Thailand. The results of this effort are intended to help promote, develop, coordinate, and monitor other similar projects. This research also uses a MOOC Professional Development (PD) project as a case study. The PD project is managed through a network of nine higher education hubs. While there are similar problems in each region, these network hubs facilitate many different types of services. Fortunately, there are universities that are ready to serve as central coordinating units or hosts that drive network hub activities for each region (thaicyberu.go.th).

There are a total of 172 institutes throughout Thailand comprising nine host institutes and 163 other higher education institutes. A map of the higher education regional network hubs is provided in Figure 13.2. The nine host institutes in the nine regions include the following:

1. The upper northern region higher education network hub with Chiang Mai University as the host institute with 17 higher education institutes.
2. The lower northern region higher education network hub with Naresuan University as the host institute with 13 higher education institutes.
3. The upper northeastern region higher education network hub with Khon Kaen University as the host institute with 15 higher education institutes.
4. The lower northeastern region higher education network hub with Suranaree University of Technology as the host institute with 17 higher education institutes.
5. The upper central region higher education network hub with Chulalongkorn University as the host institute with 47 higher education institutes.
6. The lower central region higher education network hub with King Mongkut's University of Technology Thonburi as the host institute with 33 higher education institutes.
7. The eastern region higher education network hub with Burapha University as the host institute with 8 higher education institutes.
8. The upper southern region higher education network hub with Walailak University as the host institute with 9 higher education institutes.
9. The lower southern region higher education network hub with Prince of Songkla University as the host institute with 14 higher education institutes.

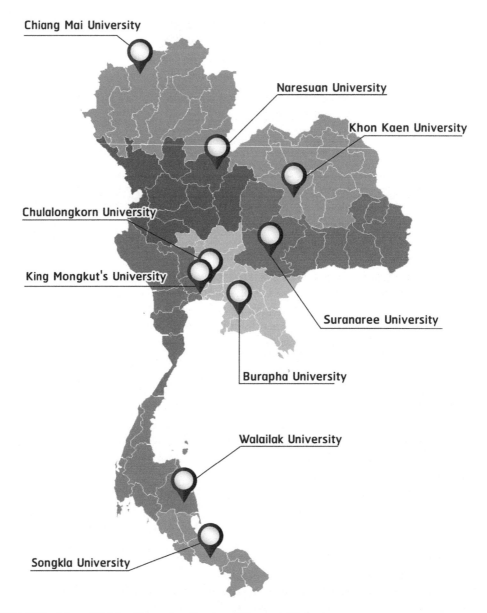

FIGURE 13.2 Map of Higher Education Regional Network Hubs

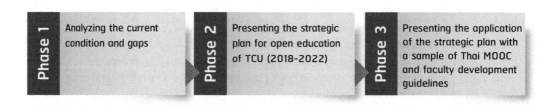

FIGURE 13.3 TCU's Institutional Research Project Consists of Three Phases

TCU works with both domestic and international higher education institutes to develop quality distance learning courses and curriculum by using a digital learning platform for formal education, non-formal education, informal education, and lifelong learning, with an emphasis on the effective use of resources, including personnel and educational media (Khlaisang, 2015). A key aspect of this chapter is to present TCU's strategic and implementation plans for promoting open education and MOOCs in Thailand using a research-based design approach to obtain a practical strategic plan that addresses the needs of users. As noted in Figure 13.3, the TCU project consists of three phases: (1) analyzing the current condition and gaps in open education which uses the Information Communication and Technology (ICT) of Higher Education Institutes (HEIs) in Thailand, (2) detailing the strategic plan for the open education of TCU (2018–2022), and (3) documenting the application of the strategic plan with a sample of Thai MOOCs and faculty development guidelines for MOOC teaching in HEIs as a case study.

Analysis of the Current Operation Conditions Relating to Open Education

Development of Online Courseware for Self-Learning

Since its establishment, TCU has promoted and supported instructors of HEIs in nine regional network hubs nationwide to produce open online courses for mutual use. According to the report on the operations of TCU (Thammetar & Khlaisang, 2018a), it was found that open courseware for self-learning in primary and secondary education, as well as for undergraduate degrees, graduate diplomas, graduate degrees, and doctoral degrees significantly developed, encompassing a total of 796 courses. Put another way, this development resulted in more than 10,746 learning hours involving over 17 different curricula.

Condition of ICT Personnel

TCU recognizes the importance of human development. Workshops and conferences have been organized continuously to help the personnel of HEIs at all levels so that they can become leaders and manage changes in the dynamics of world education and higher education. TCU has also provided opportunities to the personnel of educational institutes at all levels to gain the knowledge and skills in distance education via the digital learning platform. The impact of TCU to date is extensive. Examples of courses include: (1) the project on open courseware, including over 800 self-paced learning courses available on the TCU LMS (since 2005), and (2) the project on e-learning professional development, including courses for project managers, instructors, and e-learning courseware developers. This latter project is a full online training course with approximately 500 graduates each year since 2006. In addition, TCU also offers courses related to developing three types of educational personnel to manage e-learning, namely, the teachers, lecturers, and educational personnel of educational institutes and other organizations totalling 18,208 participants.

Condition of the Management via a Digital Learning Platform

TCU has continuously designed and developed its own learning management system (LMS). The TCU LMS has been developed to support use from all kinds of communication devices. Importantly, it supports multiple languages including Thai, English, and Japanese. By 2016, there were a total of 135 educational institutes, government organizations, and private organizations using TCU-LMS for open education, as well as online teaching and learning.

TABLE 13.1 The Thailand Cyber University Strength, Weakness, Opportunity, and Threat (SWOT) Analysis

Strengths:	Weakness:
1. Cooperation of higher education network hubs under nine host institutes in nine regions. 2. Joining the international networks related to distance education via digital learning platform continuously. 3. Organizing conferences and seminars for personnel development consciously.	Lack of specific operational targets for each strategy in each year. The measurement or assessment cannot be displayed in terms of both quantitative and qualitative data to reflect performance of the staff.
Opportunities:	**Threats:**
1. Receiving support and cooperation from government and private organizations. 2. Having an opportunity to join international networks related to distance education via digital learning platform.	A number of MOOCs have opened in other countries which offer a variety of lessons. As a result, students move to study from MOOCs of other countries rather than MOOCs developed by TCU.

The final initiative to mention is the development of the Thai Massive Open Online Course: Thai MOOC (http://thaimooc.org). The goal of Thai MOOC is to expand learning opportunities through the digital learning platform to the general public. TCU has focused on developing Thai MOOC to be a national MOOC provider. It entails collaboration among the Ministry of Education, the National Science and Technology Development Agency (NSTDA), the Ministry of Science and Technology, and the Ministry of Digital Economy and Society (formerly, the Ministry of Information and Communication Technology). The goal of the Thai MOOC initiative is to raise the quality of education in all sectors. It is also the foundation for research and development on online open education and digital learning platforms in Thailand.

Results of Gap Analysis and SWOT Analysis of Open Education Operations

In-depth interviews with 15 representatives, including the network hub president, executives, and personnel involved in online teaching, were conducted to guide the development of the strategic plan on open education via the ICT of HEIs in TCU from 2018–2022 (Thammetar & Khlaisang, 2018b). According to the existing conditions listed previously, the representatives proposed three strategic plans for TCU that focused on open education, as follows: Strategic Plan 1: Creating cooperation networking for education between domestic and international educational institutes; Strategic Plan 2: Managing distance education via a digital learning platform; and Strategic Plan 3: Researching and developing standards and quality assurance in distance education through a digital learning platform. According to gap and SWOT analyses related to TCU strategic plans and strategies during 2012–2016 (see Table 13.1.), it was found that Strategic Plan 1 was judged to be strongest and Strategic Plans 2 and 3 were weaker. A summary of the results of the interviews and the SWOT analysis follow.

Presenting the TCU 2018–2022 Strategic Plan on Open Education

Considering the qualitative data analysis, the opinions of 50 experts were collected during the focus group sessions. The opinions and recommendations of the experts can be summarized into the following three issues:

1. A vision of online instruction in the future. Because the trend of online instruction has changed constantly, the strategic plan should use neutral wording to accommodate future changes.

2. Enhancing strategies for research purposes as well as disseminating innovation, and the development of standards, quality assurance, and high quality practices. A strategic plan is proposed related to effective practice and disseminating innovation that addresses sustainability.
3. Collaboration with outside organizations. There should be collaboration with outside organizations to develop the content, train instructors, and manage the funds for the digital learning platform.

Based on the qualitative data analysis, TCU has revised the strategic plan to be more consistent with the opinions and recommendations of experts. Some of the main items in this plan are listed next.

> **Strategic Plan 1:** In the first strategic plan, there is the establishment of a collaborative network for education management among domestic and international HEIs while supporting a national digital learning platform. The objective is to create cost savings and overall effectiveness of education management by sharing personnel, educational resources, and open courseware. As shown in Figure 13.4, the strategic plan consists of seven strategies.
>
> **Strategic Plan 2**: Strategic Plan 2 is concerned with providing distance education via the digital learning platform and fostering the credit bank platform and credit transfer facilitator. The objectives of Strategic Plan 2 include: (1) cooperating with universities to provide distance learning courses that accommodate the needs of quality higher education, (2) expanding the opportunities for HEIs by adding channels and formats in education, and (3) supporting the continuing and lifelong education of the people of Thailand with distance learning via a digital learning platform. The strategic plan consists of three key strategies as shown in Figure 13.5.
>
> **Strategic Plan 3:** This plan entails research and development of standards and quality assurance in distance education via a digital learning platform and improving the strategic content provider. The two primary objectives are: (1) to improve the quality and standards of distance education via a digital learning platform, and (2) to provide quality assurance for distance education via the digital learning platform. This third strategic plan consists of four strategies as shown in Figure 13.6.

To enable TCU to develop the strategic plan 2018–2022, the researchers proposed a procedural model to formulate a strategic plan for TCU in the future. This model is illustrated in Figure 13.7. The development of the TCU SMART strategic plan consisted of five steps:

1. **Set mission/goals.** The first step in the process was to show the basic concept and objectives of the organization and to identify the scope of action.
2. **Measure the internal and external environment.** Executives must study and analyze the factors affecting the operation of each organization. This analysis can be divided into two levels: (1) external environment, and (2) internal environment. A Strength, Weakness, Opportunity, and Threat (SWOT) analysis was conducted to consider whether each factor contributes to or disrupts the organization's operations.
3. **Arrange strategic plans.** Strategic plans including strategic targets and resource allocations were defined. These were broadly defined directions to develop as a guideline for future operations of the organization. The strategy is usually designed according to the level of the organization by determining what programs should be implemented within the next five years. The important measure in this step is to determine the measurable objectives of every program, prepare a five-year plan to achieve the intended objectives, and prepare a budget for each year.

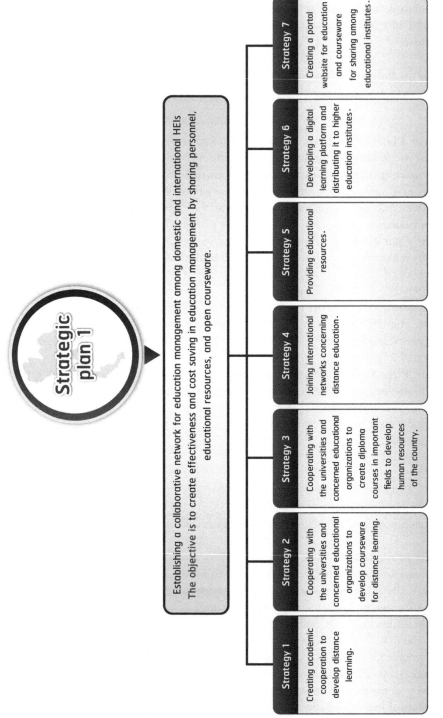

FIGURE 13.4 TCU Strategic Plan 1 Consists of Seven Strategies

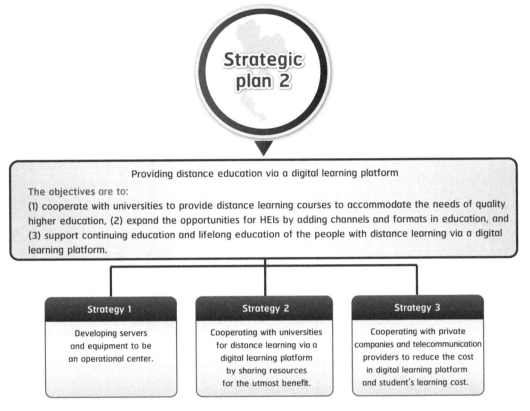

FIGURE 13.5 TCU Strategic Plan 2 consists of Three Strategies

4. **Recap and implement strategic plans.** This step is intended to implement the strategic plans for concrete operation through managing the human resource structure and systematical coordination.
5. **Test the implementation of strategic plans.** This step entails monitoring, checking, and analyzing the problems of the current strategic plans to be in line with the actual situation in order to maximize the value of the organization's operations. In addition, this step involves the evaluation of the implementation of the selected strategic plan as to whether it is successfully implemented according to the target. The result of the evaluation will be used to reconsider the development of the strategic plans. It can be seen that the strategic management process is a continuous process due to the different variables that may cause unpredictable phenomena. Whether occurring from the external environment or internal factors, executives must be alert to changes to improve and develop the strategic plans accordingly.

A Case Study on Thai MOOC

TCU has developed the Thai MOOC project to provide open learning under the Digital Economy and Society Driven Project, Plan 3: Building a Quality Society with Digital Technology. TCU, Office of the Higher Education Commission, Ministry of Education together with the Office of the Permanent Secretary, Ministry of Science and Technology, and the Ministry of Digital Economy and Society (formerly, the Ministry of Information and Communication Technology) have conducted the Thai MOOC project to be the center of the national MOOC provider to respond to the "Lifelong Digital Learning Platform" (see Figure 13.8).

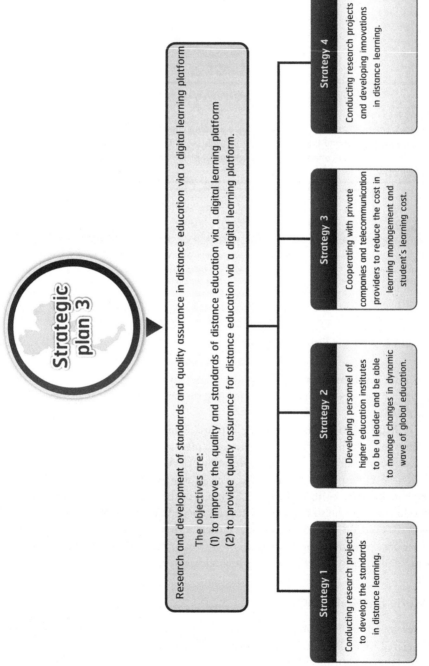

FIGURE 13.6 TCU Strategic Plan 3 Consists of Four Strategies

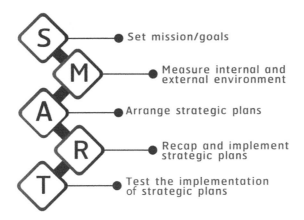

FIGURE 13.7 TCU's Procedural Model to Formulate a Strategic Plan

FIGURE 13.8 Thai MOOC: National Digital Learning Platform for Lifelong Learners (thaimooc.org)

The main purpose of the Thai MOOC project is to share learning resources between HEIs that specialize in different fields to collaborate in the development and management of the MOOC. The institutes work together to develop the central platform for instruction, measurement, and evaluation. The student database, learning records, course credits, and other related information have been stored. Cooperation between HEIs is developed to enable students to register courses and transfer course credits across universities in the future. As detailed in Table 13.2, there is currently cooperation among the nine network hubs resulting in a total of 261 courses and 2,470 learning hours.

The Thai MOOC Platform has features that support the digital learning platform with a student database, learning history, and accumulated credits. In addition, there is a credit transfer system and test bank system. In terms of standards and practice, research has been conducted on the conditions for effective and high-quality practices related to MOOC design and learning. The development of the Thai MOOC project, including learning media, learning activities, and evaluation, is in line with quality standards and learning processes. At present, it is required that instructors, instructional designers, and teaching assistants pass three courses to qualify. These courses are open and available as self-paced learning modules. After passing the courses illustrated in Figure 13.9, faculty members are qualified to open a course and teach on the Thai MOOC platform.

TABLE 13.2 Cooperation of the Nine Network Hubs Regarding the Number of Courses and Learning Hours

Higher Education Network Hubs	Number of Courses	Number of Learning Hours
Upper northern region	44	444
Lower northern region	28	230
Upper northeastern region	10	100
Lower northeastern region	14	228
Eastern region	N/A	N/A
Upper central region	89	839
Lower central region	33	270
Upper southern region	21	191
Lower southern region	22	168

The course is designed to help instructors and concerned persons in create a course to understand planning process and the design and production of MOOC courses by using Thai MOOC.	The course explains about methods and steps in developing an online MOOC course on Thai MOOC. It is suitable for instructors, staff, and those who want to develop an effective online course in a short time. This course describes the use of every tool available on Thai MOOC.	The course introduces the process of creating video for Thai MOOC. The course includes the principle in organizing the content and presenting it by camera shot, creating a video production plan under the appropriate time and resources and capabilities of the team to create quality videos.

FIGURE 13.9 All MOOC Instructors and Developer Are Required to Pass the Self-paced Learning Module Consisting of Three Courses (overview of creating an edX Course, StudioX and VideoX)

The Personal Level

The implementation of Thai MOOC focuses on the development of instructors to prepare them for teaching MOOCs; this is in line with the TCU proposed faculty development guidelines for MOOC teaching in HEIs (Level 1: Personal level). The guidelines have emphasized the professional development of instructors on three levels: (1) the personal level, (2) the teaching level, and (3) the institutional level (Thametar & Khlaisang, 2018a). *Figure 13.10* illustrates the relationships among these three levels.

Based on Figure 13.10, it is apparent that the professional development of instructors to prepare for teaching in MOOCs has several important components and levels as listed next.

Faculty Development: Personal Level

There should be a study on training programs for people involved in MOOCs. At present, TCU requires instructors, instructional designers, and teaching assistants to pass three self-paced learning courses to be qualified to open a course and teach on Thai MOOC.

Faculty Development: Teaching Level

There should be an exchange of teaching methods with other MOOC instructors who have designed various teaching activities that are relevant to online open environments. There are also plans for effective assessment of MOOC learners.

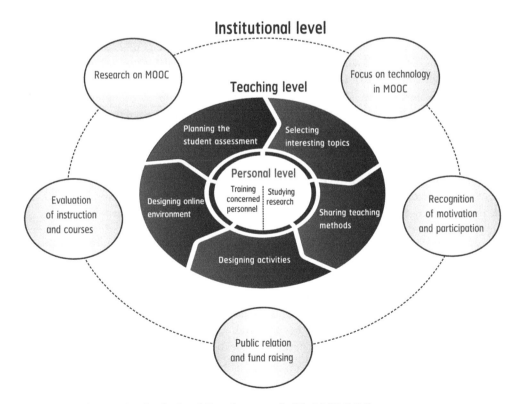

FIGURE 13.10 Continuing Professional Development for Thai MOOC Instructors

Faculty Development: Institutional Level

Faculty development at the institutional level should focus on creating recognition, motivation, and engagement in promoting and raising funds to support MOOCs. Additionally, there should be evaluation of the instruction and courses in Thai MOOC for teaching and learning standards. Instructors should also be encouraged to conduct research on MOOCs to maximize the benefits of MOOCs and perhaps further develop them.

In addition, for maximum benefit, the direction for the development of instructors to prepare for the three levels of MOOCs—personal, teaching, and institutional—should be equally important and parallel.

Discussion and Conclusion

As highlighted in this chapter, the TCU Strategic Plan (2018–2022) was designed for promoting open education and MOOCs in Thailand. The plan employs a research-based design approach with the intention of leading to a practical strategic plan that responds to the needs of its users. Among the various steps of the TCU Strategic Plan are defining strategic plans and the implementation of that plan via a case study of the Thai MOOC as a flagship project. The operations are divided into two parallel parts: (1) platform development, and (2) training instructors and system developers. All operations are in line with the TCU SMART strategic plan and the implementation plan. According to Chaim (2016), these plans will help learners to develop their competence and skills efficiently through each MOOC's interactive platform based on the learning interest. In effect, learning through the MOOCs' interactive platform will be based on the learners' interest; at the same time, it will support the learners in developing their competences and skills efficiently (Chiam, 2016).

Importantly, there are many significant implications emerging from this study. For instance, in regard to Thai MOOC, it focuses on the importance of the course instructors. It is necessary that instructors, instructional designers, and teaching assistants pass three courses to qualify. Research indicates that the instructors who become course creators of Thai MOOCs should not only be specialists in their subject matter area, but should also understand how to effectively orchestrate an online course through the Thai MOOC platform. Such skills and competencies are vital since classrooms for formal education and other online courses have different environmental structures. Secondly, instructors often need to play various roles in their courses (e.g., information deliverer, resource curator, task evaluator, etc.) to support online learner needs. Similarly, Castrillo de Larreta-Azelain (2014) emphasize the integral role of the instructor when teaching in MOOCs. Furthermore, the growth of Thai MOOCs underlines the importance of the development of instructors by paying attention to three levels: (1) the personal level, (2) the teaching level, and (3) the institutional level through the nine network organizations.

Cooperation and support among the various parties operating at each level has increased the quality of Thai MOOC courses. This finding is consistent with a study from Kovanović et al. (2015) which indicated that the success of MOOCs not only revolves around learners but also includes other stakeholders such as university professors, education policy makers, and educational technology vendors. Of course, MOOC students are not only learners but often assume the role of instructor as well. This viewpoint is similar to Loizzo, Ertmer, Watson, and Watson (2017) who pointed out the importance of professional development through MOOCs. However, although many benefits have been identified through this case, there are many challenges and issues standing in the way of MOOC instructors (Blackmon, 2018).

In addition, since the courses' instructors and instructional designers are not evaluated during or after the course, they might not have new or innovative ideas to improve the course. Naturally, these aforementioned implications for practice in Thai MOOCs might help other organizations and institutions learn how to design and develop their MOOC courses and perhaps effectively reduce or even eliminate their weaknesses. If successful, future research could investigate instructor experiences and suggestions that could lead to further Thai MOOC enhancements and improvements.

Thapanee Thammetar is the Director of Thailand Cyber University Project, Office of the Higher Education Commission in the Ministry of Education in Bangkok, Thailand. Thapanee is also an associate professor at the Department of Educational Technology in the Faculty of Education at Silpakorn University. Currently, she also serves as a member of the institute council and a member of the academic senate of the Institute of Community Colleges in the Ministry of Education in Thailand. Her latest research projects are the competency-based online professional development system for higher education officers (2018). Her ongoing research projects include strategic plans and faculty development guidelines for MOOC Teaching in Higher Education Institutes (2018–present). Her research interests include e-learning, quality assurance for online learning, open education, and MOOCs.

Jintavee Khlaisang is Associate Professor at the Department of Educational Technology and Communications, and member of Educational Invention and Innovation research unit within the Faculty of Education at Chulalongkorn University, Bangkok, Thailand. Jintavee is also the deputy director of Thailand Cyber University Project, Office of the Higher Education Commission in the Ministry of Education in Thailand. Her recent book is titled, *Ubiquitous Technology Enhanced Learning: The Outcome-Based Learning Design for 21st Century Learners* (2018). Her latest research project is the Development of Gamified Self-Regulated Learning System in Ubiquitous Learning Environments to enhance Achievement Motivation for Thai MOOCs (2018–present). Her research interests include ubiquitous learning, flipped learning, blended learning, virtual learning environments, open education, and MOOCs.

References

Blackmon, S. (2018). MOOC makers: Professors' experiences with developing and delivering MOOCs. *The International Review of Research in Open and Distributed Learning*, *19*(4), 76–91. Retrieved from www.irrodl.org/index.php/irrodl/article/view/3718

Castrillo de Larreta-Azelain, M. D. (2014). Language teaching in MOOCs: The integral role of the instructor. In E. Martín-Monje & E. Bárcena (Eds.), *Language MOOCs: Providing learning, transcending boundaries* (pp. 67–90). Berlin, Germany: De Gruyter Open.

Chiam, C. C. (2016). Benefits and challenges of massive open online courses. *ASEAN Journal of Open & Distance Learning (AJODL)*, *8*(1), 16–23.

Jones, C., & Pimdee, P. (2017). Innovative ideas: Thailand 4.0 and the fourth industrial revolution. *Asian International Journal of Social Sciences*, *17*(1), 4–35.

Khlaisang, J. (2013, August 5–6). *MOOCs pedagogy: From OCW, OER, to MOOCs—a learning tool for digital learners*. Proceeding of International E-Learning Conference Strengthening Learning Quality: Bridging Engineering and Education, Thailand Cyber University Project, Office of the Higher Education Commission, Ministry of Education, Bangkok, Thailand.

Khlaisang, J. (2015). Research-based guidelines for evaluating educational service website: Case study of Thailand cyber university project. *Procedia—Social and Behavioral Sciences, 174*, 751–758.

Khlaisang, J., & Songkram, N. (2019). Designing a virtual learning environment system for teaching twenty-first century skills to higher education students in ASEAN. *Technology, Knowledge and Learning, 24*(1), 41–63.

Kovanović, V., Joksimović, S., Gašević, D., Siemens, G., & Hatala, M. (2015). What public media reveals about MOOCs: A systematic analysis of news reports. *British Journal of Educational Technology, 46*(3), 510–527.

Loizzo, J., Ertmer, P. A., Watson, W. R., & Watson, S. L. (2017). Adult MOOC learners as self-directed: Perceptions of motivation, success, and completion. *Online Learning, 21*(2). doi:http://dx.doi.org/10.24059/olj.v21i2.889

Ministry of Commerce. (2016). *Digital development plan for the commercial economy, 2017–2021*. Bangkok, Thailand: Ministry of Commerce.

Ministry of Information and Communication Technology. (2011). *Information and communication technology policy framework, 2011–2020 of Thailand*. Bangkok, Thailand: Ministry of Information and Communication Technology.

Office of the Permanent Secretary, Ministry of Education. (2016). *12th educational development plan of the ministry of education (2017–2021)*. Bangkok: Office of the Permanent Secretary, Ministry of Education.

Sombuntham, S., & Khlaisang, J. (2013, January 21–22). *Thailand Cyber university and the best practice for open online courseware's services*. The Asia Regional OpenCourseWare and Open Education Conference 2012, organized by Japan Opencourseware Consortium and Office of the Higher Education Commission, Bangkok, Thailand.

Thammetar, T., & Khlaisang, J. (2018a). *Research report on faculty development guidelines for teaching readiness in MOOC*. Thailand Cyber University Project (TCU), Office of the Higher Education Commission (OHEC), Ministry of Education, Thailand.

Thammetar, T., & Khlaisang, J. (2018b). *Research report on TCU strategic plan for promoting open education in Thailand*. Thailand Cyber University Project (TCU), Office of the Higher Education Commission (OHEC), Ministry of Education, Bangkok, Thailand.

Thammetar, T., Theeraroungchaisri, A., & Khlaisang, J. (2018). *Thai OER, OCW, and MOOCs: Enhancing learning in higher education borderless open access education*. Country report presented at the Association of Southeast Asian Institutions of Higher Learning (ASAHIL) Conference 2016, Malaysia, December 4–6, 2016.

14
CAPACITY BUILDING OF TEACHERS
A Case Study of the Technology-Enabled Learning (TEL) Massive Open Online Courses

Sanjaya Mishra, Martha Cleveland-Innes, and Nathaniel Ostashewski

Introduction

One significant aspect of any quality teaching-learning system is the quality of the teachers themselves. Meta-analysis of several research studies (Hattie, 2003) show that the quality of trained teachers strongly influences student achievement, accounting for about 30% of the variance in results. The United Nations Educational Scientific and Cultural Organization (UNESCO) estimates that about 69 million teachers will be required to achieve Sustainable Development Goal 4 by 2030 (UIS, 2016). While such a need is mostly in the K–12 sector, the lack of training for instructors in higher education is also a matter of concern for the quality of engagement and learning (Brownell & Tanner, 2012; Hénard & Roseveare, 2012; European Commission, 2014). To perform effectively, teachers at every level need to have adequate knowledge of content, learning design, and integration of technology to deliver effective pedagogical transactions (Mishra & Koehler, 2006; Benson & Ward, 2013; Moar, 2016).

Realizing the importance of technology in teaching and learning to prepare 21st-century learners, the Commonwealth of Learning (COL) initiated a program in 2015 to support the integration of technology-enabled learning (TEL) in educational institutions, especially in conventional higher education institutions. This program required creating an appropriate environment for integrating TEL, including the development of policy and capacity building of teachers. COL followed a systematic process and undertook a baseline study focusing on the institutions' technological infrastructure, students' access to technology and its use for learning, and perceptions of teachers to use technology in teaching and learning using the TEL implementation handbook (Kirkwood & Price, 2016).

In early days of implementation of TEL in several institutions, the first author realized that the understanding of TEL in COL's partner institutions was not uniform. Also, it was impossible to follow the mainstream face-to-face workshop mode of training to reach large numbers of teachers in COL partner institutions. Thus, the idea of a massive open online course (MOOC) on TEL emerged. In taking advantage of this new educational delivery opportunity, COL entered into a strategic collaboration with Athabasca University (AU) to develop a MOOC on TEL to scale capacity building of teachers across various levels.

At the time of writing this chapter, two iterations of the TEL MOOC have been successfully delivered. In this chapter, the authors discuss the design, development, and delivery of the MOOC, and lessons learned to provide a Commonwealth-wide experience of MOOCs. We analyse the available data to present an overview of the TEL MOOC as a capacity building tool for teachers in the Commonwealth countries.

TEL MOOC: An Overview

Before design of the TEL MOOC, COL initiated a Delphi study to develop the curriculum for the course. About 60 subject matter experts from around the world participated in the two-stage Delphi process. COL developed a list of experts based on their peer-reviewed publications in the field of educational technology in the last five years. Delphi method was chosen to build consensus on the scope and coverage of the curriculum for TEL MOOC (Hsu & Standford, 2007). The two rounds of survey questions requested experts to comment on the desirability of certain issues being covered in the MOOC. After two rounds of consensus, a draft curriculum for discussion with an academic partner institution that would provide a home for the MOOC was available (Table 14.1) (Naidu, 2015).

Using the Draft outline of a curriculum for TEL MOOC, COL collaborated with the Centre for Distance Education at the Athabasca University (AU) to refine the curriculum and develop the

TABLE 14.1 Draft Curriculum for TEL MOOC Based on Delphi Study

Learning outcomes	*Key and sub-topics*

1. Describe the full range of educational technologies that are currently available for the enhancement of learning and teaching AND identify the unique affordances of these educational technologies for the enhancement of learning and teaching. **WEEKs 1–2**	• Educational technologies available now.
	  ○ Educational technologies on the horizon.
	• The value that technology can add to learning and teaching in your educational context.
	• How technologies influence the nature of learning, and perhaps make it more powerful than it would be without them?
	  ○ Critical affordances of the learning prefixes such as "e" in e-learning and "m" in m-learning.

2. Demonstrate the selection and use of educational technologies for addressing particular learning and teaching challenges in different educational contexts, including face-to-face, online, distance and blended learning scenarios. **WEEKs 3–4**	• Matching technologies to meet learning and teaching needs and challenges in your educational context.
	  ○ Use of technologies to promote student *engagement* with learning.
	  ○ Use of technologies to support *communication* among learners.
	  ○ Use of technologies to promote *cooperation* and *collaboration* among learners.
	  ○ Use of technologies to promote and support *team* or *group-based learning*.
	  ○ Use of technologies to design and support *assessment* of learning outcomes.
	  ○ Use of technologies to provide timely and relevant *feedback* to learners.
	  ○ Use of technologies to support opportunities for *error correction* and *remediation*.
	• Use of technologies to ensure integrity in online learning with devices such as webcam proctoring, photo-matching, natural language processing, keyboarding, typing pattern recognition, and signature tracking devices, etc.

3. Evaluate the impacts of these educational technologies on learning and teaching processes in their specific contexts. **WEEK 5**	• Use of technology to *evaluate effectiveness* of student learning experiences.

MOOC. Our decision to collaborate with AU stemmed from our belief that success of a MOOC is dependent upon: (1) availability of a celebrity instructor, (2) reputation of the MOOC provider (or academic home of the MOOC), and (3) availability of a robust technology platform to handle large enrolment and concurrent learning (Mishra, 2015). COL already had a partnership with the Indian Institute of Technology, Kanpur, that had developed a platform for the delivery of MOOCs—mooKIT designed as a MOOC management system for "internet novices."

MooKIT provides a robust learning analytics system and also makes it easy to upload content and deploy the course in a short time (mooKIT, 2012). The platform provides a student registration module, course uploading area utilizing YouTube video links, activities and assignment areas, a quiz feature, discussion forums, and a hangout or live chat element. One unique feature of the system is that the videos are streamed from YouTube and are not hosted within the mooKIT system. The system was available to us at almost no cost, and having decided on a delivery technology, the focus shifted to the academic host for TEL MOOC. Once AU came on board, the draft outline of the MOOC, developed using an internally developed template (Table 14.2), was shared in a two-day workshop with the other authors of this chapter. The design workshop helped develop a mutual understanding of the objectives, purpose, and delivery mechanisms for the course. This also helped us to develop a marketing plan including preparing a brochure as well as a promotional video for the MOOC. COL opened the TEL MOOC platform and marketing plan almost six months before the starting date of the MOOC as a strategy to obtain large enrolment.

TABLE 14.2 Template for Instructional Design of MOOC

Title of the Course		
Subject		
Level	*Introductory/Intermediate/Advanced*	
Fees		
Duration	*(in weeks)*	
Schedule		
Time Commitment per week	*Helps in assessing workload*	
Pre-requisites (if any)	*Normally can't be assured, but good to give to help the learners.*	
Language of Instruction		
Course Description	*In about 200 words.*	
Learning Outcomes	*After completion of this course you are expected to be able to:* *(List 3–4 main outcomes)*	
Week-wise Course Overview	*Give description of each of the weeks in about 300 words each covering what will be covered, why it is important in the context of the learning outcomes, and how this will be achieved, including the expectations from the learners.*	
Week-wise Course Detail	*Details may include links to readings, surveys, videos, quizzes, discussions, projects, etc.*	
Week 1 Outcomes:		
Contents	**Activities**	**Assessment**
Assessment Criteria		
Final Examination (if any)		
Instructors' Profile		
Course Materials	*Give links to resources included in the course.*	
Certification	*Describe who is eligible to get a certificate and how.*	

Instruction Design of TEL MOOC

In the design workshop the authors discussed the basic principles on which the TEL MOOC could be based. Both COL and AU are committed to removing barriers to learning and improving quality in education. TEL MOOC was designed to be:

- learner-centred
- highly engaging via a multi-modal, media-rich online environment
- directly instructed via video and text-based media
- facilitated via weekly opening and closing videos
- supported by roving learning-support teaching assistants throughout
- freely accessible to anyone
- a repository of relevant resources, during and after the course.

Recognising the lack of instructional rigour in early MOOC developments (Gasevic, Kovanovic, Joksimovic, & Siemens, 2014; Margaryan, Bianco, & Littlejohn, 2015), the TEL MOOC team at AU decided to utilise their inquiry-based or iMOOC model (Cleveland-Innes, Ostashewski, & Wilton, 2017). This MOOC development model utilises a Community of Inquiry (CoI) approach (Garrison, Anderson, & Archer, 1999; Garrison, 2017) for course delivery. This approach provides a learning environment with learner activities, instruction, facilitation, and support for the expected large number of learners in TEL MOOC (Cleveland-Innes, Briton, Gismondi, & Ives, 2015).

In keeping with the three presences (i.e., social presence, cognitive presence, and teaching presence), the iMOOC model offers opportunities for self-reflection, active cognitive processing, interaction, and peer-teaching (see Figure 14.1). The course content is delivered via video and text-based learning resources to read and reflect further upon content in the discussion forums. End-of-week multiple choice quizzes allow participants to take tests and measure their progress. Key to the iMOOC is the three-tiered model of instruction in TEL MOOC: (1) Instruction: lecture and instruction provided by course instructors, (2) Inspiration: the course facilitator, who serves as the inspirer to first introduce and then summarise weekly activities and highlight key lessons and experiences, and (3) Information: the roving teaching assistants in the discussion forums who provide quick responses to any doubts, questions, and comments from the participants.

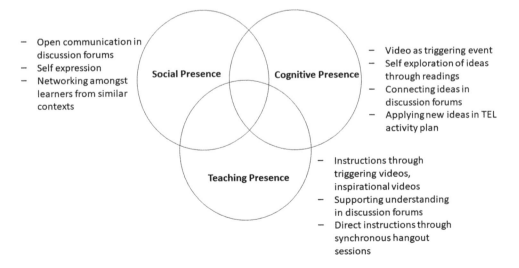

FIGURE 14.1   Community of Inquiry Model for TEL MOOC

> **Week 1: Models of Technology-Enabled Learning**
> 1.1: Community of Inquiry
> 1.2: Two Models: TPACK and TIM
> 1.3: On Teaching Presence
>
> **Week 2: Technology in Education**
> 2.1: Integrating Technology in Education
> 2.2: Benefits of Technology in Education
>
> **Week 3: Open Educational Resources**
> 3.1: Understanding OER
> 3.2: Types of Open Licenses
> 3.3: Finding Open Educational Resources
>
> **Week 4: Application of Technology**
> 4.1: Practical Application of Technology
> 4.2: Getting Help with Technology
>
> **Week 5: Creating Technology-Enabled Learning**
> 5.1: Creating Technology-Enabled Learning

FIGURE 14.2 Weekly Course Content of TEL MOOC

Participants also learn from one another in TEL MOOC through active discussions and sharing of activity plans. These activity plans form the assessment element required to receive a completion certificate. It is important to note that these TEL activity plans are available on a separate website (as open educational resources (OER) at http://telresources.org/ (Athabasca University, n.d.). A major feature of the TEL MOOC is that the course materials are permanently available online at the COL website in the true spirit of openness as OER (see http://oasis.col.org/handle/11599/2765).

The course contents of TEL MOOC were carefully chosen to accommodate the broad learning outcomes that were developed through the Delphi study. However, the focus was also on modeling participants' behaviours through exposing them to different models of TEL and the use of OER (Figure 14.2).

Delivery of TEL MOOC

In 2017, the TEL MOOC was offered twice: once in January and once in November for five weeks each. TEL MOOC 1 allowed for six months of preparation (course development) and marketing time. TEL MOOC 2 allowed for more marketing time. As a result of a multi-pronged approach to promoting the MOOC, we had 1,143 registrations in TEL MOOC 1 and 3,881 registrations in TEL MOOC 2. The two MOOCs attracted participants from 95 countries, of which 45 were from the Commonwealth. Overall, 94% of participants were from Commonwealth countries where the marketing of the MOOC was focused. In TEL MOOC 1, the majority (53.6%) of the participants were female, whereas in TEL MOOC 2, 60.7% of the participants were male. In the two MOOCs combined, 43% participants were from Africa and 31% were from Asia. Participants from the Pacific accounted for just 3%. Interestingly, in TEL MOOC 1, there were more participants from Latin America, the Caribbean, Canada, and USA in comparison to other regions. In terms of the highest education level of the participants, 44% had post-graduate degrees and 37% held a graduate degree. Impressively, doctoral degree holders accounted for 11% in the two TEL MOOC cohorts.

TABLE 14.3 TEL MOOC Learner Profile

	TEL MOOC 1	TEL MOOC 2	Total	Percentage
Africa	291	1,848	2,139	42.58
Asia	314	1,259	1,573	31.31
Europe	155	76	231	4.60
Latin America (including Canada and USA)	323	573	896	17.83
Pacific	26	125	151	3.01
No information	34	0	34	0.68
Male	488	2,358	2,846	56.65
Female	613	1,465	2,078	41.36
No information	42	58	100	1.99
Commonwealth	912	3,777	4,689	93.33
Non-Commonwealth	197	104	301	5.99
No information	34	0	34	0.68
High School	54	67	121	2.41
Graduate	217	1,660	1,877	37.36
Post-Graduate	534	1,652	2,186	43.51
Doctorate	291	283	574	11.43
Others	0	95	95	1.89
No information	47	124	171	3.40
Total	1,143	3,881	5,024	100.00

The majority of learners (93%) had advanced qualifications and roughly 4% had only a diploma or high school qualification.

The top three registrations in TEL MOOC 1 came from India, Canada, and Antigua and Barbuda in the Caribbean. In contrast, the top three registrations in TEL MOOC 2 came from Rwanda, Bangladesh, and India. The total number of registrants in TEL MOOC 2 was more than three times of that of TEL MOOC 1. Participants from five countries (i.e., Bangladesh, Barbados, India, Mauritius, and Rwanda) accounted for 70% of registrations in TEL MOOC 2, among which 33% were from Rwanda, and 22% were from Bangladesh. Such a high response rate from Rwanda and Bangladesh was partially a result of strong support from the relevant Ministries to promote the TEL MOOC to prospective teachers in their countries.

Participant Engagements

For student engagement in both cohorts of TEL MOOC, there were two types of forums: activity forums and general forums. Activity forums were based on the videos and directly related to the core learning outcomes, which not only established teacher presence, but also facilitated both social presence and cognitive presence. The general forum was for any other topics that participants might suggest. Students were encouraged to create any topic for discussion in either of these forums.

In terms of participant activity in these forums, in TEL MOOC 1, there were 259 discussion forums, of which 242 were created by the participants with a total of 2,267 messages posted. Only 12% of the messages were from instructors and teaching assistants. The average length of participants' posts to the activity forums was 95 words, whereas for the general forums the average was 44 words. Of the 2,267 recorded messages in TEL MOOC 1, 42% were in the activity forums. The fact that the posts in the activity forums were over twice as long as in the general forums suggests that the instructions in the activity forum helped elicit more developed, detailed, and reflective responses from the participants.

In TEL MOOC 2, there were a total of 2,413 discussion forums created. Only 12 of the forums accompanied the introductory message and weekly course lessons; and just seven were MOOC support forums. The remaining 2,394 forums were all created by TEL MOOC participants. Of the 13,326 discussion posts, only 437 of them (3.27%) were by the instructional team. The majority of messages, 12,889, were from TEL MOOC participants. Posts were made by 1,013 students, and the average length per post was approximately 13 words. The number of posts in both TEL MOOC cohorts shows remarkably higher levels of participation from learners due to the design of the questions in the activity forums. This could be attributed to the high level of engagement that TEL MOOCs were able to promote by applying the iMOOC design principles based on the CoI. The availability of support from teaching assistants and an instructor to summarise the discussions of the week helped MOOC learners to participate actively in the activity fourms.

In addition to watching videos, reading resource materials, and posting in the forums, participants also used the synchronous hangout sessions available in the mooKIT platform. This element of the mooKIT platform was used least by the participants. This is a synchronous element that allows learners to interact in a real-time text chat mode, so the chances of interacting with a specific peer or an instructor at any one time is relatively poor. In TEL MOOC 1, 149 participants (13%) utilised the feature, whereas in TEL MOOC 2 only 400 participants (10%) used the synchronous hangout facility. The AU team organised two live Adobe Connect sessions for the TEL MOOC 2 cohort, with 65 and 45 participants, respectively. Figure 14.3 provides a snapshot of student engagement in TEL MOOC 2, which shows a heat map of active students per day, watching videos and participating in discussion forums.

As Figure 14.3 reveals, a large number of participants were active on the TEL MOOC2 watching videos and participating in the discussion forums every day. Active students in the heat map refers to those who logged in and spent time reading the resources on the platform. In effect, the number of students logging into the platform and reading resources were more than those who watched videos and contributed to the discussion forums on any particular day.

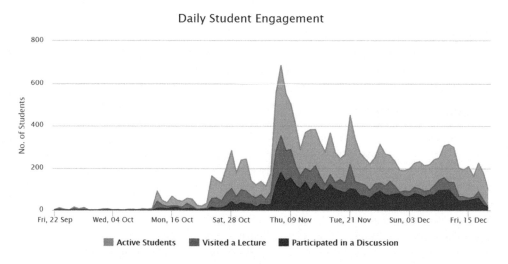

FIGURE 14.3 Student Engagements in TEL MOOC 2

MOOC Completion

TEL MOOC provides two certification options for participants who participated in TEL MOOC. A Certificate of Participation was issued to those who participated in at least three discussion forums and completed all the quizzes with 60% or more being correct. The Certificate of Completion was awarded to those who had also successfully completed the assignment on the TEL activity plan. Instructors evaluated the activity plans before issuing Certificates of Completion. In TEL MOOC 1, 9% of participants earned certificates, whereas in TEL MOOC 2, that number doubled to 18%. While the Certificate of Completion received in TEL MOOC 1 and TEL MOOC 2 was respectively 7.3% and 8.6%, a substantial number of participants in TEL MOOC 2 received certificates of participation ($n = 349, 9\%$). There was no immediately recognisable reason for this jump in participation, as there was no difference in the delivery of the TEL MOOC 1 and TEL MOOC 2, except for the use of two special Adobe Connect sessions.

Learner Experiences

To understand the participants' views and experiences in TEL MOOC, pre- and post-course surveys were conducted. Preliminary analyses of the surveys from TEL MOOC 1 and TEL MOOC 2 reveal interesting findings. In total, 343 participants (30%) completed the TEL MOOC 1 pre-course survey, and 160 (14%) completed the post survey, while 745 (19%) completed the pre-course survey in TEL MOOC 2 and 302 (8%) completed the post-course survey.

In this chapter, the authors present an overview of preliminary analyses from reports involving both the cohorts of the TEL MOOC (Cleveland-Innes, Ostashewski, Wilton, & Murphy, 2017, 2018). In TEL MOOC 1 and TEL MOOC 2, 51% and 57% survey respondents, respectively, indicated they were taking the course out of general interest in technology-enabled learning. Approximately one-third of participants took the course for professional development, with 33% in TEL MOOC 1 and 30% in TEL MOOC 2. Ninety-five per cent of respondents in both sections of TEL MOOC agreed or strongly agreed to the statement "Overall, I was satisfied with TEL MOOC." Consistently, respondents reported that "TEL MOOC met the learning objectives" and "the course material was of good quality" with very high ratings (see Table 14.5). More specifically, participants praised the TEL MOOC with quotes such as the following:

> It was a very well-structured course. The flow of work was efficient from one week to the other; it built each time. In my opinion, the best of all is the connection it provided us with, to a wealth of resources on the issue of Technology-enabled learning. I am very glad I participated. Thank you!
>
> – TEL MOOC 1 participant

TABLE 14.4 Certificate Issued in TEL MOOC

	TEL MOOC 1	TEL MOOC 2	Total
Certificate of Participation	18 (1.57)	349 (8.99)	367 (7.3)
Certificate of Completion	89 (7.79)	347 (8.94)	436 (8.68)
Total	107 (9.36)	696 (17.93)	803 (15.98)

Note: Figures in parentheses indicate percentage of certificate.

TABLE 14.5 Satisfaction With TEL MOOC

Statements	TELMOOC 1	TELMOOC 2
Overall, I was satisfied with TEL MOOC	95%	95%
TEL MOOC met the learning objectives	94%	95%
The course material was of good quality	95%	92%

> From my inner heart, I appreciate the program. Therefore, I suggest, if possible to have some more online programs so as to grow academically. Such programs are very helpful especially to us from developing countries (Tanzania) where online courses are rarely found. Thanks very very very much.
>
> – *TEL MOOC 1 participant*

> I think the TEL MOOC is good and it will help teachers in all levels of education. This is the kind of teaching experience teachers need in the 21st century. Thanks so much TEL MOOC team.
>
> – *TEL MOOC 2 participant*

> I found TEL MOOC very helpful and I will be actively recommending it to my teaching colleagues.
>
> – *TEL MOOC 2 participant*

From the level of participation, course completion, and responses, the authors believe that the TEL MOOC served the needs of the teachers for whom the course was developed. While many of the MOOC participants did not complete the course, there was active participation of over 65% of registered participants in both sections of TEL MOOC. From the perspective of professional development, even if the participants are not completing the course, such MOOCs would serve the continuous professional development by upgrading the capacity of the teachers in the Commonwealth. Interestingly, the MOOC also served participants from 40 non-Commonwealth countries as the MOOC can be taken up anywhere having access to Internet, thereby, greatly scaling-up capacity building.

Lessons Learned

MOOCs that do not put lots of emphasis on learner engagement, normally called xMOOCs, are considered to be techno-centric (Bates, 2014) with fewer challenges (McLoughlin & Magnoni, 2017). In contrast, cMOOCs or the connectivist MOOCs focus more on learning as a communication process and require 21st-century skills such as collaboration, creativity, communication, critical thinking, and information media skills (McLoughlin & Magnoni, 2017). Without these skills, learners may face difficulties in building their knowledge. The TEL MOOC has been designed and developed carefully with some similarities to xMOOC features and cMOOC features plus a dedicated focus on inquiry-based learning as represented in the CoI. There are challenges due to the diverse backgrounds and contexts of the learners. The common challenges and lessons learned through TEL MOOC 1 and 2 are summarised below.

Challenges

Participants in TEL MOOC came from various nationalities. And thus, for the majority, English was not their primary language of communication. The differences in languages resulted in different understandings and expectations as evident in the discussion forums. As effective online discussions required accurate and in-depth messages in English, they pose additional challenges for non-English-speaking learners. Therefore, despite the large number of participant-created discussions, there was a noticeable lack of critical discourse on the issues being discussed there. The technology also prohibited the creation of discussion threads and that reduced the opportunity to create meaningful and sustained course discussion. Obstacles arising from language differentials can have a significant impact on the delivery of a course and on the overall course experience for participants.

The live synchronous chat sessions, including hangouts and the Adobe Connect sessions in TEL MOOC 2, were well received by those participants who joined them. These learners expressed appreciation for the opportunity to converse with an instructor in real time. However, the low degree of participation in these sessions make them less useful in the overall context and obviously needs rethinking. One solution would be to offer multiple live sessions aligned to the different time zones of the participants.

The assignment submission and its successful assessment was a criterion for the issue of a "Certificate of Completion." While this did not prove to be a problem in TEL MOOC 1, the increase in the number of participants in TEL MOOC 2 created significant delays in the declaration of results of the participants and increased their anxiety. Caution must be exercised when planning for individual assessment of participant assignments in MOOCs, especially where enrolment numbers are expected to reach hundreds or even thousands of potential learners or more.

In the TEL MOOC, participants' contributions are shared as OER through a repository. This created some challenges during TEL MOOC 2, as the successful TEL Activity Plans were already available there. Also, the course included a component on understanding OER, and, therefore, some participants attempted to reuse existing Activity Plans without creating an original submission. Suffice to say, the practice of academic integrity is not consistent throughout the world. Though all such cases were easily detected and were very few in number, this is a real issue when registrations are in the thousands or higher.

Successful Strategies

The use of dynamic instructional videos by the instructor (as inspirer) helped focus the participants on current activities and key issues learnt in the previous week. Such an approach responded to the unique needs of the learners by clarifying concepts or other aspects of the course delivery, related updates, and posting announcements. This type of instruction demonstrates genuine interest in the participants' learning experience; hence, motivating participants to remain engaged in the course.

Most of the issues encountered in the TEL MOOC could be resolved with more sophisticated technology, which would then substantially increase the costs. COL personnel always strive to support delivering quality learning opportunities at a fraction of the conventional cost structure. As a result, the TEL MOOC operates on a shoestring budget and focuses on improving the quality of teaching in the Commonwealth by improving the quality of teacher training online using MOOC design and delivery.

Conclusion

The TEL MOOC is designed to be a strategic part of the TEL mainstreaming activity of COL in the Commonwealth. Its success so far has been quite satisfactory. Importantly, the TEL MOOC will continue to be offered until the current strategic plan of COL ends in June 2021. In the process, we are gathering massive data on learner engagements and experiences that we intend to analyse and publish as we continue to learn from these offerings. The iMOOC model and mooKIT platform used in designing the TEL MOOC provide us with a learning environment that draws on features of xMOOCs and cMOOCs with the addition of iMOOC features as drawn from the CoI model. Further analysis of the data will ideally reveal relationships between the intention of the participants and their successful completion of MOOCs, who completes a MOOC and why, and the impact of engagement in overall MOOC completion. We are also considering follow-up studies for MOOC completers, seeking to understand how they continue to use their learning from the TEL MOOC to improve the quality of student learning in their respective countries and contexts.

Sanjaya Mishra is Education Specialist, eLearning at the Commonwealth of Learning (COL) in Vancouver, Canada, since January 2015. Previously, he served COL as Director of the Commonwealth Educational Media Centre for Asia (CEMCA) from 2012 to 2014. Dr Mishra is one of the leading scholars in open, distance, and online learning. Prior to joining COL, he was Programme Specialist (ICT in Education, Science, and Culture) at UNESCO, Paris. Dr Mishra has over 25 years of experience in design, development, and management of open, distance, and online learning programmes and he is a leading advocate of open educational resources.

Martha Cleveland-Innes is Professor of Educational Innovation at Athabasca University in Alberta, Canada. She has been teaching for 35 years in all areas of education, face-to-face and online. Martha has received awards for her work on the student experience in online environments and holds a major research grant through the Canadian Social Sciences and Humanities Research Council. In 2011 she received the Craig Cunningham Memorial Award for Teaching Excellence, and, in 2009, she received the President's Award for Research and Scholarly Excellence from Athabasca University. Her work is well published in academic journals in North America and Europe.

Nathaniel Ostashewski is Associate Professor of Education Innovation at Athabasca University in Alberta, Canada. He has been utilising technology in teaching since 1990, both at the K–12 and graduate education level. For the past 20 years Dr. Ostashewski has been training teachers how to incorporate technology into "worth-it" classroom, blended, and online activities. His current research areas include iPads in the classroom, networked teacher professional development, MOOC design and delivery, and the use of collaboration technologies in teaching. His latest book is titled *Optimizing K12 Education through Blended and Online Learning* and he has several open access publications available online.

References

Athabasca University (n.d.). Technology-Enabled Learning Resources. Retrieved from http://telresources.org/

Bates, T. (2014, October 13). *Comparing xMOOCs and cMOOCs: philosophy and practice*. Retrieved from www.tonybates.ca/2014/10/13/comparing-xmoocs-and-cmoocs-philosophy-and-practice/

Benson, S. N. K., & Ward, C. L. (2013). Teaching with technology: Using Tpack to understand teaching expertise in online higher education. *Journal of Educational Computing Research, 48*(2), 153–172.

Brownell, S. E., & Tanner, K. D. (2012). Barriers to faculty pedagogical change: Lack of training, time, incentives, and . . . tensions with professional identity? *CBE—Life Sciences Education, 11*, 339–346.

Cleveland-Innes, M., Briton, D., Gismondi, M., & Ives, C. (2015). *MOOC instructional design principles: Ensuring quality across scale and diversity*. Poster presented at MOOCs in Scandinavia Conference, Stockholm, Sweden. Retrieved from www.ltlo.ca/MOOCPrinciples.pdf

Cleveland-Innes, M., Ostashewski, N., & Wilton, D. (2017). *IMOOCs and learning to learn online*. Athabasca University. Retrieved from www.thecommunityofinquiry.org/project5

Cleveland-Innes, M., Ostashewski, N., Wilton, D., & Murphy, J. (2017). *Report of the massive open online course on introduction to technology-enabled learning (TEL MOOC)*. Burnaby, BC: Commonwealth of Learning. Retrieved from http://oasis.col.org/handle/11599/2760

Cleveland-Innes, M., Ostashewski, N., Wilton, D., & Murphy, J. (2018). *Report of the massive open online course on introduction to technology-enabled learning (TEL MOOC 2)*. Burnaby, BC: Commonwealth of Learning. Retrieved from http://oasis.col.org/handle/11599/2970

European Commission. (2014). *Report to the European commission on new modes of learning and teaching in higher education*. Luxembourg: Publications Office of the European Union.

Garrison, D. R. (2017). *E-learning in the 21st century: A community of inquiry framework for research and practice*. New York: Routledge.

Garrison, D. R., Anderson, T., & Archer, W. (1999). Critical inquiry in a text-based environment: Computer conferencing in higher education. *The Internet and Higher Education, 2*(2–3), 87–105.

Gasevic, D., Kovanovic, V., Joksimovic, S., & Siemens, G. (2014). Where is research on massive open online courses headed? A data analysis of the MOOC research initiative. *The International Review of Research in Open and Distributed Learning, 15*(5). Retrieved from www.irrodl.org/index.php/irrodl/article/view/1954/3099

Hattie, J. A. C. (2003, October). *Teachers make a difference: What is the research evidence?* Paper presented at the building teacher quality: What does the research tell us ACER Research Conference, Melbourne, Australia. Retrieved from http://research.acer.edu.au/research_conference_2003/4/

Hénard, F., & Roseveare, D. (2012). *Fostering quality teaching in higher education: Policies and practices*. Paris: OECD Press.

Hsu, Chia-Chien, & Sandford, B. A. (2007). The Delphi technique: Making sense of consensus. *Practical Assessment Research & Evaluation, 12*(10). Retrieved from http://pareonline.net/getvn.asp?v=12&n=10

Kirkwood, A., & Price, L. (2016). *Technology-enabled learning implementation handbook*. Burnaby, BC: Commonwealth of Learning. Retrieved from http://oasis.col.org/handle/11599/2363

Margaryan, A., Bianco, M., & Littlejohn, A. (2015). Instructional quality of massive open online courses (MOOCs). *Computers & Education, 80*, 77–83.

McLoughlin, L., & Magnoni, F. (2017). The move-me project: Reflecting on xMOOC and cMOOC structure and pedagogical implementation. In Q. Kan & S. Bax (Eds.), *Beyond the language classroom: Researching MOOCs and other innovations* (pp. 59–69). Research-publishing.net. Retrieved from https://doi.org/10.14705/rpnet.2017.mooc2016.671

Mishra, P., & Koehler, M. J. (2006). Technological pedagogical content knowledge: A framework for integrating technology in teacher knowledge. *Teachers College Record, 108*(6), 1017–1054.

Mishra, S. (2015, September 30). *Guidelines for design development and delivery of massive open online courses*. Video presentation for the National Seminar on ODL in India: Present Status and Future Prospects. New Delhi, India. Retrieved from www.youtube.com/watch?v=FIVCS23pGOk

Moar, D. (2016). Using TPACK to develop digital pedagogues: A higher education experience. *Journal of Computers in Education, 4*(1), 71–86.

mooKIT. (2012). *Platform*. Retrieved from www.mookit.co/

Naidu, S. (2015). *A MOOC on technology-enhanced learning*. Burnaby, BC: Commonwealth of Learning (Unpublished Consultant Report).

UIS. (2016). *The world needs almost 69 million new teachers to reach the 2030 education goals*. UIS Fact Sheet No. 39. Retrieved from http://unesdoc.unesco.org/images/0024/002461/246124e.pdf

15

THE DEVELOPMENT OF MOOCs AS INCUBATION SPACE FOR PROFESSIONAL AND INSTITUTIONAL LEARNING

A View From South Africa

Antoinette van der Merwe, J. P. Bosman, and Miné de Klerk

Introduction

Stellenbosch University (SU), a research-intensive university in South Africa that aims to be globally recognised as excellent, inclusive, and innovative, and where knowledge is advanced in the service of society, aspires to be a learning organisation (Stellenbosch University, 2018b). Characteristics of a "learning organisation" include a grounding in systems thinking, valuing different types of knowledge, attempting to develop reflexivity in organisations and stressing the importance of dialogue (Senge, 2000). Aligned to the institutional vision, SU adopted a learning-centred approach to teaching (Stellenbosch University, 2018a) that is focused on learning as a partnership, where students are seen as co-creators of knowledge and learning environments. In a learning-centred approach, teaching activities facilitate knowledge-building and actively engage students in their own learning.

As part of the broader Information and Communication Technologies (ICTs) in Teaching and Learning Project funded by the University Council, SU launched its first MOOC, *Teaching for Change: An African Philosophical Approach*, in 2016 on the FutureLearn platform. At the time, SU personnel remained highly cognisant of the unique digital access challenges within the resource constraints of the (South) African context. Digital equity remains a challenge within (South) Africa both in terms of access to the Internet as well as the cost of Internet usage (Bornman, 2016).

According to the World Internet Usage and population statistics (Internet World Stats, 2018), Africa had an Internet penetration rate as percentage of its population of only 35.2%, compared to the world average of 54.4% as of the end of December 2017. Such data do not compare favourably with Internet access in Europe (85.2%) and North America (95%). It is encouraging to note that the usage has grown by a whopping 9,941% from 2000–2018 and that South Africa's Internet penetration rate is slightly under the world average at 53.7%. Coupled with these data, a study of broadband pricing in 196 countries revealed that there are vast global disparities in the cost of online access. Sub-Saharan Africa fared worst overall with almost all of the 31 countries that were measured found in the most expensive half of the table; including 16 of them in the most expensive quarter (Cable.co.uk, 2018).

This chapter provides a brief description of SU's first MOOC and then reflects on the development of this MOOC as incubation space for professional and institutional learning by using Senge's learning organisation as framework. It specifically focuses on the key capabilities required to be an effective learning organisation including aspiration, reflective conversation, and understanding complexity.

Description of MOOC

SU's first MOOC, Teaching for Change (TFC), introduced the world to a new vision for a pedagogical approach based on an African Philosophy of Education (FutureLearn, 2016). It was presented as a four-week course on the FutureLearn platform in 2016 and 2017 with over 5,000 participants (the majority in the 26–35 age group) from all around the globe over three cohorts. The rationale for the course was aimed at "engaging students in pedagogical activities that orientate them towards identifying major societal problems on the African continent and then to proceed with examining some of the implications of such problems for higher education in particular" (Waghid & Waghid, 2017, p. 2).

The TFC learning design and development was done by a small team in the Centre for Learning Technologies (CLT) who worked with the content expert and course facilitator, Prof Yusef Waghid, from the Education Policy Studies Department in the Faculty of Education at SU. In addition, learning technology advisers, a camera-team, and a multimedia designer engaged in the learning design and video-creation of the course on the FutureLearn platform with the support and oversight of FutureLearn personnel.

The course drew a healthy amount of media attention with institutional, national, and international media releases and articles (including The Conversation [Waghid, Waghid, & Waghid, 2018b]). Academic outputs from the TFC MOOC included local and national conference presentations as well as a scholarly article (Waghid & Waghid, 2017) and a book, *Rupturing African Philosophy on Teaching and Learning* (Waghid, Waghid, & Waghid, 2018a). What made the course interesting is the fact that it was the first Philosophy of Education course on FutureLearn, and the first African Philosophy of Education MOOC in the world. The innovative MOOC also contributed towards the conversation around decolonising the curriculum by situating African lived experiences as the core pedagogy.

For the institution, this initial pilot MOOC course brought with it unexpected advantages. For instance, as Waghid et al. (2018a) succinctly states: "It afforded the institute the opportunity to reaffirm its position as a leading research-intensive institution, attract international students and contribute to the knowledge economy of the world in a distinctly African way" (Waghid et al., 2018a, p. 165).

MOOC as Incubation Space

As Senge (2000) points out, universities tend to be knowing institutions—favouring familiar, tested models of operation, in a world that increasingly rewards learning institutions. Technology-focused projects are particularly met with scepticism in institutions built around traditional structures and hierarchical systems. Such scepticism is highly justifiable given that pilot tests often fail, people tend to be overly optimistic about new technologies, and complexities and difficulties invariably arise that can derail seemingly simple and predictable projects (Allenby & Sarewitz, 2011). For SU, the development of the MOOC project certainly was a step into unknown territory, deviating from its traditional model of designing and implementing curricula for formally accredited modules. Critically aware of the general hype and over-optimism about what MOOCs could offer (Zawacki-Richter, Bozkurt, Alturki, & Aldraiweesh, 2018), yet open to the opportunity to learn from a flexible and open educational model, the Division for Learning and Teaching Enhancement proposed the development and evaluation of a pilot MOOC before committing the considerable financial and operational resources required for developing a broader profile of MOOC offerings.

In addition to a small internal team, existing infrastructure and various equipment were allocated to the project. A basic level of instructional design experience certainly enabled this team to meet the quality standards set by FutureLearn. However, the SU team quickly found that less explicit attributes served them more than their prior knowledge or technical resources. In effect, the agility of a small team, a shared willingness to learn, and the resilience to creatively work with (rather than against) the boundaries of existing structures allowed the development of the TFC MOOC to pose as a rich incubation space. In the process, it was soon realised that the various lessons learned could feed back into the system to serve longer-term institutional goals, building the internal capacity and experience to plan more flexible models of course delivery. It can be argued that these separate but connected efforts are typical of a dual transformation design strategy (Gilbert, Crow, & Anderson, 2018) as the MOOC development team was able to continue its core function of optimising SU's blended learning approach within its traditional courses and programmes, whilst navigating the parallel and highly novel process related to the MOOC design.

Due to their scholarly approach related to adopting blended learning strategies for traditional courses, the MOOC team was already familiar with the type of dialogic strategies that were typically effective for teaching ever-growing student cohorts in online environments. They could effectively align these best practices to FutureLearn's social learning model, which requires facilitators to spark lively discussion and peer learning online. A mass learning model, however, requires a heightened interrogation of how to work with the massive rather than against it (Knox, 2014). The team could, therefore, not solely rely on past learning design strategies, but had to consider new ways to produce rich multimedia that would engage a massive international audience. At the same time, the MOOC design team was forced to question whether their efforts resulted in deep learning amongst the participants. The process of exploring social learning strategies on a mass scale were, in turn, of direct value to the development team's core organisational roles of supporting blended teaching and learning at SU.

This iterative approach of connecting best practices, challenges, and solutions of MOOC design to other learning formats resulted in a shift in thinking about instructional design models. Simply put, the team learned to not only acknowledge, but to directly grapple with, question, and continually learn from the necessary tension between their traditional, core offerings and novel, open educational practices. A need emerged for more "incubation spaces" (i.e., agile learning design projects) that grow from the close collaboration between academic, support, and design role players. As the MOOC development experience showed, it is an approach that requires the courage and wisdom to embrace contradiction, celebrate ignorance, and develop the resilience to keep moving forward (Allenby & Sarewitz, 2011). Embracing the complexities of adapting to emerging models of educational delivery has, and continues, to contribute to organisational learning at SU.

Capabilities of a Learning Organisation

The *five disciplines* framework, first introduced in *The Fifth Discipline* (Senge, 1990), presents tools, methods, and underlying theory for developing learning capabilities that fall into three broad areas, which are also referred to as the core capabilities that complex system leaders develop in order to maximise learning within an organisation. These three capabilities, namely aspiration, understanding complexity, and reflective conversation are evident in the organisational learning that took place as part of the development of the TFC MOOC.

Aspiration

SU has become very intentional in its teaching and learning strategic planning in the past five years shifting from a reactive problem-solving approach to a more collaborative co-creating the future approach (Senge, 2000). This collaborative approach is crucial because it involves not only building aspirational visions, but also having conversations about how the tension between vision and reality can be used to create new approaches to the use of learning technologies and more specifically the use of the MOOC as an organisational learning tool.

The MOOC project forms part of a more encompassing Information and Communication Technologies (ICTs) in Teaching and Learning project, funded over a period of five years (2014–2019) as a strategic project. This strategic project has a long-term vision of creating a holistic vision for the use of ICTs in Teaching and Learning incorporating all related aspects such as infrastructure, learning technology systems, WiFi and network provision, student support, lecturer support, and the renewal of business systems. In effect, the core focus is the possible academic and institutional implications and outcomes of this project, not simply the technological ones. As such, it acknowledges and builds upon the interconnected and complex nature of the university.

The MOOC project per se is also not the ultimate goal. Instead, energy expended on the MOOC project is inherently aligned with the SU strategic programme renewal initiative. Academic transformation, as identified by EDUCAUSE (Schmitt, 2010), is the most important issue in teaching and learning for 2018. It is also a key priority for SU. As indicated by a recent EDUCAUSE Learning Initiative (ELI) survey (Educause, 2018) this transformation includes "breakthrough teaching and learning models, innovative partnerships and alliances, and strategic transformation of the campus mission." In effect, it includes the MOOC as an incubation space that allows for experimentation in all these areas in a low-risk environment.

Understanding Complexity

The MOOC offered a chance to experiment with innovative forms of pedagogy and technology systems. Different types of partnerships emerged between professional academic support environments, teaching staff, the institution, and the external MOOC platform during the development process. Importantly, this experimentation informed institutional strategies related to the use of learning technologies for on-campus, online, and hybrid modes of learning and teaching. The process was institutionally valuable, yet, at the same time, it was a highly complex endeavour.

According to Senge (2000, p. 276) complexity in a learning organisation can be described and embraced by looking at: (a) how individual actions and *habitual ways of operating* create problems; (b) "*local solutions*" that become the source of difficulties for other parts of the institution; and (c) the *underlying interdependencies* and "systemic structures" that generate problems. To assist in understanding the complexity of the development of the MOOC as incubation for professional and institutional learning, we focus on five "actors" and describe the emerging complexity from these five perspectives (see Figure 15.1); namely: (1) the institution; (2) the academic department; (3) the MOOC platform; (4) institutional support; and (5) the design department. Aspects of these five perspectives are described next.

1. *The institution* enabled the incubation through the SU University Council by providing funding and oversight through a steering committee for a pilot MOOC project. The institutional brand of the university was at play from the start creating the expectancy that our first MOOC should be excellent and help in building the brand of the institution. Such an approach and attitude added to the complexity of not only building an exciting "course" on an African Philosophy of Education, but to also support and grow our university's image and standing of excellence among higher education institutions more globally.
2. *The academic department* provided the course expert and facilitator. Among the chief complexities was aligning the academic expert's own pedagogical views with the more social learning approach of the MOOC platform. We had to work with the educator within the confines of the MOOC platform towards creating an original course that incorporated social learning through reflection and debate on real-world African case studies. What often came up and

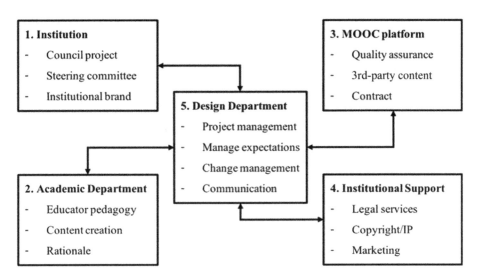

FIGURE 15.1 Visualisation of the Different Role Players and the Complex Activities They House

had to be addressed was the rationale for the course and why we as an institution as well as a department and individual professor were embarking on this new journey. Such questions added to the complexity as the answers were emerging throughout, not just during the design of the course, but indeed also during (through facilitation) and after (through reflection and research) the entire course. Such an outcome supports what Czerniewicz, Glover, Deacon, and Walji (2016, p. 293) found; namely, "participating in making and running MOOCs provides opportunities to deepen understanding of the affordances of open online learning, the potential of OER and openness. We could clearly see that this had prompted reflection on pedagogy and teaching, including changing practices."

3. *Institutional support* needed to be sought to address the legal complexities of contracting with an external academic content provider (FutureLearn). Second, institutional support also assisted in understanding and working within the confines of the university's copyright and intellectual property policies. Third, it shed light on how the MOOC would be marketed. All of these showed how local solutions (i.e., SU policies) made it very difficult to make progress. After many difficult discussions and meetings, various special arrangements had to be made to address this very new way of freely offering our knowledge to the entire world at the press of a mouse click. The main complexity is around openness. The kind of MOOC that we were designing was meant for entirely free and fully open consumption, while the original institutional mandate and organisation was, naturally, built around a "pay to open" business process. This is a fairly universal problem around MOOCs world-wide as institutions struggle with openness and new business models built around "MOOConomics" (Zawacki-Richter et al., 2018, p. 248).

4. *The MOOC platform* added to the complexity by expecting very high quality according to its set standards regarding course content (i.e., it had to address a need in the market and draw thousands of students), pedagogy (i.e., designing the course according to prescribed active and social learning principles and templates), and technology (e.g., video standards—we had to invest in new cameras to be able to produce the videos to specification). Also, as already mentioned, the contractual relationship with the university brought all the role players (indeed the whole institution) into new (complex) waters where our habitual and local ways of working were not working, leading to (difficult) change in the way we "do" things.

5. *The design department* probably experienced the most complexity as it was its responsibility to bring everything together and to make it happen. The Centre for Learning Technologies had to: (a) manage the project serving as liaison amongst and reporting to all role players 1–4; (b) manage the expectations of all the role players; (c) address and manage all the changes in the underlying systems and habitual ways of working; and (d) communicate to the institution and the world at large exactly what embarking on this new MOOC "adventure" meant for our university and higher education in South Africa and across the world. In the process, the centre itself faced problematic "local solutions," habitual ways of working and a lack of knowledge of underlying systemic structures that had to be managed. Finding out, for example, that our video standards were not up to date, learning how to meaningfully marry the pedagogical expectations of the course expert with that of the platform, and negotiating the legal waters around copyright and intellectual property was a complex learning curve.

Through all of this complexity, we experienced growth through becoming a learning organisation. As already mentioned, what we learned (and still are learning) through the pilot MOOC development process is serving us extremely well. We discovered that "In facing the challenges of profound change, there is no substitute for collaboration—people coming together out of common purpose and willing to support one another so that all can advance" (Senge, 2000, p. 278). We managed to work around the silos and embraced complexity through conversation. We integrated our local solutions into a bigger whole. We updated our "business as usual" on all levels of the organisation to (at least) being open for change. Through these various changes and continual learning efforts, we could embrace new possibilities around different future thinking academic offerings.

Reflective Conversation

Throughout the iterative process of MOOC development and the consequential education initiatives that followed, an ongoing practice of generative dialogue emerged amongst a number of SU's institutional networks. In a large, multi-stakeholder organisation, such as SU, necessary departmental and hierarchical parameters tend to inform the conversation around new innovations.

As the MOOC pilot was not explicitly linked to a single department, and as it was delivered in such a non-traditional format, it sparked productive conversation amongst individuals from a wide range of institutional subsystems that are not often drawn into shared reflection spaces. Important questions, such as *why* to develop a MOOC or *how* to measure its success, were continually revisited. Such reflective conversations have the potential to bring to light different stakeholder assumptions, to question the limits of mental models, and to learn to genuinely appreciate different points of view (Boyce, 2003; Ferguson, Scanlon, & Harris, 2016; Senge, 2000). In the case of the MOOC project, it instigated critical reflection not only amongst the development team, but also amongst those who could access and evaluate the result. Due to the open nature of a MOOC, the marketing efforts preceding its implementation, a wider stakeholder network could access, participate in, and comment on their thoughts and experiences in relation to this project.

Open access to broader markets has been, and continues to be, a major point of debate in South African higher education. The process of implementing SU's first massive open online course, however, allowed for the detailed assessment of the demographics of the audience (i.e., *who* the MOOC was really benefitting in terms of educational value), the completion rates, and data on user activity (e.g., *how* to apply social learning pedagogies for virtual learning). At the same time, over the longer term, the SU MOOC provided a window into the degree to which the financial and time investment justified the organisational learning and improved internal capacity (*why* to invest in such pilot projects, in the first place). Nevertheless, learning technologies and innovations should not only be adopted for desirable outcomes, but also to retain the underlying function and identity of *existing* practices (Weller & Anderson, 2013). The well-documented affordances and weaknesses associated with the fully online learning model stimulated thinking about potential future learning models at SU.

The institutional knowledge and improved instructional design capacity resulting from the MOOC allowed for the internal development of a number of online and hybrid learning initiatives during the ensuing two years. These projects had been the subject of ongoing discussion in broader conversation spaces, such as interdepartmental seminars, workshops, task teams, and national conversation platforms. Such engaging activities and conversations brought to light questions that were especially conflictual in the emerging market context, like the following:

- How can issues around access to Internet connectivity digital resources be addressed in a resource-thin context?
- Which universal design principles can best support a highly diverse student cohort, spanning multiple cultures and languages?
- How can teaching practitioners be enabled to explore online facilitation approaches?

Rather than limiting conversations to how technology might eventually disrupt the known, these potent conversations stimulated thinking about various options, actions, and future implications (Allenby & Sarewitz, 2011). In the process, valuable interpersonal relationships were fostered, thereby elevating and enriching the individual agency of those contributing to the conversations. When this occurs, the reach of such initiatives are enhanced (Hoover & Harder, 2015). Broadening incubation spaces, such as the MOOC development process, to include more voices continues to be a rewarding process, supporting SU stakeholders to critically evaluate and adapt to emerging modes of learning.

Conclusion and Way Forward

It is clear from the previous discussion that the three key capabilities, namely aspiration, understanding complexity, and reflective conversation have enabled professional and organisational learning as a result of using the MOOC as an incubation space within the specific SU context. Such professional and organisational learning has ramifications that can be applied to the wider and highly complex university context as a whole. Clearly, there is much to be learned.

The return on investment (ROI) of the MOOC in the resource-constrained environment of South Africa is, therefore, not calculated in terms of short-term financial gains but rather in terms of longer-term gains that include organisational learning, resilience, and sustainability. The forms of ROI include the emergence of more flexible design processes, and a heightened awareness of how online learning models can be applied in ways that could be sustainable in our local and institutional context. The development of the MOOC also increased the focus on quality and quality assurance processes for hybrid and online learning programmes.

Lastly, the experience of the MOOC has also influenced the strategic thinking around a new institutional initiative focused on the design of hybrid learning programmes. In effect, the challenges and processes that surfaced during the MOOC development have showed us how such a process could possibly work once institutionalised. The MOOC pilot as incubation has clearly proved highly useful for the planning around the institutionalisation of the MOOC delivery approach for hybrid credit-bearing academic modules and programmes.

Antoinette van der Merwe is Senior Director of the Division for Learning and Teaching Enhancement at Stellenbosch University reporting to the Vice-Rector of Learning and Teaching. After completing her bachelor's degree in French and German at Stellenbosch University, Dr van der Merwe studied at Texas A&M University, USA, obtaining another bachelor's degree in history and a master's degree in intellectual history. After returning to South Africa in 1996, she obtained a PhD from Stellenbosch University in science and technology studies and has been involved in professional academic support for the past 23 years at SU. Her main research interests include the scholarship of educational leadership, virtual learning spaces, and the effective use of learning technologies in higher education.

J.P. Bosman is Director of the Centre for Learning Technologies (CLT) at Stellenbosch University (SU) in South Africa. He trained and taught in the field of theology at SU before becoming involved in academic development work. After working at the Centre for Teaching and Learning at SU as well as a start-up educational software company, he became head (and in 2018 Director) of the CLT, a centre that spearheads and supports SU's strategies for the use of ICT in Learning and Teaching. Dr Bosman's research interests are around blended and hybrid learning, mLearning Literacy, and graduate attributes. He currently lives in Cape Town with his wife and two children.

Miné de Klerk has an MBA from the University of Cape Town and is a PhD candidate in Curriculum Studies at Stellenbosch University. She is currently an educational advisor at the Stellenbosch University Centre for Learning Technologies (CLT) in South Africa. Her professional portfolio includes the development of academically rigorous online learning offerings—ranging from formally accredited, hybrid courses to open educational resources such as MOOCs. She draws from her experience in the international e-learning and media industries, as well as the CLT's scholarly approach, to navigate the complex interface between ICTs and higher education infrastructures. She remains cautiously optimistic in her continual pursuit of developing virtual classrooms that are responsive to local contexts, enable critical dialogue, and establish learning communities that transcend geographical borders.

References

Allenby, B. R., & Sarewitz, D. (2011). *The techno-human condition*. Cambridge, MA: The MIT Press.

Bornman, E. (2016). Information society and digital divide in South Africa: Results of longitudinal surveys. *Information, Communication & Society, 19*(2), 264–278.

Boyce, M. E. (2003). Organizational learning is essential to achieving and sustaining change in higher education. *Innovative Higher Education, 28*(2), 119–136. https://doi.org/10.1023/B:IHIE.0000006287.69207.00

Cable.co.uk. (2018). *Study of broadband pricing in 196 countries reveals vast global disparities in the cost of getting online—UK ranks 62nd cheapest*. Retrieved March 26, 2018, from www.cable.co.uk/broadband/deals/worldwide-price-comparison/

Czerniewicz, L., Glover, M., Deacon, A., & Walji, S. (2016). MOOCs, openness and changing educator practices: An activity theory case study. *Proceedings of the 10th International Conference on Networked Learning 2016*, 287–294.

Educause. (2018). *Key issues in teaching and learning*. Retrieved March 14, 2018, from www.educause.edu/eli/initiatives/key-issues-in-teaching-and-learning

Ferguson, R., Scanlon, E., & Harris, L. (2016). Developing a strategic approach to MOOCs. *Journal of Interactive Media in Education*. https://doi.org/10.5334/jime.439

FutureLearn. (2016). *Teaching for change: An African philosophical approach*. Retrieved November 12, 2017, from www.futurelearn.com/courses/african-philosophy#section-overview

Gilbert, C. G., Crow, M. M., & Anderson, D. (2018). *Design thinking for higher education*. Boston, MA: Harvard Business Review Press.

Hoover, E., & Harder, M. K. (2015, November 1). What lies beneath the surface? The hidden complexities of organizational change for sustainability in higher education. *Journal of Cleaner Production, 106*, 175–188. https://doi.org/10.1016/j.jclepro.2014.01.081

Internet World Stats. (2018). *Internet usage statistics*. Retrieved May 1, 2018, from www.internetworldstats.com/stats.htm

Knox, J. (2014). Digital culture clash: "Massive" education in the e-learning and digital cultures MOOC. *Distance Education, 35*(2), 164–177. https://doi.org/10.1080/01587919.2014.917704

Schmitt, N. (2010). *Key issues in teaching and learning vocabulary*. Retrieved from www.educause.edu/eli/initiatives/key-issues-in-teaching-and-learning

Senge, P. M. (1990). *Senge, Peter M, the fifth discipline: The art and practice of the learning organization*. New York: Doubleday, Currency.

Senge, P. M. (2000). The academy as learning community contradiction in terms or realizable future? In A. F. Lucas (Ed.), *Leading academic change: Essential roles for department chairs* (pp. 275–300). San Fransisco: Josey-Bass, Inc.

Stellenbosch University. (2018a). *IF_20 June final draft teaching and learning policy*. Stellenbosch.

Stellenbosch University. (2018b). *Vision-2040-strategic-framework-2019–2024*.

Waghid, Y., & Waghid, F. (2017). Can MOOCs contribute towards enhancing disruptive pedagogic encounters in higher education. *South African Journal of Higher Education, 31*(1), 1–13. https://doi.org/http://dx/doi.org/10.20853/31-1-1329

Waghid, Y., Waghid, F., & Waghid, Z. (2018a). *Rupturing African philosophy on teaching and learning*. Cham: Palgrave Macmillan.

Waghid, Y., Waghid, F., & Waghid, Z. (2018b). What happens when you put African philosophies at the centre of learning. *The Conversation*, 2 May 2018. Retrieved from https://theconversation.com/what-happens-when-you-put-african-philosophies-at-the-centre-of-learning-95465

Weller, M., & Anderson, T. (2013). Digital resilience in higher education. *European Journal of Open, Distance and e-Learning, 16*(1), 53–66.

Zawacki-Richter, O., Bozkurt, A., Alturki, U., & Aldraiweesh, A. (2018). What research says about MOOCs—an explorative content. Analysis, *19*(1). https://doi.org/10.19173/irrodl.v19i1.3356

SECTION 4
Multi-Country Collaborations and Collections

MOOCs and Open Education are by their very nature a global phenomenon with highly diverse participants from all corners of the habitable planet. As such, in this section, attention is turned to several important collaborative initiatives involving multiple countries and participants. Our primary focus in this book is on MOOCs and open education in the "Global South" which represents the half of our planet where educational needs are the greatest. Unfortunately, the resources for the development of open resources in the Global South are the lowest.

In Chapter 16, Marianne E. Krasny, USA; Zahra Golshani, USA; Brittney López Hampton Coleman, Mexico; Juan Felipe Restrepo Mesa, Colombia; Michael Schrenk, South Africa; Masango (Massy) Roderick Warakula, Zimbabwe; Gail L. Woon, the Bahamas; and Yueyang Yu, USA, describe their individual and collaborative efforts to develop and implement MOOCs for change. Whereas early conceptions of MOOCs centered around providing universal access to high-quality education, Krasny and her colleagues intend for MOOCs to be key actors or springboards for spurring local sustainability practices. They describe how their MOOC experiences helped them to build nonprofit organizational capacity, innovate in their community engagement and environmental education practices, and launch lasting online and face-to-face networks. Design factors enabling MOOCs to contribute such public goods include facilitating and supporting online social networks and local groups, as well as final projects where MOOC participants apply what they have learned to a local sustainability practice or action. It also includes recognizing participants' local practices, such as through inviting them to co-author journal articles and e-books and facilitating ongoing social media after the course ends. In terms of social change and impact, this ambitious team has designed one of the most exciting initiatives in the history of MOOCs. Their assorted efforts demonstrate that what is learned via MOOCs can quickly impact local practices and actions.

Chapter 17 is from an ambitious team of five scholars in Japan, including Insung Jung, Gibran A. Garcia Mendoza, Jennifer Christine Fajardo, Roberto B. Figueroa Jr., and Siaw Eng (Janice) Tan. Impressively, this group purposefully conducted research to describe the development of MOOCs in Thailand, the Philippines, Malaysia, Indonesia, Vietnam, and Mexico. It is important to point out that these countries represent six emerging economies that are members of the Asia-Pacific Economic Cooperation (APEC). As such, the chapter seeks to answer three key questions: (1) When did MOOCs begin in APEC countries in Southeast Asia and Latin America? (2) How did they develop? (3) How were they supported? To answer these questions, research articles published in relevant local, regional, and international journals together with related books and reports were thoroughly examined. Furthermore, interviews of local experts were conducted to provide meaningful contexts for the research findings. This chapter begins with a review of the overall trends of MOOC growth in the six selected countries. It then discusses research findings and local experts' comments on MOOC-based learning experiences and points out various challenges currently faced as well as apparent opportunities moving forward. Finally, it concludes with several valuable lessons learned from the MOOC experiences of those emerging economies. Clearly, there is much valuable information about MOOC development, support, and lessons learned in this chapter.

In the final chapter of this section (Chapter 18), Edgar González, Antonio García, Carlos Macher, and Dou Zhang describe how the Inter-American Development Bank (IDB) is helping to develop MOOCs to improve social and economic aspects of life in Latin America and the Caribbean. This chapter presents preliminary findings of the first survey exploring how such MOOCs are impacting the academic, professional, and social life of learners in Latin America and the Caribbean. Enabling and restricting factors are identified related to use of the knowledge gained in MOOCs at the learners' workplace. Their findings show that MOOCs on social and economic topics offer valuable learning opportunities, inspire learners, and empower them to apply their knowledge to improve their lives. Such findings are especially apparent in developing countries where access to formal education is more limited and where access to skills in information and communication technology is rarer.

Overall, the data from González and his IDB colleagues are quite impressive. By the end of their chapter, it becomes quite evident that MOOCs on social and economic topics can offer many opportunities to people in emerging economies, especially within this region of the world. From a macro perspective the IDB has facilitated a MOOC success story that is continuing to unfold; hopefully such a narrative can be replicated and extended to other parts of the Global South.

16
COURSES FOR A CAUSE
MOOC Contributions to a "Better Place for All"

Marianne E. Krasny, Zahra Golshani, Brittney López Hampton Coleman, Juan Felipe Restrepo Mesa, Michael Schrenk, Masango Roderick Warakula, Gail Woon, and Yueyang Yu

Early MOOC visionaries claimed they "would establish education as a fundamental human right, where anyone around the world with the ability and the motivation could get the skills that they need to make a better life for themselves, their families and their communities" (Koller, 2012). These MOOC pioneers set out to address the gap in educational access between rich and poor, and envisioned that "the next Albert Einstein or the next Steve Jobs is living somewhere in a remote village in Africa. And if we could offer that person an education, they would be able to come up with the next big idea and make the world a better place for all of us" (Koller, 2012).

Despite the fact that Koller and her Coursera colleagues envisioned students making a better life for their communities and making the "world a better place for all," research has focused more narrowly on individual learning within MOOCs. Further, writing about MOOCs as a force for social change has focused on how to create greater access to online courses by addressing technological, cultural, and other barriers for students, particularly in developing countries (Liyanagunawardena & Adams, 2014). A few authors have suggested that MOOCs may assume a larger civic role through fostering respectful discussion across political differences (Reich, Stewart, Mavon, & Tingley, 2016), improving K–12 teaching practice (Napier, Huttner-Loan, & Reich, 2018), contributing to long-term professional development (Wang, Baker, & Paquette, 2018), or serving as a tool for public diplomacy (Hayden, 2017). In the present chapter, we broaden this focus on the social role of MOOCs to encompass MOOC participants adopting innovative sustainability practices suitable for their local context.

Previous research has used affordance theory (Greeno, 1994) as a means to understand how MOOCs and other forms of online and hybrid education can be designed to foster positive interactions and outcomes, such as collaborative learning (Jeong & Hmelo-Silver, 2016) and public diplomacy (Hayden, 2017). Although often applied to how technologies can "afford" or make possible learning, affordance theory emphasizes the *interaction* between the actor, in our case, the MOOC student, and the object, or MOOC platform (Chawla, 2006; Gibson, 1977; Sethi, 2017). Thus, affordance theory examines how MOOCs as learning platforms interact with students' expertise, skills, and cultural context (Jeong & Hmelo-Silver, 2016). Further, affordances can extend beyond how learners interact with technologies or physical objects to encompass their interactions with the social context (Clark & Uzzell, 2002), such as local groups in a hybrid MOOC. In short, affordance theory directs attention to how aspects of a MOOC interact with the capacities and context of the learner.

Next we explore how MOOCs can serve as an affordance for local sustainability practices. To do so, we first present an overview of social practice, strategic practice management, and related theories that provide insight into how sustainability practices emerge, evolve, and spread. We then present seven brief cases of how MOOCs contributed to local educational and environmental stewardship practices in developing and BRIC countries. At the end, we revisit our theoretical perspectives in light of the cases and comment on the potential of integrating these theories for informing MOOC implementation and research. Note that whereas social practice and strategic practice management theories could be used to explore MOOCs themselves as an innovative practice, we focus on sustainability practices that MOOCs facilitate rather than on MOOCs per se. In short, similar to how a government might encourage new practices through implementing supportive policies, we see MOOCs as a potential actor in facilitating not only learning, but also innovative sustainability practices.

Theoretical Background: MOOCs and Sustainability Practices

Whereas social practice and grassroots innovation theories shed light on how new sustainability practices emerge in civil society, strategic practice management and strategic niche management theories provide insight into how government and other more powerful actors strategically facilitate the emergence and diffusion of sustainability practices (Cohen & Ilieva, 2015). Here we view MOOCs as new actors, alongside governments, NGOs, and the private sector, which have the potential to facilitate the emergence and diffusion of sustainability practices.

Social practice theory (Reckwitz, 2002; Schatzki, 2000) has been used to explore the emergence of a range of practices, including home energy consumption (Gram-Hanssen, 2010, 2011), Nordic walking (Pantzar & Shove, 2010), and civic ecology stewardship (Krasny et al., 2015). It suggests that practices consist of interacting elements broadly conceived as the physical object or technology used in or the target of the practice, meanings actors attribute to the practice, and the competencies actors bring to the practice. In a previous study applying practice theory to understand how a small online course might contribute to students' local sustainability practices, we defined the physical element as the land, water, or biological resource that was the focus of sustainability practices and also included the elements meanings students attributed to their local place and the practice itself. Further, we detailed a broad suite of student communication and social competencies including the ability to articulate a vision, build collaborations, and manage volunteers. Based on the analysis of multiple practices, we suggested that technologies, ranging from modular rooftop garden planters, to do-it-yourself monitoring equipment, to social networking platforms, should also be considered as a practice element (Krasny et al., 2015).

New sustainability practices arising through the work of civil society organizations are referred to as grassroots innovations, defined as "networks of activists and organisations generating novel bottom-up solutions for sustainable development . . . that respond to the local situation and the interests and values of the communities involved . . . (and that) operate in civil society arenas and involve committed activists" (Seyfang & Smith, 2007, p. 585). Although small in scale, grassroots innovations enable people to express alternative, green values and realize tangible achievements; for example, producing food in a community garden. In that they are based on actors' values rather than market pressures, such innovations struggle to maintain themselves. Governments and other more powerful actors can offer financial and other types of support, and, therefore, help to maintain grassroots innovations (Cohen & Ilieva, 2015; Seyfang & Haxeltine, 2012). We contend that MOOCs can also support such practices through multiple strategies, including legitimizing them in the academy, helping civil society innovators understand the research and theory behind their practice, and facilitating online networks that enable the sharing of ideas about practices from diverse practitioners.

Strategic practice management and related strategic niche management theory present a lens through which to understand how MOOCs and other actors can support the maintenance and diffusion of grassroots innovations. Strategic practice management theory directs attention to the interaction of practices and policies, and suggests that given the right conditions, innovative practices can both change and be influenced by larger systems. Government actions include instituting local policies and programs that provide financial incentives for sustainability practices as well as helping shape cultural understanding of practices (Cohen & Ilieva, 2015). In a study of urban agriculture practice in New York City, Cohen and Ilieva (2015) identified a set of strategies the city and NGOs used to manage the growth of this grassroots innovation: (1) supporting related practices such as monitoring and mapping; (2) using communication tools to change dominant understandings of mainstream practices; and (3) strategically choosing practices that have broader impacts for practitioners and society, have relatively few barriers to change, are aligned with political priorities, and whose changes and outcomes can be tracked.

Strategic niche management theory similarly focuses on the diffusion of innovative practices through replication, attracting more participants, and infusing innovative ideas into mainstream settings. The growth of niches, i.e., protected spaces that enable experiments running counter to mainstream values and markets, is aided by managing expectations (or articulating clearly the value of the innovation), building social networks encompassing diverse stakeholders, and ongoing learning-by-doing (Kemp, Schot, & Hoogma, 1998; Seyfang & Haxeltine, 2012). Whereas the literature explores how governments, NGOs, and the private sector manage the growth of niches (Kemp et al., 1998; Seyfang & Haxeltine, 2012), we contend MOOCs also have the potential to facilitate these communication, social networking, and learning processes. However, in so doing, global MOOCs will face challenges in that the economic, technical, and policy barriers to niche growth vary according to practice and local context. Ways to address these barriers include helping MOOC participants adapt the course content to their local context and then creating an actor network and coordinating actions and strategies across multiple actors (Kemp et al., 1998).

Courses for a Cause

Cornell University's Civic Ecology Lab (directed by the first author) has offered multiple MOOCs over the past two years, including *Introduction to Environmental Education, Environmental Education Outcomes, Urban Environmental Education, Global Environmental Education, Introduction to Civic Ecology*, and *Climate Change Science, Communication, and Action*. In addition to standard pre-recorded lectures and readings, our MOOCs incorporate pedagogical elements informed by work on social learning (Wals, 2008), local place and cultural contexts in online learning (Jung, 2014), knowledge co-creation to address wicked sustainability problems (Krasny & Dillon, 2013), and identity threat (Kizilcec, Saltarelli, Reich, & Cohen, 2017). We focus on discussion board rather than right answer assignments, are active on course social media (Facebook, WeChat) groups, and conduct interactive webinars during the course. We also offer feedback on student final projects, and co-author articles and eBooks with online course participants (Krasny et al., 2015, 2018; Krasny & Snyder, 2016; Russ, 2015). Further we support volunteer "community leaders" who lead local, language, country, or interest-based "community groups" (Krasny et al., 2018), and participate in smaller social media groups initiated by these volunteer leaders. This high level of "instructor presence" (Garrison, Anderson, & Archer, 2000) is made possible by a core group of instructors and teaching assistants at Cornell University and in China, and may contribute to our relatively high course completion rate of 25–30%.

Our courses are guided by three foundational principles: (1) *equity*, (2) *sustainability as a wicked problem*, and (3) *action for the public good* (Civic Ecology Lab, 2018). To address *equity*, we allow anyone who is unable to pay the recommended course fee of $50, either because they cannot afford it or because they live in a country without payment transfer options (e.g., Afghanistan), to pay less or take the course for free. All students receive the same services (e.g., instructor responses to questions, PDF certificate upon completing course) regardless of ability to pay. Importantly, we attempt to address the issue of Western knowledge hegemony in MOOCs (Jung & Gunawardena, 2014) through discussions, social media, and the course final project where participants apply the course content and ideas to their local context.

To address *sustainability as a wicked problem*, or the belief that problems are addressed through integrating multiple perspectives (Brown, Harris, & Russell, 2010; Galison, 1999; Krasny & Dillon, 2013), we use social media to facilitate participants' sharing local practice, knowledge, ideas, lessons plans, and other resources. Participants are encouraged to join the course social media groups on Facebook or WeChat, as well as local, language-, or interest-based community groups that use familiar social media to share ideas and resources (e.g., WhatsApp in Nigeria, Telegram in Iran). Further, participants' final projects, in which they apply the course content and peer-to-peer learning to a local stewardship action or lesson plan, address sustainability as a wicked problem and *action for the public good*.

Our goal for our MOOCs is to spark innovative education and sustainability actions globally. The Civic Ecology Lab is not so interested in a child in Africa becoming the next Steve Jobs. Instead, we would love it if she became the next Wangari Maathai—the first African woman to win the Nobel Prize for her work launching the Green Belt Movement in Kenya. We next turn to descriptions of local actions contributed by our MOOC participant chapter co-authors.

Making a Better Place

As team leader of the Cornell Civic Ecology Lab and the first author on this chapter, I worked with our MOOC instructors and researchers to identify co-authors for this chapter. We purposefully chose MOOC participants, local instructors, and community leaders who were active in the course and had shared their local work on the course social media and in webinars and private emails. Thus, the MOOC change stories of our chapter co-authors—from Iran, Mexico, Colombia, South Africa, Zimbabwe, China, and the Bahamas—do not necessarily illustrate the norm but rather what is possible with motivated and skilled MOOC participants.

Zahra Golshani, Iran

I am an Iranian-American with a PhD in human dimensions of environmental systems living in Portland, Oregon, USA, and have conducted research on the Iranian NGO Nature Cleaners while a Cornell post-doc (Kassam, Golshani, & Krasny, 2018). When Cornell offered the *Global Environmental Education* MOOC in the winter of 2016, I was visiting family in Tehran and decided to recruit a local group. I faced multiple challenges in instructing the group of 30 or so university students, faculty, and NGO staff: the fact that Iranians were not used to learning in mixed groups of students and professionals; difficulty accessing the course Canvas platform and Facebook social media; not feeling comfortable with and having difficulty grasping discussion (as opposed to "right answer") questions; mistrust of US motivations for offering free education to Iranians; and feeling self-conscious about how the outside world would view them if they shared their final project. I overcame these challenges through our weekly meetings, which lasted up to four hours and involved sharing food and personal stories in addition to covering the course materials and helping with assignments (Krasny et al., 2018). My group and I also took a field trip to a village where we gathered information about a local doll-making tradition, which we featured in some of our final projects. In the end, the group of 20 most active Iranian students contributed eight final projects, a result of which my group participants and I were very proud.

After the MOOC, I attempted to continue working with my Iranian participants, suggesting that we concentrate on stewardship of a specific place. We focused on the Anzali wetland and students collected information, translated reports, and presented their findings to our group. Eventually, we developed ideas and I wrote a proposal so my group members could get paid for their work. We received half of the amount that we had requested so we decided to look for other funding. Having returned from Iran, I was unable to continue these efforts but I recently contacted an Iranian colleague who is willing to help us resubmit the proposal.

I was able to use what I learned in the MOOC in my subsequent position as instructor for University of Albany online courses for Iranian students. I included concepts from the Cornell MOOC including wicked problems, transdisciplinarity, systems thinking, and experiential and transformative learning. I held two real-time sessions where students shared a local wicked problem and described how they were applying systems thinking to their work and received feedback from other students and myself. Impacts of the University of Albany online courses include students using the course content in their own teaching and developing a climate change curriculum for secondary school students.

The fact that Cornell carries a prestigious international brand in Iran opened doors for me. People are always interested in collaboration with Cornell, and I was able to connect with the government Lake Urmia Council and one of the highest-ranked universities. Despite all the interest, our initial plans have not yet gone to the next level due to funding and communication challenges, but I remain committed to enhance environmental education in Iran.

Brittney López Hampton Coleman, Mexico

I earned a bachelor's degree in business in order to support myself but my passion is sustainable development. The knowledge and connections I gained through the Cornell MOOCs showed me a path to pursue my passion, which I continue to follow today.

At the time of my first Cornell MOOC, I was a volunteer at the student organization Ekolibria and at the Uppsala University Centre for Environment and Development Studies. I was also a board member of an organization that helps the LGBTQI population and refugees in Sweden. I have been a participant and led the Facebook-mediated community group "*Habla Hispana*" in five Cornell MOOCs.

I applied course concepts to strengthen my stewardship work and to start a new civil society organization, *Fusion Me We*, meaning "we are all one." Learning about the connections between positive youth development and environmental education was particularly influential because it sparked ideas about how I can connect my interests in youth and LGBT issues with my sustainability work.

The connections I made with other participants through the MOOCs have propelled me in new directions. For example, a US MOOC participant invited me to participate in a Climate Reality Project training conducted by Al Gore in Mexico City. I became a Climate Reality Leader and participated in the Mexico City Ecofest, where we screened Gore's *An Inconvenient Truth 2* and other documentaries about climate change. Through my involvement with Climate Reality, I met other Cornell MOOC participants from Mexico, and we are now collaborating on projects to reduce and classify workplace building waste. In addition, we are launching a network to promote Zero Waste events in Mexico City, create awareness of waste among businesses, and seek funding from businesses to address the Sustainable Development Goals. Through a MOOC Spanish-language WhatsApp community group, I received an invitation to participate in a Mexico City training of Jane Goodall's Roots & Shoots. Currently, in collaboration with this new network of Mexican MOOC participants, I am co-organizing Mexico City's first Sustainability Festival, where scientists and environmentalists will promote awareness of and action strategies to address climate change and the Sustainable Development Goals. Finally, partly due to my Cornell MOOC certificate, I was invited to participate in the call to cover the next COP 24 in Poland. To sum up, the MOOCs are like "magic" to me—I meet people from all over the world and from nearby in Mexico, who have worked for years on environmental education and on the protection of the planet and its life. I can now contribute to this work in Mexico.

Juan Felipe Restrepo Mesa, Colombia

I am a Montessori middle school science teacher responsible for designing, writing, and implementing our School Environmental Plan, a mandatory document required by the Colombian Government for all K–12 schools. I used MOOC concepts and contacts I made with fellow Colombian MOOC students in developing our plan. Our school is designing a project that involves multiple stakeholders. Further, based on our Montessori pedagogy, we are seeking to become the organization that other Cartagena schools turn to for environmental education.

During the *Introduction to Environmental Education* MOOC, I served as leader of an internet-mediated community group called "Montessori Environmental Education Methodology," which I opened to students in the subsequent *Environmental Education Outcomes* course. Our group now has 65 members and we continue to share ideas.

In terms of MOOC content, the simple notion of education *in, for,* and *about* the environment was particularly helpful in thinking about our school activities. Perhaps even more impactful, the emphasis on defining our program Theory of Change spurred me to start projects with the final outcome in mind, to plan backwards from intermediate outcomes to activities necessary to reach those outcomes, and to devise ways to measure if we are moving toward our final objective. Now, armed with my knowledge of Theory of Change, I am better able to prioritize my school's energy to focus on priority outcomes and activities.

I also have applied MOOC concepts about how collective conservation action is built on trust, self-efficacy, political efficacy, and multi-actor governance. As part of the "Citizenship and Biodiversity Preservation" component of our Environmental Plan, our school has embarked on multiple conservation projects in collaboration with NGOs. Our partnership with *Fundación Planeta Azul Caribe* uses a governance model known as "triad" involving education, community, and businesses in our "Manga" neighborhood. Our final outcome is to restore the mangrove ecosystems that surround the Bazurto Channel, which divides Manga Island and the continent, and to make the Island suitable for ecotourism. Important institutions that have joined us so far include City Port, National Marine Research Institute, and Manga's Community Action Board. Our role as the leading educational institution in the project is to motivate other schools in the neighborhoods surrounding the channel to join us, and to grow capacity among teachers to implement active pedagogies around channel environmental issues. We also seek to grow leadership capacity among students, who will share information that inspires and motivates environmental behavior with their peers and families.

From the MOOC, I realized our school needed to be patient with diverse views and gain the trust, confidence, and respect of stakeholders. A challenge is that some residents claim that mangroves were not here in the past, and that mangroves should be cut since they smell awful and are a place for thieves. Thus, we began organizing activities for stakeholders to share stories and, after viewing old photos of Manga from the city historical archive, residents have begun to realize that the mangroves have a story and belong here. Our motto describing our trust crusade, "Lo que no nos una, que no nos desuna," means to focus on what we share in common despite our differences. Restoring the Bazurto Channel is one of those common interests.

In addition to the concepts I learned during the course, connections I made with fellow Colombian MOOC students who I did not know previously have transformed our School Environmental Plan. In particular, I met a MOOC student working with the NGO *Fundación Titi*, which focuses on preserving the dry forest habitat of the rare titi monkey. Our students were invited to visit the urban titi population in *Parque Centarios* which motivated them to work on titi conservation. Their conservation activities entailed working with scientists to document the presence of hybrid titis in *Parque Centarios* and installing a donation box in our school to raise money for restoring dry forest corridors.

Michael Schrenk, South Africa

I am co-founder and board member of the nonprofit company Wild Serve and manage the Environmental Division, including its Urban Environmental Education and Eco-System Support subdivisions. My co-workers and I used the *Urban Environmental Education* MOOC's forward-thinking pedagogy to evolve our nonprofit organization's education program, and the Cornell connections we gained to build our organization's credibility.

Wild Serve is a young organization founded to address urban conservation issues in South Africa. We are trying to distinguish ourselves among other environmental nonprofits, in part by working on urban issues in poor townships where people struggle to maintain food security and environmental education is not viewed as important. In addition to the stigma around environmental education, we face two key issues: (1) negative views of nonprofits in South Africa, which can make corporations and academic institutions reluctant to partner with us; and (2) the gap between scientific research and organizations working on the ground.

We believe that an effective way to address these issues is to improve our skills and constantly strive to learn more about our focus areas. Coupled with this is our drive to always source the highest-level course or experience available, which is often found abroad. We understand that in order to maximize the impact of our education programs, we need to modernize, adapt, and ensure the relevance of environmental education approaches. For these reasons I encouraged four colleagues to take Cornell's *Urban Environmental Education* MOOC with me. During the course, I facilitated discussion among our Wild Serve participants, and ensured that they were actively engaged in the coursework and keeping up-to-date with all course tasks.

Our team has incorporated many of the course principles into our thinking and programs, including presentations to teachers, workshops, posters, and short-term projects. In particular, the concept of sense of place enabled me to gain a better understanding of my positionality as a white male working in black townships, whose residents experience place very differently than I do. We realized that food security and clean water were township residents' main concerns. In response, we are now in the process of partnering with a food security NGO to situate our environmental lessons within the context of food gardens and other more social-centric projects. I also decided to change the name of Wild Serve's Environmental Education division to Urban Environmental Education to highlight our focus on the urban context and the incorporation of current concepts into our practice.

The Cornell MOOC certificates and connections helped us to build organizational credibility and partnerships. We updated all our documents and proposals to potential partners and donors to include the fact that the education team had completed the course. Although we are a small and young organization, we entered into a major partnership with the Wildlife and Environment Society of South Africa (a national leader in environmental education and the national Eco-Schools implementer). We are also currently finalizing two additional partnerships with leading national organizations and a World Heritage site. The lessons learned from the course have allowed our team to converse with these partners constructively and to develop new programs that otherwise would not have come to fruition. We confidently position ourselves as thought leaders and we have yet to find ourselves behind on a conversation.

Since completing the course, I have received a National Geographic grant for an urban sustainability and education project. Not only did I mention the course in the application, but the lessons learned allowed our team to confidently draw up an innovative and comprehensive project plan. Of immense value has been meeting the Cornell Civic Ecology team including Cornell Professor Marianne Krasny, who has subsequently endorsed Wild Serve and shown a keen interest in assisting me with the National Geographic project.

Masango Roderick Warakula, Zimbabwe

I am an ordained Anglican Priest in the Diocese of Harare, and a lecturer at the National Anglican Theological College of Zimbabwe where I teach eco-theology and biblical studies (Old Testament). I was a participant in the *Climate Change Science, Communication, and Action* MOOC. The fact that the online course brought together participants from various countries and contexts enabled me to change our attempts to address climate change and how we could spread the message in our various capacities. I felt indebted to share the knowledge and experience I gained through the insightful MOOC discussions and presentations with my fellow environmental educators who did not have the opportunity to participate in the course. I believe that knowledge is power especially at a time when climate change is a threat to human security.

I have been asked by our bishop to come up with an environmental course outline that will teach youth in our churches and schools on such matters as climate change, Sustainable Development Goals, and the Earth Charter. The online course was an eye opener in explaining and engaging especially on the issue of climate change. It helped me to advance the 5th Mark of Mission for the Anglican Communion: "To strive to safeguard the integrity of creation and sustain and renew the life of the earth."

Further, my Diocese hosts a pilgrimage in commemoration of the martyred 19th-century missionary Bernard Mzeki, which attracts youth and adults within the Anglican Church in our province. I saw the pilgrimage as a befitting place to teach and advance what I learned in the Cornell MOOC, through imparting knowledge about climate change and carrying out practical gestures such as leaving the place clean and planting trees at the Bernard Mzeki shrine. The dialogue among the pilgrims formed the basis to impart knowledge and to learn how people understood the concept of climate change. As a lecturer who teaches Eco-theology, I am able to teach about climate change and how the Church can be involved in climate adaptation and mitigation. The material and ideas I obtained through the Cornell course and my other studies proved useful in part because the language was not too technical or scientific but easy for the audience I was working with to grasp.

Gail Woon, The Bahamas

I am founder and Director of EARTHCARE, an environmental education NGO in the Bahamas. Twenty years ago I became disillusioned by people's uncaring littering behaviors and abandoned any efforts to engage with community work, while continuing to teach environmental education to children. The ideas and connections I gained access to during the MOOCs have inspired me to reengage with my community, as well as enabled me to expand EARTHCARE's work with school children and build our organizational capacity.

I was a participant in the *Global Environmental Education* and *Civic Ecology* MOOCs, contributed to the webinars to support community leaders, and was community leader of Facebook-mediated groups for both courses: "Global EE EARTHCARE and Environmental Education" and "Civic Ecology EARTHCARE and Environmental Education." I still administer these groups several years after the courses ended and continue to benefit from the connections. For example, I have communicated via Skype with an American "Green Schools" (Green Schools Alliance, n.d.) teacher, and we organized a Skype call for American and Bahamian classroom students to share environmental views and actions. I also "e-mentored" a fellow MOOC participant from Nigeria.

Ideas from fellow MOOC students and from the course content have been useful to our ongoing environmental education program. Further, I was inspired to build community projects that include students and the wider public and to hold public awareness events. EARTHCARE's main community project is called EARTHCARE Eco Kids, which engages children from across the Island of Grand Bahama in weekend environmental education activities. EARTHCARE volunteers present a topic of the day such as the Importance of Mangrove Ecosystems, Why We Clean Beaches Onshore and Underwater, Sustainable Transportation, or Sharks4Kids, to name a few. Each topic is followed by a fun field trip to reinforce the information.

As a result of the MOOC experience, EARTHCARE held a community awareness event presenting films on ocean plastic pollution and participated in the first March for the Oceans in conjunction with World Oceans Day and other environmental groups. EARTHCARE facilitators prepared brightly colored signs to bring awareness to the damage that plastics are doing to our precious oceans. In response, over 100 participants met at the Lions Club Lodge for a four-mile cleanup March to Williams Town Beach. I also mention MOOC concepts in articles on our website, which sometimes are picked up by the local press. As a result of these activities, membership in EARTHCARE and our Facebook group has increased. Further, the fact that I hold a Cornell certificate was helpful in securing a grant from Awesome Without Borders to buy T-shirts for EARTHCARE Eco Kids at a time when our previous funding source had dried up. Currently, we are attempting to secure funding for a Zero Waste Demonstration Project and Educational Program.

Yueyang Yu, China

My engagement with multiple Cornell MOOCs propelled me into leadership roles through which I have been able to influence the environmental education community in China. At the time that I took my first Cornell MOOC, I was an undergraduate computer science student at Beijing Foreign Studies University. I became a Chinese MOOC teaching assistant (TA) and initially helped translate course materials. Over multiple MOOCs, my responsibilities grew to encompass leadership for the 20 Chinese MOOC TAs. These duties involved coordinating Chinese translations and our WeChat group and helping with the course Chinese registration and payment system. I also developed a template for an integrated information/registration/payment website for the Cornell online courses for my senior project. After that, I got accepted into the Cornell graduate program where I will continue my work with the online courses. Along the way, I have been fortunate to receive the "30 Under 30" award from the North American Association for Environmental Education recognizing 30 accomplished environmental educators globally who are under 30 years old.

Prior to my engagement with the Cornell courses, I had co-founded and served as president of an environmental club at my university and formed the Union of Beijing Environmental Protection Campus Clubs. Once I became engaged in the MOOCs, I implemented the Club Learning Plan, through which club members took MOOCs together. I had hoped that the students would apply the course content to their club activities; however, the English language and other barriers resulted in few students earning a certificate. Therefore, I adapted my approach to include in-person workshops in Beijing and Hangzhou, where another MOOC TA and I coached club participants on applying theory of change to their club activities. Together with two other MOOC TAs, I also launched a six-week online "camp" where club members went deeper into the course content, much of which they had not comprehended through the actual MOOC lectures and readings.

As a result of these efforts, 15 teams from 10 universities in nine Chinese provinces have engaged in video production, online discussions of course concepts, and developing their first program theory of change. These activities have had ripple effects. For instance, after the online camp, one club in Beijing consulted with me about using theory of change in applying for funding and another club in Hangzhou is applying theory of change in its work with middle school students. The camp is the first activity of the Capacity Building Network for Campus Environmental groups. In building on these successes, we currently are planning more activities and online camps for clubs.

In short, I applied the MOOC content to derive my own pedagogical strategies to enhance environmental education practice in a university club network. I also learned from several advanced course participants, both face-to-face and in online "friend circles," where we discuss topics beyond the environment such as social problems and life values.

Discussion

In addition to having different abilities and goals that impact their capacity to learn through MOOCs, participants bring to the course diverse competencies and goals related to their local work and volunteer activism. Local outcomes from participants' various projects and experiments around the world suggest that we can view MOOCs as affordances not only for learning but also for action. Clearly, MOOCs can be designed so as to leverage, support, and recognize participant capacities for action. They can also play a role in facilitating networks that enable participants to exchange diverse knowledge, ideas, and practices and to meet and collaborate with individuals with shared interests. Finally, MOOCs can help to compile through eBooks and other media participants' local sustainability practices (Krasny & Snyder, 2016). In these ways, MOOCs can assume functions important to managing and spreading grassroots innovations, including articulating outcomes, networking, and providing a platform for learning (Kemp et al., 1998; Seyfang & Haxeltine, 2012). After summarizing the types of local practices or grassroots innovations for which our MOOC participants provide leadership, we suggest how MOOCs might become more effective in managing and diffusing grassroots sustainability practices.

Local Practice Change

MOOC participants applied course content in educational, community activist, and organizational contexts. Their local practices demonstrate a range of competencies, meanings (participants used words such as faith, education, and sustainability to describe their practices), and the physical and biological resources they focused on (Schatzki, 2002).

In Iran, Zimbabwe, and China, co-authors applied the course content in their teaching in other university online courses, a Christian university and youth pilgrimage, and an online camp for university students. In South Africa, the nonprofit Wild Serve used knowledge about sense of place and environmental justice to forge partnerships with larger nonprofits, to apply for grants, and to transform its pedagogical approach in townships. And in Colombia, Juan Mesa Restrepo applied MOOC concepts like trust and governance to build school-NGO-government partnerships. The types of content also varied. For example, Masango Warakula incorporated fact-based content like climate change into his classes, while Juan Restrepo Mesa applied theory of change concepts to his school's curriculum planning process.

In the Bahamas, ideas garnered from other MOOC participants proved inspirational in planning new community activities for the nonprofit EARTHCARE, whereas in Mexico, connections formed with other participants opened up new avenues for local sustainability and climate change action. This suggests that our MOOC social learning approach (Wals, 2008), with a focus on sharing ideas and resources on the course discussion board and social media, can contribute to local action. Elsewhere, researchers found that idea sharing on the course discussion platform occurred among learners with opposing political views, suggesting that in addition to spurring action, MOOCs can have a civic mission of fostering respectful discussion (Reich et al., 2016).

In some cases, the connection with and credentials provided by a US university opened doors for local action. For example, in Iran, Zahra Golshani was able to connect with an environmental NGO and university, and in South Africa, Michael Schrenk leveraged his Cornell credentials in forming new partnerships and seeking new funding.

In addition to fostering local education and sustainability practice innovations, MOOC content, connections, and credentials helped the co-authors strengthen their organizations and launch new professional networks. For example, Gail Woon launched new initiatives based on what she learned about other MOOC participants' practices, which resulted in membership growth in her NGO EARTHCARE. In China, Yueyang Yu used the MOOCs to build capacity of a university environmental club network through "extra-MOOC" enrichment activities, including in-person workshops and an online camp.

Zahra Golshani is the only co-author who lives in the US rather than in the country in which she was teaching and hoping to make an impact. This and the fact that she lacked an ongoing institutional base presented challenges in trying to follow through on the multiple local initiatives she and her Iranian students had launched while she was visiting Iran. Although Brittney López Hampton Coleman also lacked an institutional base, she joined multiple existing local efforts, formed partnerships to organize a Sustainability Festival, and is launching her own NGO. Others, who worked at an Anglican university and diocese (Masango Warakula), K–12 school (Juan Restrepo Mesa), or as NGO or university environmental club leaders (Michael Schrenk, Gail Woon, Yueyang Yu), were able to expand existing efforts.

MOOCs as Strategic Managers of Sustainability Practice

Respecting our participants' ideas and local knowledge and practice, we view our MOOCs as helping participants understand their work in a larger research and practice context. This occurs through the course content and through sharing their work with fellow students from around the world. By compiling and disseminating participants' local sustainability practices into resources available online, our MOOCs also serve to co-create knowledge that otherwise would be inaccessible (cf. Jeong, Cress, Moskaliuk, & Kimmerle, 2017).

Drawing from strategic niche management theory, we can consider participants' local sustainability practices as "niches" outside market forces. Further, we can view our MOOCs as contributing to the growth of niches by communicating the value of the sustainability practices, building social networks encompassing diverse stakeholders, and fostering ongoing learning-by-doing (Kemp et al., 1998; Seyfang & Haxeltine, 2012). As more participants adopt local sustainability practices, our MOOCs could potentially contribute to a civic environmental movement, in which government and civil society actors work together toward sustainability goals (Sirianni & Friedland, 2005), aided by the democratic affordances of social media (Bennett & Segerberg, 2013; Loader, 2008) and MOOC discussion platforms (Reich et al., 2016). In short, we can consider MOOCs as a university actor supporting local actors, whose activities also may be buoyed by their boss, NGOs, government funders, and others. Thus, rather than forging dramatic global and societal changes by themselves, MOOCs and other forms of open education can be part of a network of resources and institutions that facilitate local innovations (Kemp et al., 1998).

Conclusion

Whereas our MOOCs may not have directly reached the next Wangari Maathai living in a remote village in Africa, they demonstrate that MOOCs can help spur local efforts to "make a better place." Participants use multiple aspects of MOOCs—including content, connections, and credentials—to facilitate their local sustainability practices. Further, MOOCs can spur ongoing networks and capture local knowledge and practice (e.g., through eBooks), and thereby support and provide examples of sustainability innovations for a broad global audience.

Based on our experience, we recommend incorporating the following MOOC elements to facilitate local sustainability or other actions to address wicked problems.

- Social networks and local groups where MOOC instructors and teaching assistants support MOOC participants, encourage them to share their practices and ideas, and model critical thinking and respectful interactions.
- Final projects where MOOC participants apply what they have learned to a local sustainability practice or action.
- In multiple communications, demonstrate respect for and interest in participants' local practices, e.g., through comments on social media and discussion boards, in webinars, and on participant final projects; through co-authoring journal articles, book chapters, and eBooks; and through providing platforms for MOOC participants to present their practices (e.g., in course webinars).

In addition to facilitating local sustainability practices, future MOOCs might play a role in the diffusion and global recognition of these practices through such strategies as:

- Facilitating active, ongoing social networks for learning and sharing resources and MOOC participant practices.
- Disseminating MOOC-participant produced "artefacts" highlighting their local practices (e.g., eBooks of final projects).
- Providing ongoing learning opportunities (e.g., webinars) for past participants from multiple MOOCs and other actors who play a role in the governance of sustainability practices.
- Recognizing that MOOCs can be one actor in fostering sustainability practices and exploring ways to form partnerships so as to have a greater impact.

Marianne E. Krasny is Professor of Natural Resources and Director of the Civic Ecology Lab at Cornell University. Her recent books include *Civic Ecology* (with K. Tidball), *Urban Environmental Education Review* (with A. Russ), *Communicating Climate Change: A Guide for Educators* (with A. Armstrong and J. Schuldt), and *Grassroots to Global*. She was director of the EPA's National Environmental Education Training Program and of the Garden Mosaics community gardening education program. She is also a Public Voices Fellow and an International Fellow of the Royal Swedish Academy of Agriculture and Forestry. Dr. Krasny particularly enjoys teaching environmental education MOOCs for international audiences, and has co-authored eBooks, journal articles, and book chapters with online course participants who implement projects that enhance their local community.

Zahra Golshani has been involved in international training and capacity building since early 2016. She obtained her PhD in human dimensions of environmental systems from the University of Illinois at Urban-Champaign, followed by a one-year post-doctoral at Cornell University. Her first international training was a collaboration with Cornell University on a course called "Global Environmental Education: Transdisciplinary Approaches to Addressing Wicked Problems." That collaboration extended itself to a new position at SUNY-Albany. Here, Dr Golshani joined an international training of trainers program, as an instructor, course developer, facilitator, and student supervisor. Her own research broadly covers the human dimensions of water resource management. She recently conducted a study that assessed minorities' participation in urban river stewardship programs in southeast Portland.

Brittney López Hampton Coleman was born in Mexico City and grew up one hour away in Atizapán. She has studied governmental institutions, accounting, and administration, and has a bachelor's degree in business. She has worked in market investigations, and networking, and was a functional trainer in a government art center. She spent two years in Sweden as a volunteer with LGBT and refugee organizations. Attending film, music, and photo festivals such as the Uppsala Sustainability Festival and the Stockholm Film Festival, Brittney was inspired to implement such events in Mexico. Recently, she has worked at Amnesty International Mexico and has enrolled in a MOOC for helping refugees.

Juan Felipe Restrepo Mesa is a marine biologist from Universidad Jorge Tadeo Lozano in Columbia, South America. He specialized in educational leadership from Universidad Tecnológica de Bolívar and obtained a master's degree in business administration from EAFIT University. He has 13 years of experience in education as a K-12 science teacher. His pedagogical approach has been based on active learning using a "think globally, act locally" perspective. He deeply believes in the student as an active agent capable of creating new significant knowledge through research and personal experiences. During the last eight years, he has been leading students' research groups of all ages from 3rd grade up to 11th grade around topics related to the environment and biodiversity preservation through a Citizen Science approach. Two of his students' research groups have been recognized as the best National School Science Projects by Colciencias, the Colombian government Investigation, Innovation, and Technology office. He has completed two of Cornell's Civic Lab MOOCs: "Introduction to Environmental Education" and "Environmental Education Outcomes," which virtually changed his perspective toward environmental education and sustainability. At the present time, he works as the Colegio Montessori de Cartagena's Environmental Education Coordinator.

Michael Schrenk obtained his degree from the School of Civil and Environmental Engineering at the University of the Witwatersrand, South Africa. At the time, he began to learn that nature and humankind can and must harmonize. An understanding of the need for these harmonies drove him to leave behind a corporate engineering career and help start the organization Wild Serve. The Wildlife Warriors program, which Schrenk co-founded, engaged over 1,000 underprivileged young students in learning about the value of wildlife and wild spaces before it was transferred to Wild Serve. Schrenk has more than five years of experience in working with a variety of urban wildlife species including mammals, reptiles, and birds. He is also a world champion martial artist and enjoys traveling.

Masango Roderick Warakula is an ordained Anglican priest in the Diocese of Harare, Zimbabwe. He is a holder of an MSc in International Relations from Bindura University of Science Education. He is a very passionate lecturer in eco-theology and a peace activist. In his spare time, he volunteers with the Scout Movement and works with youths from displaced societies. He is interested in environmental and social justice issues. Photograph by Solomon Chingono.

Gail Woon is from Grand Bahama Island. Her degrees are in environmental technology/aquaculture, oceanographic technology, and international environmental law. In addition, she has expert certificates in global environmental education, civic ecology, and biological diversity sampling techniques. In 1988, she founded an environmental NGO dedicated to environmental education called EARTHCARE. The EARTHCARE organization is active in many aspects of environmental issues affecting the nation and was instrumental in obtaining a ban on longline fishing in 1993. EARTHCARE received a grant from SWOT (State of the World's Oceans Turtles) wherein it distributed volumes on marine turtles to all of the schools and libraries on the island of Grand Bahama and has received several grants from the Florida Caribbean Cruise Association. Photograph by Tyrie Moss.

Yueyang Yu is an MS student in the Department of Natural Resources of Cornell University. She completed her BA degree in computer science at Beijing Foreign Studies University in 2018, where she began her exploration of environmental education while working closely with China campus environmental clubs. As co-founder of a club, a club union, and several club networks, Yueyang is committed to environmental education for college students and is passionate about integrating empowerment goals into her practice and research efforts. Through her leadership in a variety of online and offline activities for China campus environmental clubs, she was awarded the 30 Environmental Educators Under 30 Award by the North American Association for Environmental Education in 2018.

Acknowledgments

We thank our Cornell Civic Ecology MOOC team—Anne Armstrong, Alex Kudryavtsev, and Yue Li—for their MOOC teaching and scholarship and their advice on this chapter. We also acknowledge the Cornell Center for Teaching Innovation for launching us into MOOCs, MOOC student Karen Clarke for her support of other MOOC students and help writing this chapter, and Johanna Vega of Fundación Titi.

References

Bennett, W. L., & Segerberg, A. (2013). *The logic of connective action: Digital media and the personalization of contentious politics*. New York: Cambridge University Press.

Brown, V. A., Harris, J. A., & Russell, J. Y. (Eds.). (2010). *Tackling wicked problems through the transdisciplinary imagination*. London: Earthscan.

Chawla, L. (2006). Learning to love the natural world enough to protect it. *Barn, 2*, 57–78.

Civic Ecology Lab. (2018). *Online courses*. Retrieved from https://civicecology.org/online-courses/

Clark, C., & Uzzell, D. L. (2002). The affordances of the home, neighbourhood, school and town centre for adolescents *Journal of Environmental Psychology, 22*(1), 95–108. doi:http://dx.doi.org/10.1006/jevp.2001.0242

Cohen, N., & Ilieva, R. T. (2015). Transitioning the food system: A strategic practice management approach for cities. *Environmental Innovation and Societal Transitions, 17*, 199–217. doi:https://doi.org/10.1016/j.eist.2015.01.003

Galison, P. (1999). Trading zone: Coordinating action and belief. In M. Biagioli (Ed.), *The science studies reader* (pp. 137–160). New York: Routledge.

Garrison, D. R., Anderson, T., & Archer, W. (2000). Critical inquiry in a text-based environment: Computer conferencing in higher education. *The Internet and Higher Education, 2*(2), 87–105. doi:http://dx.doi.org/10.1016/S1096-7516(00)00016-6

Gibson, J. J. (1977). The theory of affordances. In R. Shaw & J. Bransford (Eds.), *Perceiving, acting, and knowing: Toward an ecological psychology* (pp. 67–82). Hillsdale, NJ: Lawrence Erlbaum Associates.

Gram-Hanssen, K. (2010). Standby consumption in households analyzed with a practice theory approach. *Journal of Industrial Ecology, 14*(1), 150–165. doi:10.1111/j.1530-9290.2009.00194.x

Gram-Hanssen, K. (2011). Understanding change and continuity in residential energy consumption. *Journal of Consumer Culture, 11*(1), 61–78. doi:10.1177/1469540510391725

Green Schools Alliance. (n.d.). *Green schools alliance*. Retrieved from www.greenschoolsalliance.org/home

Greeno, J. G. (1994). Gibson's affordances. *Psychological Review, 101*(2), 336–342.

Hayden, C. (2017). Technology platforms for public diplomacy: Affordances for education. In J. Mathews-Aydinli (Ed.), *International education exchanges and intercultural understanding: Promoting peace and global relations* (pp. 59–78). Cham: Springer International Publishing.

Jeong, H., Cress, U., Moskaliuk, J., & Kimmerle, J. (2017). Joint interactions in large online knowledge communities: The A3C framework. *International Journal of Computer-Supported Collaborative Learning, 12*(2), 133–151. doi:10.1007/s11412-017-9256-8

Jeong, H., & Hmelo-Silver, C. E. (2016). Seven affordances of computer-supported collaborative learning: How to support collaborative learning? How can technologies help? *Educational Psychologist, 51*(2), 247–265. doi:10.1080/00461520.2016.1158654

Jung, I. (2014). Cultural influences on online learning. In I. Jung & C. N. Gunawardena (Eds.), *Culture and online learning* (pp. 15–24). Sterling, VA: Stylus.

Jung, I., & Gunawardena, C. N. (Eds.). (2014). *Culture and online learning: Global perspectives and research*. Sterling, VA: Stylus.

Kassam, K. A., Golshani, Z., Krasny, M. E. (2018). Grassroots stewardship in Iran: The rise and significance of nature cleaners. In M. E. Krasny (Ed.), *Grassroots to global: Broader impacts of civic ecology*. Ithaca, NY: Cornell University Press.

Kemp, R., Schot, J., & Hoogma, R. (1998). Regime shifts to sustainability through processes of niche formation: The approach of strategic niche management. *Technology Analysis and Strategic Management, 10*, 175–196.

Kizilcec, R. F., Saltarelli, A. J., Reich, J., & Cohen, G. L. (2017). Closing global achievement gaps in MOOCs: Brief interventions address social identity threat at scale. *Science, 355*(6322), 251–252. doi:10.1126/science.aag2063

Koller, D. (2012). *What we're learning from online education*. Retrieved from www.ted.com/talks/daphne_koller_what_we_re_learning_from_online_education/transcript?language=en

Krasny, M. E., & Dillon, J. (2013). *Trading zones in environmental education: Creating transdisciplinary dialogue*. New York: Peter-Lang.

Krasny, M. E., DuBois, B., Adameit, M., Atiogbe, R., Baih, L., Bold-Erdene, T., . . . Yao, Y. (2018). Small groups in a social learning MOOC (slMOOC): Strategies for fostering learning and knowledge creation. *Online Learning Journal, 22*(2). doi:10.24059/olj.v22i2.1339

Krasny, M. E., Silva, P., Barr, C. W., Golshani, Z., Lee, E., Ligas, R., . . . Reynosa, A. (2015). Civic ecology practices: Insights from practice theory. *Ecology and Society, 20*(2), 12.

Krasny, M. E., & Snyder, K. (Eds.). (2016). *Civic ecology: Stories about love of life, love of place*. Ithaca, NY: Civic Ecology Lab.

Liyanagunawardena, T., & Adams, A. (2014). The impact and reach of MOOCs: A developing country perspective. *eLearningPapers Special Edition*, 38–46.

Loader, B. D. (2008). Social movements and new media. *Sociology Compass, 2*(6), 1920–1933. doi:10.1111/j.1751-9020.2008.00145.x

Napier, A., Huttner-Loan, E., & Reich, J. (2018). *From online learning to offline action: using MOOCs for job-embedded teacher professional development*. Paper presented at the Proceedings of the Fifth Annual ACM Conference on Learning at Scale, London.

Pantzar, M., & Shove, E. (2010). Understanding innovation in practice: A discussion of the production and reproduction of Nordic walking. *Technology Analysis & Strategic Management, 22*(4), 447–461. doi:10.1080/09537321003714402

Reckwitz, A. (2002). Toward a theory of social practices: A development in culturalist theorizing. *European Journal of Social Theory, 5*(2), 243–263.

Reich, J., Stewart, B., Mavon, K., & Tingley, D. (2016). *The civic mission of MOOCs: Measuring engagement across political differences in forums*. Paper presented at the Proceedings of the Third (2016) ACM Conference on Learning @ Scale, Edinburgh, Scotland.

Russ, A. (2015). *Urban environmental education*. Ithaca, NY: Cornell University Civic Ecology Lab.

Schatzki, T. R. (2000). Introduction: Practice theory. In T. R. Schatzki, K. Knorr-Cetina, & E. Savigny (Eds.), *Practice turn in contemporary theory* (pp. 1–14). Florence, KY: Routledge.

Schatzki, T. R. (2002). *The site of the social: A philosophical account of the constitution of social life and change*. State College, PA: Pennsylvania State University Press.

Sethi, R. (2017). *Studying unintended consequences of using MOOC interface: An affordance perspective to address the dropout problem in MOOCs*. Paper presented at the Proceedings of the 10th International Conference on Theory and Practice of Electronic Governance, New Delhi, India.

Seyfang, G., & Haxeltine, A. (2012). Growing grassroots innovations: Exploring the role of community-based initiatives in governing sustainable energy transitions. *Environment and Planning C: Government and Policy, 30*, 381–400. doi:10.1068/c10222

Seyfang, G., & Smith, A. (2007). Grassroots innovations for sustainable development: Towards a new research and policy agenda. *Environmental Politics, 16*(4), 584–603. doi:10.1080/09644010701419121

Sirianni, C., & Friedland, L. A. (2005). *The civic renewal movement: Community building and democracy in the United States*. Dayton, OH: Charles F. Kettering Foundation.

Wals, A. E. J. (2008). *Social learning towards a sustainable world: Principles, perspectives, and praxis*. Wageningen, The Netherlands: Wageningen Academic Publishers.

Wang, Y., Baker, R. S., & Paquette, L. (2018). *Behavioral predictors of MOOC post-course development*. Paper presented at the 7th International Learning Analytics and Knowledge Conference, Vancouver, Canada.

17
MOOCs IN SIX EMERGING APEC MEMBER ECONOMIES

Trends, Research, and Recommendations

Insung Jung, Gibran A. Garcia Mendoza, Jennifer Christine Fajardo, Roberto B. Figueroa Jr., and Siaw Eng Tan

Introduction

While online learning or open and distance learning (ODL) is not a new approach to education, massive open online courses (MOOCs) have increased the visibility of, and interest in, ODL environments to a wide range of audiences (Gasevic, Kovanovic, Joksimovic, & Siemens, 2014). When MOOCs were first introduced to the world community in 2008 and then spread more widely via global MOOC providers, such as Coursera, edX, Udacity, and FutureLearn between 2011 and 2013, they were predicted to achieve world domination and result in the complete transformation of higher education (HE). These predictions, today, seem to have been overblown; yet, we are currently observing the exponential growth of MOOCs (Shah, 2018) – certainly with respect to increasing numbers of MOOC learners across different continents, and arguably in terms of the changes it is bringing about in education more widely.

This chapter focuses on the growth of MOOCs in six emerging economies within the Asia-Pacific Economic Cooperation (APEC): Thailand, the Philippines, Malaysia, Indonesia, and Vietnam from Southeast Asia, and Mexico from Latin America. Note that APEC is a regional economic forum with 21 members, consisting of both developed and developing countries located in the Asia-Pacific region. As such, when it comes to educational initiatives, APEC is hugely influential in this region. It is also important to mention that all these APEC countries selected for the chapter, except perhaps Vietnam, are places where ODL has long been practiced and relatively well supported by local governments and other public and private sectors. However, APEC economies that are either economically well advanced, as is the case with China, South Korea, Japan, Taiwan, and Singapore, or those that have no or little experience with ODL and MOOCs such as in Chile and Peru, are excluded from discussion in this chapter.

The chapter begins with a review of the overall trends of MOOC growth in the six selected countries. It then discusses research findings and local experts' comments on MOOC-based learning experiences and various challenges currently faced as well as apparent opportunities moving forward. It concludes with some of the key lessons we have learned for future development and research. When did MOOCs begin in APEC countries in Southeast Asia and Latin America? How did they develop? How were they supported? These questions will be answered in the next section.

Trends of MOOC Development and Implementation

MOOC initiatives are strongly supported by central or local governments, together with private sectors in the Philippines, Malaysia, Indonesia, Thailand, and Mexico, but not in Vietnam, where the awareness and policy on MOOCs are yet to be developed.

The Philippines

The first country to be discussed is the Philippines where efforts to skill and reskill its population via MOOCs and MOOC-like derivatives have been nurtured strategically (Bandalaria & Alfonso, 2015). Interest in MOOCs started in 2012 with the University of the Philippines Open University (UPOU), offering a MOOC entitled "Developing Mobile Apps Using the Android Platform." A Moodle-based platform called Massive Open Distance eLearning (MODeL) was used to launch MOOCs in the Philippines (Bandalaria, 2018; Gervacio, 2015).

These MOOC projects are supported by the government through UPOU in collaboration with private institutions under the Public-Private Partnership Program. An example, the e-Service Management Program (eSMP) constitutes a series of MOOCs designed to train prospective workers of the Business Process Outsourcing (BPO) industry. Regional and international organizations like Deutsche Gesellschaft für Internationale Zusammenarbeit (GIZ) GmbH and UNICEF collaborate with UPOU to offer MOOCs related to their missions, via MODeL. UPOU and UNICEF, for instance, offer eight MOOCs under the Child Rights Protection and Promotion Program.

Indonesia

Next on the list is Indonesia with a distributed population of more than 266 million spread across more than 13,000 islands. Indonesia has been quite active when it comes to MOOCs. The first Indonesian MOOC was launched on the Open edX platform by UCEO, an online program managed by the University of Ciputra in 2013 (Berliyanto & Santoso, 2018). By 2018, UCEO had grown to include 24 courses, mainly intended for entrepreneurs.

Another Open edX-utilizing MOOC provider, IndonesiaX, had offered 27 MOOCs in collaboration with a number of Indonesia's leading universities and companies since it launched its first batch of courses in 2015 (Bandalaria, 2018; H. Handoyo, personal communication, August 11, 2018). FOCUS, another Open edX-based MOOC provider, operated by the Universitas Gadjah Mada, had 12 MOOCs in its list of offerings. A fourth MOOC option, the Universitas Terbuka (UT), a national ODL university, began offering Moodle-based MOOCs in 2015 and as of 2018 it had eight courses available.

Such opportunities signify that much is happening in Indonesia related to MOOCs, and government support for higher education has played a major role in these developments. MOOC operation in higher education institutions is supported by the government through the Ministerial Regulation Number 109, which allows students to take MOOCs and earn credits from their respective universities.

Malaysia

Next is Malaysia where the emergence of MOOCs has developed in tandem with the country's initiatives on globalizing HE courses; such goals and initiatives being specifically outlined in the Malaysian Education Blueprint 2015–2025 (Ministry of Education Malaysia, 2015). In 2013, the first MOOC, entitled "Entrepreneurship," was offered by the private institution, Taylor University, through the OpenLearning platform. In 2014, four public universities listed MOOCs for compulsory subjects, making Malaysia the first country to implement MOOCs in public universities that allowed credit transfer (Fadzil, Latif, & Munira, 2015; Nordin, Embi, & Norman, 2015).

To date, OpenLearning has a total of 67 providers including public and private universities, 612 courses, with almost 400,000 learners in two languages (Malay and English). With the aim of offering local expertise to a global audience, some universities provide courses such as Islamic Banking, Tropical Infectious Diseases, and Ethnic Relations. Unfortunately, these courses have not attracted learners from other parts of the world, most likely due to the use of a local platform like OpenLearning (Nordin et al., 2015). This may change as Open University Malaysia now offers MOOCs via iTunesU, and Universiti Malaya is providing MOOCs on the FutureLearn platform developed at the Open University in the UK.

In addition to the funds used by individual institutions, the Malaysian Ministry of Education has also allocated US$138.6 million to sustain the cost of development and implementation of MOOCs between 2016–2020 (Fadzil et al., 2015). With such a steady and significant source of funding, it is likely that MOOCs will continue to have a notable impact in Malaysian education.

Thailand

The development of MOOCs in Thailand was likewise examined. Its first MOOC-style online course, titled "e-Learning Professional Development," was launched in 2006 under the Thai Cyber University (TCU) Project through the TCU's Open Courseware (Theeraroungchaisri, 2018). More recently, other Thai universities have successfully delivered MOOCs through a combination of learning management systems and other media platforms (Nasongkhla, Thammetar, & Chen, 2015). Since the TCU Project introduced an Open edX-based platform called Thai MOOC in 2017, it has then invited MOOC developers, via the Thai University Network. To date, this network of developers has created 195 courses using a US$6 million government budget (Bandalaria, 2018; Theeraroungchaisri, 2018). Sukhothai Thammathirat Open University, a national ODL university, is one of the leaders in offering several MOOCs on AAOU's Asian MOOCs.

Vietnam

Although MOOC initiatives in Vietnam have not been supported by central or local governments as in the Philippines, Indonesia, and Malaysia, there has been some recent progress. For instance, with the purpose of bringing a high level of knowledge to all, GiapSchool, an online education portal, started the first MOOCs in Vietnam in 2013. As of 2018, it offered 24 courses with more than 10,000 users enrolled. Most of the courses are developed by one person, Dr. Giap Van Duong, who is the founder of GiapSchool. In addition, Hanoi Open University, a government-funded ODL university, offers a MOOC entitled "Basic Topics in Vietnamese for Foreigners" on the Asian MOOCs site where member institutions of the Asian Association of Open Universities (AAOU) can list their MOOCs.

Collaboration for MOOCs in Southeast Asia

Given their common location in Southeast Asia, the Philippines, Indonesia, Malaysia, Vietnam, and Thailand have developed strong collaborative ties in education through regional organizations such as the Association of Southeast Asian Nations (ASEAN) and Southeast Asian Ministers of Education Organization (SEAMEO). As such, they can exchange knowledge, best practices, and innovations in MOOCs and open education through regional summits, conferences, and other events.

Recently, SEAMEO Regional Open Learning Centre (SEAMOLEC), one of the 24 centers under SEAMEO focusing on ODL in the region, established the SEA MOOCs Network, which is aimed at promoting capacity-building of the MOOC providers in the region via a community of practice (SEAMEO, 2018). Such initiatives are vital to the promotion and growth of MOOCs as well as other emerging forms of educational delivery in this region. Moreover, sharing of these practices and knowledge can provide more contextualized scenarios to meet the educational needs of its citizens.

The majority of MOOC providers from those Southeast Asian countries are members of AAOU. The AAOU's Asian MOOCs site lists MOOCs offered by its member universities. The Asian Learning Portal serves as AAOU's official MOOC platform and can be utilized by member universities that have no technical capacity for hosting their own MOOCs (Bandalaria, 2018). Such services can serve to nurture the development and delivery of MOOCs and open education to people living in educationally underserved areas.

Mexico

Besides these five Southeast Asian countries, MOOCs have also impacted countries on the other side of the Pacific Rim. For instance, platforms such as MiríadaX, MéxicoX, and Académica in Mexico emerged to provide MOOCs to different countries across Latin America (Muñoz Muñoz & Ramió Aguirre, 2013; Zubieta García, 2015). These platforms were born after Spain's Universidad Politécnica de Madrid had developed the first MOOC in the Spanish language, "El algoritmo RSA," which was released on the platform Crypt4you in 2012.

The National Autonomous University of Mexico (UNAM) introduced its first MOOCs with Coursera in early 2013, which led to the development of MiríadaX. MiríadaX, the first non-American MOOC provider, tapped into the large Spanish-speaking market worldwide and attracted over a million users for its first four MOOCs (Shah, 2014).

Later in 2013, the Monterrey Institute of Technology and Higher Education (ITESM) joined Coursera and became the first private university in Latin America to offer MOOCs in both Spanish and English. According to the Observatory of Educational Innovation Tecnológico de Monterrey report (2014), the partnership produced seven courses and reached 137,000 users from 142 countries in 2013.

Furthermore, Televisión Educativa signed an agreement with edX in 2013 to develop and offer online interactive classes and MOOCs from well-known universities worldwide. In 2015, MéxicoX, an Open edX-based platform, began to be operated by Televisión Educativa, focusing on areas such as fundamental academic abilities and specialized professional training. The latest figures reveal that it has 57 partners, including public and private universities and institutions, 235 courses, and over 1.5 million users.

In 2015, another platform called Académica was released. Developed by TELMEX and the Carlos Slim Foundation, it had the initial aim of promoting TELMEX's internet services in major universities. Currently offering 150 courses in Spanish, Académica focuses not only on providing quality content but also on promoting user interaction and improving learning experiences (A. Vázquez, M. Serrano, R. López, S. Velázquez Castillo, personal communication, April 11, 2018).

Findings From MOOC Research and Local Experts

For this chapter, research articles published in a number of local, regional, and international journals were analyzed, together with related books and reports, as well as interviews of a number of local experts. The following section discusses major findings from these analyses.

Learners and Learning Experiences

Some of the MOOC studies included in the analyses detail general MOOC learner characteristics and their learning experiences as follows.

Demographics

In the Philippines, MODeL's user registrations reached 10,000 as of 2018. However, the only demographic data available was for eSMP, one of its programs. eSMP had 2,000 learners (51% female, 49% male) as of 2016. The majority were 20- to 31-year-olds, with 20% having a high school diploma and others an associate or bachelor's degree. The majority of the enrollees were Filipino.

Thai MOOC currently has about 121,000 enrollments across all courses. According to the deputy director of TCU (Theeraroungchaisri, 2018), around 70,000 new registrations were added in the period from March 1, 2017, to July 18, 2018, alone, confirming the observation that interest in Thai MOOC has been increasing (B. Siritarungsri, personal communication, August 11, 2018). The median age of learners is 31, and 57.7% have a college degree. Based on the data from two of the most popular courses, 1–2% of the learners came from countries like Canada, the USA, and Laos, while the vast majority were Thai.

In Malaysia, most MOOC learners are university students due to the fact that several MOOCs are compulsory in public universities. MOOCs offered by private universities, such as Taylor's University, are undertaken mostly by their full-time students (Fadzil et al., 2015).

MéxicoX website reports that in 2017 it had 1,575,010 users; 55.38% female, 44.62% male, of which 38% held a bachelor's degree, and 35% a high school diploma. Ages ranged from 16 to 35 years old (21–25 being the largest group). MiríadaX's 4,071,483 users are not solely from Mexico, Central and South America but come also from the US, Spain, France, Italy, and India. Zubieta García (2015) reports that in 2013, most of MiríadaX's learners were students, followed by professionals, enthusiasts, and academics.

The data show that the general characteristics of the MOOC learner in emerging APEC countries (e.g., age, gender, and education) are not so different from those of the global MOOC learners reported in Chuang and Ho (2016). However, in the APEC countries, more university students are taking MOOCs as part of their coursework, compared with other parts of the world.

Learner Perception and Acceptance

Experiences with MOOCs by Southeast Asian learners are generally seen to be positive. Manalo (2014) reported positive responses from learners towards the first MOOC in the Philippines. Similarly, Gervacio (2015) reported positive evaluation of another MOOC on MODeL. Over 90% of respondents expressed satisfaction with course content, working and learning approach, participants, achievement of objectives, and course organization. In Malaysia, a survey of 1,055 students of an ethnic relations course by Nordin, Norman, and Embi (2015) found positive learner acceptance towards MOOCs; however, caution should be taken when generalizing these findings due to the relatively small number of survey participants.

Cultural Influence

Not all studies conducted report positive experiences with MOOCs. MOOC learners, and even instructors in Ho Chi Minh City Open University of Vietnam, who were so accustomed to traditional instructor-led teaching and learning, spent more time on passive reading and video watching than they did on interaction while taking a MOOC (Dang, Watts, & Nguyen, 2017). In Thailand, Thaipisutikul and Tuarob (2017) reported resistance from conservative instructors in sharing teaching techniques on public platforms. As Connolly (2016) and Dang et al. (2017) indicated, a teacher-centered culture in Asia could be a huge barrier for online learning which requires learners' active interactions with the instructor as well as other learners together with their self-directed learning.

Challenges

The analyses have revealed major challenges such as the following.

Lack of Technological Infrastructure

One of the most common challenges faced by the Southeast Asian MOOC providers is the uneven Internet coverage and relatively slow connection speeds which inhibit the opportunities for equitable education via MOOCs. A good example of this is Vietnam. Although in Vietnam, approximately 52% of its population are Internet users, Vietnam has a network capacity insufficient for multimedia-based MOOC learning (Dang et al., 2017). The problem is similarly reported in the Philippines, Indonesia, and Thailand. Bandwidth limitations remain a formidable barrier to more widespread uptake of MOOCs in many developing countries (Patru & Balaji, 2016).

Lack of Digital Literacy

Another common challenge faced is the lack of digital literacy, technological competence, or e-learning efficacy of both instructors and learners. For instance, a study from Hanoi Open University found low levels of learners' e-learning readiness which was a key barrier to successful MOOC learning in Vietnam (Le & Nguyen, 2015). Similarly, Berliyanto and Santoso (2018) report that the Indonesian MOOCs are open but not massive due to the relatively low English and technical skills of learners, and poor technological infrastructure in homes.

In a survey from 33 higher education institutions in Malaysia, Kumar and Al-Samarraie (2018) found that instructors felt ill-equipped to design MOOCs. They also reported that these instructors are further burdened with handling two modes of instruction, via face-to-face and online, as MOOCs are credit-compulsory. Culquichicón et al. (2017) point to instructors' lack of content expertise as one of the major problems with MOOCs from Latin America, including Mexico. Measures aimed at improving training support and facilities were among the suggestions put forward by researchers in an effort to alleviate such problems. Another key suggestion was to invite contributions from top content experts.

Poor Course Design

Another challenge is related to the design of courses and their subsequent development. For example, Taib, Chuah, and Aziz (2017) report issues with teacher-centered design and the lack of collaborative elements in some Malaysian MOOCs. In a study from Latin America, conducted with MOOCs on health science, Culquichicón et al. (2017) revealed serious problems with poor course content and design as well as a lack of expertise on the part of MOOC developers.

Moreover, a face-to-face learning culture in the region has not been fully considered in the MOOC design and delivery process, which may have affected low retention and completion rates. One suggestion was to promote voluntary meet-ups or clubs of MOOC learners where learners can meet others face-to-face in physical spaces or build virtual communities (Firmansyah & Timmis, 2016). This may lead to an increase in motivation, online interactions, and, most importantly, a sense of belonging to a MOOC community.

Unbalanced Content Areas and Languages

In the APEC region, substantial use of MOOCs is observed in conventional HE contexts. Mexico UNAM's courses, hosted on the Coursera platform, primarily focus on business and social science, while ITESM MOOCs on edX mostly focus on engineering and science. As Pérez Sanagustín, Maldonaldo, and Morales (2016) conclude, natural sciences are seemingly left unattended.

In Thailand and Indonesia, most MOOCs are offered in their native language to attract local enrollees. However, the opposite is true for the Philippines and Malaysia, where most of the MOOCs are offered in English for global participants. While this difference could be explained by each nation's purpose in offering MOOCs, there is a need to closely review changes in MOOC learner demographics and choose the language(s) in which they are offered accordingly.

Lack of Sustainable Business Models

Yet another challenge is the lack of a mature business model for MOOCs, as is indicated in case studies of an Asian MOOC project (Kim, 2015). One promising example can, however, be found in the Philippines where grants from governmental and international organizations, such as UNICEF and the Asian Development Bank, are used for UPOU's development of MOOC materials while giving MOOC instructors teaching load credits (M. Bandalaria, personal communication, August 5, 2018). Unfortunately, the partnerships between HE institutions and businesses are still not visible in most MOOC projects in the APEC region, which is most likely due to weak legal, policy, and regulatory frameworks that are necessary to involve both the public and private sectors effectively.

Opportunities

Despite the limited evidence to date of positive impacts made by MOOCs in the six countries examined in this chapter, several studies as highlighted in the succeeding paragraphs have revealed promising opportunities for MOOCs that could effectively address persistent educational issues, and thereby improve the social and economic development of individuals living this region and beyond.

Strong Governmental Support

The Malaysian and Filipino MOOC projects are viewed as a key national initiative to improve the accessibility and quality of higher education, and, as such, are strongly supported by their respective governments (Bandalaria, 2018; Bandalaria & Alfonso, 2015; Fadzil et al., 2015). At the same time, the Indonesian MOOC initiative is also supported by its government to serve as a link between formal and non-formal education systems (Berliyanto & Santoso, 2018). Additionally, the Thai MOOC initiative has moved into mainstream education since the government allowed credit transfer among participating universities and continuously increased MOOC development funds (Theeraroungchaisri, 2018). In Mexico, MOOC initiatives are supported by local governments or developed collaboratively with other Latin American countries, often with support from the EU, to provide quality higher education to Spanish-speaking peoples.

Growing Number of Potential MOOC Learners

The rapidly growing demand for higher education in Southeast Asia, the large Spanish-speaking population in Latin America, and the fast development of connectivity in the emerging economies definitely offer a good opportunity for MOOCs in the six countries studied. Significant inroads are being made despite the scale of current MOOCs in this region typically not as "massive" as reported in the literature (e.g., Jordan, 2014). With regard to the issue of connectivity, the Philippine government launched its project "Free Wi-Fi Internet in Public Places," which provides that all public places such as parks, hospitals, schools, universities, and others will have free Internet access (Gervacio, 2015).

Association With Global MOOC Providers

Alliance with top MOOC providers, like Coursera and edX, as seen in Mexico, together with the adoption of Open edX as the basis of local MOOC platforms in Southeast Asian countries, brings promising opportunities for emerging countries to offer their MOOCs to a wider and more global audience.

Conclusion: Lessons for Future MOOC Development and Research

The chapter shows that the six emerging APEC countries studied have utilized MOOCs as a means to achieve the UN's global goals of ensuring inclusive and quality education for all. These six nations also promote lifelong learning and bringing about innovation in higher education based on their long experience with open and distance learning. What follows are the key lessons that have emerged from their MOOC experiences previously analyzed.

- *Policy support and funding from the government are critical, especially in the early stages of MOOC development*, as shown in the successful cases of Indonesia and Malaysia which allowed credit transfer of MOOCs and funding for course materials. In some APEC countries and HE institutions where ODL is still considered as a second-rate mode of education, gradual integration and recognition of MOOCs in HE institutions with a strong quality assurance system may not only boost MOOCs adoption among students but may also contribute to promoting a culture in which MOOCs can be perceived as part of and not just an alternative to the standard academic program requirements.
- *Development of sustainable business models, in collaboration with HE institutions, the private sector, and other organizations, is important* for the future of MOOC development, as seen in the Philippines working together with governmental institutions and international/regional organizations. To overcome a lack of sustainable partnerships between public and private sectors in APEC MOOC projects, all parties involved in the MOOC business need to take ownership of their roles. MOOC providers should find effective ways to validate their certifications in the job market. It is critical for MOOC learners, especially for those who are not enrolled in HE institutions, to be able to receive feasible and real benefits from their MOOC certifications such as enabling them to apply for a job or get a promotion in their companies. Governments need to create an enabling environment for other public and private parties and establish an appropriate mechanism to assure the quality and accountability of MOOC development and delivery. Finally, companies should see MOOCs as an additional way to provide professional development or career development to their employees.
- *Encouraging and rewarding instructors and researchers for MOOC development, facilitation, and research are important to sustain quality MOOC projects*, as shown in the Philippines which assigned teaching or workload credits for MOOC-related courses and research activities. With the rapid changes and developments in HE, especially in the emerging economies in the APEC region, much more is expected and demanded of instructors. However, there is still a lack of clarification concerning their transforming roles without any real plans for systemic change. To bring about desirable results with MOOCs including more support for instructors in their shifting roles while enhancing their status and capacity, there is a need for a systemic plan of action for change.

- *An alliance with global MOOC providers will promote lifelong learning and the globalization of local MOOCs*, as seen in Mexico which collaborated with such providers as edX and Coursera and reached out to both English- and Spanish-speaking populations across different countries. In several APEC countries, it is observed that MOOCs have opened up opportunities for free online study mostly for university students and young generations within each local context. Unfortunately, there is little evidence that MOOCs have reached out to a wider range of learners of all ages beyond the border of each country. There is a need to examine various ways to expand access to HE and lifelong learning via MOOCs.
- *More and better-designed empirical studies on MOOCs are needed* to explore the future potential of MOOCs. Rigorous research on MOOCs in the emerging APEC countries is quite limited. Additional studies are needed in a variety of areas; including, but not limited to, learner characteristics, non-completion issues, cost-effectiveness, instructional design, pedagogical dimensions, assessment strategies, and short- and long-term impact evidence using learning analytics and accumulated MOOC data.

As is clear, these are exciting yet challenging times for educational delivery in the Asian Pacific region and Mexico. MOOCs are providing a unique and evolving mechanism for addressing the diverse educational needs of learners of a wide range of ages and cultural backgrounds. Each of the countries reviewed in this chapter may continue to refine its existing MOOC solutions as well as create new ones which can provide countless individuals not only with access to higher education but also to primary education. Continuous collaboration among public and private educational institutions along with the support of local governments and the private sectors accompanied by consistent and improved quality are therefore needed and significant in utilizing MOOCs.

Insung Jung is Professor of Educational Technology at the International Christian University in Tokyo, Japan. She has served as an editorial board member of several journals including *International Review of Research in Open and Distributed Learning*, *Distance Education*, and *Journal of Online Learning and Teaching*. She is currently an editor of *SpringerBriefs* in the Open and Distance Education series. Her recent books include *Quality Assurance in Distance Education and E-learning* (Sage), *Distance and Blended Learning in Asia* (Routledge), *Quality Assurance and Accreditation in Distance Education and E-learning* (Routledge), *Online Learner Competencies* (Information Age Publishing), and *Culture and Online Learning* (Stylus). For details, visit http://epiaget.com.

Gibran A. Garcia Mendoza holds a doctoral and a master's degree in education from the International Christian University in Tokyo, Japan, and a bachelor's degree in teaching English as a foreign language from the Benito Juárez Autonomous University of Oaxaca, Mexico. He worked for the SEPA-Inglés program of the Latin American Institute of Educational Communication training teachers who worked for the *Telesecundaria system* (a distant secondary school learning system with television support in Mexico). He has worked as a Spanish teaching assistant at Albion College, USA, through the Fulbright Foreign Language Assistant Program of the Institute of International Education.

Jennifer Christine Fajardo is currently a doctoral candidate of the International Christian University in Tokyo, Japan. She obtained her Master of Arts in Education and Bachelor of Science in Development Communication degrees from the University of the Philippines. Prior to joining the academe, she was a corporate trainer in various business process outsourcing (BPO) companies. She has five years of experience teaching at San Beda University in the English and Foreign Languages Department prior to coming to Japan as an MEXT scholar. In addition, she served as a corporate trainer for top business process outsourcing companies in Manila. Her research interests are MOOCs, learner support, and pedagogical approaches in ODL.

Siaw Eng (Janice) Tan is currently a doctoral candidate of the International Christian University (ICU) in Tokyo, Japan. She holds a master's degree in mathematics and bachelor's degree in education, science and computer from the University of Technology, Malaysia. She was an Assistant Professor of Mathematics at the University of Nottingham, Malaysia Campus. Tan was also a mathematics lecturer, program coordinator, and head of the university placement team during her career with Sunway College, Johor Bahru, Malaysia. She is currently a student coordinator of Education Joint Seminar for the Department of Education and Psychology, ICU. Her research interests are psychology and cognition in technology-enhanced environments.

Roberto B. Figueroa Jr. is a doctoral candidate of the International Christian University in Tokyo, Japan. He obtained his Master of Science in Computer Science and Bachelor of Science in Computer Science degrees from the University of the Philippines (UP). In his capacity as Assistant Professor at UP, he took an active role of a technical lead in educational research and extension projects funded by international organizations such as AusAID, ADB, and UNICEF. His primary research interests revolve around immersive-technology enhanced learning environments. More of his work can be found in http://bobfigueroajr.com.

References

Bandalaria, M. D. P. (2018). Open and distance elearning in Asia: Country initiatives and institutional cooperation for the transformation of higher education in the region. *Journal of Learning for Development, 5*(2). Retrieved from www.jl4d.org/index.php/ejl4d/article/view/301

Bandalaria, M. D. P., & Alfonso, G. A. (2015). Situating MOOCs in the developing world context: The Philippines case study. In C. J. Bonk, M. M. Lee, T. C. Reeves, & T. H. Reynolds (Eds.), *MOOCs and open education around the world* (pp. 243–254). New York: Routledge.

Berliyanto, B., & Santoso, H. B. (2018). Indonesian perspective on massive open online courses: Opportunities and challenges. *Journal of Educators Online, 15*(1). Retrieved from https://files.eric.ed.gov/fulltext/EJ1168947.pdf

Chuang, I., & Ho, A. (2016). *HarvardX and MITx: Four years of open online courses—Fall 2012-Summer 2016*. Retrieved from https://ssrn.com/abstract=2889436

Connolly, R. T. (2016). *Barriers to the adoption of online education at Vietnam National University-Ho Chi Minh City* (Doctoral dissertation). Retrieved from Creighton Theses and Dissertations, Creighton University.

Culquichicón, C., Helguero-Santin, L., Labán-Seminario, L. M., Cardona-Ospina, J., Aboshady, O., & Correa, R. (2017). Massive open online courses in health sciences from Latin American institutions: A need for improvement. *F1000 Research, 6*(940). Retrieved from www.ncbi.nlm.nih.gov/pmc/articles/PMC5499794/

Dang, L., Watts, S., & Nguyen, T. Q. (2017). *Massive open online course: International experiences and implications in Vietnam*. Proceedings from Informing Science and Information Technology Education Conference (pp. 97–115). Informing Science Institute, Santa Rosa, CA.

Fadzil, M., Latif, L. A., & Munira, T. A. (2015). *MOOCs in Malaysia: A preliminary case study*. Paper presented at the E-ASEM Forum, Renewing the Lifelong Learning Agenda for the Future. Bali, Indonesia.

Firmansyah, M., & Timmis, S. (2016). Making MOOCs meaningful and locally relevant? Investigating IDCourserians—an independent, collaborative, community hub in Indonesia. *Research and Practice in Technology Enhanced Learning, 11*(1), 11. http://doi.org/10.1186/s41039-016-0032-6

Gasevic, D., Kovanovic, V., Joksimovic, S., & Siemens, G. (2014). Where is research on massive open online courses headed? A data analysis of the MOOC research initiative. *International Review of Research in Open and Distributed Learning, 15*(5). Retrieved from www.irrodl.org/index.php/irrodl/article/view/1954/3099

Gervacio, J. (2015). MOOCs in the Philippines. In K. Bowen (Ed.), *MOOCs and educational challenges around Asia and Europe* (pp. 103–120). Seoul, South Korea: KNOU Press.

Jordan, K. (2014). Initial trends in enrolment and completion of massive open online courses. *The International Review of Research in Open and Distributed Learning, 15*(1). doi:10.19173/irrodl.v15i1.1651

Kim, B. (Ed.) (2015). *MOOCs and educational challenges around Asia and Europe*. Seoul, South Korea: KNOU Press.

Kumar, J. A., & Al-Samarraie, H. (2018). MOOCs in the Malaysian higher education institutions: The instructors' perspectives. *The Reference Librarian*, 1–15.

Le, V. T., & Nguyen, V. Q. (2015). *E-readiness of learners for massive open online courses at Hanoi Open University*. Proceedings from ICSR 2015: Role of Distance Education Human Research Development. Hanoi Open University, Hai Ba Trung, Hanoi.

Manalo, J. M. A. (2014). An evaluation of participants' levels of satisfaction and perceived learning regarding the MOOC in@ RAL platform. *Malaysian Journal of Distance Education, 16*(1), 101–121.

Ministry of Education Malaysia. (2015). *Blueprint 2015–2025 (Higher Education) executive summary*. Putrajaya: Kementerian Pendidikan Malaysia.

Muñoz Muñoz, A., & Ramió Aguirre, J. (2013). CRYPT4YOU and the MOOCS usefulness in Spanish e-learning. *Innovación Educativa, 23*, 231–240.

Nasongkhla, J., Thammetar, T., & Chen, S. H. (2015). Thailand OERs and MOOCs country report. In K. Bowen (Ed.), *MOOCs and educational challenges around Asia and Europe* (pp. 121–135). Seoul, South Korea: KNOU Press.

Nordin, N., Embi, M. A., & Norman, H. (2015). Malaysia MOOCs: The way forward. In K. Bowen (Ed.), *MOOCs and educational challenges around Asia and Europe* (pp. 87–102). Seoul, South Korea: KNOU Press.

Nordin, N., Norman, H., & Embi, M. A. (2015). Technology acceptance of massive open online courses in Malaysia. *Malaysian Journal of Distance Education, 17*(2), 1–16.

Observatory of Educational Innovation Tecnológico de Monterrey. (2014). *EduTrends MOOCs*. México: Tecnológico de Monterrey. Retrieved from https://observatorio.itesm.mx/edutrendsmooc/

Patru, M., & Balaji, V. (2016). *Making sense of MOOCs: A guide for policy-makers in developing countries*. Vancouver, BC: Commonwealth of Learning. Retrieved from http://unesdoc.unesco.org/images/0024/002451/245122E.pdf

Pérez Sanagustín, M., Maldonaldo, J., & Morales, N. (2016). *MOOC-maker building management capacity for MOOCs in higher education: Status report on the adoption of MOOCs in higher education in Latin America and Europe*. Retrieved from www.moocmaker.org/?dl_id=30

SEAMEO. (2018, March 19). *SEAMEO massive open online courses (MOOCs) network*. Retrieved from www.seameo.org/SEAMEOWeb2/index.php?option=com_content&view=article&id=676&Itemid=689

Shah, D. (2014). MOOCs in 2014: Breaking down the numbers. *edSurge*. Retrieved from www.edsurge.com/n/2014-12-26-moocs-in-2014-breaking-down-the-numbers

Shah, D. (2018, January 22). A product at every price: A review of MOOC stats and trends in 2017. *Class Central*. Retrieved from www.class-central.com/report/moocs-stats-and-trends-2017/

Taib, T. M., Chuah, K. M., & Aziz, N. A. (2017). Understanding pedagogical approaches of UNIMAS MOOCs in encouraging globalised learning community. *International Journal of Business and Society, 18*(S4), 838–844.

Thaipisutikul, T., & Tuarob, S. (2017, August). *MOOCs as an intelligent online learning platform in Thailand: Past, present, future challenges and opportunities*. Proceedings from Ubi-media Computing and Workshops (Ubi-Media), 2017 10th International Conference (pp. 1–5). IEEE.

Theeraroungchaisri, A. (2018, July). *Transformation of Thai MOOC and future of Thai education*. Keynote session presented at The 9th TCU International e-Learning Conference 2018. Bangkok, Thailand.

Zubieta García, J. (2015). La universidad a la vanguardia tecnológica: Los cursos masivos abiertos en línea (MOOC). In J. Zubieta García & C. Rama Vitale (Eds.), *La educación a distancia en México: Una nueva realidad universitaria* (pp. 175–199). México: Universidad Nacional Autónoma de México.

18

A GLIMPSE ON HOW MOOCs FROM IDB ARE IMPACTING LEARNERS IN LATIN AMERICA AND THE CARIBBEAN

Edgar González, Antonio García, Carlos Macher, and Dou Zhang

Introduction

The Inter-American Development Bank (IDB) works to improve lives in Latin America and the Caribbean (LAC). The IDB is the leading source of development financing for this region and provides loans, grants, and technical assistance. It is also conducting extensive research. As a multilateral development agency, the IDB maintains a strong commitment to achieving measurable results and the highest standards of increased integrity, transparency, and accountability (IDB, 2019).

The IDB is also committed to sharing knowledge on economic and social development topics to strengthen the capacity of decision-makers and development actors in the region and to provide evidence of what works and what does not work in terms of development policies, programs, and projects. This knowledge is the result of thousands of development operations implemented over the years. This knowledge has been collected and distilled through project evaluations, research findings, publications, lessons learned, and case studies. In addition to the open educational resources as well as online tutor-led and face-to-face courses, the IDB is offering a series of massive open online courses (MOOCs), available through IDBx, its training initiative that uses the edX platform.

The objective of this chapter is to discuss our preliminary findings on how IDBx MOOCs are impacting learners in LAC countries.

The IDBx Program

The IDBx Program was created in 2013 with the objective of disseminating openly and massively the knowledge generated by the IDB. A key goal for the establishment of the IDBx program was to improve the capacity of development actors in the LAC region through MOOCs. Accordingly, a learning outcomes and impacts results framework was progressively developed, which has been guiding the general operation of the program, the instructional design of each MOOC in particular, as well as the evaluation of results (see Figure 18.1).

MOOCs Offered

The IDBx Program launched its first MOOC on September 30, 2014. As of late February 2019, it has offered a total of 103 MOOCs (34 new courses and 69 re-runs). Those MOOCs have been offered in the four official languages of the Inter-American Development Bank (77 in Spanish, 15 in English, 8 in Portuguese, and 3 in French by February 2019). Nearly 85% of the enrollments in those MOOCs come from Latin America and the Caribbean (see Figure 18.2).

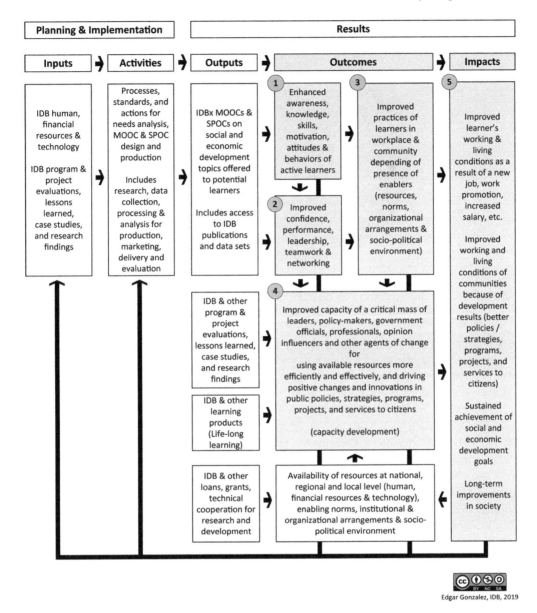

FIGURE 18.1 IDBx Learning Outcomes and Impacts Results Framework

The top IDBx MOOCs by enrollment include project management, sustainable development of cities, data for effective policy-making, urban development, management for development results, and new trends in trade agreements. Other MOOC topics that have attracted thousands of learners include digital economy, macroeconomics, early childhood development, agricultural policy food safety and climate change, public-private partnerships, pensions, management of water resources, and social development landscape (IDBx, 2019).

IDBx Learners

As of late February 2019, a total of 1,042,441 learners had enrolled in IDBx MOOCs. Impacting more than one million potential learners is a clear sign of impact. Importantly, some 501,856

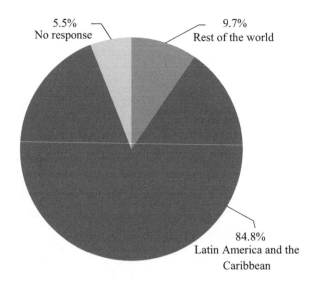

FIGURE 18.2 Distribution of Enrolled Learners

enrolled learners (i.e., nearly 49%) in those MOOCs actively participated in those courses by accessing learning resources such as videos, readings, discussion forums, infographics, case studies, and assessments, among other course resources.

However, as seen in other research, there were varied degrees of MOOC participation. Of the 501,856 active learners (participants), 396,755 were labeled "Exploring Participants" (38% of enrolled learners) who took advantage of up to 49% of the available learning resources. In addition, 105,101 were "Advanced Participants" (10% of enrolled learners) who took advantage of 50% or more of the course resources, and 83,532 participants (8% of enrollments) completed the course and obtained a passing grade of 65 or more points out of 100 and were eligible to obtain a certificate. Of that total, 58,111 (6% of enrollments) obtained a certificate; such certificate options included a free honor code certificate until the end of 2015 or a verified certificate starting in 2016, which was obtained by confirming their identity and paying US$25.

Country of Residency of Enrolled Learners

The number of countries and territories in which IDBx enrolled learners lived ranged from 45 to 193 depending on the course. However, as shown earlier in Figure 18.2, 84.8% of all enrolled learners lived in the 26 borrowing member countries of the IDB in LAC. Figure 18.3 presents the top 10 countries of residency by the number of enrolled learners in all MOOCs, whereas Figure 18.4 presents the top 10 countries of residency by the number of enrolled learners as a ratio of their Economically Active Population (EAP) per 100,000 inhabitants (World Bank, 2018).

Course Completion per Country and Human Development Index (HDI)

When plotting course completion per country with their respective HDI, a statistic composite index that includes life expectancy, education, and per capita indicators (UNDP 1990–2017), our data shows that learners in the less developed of the 26 countries in the LAC region are taking greater advantage of the MOOCs offered. Those countries have a higher ratio of learners who completed the course in relation to enrolled users when compared with countries with higher HDI (see Figure 18.5). This suggests that MOOCs are more appreciated in those countries where learning opportunities are more limited.

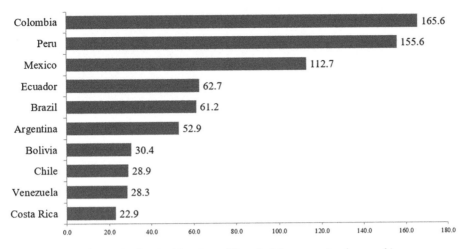

FIGURE 18.3 Top 10 Countries by the Number of Enrolled Learners (in thousands)

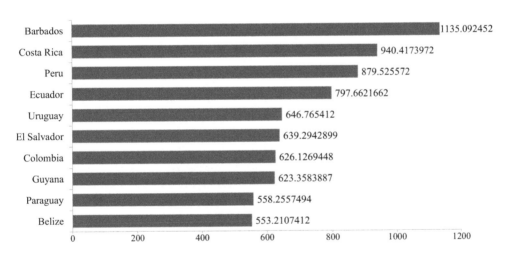

FIGURE 18.4 Top 10 Countries by the Number of Enrolled Learners as a Ratio of EAP per 100,000 Inhabitants

Age, Gender, and Level of Education of Enrolled Learners

Out of all enrolled learners in IDBx, 47.21% identified as male, while 39.92% identified as female. In addition, 98% were within economically active age (between 18 and 64 years old). In terms of educational level attained, 33.8% had a bachelor's degree and 29.3% had a master's degree. Figure 18.6 and Figure 18.7 present more detail about participant demographic characteristics.

Occupation of Enrolled Learners

In line with the intended target audience, the largest percentage of learners enrolled in IDBx MOOCs were development practitioners working in the public sector (33.2%). The second-largest

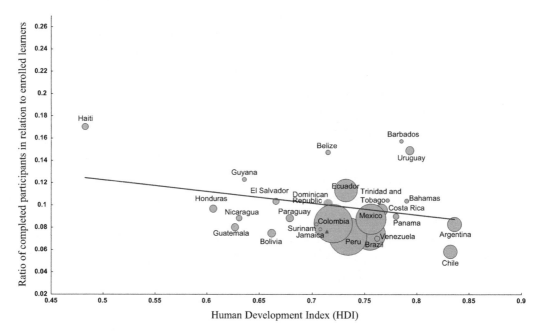

FIGURE 18.5 Ratio of Completed Participants in Relation to Enrolled Learners Plotted by HDI of 26 IDB Borrowing Countries (the size of each circle represents the number of enrolled learners in that country by October 2018)

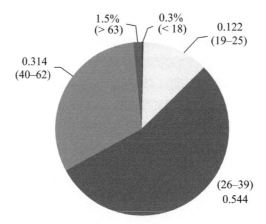

FIGURE 18.6 Age Group of Enrolled Learners

percentage were in the private sector (22.3%). Still others were consultants or some other type of independent occupation (11.2%), worked in NGOs (8.7%), or were part of other types of international organizations (3.6%).

Approximately, one in five (21.0%) of enrolled learners came from academia. We found that a large number of teachers are using our courses to improve their professional practice and that an increasing number of graduate and postgraduate students are interested in development issues (see Figure 18.8). These data are hopeful for positive change to educational opportunities in this region.

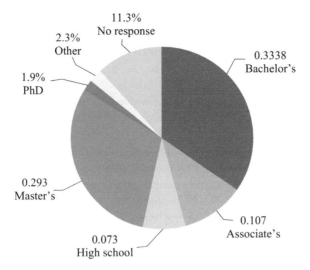

FIGURE 18.7 Education of Enrolled Learners

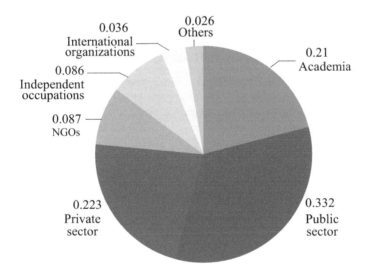

FIGURE 18.8 Occupation of Enrolled Learners

Learners' Satisfaction With IDBx MOOCs

The IDBx Program conducted Kirkpatrick Level-1 surveys (Kirkpatrick & Kirkpatrick, 2006), also known as reaction or satisfaction surveys, weekly during course delivery. There was also a final survey at the end of each course to evaluate learners' perceptions of the course, including the achievement of learning objectives (i.e., course and module objectives); the sufficiency, appropriateness, relevance, and currency of course content; and the quality of learning resources and activities (e.g., videos, readings, interactive forum, formative and summative evaluations, etc.). In addition, in terms of their contribution to the learning process, surveys were also utilized to determine the usefulness of each course in relation to the applicability of its contents to the learner's context.

The response rate of the weekly surveys ranged from 14.9% to 17.2% of participants. However, the response rate for the final survey ranged from 10.9% to 13.3% of participants. The IDBx MOOC Quality Index (MQI), the simple average of those indicators rated by learners in all courses delivered during 2014–2018, was 4.56 out of 5.0, which indicates a high level of learner satisfaction.

In that cultural context, relevance, and practicality are critical for adult learning, IDBx MOOCs are designed and developed considering regional and cultural complexities as well as the similarities and differences among LAC countries, including offering the courses in national languages. This approach creates a positive sense of belonging and social identity for participants of the region, which is conducive to learning. Of course, such an approach is in contrast with findings reported for MOOCs not tailored to the regional culture and offered only in English (Kizilcec, Saltarelli, Reich, & Cohen, 2017). Following sound principles of instructional design and based on a learner-centered approach shared by experts in the field (MacKeracher, 2004). IDBx MOOCs intend to provide guidance, inspiration, tools, methodologies, case studies, and examples relevant and useful to the development of practitioners in LAC countries. IDBx MOOCs are also designed to promote the use of knowledge and put course participants in the mindset of viewing themselves as agents of change of their own reality; including personal, organizational, institutional, and social issues and challenges.

Impact of IDB MOOCs on Learners in Latin America and the Caribbean

Objective and Characteristics of the First Survey

In line with the learning outcomes and impacts results framework presented in Figure 18.1, the goal of the first survey was to collect some evidence about the short-term results achieved by the IDBx program on learners' academic life, professional/work life, including the impact in their workplace, and their social/community life:

1. Enhanced awareness, knowledge, skills, motivation, attitudes, and behaviors of active learners.
2. Improved confidence, performance, leadership, teamwork, and networking.
3. Enhanced practices of learners in their workplace and communities.
4. Expanded capacity of a critical mass of leaders, policy-makers, government officials, professionals, opinion influencers, and other agents of change for using available resources more efficiently and effectively, and driving positive changes in public policies, strategies, programs, projects, and services to citizens.
5. Improved learner's working and living conditions as a result of a new job, work promotion, increased salary, and so on.

In July 2017, the IDBx Program sent its first Kirkpatrick Level-3 survey to 53,582 learners who accessed 30% or more of the available learning resources of 32 MOOCs. These MOOCs were offered in Spanish, English, Portuguese, and French from 2014 to 2016.

Results of the Survey

Through a series of closed and open questions, the Level-3 survey explored the impact of MOOCs on learners' academic life, professional/work life, including impact in their workplace, and their social/community life. A total of 7,655 learners answered the survey (González, García, Macher, & Zhang, 2018a). This reflected a response rate of 14.3%, which was deemed more than acceptable for an opt-in online survey (Cho & LaRose, 1999). Presented next are some of the data collected through the closed survey questions.

Impact on Learners' Academic Life

According to the survey results, 74.7% of learners agreed that the MOOC helped them to decide what to study or research in the future and 64.5% reported that MOOCs improved their academic performance. In addition, 61.9% of MOOC learners reported that the course inspired them to initiate or reinitiate their studies (González, García, Macher, & Zhang, 2018a). Such findings indicate that the IDBx Program is making a significant impact on careers of most people who enroll. In effect, MOOCs are providing a sense of direction and academic goals to accomplish.

Impact on Learners' Professional/Work Life

The most noticeable impacts reported were on improving knowledge and skills for their current job (92.7%) and improving professional performance (91.3%). Other areas of high impact included increasing leadership and influence in the workplace (78.7%). MOOCs also had a positive influence on their professional career (66.9%) as well as improving their standing for a new job (59.9%) (González, García, Macher, & Zhang, 2018a). These are very encouraging findings about the potential of MOOCs for closing existing skill gaps, both among employees, senior management, and decision-makers in public and private organizations; for reducing the impact of high turnover, as well as addressing current and future needs for reskilling and upskilling to keep pace with technological change and modernization of public management.

Impact on Learners' Workplace

The impact was also felt directly in their work settings. In fact, 87.83% of the learners who answered the survey reported using the knowledge gained in IDBx MOOCs to improve their workplace or organizational setting. When analyzing the knowledge use per country in relation with their respective Information and Communication Technology (ICT) Development Index (IDI), which integrates ICT readiness, use, and capability (International Telecommunication Union, 2015), we observed that a higher percentage of learners used their knowledge in countries with lower IDI in relation with learners in countries with higher IDI (see Figure 18.9). Such results suggest that

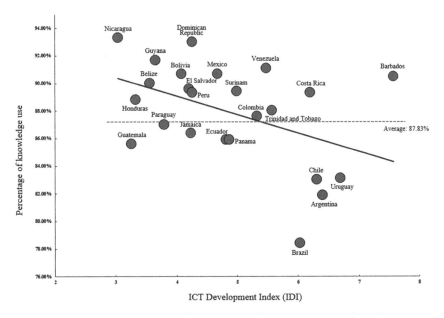

FIGURE 18.9 Knowledge Use per Country Plotted by ICT Development Index (IDI)

learners in less developed countries were more eager to take advantage of their learning opportunities and use the knowledge gained to face the restrictions and challenges that they have.

Of the learners who reported using their knowledge to improve their workplace or organizational setting, over 90% agreed that they were more productive or more efficient. In addition, 88.3% applied new or innovative methodologies or technologies in their work, while just slightly fewer (i.e., 86.9%) were able to advance existing or new initiatives, projects, or programs. Also, of importance, 78.3% improved their leadership and influence at work (González, García, Macher, & Zhang, 2018a). We believe that these findings are associated with the improved knowledge and confidence of MOOC participants after learning not only about fundamentals, concepts, and theories of a particular development topic, but also after learning from the experience, successes, and failures of expert practitioners working in different LAC countries. It seems that instructional design of IDBx MOOCs, which integrates theory (why, what), and expert know-how (how, when, where), with context-based learning activities and calls-to-action, is working effectively to motivate and empower participants to view themselves as agents of change of their own reality.

Enabling Factors to Use Knowledge in Learners' Workplace

Participants reported that the main enabling factor was related to the tools and methodologies provided by the MOOC (94.7%), followed by the availability of time at work (83.6%), and the flexibility of existing norms and procedures (62.2%). Also important to knowledge use was the support from supervisors and coworkers (54.3%) as well as the availability of financial resources (42.2%) (González, García, Macher, & Zhang, 2018a). Finding that the main enabling factor to use knowledge in the workplace was the tools and methodologies provided by IDBx MOOCs confirms the importance of practicality for adult learning. This result has been achieved by including toolkits, step-by-step methodologies, roadmaps, checklists, worksheets, and templates that participants can adapt, localize, use, reuse, and share as open educational resources (OER).

Restricting Factors to Use Knowledge in the Learners' Workplace

For those learners who reported not being able to use their knowledge in their workplace, the main reported restricting factor was the rigidity of norms and procedures (34.4%). This lack of flexibility issue was followed by the lack of financial resources (24.2%), lack of time at work (22.4%), lack of support from supervisors or coworkers (20.5%), and the lack of tools/methodologies to use their knowledge (8.8%) (González, García, Macher, & Zhang, 2018a). Innovation in the public sector is not easy to achieve due to several factors including among others, outdated laws and regulations, risk aversion culture, hierarchical structures, organizational silos, and lack of incentives. However, we believe in the power of data, information, and knowledge to progressively overcome those barriers and foster the ability, motivation, and opportunity to innovate in public sector organizations, so they can continually improve and adapt to address the challenges facing their societies.

Impact on Learners' Social Life

Of high importance, 63% of learners reported that people in their communities benefited from initiatives, projects, or programs implemented by them. In addition, 57.9% reported that people in their families, workplaces, or communities changed their behavior because of those initiatives, projects, or programs. And 45.6% reported that family and friends also benefited from those initiatives, projects, or programs implemented by learners. These findings are indicative of the potential of MOOCs for increasing leadership and social influence as well as service orientation, which are essential skills for capacity development.

Testimonials About Outcomes and Impacts

In addition to the responses given to the survey's closed questions, we also received 2,506 responses to the open questions with specific details on how MOOCs enriched learners' academic lives, professional/work lives, and their social/community lives. These testimonials are evidence of the value of MOOCs for fostering ideas to introduce something new in their practice to improve their lives. Clearly, MOOCs offered by the IDBx Program serve a vital role in LAC countries for adapting, adopting, and improving existing processes, methodologies, tools, and technologies. They also can foster the creation of entirely new and highly innovative products or services. Such results and feedback give us at the IDB much optimism and hope for MOOCs and other forms of open education in the future.

Consistency of the Results Between 2017 and 2018 Surveys

In July 2018, the IDBx Program sent its second Kirkpatrick Level-3 survey to additional 40,460 learners who accessed 20% or more of the available learning resources of 27 MOOCs offered during 2017 and 2018. A total of 4,208 learners answered this second survey (10.4% response rate) (González, García, Macher, & Zhang, 2018b). The percentages of responses to the closed questions in 2018 survey were very similar to the percentages of responses of the 2017 survey presented in this chapter, although the learners and the MOOCs in which they participated were different between the two surveys.

Discussion and Conclusions

Further analysis of current data as well as additional surveys are necessary to better identify possible patterns in the data. However, it is clear, even at this early stage, that MOOCs are significantly and positively impacting the academic, professional, and social lives of learners in LAC countries.

Our findings show that MOOCs covering social and economic topics offer valuable learning opportunities, inspire learners, and empower them to apply their knowledge to improve their lives. Such results are especially true in less developed countries where access to formal education and access to, use of, and skills in information and communication technology are more limited. This is consistent with previous research in which learners with lower levels of socioeconomic status and education are significantly more likely to report tangible career benefits (Zenghao, Alcorn, Christensen, Eriksson, Koller, & Emanuel, 2015).

In our research, knowledge use was reported higher in less developed LAC countries. One hypothesis to explain this phenomenon could be that, although possibly counterintuitive, learners in these countries were more eager to take advantage of these learning opportunities because they simply saw the inherent value in such free and open courses. In effect, free and open education was relevant to the improvement of their life situations.

The survey respondents also cited in their responses that both time and flexibility were important factors in exploring such opportunities to use their acquired knowledge. It could also be argued that learners in less developed LAC countries have more room to be more productive and efficient, to apply new and innovative methodologies or technologies in their work, to advance existing or new initiatives, projects, or programs, and to improve their leadership and influence at work. If such views are accurate, MOOCs could be considered as an effective open knowledge tool for leveling the playing field in terms of educational opportunities among various LAC countries. In addition, they can also strengthen organizations and promote social and economic development.

In line with the findings in previous research (Deboer, Ho, Stump, & Breslow, 2014; Kizilcec, Piech, & Schneider, 2013), we have observed that many learners in IDBx MOOCs stay engaged and committed to learning without taking all of the assessments nor with the intention of completing the course or getting certified. In fact, so far, we have not found any statistical difference between learners who were able or were not able to use their knowledge as a function on the amount of learning resources consumed in each MOOC. Such results include exploring learners who consumed more than 30% of learning resources, advanced learners, and completing and certified learners (González, García, Macher, & Zhang, 2018a, 2018b).

In summary, our findings are consistent with the expected outcomes and impact of our Learning Results Framework presented in Figure 18.1. Based on those findings we believe that IDBx MOOCs can be an effective tool to foster capacity development in LAC countries, this is, to improve capacity of a critical mass of leaders, policy-makers, government officials, professionals, opinion influencers, and other agents of change for using available resources more efficiently and effectively and for driving positive changes and innovations in public policies, strategies, programs, projects, and services to citizens. Based on the responses received in our survey, and in line with previous findings (Bogdan, Holotescu, Andone, & Grosseck, 2017), we also believe that MOOCs can be a cost-effective solution for training employees in the private sector, independent professionals, entrepreneurs, and staff members of start-ups.

Notwithstanding these promising findings, much more work needs to be done from MOOC providers, international organizations, governments, and academic institutions for reaching that critical mass of learners in the public and private sector to bring to fruition the potential outcomes and impact of MOOCs in LAC countries, in terms of capacity development and socio-economic development. Recognizing human capital investment as an asset rather than a liability is imperative to address the changes that will impact millions of workers, according with a recent report on the future of job (World Economic Forum, 2018).

A key action in this regard is disseminating massively the good news about MOOCs not only to potential learners but also to employers and recruiters in the public and private sectors. According with a recent survey (Gatuguta-Gitau, 2017), 77% of graduate recruiters in Latin America were not aware of MOOCs. This region, as well as Western Europe, evidenced the greatest proportion of graduate recruiters who were unaware of MOOCs. This proportion was lower in Asia Pacific (70%), Africa and the Middle East (66%), the US and Canada (55%), and Eastern Europe (44%).

It is also essential that employers and recruiters in LAC countries recognize MOOC certificates and other alternative credentials as credible evidence of knowledge and skills gained by current and potential employees. Lifelong learners will be much more likely to invest in training if it confers a qualification that potential employers will recognize in line with their needs. According with recent findings on demographic shifts in educational demand and the rise of alternative credentials, professionally focused learning goals require smaller, simpler, more applied learning programs that are shaped by industry need, less expensive than degrees and sometimes more smaller than traditional courses (Fong, Janzow, & Peck, 2016).

MOOC providers, employers, universities, accreditation bodies, and governments should collaborate to develop a credentialing ecosystem of stackable open digital badges useful to recognize competences and skills relevant for employers in the public and private sector to address current and future challenges in the work environment. Transparency, trust, and value of these alternative credentials can be built progressively in LAC countries by using recognized standards for learning assessment in MOOCs, identity verification, and adequate metadata in line with the Open Badges specification, coupled with the reputation of those institutions issuing the credentials.

So far, enrollments in MOOCs are the result of individual decisions to learn more about a particular topic of interest for those learners who are well informed about the existence of these open learning opportunities. However, it is necessary to complement this bottom-up approach with top-down initiatives in which government authorities, CEOs, and middle-level supervisors in the public and the private sectors purposefully use and recognize MOOCs as a cost-effective alternative to improve their employees' performance towards achieving their organizational goals, in comparison with traditional on-the-job training. This is particularly critical in governments, which must continually adapt and innovate to address new and ever more complex challenges facing their societies (OECD, 2017).

Private and public organizations in LAC countries should implement a series of actions to take advantage of MOOCs to improve their employees' performance including: (1) define and make explicit medium- and long-term organizational priorities and goals; (2) appoint selected personnel to curate available MOOCs based on their usefulness to address organizational priorities and goals; (3) include provisions in their administrative norms and procedures to recognize alternative credentials like MOOC certificates and digital badges, not only for recruiting and hiring but also for recognition of employees' continuous development and for career advancement opportunities; (4) establish adequate work arrangements and incentives for employees willing to take organizational curated MOOCs, get certified, and apply gained knowledge and skills to improve organizational performance and drive innovations into the workplace; and (5) cultivate an organizational culture that nurtures and rewards lifelong learning, creativity, and innovation.

The coming decades will likely see many more initiatives and pilot testing of innovative learning programs with alternative credentials that can play a role in the social and economic development of different LAC countries. The Inter-American Development Bank intends to continue to play a leading role in such efforts in collaboration and partnership with governments, universities, and other organizations. We will continue offering open knowledge through MOOCs and searching for ways to not only increase their effectiveness as a tool for development, but also to dramatically extend and multiply their impact throughout the countries of LAC and beyond.

Disclaimer: The opinions expressed in this chapter are those of the authors and do not necessarily reflect the views of the Inter-American Development Bank, its Board of Directors, or the countries they represent.

Edgar González has contributed for 30 years to social development in Latin America formulating and implementing policies in health and social protection, managing projects, and strengthening institutional capacity through face-to-face training programs and online courses. He works as a lead specialist in learning and knowledge management at the Inter-American Development Bank (IDB) in Washington, DC. Currently, Edgar is acting as the IDBx Program Manager, the IDB training initiative in edX. Prior to joining the IDB, he worked as a PAHO/WHO consultant, General Director of Services Development of the Ministry of Health, Director and Professor of the Health Services Management Program of the ESAP and Health Advisor of the Presidency of the Republic of Colombia. He is a doctor in medicine and surgery from the University of Santander and has a master's in community medicine from the University of London and is certified in knowledge management from the Knowledge Management Institute.

Antonio García is a project management professional with over a decade of experience in knowledge and learning. He has worked at the Inter-American Development Bank (IDB) in Washington, DC (USA) since 2012. He initially joined the Country Department for Central America (CID), Mexico, Panama, and the Dominican Republic and later the Integration and Trade sector. Currently, Antonio is Operations Coordinator of the IDBx program, the IDB training initiative in edX. Prior to joining the IDB, he worked in the Chamber of Commerce and Industry of Toledo in Spain as a foreign trade specialist providing training programs in business internationalization for small and medium enterprises. He is a lawyer with an MBA, with a focus on multilateral projects from the Center for Economic and Commercial Studies (CECO). He also holds a master's degree in international business from the School of Industrial Organization (EOI).

Carlos Macher is an e-learning technologist and audiovisual producer for the IDBx Program of the Inter-American Development Bank. He has worked for more than eight years in the management of information technology, data analysis, audiovisual productions, and multimedia interactive innovation in online education initiatives for the social development of Latin America and the Caribbean. Prior to joining the IDB, he worked for five years as a communications, multimedia, and e-learning specialist at the Organization of American States and in Peru as a producer and director for different TV and film projects. He has a Bachelor's in Communications and a specialization diploma in audiovisual production from the University of Lima in Peru. Macher currently is a candidate for a Master's in Fine Arts in Film and Electronic Media at American University.

Dou Zhang is a policy analyst and researcher. Dou is currently working at the Doing Business team of the World Bank Group. Prior to the World Bank, Dou was working at the Inter-American Development Bank on evaluations and data analytics that relate to e-learning. Dou holds a Master's of Public Policy degree (MPP) from George Washington University and is currently pursuing a PhD of Public Policy and Public Administration degree from the same university. Originally from China, Dou currently lives in Washington, DC.

References

Bogdan, R., Holotescu, C., Andone, D., & Grosseck, G. (2017, April 27–28). *How MOOCs are being used for corporate training?* The 13th International Scientific Conference eLearning and Software for Education, Bucharest.

Cho, H., & LaRose, R. (1999). Privacy issues and internet surveys. *Social Science Computer Review, 17*(4), 421–434. doi:10.1177/089443939901700402

Deboer, J., Ho, A. D., Stump, G. S., & Breslow, L. (2014). Changing "course". *Educational Researcher, 43*(2), 74–84. doi:10.3102/0013189x14523038

Fong, J., Janzow, P., & Peck, K. (2016). *Demographic shifts in educational demand and the rise of alternative credentials.* Retrieved from https://upcea.edu/wp-content/uploads/2017/05/Demographic-Shifts-in-Educational-Demand-and-the-Rise-of-Alternative-Credentials.pdf

Gatuguta-Gitau, S. (2017). QS intelligence unit. *MOOCs: Employers View, a Brief Snapshot.* Retrieved from www.qs.com/moocs-employers-view-a-brief-snapshot/

González, E., García, A., Macher, C., & Zhang, D. (2018a). *IDBx initial survey 2014–2017.* Washington, DC: Inter-American Development Bank. Unpublished raw data.

González, E., García, A., Macher, C., & Zhang, D. (2018b). *IDBx 2017 and 2018 level 3 survey in Spanish, English, French, and Portuguese.* Washington, DC: Inter-American Development Bank. Unpublished raw data.

Inter-American Development Bank (2019). *About us.* Retrieved from www.iadb.org/en/about-us/borrowing-member-countries

IDBx, Inter-American Development Bank (2019). https://www.edx.org/school/idbx

International Telecommunication Union. (2015). *Measuring the information society report 2015* (Rep. No. ISBN 978-92-61-15791-3). Geneva, Switzerland: Place des Nations CH-1211.

Kirkpatrick, D. L., & Kirkpatrick, J. D. (2006). *Evaluating training programs: The four levels.* San Francisco, CA: Berrett-Koehler.

Kizilcec, R. F., Piech, C., & Schneider, E. (2013). *Deconstructing is engagement*. Proceedings of the Third International Conference on Learning Analytics and Knowledge—LAK 13. doi:10.1145/2460296.2460330

Kizilcec, R. F., Saltarelli, A. J., Reich, J., & Cohen, G. L. (2017). Closing global achievement gaps in MOOCs. *Science, 355*(6322), 251–252. doi:10.1126/science.aag2063

MacKeracher, D. (2004). *Making sense of adult learning*. Canada: University of Toronto Press. ISBN 0-8020-3778-X

OECD. (2017). *Fostering innovation in the public sector*. Paris: OECD Publishing. http://dx.doi.org/10.1787/9789264270879-en. ISBN 978-92-64-27087-9

United Nations Development Programme. Human development reports. *Human Development Data (1990-2017)*. New York. Retrieved from http://hdr.undp.org/en/data

World Bank. (2018). *World development indicators*. Retrieved from http://data.worldbank.org/data-catalog/world-development-indicators

World Economic Forum. (2018). *The future of jobs report*. Geneva, Switzerland. ISBN 978-1-944835-18-7

Zhenghao, Z., Alcorn, B., Christensen, G., Eriksson, N., Koller, D., & Emanuel, E. J. (2015, September 22). Who's benefiting from MOOCs, and why? *Harvard Business Review, 25*. Retrieved from https://hbr.org/2015/09/whos-benefiting-from-moocs-and-why#

SECTION 5
Government Policies and Strategies

Although most of the early MOOCs and open education initiatives can be traced back to individual universities or relatively small consortia of institutions, there have also been larger developments at national or regional government levels. This is the focus of this fifth section.

In the first chapter of this section, Chapter 19, Tel Amiel and Tiago Chagas Soares from Brazil argue that Brazil has made significant strides in advancing open education policies in recent years. One of the most significant developments has been the adoption of an open license policy for the Open University of Brazil (UAB), a consortium of over 100 public higher education institutions. Amiel and Soares report on a survey conducted with a large sample of participants from these institutions. This research was developed as part of an ongoing review on OER projects and policies (both national and internationally). The survey data identified the need for increased awareness and understanding of the meaning of openness and what effectively constitutes an OER. These data also indicate categories related to institutional encouragement for OER production as well as significant interest in the implementation of policies to advance openness; however, progress on actual policy implementation has been quite limited. The authors of this chapter argue that although open education is often seen as "incipient" in Latin America, significant developments are now actually taking place. Such developments could offer an opportunity to reflect on the local conditions and levers to advance policy design and implementation.

In Chapter 20, Purushothaman Ravichandran from Malaysia discusses the economic challenges inherent in sustaining the development of MOOCs in the Malaysian context. As he notes, massive open online courses (MOOCs) in Malaysia has been the primary focus of many universities since they first launched in September 2015. According to Global E-Learning Market Analysis and Trends in 2017, the global eLearning market is poised to grow at a compound annual growth rate of around 7% over the next decade to reach approximately $330 billion by 2025. However, it is not entirely clear how the MOOC approach to online education can be fiscally sustained. Such financial concerns also need to be viewed from the standpoint that the Malaysia government intended to have 15% of all Malaysian public university courses taught online as MOOCS by the end of 2015 and 30% of all university courses by the year 2020.

Given the various reasons to learn from MOOCs, whether intrinsic or extrinsic, there needs to be a clear understanding of how governmental strategies can influence institutional policies and practices toward sustainable MOOC development. As such, this chapter discusses the global trends as well as policy-related strategies and their implications for the sustainable and continually expanding development of MOOCs in the Malaysian context.

Chapter 21 comes from Melinda dela Peña Bandalaria, who is now the Chancellor of the University of the Philippines Open University. As Chancellor Bandalaria explains, developing countries are often perceived as resource-poor and on the receiving end or recipients of initiatives by developed countries. The same perspective is usually applied to education and is usually concretized in the outbound internationalization especially among higher education institutions (HEIs). When massive open online courses (MOOCs) and open educational resources (OERs) were initially introduced, there seemed to be no reason why developing countries would have to "reinvent the wheel" and think of developing their own MOOCs and OERs.

The Philippines provides a case study wherein MOOCs and OERs were developed, produced, and offered by a developing country under the framework Open Educational Resources for Development (OERs4D). The framework provided the imperatives and considerations for the development of original OERs and MOOCs within the Philippines. It also fostered the redefinition of MOOCs as practiced and contextualized in the country, the MOOCs as OERs model, and the integration of Universal Design for Learning principles for both MOOCs and OERs. This model addresses the challenge of sustaining the initiative and ensuring that both MOOCs and OERs will be fully utilized. Initial implementation of the OERs4D Framework shows promising results while unraveling key areas in need of improvement and refinements.

Finally, Chapter 22 from Abtar Darshan Singh, Sumayyah Abuhamdieh, and Shriram Raghunathan turn the reader's attention to the Middle East where enormous potential for open education is seemingly matched by difficult, but surmountable, challenges. As revealed in this chapter, there are highly interesting dynamics being played out today in terms of MOOCs in the Middle East. It is important to point out that this is a part of the world with a very young and growing population. The Middle East is also a mix of regions with extremes in technological connectivity ranging from fully modern to scarce availability. In addition, there are refugee camps where traditional education systems cannot work. Add to that, there is a preference for local language content for educational delivery and the need for non-traditional skill-based offerings. Not too surprisingly, then, there is diverse participation in MOOCs offered in the Middle East with proliferating public and private support.

Clearly, the Middle East MOOC landscape has tremendous potential to grow and meet the needs of its population provided that accreditation requirements are met along with common standards across the region. According to the authors, there is also a need for increased governmental involvement and support as well as a need for diverse skill education offerings in Arabic. They also point out that MOOCs in the Middle East also require increased employer involvement. Finally, this chapter highlights the opportunity for focused studies that trace current MOOCs in depth and analyzes the factors that are involved. It ends with vital recommendations for Arab-MOOC (A-MOOC). What becomes clear from their insightful analysis is that governments, business interests, and universities will need to cooperate more seriously if the vision of an Arab-MOOC (A-MOOC) is to be realized.

19
ADVANCING OPEN EDUCATION POLICY IN BRAZILIAN HIGHER EDUCATION

Tel Amiel and Tiago C. Soares

Introduction

Brazil is in a peculiar spot when it comes to the development and implementation of Open Education (OE) policies. The country faces a considerable gap from what could be considered high-level access to educational technology while operating with limited equipment/infrastructure and unequal distribution. In terms of open content, the level of knowledge and awareness related to open education resources (OER) is still limited in Brazil. Moreover, much high-level content is made available by simple translation to Portuguese, and/or is ill adapted to local contexts. On the more positive side, most OER initiatives in Latin America are maintained by governmental funding on municipal, state, or federal levels (Amiel & Soares, 2016).

Such trends are understandable when governmental policies articulate the many dimensions addressed by open education. Governments have the resources to deal with institutional cultures, mapping and adjusting expectations and rewards. Also, it is through the state that technical requirements and blind spots (in terms of devices, cables, bandwidth, software, etc.) may be evaluated and corrected on the scale expected for the wide creation, refinement, and circulation of OER. In addition, such technological infrastructures demand technical training and maintenance; something that governments are able to engage in through concerted efforts and the implementation of bureaucratic and scientific guidelines.

Under such governmental oversight and influence, Brazil has managed to significantly advance its high-level OER policies during the past few years (for a review, see Amiel, Gonsales & Sebriam, 2018). Recent regulation by CAPES (Coordination for the Improvement of Higher Education Personnel, part of the Ministry of Education) in Brazil now demands that anyone receiving funds at the Open University of Brazil (UAB) in the form of scholarships, assistantships, and the like must choose an open license for the products of their work. This mandate was part of a series of actions aimed at promoting openness, and particularly OER, within the UAB. Importantly, the UAB is an initiative by the Brazilian government to further higher education through the networking of over 100 existing public higher education institutions in Brazil (which are, generally, more selective and prestigious than private institutions). Though such institutions stand for a relatively small part of the Brazilian higher education structure (recent data accounts for a total of over 2,400 institutions of higher learning in the country, with about 8 million students [INEP, 2017]), the faculties networked through the UAB system encompass a significant share of the public institutions maintained at the state and federal levels.

In this chapter, we present a study based on data collected from more than 100 public higher education institutions in Brazil, specifically, members of the UAB system. The goal was to understand their current perspectives and practices in relation to OER and open education. The study itself was part of a systematic set of actions that were put in motion in tandem with the policy changes, including the development of an awareness campaign, an online course on OE/OER, the launch of an OER portal, and several other initiatives by CAPES and partners.

It is important to mention that we were directly involved in many of these activities through our work in the Open Education Initiative (IEA) and the UNESCO Chair in Open Education (NIED/Unicamp), which was led by the first author. We present the collected data, and describe its relationship to policy change and future work, together with implications for the development of an OE/OER agenda for the region.

Open University of Brazil

The Open University of Brazil (UAB) was officially created in 2006. Inspired by a number of previous experiences in distance education in Brazil and abroad (Costa, 2007), the primary goal of the UAB was to provide opportunities for higher education in regions not served by traditional institutions. Moreover, it focused on serving in-service teachers in order to provide higher and continuing education to meet the demands of the teaching profession. Brazil had (and continues to have to a smaller degree) many teachers without a higher education diploma, or without a diploma in one's actual area of activity.

Only in 1996, through enactment of an education bill (BRASIL, 1996; known as *Lei de Diretrizes e Bases*) did Brazilian legislators seriously recognize the importance of distance education and begin a movement towards defining how it should function. Early on distance education was seen as potentially making significant contributions towards providing the necessary qualifications and professional development opportunities for in-service teachers. It is important to remember that such goals were taking place in a country with continental dimensions, while operating with a strong concentration of population and educational opportunities in large cities and metropolitan regions.

In order to answer these substantial demands, UAB functions as a consortium that includes over 100 institutions of higher education (HEIs), such as the federal universities, which are responsible for the pedagogical and operational aspects of courses. Local and state offices have the role of providing support to students and an institutional presence, in the form of a local center (buildings know as *polos*) with appropriate connectivity, personnel, and infrastructure to provide face-to-face support, resources, tutoring, access to the Internet, and evaluation of learning. These are established in towns that are usually not served by HEIs. The staff of each *polo* is usually composed of technicians, support and maintenance personnel, and a local coordinator. The federal government, in particular CAPES, is responsible for establishing official regulations as well as funding (including the necessary costs associated with infrastructure and personnel at all levels).

The local and national infrastructures articulated by the system are linked by the SisUAB platform, which is an online database through which the execution and follow-up of processes are managed by local coordinators and government personnel. The system is also served by the EduCapes repository (a website created to permit sharing of open and closed content; see http://educapes.capes.gov.br), which is designed to foster the sharing and circulation of open educational resources developed by the UAB community.

In light of this complex structure, we conducted our study with a subsection of the system. Our focus was on the perspectives and responses of actors involved with the HEIs. We present the study and the findings in the following sections.

Methodology

In order to create a survey for UAB, we analyzed items that had been included in various recent surveys and questionnaires that focused on open educational resources and open education. We also reviewed a selection of recent literature in this area (Allen & Seaman, 2014; Camilleri, Ehlers, & Pawlowski, 2014; Conrad, Mackintosh, McGreal, Murphy, & Witthaus, 2013; De Beer, 2012; De los Arcos et al., 2014; Hoosen, 2012; Hylén et al., 2012; Inamorato dos Santos, 2013; Mishra & Kanwar, 2015; McGreal, Conrad, Murphy, Witthaus, & Mackintosh, 2014; Orr, Rimini, & Van Damme, 2015; Punie, Inamorato dos Santos, Mitic, & Morais, 2016; Santos-Hermosa, 2014; UNESCO, 2015; Venturini, 2014). Based on this review, we created a table to identify questions and indicators that were present in multiple surveys as well as those that were unique and particularly relevant to our research needs. Based on this analysis, we created a framework for our survey that included the following three key sections:

1. **Educational resources**: perceptions related to access, sharing, remix of educational resources (not focusing on OER);
2. **Open practices and resources**: perceptions, expectations, and critical evaluation of knowledge of OER, open practices, and associated fields;
3. **Institutional aspects**: perceptions and evaluation of the relationship between openness and institutional demands, needs, and outlook.

The questionnaire was sent to persons involved with the Open University of Brazil (i.e., professors, researchers, and technical staff), who were contacted directly by the Ministry of Education (CAPES) based on their registry. A total of 2,660 valid responses were computed, representing 103 public higher education institutions from all regions of Brazil. In this chapter, we focus on the third element, institutional aspects, which offers a wide-angle view of current practices and challenges for open policy in Brazilian higher education.

Findings

We asked participants questions about their engagement with Open Access (OA), since it has a longer history as a movement, and it is often considered a precursor or contributor to the open educational resources movement. When asked whether they had published an article in an open access journal during the preceding five years, 59.5% responded positively. Considering that many pressures exist for publishing in closed journals (usually measured by journal-level, traditional impact factors), the high exposure to OA journals was a positive finding.

When asked about policy, only 18.2% stated that their institutions had an OA policy, 16.1% did not have an OA policy and 71% responses were "don't know". When asked about OER, the scenario was similar: 12.3% acknowledged that their institution had an OER policy, 21.3% responded no, and again the majority (59.9%) stated that they didn't know.

Since this response had greater pertinence to our study, we conducted a review of previous studies and concluded that the reported number was optimistic. Respondents who pointed out the existence of OER policies were invited to indicate a site we could visit and investigate further. We received 134 responses. Of these, 72 were identified as valid after screening them; 14 promising OER-related policies were identified. A reading of each of these policies resulted in only two institutional policies that addressed OER specifically (Federal University of Paraná – UFPR and Fundação Oswaldo Cruz—FIOCRUZ). The analysis indicated a large number of links that led to institutional open access (OA) websites (e.g., student theses/dissertations), and sometimes to the site of the institutional library.

This analysis indicates that there is some difficulty in understanding the specific domain of OER among the academic community in Brazil. In fact, much of what is considered an example of "open" is simply something made available "online" by Brazilian and other institutions of higher learning. When asked whether *a policy should exist* regarding OA and OER, the response was overwhelmingly positive on a scale of 1 (low) to 5 (high). In fact, 88% of respondents were in favor of establishing an OER policy, while 89% were in favor of enacting such a policy for OA. Additionally, 80% considered it important to have an open source software policy. While there may be misunderstandings related to exactly what qualifies as OER or OA, there is strong support for institutional open policies in general.

When queried about current initiatives in their HEIs aimed at encouraging creation and use of OER, respondent data indicated that the following:

- 39.1% of respondents indicated the existence of training and awareness-raising;
- 31.9% indicated support in the form of human resources (e.g., assistantships);
- Nearly 20% indicated financial support (e.g., calls for production of open resources, or requiring open publication);
- 19.2% indicated formal incentives (e.g., points for career progression);
- Around 15% mentioned informal incentives (e.g., recognition, awards).

Though the first two numbers might seem substantial, we read them in light of a broad view of what support means, and a wide interpretation of OER and openness. In any case, there still seems to be a large margin for growth in terms of encouraging OER development at HEIs in Brazil.

Training and awareness seem to be particularly important, especially in light of a number of other findings: though nearly 50% of the respondents said they would be comfortable explaining OER and associated practices to a colleague, the number drops substantially (28%) when asked if they would be comfortable helping someone choose a CC license.

There seems to be an extensive demand for support. When asked if they were in favor of CAPES taking the lead on a series of OER-related activities, the answers were all in favor of such leadership (Figure 19.1). Not surprisingly, financing of collaborative production of OER

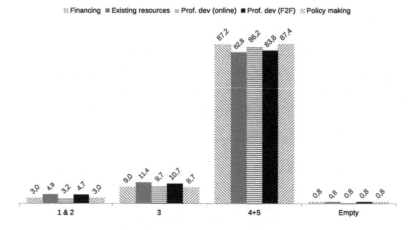

FIGURE 19.1 Support for CAPES

among multiple institutions was viewed favorably by 87.2%, as was providing financing with a clause incentivizing the reuse/remix of existing UAB resources—viewed favorably by nearly 83% of the study participants. Professional development for the production, dissemination, and reuse of educational resources was also positively viewed by 86.2% (online versions of courses) and 83.8% (face-to-face). Finally, nearly 87.4% were in favor of CAPES assisting their institutions in building OER-related policies.

Discussion

Some scholars argue that the development of open education policies in Latin America is still in the "early stages" (Yang & Kinshuk, 2017). Based on our findings, we further note that the development of policies around OE and OER, specifically, have been rather slow in most countries, states, municipalities, and even institutions. There have been many exceptions and substantial advances in some countries around the world, but extensive policy development and practices is by no means the standard even in richer nations (COL, 2017). Examples of advanced work on OER policy include the country of Fiji, a comprehensive national strategy in Slovenia, and various state-level policies in the United States.

The UAB policy is part of a suite of recent policy changes in Brazil that affect the way educational resources are purchased or licensed in many governmental programs using public funds, effectively making Brazil one of these exceptions (for a review of these policies, see Amiel et al., 2018).

The results from this initial analysis of survey data indicate that, even though advances have been reached, the practices that foment openness in higher education in Brazil are still limited. The findings also reveal that there is high demand for both training and awareness around the topic of open education and OER. As a result, it is not too surprising that there seems to be substantial awareness of the need for policies aimed at promoting open education at the institutional level in Brazil.

The build-up and integration of OER demands a very concrete, and, at times, potentially contradictory articulation of action and infrastructure development. The challenge goes beyond the implementation of top-down policies. Even though the OE community goes to great lengths to establish common ground, tensions and grey zones remain. And even if a certain common ground (such as CC licenses) may serve as an interface between different institutional players, the time demanded for the development and crystallization of open practices and policies follows the (unpredictable) time demanded by the negotiation and accommodation of institutional cultures, tools, and techniques.

In this brief chapter we presented the UAB as perhaps the most significant example of systemic actions to promote OE in Brazil. The subset of data presented here indicate a significant level of engagement with openness, particularly in OA, but an important margin for better understanding OER (repositories, licenses, and the like). Positively, there is clear demand for the definition of policies for openness at HEIs, and interest in receiving support from the government to advance open practices at the institutional level. These data have helped support policies and decisions by CAPES (courses, awareness-raising, financial support for the remix of existing resources), as it aims to promote openness in the UAB. We hope that the pioneering work done by UAB in navigating the bumpy and sometimes complex terrain of promoting openness can help others reflect about the potentials for openness in their organizations, institutions, and systems in Brazil.

Tel Amiel completed his PhD in Instructional Technology at the University of Georgia. He currently is Professor at the School of Education at the University of Brasília where he coordinates the UNESCO Chair in Distance Education. He was previously Coordinator of the UNESCO Chair in Open Education (Unicamp). He has also been a visiting fellow at the University of Wollongong as well as Stanford University, and a visiting professor at Utah State University. His interests are in the areas of open education and educational technology, with particular focus on schooling and teacher professional development.

Tiago C. Soares is currently finishing his PhD in Economic History at the University of Sao Paulo. He is conducting research with the UNESCO Chair in Distance Education (University of Brasilia) and the Latin American Network of Surveillance, Technology and Society Studies (Lavits). A longtime activist in Brazil, his research follows historical and contemporary developments between political economy, technology, and society. Previously, he carried out projects with institutions such as the UNESCO Chair in Open Education (Unicamp), Open Knowledge Foundation Brazil, and the World Social Forum. As a writer, his work has been published by Le Monde Diplomatique (Brazil) and Vice Media, among others.

References

Allen, I. E., & Seaman, J. (2014). *Opening the curriculum: Open educational resources in US higher education*. Babson Survey Research Group. Retrieved from www.onlinelearningsurvey.com/reports/openingthecurriculum2014.pdf

Amiel, T., Gonsales, P., & Sebriam, D. (2018). Recursos Educacionais Abertos no Brasil: 10 anos de ativismo. *EmRede*, 5(2), 246–258. Retrieved from www.aunirede.org.br/revista/index.php/emrede/article/view/346

Amiel, T., & Soares, T. C. (2016). Identifying tensions in the use of open licenses in OER repositories. *The International Review of Research in Open and Distributed Learning*, 17(3). Retrieved from www.irrodl.org/index.php/irrodl/article/view/2426/3688

BRASIL. (1996). *Lei de diretrizes e bases*. Retreived from www.planalto.gov.br/ccivil_03/LEIS/L9394.htm

Camilleri, A. F., Ehlers, U. D., & Pawlowski, J. (2014). *State of the art review of quality issues related to open educational resources (OER)*. Luxembourg: Publications Office of the European Union 2014 – (JRC Scientific and Policy Reports).

COL. (2017). *Open educational resources: Global report*. Retrieved from http://oasis.col.org/handle/11599/2788

Conrad, D., Mackintosh, W., McGreal, R., Murphy, A., & Witthaus, G. (2013). *Report on the assessment and accreditation of learners using OER*. Unesco/Commonwealth of Learning. Retrieved from http://oasis.col.org/handle/11599/232

Costa, C. J. Da. (2007). Modelos de educação superior a distância e implementação da Universidade Aberta do Brasil. *Revista Brasileira de Informática Na Educação*, 15(2), 9–16.

De Beer, T. (2012). *SCORE library survey report*. The Open University. Retrieved from www.open.ac.uk/score/files/score/file/Library%20Survey%20Report%20final%2014022012.pdf

De Los Arcos, B., Farrow, R., Perryman, L. A., Pitt, R., & Weller, M. (2014). OER evidence report 2013–2014. *OER Research HUB*. Retrieved from https://oerresearchhub.files.wordpress.com/2014/11/oerrh-evidence-report-2014.pdf

Hoosen, S. (2012). *Survey on governments' open educational resources (OER) policies*. Unesco/Commonwealth of Learning. Retrieved from www.unesco.org/new/fileadmin/MULTIMEDIA/HQ/CI/CI/pdf/themes/Survey_On_Government_OER_Policies.pdf

Hylén, J., et al. (2012). *Open educational resources: Analysis of responses to the OECD country questionnaire*. OECD Education Working Papers, No. 76, OECD Publishing. http://dx.doi.org/10.1787/5k990rjhvtlv-en

INEP. (2017). *MEC e Inep divulgam dados do Censo da Educação Superior 2016*. Retrieved from http://portal.inep.gov.br/artigo/-/asset_publisher/B4AQV9zFY7Bv/content/mec-e-inep-divulgam-dados-do-censo-da-educacao-superior-2016/21206

McGreal, R., Conrad, D., Murphy, A., Witthaus, G., & Mackintosh, W. (2014). Formalising informal learning: Assessment and accreditation challenges within disaggregated systems. *Open Praxis*, 6(2). Retrieved from http://openpraxis.org/index.php/OpenPraxis/article/view/114

Orr, D., Rimini, M., & Van Damme, D. (2015). Open educational resources: A catalyst for innovation. *Educational Research and Innovation*. Paris: OECD. Retrieved from http://dx.doi.org/10.1787/9789264247543-en

Mishra, S., & Kanwar, S. (2015). Quality assurance for open educational resources: What's the difference? In C. J. Bonk, M. M. Lee, T. C. Reeves, & T. H. Reynolds (Eds.), *MOOCs and open education around the world* (pp. 119–129). New York: Routledge. Retrieved from http://oasis.col.org/handle/11599/881

Inamorato dos Santos, A. (2013). *Recursos Educacionais Abertos no Brasil: o estado da arte, desafios e perspectivas para o desenvolvimento e inovação*. São Paulo: Comitê Gestor da Internet no Brasil. Retrieved from http://unesdoc.unesco.org/images/0022/002279/227970por.pdf

Punie, Y., Inamorato dos Santos, A., Mitic, M., & Morais, R. (2016). *How are higher education institutions dealing with openness? A survey of practices, beliefs and strategies in five European countries*. Institute for Prospective Technological Studies. JRC Science for Policy Report. doi:10.2791/709253. Retrieved from http://publications.jrc.ec.europa.eu/repository/bitstream/JRC99959/reqno_jrc99959.pdf

Santos-Hermosa, G. (2014). ORIOLE, in the search for evidence of OER in teaching: Experiences in the use, re-use and the sharing and influence of repositories. *Qualitative Research in Education*, 3(1), 232–268. doi:10.4771/qre.2014.46. Retrieved from http://dx.doi.org/10.4471/qre.2014.46

UNESCO. (2015). *Diretrizes para Recursos educacionais abertos (REA) no Ensino Superior*. Paris. Retrieved from http://unesdoc.unesco.org/images/0023/002328/232852por.pdf

Venturini, J. (2014). *Recursos educacionais abertos no Brasil: o campo, os recursos e sua apropriação em sala de aula* (vol. 11). São Paulo: Ação Educativa. Retrieved from www.cest.poli.usp.br/wp-content/uploads/sites/26/2014/05/Jamila-REA-Apresenta%C3%A7%C3%A3o-USP.pdf

Yang, J., & Kinshuk. (2017). Survey and reflection of open education policies. In M. Jemni, Kinshuk, & M. K. Khribi (Eds.), *Open education: From OERs to MOOCs* (pp. 23–37). Berlin: Springer.

20

GLOBAL TRENDS AND POLICY STRATEGIES AND THEIR IMPLICATIONS FOR THE SUSTAINABLE DEVELOPMENT OF MOOCs IN MALAYSIA

Purushothaman Ravichandran

The much-anticipated Malaysian Education Blueprint for Higher Education (2015–2025), released by the Malaysian Ministry of Education (MOE) in April 2015, targeted 15% of all courses offered by public universities in Malaysia to be delivered via an online platform (specifically Massive Open Online Courses or MOOCs) by the end of 2015. This aim by the government to teach 15% of all Malaysian public university courses online as MOOCs by the end of 2015 was part of the strategy to eventually reach 30% of all university courses by the year 2020 (Jacqueline, 2017, p. 9). However, given issues related to MOOC retention and completion rates, the benefits of online learning, especially in the context of MOOCs, pose huge challenges for higher education (HE) (Ho, Chuang, Mitros, & Pritchard, 2015; Koller, Ng, Do, & Chen, 2013). This low percentage of students' completion was not good news for the MOE, whose intention was and is to leverage MOOCs as a means to take advantage of the technology to improve quality and widen access to education (MOE, 2014). Thus, there seems to be a need to analyse policies and programs to determine "what works" best with the particular focus on MOOCs offered for credit, based on the global trends, strategic policies, and implications for a sustainable development of MOOCs in Malaysia.

Global Trends and Strategies for Sustainable Development of MOOCS in Malaysia

According to Global E-Learning Market Analysis and Trends (2017), the global eLearning market is poised to grow at a compound annual growth rate (CAGR) of around 7% over the next decade to reach approximately $331 billion by 2025. However, it is not entirely clear how the MOOC approach to online education can be fiscally sustained. Some common approaches to generate revenue are used by Coursera and other start-ups working in partnership with higher education institutions (HEI), such as charging students a fee for certificates of participation, certificates of completion, or transcripts indicating the timing of enrolment and performance. Revenue can also be generated by selling premium services such as recruiting tools that link employers with students who have shown ability in a given area; or by obtaining philanthropic donations from individuals and companies (Alumu & Thiagarajan, 2016).

However, it is a significant challenge for partner universities to generate income in such ways to sustain and perhaps elevate the use of MOOCs. In established business models universities have control of the customer value proposition in that they control and regulate any recognition of learning and set tuition fees. For MOOCs, most participating institutions have decided that they will not offer credits as part of traditional awards for these courses, probably as a result of concerns about the quality of the courses and the downside risks posed to their branding. At the same time, it would also be against the initial ideals of MOOCs if universities started to charge tuition fees for their courses. Therefore, at present, many institutions participating in MOOCs consider the courses that they offer to be a branding and marketing activity to sustain the market (Alumu & Thiagarajan, 2016).

In Malaysia, the MOE has allowed Credit Transfer for MOOCs via Accreditation of Prior Experiential Learning Credit (APEL-C) guidelines, which grant individuals with work experiences and who complete various short courses to be entitled to credit transfers taken in the respective academic programmes offered in higher education institutions. Such practices can effectively decrease the duration of studies compared to regular studies. APEL (C) encompasses assessment on prior learning experiences (non-formal and informal) for the purpose of awarding credits, including learning through MOOCs and other self-learning methods in the Malaysian Qualifications Framework (MQF). Although this may sound like an indirect strategy enforced by the Ministry for a sustainable development of MOOCs among the private universities, when this study began in 2018, there was only a low percentage of universities and colleges that had sought APEL (C) centre recognition. These results are not positive news for the sustainability of MOOCs at Malaysian universities.

MOOCs Strategies and Policies in Malaysia

As of January 2015, Malaysia MOOCs had an enrolment of about 55,000 learners where approximately 54,000 were university students, while the remaining were not associated with any higher educational institution. In terms of specific MOOCs, around 22,000 learners were enrolled in the Asia and Islamic Civilisation MOOC, around 17,000 were using the xMOOC format for the Ethnic Relations course, and over 10,000 were in the Introduction to Entrepreneurship MOOC. The remaining 5,600 were in the ICT Competency MOOC. In general, research shows that the application of MOOCs is accepted by lecturers and students of HEIs as an effective means of communication (Norazah, Amin, & Helmi, 2015). However, as of November 2017, there are a total of 226 MOOCs and almost 250,000 users enrolled in Malaysia MOOCs. OpenLearning is the learning platform chosen for implementation of Malaysia MOOCs and the courses can be found at https:// www.openlearning.com/malaysiaMOOCs.

This data needs to be viewed in the context of a statement made by Second Education Minister Datuk Seri Idris Jusoh, who declared Malaysia as the first country in the world to implement MOOCs in all public universities in September 2014. He also mentioned that Malaysia is also currently the only country where MOOCs are implemented at a national scale through the government; the United States, the UK, Australia, Japan, or Korea, which have been leaders in the MOOC space, cannot make such a claim. Such an announcement can give the people of Malaysia a source of national pride when it comes to the education of its citizenry. This announcement was made in relation to the September 2014 launch of four pilot MOOCs by four public universities (Fadzil et al., 2015):

- Islamic and Asian Civilisations (UPM);
- Ethnic Relations (Universiti Kebangsaan Malaysia [UKM]);
- Entrepreneurship (Universiti Teknologi Mara [UiTM]); and
- ICT Competence (Universiti Malaysia Sarawak [UNIMAS]).

The four institutions listed have been tasked by the MOE in Malaysia to coordinate and develop the official portal for MOOCs by public universities (known collectively as Malaysia MOOCs). All course instructors teaching the four courses previously mentioned were recommended to utilise MOOCs as learning content in a blended learning mode, according to course instructors in their respective universities (Ministry of Education Malaysia, 2015). OpenLearning was the learning platform chosen for the implementation of the Malaysia MOOCs. These courses can be found at www.openlearning.com/malaysiamoocs. Even private universities, such as University College Fairview (UCF), which started its operation in 2017, began to use OpenLearning for Continuous Professional Development (CPD) for their teachers using MOOCs.

Further, all MOOCs by Taylor's University, UPM, UKM, UiTM, and UNIMAS are offered via OpenLearning, a MOOC platform based in Sydney, Australia. Unlike the five other institutions offering MOOCs, OUM has collaborated with Apple to offer MOOCs via iTunes U, available for iPad and iPhone users. OUM considers MOOCs as a platform for institutional promotion and branding as well as part of the university's continuing efforts towards widening access through open distance learning. As of 2017, MOOCs were adopted in numerous educational institutions in Malaysia. Malaysian institutions are adopting MOOCs in the higher education landscape due to the large and rapidly growing number of schools. During the past several years, institutions of various sizes as well as structures have been rushing to integrate MOOCs into their curriculum. In many instances, the courses available as MOOCs are similar to existing undergraduate courses offered live at elite, prestigious universities across Malaysia. Twenty-eight higher education institutions are involved in MOOCs development in Malaysia (Umniya, 2017).

Added to the previously mentioned online learning approaches followed in MOOCs, there are several benefits perceived for online approaches. According to Fadzil et al. (2015), MOOCs as an online learning approach can offer the following benefits for Malaysia:

- An interactive and engaging delivery that encourages high-degree collaboration and international interactions;
- Global visibility of and access to Malaysian expertise in niche areas (e.g., Islamic Finance and Tropical Diseases); and
- An opportunity for Malaysian higher education institutions to showcase their best programmes and research areas.

Ideally, online learning approaches can provide better benefits for quality education to all students via MOOCs and eventually contribute towards bringing meaningful differences among their lives as they journey from university to careers. In order to bring these meaningful differences, the Malaysia Education Blueprint (Higher Education) (2013–2025) outlines 10 key shifts that will spur continued excellence in the higher education system. All 10 shifts address key performance issues in the system, particularly with regard to quality and efficiency, as well as global trends that are disrupting the higher education landscape. Specifically, these shifts relate to: (1) holistic, entrepreneurial, and balance graduates; (2) talent excellence; (3) nation of lifelong learning; (4) quality TVET graduates; (5) financial sustainability; (6) empowered governance; (7) innovation ecosystem; (8) global prominence; (9) globalised online learning; and (10) transformed higher education delivery. The ninth shift relates to the Global Online Learning (GOL) initiative of the MOE (Ministry of Education, 2015). In realising the GOL initiative and as part of the long-term plan for Malaysia online learning, the Malaysian MOE has developed a National e-Learning Policy, which is revised every three to five years. It involves three phases of implementation: (1) year 2015 to 2016; (2) year 2017 to 2019; and (3) year 2020 to 2025. The plan involves six domains, which are the Infrastructure and Infostructure, Governance, Pedagogy Online, e-content, Professional Development, and Enculturation.

Shift nine lists seven key initiatives (strategies) related to MOOCs development in Malaysia:

1. Infrastructure: Establish dedicated independent infrastructure network for Malaysian higher education and any technology necessary for delivering globalised online learning;
2. Awareness: Launch MOOCs in subjects of distinctiveness for Malaysia, targeting 50% international enrolment, and promoting MOOCs initiatives to the Malaysian public;
3. Capacity building: Improve training programmes for academic and support staff to enable effective utilisation of the best pedagogical models;
4. Governance: Promote online programme development by establishing a national platform, shared services, and the coordination of MOOC development while building the necessary partnerships;
5. Policy: Provide an implementation framework for successful deployment of globalised online learning based on international best practices; establish online learning as an integral component of higher education, with 70% of courses using blended learning by 2025;
6. Credit transfer: Establish mechanisms to allow credit transfer of courses completed by students via MOOCs and other online learning platforms; and
7. Lifelong learning: Develop a common platform to enhance the utilisation of MOOCs for lifelong learning.

In addition to the identification of these seven initiatives, student engagement is considered a necessary prerequisite for effective e-learning (Guo, Kim, & Rubin, 2014). In the context of MOOCs, the challenge of engaging students is made much more difficult due to a large and diverse student body. There are, of course, students who find a MOOC engaging or satisfying due to their personal interest or curiosity in the topic or subject, or if they see extrinsic value in terms of gaining a MOOC certificate or knowledge and skills for potential work advancement (Agarwal, 2012; Allon, 2012; Breslow et al., 2013).

Today there are millions of individuals who are simply curious about some learning content and find themselves obsessed with MOOCs. For them, participation in MOOC-related activities such as viewing video lectures is similar to a hobby or a way to spend their open moments of the day (Young, 2013). In effect, most MOOC participants believe that openness of platforms and free courses encourage people to learn through such platforms (Hakami, White, & Chakaveh, 2017). If platforms were not free, the number of learners would surely decrease precipitously. However, while free education encourages enrolment, there is an associated decrease in the commitment of learners to complete such free and open courses (Hakami et al., 2017; Shrader, Wu, & Owens-Nicholson, 2016). In addition, free courses may convey negative impressions for some people who might conclude that they are not of sufficient quality, and hence, are less valuable (Hakami et al., 2017). Given the various reasons to learn from MOOCs, whether intrinsic or extrinsic, there needs to be a clear understanding of how the government strategies and polices influence institutional policies of MOOCs usage for a sustainable development of MOOCs.

Strategic Opportunities and Trends in MOOC Usage

Taking a strategic direction implies the need to develop corresponding capabilities as determined by the outcome desired. At an operational level, this can be captured in the components of a business model. Strategically, the significant question for HEIs is the extent to which they should rely on external partners and suppliers to provide elements of the business model—elements that they are not equipped to do or interested in undertaking. This could feasibly result in some form of disaggregation or unbundling of the learning delivery model. Or, they could decide to internally develop such capabilities and deliver the full-business plan without external support or reliance on outside partners (Yuan et al., 2014). Such decisions are never easy or straightforward.

Perhaps most importantly, there is also a need for effective pedagogical principles in trying to address learning in MOOCs. As stated by Anderson, Collier, and Horii (2013), one needs to consider general design principles of good pedagogy, the barriers and constraints posed by online learning in general, and the specific challenges of MOOCs, which include the large number and diversity of students' cultures, languages, ages, experiences, educational backgrounds, and motivations for participating.

Pedagogical Approaches and Pedagogical Appropriateness for Sustainability of MOOCs

Malaysia higher education institutions need to identify more such sustainable elements of MOOCs based on solid pedagogical approaches by conducting effective research within their respective universities. For instance, they might study student acceptance of and engagement with MOOCs. They might also explore differences in pedagogical approaches and course activities of MOOC instructors in different disciplines as well as changes in pedagogical approaches over iterations of the same MOOC or across several MOOCs designed by a common instructor or instructional design team. Such researches might also explore the manner in which MOOCs might be better personalised (Bonk et al., 2018) and adapted to those from varying cultures and backgrounds. Researchers can also evaluate adopting some of approaches used outside of Malaysia (cf. Conole, 2015; Mayes & De Freitas, 2004). Such research could be based on the five different types of MOOCs discussed in Conole (2015).

MOOC #1: Associative: In this type of MOOC, the focus is on the individual. It is about associating a stimulus with a response or in other words operant conditioning. Examples of ways in which technologies can facilitate associated pedagogies include drill and practice and e-assessment. An example of an associative MOOC is a course on Chinese language learning provided by the Open University UK. That particular MOOC is based around a series of podcasts and interactive assessment elements to test participant's knowledge and understanding.

MOOC #2: Cognitive: In a cognitive MOOC, the emphasis is on learner reflection and linking what they know to prior knowledge. Resources are provided to reduce working memory limitations and bottlenecks. As part of this process, learners experience various stimuli and are encouraged to reflect on their learning. An example of a cognitivist MOOC is a Coursera's course on song writing. The MOOC starts from the learner's current level of experience and attempts to build on it.

MOOC #3: Constructivist: As might be expected, in a constructivist MOOC, a key goal is to build on prior knowledge; in effect, activities in the MOOC should apply meaning to and build on what the learner already knows. This type of MOOC is more active and task-orientated. Examples of ways in which technologies can facilitate constructivist pedagogies include problem-based learning (PBL) and other inquiry-based forms of learning. An example of a constructivist MOOC is a course on learning design run by the Open University in the UK. The course begins by examining participants' existing level of knowledge of teaching and design and builds on such prior knowledge as the course progresses.

MOOC #4: Situative: In a situative MOOC, the focus is on learning in a context and through dialogue. Examples of how situative pedagogies can be facilitated include learning through virtual worlds. An example of a situative MOOC is a Coursera course on clinical neurology. This particular course is an applied, contextual course intended to provide continuing professional development to professionals working in the field.

MOOC #5: Connectivist: As the name implies, a connectivity MOOC will be apparent when there is an emphasis on learning in a networked context, through a distributed community of peers. Learners create their own personal learning environment and repertoire of digital tools. Such an approach encourages reflective, personalised learning. An example of a connectivist MOOC is the Connectivism and Connective Knowledge course from George Siemens and Stephen Downes (Downes, 2012, May).

In spite of the various pedagogical approaches being available for MOOCs (Zhu, Bonk, & Sari, 2018), these designs are still not extensively employed in Malaysia (Sari, Bonk, & Zhu, 2018). Part of the problem is that teachers lack the necessary digital literacies (Jenkins, 2006, 2009) to make effective use of technologies in their teaching. What is needed is a clear learning design for MOOC teachers to make pedagogically informed decisions that result in more appropriate uses of MOOCs. The hope is for MOOC learning designs that are sustainable and reusable by new generations of adult learners. In the Malaysian context, even though many universities have contributed towards MOOC research, still there is no concrete evidence of the acceptance of MOOCs and MOOC-like derivatives among adult learners at universities in Malaysia. Therefore, there is a need to investigate the factors for sustainable growth of MOOCs in the Malaysia context and beyond.

Use of Strategic Business Models for Sustainable Development of MOOCs

Higher education has remained relatively stable for many years, comprising teaching services and research activities in different proportions depending on the characteristics of any particular institution. However, the financial model that supports teaching has changed significantly in recent times in countries like England and Australia, as state funding has been largely withdrawn and replaced by student fees backed by state loans. The opportunity and challenge presented by MOOCs is how to develop a viable business model that includes open online learning that is attractive to students and fits the characteristics and needs of a particular institution or program (Yuan, Powell, & Olivier, 2014).

Figure 20.1, Framework for Assessing and Designing New Business Models, represents a starting point for identifying an appropriate strategy for the development of MOOCs. Reading from the left, three external strategic challenges and opportunities are followed by an organisational response that in turn produces an appropriate business model. For some, such a model could foster an institution to review how it interprets its mission, purpose, and values, especially if a new strategic direction is proposed. Even where the strategy fits well within existing institutional policies and practices, it is still likely that there will be significant implications for developing a new business model (Yuan, Powell, & Olivier, 2014). Thus, the experience of the sector is that for successful online provision to grow, substantial investment is required to develop new capabilities. Alternatively, the institution could build new external partnerships to bridge any internal capability gaps in technology, institutional processes, and working practices. Given the uniqueness of MOOCs and MOOC-like derivatives, there must also be some attention paid to the development and teaching of new types of courses that MOOCs allow.

Publication of MOOCs

Strategic challenges and opportunities	Organisational Response	Business Model
* Internationalisation * Increased, world-wide demand * Technological developments * Learner affordability * Competition from new public & private providers * Reduced central government funding	Mission, purpose, and values ↓ Informs Strategic directions ↓ Determines Capability building	Customer Value Proposition Revenue Streams: * Customer relationships * Customer segments * Delivery channels Cost structure: * Key resources * Key activities * Key partnerships

FIGURE 20.1 Framework for Assessing and Designing New Business Models

Conclusion

While there is still much debate surrounding the pros and cons of MOOCs, sustainable development of MOOCs in Malaysia requires a fundamental re-thinking in the context of developing a wider strategy for MOOCs. This chapter attempts to provide an insight into global trends, policy goals, and strategies that are essential for a sustainable development of MOOCs in the context of Malaysian universities.

High intention to continued usage of eLearning can lead to lower dropout rates, higher persistence, and greater commitment to the program (Wu & Chen, 2016). Considering these potential benefits, it is important to examine how to retain MOOC learners by proving appropriate pedagogical approaches and benefits from APEL (C) credit transfers towards experiential learning. At the same time, for a sustainable growth of MOOCs, a substantial investment is required to develop new capabilities, such as addressing any internal capability gaps in technology as well as developing new external partnerships to bridge internal capability gaps. Further, higher educational institutions in Malaysia should have institutional-based business models to bring MOOCs into their regular system not only for the compulsory courses which are under the Ministry's Malaysian Studies Course, but also for other regular courses.

In order to achieve such goals, there needs to be sufficient support from MOOC practitioners, policy makers, and associated MOOC content developers to provide flexible learning opportunities for MOOC participants within Malaysia and beyond for sustainability. This flexibility of learning opportunities in turn may get amplified when institutionally based action plans are initiated to develop additional MOOCs that not only support MOE policies in Malaysia to achieve its goal in 2020 but that do so in a way to attract and sustain Malaysian MOOCs learners and developers for lifelong learning by reskilling and upskilling on demand and just in time. Such are my hopes and dreams for the sustainable development of MOOCs in Malaysia as well as emerging economies spanning the globe.

Purushothaman Ravichandran is currently Acting Dean at the University College Fairview, Malaysia. His work experiences include teaching a wide spectrum of students ranging from pre-university to the PhD level for the past 30 years. He has a PhD in Education with a specialisation of Pedagogical Leadership and has completed his second PhD in Information Technology with a specialisation in student modelling for Intelligent Tutoring System (ITS). He had taken several roles in the field of education as an author, researcher, keynote speaker, teacher trainer, curriculum designer, module writer, and external examiner for PhD students.

References

Agarwal, A. (2012). Circuits and electronics: MITx. *Chronicle of Higher Education, 59*(6), B10.

Allon, G. (2012). Operations management: Udemy. *Chronicle of Higher Education, 59*(6), B10–B11.

Alumu, S., & Thiagarajan, P. (2016). Massive open online courses and e-learning in higher education. *Indian Journal of Science and Technology, 9*(6), 10. doi:10.17485/ijst/2016/v9i6/81170

Anderson, S., Collier, A., & Horii, C. V. (2013, April). *Designing and implementing MOOCs to maximize student learning*. Online presentation delivered as part of the EDUCAUSE Learning Initiative Spring Focus Session. Presentation slides, recording, and transcripts. Retrieved from www.educause.edu/eli/events/eli-online-spring-focus-session/2013/2013/designing-andimplementing-moocs-maximize-student-learning

Bonk, C. J., Zhu, M., Kim, M., Xu, S., Sabir, N., & Sari, A. (2018, September). Pushing toward a more personalized MOOC: Exploring instructor selected activities, resources, and technologies for MOOC design and implementation. *The International Review of Research on Open and Distributed Learning, 19*(4), 92–115. Retrieved from www.irrodl.org/index.php/irrodl/article/view/3439/4726

Breslow, L., Pritchard, D. E., DeBoer, J., Stump, G. S., Ho, A. D., & Seaton, D. T. (2013). Studying learning in the worldwide classroom. *Research into edX's First MOOC: Research & Practice in Assessment, 8*, 13–25.

Conole, G. (2015). Designing effective MOOCs. *Educational Media International, 52*(4), 239–252. Retrieved from https://doi.org/10.1080/09523987.2015.1125989

Downes, S. (2012, May). *Connectivism and connected knowledge: Essays on meaning and learning networks*. Retrieved from www.downes.ca/files/Connective_Knowledge-19May2012.pdf

Fadzil, M., Latif, L. A., & Azzman, T. A. M. T. M. (2015). MOOCs in Malaysia: A preliminary case study. *E-ASEM Forum: Renewing the Lifelong Learning Agenda for the Future*, 1–17.

Global E-Learning Market Analysis and Trends. (2017). *Global e-learning market research report and forecast to 2017–2022*. Retrieved from www.reuters.com/brandfeatures/venture-capital/article?id=11353

Guo, P., Kim, J., & Rubin, R. (2014). *How video production affects student engagement: An empirical study of MOOC videos*. Proceedings of the first ACM conference on learning @ scale conference (pp. 41–50). ACM, New York.

Hakami, N., White, S., & Chakaveh, S. (2017). *Identifying the motivational factors that influence learners' intention to continue use Arabic MOOCs*. Proceedings of 81st The International Conference (pp. 5–13). Edinburgh, UK.

Ho, A. D, Chuang, I., Mitros, P., & Pritchard, D. E. (2015). Who does what in a massive open online course? *Communication of the ACM, 54*(7).

Jacqueline, K. (2017). *Current state of massive open online courses in Malaysia*. Retrieved from www.opengovasia.com/current-state-of-massive-open-online-courses-in-malaysia/

Jenkins, H. (2006). *Convergence culture: Where old and new media collide*. New York: New York University Press.

Jenkins, H. (2009). *Confronting the challenges of participatory culture: Media education for the 21st century*. Cambridge, MA: MIT Press.

Koller, D., Ng, A., Do, A., & Chen, Z. (2013). Retention and intention in massive open online courses. *EDUCAUSE Review, 48*(3), 62–63. Retrieved from https://er.educause.edu/~/media/files/article-downloads/erm1337.pdf

Mayes, T., & de Freitas, S. (2004). *Review of e-learning theories, frameworks and models* (p. 43). London: Joint Information Systems Committee. Retrieved from https://curve.coventry.ac.uk/open/file/8ff033fc-e97d-4cb8-aed3-29be7915e6b0/1/Review%20of%20e-learning%20theories.pdf

Ministry of Education Malaysia. (2014). *Malaysian Education Blueprint on Higher Education [Discussion Document] – Shift 10: Globalised Online Learning*. Retrieved January 29, 2015, from http://moe.gov.my/cms/upload_files/files/Chapter%2010-Globalised%20Online%20Learning%20FINAL%20EN_2.pdf

Ministry of Education Malaysia. (2015). *Malaysia education blueprint 2015–2025 (Higher Education)*. Retrieved from https://www.um.edu.my/docs/default-source/about-um_document/media-centre/um-magazine/4-executive-summary-pppm-2015-2025.pdf?sfvrsn=4

Norazah, M. N., Amin, E. M., & Helmi, N. (2015, December). Malaysia MOOCs: The way forward. *MOOCs and Educational Challenges Around Asia and Europe*, 87–102.

Sari, A., Bonk, C. J., & Zhu, M. (2018, October 25). *The design challenges of MOOCs: A case study of Indonesian and Malaysian MOOCs*. Paper presented at the 2018 Association for Educational Communications and Technology (AECT) Annual Meeting, Kansas, MO.

Shrader, S., Wu, M., & Owens-Nicholson, D. A. K. (2016). Massive Open Online Courses (MOOCs): Participant activity, demographics, and satisfaction. *Online Learning, 20*(2).

Wu, B., & Chen, X. (2016). Continuance intention to use MOOCs: Integrating the technology acceptance model (TAM) and task technology fit (TTF) model. *Computers in Human Behavior, 67*. doi:10.1016/j.chb.2016.10.028.

Young, J. R. (2013). What professors can learn from "hard core" MOOC students. *Chronicle of Higher Education, 59*(37), A4.

Yuan, L., Powell, S., & Olivier, B. (2014). *Beyond MOOCs: Sustainable online learning in institutions*. doi:10.13140/2.1.1075.1364.

Zhu, M., Bonk, C. J., & Sari, A. (2018, December). Instructor experiences designing MOOCs in higher education: Pedagogical, resource, and logistical considerations and challenges. *Online Learning, 22*(4), 203–241. Retrieved from https://olj.onlinelearningconsortium.org/index.php/olj/article/view/1495

21
OERs FOR DEVELOPMENT (OERs4D) FRAMEWORK AS DESIGNED AND IMPLEMENTED IN THE PHILIPPINES

Melinda dela Peña Bandalaria

Introduction

Developing countries are often perceived as resource-poor. As a result, they are too often considered to be on the receiving end or the ultimate recipients of initiatives designed and promulgated by more developed countries. The following observation almost always accounts for the usual perception:

> Scientific advances, the evolution of technology and the transformation of productive and service activities have become closely intertwined in the dynamic sectors of the world economy, which are an almost exclusive preserve of the highly industrialized nations. In the rest of the world, knowledge, technology and production have remained wide apart, with local forms of knowledge generation relegated to a marginal role at best.
>
> *(Times Higher Education, 1997)*

The benefits to developing countries of the scientific and technological advancements from the highly industrialized nations could not be denied. In fact, they were often reflected in the various thrusts and priorities of these countries, including the Philippines (Bandalaria & Alfonso, 2015). For instance, as per the Commission on Higher Education (2016) or CHED in the Philippines, cross-border education as exemplified by outbound academics pursuing advanced studies in other countries is an important initiative (see, for example, the 2016 CHED Memorandum Order (CMO), No. 55 s. 2016; Commission on Higher Education, 2016). As the government agency in charge of supervising and regulating all higher education institutions in the Philippines, CHED holds immense responsibility and power, especially in regard to educational change initiatives.

As seen in CHED memoranda and higher education agencies spanning the globe, with the advancements in information and communication technologies, there has been a marked change in world views about education. Specifically, the Internet has opened education in expansive and meaningful ways to individuals that too often were left out of the educational process. Increasingly, through the digitization of books and other media, online resource portals, online collaboration and social networking, mobile learning, and blended and fully online learning, many aspects of education have become open (Bonk, 2009). Today, the World Wide Web offers a seemingly unlimited space for educational contents and activities as well as an audience for all sources of knowledge including those which are locally generated or produced from the developing world (Krasny, 2018).

One of the major components of open education is the open educational resources or OERs which UNESCO defined as "teaching, learning and research materials in any medium—digital or otherwise—that reside in the public domain or have been released under an open license that permits no-cost access, use, adaptation and redistribution by others with no or limited restrictions" (AIMS Team, 2018; UNESCO, n.d., 2018). The World OER Congress held in June 2012 in Paris released the 2012 Paris OER Declaration which "calls on governments worldwide to openly license publicly funded educational materials for public use" (UNESCO, 2012) (AIMS Team, 2018; UNESCO, n.d.). The declaration provided the much-needed impetus for the growing open education movement to disrupt traditional educational conventions and worldviews.

The Conflicting Discourses

With the growing adoption of open education practices and the proliferation of open educational resources, there also came about the conflicting discourses on how educational institutions, especially those from developing countries, would position themselves. For many, it is a welcome opportunity that knowledge and education can now be freely transferred across borders with a minimal cost to the recipients (i.e., both the learners and the educational institutions) and from among the best universities in the world. For instance, the OpenCourseWare (OCW) Project, which was initiated by the Massachusetts Institute of Technology (MIT) in 2001 and later evolved into the Open Education Consortium, has made available "many thousands of courses, open textbooks and other resources" from "nearly 300 educational institutions and related organizations" and has become a highly "trusted resource for both teachers and students" (MIT News, 2016). Hence, for this school of thought, there seemed to be no reason why developing countries would have to "reinvent the wheel" and think of producing their own OERs and MOOCs (Friedman, 2013; Pappano, 2012). For some, however, OCW reflects the long tradition of perceiving and concretizing internationalization as cross-border education.

Increasing concerns are being raised related to these viewpoints. Opposing perspectives consider the various dynamics, challenges, and concerns that the education sector needs to contend with (Mishra & Kunwar, 2015; Wiley, 2015). Such views might view open education as an opportunity to provide relevant educational content and practices among its various groups of learners, especially in the context of a developing nation (Arinto, Hodgkinson-Williams, King, Cartmill, & Willmers, 2017; Venkataraman & Kanwar, 2015). According to Arinto et al. (2017):

> Education in the Global South faces several key interrelated challenges for which OER are seen to be part of the solution and against which use of OER might be evaluated. These challenges include: unequal access to education; variable quality of educational resources, teaching and student performance; and increasing cost and concern about the sustainability of education.
>
> *(p. 6)*

Given the fast-changing world of work, any sustained efforts to provide continuing education opportunities is another challenge to the educational system; especially, at the level of higher and continuing education while society is being transformed by the Fourth Industrial Revolution 4.0 (Schwab, 2017). The demands of this Fourth Industrial Age require individuals to continuously upgrade their knowledge and skills to remain productive and relevant as members of the workforce. The opportunity to also provide space for the sharing of local or indigenous knowledge was verbalized in a special report on the role of open educational resources by the editor of the *International Review of Research on Open and Distributed Learning*, Rory McGreal (2017):

> OER can also be used to preserve and distribute Indigenous knowledge, which is being supported now in many countries. OER can be used to support the "participatory principle"

that is common in many Indigenous communities, as well as preserving and distributing Indigenous knowledge that has traditionally been open. Indigenous knowledge is seen as belonging to the community as a whole and like OER, it can be continually enhanced and expressed in many forms such as in stories, dance, songs, and through the wisdom of elders.

(p. 293)

The Philippines OER Journey

The Philippines is a developing country whose educational system is faced with many challenges (Arinto et al., 2017) and opportunities. Available documents on the Philippines' OER journey showed that it started in 2006 with the Vibal Foundation's initiative on open knowledge (Garcia, Alip, & Serrano, 2013) to achieve its vision of "free and open repositories of learning." The Vibal Foundation was established by the Vibal Publishing House, a major player in the Philippine educational publishing industry. The Vibal Foundation's OER initiatives include an online digital library and a research portal called Filipiniana.net. It also contains WikiPilipinas which is a free online encyclopedia written collaboratively by volunteers around the world featuring articles about government and politics, Philippine history, media, and entertainment among others. Vibal's other OER initiatives include The Philippine Online Chronicles, an online publication that features both mainstream news sources and alternative sources of information like blogs. Finally, it has a network of free and open educational resources that users can download, share, modify, and print called e-Turo (Garcia et al., 2013).

Other early OER initiatives in the Philippines were undertaken at the University of the Philippines Open University (UPOU) and which included the use of OERs in course materials development and open access software, like Moodle, as well as the establishment of a repository for the open access multimedia materials (Arinto, 2010). Also documented was the UPOU Networks (www.upou.networks) (Arinto, 2010), which is an online repository of various multimedia resources that the UPOU designed. UPOU Networks is a type of online portal to a wealth of information about different types of media.

A more concrete initiative by UPOU was the Round Table Discussion on OER in September 2011. This particular effort provided a venue for the expression of the varying perspectives on OERs, Intellectual Property Rights (IPR), and Creative Commons licensing by the different groups of academics and artists. Discussions of each of these three topics remains vital today.

The following year, the Commonwealth of Learning (COL) conducted a survey among the education ministries in Asia with regard to the respective policies on OERs (COL, 2012). The results for the Philippines indicated the intent to "articulate and formulate an OER policy for tertiary education" (COL, 2012). At around the same time, November 2011 to April 2012, another survey was conducted but with the faculty members from different universities as respondents. Results of this survey revealed a "high percentage of respondents using digital resources (83%), but only 48% said that they are using OERs" (Arinto & Cantada, 2013, p. 146).

An effort to put in place a national policy on the use of OERs was started in 2015 through a two-day policy forum (SEAMEO INNOTECH, 2015) that was followed by another two-day consultation with the different stakeholders in 2016 to finalize the policy draft (SEAMEO INNOTECH, 2016). To date, however, the policy is yet to be finalized and signed by the concerned agencies.

Going Beyond OERs: Towards the Development of the OER4Development Framework

As an open university, the University of the Philippines Open University (UPOU) actively engaged in OER discourse and advocacy of use. Hence, soon after being convinced of the necessity to produce and/or contextualize OERs to address local needs, the OER initiative was further interrogated and evaluated at the UPOU in terms of producing or resulting in the expected impact. Of particular interest to the UPOU was the level of use by teachers and learners with digital access. During this evaluation, the realization that "an OER randomly produced will not have many users" came to the forefront. Such results indicated a need for a new framework for OER development.

Going back to the drawing board with the question "what exactly is it that we want to see with regard the use of OERs?," two primary responses surfaced. First, the use of OERs should directly contribute to the improvement in the quality of instruction as well as in facilitating equity in learning outcomes as a result of providing equal opportunities to learners to access educational resources required by the teachers. Second, the OERs should provide the content for the MOOCs identified as needing to be developed as a response to the learning needs of the various sectors of the Philippine society. With these directions, the OER4D (Open Educational Resources for Development) Framework was developed to respond to the identified imperatives.

Imperative #1: Directly contribute to the improvement of the quality of instruction and equity in learning outcomes.

To achieve this purpose, OERs should provide quality learning resources for both teachers and students and/or fill gaps in content availability. As such, OERs should be directly related to the courses/subjects that the instructors are teaching and students are enrolling in as part of their academic journey. If there are existing OERs that suit local needs, then there will be no need to produce another OER. If additional contextualization for existing open resources is necessary, then that direction should be taken.

To be more systematic and relevant under this strategy, new academic programs covered by the Policies, Standards and Guidelines (PSG) released by the Commission on Higher Education (CHED) in the Philippines became a key component in deciding what OERs to produce and when. The OERs produced should correspond to the lessons contained in each of the courses comprising the academic program. Examples of OERs developed under this initiative were courses based on those found in the Service Management Program as per CMO No. 34 s.2012 (Commission on Higher Education, 2012b) and CMO No. 06 s.2012 (Commission on Higher Education, 2012a). Other examples were the OERs for the courses in business analytics as per CMO No. 11 s. 2013 (Commission on Higher Education, 2013a) and CMO No. 12 s. 2013 (Commission on Higher Education, 2013b). Accordingly, those courses were put in place as accredited courses in relevant degree programs in support of the Business Process Outsourcing (BPO) industry in the Philippines.

For example, under CMO No. 12 s. 2013, one course identified was "Fundamentals of Learning Analytics." Based on the learning outcomes specified in the Memorandum Order, the course syllabus was developed to identify the lessons/content that should be taught to the students. Following is the list of lessons developed by the university for the course.

MODULE 1. Overview of Big Data and Business Analytics

Introduction to Business Analytics
History of Business Analytics
Big Data and Business Analytics
Big Data Investments by the Numbers
Providers of Big Data Services

MODULE 2. Business Analytics Framework

Framework for Business Analytics
Types of Analytics

MODULE 3. Data and Database Management

Data, Information, and Knowledge Management
Database
Database Management
Functions and Components of a Database System

MODULE 4. Applications of Business Analytics

Types of Analytics
Applications of Business Analytics in Finance
Applications of Business Analytics in Human Resource
Applications of Business Analytics Marketing

MODULE 5. Ethics Issues in Business Analytics

Ethical Issues
Ethical Implications of Business Analytics

Each topic or lesson became the subject of an OER-produced content resource. An example is the OER on "Introduction to Big Data and Business Analytics" which is a 9-minute, 35-second video introducing the course that potential learners can locate in YouTube (UP Open University, 2018). All OERs developed by the university were made available through the university's OER repository titled UPOU (UP Open University, 2019) (see Figure 21.1).

Specific to the Business Analytics, the OERs produced were not just the video materials on the lessons but the whole syllabus developed, which consists of learning resources (the OERs), learning activities, and sample assessments; these were also shared as OERs with CC-BY-NC-ND license. Providing learning content through OERs, however, did not become the end goal.

Considering that the courses were relatively new, instructors for these courses needed training on the content of the course, how to teach the content, and how to assess learning. Realizing this need, MOOCs were developed using the OERs that had been previously produced initially for the purpose of training the instructors. These MOOCs were made accessible through the university's MOOC Portal found at model.upou.edu.ph (see Figure 21.2).

In the Philippine Higher Education System, a 3-unit credit course would comprise learning content to be taught for 48 to 54 contact hours of formal learning. Putting this much content into

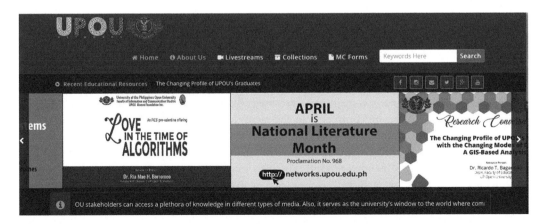

FIGURE 21.1 Screenshot of UPOU's OER Repository

FIGURE 21.2 Screenshot of UPOU's MOOC Portal MODeL

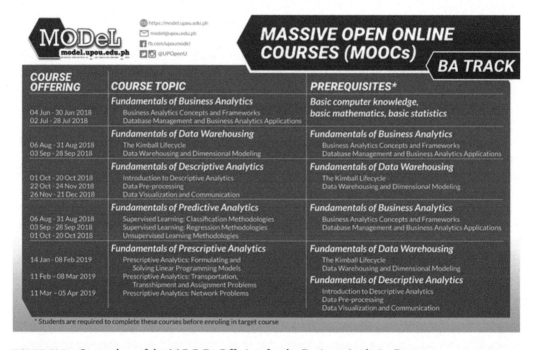

FIGURE 21.3 Screenshot of the MOOCs Offering for the Business Analytics Program

one MOOC was deemed not to be a good idea; hence, the equivalency of one MOOC with the duration of 6 weeks (i.e., 16 hours of contact sessions) was established to correspond to 1-credit unit of the formal credit course. In most cases, three MOOCs will be equivalent to one 3-credit course for students and can be completed in the same duration of 16 to 18 weeks/one term (see Figure 21.3).

Importantly, to complete the envisioned impact of OERs, Filipino teachers were also trained how to use the OERs in a blended teaching and learning strategy. To facilitate this process, another MOOC was developed on "Blended Teaching and Learning Using OERs" (see Figure 21.4).

To further maximize the MOOCs developed, they were also offered as OERs in a blended teaching and learning mode of instructional delivery. Under this model, students enrolled in a

FIGURE 21.4 Screenshot of the MOOC "Blended Teaching and Learning Using OERs"

formal course are simultaneously enrolled in the MOOC that corresponds to the formal credit course. This way, the learning environment is made richer since the students interacted with other learners who could come from different parts of the world. The schedule of offering MOOCs is synchronized with the semester-related schedule of the universities to closely simulate the planned schedule of teaching the lessons (Bandalaria, 2019). And since MOOCs were designed to be stand-alone courses, they were also made available to other learners who may be interested to enroll for various reasons such as continuing education for professional advancement.

Imperative #2: The OERs should provide the content for the MOOCs identified to be developed as a response to the learning needs of the various sectors of the Philippine society.

The second imperative for developing OERs is the need to provide content to the other MOOCs identified by the university as its response to providing lifelong learning opportunities for all.

Positioning MOOCs as a "training program delivered online," MOOC Certification Programs were offered starting in 2018. Each certification program consists of three to four related MOOCs that the learner has to complete to earn the certification. For each MOOC completed, the learner earns a certificate or badge through the implementation of the "Open Badge System." To earn the certification, after completing all the requisite MOOCs in the program, learners must pass a required capstone comprehensive assessment of learning. To date, UPOU offers the MOOCs Certification Programs in the following areas (https://model.upou.edu.ph):

a. eService Management
b. Business Analytics (for IT)
c. Business Analytics (for Business majors)
d. Technology for Teaching and Learning
e. Open Distance eLearning Teaching
f. Open Distance eLearning Technical Staff
g. Open Distance eLearning for School Administrators
h. Child Rights Protection and Promotion
i. eFilipiniana
j. Sustainable Development

Certifications issued by the university can form part of an individual's portfolio/credentials when applying for work or professional advancement. For MOOCs designed to train the teachers, endorsement from the CHED was also sought for training accreditation purposes (Figure 21.5).

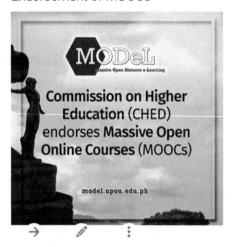

FIGURE 21.5 Screenshot of the MOOCs Endorsement From the Philippine Commission on Higher Education

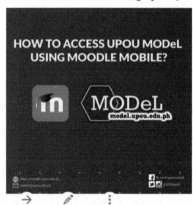

FIGURE 21.6 Making the University MOOCs Accessible Through the Mobile Phone

Importantly, these MOOCs were made more accessible through the integration of the basic features of the Universal Design for Learning (UDL) and the Website Content Accessibility Guidelines (WCAG) in the MOOC Learning Platform. In addition, these MOOCs were made "mobile responsive," and, as such, can be accessed by anyone using their mobile phone. Considering the high ownership of mobile phones among Filipinos (68.6%) (Statista, 2019), this move was intended to directly address technology barriers as a constraint to MOOC access and use (Figure 21.6) (Bandalaria, in press).

Expected Impact of the OERs4D Framework

Much is expected from this initiative. First of all, many improvements in the quality of education in the Philippines are anticipated from the OERs4D Framework. Such improvements can lead the country in many interesting directions. Second, lifelong learning for all could result in a social transformation for individual learners. A third outcome might be a greater alignment with and potential achievement of the Sustainable Development Goals from UNESCO as some of the MOOCs developed and planned to be developed would contribute to the learning component to achieve the different SDGs. Finally, knowledge generation can result in refinements and improvements with open education practices.

It is truly an exciting time to be an educator in this era of open education. As shown in many of the chapters of this book, frameworks like OERs4D are a start. However, much more needs to be undertaken in the coming decade for open education to create the impact that has been promised. In my role as chancellor of the UPOU, I intend to continue to support the development, implementation, and evaluation of different MOOC and OER initiatives in the Philippines.

Melinda Bandalaria is Chancellor and Professor at the University of the Philippines Open University. Previously, she served as Dean of the Faculty of Information and Communication Studies. Dr Bandalaria has developed and handled distance e-learning courses both at the undergraduate and graduate levels as well as massive open online courses (MOOCs). She has also been actively involved in research and community development projects. From 2017–2019 Professor Bandalaria served as President of the Asian Association of Open Universities. She has also been chairing the Asian Massive Open Online Course (MOOCs) Steering Committee since 2016. In these capacities, Bandalaria has helped coordinate international conferences on open education and written extensively on e-learning in the Philippines.

References

AIMS Team. (2018, April 21). Open invitation to contribute to the draft of OER recommendation text. *AIMS Blog*. Retrieved from http://aims.fao.org/activity/blog/contribute-unesco-open-educational-resources-oer-recommendations

Arinto, P. B. (2010, October 25). *OER in the Philippines*. Presented at Sub-Project 7 Inaugural Workshop at the Vietnam National University, Hanoi, Vietnam. Retrieved from https://oerasia.org/index.php?option=com_content&view=article&id=9&Itemid=11)

Arinto, P. B., & Cantada, R. (2013). OER in Philippine higher education: A preliminary study. In G. Dhanarajan & D. Porter (Eds.), *Open educational resources: An Asian perspective* (pp. 141–158). Published by the Commonwealth of Learning and OER Asia, Vancouver. Retrieved from www.researchgate.net/publication/258498612_Open_educational_resources_an_Asian_perspective

Arinto, P. B., Hodgkinson-Williams, C., King, T., Cartmill, T., & Willmers, M. (2017). *Research on open educational resources for development in the Global South: Project landscape*. Retrieved from https://open.uct.ac.za/bitstream/handle/11427/26435/ROER4D-ch1-final.pdf?sequence=7

Bandalaria, M. D. P., & Alfonso, G. A. (2015). Situating MOOCs in the developing world context: The Philippines case study. In C. J. Bonk, M. M. Lee, T. C. Reeves, & T. H. Reynolds (Eds.), *MOOCs and open education around the world* (pp. 243–254). New York: Routledge.

Bandalaria, M. D. P. (2019). Massive open online courses as open educational resources in a blended teaching and learning mode of instructional delivery in higher education. *International Journal on Innovation and Learning, 25*(2), 156–169.

Bandalaria, M. D. P. (in press). Universal access in online distance education: A case study from the Philippines. In S. L. Gronseth & E. M. Dalton (Eds.), *Universal access through inclusive instructional design: International perspectives on UDL*. New York: Routledge.

Bonk, C. J. (2009, July). *The world is open: How Web technology is revolutionizing education*. San Francisco, CA: Jossey-Bass.

Commission on Higher Education. (2012a). *CHED memorandum order, no. 06 2012: Addendum to CMO No. 39, S. 2006 entitled, policies, standards and guidelines for Bachelor of Science in business administration prescribing additional electives on service management for business process outsourcing*. Republic of the Philippines. Retrieved from https://ched.gov.ph/cmo-6-s-2012/

Commission on Higher Education. (2012b). *CHED memorandum order, No. 34, s. 2012, addendum to CMO No. 53, s. 2006 revised policies, standards and guidelines for information technology education (ITE) programs prescribing specialization track on service management for business process outsourcing*. Republic of the Philippines. Retrieved from https://ched.gov.ph/cmo-33-s-2012-2/

Commission on Higher Education (2013a). *CHED memorandum order, no. 11 2013: Addendum to CMO No. 39, S. 2006 policies, standards and guidelines for Bachelor of Science in business administration prescribing specialization track on business analytics*. Republic of the Philippines. Retrieved from https://ched.gov.ph/cmo-11-s-2013/

Commission on Higher Education. (2013b). *CHED memorandum order, no. 12 2013: Addendum to CMO No. 53, S. 2006 policies, standards and guidelines for information technology education (ITE) programs prescribing specialization track on business analytics*. Republic of the Philippines. Retrieved from https://ched.gov.ph/wp-content/uploads/2017/10/CMO-No.12-s2013.pdf

Commission on Higher Education. (2016). *CHED memorandum order, no. 55 2.2016: Policy framework and strategies on the internationalization of Philippine higher education*. Republic of the Philippines. Retrieved from https://ched.gov.ph/wp-content/uploads/2017/10/CMO-55-s.-2016.pdf

Commonwealth of Learning. (2012). *Survey on governments' open educational resources (OER) policies*. COL 2012. Retrieved from https://en.unesco.org/sites/default/files/survey_on_government_oer_policies.pdf

Friedman, T. (2013, January 26). Revolution hits the universities. *The New York Times*. Retrieved from www.nytimes.com/2013/01/27/opinion/sunday/friedman-revolution-hits-the-universities.html?_r=0

Garcia, P. G., Alip, A. S., & Serrano, J. (2013). Open knowledge initiatives in the Philippines: The vibal foundation. In G. Dhanarajan & D. Porter (Eds.), *Open educational resources: An Asian perspective* (pp. 195–206). Vancouver: Published by the Commonwealth of Learning and OER Asia. Retrieved from www.researchgate.net/publication/258498612_Open_educational_resources_an_Asian_perspective

Krasny, M. E., et al. (2018, June). Small groups in a social learning MOOC (slMOOC): Strategies for fostering learning and knowledge creation. *Online Learning, 22*(2), 119–140. Retrieved from https://olj.onlinelearningconsortium.org/index.php/olj/article/view/1339

McGreal, R. (2017, November). Special report on the role of open educational resources in supporting the sustainable development goal 4: Quality education challenges and opportunities. *International Review of Research in Open and Distributed Learning, 18*(7), 292–305. Retrieved from www.irrodl.org/index.php/irrodl/article/view/3541/4485

Mishra, S., & Kunwar, A. (2015). Quality assurance for open educational resources: What's the difference? In C. J. Bonk, M. M. Lee, T. C. Reeves, & T. H. Reynolds (Eds.), *MOOCs and open education around the world* (pp. 119–129). New York: Routledge.

MIT News. (2016, April 4). MIT open course ware celebrates 15 years of open sharing. *MIT News*. Retrieved from http://news.mit.edu/2016/mit-opencourseware-celebrates-15-years-open-sharing-0404

Pappano, L. (2012, November 2). The year of the MOOC. *The New York Times*. Retrieved from www.nytimes.com/2012/11/04/education/edlife/massive-open-online-courses-are-multiplying-at-a-rapid-pace.html?pagewanted=all&_r=0

Schwab, K. (2017). *The fourth industrial revolution*. New York: Crown Publishing Group.
SEAMEO INNOTECH. (2015, October 8). *SEAMEO INNOTECH conducts OER policy forum*. Retrieved from www.seameo-innotech.org/news/seameo-innotech-conducts-oer-policy-forum/
SEAMEO INNOTECH. (2016, April 5). *DepEd, CHED, TESDA, UPOU finalize joint circular for OER policies*. Retrieved from www.seameo-innotech.org/news/deped-ched-tesda-upou-finalize-joint-circular-for-oer-policies/
Statista. (2019). *Share of the population that uses a mobile phone in the Philippines from 2014 to 2020*. Retrieved from www.statista.com/statistics/570389/philippines-mobile-phone-user-penetration/
The Times Higher Education. (1997, April 11). *The knowledge monopoly*. Retrieved from www.timeshighereducation.com/features/the-knowledge-monopoly/101356.article
UNESCO. (2012, June 20–22). *The Paris OER declaration. 2012*. Paris, France: World Open Educational Resources (OER) Congress, UNESCO. Retrieved from https://en.unesco.org/oer/paris-declaration
UNESCO and Commonwealth of Learning. (2011). *A basic guide on open educational resources* (OERs). Butcher, Neil, Kanwar, Asha, and Uvalic'-Trumbic', Stamenka (editors). Retrieved from https://unesdoc.unesco.org/ark:/48223/pf0000215804
UP Open University. (2018, May 31). Introduction to big data and business analytics by Prof. Erik Paolo Capistrano. *YouTube*. Retrieved from www.youtube.com/watch?v=nVifzj0zM1Y&t=0s&list=PLiqeNUxu5x2HplGrEaxWMGlb_h9MVEo6I&index=59
UP Open University. (2019). *University of the Philippines commons*. University of the Philippines Open University. Retrieved from http://networks.upou.edu.ph
Venkataraman, B., & Kanwar, A. (2015). Changing the tune: MOOCs for human development? In C. J. Bonk, M. M. Lee, T. C. Reeves, & T. H. Reynolds (Eds.), *MOOCs and open education around the world* (pp. 206–217). New York: Routledge.
Wiley, D. (2015). The MOOC misstep and the open education infrastructure. In C. J. Bonk, M. M. Lee, T. C. Reeves, & T. H. Reynolds (Eds.), *MOOCs and open education around the world* (pp. 3–11). New York: Routledge.

22
DISRUPTIVE LEARNING

Inspiring the Advancement of MOOCs in the Middle East

Abtar Darshan Singh, Sumayyah Abuhamdeih, and Shriram Raghunathan

Introduction

Massive open online courses (MOOCs) have yet to create a disruption in the learning landscape of the Middle East in terms of scalability and new approaches in learning despite the huge advancements made in online and e-learning as well as investments in technological devices. This is understandable owing to two key factors: (1) MOOC take-up started rather late and (2) there initially were not many MOOC providers. MOOCs started in Middle East in 2011 as video-based lectures and emerged in a full-fledged manner in 2013. However, despite the efforts made in the propagation of MOOCs, a major disruption in terms of adoption, participation, and research in MOOCs in the Middle East has yet to visibly transpire.

This chapter will report on the successes, challenges, and opportunities related to MOOCs and other open forms of education that Middle Eastern economies need to address as well as capitalize on to make a more significant impact on its citizenry. With proper foresight and planning, MOOCs can be a disruptive technology that both opens up and enhances learning across educational sectors. Taking advantage of this situation is imperative as Middle Eastern economies are beginning to realize the influence informal learning has on formal learning. In the midst of increasingly open and informal learning content, there is a pressing need to enhance competencies related to autonomy, responsibility, and self-development. There is also a need to include accreditation of prior experiential learning as well as recognition of prior learning into the total learning realm of an individual.

As information and knowledge proliferate in the World Wide Web, online courses that provide validated and accredited learning courses will enable Middle Eastern learners to allay their fears of taking courses not accepted by their local accreditation bodies. Further, it is also crucial that Middle Eastern countries capitalize on emerging trends in learning to ensure their students are not left behind in preparing themselves to face learning challenges of the 21st century.

MOOCS in the Middle East

The key statistics of the MOOCs relevant to the region (MoocLab Report, 2017) are as follows.

- 30% of MOOC platforms is in the Middle East. Asia and the Middle East account for 37% of all courses offered globally. Arabic accounts for 3% of the MOOC platforms locally. This is a growth from a study (Stratton and Grace, 2016) held across three years (2013–2016) where Arabic was represented in 1% of all courses. Stratton and Grace (2016) also mention a unique opportunity. MOOCs in Arabic (13%) and French (14%) present greater proportions of opportunities for credentialing than English MOOCs (10%).

According to the Docebo report (2018) the self-paced eLearning market in the Middle East will hit close to $690M by the end of 2016. QS Intelligence Unit surveyed employers in 2017 about their awareness about MOOCs in their Global Employer survey (Gatuguta-Gitau, 2017) and found that 34% of the employers in Africa and the Middle East (Table 22.1) were aware of MOOCs. The major providers in the Middle East according to the MoocLab comparison report (2018) based on the league table (Table 22.2) are as follows.

The success of Edraak is due to two factors. When it was launched in 2013, one of the key decisions was to partner with edX to create the platform. Regional talent with the technology of edX helped it get established quickly. The platform offered Arabic translated courses from edX.

According to Alshahrani and Ally (2016), Rwaq is the first MOOC popularized by Saudi Arabia and is popular among both Saudis and Egyptians. These researchers attribute the reasons for that to the ratio of population in the two countries, the availability of Internet access, and to the language used given that the platform offers courses in Arabic; however, the MOOC certificates awarded by Rwaq are not accredited by universities.

One of the interesting offshoots of Rwaq is the Maharah (Almuhanna, 2018) platform which was launched as many lecturers could not meet the guidelines prescribed in the Rwaq. To cater to this demand and enable anyone to offer courses, Maharah was launched. Zadi, a MOOC for Islamic law courses, is also highlighted in the work. Nadrus (www.nadrus.com/) is a platform offering Arabic-only courses reaching around 600,000 users in a short period of time. The platform has reported success in corporate training across the Middle Eastern region. Dawrat (www.dawrat.com/ae/en/about) is a market place out of Kuwait that combines training centers, trainers, educational event organizers, and online course providers in one place. It claims 47,000 users and

TABLE 22.1 Employers' Awareness of MOOCs

Africa and Middle East	34%
Asia Pacific	30%
Eastern Europe	56%
Western Europe	23%
Latin America	27%
US and Canada	45%

Source: Summarized From Gatuguta-Gitau (2017)

TABLE 22.2 MOOCs in the Middle East: A Compilation

Platform	Location	Launched	N° Users	N° Courses	Free Courses	Paid Courses	Subjects	Credit	Course Type	Language
Nadrus	Dubai	2015	100,000+	150	Yes	Yes	Professional skills	No	On-Demand	Arabic
Edraak	Jordan	2014	1,200,000+	70+	Yes	No	Varied	College	Scheduled & On-Demand	Arabic
Rwaq	Saudi Arabia	2013	600,000+	200+	Yes	No	Varied	No	Scheduled	Arabic

5,000 registered courses and workshops. An-Najah University (https://elc.najah.edu/node/304) has launched a MOOC in its portal.

Madrasa is a leading e-learning platform for the "Life-long-Learning (LLL)" MOOC. The platform provides Arabic-language educational content at all levels of science and mathematics and is available free of charge to more than 50 million Arab students. This innovative idea and site was launched on October 16, 2018. The LLL platform is one of the initiatives of the Mohammed bin Rashid Al Maktoum International Initiatives Foundation, with 5,000 video lessons, including physics, chemistry, biology, mathematics, and general science covering the curriculum from kindergarten to grade 12 (https://madrasa.org/).

Edlal is an interesting Omani e-learning platform that was launched in 2016 (Sekka Editorial, 2017). In 2017, it claimed to have 22 courses with 15,000 users. The interesting strand focused on by Edlal was the emphasis on micro-courses. The majority of the courses in the platform were of short duration. Aydin(2017) traced the MOOCs in Turkey and outlined the following status as in Table 22.3.

One of the interesting insights from the article was that while design of the MOOCs in the universities was to reach their own students (55%), the impact of the MOOCs on their major operations and stakeholders was around 37.5%. These are two interesting strands for further research exploration. Another nugget brought out was the fact the institutions outsourced their operations related to the MOOCs in a significant way. The article stressed the problems like recognition of prior learning and MOOC certificates, creation of norms for transfer of credits from the MOOC programs into formal settings. Farhat (2017) postulated that training courses provided by MOOCs can boost skills of learners in the Middle East. Sarhan (2016) views the creation of MOOCs as an opportunity in the Arab world to quicken the pace of advancement and sharpen the skills of learners in the labor market. Al-Zoubi and Al-Rousan (2017) mentioned that the Ministry of Higher Education and Scientific Research (MoHESR) formed a committee for e-learning, but upon checking their strategy and priorities, it was revealed that it is still not the focus of higher education in Jordan. As they noted, "E-learning was first presented in Jordan by the Arab Open University (AOU) – Jordan branch which was set up in 2002" (p. 8). Through the years, the graduates of e-learning in Jordan struggled due to the lack of accreditation of their certificates by MoHESR. At the time, the Arab States were beginning to look at online certification seriously. The two authors reviewed several different studies that documented the importance and the acceptability of online learning in the region. In concluding their research, they note that such projects need support from those at or near the top of the decision-making process. For any change to be taken seriously and to pick up the pace, it should be supported by the key decision leaders and policy makers of a country.

Laurillard and Kennedy (2017) investigated the scaling of MOOCs in the Global South and emphasized the importance of providing "equitable higher educational opportunities to all ... of high quality ... and achieve efficiency of scale to ensure sustainability." After the analysis of MOOCs and what they provide, the issue of "quality" is still prominent, provided that sufficient connectivity and infrastructure is available in the countries to host MOOCs platforms. One of the more

TABLE 22.3 Status of MOOCs in Turkey

AKADEMA (Anadolu University)	48 courses in Turkish and 1 course in English
Atademix (Erzurum Ataturk University)	14 courses
Yaşar University	17 courses
Koç University	6 courses in Coursera, 3 courses in edX
UniversitePlus	46 courses in partnership with 4 universities

Source: Aydin, 2017

interesting research in the domain is from Ruipérez and Reich (2018) who surveyed the enrollment in MITx and HarvardX courses between 2012–2018 and found that 3.82% of the population (140,994 students) were from the 22 Arab countries. They highlighted a correlation between the human development index and the enrollment. Thus UAE, Qatar, and Bahrain lead the enrollment whereas Comoros, Yemen, and Mauritania lag behind. The report highlights a revealing statistic in that the average Arab learner enrolls in 2.47 MOOCs while the value for the rest of the world is of 2.25 MOOCs. The completion percentage aspect is left open to further exploration in that the average completion of the Middle Eastern learner is worse than the rest of the world.

Clark (2016) explains that course completion rates for MOOCs are a flawed and inappropriate measure. As he noted, studies show that MOOC participants often state that they never intended to finish the course but were there out of curiosity or needing some limited piece of information. Perhaps MOOC certificates and micro-credentials can inform potential as well as current employers that the participant is attempting to personally grow and develop a range of skills, rather than being overly concerned with the acceptability of such certificates as a formal education degree. In effect, MOOC certificates might simply be viewed by employers as a training supplement until issues like cheating and plagiarism, for example, can be resolved. In one study, Kursun (2016) found participants who aimed to gain credit from MOOCs actually performed significantly better. Given these results, he suggested that, "various possible models can be adopted by higher education institutions to integrate MOOCs as a credit."

To MOOC or NOT to MOOC in the Arab World

Education is becoming an expensive affair for most Middle Eastern learners as traditional learning paradigms are still popular and there is a huge void that can be filled by MOOCs which has yet to be extensively tapped. Currently, the largest percent of the budget for Ministries of Education is consumed by salaries of teaching staff. What is too often left out of such budgets is any mention of resources for innovative ideas related to advancing teaching and learning in the Arab world.

With the phenomenal progress in online learning technologies combined with the rapid adoption of such technologies by younger generations of learners, there is much hope for the future emergence of unique and effective learning avenues (Jones (2010). For example, it is a well-known fact that in the UAE, some private schools, including GEMS and InterHigh, provide distance learning for their students. While this is still not widespread among the Arab States, the utilization of online platforms is picking up among education providers across all levels of education.

At the higher education levels, Sallam (2017) concluded in his research that the contributions by Arab universities to the MOOC movement can be improved. A study of the Class Central website (www.class-central.com/) reveals that among the 883 universities offering free MOOC courses, to our knowledge, 22 are from the region as shown in Table 22.4. This table is confined to MOOCs referenced by Class Central alone.

One of the reasons for the low number of courses and participation is the accreditation of programs across the Arab States (Creelman, 2017; Hamid, 2014). This one issue has led potential learners to avoid seeking MOOCs created by other Arab universities. At the same time, this avoidance is somewhat ironic given the high propensity for Arab learners to participate in MOOCs offered by universities from other countries. Another high probability for why MOOCs have not been more embraced in the Arab States is due to language concerns. Except for MOOC resources available on the Rwaq and Edraak platforms, most available MOOC materials are in English. The following statistics by Music (2016) show that the share of MOOCs offered in English, across all MOOC courses, still commands a high percentage. More specifically, 76% of MOOC materials were in the English language in 2015, followed by Spanish 8%, French 5%, and Arabic 1% (Music, 2016).

TABLE 22.4 Free Online Courses in MOOCs Offered by Universities in the Middle East in MOOC Portals

S.No	Name of University	No. of Free Online Courses	Platform	Nationality
1	Heliopolis University	1	Canvas Network	Egypt
2	Weizmann Institute of Science	4	1 on edX and 3 on FutureLearn	Israel
3	Tel Aviv University	19	15 on Coursera, 2 on edX, and 2 on FutureLearn	Israel
4	Technion—Israel Institute of Technology	16	12 on Coursera, and 4 on edX	Israel
5	Ben-Gurion University of the Negev	1	Canvas Network	Israel
6	Shenkar College of Engineering	1	edX	Israel
7	University of Haifa	1	edX	Israel
8	Holon Institute of Technology	1	edX	Israel
9	Bar-Ilan University	1	edX	Israel
10	Kuwait University	1	OpenLearning	Kuwait
11	AUB: American University of Beirut	3	All on Edraak	Lebanon
12	Université La Sagesse	1	France Université Numerique	Lebanon
13	Hamad Bin Khalifa University (HBKU)	2	Both on edX	Qatar
14	Qatar Faculty of Islamic Studies	1	Rwaq	Qatar
15	King Abdulaziz University	1	Rwaq	Saudi Arabia
16	King Faisal University	1	Rwaq	Saudi Arabia
17	Taibah University	1	Rwaq	Saudi Arabia
18	Princess Nora bint Abdul Rahman University	1	Rwaq	Saudi Arabia
19	King Saud University	4	All on Rwaq	Saudi Arabia
20	King Fahd University of Petroleum and Minerals	3	All on Rwaq	Saudi Arabia
21	Arab East Colleges for Graduate Studies	2	Both on Rwaq	Saudi Arabia
22	Koç University	7	All 7 courses offered on Coursera	Turkey

There is a lack of demonstrable success of MOOCs due to lack of accreditation, norms, and expectations. Other factors that hinder the completion of MOOCs in the Arab world are often related to family and social factors. Arab families, historically, are very family-centric; as such, giving up a social event to allocate time to studies is a serious challenge (Gais, 2014).

Adapting to technological advances and innovations is often quite natural for younger generations, while, for those more senior, it can be a huge challenge. Karr (2017), founder of The MarTech Blog, presented the characteristics of each age group and how they use the technology. While Karr is interested in the technology for business purposes, the classifications fit the type of users expected for MOOCs. Various technological advancements not only provide the possibility of offering effective digital materials for learners to choose from, react to, and share, but also the ability to interact virtually with other MOOC learners adds engagement and novelty to the process. For example,

Conole (2016) suggested that these "interactive communities" (p. 7) or MOOCs be in tune with the demands of the masses, who want to be involved and have their voice heard.

Are Current MOOCS a Disruptive Innovation?

According to Al-Imarah (2018), there is yet to be sufficient evidence to indicate that MOOCs are a disruptive innovation. "MOOCs may be . . . innovation that establishes new markets for learners who are not served by universities" (p. 1). However, the notion of disruption can surface in various forms to suit the needs of the population. In order to better understand disruption, it is important to simply ask, do MOOCs make an impact on learning and employability? Conole (2016) debated what is high-quality learning before exploring MOOCs and similar forms of open e-learning. She concludes that MOOCs are challenging traditional higher education and may lead to improvements in the delivery of education. MOOCs may not be a disruptive innovation as of now; nevertheless, MOOCs may disrupt the manner in which higher education will be delivered in years to come.

In the Arab States, the accreditation of certificates obtained online is yet to be accepted. At present, Hamdan Bin Mohamed Smart University (Dubai, UAE) and Saudi E-University (SEU, Saudi Arabia) are two universities that run blended and fully online programs that are endorsed by their governments. In contrast, Jordan has begun to acknowledge such certification but for a limited number of issuers. One key barrier is that online education is still new to many Arab States. Al-Zoubi and Al-Rousan (2017) confirmed that the universities under the Jordanian Ministry of Higher Education and Scientific Research offer online courses to students. Although the two researchers listed many benefits related to online studies, students are hesitant due to issues raised by accrediting bodies and ministries about the validity of the certificates issued.

Swedish researcher Alastair Creelman (2017) argued that studies show that MOOCs have the potential of offering higher education of quality and affordability to millions in the Middle East. In addition to having the potential to help refugees, MOOCs should be tweaked to attract more of the youth population residing in the Arab world, especially since "the Arab region has one of the highest rates of young population" (Alshahrani and Ally, 2016, p. 17). There is also a huge youth market for MOOCs in the Arab region, especially displaced youth or NEETs (neither in education nor employment). The Jamiya Project is another project that works with refugees (Coluci et al., 2017) that is in the realm of Small Private Online Courses (SPOCs, not MOOCs) in Applied IT and Global Studies, delivered in Arabic in blended mode and certified by the University of Gothenburg. These are being delivered in collaboration with a small team of Syrian academics and NGOs in the field—Norwegian Refugee Council and Jesuit Refugee Service, both in Jordan.

According to Saleh (2016), the UN's Arab Human Development 2016 report forecasted that the number of young people in the region living in countries with a high risk of conflict is projected to grow from about 250 million in 2010 to over 305 million by the end of the decade. In response, higher education institutes are often tasked with finding ways to effectively utilize MOOCs as a disruptive innovation and offer them in a way that would not compromise their reputation yet would help these youth who cannot afford regular education to attain the proper knowledge and skills ultimately needed for gainful employment in the labor market.

Freihat and Al Zamil (2014) conducted an experiment to evaluate the impact of using MOOCs on a specific topic and specific target group. The researchers conducted their research on Saudi females studying the English language, and, in particular, listening skills. The researchers found it pertinent "to integrate MOOCs in English listening courses." Enhancing girls' education is very important in the MiddleEast. As such, this effort is seen as an important step forward for the development of MOOCs. Apart from the KSA and Jordanian MOOCs, Lebanon and Egypt are two countries that have taken on leadership related to MOOCs in the Middle East. For instance, Adham and Lundqvist (2015) explored the Lebanese MOOC, Mena Versity, a platform with courses targeting those up to age 40. In addition, the Egyptian Skill Academy launched in 2013 managed to present high-level courses with certificates that could be authenticated to reduce the high cost of higher education, alleviate the over-crowdedness in classrooms, and provide well-trained human resources. Thus, this MOOC is focused on training, which is another important milestone for the advancement of MOOCs in the MiddleEast. After measuring trends in the world related to MOOCs, Arya (2017) stated that to guarantee the success and utmost utilization of disruption that MOOCs can offer, governments should take charge of MOOCs. One example to follow is the country of Norway where there is a government-appointed MOOC Commission (Tømte, Fevolden, & Aanstad, 2017). Governments might not only offer MOOC-related policies and vital resources, they can also offer important incentives. For instance, Al-Shboul and Alsmadi (2010) also recommended training for faculty members of universities as well as other incentives. They stated that "for implementing e-Learning systems in public universities in Jordan, faculty need financial incentives to encourage them to use e-Learning systems tools; faculty need training, technical assistance, and institutional support to enable them to use e-Learning systems tools" (p. 9).

Doroob, which was created due to a partnership between the Saudi government and edX to create a MOOC especially for the labor market, is one step in this direction. The Human Resource Development fund website (https://hrdf.org.sa/) lists the acceptance of the Doroob certificates for employability. Similarly "IsraelX is a national consortium of higher education institutions in Israel, led by the Council for Higher Education and the Ministry for Social Equality. IsraelX is the international arm of Campus—the Israeli National Project for Digital Learning, whose goal is to promote general, academic and professional education in Israel in order to reduce social gaps and accelerate economic growth" (www.edx.org/school/israelx). A set of MOOCs has been launched by the consortium.

An interesting initiative of which little is written in the academic world is the ta3mal platform. This is an employability portal offering courses online. The portal (www.ta3mal.com) says that it has 99 training courses around 4,20,000 members working overall. This was born out of a partnership between ALISON and Silatech (Cahill, 2013) to create employability-related courses (Blumel, 2014) in Arabic. This one used the Microsoft platform. More information about the portal and initiative is given in Avina and Russell (2016). Similarly, the partnership between Taghreedat and Coursera for translation of the content in the Coursera platform is reported (Al Arabiya, 2013) but not much is known of the impact. The preceding shows that there is work started on the MOOCs with support from the government on one hand and also through separate initiatives on the other.

In analyzing the future of MOOCs, the following strands are emerging.

- There is increasing acceptance in the minds of the learners on the value of MOOCs. In a survey of 52,000 respondents by Coursera, 72% reported benefitting from the MOOCs (McIntyre, 2017).
- There are around 9,000 students enrolled in MOOC-based online degrees and 1,000 have already graduated. With bachelor's degrees now being offered, the market is going to be disrupted in a second wave now (Shah, 2018).
    - This is potentially going to have a worldwide disruption. If this succeeds, the bright students with resources will no longer be dependent on their national and regional borders but will have access to accredited high-quality education on their own pace and at their doorstep. The success here will be known after a few years but universities must watch this phenomenon and be ready to capitalize on this in a big way.
- There is a shift to the OPM (Online Program Management) model. In this, companies sit between the universities and the consumer with resources for services which the universities

alone cannot provide like "marketing & recruitment, enrollment management, curriculum development, online course design, student retention support, technology hosting, and student and faculty support" (Hill, 2016). The OPM market itself is in a consolidation phase with MOOC providers and LMS vendors like Blackboard themselves competing with the OPMs for the market (Kronk, 2018). One of the interesting messages of this article from a UC Berkeley report is that the student retention rate has been very high and the financial cost of the program was covered.

- One of the biggest reasons for non-participation by universities worldwide in the MOOCs is the high initial cost. Partnering with organizations who specialize in the end-end spectrum of expertise in service provision and already proven capacities will remove this while bringing in benefits of additional students and economies of scale.

- There is a push from the employees to upskill themselves while in the marketplace. This trend is worldwide and not specific to the Arab region alone. A study of employers by Raish and Rimland (2016) of 115 employers in the US found that 62% of them were interested in the digital badges. But they needed to know more about them. There is a trend by companies to upskill their employees in MOOCs.

  - In areas where education has been disrupted, the industry has been a prime driver in the change. With the changing job roles due to advances in technology, there is a tremendous need for courses which will cater to this gap. This will be felt in the Middle East also. For many employees, MOOCs can emerge as the only option due to the cost barrier in the traditional degrees. Here there is a need for the MOOCs to accredit and certify prior learning also.

- There is a trend towards the MicroMasters degree as a bridge between the student and the employee and also the Master's degree program. This is to be validated further. Even in the existing MOOCs, there is a trend towards micro-courses especially in providers like Udemy. These micro-courses solve a specific need.

  - There is a need for universities to come out of the MOOC course mindset and focus on specific skills that the students and industry want. This will help drive up enrollment and reduce the attrition rates.

Immersive Learning and Its Potential to Disrupt MOOCs

Horn (2014) discussed disruption theory in education and believes that it is the way to "transform teaching and learning to better serve each individual student within each school by personalizing and humanizing learning—and undo the factory-model assumptions." Horn makes a distinction between disruptive education at the school level (K–12) and university education, where innovations are more welcomed. Arnett (2014) sees it as an "equitable access to high-quality education," whereas Sagenmüller (2017) reiterates that disruptive education will revolutionize education. She argues that virtual reality (VR), collaboration platforms, augmented reality (AR), and artificial intelligence (AI) will soon be affordable and once obtained, quality education become the norm.

Educators, whether engaged in face-to-face teaching or online or blended environments, are tasked with making the learning experience informative and impactful, and, to some degree, enjoyable and engaging. Another issue facing educators is how to immerse their learners into high-fidelity learning situations that approximate real life thereby. The learning challenges faced by most graduates from schools and universities is that much of their previous learning is highly theoretical.

As a consequence, far too often they find themselves unable to apply the knowledge that they gained.

MOOCs utilizing new technologies can provide the types of immersive experiences that face-to-face learning environments too often fail to provide. However, online learning in the form of MOOCs can provide many learners throughout the world with the affordability of "real experiences" through virtual labs, field trips, educational tours, holograms, and other applications—all of which are representative of immersive learning (Pagano, 2013, p. 3). Immersive learning is the process of learning with the use of a simulated or artificial environment. Immersive learning enables learners to be deeply involved in the learning process. Some notable examples of an immersive environment are Thrive (Memon, 2015) and The Void (Tickle, 2015). Such a type of learning is based on gamification (Memon, 2017). It should have varied levels of complex elements that attempt to consume 100% of the participants' mental capacity.

Scenarios that immerse learners in the environment using ubiquitous technology are also another useful strategy for disruptive MOOCs. Singh and Hassan (2017) shared the following scenario as an example of immersive learning:

> Consider a learner, John, who is going home after school. As John passes through a garden, the learning system identifies that one of the trees is related to what he has learned in school during his natural science course. Moreover, John has mentioned that he would like to see the real tree if possible. As there is still plenty of time for John to get home for dinner, the learning system reminds him to note the tree and provides him with some relevant learning materials. In addition, the learning system recommends that he does a learning task, that is, to complete a concept map about the ecology of the target tree based on his observations of the tree as well as what he has learned from the textbook.
>
> *(p. 13)*

In that students are currently using their mobiles and tablets in and out of classrooms, it is evident that technology is no longer creeping into the educational system but that it is a pervasive part of it and can no longer be ignored (Tan, 2011). Augmented reality and virtual reality, as mentioned in VR Focus (iVROX, 2018), are the next step in making MOOCs more disruptive. Such tools can make the learning experience rich and would enable learners to better comprehend the subject matter. Although the technology is still quite expensive, its implementation would revolutionize learning inside as well as outside classroom settings. When MOOCs and other forms of online learning are added to the revolution equation, there is much hope for improving the educational experience in the Middle East and beyond, and even changing online learning providers' pedagogical approaches. Experiential immersive learning (EIL), constructivist learning methods, and social and collaborative learning could take advantage of such technologies to implement more immersive learning (Ly, Saade, & Morin, 2017).

Suggestions for AMOOCs—The Disruption

The following table (Table 22.5) summarizes proposed ideas for AMOOCs (Arab MOOC) as compared to current MOOCs in terms of the disruption factor.

The preceding framework proposed for AMOOCs can be a positive improvement of existing MOOCs and also aligned to the needs of the community. The idea for the AMOOC is for institutions in the MiddleEast to come together and collaboratively plan and create pedagogical interactions in MOOCs that are consistent with emerging technologies and suited to the younger generations of learners who are very comfortable with online forms of learning and who interact intuitively with advance technologies.

TABLE 22.5 Disruption of AMOOC Versus Current MOOCs

	AMOOC	Current MOOCS
1	Learner-driven outcomes. It is important that learners be given broad goals and within these, that they plan their own "learning paths" to attain the learning goals.	Instructor-driven outcomes. Currently, the design of MOOC courses are driven almost completely by the instructor. If they are not adaptable to different learner needs, they may quickly lose the novelty of learner-centered learning which is becoming increasingly important.
2	Task-based activities. The learning process ideally should be driven by real-world tasks, whereby the learner plays the role of an "apprentice." In solving real-world problems, the learner has access to experts and "smart intelligent agents" whereby they can post dedicated questions related directly to the challenges they face whilst addressing the real-world problem.	Instructor-designed activities and assignments which are directly related to what was learned. These activities/assignments are normally centered around facts, theories, and concepts which often do not allow for extensive displays of creativity or opportunities for other forms of higher-order thinking.
3	High use of artificial intelligence and agent technology resulting in personalized adaptive learning and assessments.	Low or no use of artificial intelligence and agent technology.
4	Learners create learning assets to demonstrate their learning experiences. These learning assets will form the new learning culture. Learners demonstrate their learning by re-creating knowledge. This will enhance social collaborative learning.	Instructor creates learning resources and curates learning events. Whilst these activities are useful, it is important to re-strategize such events to include as much learner input as possible. Allow learners to be their own learning architects.
5	Learner is constantly in an immersive contextualized learning environment through the use of emerging technological innovations such as holograms and virtual and augmented realities. Sensing technologies will also enable a learner to learn from a dynamic real-world environment. The environment should be flexible enough to allow the learners to acquire knowledge and meet course objectives through formal as well as informal means.	Learner is in a static learning environment (the learning management system) which is normally "one-size-fits-all."
6	Support for micro-content and wherever possible offering systematic micro-degrees. Many MOOC users report that they are looking for specific topics to be taught in a systematic manner. In this, the emphasis is slightly more systematic than a YouTube video but to be completed in less time than a MOOC.	Many MOOCs offer content for which the duration is slightly longer. Users may only be interested in specific aspects of the content after which they may discontinue, which basically skews the completion rate of the MOOC but helps the user. Use of analytics in the MOOC can help analyze which specific parts of the MOOC are most popular and then a study can be done as to why. This can be branched off as a separate micro-MOOC.
7	Support for the Arabic language within the system by enabling cross-lingual information systems as a base in the system through technology.	The statistics worldwide show a clear orientation towards English. But in a regional context, more can be done.

Conclusion and Future Work

The work has so far outlined the status of MOOCs in the Middle East, tracing the reason for success, and outlining the key issues in the present scenario such as lack of participation by leading universities and lack of accreditation of existing courses. The potential exists in terms of enhancement of skills of the young population, knowledge and proper education of displaced people, enhanced participation of the private sector and the need for governments to invest in the MOOCs landscape. We also trace the trends that are emerging in the MOOCs landscape now and trace its impact on the Middle East. From these trends, a set of suggestions for the Arab MOOCs is given. There are some areas of research that have emerged which are worth exploring as future research. There is a need for surveys of all the MOOCs in the region with statistics like analysis of completion percentage of students, whether the local language courses of the same subject are more popular than the similar courses in English, and so on. There is also a need to trace the participation of Arab universities in the MOOCs era and their experiences. There needs to be a focus on skill training and MOOCs and examination of this specific aspect in the Middle Eastern context.

Abtar Darshan Singh is Dean of the School of E-Education at Hamdan Bin Mohammed Smart University, Dubai, UAE. She has published widely in instructional design, multimedia, online learning, blended learning, learning objects, MOOCs, and smart learning. Her current research interests are learning design, smart learning environments, next-generation digital learning environments, and design thinking. Abtar is a recipient of numerous awards such as a Fulbright Scholarship, a Blackboard Excellence in e-Learning Award, and an Innovative Excellence in Teaching Award. She has consulted widely with impactful projects related to e-learning under world bodies such as UNESCO and the Commonwealth of Learning (COL). She is on the International Advisory Board for the *Educational Technology in Higher Education (ETHE)* journal. She recently co-edited a book with IGI Global titled *Cases on Smart Learning Environments*.

Sumayyah Abuhamdieh is an Education Specialist who worked in the field of education for 20 years as a K–12 teacher, university lecturer, interpreter, and translator in the private sector. She later moved to UNESCO where she worked on educational projects such as teacher professional development, informal education, developing educational strategies for the Ministry of Education and Vocational Education. Currently, Sumayyah is involved in an IIEP project in Jordan for developing the capacities of Ministry of Education staff in Crisis Risk Management planning. Sumayyah has a BA in English Language and Literature and an MA in Curriculum and Teaching Methods from the University of Jordan. She can be contacted at sumayaabuhamdeih@yahoo.com.

Shriram Raghunathan works on natural language processing, instructional design, and gaming. He completed his PhD in computer science and engineering in 2008 and received his master's degree in Instructional Design (online) from the Open University of Malaysia. He set up India's first Centre of Excellence in Pervasive Computing in 2007. He also completed several funded projects (e.g., mobile Tamil interfaces, mobile keypad standardization, and plagiarism checking) in Tamil computing. Shriram has published widely in the domains of cloud computing, natural language processing, and instructional design. He recently co-edited a book with IGI Global, titled *Cases on Smart Learning Environments*. He currently is Associate Professor and Programme Chair of the Gaming Technology Division in the School of Computing Science and Engineering (SCSE) at VIT Bhopal.

References

Adham, R., & Lundqvist, K. (2015). MOOCS as a method of distance education in the Arab world—a review paper. *European Journal of Open, Distance and E-Learning, 18*(1), 123–138. doi:https://doi.org/10.1515/eurodl-2015-0009

Al-Imarah, A. A., & Shields, R. (2018). MOOCs, disruptive innovation and the future of higher education: A conceptual analysis. *Innovations in Education and Teaching International*, 1–12. doi:10.1080/14703297.2018.1443828

Almuhanna, M. (2018). *Participants' perceptions of MOOCs in Saudi Arabia* (Doctoral dissertation). University of Sheffield. http://etheses.whiterose.ac.uk/21573/1/Manal%27s%20dissertation.pdf

Alshahrani, K., & Ally, M. (2016). MOOC in the Arab world: A case study. In *Transforming education in the Gulf region* (pp. 206–215). New York: Routledge.

Al-Shboul, M., & Alsmadi, I. (2010). Challenges of utilizing e-learning systems in public universities in Jordan. *International Journal of Emerging Technologies in Learning (iJET), 5*(2), 4–10. doi:10.3991/ijet.v5i2.1147

Al-Zoubi, D. M., & Al-Rousan, N. M. (2017). *E-learning in Jordanian institutions-the latest experience (Edraak platform-the MOOC)*. Retrieved from www.researchgate.net/publication/323454960_E-_LEARNING_IN_JORDANIAN_INSTITUTIONS_-_THE_LATEST_EXPERIENCE_EDRAAK_PLATFORM-_The_MOOC

Arabiya, A. (2013). *Top global university courses to be available in Arabic for free*. Retrieved from: http://english.alarabiya.net/news-renderer?mgnlUuid=dffd57d3-5a7c-42c5-bfb9-fc611fb2c583

Arnett, T. (2014, January 6). Why disruptive innovation matters to education. *The Clayton Christensen*. Retrieved from www.christenseninstitute.org/blog/why-disruptive-innovation-matters-to-education/

Arya, U. (2017, June). The rise of MOOCs (massive open online courses) and other similar online courses variants—analysis of textual incidences in cyberspace. *Journal of Content, Community & Communication, 6*, 26–35. Retrieved from www.amity.edu/gwalior/JCCC/pdf/JCC-Journal-December-2017-26-35.pdf

Avina, J. M., & Russell, P. (2016). *IT solution to Arab youth unemployment*. Middle East Institute, Policy Focus Series. https://www.mei.edu/sites/default/files/publications/AvinaRussell_ITArabyouthemployment.pdf

Aydin, C. H. (2017). Current status of the MOOC movement in the world and reaction of the Turkish higher education institutions. *Open Praxis, 9*(1), 59–78.

Blumel, C. (2014). *Trends in ICTs youth workforce for development*. Retrieved from www.fhi360.org/sites/default/files/media/documents/TechLab_TrendsInICTs_v8-508.pdf

Cahill, S. (2013). *ALISON And silatech deliver Arabic MOOC to tackle youth unemployment in the Arab world*. Retrieved from www.einpresswire.com/article/153232188/alison-and-silatech-deliver-arabic-mooc-to-tackle-youth-unemployment-in-the-arab-world

Clark, D. (2016, February 27). MOOCs: Course completion is wrong measure. *Plan B* [Blog post]. Retrieved from http://donaldclarkplanb.blogspot.com/2016/02/moocs-course-completion-is-wrong-measure.html

Coluci, E., Smidt, H., Devaux, A., Vrasidas, C., Safarjalani, M., &Muñoz, J. C.(2017). Free digital learning opportunities for migrants and refugees. In J. C. Muñoz, S. Carretero, & Y. Punie (Eds.), *JRC science for policy report* (pp. 1–42). Luxembourg: Publications Office of the European Union. Retrieved from http://publications.jrc.ec.europa.eu/repository/bitstream/JRC106146/jrc106146.pdf

Conole, G. (2016, July 15). MOOCs as disruptive technologies: Strategies for enhancing the learner experience and quality of MOOCs. *RED: Revista de Educación a Distancia, 50*(2), 1–18. doi:http://dx.doi.org/10.6018/red/50/2

Creelman, A. (2017, June 1). MOOCs for refugees—work in progress. *The Corridor of Uncertainty: Assorted Thoughts and Reflections on Technology in Education* [Blog Post]. Retrieved from http://acreelman.blogspot.com/2017/06/moocs-for-refugees-work-in-progress.html

Docebo Report. (2018). *eLearning trends for 2018*. Retrieved from www.docebo.com/resource/whitepaper-elearning-trends-2018/

Farhat, R. (2017, December 11). *The rise of the Arab MOOCs: Will education in the Arab world ever be the same?* Retrieved from www.wamda.com/2017/12/rise-moocs-education

Freihat, N., & Al Zamil, A. J. (2014, December). The effect of integrating MOOC's on Saudi female students' listening achievement. *European Scientific Journal, ESJ, 10*(34). Retrieved from http://eujournal.org/index.php/esj/article/viewFile/4828/4537

Gais, H. (2014, September 2). Saudi Arabia gets MOOC'd up. *Al Jazeera America Online*. Retrieved from http://america.aljazeera.com/opinions/2014/9/saudi-arabia-massiveopenonlinecoursesgendersegregation.html

Gita, G. (2017). *MOOCs: Employers view, a brief snapshot.* Retrieved from www.qs.com/moocs-employers-view-a-brief-snapshot/

Hamid, T. (2014, March 19). Massive open online courses make strides across region. *The National* [Blog Post]. Retrieved from www.thenational.ae/business/massive-open-online-courses-make-strides-across-region-1.305349

Hill, P. (2016). *Online program management: A view of the market landscape.* Retrieved from https://mfeldstein.com/online-enablers-a-landscape-view-of-the-market-for-higher-education/

Horn, M. (2014, July 2). Disruptive innovation and education. *Forbes* [Blog Post]. Retrieved from: www.forbes.com/sites/michaelhorn/2014/07/02/disruptive-innovation-and-education/#1b8a8fcf3c6e

iVROX. (2018, April 16). Immersive learning: How VR is changing the nature of education. *VRFocus.* Retrieved from www.vrfocus.com/2018/04/immersive-learning-how-vr-is-changing-the-nature-of-education/

Jones, C. (2010). A new generation of learners? The net generation and digital natives. *Learning, Media and Technology, 35*(4), 365–368. doi:10.1080/17439884.2010.531278

Karr, D. (2017, September 13). How each generation has adapted to and utilizes technology. *Martech* [Blog Post]. Retrieved from https://martech.zone/generation-technology/

Kronk, H. (2018, April 4). *How the OPM market is slowly shifting out of the profit-sharing model.* Retrieved from https://news.elearninginside.com/opm-market-slowly-shifting-cost-sharing-model/

Kursun, E. (2016, April). Does formal credit work for MOOC-like learning environments? *The International Review of Research in Open and Distributed Learning, 17*(3). Retrieved from www.irrodl.org/index.php/irrodl/article/view/2403/3686

Laurillard, D., & Kennedy, E. (2017). The potential of MOOCs for learning at scale in the global South. *Centre for Global Higher Education,* working paper series, Lancaster (p. 42). Retrieved from www.researchcghe.org/perch/resources/publications/wp31.pdf

Ly, S. L. S., Saade, R. G., & Morin, D. (2017). Immersive learning: Using a web-based learning tool in a PhD course to enhance the learning experience. *Journal of Information Technology Education: Innovations in Practice, 16*, 227–246. Retrieved from www.jite.org/documents/Vol16/JITEv16ResearchP227-246Ly3172.pdf

McIntyre, C. (2017). Are MOOC certificates from Coursera and edX helpful in getting jobs? *LinkedIn.* Retrieved from www.linkedin.com/pulse/mooc-certificates-from-coursera-edx-helpful-getting-jobs-mcintyre/

Memon, M. (2015). Immersive learning vs experiential learning (what's the difference?). *LinkedIn.* Retrieved from www.linkedin.com/pulse/immersive-learning-vs-experiential-whats-difference-mohsin-memon/

Memon, M. (2017). Gami-what? Gamification or gamified learning. *LinkedIn.* Retrieved from www.linkedin.com/pulse/gami-what-gamification-gamified-learning-mohsin-memon/

MoocLab. (2017). *MoocLab report: The global MOOC landscape—2017.* Retrieved from www.mooclab.club/resources/mooclab-report-the-global-mooc-landscape-2017.214/

MoocLab. (2018). *MOOC platform comparison table—2018.* Retrieved from www.mooclab.club/pages/mooc_comparison_2018/

Music, A. (2016, November). *Massive open online courses (MOOCs): Trends and future perspectives.* Retrieved from www.oecd.org/officialdocuments/publicdisplaydocumentpdf/?cote=EDU/CERI/CD/RD(2016)5&docLanguage=En

Pagano, K. O. (2013). *Immersive learning.* American Society for Training and Development. https://www.oreilly.com/library/view/immersive-learning/9781607286431/

Raish, V., & Rimland, E. (2016, January). *Employer perceptions of critical information literacy skills and digital badges.* Retrieved from https://pdfs.semanticscholar.org/1562/0955a8c6d14b068423007b7a98e9221d5451.pdf

Ruipérez-Valiente, J. A., & Reich, J. (2018, September). *Participation of the Arab world in MOOCs.* 2018 Learning with MOOCS (LWMOOCS) (pp. 47–50). IEEE.

Sagenmüller, I. (2017, June 29). *4 disruptive education technologies poised to change higher learning* [Blog Post]. Retrieved from www.u-planner.com/blog/disruptive-education-technologies-poised-to-change-higher-learning

Saleh, Y. (2016, November 30). Arab youth unemployment could trigger more unrest by 2020, UN report warns: Arab economies may not be able to find 60 million new jobs needed by 2020. *Zawa.* Retrieved 2018, from www.zawya.com/mena/en/story/Arab_youth_unemployment_could_trigger_more_unrest_by_2020_UN_report_warns-ZAWYA20161130113340/

Sallam, M. H. (2017). A review of MOOCs in the Arab world. *Creative Education, 8*, 564–573. doi:10.4236/ce.2017.84044

Sarhan, E. (2016, 18 June). All you need to know about open education. *Taelum* [Blog Post]. Retrieved from https://taelum.org/mooc

Sekka Editorial. (2017, October 18). *First e-learning platform in Oman is bringing knowledge to all*. Retrieved from www.sekkamag.com/article/first-e-learning-platform-in-oman-is-bringing-knowledge-to-all

Shah, D. (2018, May 21). *The second wave of MOOC hype is here, and it's online degrees*. Retrieved from www.edsurge.com/news/2018-05-21-the-second-wave-of-mooc-hype-is-here-and-it-s-online-degrees

Singh, A. D., & Hassan, M. (2017). *In pursuit of smart learning environments for the 21st century (Current and critical issues in curriculum series, No. 12, IBE/2017/WP/CD/12)*. Geneva: UNESCO. Retrieved June 17, 2018, from http://unesdoc.unesco.org/Ulis/cgi-bin/ulis.pl?catno=252335&set=005977E89F_0_165&gp=0&lin=1&ll=s

Stratton, C., & Grace, R. (2016, October). *exploring linguistic diversity of MOOCS: Implications for international development*. Proceedings of the 79th ASIS&T Annual Meeting: Creating Knowledge, Enhancing Lives through Information & Technology (p. 71). American Society for Information Science.

Tan, F. (2011, July 4). South Korean schools to replace all textbooks with tablets. *The Next Web* [Blog Post]. Retrieved from https://thenextweb.com/asia/2011/07/04/south-korean-schools-to-replace-all-textbooks-with-tablets/

Tickle, G. (2015, May 7). *The void, a real-world environment combined with virtual reality for an immersive experience*. Retrieved from https://laughingsquid.com/the-void-a-real-world-environment-combined-with-virtual-reality-for-an-immersive-experience/

Tømte, C. E., Fevolden, A. M., & Aanstad, S. (2017). Massive, open, online, and national? A study of how national governments and institutions shape the development of MOOCs. *The International Review of Research in Open and Distributed Learning*, *18*(5). Retrieved from www.irrodl.org/index.php/irrodl/article/view/2751/4282

SECTION 6
Organizational Innovations

In addition to country-wide government policy initiatives, there are also important innovative projects taking place within individual organizations. This section offers four interesting chapters focused on innovations emanating from various organizations such as the World Bank and the African Virtual University.

The first chapter in this section, Chapter 23, is from Sheila Jagannathan who is Head of the Open Learning Campus at the World Bank. Readers of this chapter will discover that the World Bank Group (WBG) has invested significantly in digital and blended development learning through an open, interactive, and virtual ecosystem called the Open Learning Campus (OLC). As Jagannathan contends, the OLC's potential to support continuous learning and to build skills to prepare for future job opportunities and workplace settings in the context of the Fourth Industrial Revolution (Schwab, 2017) are considerable. Massive open online courses (MOOCs) are a major catalyst of such societal changes due to their broad global reach and democratization of knowledge. Lessons from delivering MOOCs for global audiences on development topics are highlighted as they have widespread applicability for learning providers.

In her chapter, Jagannathan describes lessons learned in the process of designing and delivering MOOCs for global audiences on critically important development topics. In the past, MOOC topics from the World Bank have included climate science to action, digital technologies, managing risk for development, citizen engagement, financing for development, public-private partnerships, and the future of work. Next up are MOOCs on maternal health and learning to realize education's promise.

Next, in Chapter 24, Atieno Adala from Kenya explains the efforts of the African Virtual University (AVU) to provide an innovative multinational teacher education degree program in math and science using open educational resources (OERs). It is important to point out that the AVU is an organization that works through a consortium of universities in Africa to help them build their capacity to exploit ICTs for the delivery of distance and eLearning programs. Adala attempts to answer the question of whether the adoption of open education resources (OER) can lead to the emergence of open educational practices (OEP). Included in this chapter are stories of OER adoption and challenges to such adoption in Uganda, Zimbabwe, Kenya, Tanzania, Zambia, and Somalia.

According to Adala, a central component of this project was that the course instructional modules be developed as OER textbooks. Creation of these open materials took place at the level of the consortium. The AVU OER authors were faculty members drawn from participating universities. Adala found that the practice of OER use tended to occur at the institutional level and was especially facilitated by the fact that they were introduced as instructional resources for a degree program. Faculty used OER as a resource for course development, for training new faculty, for lesson preparation, and for student readings. Use of OER also led to practices related to repurposing, creation, and sharing. Accessibility, institutional policies, and appropriate knowledge were some of the factors considered important in promoting moves toward OEP. Given the breadth and depth of this chapter, there is much for those exploring the use of OER to grasp and reflect upon.

In the third chapter of this section, Chapter 25, Balaji Venkataraman from Canada and Tadinada V. Prabhakar from India collaborate to describe the innovative work behind the provision of agriculture-oriented MOOCs in conditions with at best marginal bandwidth capabilities. In their chapter, Venkataraman and Prabhakar explore these concerns and demonstrate that the way forward is through learning delivery innovations. They present a case study involving MOOCs in food and agriculture in India. As a sector that is among the least influenced by online learning, there is much potential for MOOCs in agriculture. Most students and faculty in agricultural universities in the developing world live and work in situations of inadequate bandwidth. In response, the authors present their results and insights from experiences with 16 MOOCs in agriculture. Their findings reveal that innovative deployment of messaging systems and opportunities to access content offline can increase engagement in the learning process.

Once people realize how MOOCs can serve farmers in India, their perspectives expand. Can they also benefit fisherman in the South Pacific? How about ship mariners in Antarctic waters? Or perhaps yak herders in Mongolia? Yes. Yes. And Yes!

Finally, in Chapter 26, Michael Mayrath, Craig Brimhall, Graham Doxey, Scott Doxey, and Joshua Stroup, all from the USA, provide an example of a creative solution to an educational problem. When prospective MOOC learners in Kenya were found to lack the technological skills to successfully learn online, a 10- to 14-day, face-to-face onboarding program was designed and implemented to help prepare students to successfully learn online via MOOCs and OER. It is important to think about ways that the lessons learned from this one case can be quickly and successfully replicated in other countries of the Global South. In some ways, this particular chapter as well as the others in this section, also have applicability for the final section of this book on the future of MOOCs and open education.

Reference

Schwab, K. (2017). *The fourth industrial revolution*. New York: Crown Publishing Group.

23
OPEN EDUCATION IN THE WORLD BANK

A Significant Dividend for Development

Sheila Jagannathan

Recent literature has highlighted the fact that the difference between rich and poor countries can often be traced to a human capital gap. World Bank President Jim Yong Kim has explained this eloquently in a recent essay in *Foreign Affairs*. The message is that the human capital gap is not because developing countries are not investing heavily in education, but rather because the quality of instruction varies considerably from country to country.

With the Internet and mobile telephones becoming ubiquitous in more and more geographies, significant opportunities are arising to disrupt the status quo. As this occurs, a dividend for development is generated by making many more high-quality educational opportunities freely available and easy to access, including using mobile devices almost wherever one happens to be at the time.

This chapter reviews how open education could play a pivotal role in achieving the Sustainable Development Goals (SDGs), which are a comprehensive set of goals and targets set by all nations of the world to be achieved by 2030. The chapter builds on the experiences gained through the World Bank's Open Learning Campus (OLC), which has already become a significant destination for development learning.

Urgency of Achieving the Sustainable Development Goals (SDG) – 12 Years and Counting!

In 2015, the United Nations declared 17 Sustainable Development Goals (SDGs) that most of the countries of the world endorsed for achievement by 2030. These goals were established as a more comprehensive framework for eradicating poverty, compared to the earlier Millennium Development Goals (MDGs), which were under implementation between 1995 and 2015 but with mixed success. The achievements of MDGs on a global scale were:

- The number of people living in extreme poverty declined by more than half.
- The percent of undernourished people fell by almost half.
- The number of out-of-school children of primary school age fell by almost half.
- More girls were educated.
- The global under-five mortality rate declined by more than half.
- The maternal mortality ratio declined by 45%.
- New HIV infections fell by approximately 40%.

FIGURE 23.1   Sustainable Development Goals

Source: www.un.org/sustainabledevelopment/news/communications-material/

However, 13% (or 950 million people) of the world's population still live in extreme poverty on roughly less than $1.90 per person, per day. Sub-Saharan Africa and South Asia account for about 80% of the extremely poor, and these are the geographies where achieving the ambitious and time-bound SDG goals are most challenging. The glass, therefore, is at best half full; however, the empty half cannot be allowed to continue.

The SDGs build upon lessons learned from implementing the MDGs: most significantly, they emphasize the point that eradicating poverty requires moving beyond solely numeric targets. As illustrated in Figure 23.1, these 17 SDGs represent a set of development goals. In addition, there is a subset of 169 specific targets to help end poverty by 2030. Eliminating any form of discrimination because of gender, age, disability, or ethnicity is also a major aim of the SDGs.

The SDGs and their specific targets were formulated through an intensive process of consulting with a cross-section of stakeholders that included those in civil society, the private sector, academia, and various levels of government. It is important to point out that these goals have been derived through consensus for the people and planet to achieve by 2030. Whereas some of the SDGs require modifying existing business practices of governments, others rely on working collaboratively with civil society and communities, and yet others with more active engagement from the private sector. Most significantly, given that the SDGs are inter-related, the SDGs require the ability to appreciate the "holistic" nature of sustainable development.

Why Are SDGs Being Highlighted NOW?

Apart from their universal benefits, there is a valid concern about the very limited time available to meet these bold yet vital goals; in fact, there are less than 12 years left to achieve the SDGs. The consequence of not achieving the various goals and targets could be devastating. The following are some highlights of the possible outcomes if the SDGs are not achieved in a timely manner.

- Sea level rise could cause 20 of the largest ports of the world to go under water, affecting global trade.

- Over a billion people could be living in extreme poverty, while more than a third of the food produced is wasted.
- More than 1.5 million children under age 5 will die each year due to avoidable reasons.
- A billion people may not have sustained access to a reliable water supply and 2 billion people will lack access to safe sanitation, giving rise to all sorts of diseases and pervasive global migration.
- One in four of the world's children will suffer from stunted growth due to poor sanitation, which may actually become one in three in the least developed countries.
- More than half of the global urban population will remain exposed to air pollution levels at least 2.5 times higher than the benchmarks the World Health Organization has established.
- Over 265 million children are currently left out of school; 22% of them are of primary school age. Moreover, millions more children who are attending schools are not attaining basic skills in reading and math.
- 617 million youth worldwide will lack sufficient basic education to compete for well-paying jobs.
- 13% of the global population will lack access to modern electricity. *Energy poverty* in many countries is a fundamental barrier to reducing hunger and increasing education opportunities.

Climate change forecasts add to the urgency of achieving the SDGs. Already many parts of the world are experiencing unprecedented natural disasters in the form of devastating floods, hurricanes, forest fires, and droughts. Entire communities find their livelihoods disrupted and assets destroyed. Achieving the SDGs are critical building blocks to enhance our capacity to address climate change beyond 2030. While much is known to address these problems and issues, much more knowledge is required. As elaborated upon in the next section of this chapter, discovering solutions through an open learning process is now a critical ingredient for sustainable development. The possibilities are exciting to think about.

The Crucial Role of Capacity Building in Achieving the SDGs

Capacity development is the process by which individuals and organizations enhance their skill, knowledge, and experiences to improve job performance and effectively respond to new challenges including climate change, resource fragility, fast-changing educational requirements, and so on. Achieving the SDGs is particularly challenging in Sub-Saharan Africa because many countries face dual challenges: (1) adapting to climate change, and (2) building institutional frameworks that respond to fragility, conflict, and violence. The capacity of these countries to respond and adapt requires a suite of enabling policies and investment programs aimed at building awareness, deepening adaptive competencies/skills, and building accountability of service providers to users.

Capacity building is, therefore, a multifaceted concept that includes providing support for leadership development, building a culture that promotes risk taking, and creating incentives for continuous innovations, all of which contribute to robust and sustainable development. If the SDGs are to be achieved within the next 12 years, institutional and human capacity in the least developed countries must be accelerated.

Who Are the Relevant Players Who Can Accelerate Achievement of SDGs?

The hallmark of successful capacity building programs is observable changes in the way business is conducted within institutions, and behavior change that occurs among individuals working on development issues. These pervasive changes are necessary to accelerate progress toward achieving the SDGs. For this to happen, inclusion should be the cornerstone of capacity building efforts, facilitated through an open dialog involving all stakeholders, so that their perspectives and concerns are heard and acted upon. The key players include:

- Policy makers from the various sectors relevant to SDG implementation because policy frameworks often need to be reviewed and adapted.
- Practitioners, representing the professional staff (e.g., doctors, engineers, school teachers, etc.) who implement policies, as well as requisite financiers, planners, and designers who are responsible for designing the various interventions with innovative projects and programs.
- NGOs, who often work at the community level to organize and empower citizens to seek out information and demand their rights.
- Universities and research institutions, which play a key role in research and data analysis and have deep insights from several decades of experiences. As Professor Jeffrey Sachs has stated:

  We can use the global network of universities, to be an active 'solutions network to help governments, business, and civil society to chart out the pathways to successful sustainable development, and also to be the incubators for the rapid development and rapid fusion of sustainable development technologies. Universities around the world should be in the lead of helping society to find the technical solutions to achieve these goals'.

- The private sector representing business interests relating to specific SDGs, and who are knowledgeable about future market conditions.
- Youth, as citizens of the post-2030 world, need to be engaged, both to more fully appreciate why achievement of the SDGs is so important, and to become catalysts to reshape the development agenda, including the advocacy of climate mitigation and adaptation.
- Last but not the least, the ultimate beneficiaries of policy changes are the citizens owning the proposed action plan to achieve the SDGs.

Importance of "Integrated" Capacity Building to Achieve the SDGs

The need to achieve the SDGs in the limited time frame available has resulted in a transformative development agenda, affecting both existing institutions and individuals working through those institutions. One of the key requirements is to think, plan, and implement holistic solutions that cut across professional or academic boundaries.

Unbundling the SDGs for Capacity Building and Policy Action

Learning and capacity building about SDGs could benefit from unbundling the SDGs into more manageable units (see Figure 23.2). As shown in Figure 23.2, there are three pillars for unbundling the SDGs for capacity building: namely, the economy, the environment, and the social community (i.e., society). The concept was first identified in the seminal "Our Common Future" or the Brundtland Framework.

- The economy describes the financial and economic ability to generate GDP or economic growth and invest in physical and social infrastructure necessary to sustain progress.
- The social community recognizes the importance of societal norms and cultural structures within which communities are organized, and the disruptions which usually end up exacerbating conflict and violence.
- The third pillar of the environment describes the various social costs arising out of pollution and degradation from human interactions with nature. Untreated wastes from cities and industries, for example, affect surface and ground water and the habitats of various species living in

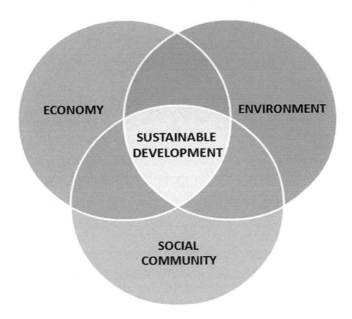

FIGURE 23.2 Unbundling the SDGs for Capacity Building

Source: Image adapted from www.yourarticlelibrary.com/environment/what-is-the-importance-of-sustainable-development/9910

the ecosystem. Also highly problematic is the clearing of rainforests which affects the size of carbon sinks, and, thereby, releases dangerous amounts of greenhouse gases to the atmosphere. Add to that the dilemmas brought about by coal-based power plants, which are key contributors to global warming, unregulated deep-sea fishing that destroys the habitats of many aquatic creatures, and the various perplexities faced by both man and animals with the rapidly thinning of the Arctic ice. Worse, climate change can exacerbate these social costs across regions and even continents with the unpredictability in the frequency and timing of severe droughts, floods, and hurricanes. Such news is indeed quite grim.

A key role of development practitioners is to engage people beyond the typical academic silos and comfort zones that too often are formed around the knowledge gained from prior research. For example, an urban transport planner may be committed to looking at ways to improve mobility and develop affordable mass transit in cities, whereas a gender specialist may seek to track the challenges for working women to balance their work and home environments. Yet, in many situations, these two specialists are dealing with a set of interlinked challenges. If bus routes are not appropriately designed, the home maker living in a slum may find it impossible to participate in the job market in more affluent parts of the town because of difficulties in commuting between the home and the job opportunity. However, capacity building does not always take place in a linear pathway, one issue at a time. Instead, it often evolves in a holistic manner, integrating cross-sectoral learning.

Take, for example, the SDG 4, which is education for all. In many societies, this requires overhauling the way education for girls is being offered, not only in terms of better facilities, including school toilets, but also in terms of Gender Equality (SDG 5). This goal involves changing societal norms and conventions on the roles and responsibilities of girls as well as building the trust and support from parents. It also requires providing nutritious meals so that girls from very poor families are incentivized to come to school rather than scraping a living to just feed themselves. Finally, part of this goal entails ensuring safety in their commutes from the home to the school and back.

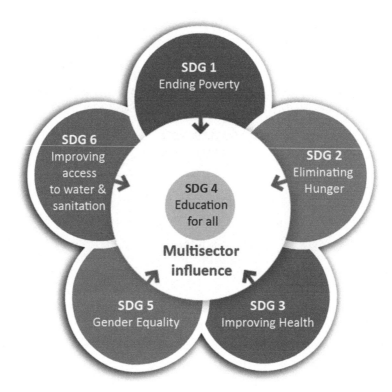

FIGURE 23.3 Multi-sector Influence

Ending poverty (SDG 1), eliminating hunger (SDG 2), improving health (SDG 3), and improving access to water and sanitation (SDG 6) are all important building blocks. Without a doubt, capacity building needs simultaneous strengthening across several sectors. A gender specialist tasked to develop a program for SDG 5 (Gender Equality) needs to be fully aware of her critical role in achieving SDG 4 as illustrated previously. The education specialist working on SDG 4 (Quality Education) needs to be equally aware of the linkages between human capital formation issues, skill upscaling, and continuous learning concepts. Figure 23.3 illustrates these inter-relationships.

Open Learning: An Instrument to Unlock Global Knowledge to Deliver Local Solutions

Open learning facilitates the diffusion of best practices both through institutions and individuals, while breaking down barriers of affordability and accessibility. Through open learning repositories, capacity building and training institutions in developing countries acquire access to high-quality learning products that can be customized to local contexts. Open learning also serves individual learners with several advantages, including the following:

- *Learn anywhere and anytime*: The profile of the learner is typically that of an adult who is already juggling a complicated work-life balance. Open learning offers the advantage of being able to digitally access the required knowledge and learning flexibly.
- *Scale-up capability across geographies and cultures cost effectively*: Open learning is available at relatively lower cost than traditional instructional interventions, and now high-quality translation through software is becoming increasingly available. In addition, open learning saves the learner the costs of acquiring textbooks and other printed materials.

- *Rich library of supplementary learning materials*: Open learning makes available publicly accessible learning materials that are invaluable supplements to materials given in the classroom. Such supplemental content resources enable interested and curious learners to undertake "deeper dives" into the materials if there is interest. Moreover, blogs, videos, audio recordings, and other applicable multimedia can greatly enrich and enhance the learning experience.
- *Building communities of practice*: Many mid-career learners from developing countries appreciate the opportunity to share challenges and solutions as well as experiences. Fortunately, open learning often results in a long-term professional exchange of insights that lead to virtual communities of practice.
- *Opportunities to improve quality of content*: Wikipedia has demonstrated the power of group authoring and co-creation of content. If a feedback loop is provided, as in Wikipedia, the quality of content could be continuously improved.

The 12-year countdown remaining to achieve the SDGs is taking place at a time when a parallel opening up of pathways to learning, unimaginable even a few years ago, is occurring. As highlighted in the 2018 Mobile Congress held in Barcelona, the mobile Internet will be accessible in every part of the world by 2023—or within just five years. Equally significant is the dramatic lowering of costs with a simultaneous increase in functionality of smart hand-held devices that can be inexpensively and rapidly recharged.

However, the process of leveraging technology breakthroughs for learning requires pedagogical innovations that build on these emerging opportunities. In its absence, the default mode is for software apps to provide games and entertainment to owners of hand-held devices in developing countries. If, as an alternative, open learning is promoted for achieving the SDGs, suitable learning material must be made available in attractive, engaging, and interactive formats. The effectiveness of such open learning interventions depends on the quality of pedagogical design and packaging; notably on how effectively it fosters interactivity and sustained interest among learners.

World Bank Group's Open Learning Campus (OLC)

In response to these developments in open learning as well as the revolution currently unfolding in instructional design and educational technology in the US and elsewhere, the World Bank established the Open Learning Campus (OLC) as a single destination for development learning for Bank Group clients and staff alike. The OLC offers digital and blended learning on a variety of development topics to a cross-section of policy makers, practitioners, academics, and NGOs as well as to the public.

Those accessing the OLC will find learning on a broad range of development topics from health systems for the poor that promote rural development to the use of artificial intelligence to revolutionize economic development. Importantly, the OLC enables geographically distributed staff to refresh their skill-sets while working in teams to deliver on the SDGs. World Bank Group (WBG) clients also learn about various ongoing innovations aimed at improving service delivery outcomes for each of the SDGs. These clients represent a cross-section of society, ranging from senior officials to civil society groups, academia, organized labor, and the ordinary citizen. The OLC also offers courses for civil society to learn about their rights and obligations, such as how women can be empowered through education and labor participation, how local governance can be improved through civic participation, how accountability can be enhanced among civil servants, and so on.

The OLC is an open educational resource for anyone at any place and at any time. It offers a range of products, from blended courses (offered on a cohort basis, at fixed time frames of 4–6 weeks) to bite-sized learning nuggets that are available as needed. The OLC is also a virtual repository of WBG knowledge; it has begun converting more and more of WBG's knowledge products and flagship reports (such as the World Development Report and country and regional technical reports) into learning products that are easily accessible through the Internet. Through these processes, the WBG's tacit knowledge is unlocked, and often re-packaged into absorbable content and made available to its staff, clients, and partners.

Since its launch more than 4 million learners from 190 countries have visited the OLC. It is also important to point out that approximately 7,000 digital learning activities have been designed and curated. Gradually, the vision of the OLC is beginning to be realized although much work remains. In the years to come, the OLC will continue to convene, connect, contextualize, and co-create learning for and with our clients and development partners. When successful, the OLC will not simply be a destination for just-in-time content, but perhaps, more importantly, it will evolve into a vibrant destination for problem-solving conversations and communities.

Flexible Learning Pathways for the Busy Professional

The OLC leverages advances in pedagogy and technology to provide distinctive formats to match the evolving needs of learners through structured courses, bite-sized lessons, and vibrant communities of practice. It harnesses a wide array of educational technology including mobile capabilities, cloud-computing, and innovations in e-learning to produce a world-class learning ecosystem through three schools of learning. Among the key principles are offering robust content, innovative delivery methods, and access to the course resources and tools from anywhere and at any time.

- The first school, WB Talks, enables the busy professional to explore nuggets of knowledge through talks, podcasts, videos, and games.
- The second school, WB Academy, helps the learner to unpack deep learning related to development challenges and solutions through virtually facilitated or self-directed e-courses, MOOCs, and blended learning.

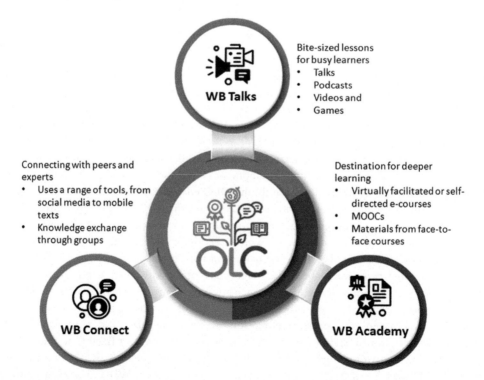

FIGURE 23.4   Flexible Pathways to Learning

FIGURE 23.5 Examples of WB Talks—Bite Sized Learning

- The third school, WB Connect, enables learners to engage with others to find crowd-sourced solutions to development challenges. Using a range of tools, from social media to mobile texts, knowledge exchange can be promoted between clients, partners, and global citizens. Examples of such communities include urban floods, Smart Cities, and integrated water management and land and house thematic groups.

Open Learning in Action

Open learning on what works and what doesn't work is critical to help development practitioners appreciate the challenges and opportunities of innovations that could expedite the elimination of extreme poverty and enhance shared prosperity. The two examples to come illustrate how open learning using digital technologies helps building capacity on SDGs in a much more cost-effective way than more traditional reliance on only face-to-face training.

Example 1: *No More Business as Usual With Climate Resilience*

This course provides guidance on supporting the integration of weather and climate services. Timely information on rainfall and temperatures is of critical importance to small farmers in making decisions on when to plant, what types of crops to grow, and when to harvest.

This facilitated e-course helps teams and project managers integrate weather and climate services considerations into their projects, from concept to delivery. The course is divided into four modules: (1) an introduction to the benefits of weather and climate services and the value-chain approach; (2) a deeper dive into the value chain, from the collection and management of water and weather data to the delivery of climate information to end-users, as well as all of the institutional actors involved along the way; (3) how the range of investment options is applied in the context of a real-world project; and (4) an examination of Satellite Earth Observations, to learn about its potential for modernizing weather and climate services in developing countries.

Example 2: *Getting People Where They Need to Go: Learning About Transit System Maps and Data Feeds*

This interactive e-course shows how to set up and use the General Transit Feed Specification (GTFS). It enables transit planners to utilize an open data standard for organizing transportation data so that it can be easily accessed via applications and websites, such as Google Maps. It is an extremely useful format for transit data in developing country cities, both for public transit agencies trying to keep up with transit planning and operations, and for passengers accessing transit services. GTFS "feeds" enable agencies to publish transportation schedules and geographic and fare information in a format that can be easily accessed, updated, and used by citizens as well as service providers.

Learning modules cover the history and file structure of GTFS, setting up a GTFS feed, GitHub and Open Source tools, stories from the field, how to map transit data, how to collect data for a city's first feed, App surveys, and GTFS Realtime. This course is intended to raise awareness of best practices for mapping informal transit systems and provides the tools and knowledge that transit agency staff need to make evidence-based planning, policy, and investment decisions.

The OLC provides a rich library of learning courses and content across all sectors and regions that is curated from operational groups within the WBG and includes external global knowledge. The learning focuses on best practices and lessons from failures and is facilitated by global and regional experts on development topics from the WBG and the broader development community.

A Possible Framework for Capacity Building to Achieve the SDGs

SDGs are ambitious targets set by the global community. Achieving them requires multiple layers of capacity building across different geographies and constituencies (such as policy makers, practitioners, academia, civil society, and every individual). In Figure 23.6, six areas are identified for capacity building.

Take the example of building capacity to achieve SDG 6 (i.e., clean water and sanitation). A recent World Bank evaluation study estimates that about 660 million persons are without access to improved sources of water, and 2.4 billion people are without improved sanitation facilities. Strikingly, a majority of these individuals reside in Sub-Saharan Africa and South Asia.

Bridging the gap in access to improved water and sanitation is a core concern of SDG 6, which seeks "to ensure availability of sustainable management of water and sanitation for all." There are several areas of support needed by stakeholders if this goal is to be achieved.

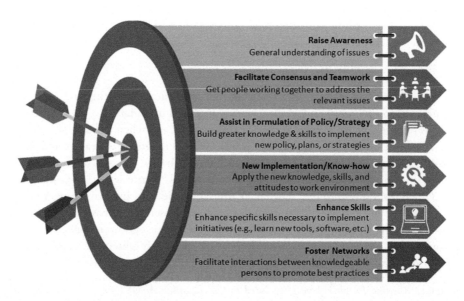

FIGURE 23.6 Areas for Capacity Building

- The first column, raising awareness, provides learning that communicates some core messages that are targeted to reach all constituents. For example, to eradicate open defecation practices, apart from building toilets, health-related and other risks need to be communicated among stakeholders who currently are unwilling to change their lifestyles. Increased awareness is the first step in the process.
- The next three columns describe some key elements relevant for effective delivery of the SDGs; such as greater engagement with beneficiaries in decision making, sharing effective practices from other parts of the world, and applying the learning to real-world challenges to effect change in policies.
- The fourth column focuses on specific skills required to achieve the SDGs. For example, if villages are to operate and manage piped water supply systems through water user associations, villagers should acquire the skills to maintain a pressurized network, learn how to manage billing and collections, and provide customer-focused services.
- The last column aims at building networks or communities of practice that can share and learn from each other. For example, in Sub-Saharan Africa, Uganda is often identified as a quality model for developing urban water utilities; as a result, other countries have been learning from their experiences.

Summing Up

As open learning matures, it redefines the way educational certification and credentialing can be acquired. Such trends toward open online learning enable educators and policy makers to reimagine education from the ground up, while helping to customize learning to suit existing as well as emerging job needs. One could visualize a future scenario in which degrees are not as important as acquiring specific skills that could be learned through modular programs that are much more cost-effective than earning graduate and post-graduate degrees. MIT's edX, for example, already offers a MicroMasters credential that is worth about 25% of a Master's degree but at a fraction of the cost. A prerequisite at the policy level is to introduce continuous learning on a variety of topics.

The menu of open learning choices is already expanding from MOOCs to micro-courses, and even shorter bite-sized learning and self-paced courses that focus on specific skills a learner would like to learn. Along with the expansion of offerings, there needs to be a quality vetting process through accreditation or certification that is recognized by employers and academic institutions. Finally, a business model that balances the free part of open learning with minimum cost recovery necessary to sustain the services is required. For young learners facing challenges of financing quality education, funding from charitable foundations and CSR allocations could bridge the cost gap. By contrast, capacity building among workforce participants, interested in reskilling and upskilling, could recover costs by charging for the course assessments or any resulting certification or both.

Without a doubt, open learning in the age of the mobile Internet will attract a substantially higher proportion of bite-sized learning than in the past. Attention spans today are shaped by the small screens of handheld devices. With such tools at the ready, there is a preference for brief, focused, and engaging learning materials that mimic the audiovisual feel of a variety of digital media and resources, including YouTube, Wikipedia, TED talks, Tweets, Facebook, and other social media. Such on-demand digital content can be delivered through any medium and is particularly relevant for formats such as video talks, podcasts, caselets, infographics, short talks, and policy briefs.

With a plethora of such content now available and supported, deeper learning opportunities are possible in open online learning such as through MOOCs and other innovative types of learning offerings. Needless to say, the World Bank will continue to experiment with various forms of open online learning as well as other disruptive pedagogies and technologies for learning in the coming decade. Society, the global economy, and the environment are counting on innovations and breakthroughs of leveraging open education in developing countries to meet the SDGs, notably the challenge from climate change and fragility among the poorest countries.

Sheila Jagannathan is the Head of the Open Learning Campus at the World Bank Group in Washington, DC. She serves as the organization's focal point on digital learning and issues at the intersection of technology use and education in emerging countries. She is an innovative and strategic educational leader with over 30 years of experience in designing and managing distance learning programs/knowledge products and transforming the use of online and classroom pedagogies and technology. Sheila also provides policy advice and technical assistance to World Bank country-level capacity building programs in East Asia, China, Africa, the Middle East, and South Asia. She is on the advisory board and planning committees of major professional associations of e-learning such as the E-learning Africa and the International Conference on E-Learning (ICEL).

References

Agarwal, A. (2013). Why massive open online courses (still) matter. *Ted.com* [online]. Retrieved from www.ted.com/talks/anant_agarwal_why_massively_open_online_courses_still_matter?language=en.

Boerner, H. (2018). "Our common future" – the masterpiece of Gro Harlem Brundtland, also known to many as the influential "brundtland report" | sustainability update. *Ga-institute.com* [online]. Retrieved from https://ga-institute.com/Sustainability-Update/2016/02/19/our-common-future-the-masterpiece-of-gro-harlem-brundtland-also-known-to-many-as-the-influential-brundtland-report/

Carvalho, N. B. (2018). Mobile world congress 2018 [around the globe]. *IEEE Microwave Magazine, 19*(6), 120–121.

Collins, A., & Halverson, R. (2018). *Rethinking education in the age of technology: The digital revolution and schooling in America* (2nd ed.). New York: Teachers College Press.

eLearning Inside News. (2018). *MOOCs from a learner's perspective: A conversation with Dhawal Shah, Founder of Class-Central.com | eLearningInside News* [online]. Retrieved from https://news.elearninginside.com/moocs-learners-perspective-conversation-dhawal-shah-founder-class-central-com/.

Google Developers. (2018). *GTFS realtime overview | realtime transit | google developers* [online]. Retrieved from https://developers.google.com/transit/gtfs-realtime/

Gordon, A. (2018). "MicroMasters" surge as MOOCs go from education to qualification. *Forbes* [online]. Retrieved from www.forbes.com/sites/adamgordon/2018/02/13/voice-of-employers-rings-out-as-moocs-go-from-education-to-qualification/#45c9f05a564b

Griggs, D., Stafford-Smith, M., Gaffney, O., Rockström, J., Öhman, M. C., Shyamsundar, P., . . . Noble, I. (2013). Policy: Sustainable development goals for people and planet. *Nature, 495*(7441), 305.

Kim, J. (2018). The human capital gap. *Foreign Affairs* [online]. Retrieved from www.foreignaffairs.com/articles/2018-06-14/human-capital-gap

Sachs, J. D. (2015). Achieving the sustainable development goals. *Journal of International Business Ethics, 8*(2), 53–62, 61.

SDSN Australia/Pacific. (2017). *Getting started with the SDGs in universities: A guide for universities, higher education institutions, and the academic sector* (Australia, New Zealand and Pacific ed.). Melbourne: Sustainable Development Solutions Network—Australia/Pacific [online]. Retrieved from http://ap-unsdsn.org/wp-content/uploads/University-SDG-Guide_web.pdf

UNDP. (2015). *The millennium development goals report 2015* [online]. Retrieved from www.undp.org/content/undp/en/home/librarypage/mdg/the-millennium-development-goals-report-2015.html

World Bank. (2011). *Overview of WBI's capacity development and results framework: Approach to guide the assessment, design, monitoring, and evaluation of capacity development efforts (English)*. World Bank Institute Capacity Development and Results Practice. Washington, DC: World Bank Group. Retrieved from http://documents.worldbank.org/curated/en/106621467998824685/Overview-of-WBI-s-capacity-development-and-results-framework-approach-to-guide-the-assessment-design-monitoring-and-evaluation-of-capacity-development-efforts

World Bank. (2018). *Atlas of sustainable development goals 2018: From world development indicators*. World Bank Atlas. Washington, DC: World Bank. © World Bank. Retrieved from https://openknowledge.worldbank.org/handle/10986/29788 License: CC BY 3.0 IGO.

24

FROM OER TO OEP

The Case of an OER-Integrated Teacher Education eLearning Program in Africa

Atieno Adala

Introduction

This chapter is based on a study that sought to explore whether the availability of open education resources (OER) could lead to the emergence of open educational practices (OEP). This proposition was informed by the argument in the literature that there has been an undue and disproportionate focus on building more access to digital content, with too little consideration given to whether access alone will support innovative educational practices in teaching and learning (Camilleri, Ehlers, & Pawlowski, 2014). OEP seeks to build on OER and moves on to the development of concepts of how OER can be used, reused, shared, adapted, and created. The underlying assumption is that with the appropriate structures and policies, availability of OER has the potential to lead to open education practices (Camilleri et al., 2014; Ehlers, 2011).

Context of Adoption

The context of adoption of the African Virtual University (AVU) OER was the development and implementation of a teacher education program in Math and Science that integrated ICT and OER in its design and delivery. A number of the universities in the AVU consortium already had some form of distance learning programs, but ICT-integrated delivery of courses was still in the early stages. The AVU project was instrumental in the use of interactive online, open, distance, and eLearning methods that collectively came to be known as ODeL.

The faculty that participated in the project cited ICT-integration as one of the major benefits of the AVU project. An administrator from one of the consortium universities who was involved in the project at its inception stated that "initially the Faculty of Sciences was hesitant to adopt an open, distance and eLearning teaching mode for the science courses, as they felt that science courses could not be taught online (ODeL)." Their stance, however, was altered when they participated in the AVU project, admitting that it led to a *"paradigm shift."* In fact, the project not only convinced the leadership that online and distance teaching of science courses was feasible, but it also led faculty to endorse the importance and impact of ICT-integration from infrastructure to design of learning materials.

The importance and impact of ICT-integration was echoed by most of the faculty in the study. A director of distance learning at one institution noted the following, "[ICT] integration element is the strongest aspect of AVU and I believe that I would still support integrating of ICT into the teaching of anything [as that] is the strongest point that AVU made." Giving the example of the animation of the heart, he highlighted how integrating technology in teaching brought instruction to life. He noted that following the lead of the AVU, his institution had now incorporated ICT integration in the development of its courses.

OER Module Development Process

The OER content was developed and authored by subject matter faculty from the consortium universities. They were trained in the skills of identifying and presenting e-learning content, a process that was facilitated by ICT integration in education experts. A module development template was provided to guide authors in how to insert subject content such as links to online and multimedia resources, learning activities, assessment activities, and reading references. The template also provided instructions on how each section of a module was to be written with regards to content and teaching methods.

The use of "open content" was mandatory in the creation of the modules. Although the use of the term "OER" was not particularly widespread when the project began, participants came to know that OER could include software tools such as open office, content management systems, open journal articles in the Directory of Open Access Journals (DOAJ), worksheets, and repositories such as MERLOT. Many of these resources were projects started by universities mostly from the North, such as the University of California, Michigan State University, and the University of West Indies. A number of the suggested sites and resources were from Canada, especially, for French-bilingual resources. Unfortunately, many of the sites suggested at that time no longer exist.

Process for the Adoption of an Open License

One of the concerns for the creation of OER is that the licenses adopted allow for the free use, repurposing, and sharing of OER (Hilton, Wiley, Stein, & Johnson, 2010). In the creation of the AVU OER, certain strategies were undertaken to enable the modules to be released as open. First of all, these included the stipulation that members of the consortium agree to assign intellectual property rights to one institution or to the consortium overall in order to allow the resources to be released under a Creative Commons license. Secondly, individual module authors and peer reviewers had to waive their intellectual property rights to AVU by signing a Creative Commons agreement. And thirdly, in the development of the modules, authors were directed to use and repurpose relevant OER readily available online or create their own original materials. Consequently, this approach made it possible for AVU to release the modules as OER under the Creative Commons license; hence, allowing users to freely access, use, repurpose, and share the resources.

Once the AVU OER modules were developed, they were submitted to a peer review process, then sent back to the authors for preparation of the final draft. Next, they were sent to the materials development coordinator who worked with a team of editors and instructional designers. In addition to the AVU OER modules developed for the degree programs, other modules were developed for use in short certificate courses in ICT Basic Skills and ICT-Integration (in teaching of science subjects) for use by the consortium universities to train faculty and student teachers.

OER-Integrated Degree and Certificate Programs

The consortium universities were to take the jointly developed degree program and offer it at their own institutions in conformity with their own accrediting (awarding) structures. However, this goal proved to be a challenge, and of the six institutions represented in the study, only two offered

TABLE 24.1 Institutional Context of Adoption and Use of AVU OER

University (pseudonym)	OER-integrated degree program in Math & Science	OER-integrated short certificate courses in ICT Integration	Instructional resource for existing programs
UC Uganda	Yes. Bachelor of Education (ODeL) Science	No	Yes
UE Zimbabwe	Yes. Bachelor of Education (Science & Maths) ODeL program	No	Yes
UA Kenya	No	Yes	Yes
UB Tanzania	No	Yes	Yes
UD Zambia	No	Yes	Yes
UF Somalia	No	Yes	Yes

the OER-based joint degree program. The faculty from a university in Uganda mentioned that their institution offered a Bachelor of Education (ODeL Science) based on the OER-integrated program, and the faculty from a university in Zimbabwe noted that their institution offered a Bachelor of Education (Maths and Science) ODeL program. Even though participating faculty had indicated that the OER-integrated degree program was offered at their institution, they noted that "the modules are heavily supplemented and complemented by other OER sources, sometimes to the extent that they may not necessarily take a primary position," explaining that it really depended on the particular lecturer giving the course (see Table 24.1).

The certificate courses were offered at four of the universities; still, all used the resources to varying degrees. The resources that were released as AVU OER were also made available via the AVU website. These programs were also being offered in the Francophone and Lusophone countries/universities; however, in this study, the focus was on the Anglophone countries.

Methodology

This study sought to get an in-depth understanding of the impact of OER on the emergence of OEP in a specific context of implementation. The units of analyses in this qualitative case study are four specific dimensions of OEP being investigated: (1) use of OER, (2) repurposing OER, (3) process for creation of OER, and (4) degree of sharing of OER. The levels of analysis are also derived from the OEP conceptual framework that identified four main categories of stakeholders including policy makers, management and administration of educational organizations, educational professionals (such as faculty, instructional designers, course developers, etc.), and learners. In the case of this study, three levels of analysis were delineated—namely, the level of the AVU network (consortium), and the level of the participating institution, and the level of faculty. Data collection methods included face-to-face interviews and an online questionnaire.

Face-to-Face Interviews

The face-to-face interviews formed the pilot study that helped inform the design of subsequent instruments. A semi-structured questionnaire was developed and was administered to the respondents during face-to-face interviews. While the questionnaire offered some structure, follow-up questions to obtain an in-depth understanding or clarification was used throughout the interviews.

The sampling of respondents was purposive in that they were identified from AVU records, but also respondents suggested other respondents. The respondents were representative of both administration and faculty. For example, the institutional level of the partner institution was represented by respondents that were acting in some administrative capacity such as a Director of the Center for Open and Distance Learning, Coordinator of Open, Distance and eLearning (ODeL), or Head of the Mathematics Division. The individual level was represented by the individual faculty members. The ones selected for interview were in some way familiar with the AVU OER.

Online Questionnaire

A questionnaire was developed and administered online using Survey Monkey and completed by 16 people. The questions covered four dimensions of OEP, namely—extent of use, extent of repurposing, availability of a process for OER creation, and degree of sharing of OER. Under each dimension there were sub-questions related to the impact of AVU OER on these dimensions as well as the barriers, quality assurance and research personnel, and the degree of institutional support and recommendations.

Research Sites and Respondents

The study respondents included six people from Tanzania, five from Uganda, three from Zambia, one from Zimbabwe, one from Somalia, and 10 from Kenya. They were deans, department heads, directors of Open and Distance Learning, e-learning project leaders, coordinators of programs, directors, and authors as well as peer reviewers of AVU OER module.

Open Resources: Cost Issues

While the consortium universities adopted the AVU OER modules and the ODeL mode of delivery, when it came to implementing OER-integrated degree programs, not all the institutions offered the program. For example, an author of AVU OER in Kenya noted that in participating in the project, his understanding was that his institution would offer the ODeL degree program, but he was not clear why that did not happen. The following explanation from an ODeL administrator in Kenya may shed some light on why that was the case. The administrator admits that even though participating in the development of the OER integrated joint-degree program meant that his university did not have to develop its own program in that area, there were a number of factors why the institution did not offer the ODeL program. He pointed to the fact that, "they were only in four broad subject areas [math, biology, chemistry and physics], therefore, they were going to exclude several other areas."

The second drawback was the cost-sharing arrangement. The expectation was that a percentage of student fees (about 33% of US$1,000 per student) be remitted back to AVU. For the administrator, the contention was that even if his institution signed on to this agreement, they would still have to use their own resources and materials. He advised against the cost-share, contending that the resources were already open and free, "because it is going to cost us money yet we have adequate resources we can use [to teach] our students by distance mode without having to sign into this [agreement] other than *openness* [yet the resources] are available for accessing and for which we don't have to pay."

Faculty from the other institutions also had varying explanations why their institutions had not offered the OER-integrated degree program, mostly to do with alignment to the curriculum. Nonetheless, whether the institution offered the OER-integrated degree program or not, the AVU OER modules were still adopted by individual faculty members at these institutions and incorporated in various ways that suited their purposes.

Impact of AVU OER on the Practice of Use

In the OEP guiding framework it is argued that finding and using OER is often the first step towards OEP (Camilleri et al., 2014). In this case study, the availability of OER happened within the context of the implementation of the OER-integrated teacher education program outlined previously. Access to the AVU OER had implications for the dimension of use. Faculty indicated using the AVU OER content in a variety of ways. There were those who noted that the AVU OER formed part of the readings for students in the degree program. An author of AVU OER from Zimbabwe noted that OER formed part of the required reading texts for most of the courses offered in the Bachelor of Education (ODeL) degree program. A Uganda instructor who has used AVU OER models noted that the soft copies of the AVU OER on CD were extremely helpful as they avail the materials to the students before they [meet] face-to-face. A math author of AVU OER from Kenya noted that they used [the OER] to reinforce the distance learning program and recommend "the books [to] our distance learners."

The use of OER in lesson preparation was cited by most of the faculty. More specifically, they indicated consulting OER when preparing their own courses and lecture notes. For instance, a Tanzanian respondent noted using AVU OER modules "as a guide for preparation because the contents are highly organized," while another noted that the modules were very good for topic introduction and improved students' understanding.

A number of faculty noted that the AVU OER was being used as a resource in the development of their distance learning materials. As an example, an ODeL administrator from Kenya submitted that the use of OER was embedded into the practice of the institution; in particular, in areas where it was developing distance and open learning materials. He noted that AVU OER and other OER materials were being used as resources to train faculty and in the development of courses for distance learning. As he stated, "we use resources that are in familiar areas and from familiar institutions."

The resources for this training and development included the AVU OER, the Commonwealth of Learning, and Teacher Education in Sub Saharan Africa (TESSA) program (Wolfenden, Buckler, & Keraro, 2012). Importantly, compared to the other two, the AVU OER were particularly the closest to their curriculum; a factor that could be partly due to the fact that UA faculty did participate in the creation of some of the AVU OER modules. In terms of the interviews, an assistive special technologies instructor from Tanzania noted that he used OER when developing course materials as did an instructor from Tanzania who mentioned using OER in the course development.

Most indicated using the AVU OER to supplement their existing programs and courses. For instance, one respondent in Tanzania pointed out that the AVU OER was mainly used by lecturers and students as supplementary resources. Additionally, one respondent in Uganda indicated that the modules have extensive supplementary information, while another person in that country noted that the modules were used alongside the university curriculum. At the same time, a respondent from Zambia added that his institution uses OER not only from AVU Teacher Education, but also from other sources such as TESSA. A similar perspective was mentioned by someone from Zimbabwe who shared that they are used "in conjunction with other OER sources as supplements and complements." On the other hand, an author of AVU OER from Kenya whose institution did not offer the OER-integrated degree program indicated that the AVU OER were being used as a primary resource in their existing Bachelor of Education program. The fact that extent of use really depended on individual faculty seemed to hold true whether an institution offered the newly developed OER-integrated degree and used the OER as primary resources or incorporated the use of the AVU OER to supplement existing programs.

Level of use and integration whether at the level of the individual or the level of the institution seemed to have implications as to how all the other practices were adopted. When comparing the extent to which all the practices were employed, using OER at the level of the individual faculty was the most pronounced. And the practices were higher at the level of the individual than at the level of the institution.

Impact of AVU OER on Practice of Repurposing

Integrating an OER into one's own teaching and learning is called repurposing. Repurposing often involves dismantling the original resource and taking what is useful and setting aside the unnecessary. Repurposing was done by faculty using the OER to contextualize the OER to the requirements of the context, such as any prevailing standards in the syllabus or industry requirements. Faculty members in this study also indicated that they customized the modules to suit the university's standards and to conduct lessons.

Repurposing—Need to Adapt to Contextual Conditions

Faculty indicated that they repurposed the AVU OER to adapt them to certain contextual standards or conditions. One respondent from Tanzania noted that adaptation was done in recognition of differences in local contexts. He argued that the AVU OER modules provided insight for development of his own modules and that he freely uses them when developing courses. An administrator from Uganda indicated that the teaching staff had customized modules to suit the university's standard, and that they customized the modules to conduct lessons. Another respondent from Kenya stated that depending on industry and stakeholder requirements "repurposing OER to align with the syllabus is certain," indicating that they picked the relevant content and methodologies and improved them by "inserting new developments in our syllabuses." As an example, an ODeL administrator from Kenya explained that in the development of courses, the OER were not being used as is, but were being repurposed by the course writers when developing their own instructional materials. Along these same lines, a dean from Uganda cited adapting the modules by adding supplementary content to the AVU OER.

Repurposing—Need for Collaboration and Stakeholder Involvement

The need for collaboration and stakeholder involvement in repurposing was cited by faculty.

Among those mentioning repurposing, a respondent from Tanzania recommended the need to arrange for joint review to update some materials, while another from Uganda suggested that inter-university physical visits be encouraged. Additionally, a respondent from Zambia argued that the AVU program organizers at their institution should work with instructors to begin the process of repurposing, which in turn can spread to others. Also, a respondent from Kenya indicated that they are given the liberty to fit industry and stakeholder proposals into the syllabi and thought that stakeholder and industry recommendations should be included. He pointed to brainstorming sessions as a strategy. Finally, a respondent from Uganda identified low involvement of the key stakeholders as a barrier and recommended that such stakeholders be involved in the repurposing of the OER.

Repurposing—Need for Appropriate Knowledge and Skills

There was the recognition of the need to acquire knowledge and skills, which was seen to have implications for repurposing. Faculty cited the need to organize workshops, train staff, and avail more resources for training. One of the study respondents from Tanzania identified the lack of knowledge and skills as barriers and recommended that the available materials be taught to community members, while another from that country indicated that the institution should organize a workshop on AVU OER. Respondents from Uganda recommended the training of staff while also acknowledging that staff training was being carried out.

Constraints to Repurposing

Access to OER online had implications for repurposing. Those who indicated high extent of repurposing pointed to the fact that the AVU OER were on the university website for members to access. As an example, a curriculum coordinator from Tanzania indicated that materials are freely available in the university library as a matter of policy. Conversely, a dean of science from Uganda noted that accessibility of online resources is not easy. At the same time, one instructor in Tanzania identified that a lack of bandwidth was a barrier, and an ODeL center director from Uganda cited that the extent of repurposing was low, noting that his "university has not bought computers to control scarcity of media," and recommended the need to buy computers.

Time and motivation were also cited as having implications for repurposing. Prominently, the Ugandan ODeL center director indicated that some [of the] teaching staff were overwhelmed with work and also this was due to end user attitudes as a factor. Another interviewee from Uganda cited time limitations and yet another pointed to the need for more resources.

Issues that cut across all the practices such as awareness, access to ICT, and knowledge and skills are discussed next.

Impact of AVU OER on the Practice of Creation

In the OEP guiding framework (see Camilleri et al., 2014), the availability of a process for OER creation is key. In order for an organization to progress towards OEP, it is important to define a process whereby educational resources are made available under free license schemes to become open educational resources. Only then will these resources be available for others to use and/or repurpose internally as well as externally. Suffice to say, a comprehensive organization-wide process for OER boosts progress towards OEP.

Impact of AVU OER on the Practice of Creation

A number of the faculty indicated that adoption of AVU OER did have an impact on their practice of creation, although they were at various stages from having created OER (i.e., "e-content)" to being inspired. Some of these course instructors had participated in authoring the AVU modules. Among them, an instructor in Tanzania noted that he had developed a course on Academic Integrity, whereas an author of AVU OER from Uganda pointed to developing a module on simulations and field data. Along these same lines, a different instructor in Tanzania explained that he was in the process of creating an OER course by using available OER materials, while another in Tanzania specifically mentioned articles he had published in open access journals. Still further inroads were made by an instructor in Kenya who pointed to the fact that they use AVU OER to write other modules for their distance education program as did a Tanzanian instructor who pointed out that teachers use them to update their lectures.

An instructor in Uganda referred to developing "e-resources" and other e-content that he had developed and uploaded to the LMS platform. Additionally, an instructor in Uganda spoke of having designed "e-resources" and they were being used. Others mentioned being inspired, such as an instructor un Zimbabwe who stated that, "the OER had an inspiring effect and opened the possibility that was never apparent to me before." To the north, an instructor in Uganda stated that he had developed an interest in designing an OER module for the Bachelor of Education online program through a "Faculty of Education" project supported by the Commonwealth of Learning (COL) at his institution.

Institutional Efforts to Support Practice of Creating OER

Some of the faculty pointed to the efforts by their institutions towards developing a process for creating OER. One person in Tanzania indicated that there is a move by his institution to transform all its courses into OER. Similarly, a Ugandan instructor indicated that efforts are being made to make online resources part and parcel of teaching and learning and to institutionalize the use of online materials. An instructor from Kenya indicated that his university encourages that each course should have an OER module, although these are still restricted to the university use. One interviewee in Zimbabwe indicated that "individuals are free, actually heavily encouraged to create and utilize OER, but this depends on individual will and skill."

Permissions to Open Resources

Issues related to obtaining permissions to open instructional resources were raised by a respondent from Kenya. He explained that the adoption of the AVU OER modules influenced the institution into wanting to create and make their resources open. He cited academic visibility as a benefit of making resources open by showing the kind of academic information being provided to students in the various programs. He mentioned that such transparency can mean the promotion of staff members, and also opportunities to consult and collaborate with peers. However, he argued that opening up the institution's courses required addressing issues of intellectual property. The current terms at his institution were that course authors "surrender the courses to the institution to use but [the authors] retain the intellectual property right." This is a serious scholarly and political matter, as he explained that if his institution in Kenya wanted to open and share its resources, it would require a change in policy to allow for the institution to open up its resources globally.

Constraints to Practice of Creation

Conversely, limited access to OER was seen to hinder the dimension of creation. An instructor in Uganda noted that even the existing OER content was not readily available to the lecturers, whereas another in Tanzania pointed to unreliable power and Internet connectivity. He recommended that the infrastructure be improved. Similar to the practice of repurposing, the lack of appropriate skills was highlighted by some faculty including those in Uganda and Tanzania who noted that facilitation was inadequate and that there was a lack of procedures for creating OER. There was a general lack of exposure to the necessary information for creating OER content. At the same time, an instructor from Uganda insightfully pointed to the need for alignment with the university curriculum so that content did not deviate much from the university curriculum.

The Practice of Sharing of OER

The guidelines reveal that the most successful use of OER is where there is some type of a sharing process. Not too surprisingly, the *openness* required for sharing educational resources is a key success factor for OEP. In addition to a culture of sharing among practitioners and management, tools for sharing resources and experiences within the organization and with actors from other organizations must exist. It is as important to share resources as it is to share the experiences of what works and what does not within OEPs. Social network tools, therefore, play an essential role in any OEP strategy.

Impact of Sharing on Updating Curriculum

The AVU OER was shared (distributed) through the various ways already described earlier. Faculty indicated that being able to access OER had an impact on their practices with regards to its use, repurposing, and creation as well as sharing. Access to the resources afforded instructors the opportunity to review and develop new courses and programs. One instructor and author of AVU OER from Zimbabwe noted his department's participation and use of the AVU model for its BEd program. At the same time, faculty from the Open University of Sri Lanka have been known to refer to the AVU OER in the development of their own program.

Resources Mostly Shared With Students

When it came to sharing the OER, faculty mainly shared with their students. An instructor in Tanzania indicated that he directed students to access the learning resources through the AVU website, whereas a department head from Kenya mentioned that they usually recommend the AVU OER to their distance learners as additional reading and learning resources. These instructors urge their junior faculty to use them alongside other distance learning resources in order to enhance their teaching. For example, an instructor in Zambia indicated that he has mainly shared AVU and TESSA OER with other colleagues, and recommended sharing with all his students and fellow colleagues.

With regard to print copies, an instructor and administrator from Kenya explained that when the AVU OER was distributed to their institution, they shared them with students and the teaching staff. Some copies were also taken to the library so that people who needed to use them could have access. In Kenya, the first batch of students were given the original print textbooks while for the subsequent groups, the institution reproduced copies of the textbooks and distributed them to the students.

Sharing as Collaborative Practice

Sharing as a practice among faculty is also considered key to developing collaborative practice that has implications for quality of teaching and learning. An instructor in Zambia mainly shared AVU and TESSA OER with other colleagues. Similarly, an instructor from Kenya stated that apart from sharing the original copies of the AVU OER, he shared his notes with other tutors. At the same time, a fellow instructor in Uganda advised that collaborations be established and recommended the need to work in teams.

Further still, an instructor in Zimbabwe proclaimed that the modules were inspirational when it came to sharing and noted that working in teams was critical in his department. He also posted the notes on the AVU LMS so that others could see and make their comments – "For AVU I think I was sending the notes that I repurposed and my notes were being shared by other tutors elsewhere so that they could go through them ... Even in the LMS there was a place we were posting notes so that others could see and if there was any issue they could comment."

Tools for Sharing

ICT tools and infrastructure were particularly key for the dimension of sharing. The following themes were identified—existence of a platform for sharing, such as a repository or LMS, social network tools, Internet connectivity, ICT learning facilities, and access to computers. Conversely, a lack of access to IT resources led to low impact on the practice of sharing.

A study respondent from Zambia mentioned that he shares OER using social networking tools. Similarly, an instructor in Kenya noted that he was able to share and redistribute AVU OER because of the use of social media tools such as YouTube videos, Facebook, email, and blogs that support sharing and exchange of information about OER. Furthermore, he noted that use of such social media tools that support sharing and exchange were a widespread reality among him and his colleagues. An instructor in Tanzania revealed his university was creating a repository for sharing OER. Similarly, a Zambian instructor indicated that faculty shared OER through the institutional repository online, whereas a respondent from Uganda noted that his university had built an LMS and had free WiFi that fostered his ability to share resources on his university LMS platform. Another study respondent from Uganda mentioned the introduction of "e-campus" platform that made it possible to share materials more readily.

Constraints on Sharing

The low extent of sharing was implicated in instances where the mode of teaching was perceived to not support the practice, or the content was considered inadequate. For example, there was a complaint in Uganda that sharing was low because "lecturers have stuck to traditional way[s] of teaching." In addition, poor Internet connectivity, inadequate ICT teaching and learning facilities, and a lack of computers for students' use were cited as major barriers to sharing.

Cross-Cutting Issues for All the Practices

Although some factors were unique to each of the dimensions, there were also factors and conditions that cut across and had implications for the extent to which all the practices—use, repurposing, creation, and sharing—were performed. These factors included perceived relevance of the resources, access to connectivity and ICT tools, freedom to practice OEP, lack of awareness, need for appropriate skills and training, need for stakeholder involvement and collaboration, and institutional policies to support OEP.

Low Use and Other Practices Due to Inadequate Content

While faculty highlighted the various ways the AVU OER content was useful as an instructional resource, they also pointed to some limitations. The perceived lack of relevance of the content was considered to have implications for low emergence of all the practices. While an instructor in Uganda noted the modules were good for introduction, they were not adequate for the distance education degree program that was aligned to the full-time degree program at the university. He indicated that the modules "don't provide all the content as in the curriculum." He recommended to revise modules in line with the BEd curriculum. Another Ugandan respondent stated that it was a challenge to blend the AVU materials with the university curriculum. Perhaps worse, a third instructor from Uganda was concerned that the modules were developed about 10 years ago and needed significant revising. He noted that, "the modules were fairly used in the first five years but now the lecturers" had access to more current information and publications "which is demanded by students." The need for revision was also echoed by an instructor from Zimbabwe who stated that continuous improvement on the AVU OER is encouraged at his institution. He argued that the AVU OER modules should be considered foundational and then there is a need to "modify, refine or adapt them for one's purposes in sensitivity to the context." Obviously being able to revise, repurpose, and update OER is an important step to move towards OEP.

OEP Requires Access to Connectivity and ICT Resources

Faculty who cited the high extent of use pointed to having access to the AVU OER or other OER online, while pointing out that they were available electronically and readily accessible to all. In Tanzania, the AVU OER are on the university website for all to access; in particular, in the university library. Instructors in Zambia could access the Internet in their offices and it was easy to access online materials when it was working well. Access to the AVU OER had implications for all the practices of use, repurposing, creation, and sharing, and faculty who cited low extent of use also detailed limitations as far as access to OER. Clearly, there was a pressing need for reliable access to the Internet and ICT infrastructure and tools. Though lack of reliable ICT tools was not the only cause, it was a key issue that was mentioned.

Technology-Related Barriers to OEP

Lack of access to adequate technology infrastructure and resources such as Internet connectivity and computers was cited by most as a barrier to OEP. In Zambia, there is often a challenge with the Internet facility so that instructors cannot access the OER when they need it. Limited access to Web-based materials due to poor connectivity was also noted in Uganda, as exemplified the following quote, "inadequate supply of network in the university especially in lecture rooms and computer labs." Even those who had identified being able to readily access OER online cited poor Internet connectivity as a barrier to accessing OER. Limited computer facilities and unavailability or high cost of Internet connectivity was also apparent in Zambia and Somalia.

Alongside poor connectivity, lack of access to computers was also cited as a barrier to accessing OER. In Uganda, some lecturers do not own computers and are not connected in their homes. As one Ugandan instructor put it, "many students still do not have computer[s]." The situation seems not much better in Kenya where most people use personal laptop computers but not everyone has them. A respondent from Zambia stated that the lack of computer facilities to support the students in their homes and schools was a barrier to use.

Across these countries, most of those who cited limitations in accessing OER pointed to technological constraints. Nevertheless, there were other issues such as lack of awareness, knowledge, and skills as well as a lack of sound institutional policies and practices.

Lack of Awareness

Lack of awareness of the AVU OER was one of the themes that emerged especially in response to barriers to use and the extent of institutional support. A number of faculty who cited use and repurposing as low made recommendations on the need to create awareness and promote OEP. One instructor stated that he found the AVU OER on the bookshelves and started using them but was never informed by his institution of their availability, and another one stated that he had never been officially informed of AVU OER. He suggested that the university should inform course instructors on the availability of OER materials that can be used in their courses. He further recommended that the university repository should be promoted to the general public. Still another instructor stated that his administration fully supported AVU OER programs and the materials were available, but that awareness was not at the desirable level.

In Zambia, an instructor mentioned that his institution rarely designs OER due to the fact that many of the AVU OER modules are not known, and, therefore, they cannot tell which sections of the modules should be repurposed. He noted the need to popularize the modules so that more people at the institution can know about them and use them in lessons. He recommended trying out the OER in various classes of pre-service students of biology, chemistry, physics, and mathematics who were not part of the select groups that participated in the AVU Teacher Education project.

If the OER are found to be helpful to the learners, then recommendations should be made to the institution to make them part of the materials used in teaching and learning.

Freedom to Use OER

While most faculty indicated a lack of institutional policies in place to integrate the practices, they pointed to having the freedom to use, repurpose, create, or share OER. Instructors in Tanzania stated that they are free to use the AVU OER modules and that AVU OER are freely utilized, provided that they are appropriately acknowledged. An instructor in Zimbabwe claimed that the use of OER is left to the discretion of the individual lecturer. As he stated, "individuals are free and actually heavily encouraged to create and utilize OERs, it really [is] left to individual will and skill." Similar practices exist in Kenya where each lecturer has the liberty to use OER from AVU and other recognized institutions that can help enrich the learner experience. As such, one Kenyan respondent noted that "any lecturer who is ICT compliant [literate] has no problem in using OER at whatever level." He also noted that they are free to repurpose content and are given the "liberty to fit industry and stakeholder proposals into the syllabuses." A study respondent from Somalia indicated that like in most other universities, faculty are very autonomous in their operations. He stated that the administration fully supports AVU OER modules but noted a lack of implementation capacity which needs to be addressed for impact of the AVU OER modules to be truly felt.

What these quotes and stories reveal is that freedom and autonomy to adopt OER is distinctly different from lower levels of the educational system that is dominated by textbook publishers and the use of OER may not be readily encouraged or supported. Nevertheless, as detailed in this chapter, with proper planning and support, significant change may be in the offing in the coming decade.

Knowledge and Skills

Having the requisite knowledge and skills to use, build, and refine OER was seen to have implications for all the OEP practices. Stated the other way, not having the appropriate knowledge and skills was considered a serious constraint to the emergence of OEP. The need for training across all the dimensions was identified alongside the need to involve all stakeholders. A Tanzanian instructor recommended that all course instructors should undergo training on creation of OER, while one in Zambia recommended sensitization of staff on the benefits of OER as well as capacity building activities. Over in Kenya, a suggestion was made that each person should be trained to write self-instructional content. Similarly, someone in Uganda made an appeal to management to increase the number of staff training sessions on the use of the LMS platform.

Lack of motivation

In many interviews, motivation was also cited as having implications for the practice. Factors cited for the lack of motivation included lack of time, high workload, lack of interest, and negative attitudes.

Conclusion

In the OEP guiding framework, it is argued that finding and using OER is often the first step towards OEP. The key assumption is that the other practices, such as repurposing, creation, and sharing, should follow from there. Indeed, that was confirmed by this study. The AVU OER were being used in a variety of ways, notably in the development of course materials, for the purpose of training faculty when developing their own courses, for lesson preparation, for student readings, and to enrich the curriculum. The availability of the AVU OER led to use, with the extent of use cited as ranging from high to low depending on the faculty and other prevailing conditions.

In addition to factors that were unique to each of the dimensions, there were factors that cut across and had implications for the extent to which all the practices—use, repurposing, creation, and sharing—were performed. These factors included the perceived relevance of the resources, access to connectivity and ICT tools, freedom to practice OEP, lack of awareness, need for appropriate skills and training, need for stakeholder involvement and collaboration, and institutional policies to support OEP.

Except in some instances where it was indicated that the AVU OER were used to develop other courses and programs, the practices were taking place more at the level of the individual faculty than at the institutional or organizational level. Such savviness with OER ultimately depended on the knowledge, experience, and interest of the faculty in relation to the OER. For OEP practices to take root at partner institutions, there needs to be a higher level of integration of OER into the curriculum. As indicated, it is essential that OER integration occur at the institutional level, not solely at the individual faculty level. Appropriate policies to support such efforts must be developed and refined during the coming decade for fuller impact of OER to take place across the African continent and beyond.

A. Atieno Adala is Director of the Centre for Excellence in Learning and Teaching, and Associate Professor at the United States International University (USIU) Africa located in Kenya. She is Research Mentor for the International Research Collaborative for Established and Emerging Scholars [IRCEES] in Educational Technology, a collaboration between e/merge Africa and the AECT Culture, Learning and Technology division. She is currently an instructional design consultant and lead evaluator for the Sexual and Reproductive Health and Rights (SET-SRHR) project being implemented in Uganda by the Institute for Social Studies at Erasmus University as part of the Netherlands Initiative for Capacity Building in Higher Education (NICHE). Before that, Dr Adala was with the African Virtual University (AVU), Kenya, as Manager of Research where she led the AVU research and development agenda in open, distance, and eLearning. She received her PhD in Instructional Systems Technology and Master of Public Health from Indiana University, Bloomington.

References

Camilleri, A. F., Ehlers, U-D., & Pawlowski, J. (2014). *State of the art review of quality issues related to open educational resources (OER)*. Seville: Joint Research Centre, European Commission. Retrieved from http://is.jrc.ec.europa.eu/pages/EAP/documents/201405JRC88304.pdf

Ehlers, U-D. (2011). Extending the territory: From open educational resources to open educational practices. *Journal of Open, Flexible and Distance Learning, 15*(2), 1–10. Retrieved from www.jofdl.nz/index.php/JOFDL/article/view/64

Hilton III, J., Wiley, D., Stein, J., & Johnson, A. (2010). The four 'R's of openness and ALMS analysis: Frameworks for open educational resources. *Open Learning: The Journal of Open, Distance and E-Learning, 25*(1), 37–44.

Wolfenden, F., Buckler, A., & Keraro, F. (2012). OER adaptation and reuse across cultural contexts in Sub Saharan Africa: Lessons from TESSA (Teacher Education in Sub Saharan Africa). *Journal of Interactive Media in Education*, (1). Retrieved from http://doi.org/10.5334/2012-03

25
RESPONSIVE INNOVATIONS IN MOOCs FOR DEVELOPMENT

A Case Study of AgMOOCs in India

Balaji Venkataraman and Tadinada V. Prabhakar

Introduction

The mainstream media in the OECD countries was once particularly interested in the sudden phenomenon known as MOOCs, going so far as to call the year 2012 the Year of the MOOC (Pappano, 2012). While media interest in MOOCs has declined significantly over the years, by 2019, the MOOC paradigm has rapidly matured. A number of universities in the OECD countries now offer degree programs online, largely based on the success of MOOCs. The MOOC paradigm is more relevant today than it was six years back. Its relevance is more due to the usefulness of MOOCs and MOOC-like derivatives in advancing the paradigm of Open Online Learning.

The international community is committed to achieving the United Nations "Sustainable Development Goals" (SDGs; United Nations General Assembly [UNGA], 2015). Sustainable Development Goal 4 (SDG4), whose aim is to "ensure inclusive and quality education and lifelong learning opportunities for all" (UNGA, 2015, p. 14) places education and lifelong learning at the same level. One of the many challenges faced by developing countries in achieving SDG4 is the need to build viable human capacities on scale and at speed. There is an increasing realisation among policy makers in education that existing or conventional structures and processes alone will not be adequate. The MOOC can become an ally in this quest for a quality-oriented solution that combines scale and speed in building capacity. In this chapter, we will offer a few examples to show how the MOOC can be suitably re-engineered and adapted to serve as an auxiliary tool in support of achieving the SDGs, especially SDG4. We term this group of efforts "MOOCs for Development" (Venkataraman & Kanwar, 2015a, 2015b).

The Commonwealth of Learning has brought out a number of publications where the potential of MOOCs to contribute to increasing access to learning has been highlighted and explained (Boga & McGreal, 2014; Patru & Venkataraman, 2016; Porter & Beale, 2015; Prabhakar, 2012; Venkataraman & Kanwar, 2015a, 2015b). Importantly, all these publications have developing countries as the focus of interest. In addition, we have noted the interest of academics in Sub-Saharan African countries in making use of MOOCs to increase the reach of academic institutions (Castillo, Lee, Zahra, & Wagner, 2015).

In an earlier time, it was usual to view the MOOC as a package of online services that particular brands were able to offer to the global public. That has led to a trend that is relatively sceptical of the usefulness of MOOCs in the Global South (see, for example, Altbach, 2014; Sharma, 2013). In the non-OECD world, however, a different approach to MOOCs has emerged. In China, for instance, the XuetangX, which is now one of the largest MOOC providers in the world, uses Open Source software codes of edX with substantial additions of its own to operate its platform. The SWAYAM and National Programme for Technology Enhanced Learning (NPTEL) MOOCs in India make use of customised platforms designed by Internet companies such as Microsoft or Google. Rather than contextualise courses offered by global MOOC brands, these initiatives have proceeded with building their own platforms as well as courses.

To reach a typical learner in a developing country, especially in semi-rural areas, it would be necessary to make serious adaptations in a typical or "industry-grade" MOOC platform. There are a massive number of aspiring learners who are faced with serious limitations in access to viable data connectivity for socialising (Tarus, Gichoya, & Muumbo, 2015; Touray, Salminen, & Mursu, 2013; United Nations International Children's Emergency Fund, 2018). Therefore, most of them are unfamiliar with the ethos of the online world, such as online peer-to-peer discussions, communities of practice, or purposive online. They unfortunately find themselves in the "last mile" zone in the online paradigm. Moreover, a teacher in a typical university in a developing country requires a reasonable amount of effort at induction into the world of online teaching, mentoring, and facilitation (e.g., Koneru, 2019). Lower the barrier to induction and greater is the chance of more teachers and learners participating in the online paradigm, thereby opening educational opportunities for countless millions of potential learners and instructors.

Overcoming Limitations Through Innovations

A variety of such limitations have been analysed in a recent review by King, Pegrum, and Forsey (2018) of issues as well as possibilities related MOOCs and OER in the Global South. These limitations can be overcome through a process that combines responsiveness to contexts with innovations in online technologies. It is in this background that the Indian Institute of Technology in Kanpur (IITK) and Commonwealth of Learning (COL) found it useful to build an entry-level online platform to access or manage MOOCs in an easy as well as effective manner. The platform, called "mooKIT," was launched in 2015 and has been deployed in 61 course offerings as of January 2019. Of these MOOCs, 21 were offered in partnership with COL. The mooKIT has also been offered by COL and IITK as a service to the University of the South Pacific, Athabasca University, and the National Open University of Nigeria to offer their own MOOCs. A number of innovations were incorporated in the mooKIT platform over a period of 44 months to overcome at least some of the limitations.

Scalability of the Technology Platform

In the period 2015–2018, a total of 155,914 enrolments were handled by the mooKIT platform. Approximately 52,000, or about one-third of the enrolments to date on mooKIT, occurred in a single offering of a MOOC meant for high school and college students. During this time, the platform performed reliably and delivered services to learners, faculty, and the course management team for the duration of the course (eight weeks) without interruption. In effect, this was a valuable demonstration of the scalability and viability of the mooKIT platform.

Supporting Access to MOOC Services at Relatively Lower Bandwidth

This goal is partly achieved through use of YouTube as the video streaming service which is known to optimise its delivery based on the bandwidth available at the browser's end. The mooKIT further provides its own user interface to enable the user to vary the speed of the video. A user can also opt to listen to just the audio track while browsing the slides as downloadable PDF files. If the user bandwidth is such that even audio cannot be streamed, a user can opt to use her/his phone to receive the audio track as a voice call. An offline version of mooKIT has been available since 2017 for use by learners who are operating in conditions of extremely limited bandwidth.

Compatibility With Mobile Communications Paradigm

The mooKIT has been designed, from the beginning, as a mobile-responsive platform. It is known that in developing countries, Internet traffic from mobile devices is greater than that from desktop or laptop computers (Meeker & Wu, 2013). Further, messaging, a typical activity in mobile devices, has more users annually compared to users on Web-based social media platforms (Meeker, 2016). Messaging as a service tends to use relatively lower amounts of bandwidth compared to browsing the Web. Since 2017, the mooKIT has provided an app via the Google Play Store as well as the App Store. Importantly, it is made available free of cost. A learner can opt to access the course using this app which uses messaging protocols that require relatively less bandwidth.

Making It More Affordable for Institutions to Offer

Cost is a factor for institutions that intend to offer MOOCs. There are at least two groups of costs: (1) First of all, there is the cost of access to a MOOC management platform; (2) Second is the cost of computer processing power for scalability if an institution deploys its own platform. An early MOOC study from Hollands and Tirthaly (2014) cited a figure ranging from US$70,000 to US$325,000 as the cost of producing and delivering a single offering of a MOOC using a branded platform. Such financial resources are well beyond the means normally available to an institution in a developing country. To address this dilemma, the mooKIT does not have access costs. Currently, it is at the release stage as an Open Source application. The mooKIT is also designed to work with relatively smaller amounts of processing power, thereby contributing to lower operating costs. As a result, at the level of 10,000 users, mooKIT will require much less of the processing power typically needed in a branded MOOC management system with the same number of users.

Providing Easy-to-Use Interfaces for Faculty to Manage the MOOC

These interfaces are developed specifically for those that are unfamiliar with management of processes and events online. The mooKIT is also designed to integrate with Web-based social media platforms such as Facebook. The idea is to enable faculty and learners to participate in course discussions in spaces that they may be more familiar with in their daily lives.

Integration With a Public Blockchain

A significant development recently is the integration of mooKIT with a public Blockchain (Grech & Camilleri, 2017). In 2018, *mooKIT Wallet* was made available free of cost (via Google Play Store as well as the App Store) to learners to keep their certificates and records in an immutable fashion using the public Blockchain.

In summary, mooKIT is a platform that has incorporated a number of technological innovations that are useful in overcoming a number of limitations known in making use of the MOOC in the Global South. Developed in response to inputs gathered from learners and faculty, these innovations are useful in helping learners and faculty unfamiliar with the world of online learning to participate easily in the MOOC paradigm. A number of mooKIT details have been described elsewhere (Prabhakar, Venkataraman, & Revathy, 2018).

AgMOOCs: A Case Study in MOOCs for Development

A large subset of MOOCs offered by COL and IITK focus on topics in the food and agriculture sector. Numerically speaking, the general presence of this sector in the MOOC paradigm is relatively minor. For example, among the 11,400 courses catalogued in Class Central (www.class-central.com) in early 2019, less than 100 were related to agriculture. In 2014, COL organised a consultation with the Indian National Academy of Agricultural Sciences to gain a perspective on the usefulness of MOOCs in the food and agriculture sector (Devakumar, Venkataraman, & Yaduraju, 2014). The consultation revealed that there was considerable scope of possibilities that needed to be addressed. There was a clearly felt need to build human capacities in different areas in the sector. As an example, there was a gap in training research professionals in emerging topics as well as training extension personnel to solve new problems in the field quickly. There was also a pressing need to provide training on the job to personnel in agro-industry and in agri-businesses. In particular, there was a widely felt need for training farmers in emerging techniques in agricultural production, protection, and processing. The scale of these issues and opportunities was massive given the potential number of people involved. Following this consultation, IITK launched the AgMOOCs India consortium jointly with COL. The purpose of the consortium was to explore and establish the viability of the MOOC paradigm in food and agriculture through the organisation of a series of MOOCs aimed at developing countries (see Commonwealth of Learning, 2015).

The consortium members met every year during 2015–2017 to decide on the topics that needed to be addressed in the AgMOOCs and to conduct capacity strengthening programs for the faculty volunteers. Any interested faculty could propose a course and it was assessed for suitability as an offering from the consortium. Relevance of the topic was a major consideration. Every course was designed at the mid-level of an undergraduate program in an agricultural university. In addition, the courses would be supplementary in their approaches and scope and would not repeat what was already taught in most university curricula. Faculty capacity strengthening sessions allowed interested faculty to build segments through extensive trials that were peer-reviewed by consortium members. During these sessions, they worked with experts in online pedagogies, mentoring, and assessment as well as with advanced practitioners in online media production. A multidisciplinary course team based at IITK provided the engineering and communications support for the AgMOOCs that were designed and delivered.

A key activity in the consortium was to promote the courses through multiple channels. Standard digital media channels were used extensively, including email and social media campaigns. Team members at IITK also mailed out announcements and posters to hundreds of campuses, especially those located in the northern regions of India which were mostly rural. Additionally, IITK personnel occasionally visited some of the campuses to conduct special orientation sessions.

During 2015–2018, the AgMOOCs consortium offered 16 MOOCs. Twelve were unique while the remainder were repeat offerings. The specific topics of these MOOCs included therapeutic nutrition, functional foods, crop diseases, and pest management. Other topics involved IT and geographic information systems in agriculture. A list of all these courses is available at www.agmoocs.in/courses. Each MOOC was of six to eight weeks in duration. Importantly, every MOOC was open to anyone interested. No pre-requisites were stipulated. No fee of any kind was levied on the learner for accessing the course or for assessments or certificates if found eligible. Adherence to an honor code was mandated for anyone that enrolled.

Each course offered two types of certificates. One certificate was based on a learner completing a threshold level of participation as measured in terms of the number of videos viewed completely and on the number of posts that he or she made in the course forums. The other was called a "competency certificate." In effect, this competency certificate required a learner to complete assignments and secure a minimum score in the assessments. The certificates were awarded by IITK and COL as founding partners.

At the end of each course, participants were invited to respond to a survey which was online and offered anonymity. An average of 25% of the active learners participated in these surveys. The results are summarised and presented in a set of public online folders (www.agmoocs.in/feedbacks). The partners also conducted a series of large-scale trials that entailed delivering learning services to practicing farmers that used a basic cell phone to access the courses. Results from these trials that covered about 2,000 users have been reported elsewhere (see Moloo, Prabhakar, Venkataraman, & Khedo, 2018).

Overview of AgMOOC Results

We present results from the analytic modules (aggregates) as well as from the surveys of participants noted earlier. The AgMOOCs had a total of 44,301 enrolments in 48 months, of which over 10,200 were issued certificates. About 28% of the survey respondents were women and approximately 65% of the enrolments were deemed active. Participants signed up from 94 countries. India, Nigeria, Kenya, Nepal, Egypt, and Afghanistan were the top six countries. Partners invested a total of US$110,000 over 48 months which translates as an investment of about US$11 per certificate. Almost 95% of the learners were students or faculty in agricultural colleges and universities. For most of the learners, the purpose of joining the MOOC was knowledge enrichment.

The overall results were encouraging. Among the positive signs was that most participants were satisfied or highly satisfied with the content (87%) as well as competence of the instructors (90%). Nearly 95% of the participants were of the view that the course management system helped them meet the course objectives. Additionally, about 90% agreed that the pace of the courses was comfortable for learning. Of key importance, over 95% noted that they would recommend these massively open courses to others. Somewhat surprisingly, almost 66% indicated that they would have taken the course even if no certificate was offered. Nevertheless, the rates of certification increased from about 9% of enrolments in 2015 to 23% in 2018.

We were delighted that the course platform, mooKIT, functioned well in all the offerings. Of particular importance, the mooKIT was accessible 24/7 for the course duration without interruption. Maintenance tasks were carried out in such a way that no interruption in platform access or services ever occurred. At the same time, about 88% of the learners considered the platform to be easy to use. As an indicator of this deemed ease of use, almost 90% of participants accessed the course videos, and almost all accessed them within the course space (that is, without using YouTube services). About one-fourth of the learners used just the audio track possibly due to limitations in local access to the Internet.

We were also interested in how learners accessed our AgMOOCs. Per the 2015–2016 data, the access device that they employed at that time was mostly a desktop or laptop computer. By 2017–2018, however, almost half of the learners were using a mobile device to access the AgMOOCs. The increase in the use of mobile devices in AgMOOCs from 2016 onwards may be due to the increased availability of high-speed mobile networks in India where most of the learners were located. More recently, the mooKIT mobile App released in 2017 has come into wider use. In 2018, almost half of the participants that used mobile devices were using the App at least occasionally. About 82% indicated that the availability of the App led to increased engagement in the course.

Lessons and Limitations in Building at Scale

The AgMOOCs project 2015–2018 provides a case study in deploying MOOCs for development. The AgMOOCs coverage is mainly oriented towards developing countries. Secondly, this project was designed to conduct advanced trials in scalable open learning in the food and agriculture sector which is not served by major players in online learning. Sustainable Development Goal 2 (UNGA, 2015) is concerned with ending hunger and promoting sustainable agriculture. A critical process in achieving this goal is building adequate human capacity. Deploying the advantages of scalable learning technologies in support of this process is meaningful and relevant.

The results show that the MOOC paradigm can indeed be harnessed in support of building capacities at scale in the food and agricultural sector. Our results also show that through sustaining in the MOOC space, institutions can hope to increase enrolments as well as rates of certification. Some of the insights gained from our MOOC offerings to date are listed next.

Barriers to Entry in MOOCs Can Be Lowered for Faculty and Learners in Developing Countries

Results from AgMOOCs demonstrate that a platform such as mooKIT can be designed and operationalised to reduce barriers related to cost as well as familiarity. The mooKIT interfaces and assessment systems are easy for even first-time MOOC faculty to work with. In addition, learners have found the mooKIT consistently easy to manage the process of learning because unfamiliar processes of online socialising are not mandatory as seen in many other MOOC courses and offerings.

Limitations in Access to MOOCs Can Be Overcome

The most optimal way to overcome limitations is to generate practical innovations along the way. In the developing world, one quick route to such innovations is via the rapid increase in access to the Internet using mobile devices. The design of mooKIT took this emerging trend into consideration. Messaging can work under conditions of lower bandwidth. The mooKIT uses messaging protocols in the design of the App. There is an offline version available as well. We are delighted to report that high levels of learner engagement and satisfaction resulted from such mobile messaging innovations with the mooKIT.

Faculty Capacity Development Is Essential

Successful researchers and well-regarded instructors in particular disciplines may not always be successful to the same extent while delivering courses in a more interactive or online medium such as a MOOC. As a result, re-orientation and retooling of such scholars through professional development courses and experiences is a must. The MOOC is a media-heavy online event. The faculty members and instructional design staff involved should understand the nuances of managing a MOOC as an online event with potentially huge participation rather than a conventional face-to-face class with more restricted enrolments and confined learning opportunities.

Mentoring of Learners Is of Critical Importance

A significant proportion of enrolled learners are unlikely to be familiar with being purposive while in cyberspace. Our experience is that investing faculty time in different mentoring tactics and instructional advice would add value to the efforts of the MOOC learners. For example, use of a live "hangout" with the faculty on a few occasions during the course does contribute to improved engagement in the course.

Emphasise Quality and Relevance of Content, Not the Celebrity Status of the Faculty

We found that carrying out research on the potential audience for a course is valuable in identifying relevant topics and content resources. As would be expected, determining relevance to the context is a key factor in gaining a larger number of learners. Ability to deliver quality in content, assignments, and mentoring is also a critical factor in MOOC scalability and overall success. The celebrity status of a faculty member placed in a developing country context is not easy to communicate across the regions and typically is not material to the viability of the course offering.

Certification Is Valued

Participants in our MOOCs often operated under difficult conditions including facing infrastructure limitations and needing to spend their own resources to overcome them. Many participants faced serious demands on their time because they were enrolled in challenging curricula in university/college courses as full-time students. Extension or industry personnel also operated in difficult environments. For all of these learners, a certificate is a significant and highly valuable outcome of the investment of their limited resources and time. Such personal rewards are why any guarantee of a free-of-cost assessment and certificate for eligible performers is important in innovative initiatives such as MOOCs for development.

Strategic and Multi-Modal Promotion of Courses Is Helpful

A number of self-directed learners in developing countries do not have access to channels of information on emerging learning opportunities online. Hence, a pro-active, targeted campaign in the digital and social media space is helpful. Our surveys show that word-of-mouth among peers is still a dominant channel.

Final Reflections

Building human capacities at scale, at speed, and with quality is priority in policy for organisations, institutions, and entire governments. In fact, for close to a decade now, the MOOC paradigm and associated inroads into technology-enabled learning in general have attracted the attention of policy makers from all corners of the planet, whether representing developing nations or more developed countries. In a recent triennial meeting of the Commonwealth Ministers of Education, the Ministers sought to learn about the ways that MOOC programs have been operationalised in member countries (e.g., see Commonwealth Secretariat, 2018).

The current trend of universities offering full-fledged degree programs using scalable learning technologies is a further indication that the MOOC paradigm is past the phase of unrealistic expectations. As our results from the AgMOOCs project indicate, some of the development priorities in developing countries can be addressed with the MOOC paradigm serving as an ally.

This inference is at variance with opinions recently expressed by Reich and Ruiperez-Valiente (2019) based on an analysis of massive amounts of learner analytic data obtained from the edX platform. Their large-scale data of more than 1 million MOOC registrations contends with the notion that MOOCs will disrupt the higher education space through providing avenues to high-quality education that can help democratise higher education as was advocated by early MOOC adopters and proponents. Instead, two-thirds of MOOC enrolments in that study came from developed parts of the world and just slightly over 3 percent of MOOC participants completed their courses in 2017–2018. However, others like Rascoff and DeVaney (2019) have quickly rebutted such views by arguing that MOOCs have enabled "stackability" in learning, wherein MOOC courses, micro-credentials, and certificate programmes offer a new learning ecology of credentials that opens access to learning in ways that Reich and Ruiperez-Valiente (2019) and other MOOC critics too often ignore or neglect in their analyses. They argue that such programs may be perfect solutions for the "lifelong and lifewide" learning needs and credentials that may be highly valued in the labour market. Accordingly, it would be useful to facilitate the development of national and international support systems for MOOCs to enable institutions to make the right choices in MOOC platforms and testing, course design, learner assessment, and credentialing systems (Patru & Venkataraman, 2016). For smaller countries, a common facility of this nature can be built through international cooperation. Until then, AgMOOCs from COL and similar programmes documented in this particular book and elsewhere will serve as examples of what is possible to educate those in the developing world through MOOCs and other related open forms of online learning.

Acknowledgments

Technical advice and support provided by Dr. Neeta Singh, Mrs. K.T. Revathy, Mr. Deepak Kumar (all three at the IITK), and Ms. Kexin Feng (COL) is gratefully acknowledged.

Balaji Venkataraman is Vice President of the Commonwealth of Learning (COL), Vancouver, Canada. He is a worker in the area of IT applied to agricultural development and learning. His current interests are in deploying new-generation mobile devices in rural learning and in examining the advantages of MOOCs in support of skill development. Balaji received his master's and doctoral degrees from the Indian Institute of Technology and the University of Madras.

Tadinada V. Prabhakar (TVP) has a PhD in Computer Science from IIT Kanpur and has been teaching there since 1986. His research interests are in the areas of software architecture (which is about building large-scale software), knowledge management, and Indian-language computing. Suffice to say, he loves to build software systems. Currently, TVP is working in the field of online education where he has built a MOOC Management System called mooKIT with several innovative features for developing countries. To date, the mooKIT has been used in more than 60 courses. His other area of interest is in ICT in agriculture where he built systems like Agropedia, AgroTagger, and Agriculture Advisory delivery systems. He is currently running an initiative called AgMOOCs which has delivered 16 MOOCs in agriculture.

References

Altbach, P. G. (2014). MOOCs as neocolonialism: Who controls knowledge? *International Higher Education*, *75*(Spring), 5–7. doi:10.6017/ihe.2014.75.5426

Boga, S., & McGreal, R. (2014). *Introducing MOOCs to Africa: New skills for economy programme-ICT*. Commonwealth of Learning (COL). Retrieved from http://hdl.handle.net/11599/613

Castillo, N. M., Lee, J., Zahra, F. T., & Wagner, D. A. (2015). MOOCs for development: Trends, challenges, and opportunities. *Information Technologies & International Development*, *11*(2), 35–42. Retrieved from http://itidjournal.org/index.php/itid/article/view/1396

Commonwealth of Learning. (2015). India AgMOOCs consortium launches five new MOOCs. *Connections*, *20*(3), 12. Retrieved from http://hdl.handle.net/11599/1743

Commonwealth Secretariat. (2018). *Nadi declaration: Education can deliver*. 20th Conference of Commonwealth Education Ministers, Nadi, Fiji. Retrieved from http://thecommonwealth.org/sites/default/files/inline/20CCEMNadiDeclaration.pdf

Devakumar, C., Venkataraman, B., & Yaduraju, N. T. (2014). *MOOC for capacity building in Indian agriculture: Opportunities and challenges*. Policy Paper 70, National Academy of Agricultural Sciences, New Delhi, India. Retrieved from https://drive.google.com/file/d/0B2ESp7vQtAoZam9VVW8wLTl1R28/view

Grech, A., & Camilleri, A. F. (2017). *Blockchain in education* (A. Inamorato dos Santos, ed.). EUR 28778 EN; doi:10.2760/60649

Hollands, F. M., & Tirthali, D. (2014). Resource requirements and costs of developing and delivering MOOCs. *International Journal of Research in Open and Distributed Learning*, *15*(5), 113–133. Retrieved from www.irrodl.org/index.php/irrodl/article/view/1901

King, M., Pegrum, M., & Forsey, M. (2018). MOOCs and OER in the global South: Problems and potential. *International Journal of Research in Open and Distributed Learning, 19*(5), 1–20. Retrieved from www.irrodl.org/index.php/irrodl/article/view/3742/4825

Koneru, I. (2019). *The impact of technology-enabled learning implementation at Rajiv Gandhi university of knowledge technologies*. Retrieved from http://oasis.col.org/handle/11599/3119

Meeker, M. (2016). *Internet trends 2016* [Powerpoint Slides]. Retrieved from www.kleinerperkins.com/perspectives/2016-internet-trends-report

Meeker, M., & Wu, L. (2013). *Internet trends 2013* [Powerpoint Slides]. Retrieved from www.slideshare.net/kleinerperkins/kpcb-internet-trends-2013/32-Mobile_Traffic_as_of_Global

Moloo, R. K., Prabhakar, T.V., Venkataraman, B., & Khedo, K. (2018). Successful delivery of a MOOC via basic mobile phones: A case study of mobile learning in India for increasing awareness of science-based production practices among semi-skilled horticultural farmers. In S.Yu, M. Ally, & A. Tsinakos (Eds.), *Mobile and ubiquitous learning: An international handbook* (pp. 279–303). doi:10.1007/978-981-10-6144-8_17 Singapore: Springer

Pappano, L. (2012, November 2). The year of the MOOC. *New York Times*. Retrieved February 20, 2019, from www.nytimes.com/2012/11/04/education/edlife/massive-open-online-courses-are-multiplying-at-a-rapid-pace.html

Patru, M., & Venkataraman, B. (2016). *Making sense of MOOCs: A guide for policy makers in developing countries*. UNESCO and Commonwealth of Learning (COL). Retrieved from http://hdl.handle.net/11599/2356

Porter, D., & Beale, R. (2015). *A policy brief on MOOCs*. Commonwealth of Learning (COL). Retrieved from http://oasis.col.org/handle/11599/825

Prabhakar, T.V. (2012). *Massive open online courses for development: A video series*. Commonwealth of Learning (COL). Retrieved from http://hdl.handle.net/11599/740

Prabhakar, T.V., Venkataraman, B., & Revathy, K.T. (2018). *mooKIT—A MOOC platform for developing countries*. Proceedings of the 2018 International Conference on Multidisciplinary Research (pp. 324–334). Mauritius. Retrieved from http://myres.net/MyRes%202018%20Proceedings.pdf

Rascoff, M., & DeVaney, J. (2019, January 20). Guest post: Stackability is a learning strategy. *Inside Higher Ed* [Web log post]. Retrieved February 20, 2019, from www.insidehighered.com/blogs/technology-and-learning/guest-post-stackability-learning-strategy

Reich, J., & Ruiperez-Valiente, J.A. (2019). The MOOC pivot: From teaching the world to online professional degrees. *Science, 363*(6423), 130–131. doi:10.1126/science.aav7958

Sharma, G. (2013, July 15). *A MOOC delusion: Why visions to educate the world are absurd* [Blog post]. Retrieved February 20, 2019, from http://chronicle.com/blogs/worldwise/a-mooc-delusion-why-visions-to-educate-the-world-are-absurd/32599

Tarus, J. K., Gichoya, D., & Muumbo, A. (2015). Challenges of implementing e-learning in Kenya: A case of Kenyan public universities. *The International Review of Research in Open and Distance Learning, 16*(1). doi:https://doi.org/10.19173/irrodl.v16i1.1816

Touray, A., Salminen, A., & Mursu, A. (2013). ICT barriers and critical success factors in developing countries. *The Electronic Journal on Information Systems in Developing Countries, 56*(1). doi:10.1002/j.1681-4835.2013.tb00401.x

United Nations General Assembly. (2015, October 21). *Transforming our world: The 2030 agenda for sustainable development* (A/RES/70/1). Retrieved February 20, 2019, from https://undocs.org/A/RES/70/1

United Nations International Children's Emergency Fund. (2018). *The state of the world's children 2017, children in a digital world*. Retrieved on February 20, 2019, from www.unicef.org/publications/files/SOWC_2017_ENG_WEB.pdf

Venkataraman, B., & Kanwar, A. (2015a). Changing the tune: MOOCs for human development? In C. J. Bonk, M. M. Lee, T. C. Reeves, & T. H. Reynolds (Eds.), *MOOCs and open education around the world* (pp. 206–217). New York: Routledge. Retrieved from http://hdl.handle.net/11599/882

Venkataraman, B., & Kanwar, A. (2015b). *MOOC for development*. Presentation made at the Ministerial Round Table on MOOCs, 19th meeting of the Council of Commonwealth Education Ministers (19CCEM), the Bahamas. Retrieved from http://hdl.handle.net/11599/1004

26

IMPLEMENTING A SKILLS ACCELERATOR TO PREPARE STUDENTS IN KENYA FOR ONLINE-ONLY BACHELOR'S AND MBA PROGRAMS THAT REQUIRE MOOCs AND OER

A Case Study

Michael C. Mayrath, Craig Brimhall, Graham Doxey, Scott Doxey, and Joshua Stroup

According to the International Labour Office (ILO; Kühn, Milasi, Yoon, Mourelo, & Viegelahn, 2018), the number of individuals across the globe who are unemployed is over 190 million with the most glaring unemployment rates occurring in emerging economies. Unfortunately, the employment prospects in these countries do not appear to be improving. Kühn et al. (2018) estimate an increase of 1.2 million in the number of unemployed in emerging countries by 2019. The expected growth in unemployment is attributed to the persistence of poor-quality employment opportunities and to working poverty. According to Kühn et al. (2018), the lack of access to skill development opportunities is among the greatest challenges facing countries, enterprises, and individuals around the globe in combating the rising unemployment rates.

There is a paradoxical relationship between global unemployment and employers around the globe expressing a disturbing trend of being unable to find the talent necessary to fill skilled positions (Dobbs et al., 2012). A McKinsey Global Institute report titled *Education to Employment: Designing a System That Works* estimated by 2020 there will be a shortage of 38 to 40 million college-educated workers globally. In the same report, the estimated shortfall of high- and middle-skilled workers is expected to be 85 million by 2020 (Barton, Farrell, & Mourshed, 2013, p. 9).

Bessen (2014) argues this "skills gap" between the unemployed and employment opportunities is not about deficiencies in reading and math skills. Rather, the problem is employers are having difficulty recruiting candidates that have the requisite technological and soft skills required to adequately perform job tasks. The skills gap is especially pernicious in developing countries where poor educational systems—especially systems of higher education—and the lack of access to high-quality technological instruction is hamstringing the skill development of potential employees. Given the pressing need for skill development in countries with poor education systems, massive open online courses (MOOCs) and open-education resources (OERs) can potentially be used to fill the gaping void in skill development education.

MOOCs and OER—A Potentially Transformative Solution

As pointed out in Bonk, Lee, Reeves, and Reynolds (2015), the term "open education" has a history going back over 50 years and that the modern conception of "open education" is generally applied to higher education and adult learning as well as to the Web-based delivery of education (a definition of which MOOCs fall under). The *New York Times* labeled 2012 the "Year of the MOOC" (Pappano, 2012) due to the rapid proliferation of free online courses providing access to anyone with an Internet connection, a device, and the interest to enroll in a course, often offered by a top-tier university. Despite the high level of excitement, there were numerous questions about MOOCs, many of which remain unanswered today including those related to participant motivation and low completion rates (Ho et al., 2014; Perna et al., 2014) and how to create more sustainable economic models and programs (Hoxby, 2014). And, given the skills gap and employment data presented earlier, there are also vital questions whether the learning taking place in MOOCs develops real-world skills and ultimately improves employment outcomes (Calonge & Shah, 2016).

In developed countries, such as the United States, technology ownership among college students is pervasive. University students in these countries are frequently required to bring their own device to class. Often, these students have a smartphone, a laptop, *and* a tablet. However, despite being technologically equipped, the United States' MOOC completion rate is not much different from that found in developing countries (Liyanagunawardena, Adams, & Williams, 2013), suggesting that having easy access to technology and generally enjoying stable high-speed Internet connectivity does not equate to high MOOC completion rates. Part of the problem may be that these students, despite having nearly ubiquitous access to technology, lack sophisticated digital literacy skills (Johnson et al., 2016). In any case, it is worth asking, how can MOOCs and OER be successfully utilized to fill an educational void in regions of the world with limited access to technological devices and unstable Internet connections (Younous, 2012)?

Access to MOOCs and OER in Kenya

As a country with a high number of students unable to access higher education and subsequently professional employment, Kenya and similar emerging economies around the world have an opportunity to utilize MOOCs and OERs as a free or low-cost means for relatively high-quality instructional content. Considering Kenya is classified as an emerging country by the ILO (see Barton et al., 2013), the country can serve as a case study for the implementation and impact of MOOCs in an emerging economy.

Kenya's Potential

The World Bank report (2016) on Kenya, titled *From Economic Growth to Jobs and Shared Prosperity*, states that even though Kenya has great potential, young people face challenges accessing post-primary education due to a lack of financing.

> Putting Kenya's human capital to productive use has proven to be a major challenge. Between 2009 and 2013, three million youth became of working age, yet the economy was able to add only 2.6 million non-farm jobs, and the growth in employment (24 percent) could not keep up with GDP growth (26 percent).
>
> *(World Bank, 2016, p. 22)*

The fastest-growing sectors in the Kenyan economy have been increasingly hard-pressed to find employees whose skill sets meet the demands of the job. In striking contrast, in 2007, only 2 percent of service firms in Kenya identified skills as a major constraint to their operations; however, by 2013, more than a third of service firms identified the lack of qualified workers as a major operational concern. To remedy the growing need for skilled workers, access to quality education needs to improve—including the mastery of basic foundational skills and key competency outcomes—and educational programs need to be relevant to potential employment.

Data from the World Bank (2016) positions Kenya as an entrepreneurial country with great potential when compared to other emerging economies like Ghana and Uganda. However, the lack of skilled workers is an albatross limiting its economic growth and curtailing its economic potential. The key component to gaining skilled employment begins by acquiring job-relevant technical skills such as being able to use computers to access and utilize new information. This learning can be accomplished through technical and vocational education, higher education, pre-employment training, or on-the-job training. It is often equally important for potential employees to build additional soft skills that are valued by employers, such as knowing how to interact professionally with clients, solving complex problems, and learn while on the job. According to this report from the World Bank (2016),

> The present [Kenyan] system has several deficiencies: it is not flexible to labor market needs, capacity is limited, and there is limited successful measurement of quality and outcomes. Overall, the main priorities for improving the employability of youth are ... improved design of training programs to meet employers' needs.

(p. xv)

MOOCs and Kenya

John, Bundi, Riungu, and Anondo (2016) state that "MOOCs have been identified as a new revolution in the use of technology to deliver content for University education" (p. 206). Despite the potential of MOOCs to supplement university-level education with increased flexibility and collaborative delivery of content seemingly designed to overcome the shortages of qualified faculty and limited facilities, there exist hurdles to implementation in the existing education policy structures (Karaim, 2011). Namely, there is no policy framework in place for the adoption and implementation of MOOCs into the current Kenyan educational system. To help expedite the adoption of MOOCs in Kenyan higher education, John et al. (2016) outlined three research questions for empirical research to examine: First, will the implementation of MOOCs reduce the cost of university education? Second, will the implementation of MOOCs lead to improved skill sets acquired in university education? Third, do the current policies for university education serve as barriers to implementation of MOOCs? In this chapter, we are primarily concerned with the second question focused on using MOOCs to improve learning outcomes for students. More specifically, our study examines the importance of technology readiness for beginning an online-only higher education program (e.g., bachelor of business or MBA).

MOOCs and OER as Primary Content for Employer-Engaged Project-Based Learning

In 2013, Knod—a United States-based organization with the mission of addressing the skills gap in developing countries—was launched to provide Employer-Engaged Project-Based Learning (EE-PBL) experiences to students seeking their first degree and first job. The EE-PBL projects were designed to provide authentic work experiences for students that could be used on their resumes and CVs to help them obtain their first job in a professional organization. To meet their mission, Knod relied heavily on MOOCs and OERs as the primary content used for the EE-PBL experiences and associated course work. In addition, mentors and faculty scaffolded students on their journey from novice to experts in their fields.

Knod launched in Kenya in May 2014. Unfortunately, many Kenyan students lacked experience with and access to technology that severely restricted their ability to participate effectively in the EE-PBL projects, which were conducted almost entirely in an online environment that required synchronous and asynchronous participation. To address this potential barrier to learning, Knod created a one- to two-week onboarding and training program for new students named the "21st Century Skills Accelerator." The primary instructional objective of the Accelerator was to prepare students for online-only courses that required them to work in teams on EE-PBL projects. Students had to become fluent in online systems ranging from Google Docs to Skype to the Canvas Learning Management System (LMS). See Appendix 26.A for the list of instructional objectives and skills to be developed by the students.

Throughout the Accelerator, students worked in teams and simulated solving problems at a distance using technological systems. In these simulations, students researched and presented strategies for being self-regulated online students. Many new students had never taken an online course; thus, it was crucial for them to receive foundational technological scaffolding and support while at the Accelerator. For example, students were shown and then practiced how to use tools like Evernote and Google Calendar to manage their academic life.

Knod relied on upperclassmen who had demonstrated the ability to succeed in an online environment to provide critical support and to mentor the new, incoming students. Each mentor underwent six to eight weeks of training prior to the start of an Accelerator. Each day of the Accelerator was carefully planned to be interlaced with the previous days' experiences so students could progressively develop the foundational knowledge and training on the topics outlined in Appendix 26.A.

Teams Focus on Technology Fluency, Problem Solving, and Communication

Using a flipped classroom approach meant there were no lectures. Rather, students engaged in a series of carefully designed learning opportunities where individuals worked in teams to collaborate and communicate using technologies. Teams also simultaneously practiced soft skills such as creative problem solving, critical thinking, professional presentations, public speaking, and leadership.

Teams Practice Online Team-Based Collaboration and Presentation Skills

To scale a face-to-face learning experience focused on developing technological and soft skills, Knod instructional designers sought to leverage its best asset—the students. Upperclass students led breakout sessions where new learners worked in teams to solve problems.

Teams were required to use the same cloud-based technologies to communicate that they would be using once the Accelerator finished and they returned to work remotely from home. Teams were assigned questions and were required to create slides that they then used to practice presenting both online and in-person. For example, a team of four students taking a Microeconomics course was required to split into two groups and work from different locations. The

TABLE 26.1 Descriptions of Key Accelerator Instructional Activities

Instructional Activity	Description
Individual Research	For 5 minutes, each individual team member researches answers to questions provided by the Mentor and/or LMS.
Team Discussion	For 15–20 minutes, discuss as a team the answers to each question. All team members need to equally contribute to the team's discussion.
Individual PowerPoint Slides	For 15–20 minutes, work on PowerPoint slides that address the questions.
Team Selects Slides for Presentation	Teams present the best slides from their group. Teams present face-to-face and/or using LMS Conference or Webinar. All team members are required to speak. The questions given to the teams during these sessions cover a range of topics.

split-team then had to use Skype to meet and prepare for a presentation to be given in one hour. The subsequent presentation took place using the LMS's Web conferencing system. After presenting to their teams, the students then presented to Knod faculty and partner employers in locations ranging from Malaysia to Kenya to Texas. Table 26.1 lists key Accelerator instructional activities.

Every team-based activity was designed using the uniting concept of the Knod mission that students should be regularly engaging with local employers. Engagement with local employers is the most important part of the Accelerator because it provided students an opportunity to interface with multiple potential employers. To ensure regular exposure to employers, Knod brought in business veterans and senior executives from Nairobi to guest coach each day during the Accelerator. The guest coaches would discuss how to secure employment in the current labor markets. Having employers and working professionals at the Accelerator interacting with and mentoring students allowed the students to network and to contextualize the process of employment from actual potential employers. For Knod's employer partners, the Accelerator was an opportunity to meet potential talent.

Offline Redundancy Plan

One of the challenges of using MOOCs in emerging countries is connectivity (Liyanagunawardena et al., 2013) and the Accelerators were not immune to this difficulty. Regular loss of Internet connectivity was common. In anticipation of lost connectivity, Knod created redundancy plans that still allowed students to develop familiarity with technologies in a scaffolded environment. For example, if teams could not collaborate and present online using Skype, they would instead create slides for a given set of questions or problems prepared by faculty. Teams were still required to collaborate to create solutions that were communicated using the slides, which were then presented to their peers in person. Peers subsequently gave feedback.

Research Questions

To explore the potential of MOOCs and OER in an emerging economy, we aimed to answer the following research questions:

- Research Question 1: What are students' attitudes towards computers and the Internet prior to starting an online-only degree program?
- Research Question 2: What are the levels of student technology fluency and experience using computers, using the Internet, and using online communication tools?
- Research Question 3: What is the student feedback after completing an Accelerator?

TABLE 26.2 Academic Enrollment of Participants by Program

Academic Program	Count
Bachelor's of Business Management/Leadership	124
Bachelor's of Information Technology	59
MBA—IT	18
MBA—Finance	10
MBA—Management	13
MBA—Marketing	9
Total	233

Note: These enrollment numbers represent the total enrollment of students across all intakes in the study.

Method

Participants

This study included 233 Kenyan students enrolled in Bachelor of Business, Bachelor of IT, or MBA programs in an online university coupled with a skills development program both offered by Knod (see Table 26.2). The students were from various regions of Kenya with concentrations in Nairobi, Kisumu, and Eldoret. Knod offered accredited degrees in partnership with universities in the USA and Malaysia. Prior to starting their degree program with an emphasis on employability, each student completed an online survey. The data presented in this study is the intake survey collected from three cohorts who started during 2016. The average age of students was 25 with a range of ages from 18 to 55.

Instrumentation

An online survey including Likert-type rating questions and open-ended questions was administered to all incoming students designed to assess individual exposure to and comfort with technology as well as their technology skills and past academic experience. The survey included numerous sections of questions. A limited portion of the data is presented here that is pertinent to students' technology readiness to start online courses that use MOOCs and OER.

Computer and Internet Self-Efficacy, Anxiety, and Attitudes Survey

To assess comfort with computers and the Internet, we used Durndell and Haag's (2002) *Computer self-efficacy, computer anxiety, attitudes towards the Internet and reported experience with the Internet* survey. That survey was minimally adapted to better meet the needs of our target population.

Technology Experience and Fluency Survey

A technology experience and fluency survey was created by Knod that asked very specific "Yes" or "No" questions about whether a participant had experience with specific technologies they would use during their Knod experience. For example, one of the questions asked was whether students had ever used a laptop computer before starting the program.

Evaluation of the Accelerator Onboarding Program

An online survey was also administered requesting feedback from students about the Accelerator after it was completed.

Results

Research Question 1: What Are Students' Attitudes Towards Computers and the Internet Prior to Starting an Online-Only Degree Program?

Overall, the students reported to have highly positive perceptions of technology. For example, the mean response to the statement "I feel comfortable working with computers" was 4.3 on a 5-point Likert scale with 1 being "strongly disagree" and 5 "strongly agree." Additionally, the mean response was 4.5 for the statement "Technology makes school more interesting." Statements that were negatively framed like "I think technology is scary," and "Technology is too difficult for me" had mean responses of 2.1 and 1.6, respectively. From the results of the attitudes towards technology

TABLE 26.3 Mean Responses to the Attitudes Towards Technology Survey

Attitudes towards technology	Mean
I feel comfortable working with computers.	4.3
I think technology is a little scary.	2.1
Technology makes school more interesting.	4.5
Technology is too difficult for me.	1.6
I am worried about charging my laptop.	1.7
I am worried about poor Internet access affecting my Knod work.	2.7

Note: All questions were rated on a 5-point Likert scale (0 as completely disagree and 5 as completely agree).

measure, the students in the incoming cohorts mostly had positive attitudes towards technology (see Table 26.3). This enthusiasm towards technology quickly became evident when the students actively engaged with various technologies throughout the Accelerator.

However, positive attitudes towards technology do not always equate to technological competence. The second research question aimed to assess the students incoming technological competencies.

Research Question 2: What Are the Levels of Student Technology Fluency and Experience Using Computers, Using the Internet, and Using Online Communication Tools?

Most of the incoming students confirmed that they had had at least some minimal exposure to computers (79 percent responded "no" to the statement "I have never used a computer"), 25 percent responded that they owned their own computer, and 81 percent responded that they had a Facebook account. Despite the broad use of technology across the cohorts, the exposure to software programs the students would be using to complete employer-engaged projects was less pronounced. Only 32 percent had ever used Skype, 51 percent reported having used Microsoft PowerPoint, and 57 percent reported having used Microsoft Excel (see Table 26.4).

Undoubtedly, exposure to any type of technological device whether a laptop, desktop, or handheld device reduced the learning curve for these students. However, training on specific technologies like Skype, Canvas LMS, and Microsoft Office were critical to the success of the students once they returned to their homes. Because of the fairly ubiquitous low-level exposure to these technologies among the students, the Accelerator focused more on training on software rather than on orienting students towards the basics of computers.

Research Question 3: What Is the Student Feedback After Completing an Accelerator?

At the completion of each Accelerator, the students completed another survey responding to open-ended questions about their experience with the Accelerator. Overall, students had positive responses regarding the Accelerator. For example, one student wrote, "it was awesome, exciting, and life changing." A student named Catherine stated, "The learning approach has nurtured me to become a self-regulated student."

Many of the students mentioned learning both soft skills and technological skills. One student expressed gaining comfort with the LMS as well as building his skills as a self-regulated student. Another explicitly expressed an increased ability to leverage technology to improve her presentations while she simultaneously built her presentation skills at the Accelerator.

TABLE 26.4 List of Technology Fluency Questions and the Student Responses

Technology Fluency	n	"Yes" %	"No" %	"Yes" Count	"No" Count
I have used Skype.	234	32.17%	67.83%	96	138
I have a Facebook account.	234	81.01%	18.99%	207	27
I can attach a file to an email and send.	235	67.34%	32.66%	178	57
I can copy and paste text.	234	80.30%	19.70%	201	33
I have used Windows to create a folder.	232	68.78%	31.22%	176	56
I have used Microsoft Excel to create a spreadsheet.	234	57.07%	42.93%	145	89
I have used Microsoft PowerPoint to create a presentation.	235	51.14%	48.86%	142	93
I have used Microsoft Word to create a document.	234	69.70%	30.30%	179	55
I have never used a laptop before starting at Knod.	232	41.87%	58.13%	68	164
I have never used a computer.	233	20.99%	79.01%	36	197
I own my own computer.	232	24.51%	75.49%	60	172

Note: All questions were asked in yes/no format.

One of the weaknesses of our study is that it did not include behavioral outcomes assessing if the students did, in fact, learn as much as their responses to the open-ended questions suggested. Indeed, a key finding and instructional activity that evolved over two years of delivering the Accelerator was that students needed to practice the most complex, technology-based task that was required of them within the scaffolded environment of the Accelerator.

Discussion

This chapter seeks to provide data and lessons learned from implementing an onboarding a program designed to prepare students to engage in online-only project-based learning. The onboarding program included exposure to and skill development in the necessary technologies as well as soft skills. The Accelerator was designed as a hybrid program utilizing both face-to-face instruction and online pedagogy. The critical piece of the experience was the scaffolding provided by Knod faculty, upperclass students, and local business executives to prepare new students for the rigors of the online-only program.

Eight essential learning dimensions specified by Reeves (2006) (i.e., objectives, content, instructional design, learning tasks, student roles, instructor roles, technological affordances, and assessment) were used as a framework for portraying how we leveraged the affordances of low-cost or free instructional materials—MOOCs and OERs—to assist people in emerging economies seeking to build a bridge to prosperity.

Learning Dimension—Objectives

The primary objective of the Accelerator was to prepare students for Knod's Employer-Engaged Project-Based Learning (EE-PBL) method; specifically, how to use Web-based and mobile tools to collaborate on projects for real clients. Core areas of focus included: (1) Professional Communication, (2) Collaboration and Leadership, (3) Critical Thinking/Problem Solving, (4) Creativity, (5) Technology Fluency, and (6) Project Management. Appendix 26.A has detailed objectives for each of the meta-level objectives listed.

Learning Dimension—Content

MOOCs and OERs were primary sources of content for the Accelerator. Employer-Engaged PBL (EE-PBL) project requirements created by partner businesses and Knod's instructional designers, with all identifying and confidential information from an Employer Partner being removed, were used as content for simulated team projects during the Accelerators.

Learning Dimension—Instructional Design

The Accelerator's instructional design approach was based on authentic tasks that required students to get training on and practice using the technology-based tools required for their online-only courses and team projects.

Learning Dimension—Learning Tasks

During the Accelerator, students had to work in teams to design solutions to employer-relevant problems provided by the instructors like creating an IT Plan for a new retail business or creating a slide deck to pitch a new business idea to judges, similar to the TV show *Shark Tank*. The teams had to research solutions to problems and present them to their classmates. With over 100 students present at the Accelerator, it was often a transformative experience for students having to practice public speaking and present multiple times a day in a team with the goal of being professional and solving the simulated client problem scenario. The goal of these types of learning tasks was to support the students' development in multiple ways:

- Increase their confidence in face-to-face, professional communication—presenting in teams, creating PowerPoint presentations, conducting inquiry to solve an ill-structured problem.
- Establish professional relationships and social cohesion within their cohort while face-to-face for one to two weeks working on team projects every day.
- Model exemplary performances of desired skills, ranging from how to give engaging team-based presentations in front of 100 people to working remotely to deliver projects.
- Become technology-fluent with the tools of the trade for the industry and career they want to pursue.

Learning Dimension—Student Roles

New students who were starting with Knod would attend the Accelerator to develop new skills and move from novice to experienced in many skill areas. Students that had successfully completed the Accelerator in the past and were in good standing at Knod were allowed to become Accelerator student mentors.

Student mentors were a critical component of scaling the Accelerator to having over 120 students. Some EE-PBL practice projects completed during the Accelerator put the 120-plus students into teams with 4–5 students in each team. Thus, there would be 20–25 teams that needed to present in a 1–2 hour session. Student mentors allowed for scaling because 1–2 mentors would be overseeing the work of 5–6 teams. Thus, each breakout room could have teams complete their 10–20 minute presentations. The mentors in the breakout rooms would give feedback to the team and report on team progress to the Accelerator faculty.

Similarly, student mentors provided hands-on training for new students that had very low levels of prior experience using technology. Each Accelerator would have at least 5–10 students who had never used a laptop. Student mentors were individually assigned to students who reported on the Day 1 survey that they had never used a laptop.

TABLE 26.5 Eight Essential Learning Dimensions Applied to 21st Century Skills Accelerator

Learning Dimension	
Objectives	• Prepare students for Knod's Employer-Engaged Project-Based Learning (EE-PBL) method, including Web-based tools. • Meta-Level Objectives: (1) Professional Communication, (2) Collaboration and Leadership, (3) Critical Thinking/Problem Solving, (4) Creativity, (5) Technology Fluency, and (6) Project Management. • See Appendix 26.A—Accelerator Learning Objectives
Content	MOOCs and OER were primary sources of content for Accelerator. Employer-Engaged PBL (EE-PBL) project requirement docs were used as content for simulated team projects during Accelerators.
Instructional design	Get trained on and practice using the technology-based tools that they will use for their online-only courses and team projects.
Learning tasks	Students worked in teams to solve projects. Teams would present in face-to-face and online modalities.
Student roles	New students participated in team-based projects. Student mentors were key to scaling the Accelerator's presentation-heavy schedule and helping technology inexperienced students skill up.
Instructor roles	Accelerator instructors and student mentors served as coaches and facilitators by scaffolding the students and teams during EE-PBL.
Technological affordances	Immersed students into a variety of free technologies that would be used for their online programs. Required students to practice synchronous and asynchronous team presentations.
Assessment	Accelerator's assessments included short team presentations, individual projects, reflection discussions, retention quizzes, and lesson discussions.

Learning Dimension—Instructor Roles

Instructors, including student mentors, served as facilitators consistent with best practices of project-based learning. "The teacher's role should be to challenge the learner's thinking—not to dictate or attempt to proceduralize that thinking" (Savery and Duffy, 1995, p. 35). Instructors would start each session with clear objectives for students in breakout rooms. Instructors and mentors would scaffold students' communication skills, such as presenting and public speaking, and providing support with technology, ranging from how to use the Canvas LMS to how to present as a team using Skype.

Learning Dimension—Technological Affordances

The Accelerator immersed the students into all of the technology that they would need once they transitioned to their EE-PBL experiences, which required extensive synchronous communication using Skype and other tools. During the Accelerator, teams would practice asynchronous presentations. Each team member would remotely record his or her part of the presentation then upload the file to a shared folder on Google Drive. One team member would download all of the team members' videos and assemble the parts into a complete video presentation. The final team presentation video was submitted to the Canvas LMS for grading by Accelerator instructors. The process of team-based asynchronous presentations was necessary because of (1) scale—if 100 students are in a course with 5 students in each team, then 20 teams have to present during a Web conference synchronous session; and (2) technology stability—teams had more control over the presentation.

Learning Dimension—Assessment

The Accelerator's assessments included a mix of synchronous and asynchronous measures. The types of assessments included in the Accelerator's assessment mix are:

1. Short team presentations—teams presented both face-to-face in breakout rooms or in front of other students or remotely present using online tools. Online team presentations were rehearsed both using synchronous and asynchronous technologies.
2. Individual projects—individual students had to practice creating work products, like a mission statement as well as practice having to upload files to Canvas LMS assignments.
3. Reflection discussions—individual students were required to post an asynchronous discussion. Questions in reflection discussions required students to be meta-cognitive and consider their progress and understanding of the content.
4. Retention quizzes—students were required to read articles and watch videos with instructional content. Students' retention and understanding of this content was assessed using quizzes.
5. Lesson discussions—students were required to post and participate in asynchronous discussions about the lesson topics, such as self-regulated learning or EE-PBL.

This mix of assignment groups each contributed to a student's final grade for the Accelerator course. Engagement in the LMS on a daily basis was not required but frequent engagement in the discussions was expected along with weekly team meetings and weekly synchronous sessions with the course Instructor via the Web conferencing tool found in the LMS. Table 26.5 summarizes how the Knod 21st Century Skills Accelerator applies to the eight essential learning dimensions.

The purpose of Knod's educational program in Kenya was to close the skills gap between employers and potential employees. The Accelerator served as a springboard for students to gain the necessary exposure and skills with technology to succeed in a collaborative online-only learning environment designed to develop their employability skills. This chapter provides findings from data gathered over two years of providing Accelerators for incoming students. Overall, the key finding is the Accelerator effectively prepared students with limited past experience with technology to engage in collaborative project-based learning entirely online. Our findings tentatively suggest that training students for a week in a scaffolded, face-to-face environment can have a large impact on their ability to engage and succeed in online learning.

Conclusion

This chapter provides a case study with data and an instructional framework for onboarding students with low technology fluency and limited exposure for online-only higher education programs delivered to students in Kenya. The express goal of the onboarding was to address the inability of individuals with low technology fluency to successfully engage with online learning, specifically with MOOCs. The potential of MOOCs to impact global employment readiness is contingent on individual abilities to effectively navigate and utilize various technologies. Importantly, our research data suggest that scaffolding an introductory experience may increase the MOOC completion rate among students in emerging economies.

Generalizability Limitations

The results presented are limited to this specific case study in Kenya; however, we hope that the design of the Accelerator and the findings from implementing the Accelerator over two years will be of value and interest to those tasked with improving online learning outcomes for those in emerging economies.

Additionally, most of the incoming students reported at least low levels of familiarity with computers and technology. Although we are confident technological neophytes will benefit from some sort of introductory onboarding experience, our data does not answer if an Accelerator-like experience will be enough to prepare students with no exposure to technology for successful engagement with MOOCs.

Future Research Directions

The future direction of this research is to investigate how an Accelerator-like experience can be scaled. The Accelerator program described in this chapter required in-person, scaffolded experiences that were labor- and capital-intensive while simultaneously requiring students to travel to a central location. It still needs to be determined if an Accelerator-like program is possible to conduct entirely online or how the current model of the Accelerator can be scaled without needing such a large investment.

APPENDIX 26.A
Accelerator Learning Objectives

Professional Communication

- Presentation Skills
    - Teams practice presenting F2F and online using the technology for their courses/projects. Each individual is required to participate so that they get to practice using the conferencing and webinar technologies before going home and being remote.
- English Writing Proficiency
    - Individuals take a baseline English quiz and are provided support. Plagiarism is taken very seriously. Modules for APA Style, Citations, and References, etc. are provided.

Collaboration and Leadership

- Leadership Practice/Team Work
    - From the very beginning of the Knod Experience, students are put into teams and required to collaborate. They are provided with readings and videos on how to best collaborate, but they are told that deep learning that lasts occurs through application, such as practicing leadership by pulling a team together to complete a project.

Critical Thinking/Problem Solving

- Evidence-Based Decision Making
    - Knod students are trained to find their own answers rather than to expect an answer from the coach. Further, teams are strongly encouraged to include evidence and citations in their slides to bolster their argument.

Creativity

- Innovative
    - Knod students are told that projects do not have a right answer, and to be creative in determining the best solution for the client. Their value is partially a unique perspective.
- Technology Fluency
- Project Management

Michael C. Mayath is Vice President of Learning and Product Development at Tiber Health/Ponce Health Sciences University. Dr Mayrath's professional mission is to integrate educational psychology and innovative technology to increase learning, motivation, and assessment outcomes. He leads product development for Tiber Health/Ponce Health Sciences University where he is focused on improving healthcare and medical education. Dr Mayrath has conducted research and development for leading organizations, including the US Air Force, Harvard, and Cisco. He received a PhD in Educational Psychology and a Master's in Program Evaluation from the University of Texas at Austin. He is the lead editor of the book *Technology-Based Assessments for 21st Century Skills: Theoretical and Practical Implications From Modern Research* published by Information Age Publishing in 2012.

Craig Brimhall is a PhD student in organizational behavior at the David Eccles School of Business at the University of Utah. His current research focuses on how employees and organizations learn from experience. Prior to beginning his doctoral studies, Craig was the managing director of learner engagement and an instructional designer at Knod. He has a Master's of Education degree from the Harvard Graduate School of Education and a Bachelor of Science in Finance from Utah Valley University.

Graham Doxey is Founder and CEO of Knod. Graham has over 30 years of global experience successfully building and managing small and large enterprises, with the most recent 15 years focused on higher education. Currently, Graham and his team are building globally scalable solutions related to the education to employment skills gap through an innovative experiential learning model. As a co-founder of Neumont College of Computer Science, Graham began a decade of creating innovative solutions to close the skills gap between higher education outcomes and industry needs. Exemplary results have been achieved through engaging employers in the learning process, implementing experiential learning pedagogies, and mapping regulator required learning outcomes with industry required skills.

Scott Doxey is Managing Director of Student Life Engagement at Knod. Scott is a higher education and information technology executive known for his ability to create and implement new ways of doing business and increasing efficiencies. Scott has a master's degree in business information systems and education. He was part of the executive team at Knod managing the student services experience. Before Knod, Scott was the Vice President of Student Services and Operations at Southern Virginia University. Scott was also part of the executive team at Neumont University as Vice President of Academic Affairs and Operations.

Joshua Stroup is an edupreneur whose passion for education started while working as a K–12 platform product manager at Apple Inc. Joshua then pursued a BS degree in Computer Science and a Master's degree in Cybersecurity, with a published thesis titled *A Conceptual Modeling Language for the Conceptions and Misconceptions of Cybersecurity*. Joshua has worked to establish himself in the education entrepreneurial community and has taught at various higher education institutions and pursued several startups in an effort to combine his deep technical knowledge and educational experiences to construct a modern, transformational, world-class 21st-century educational experience.

References

Barton, D., Farrell, D., & Mourshed, M. (2013). *Education to employment: Designing a system that works*. Washington, DC: McKinsey Center for Government. Retrieved from www.mckinsey.com/industries/social-sector/our-insights/education-to-employment-designing-a-system-that-works

Bessen, J. (2014). Employers aren't just whining—the "skills gap" is real. *Harvard Business Review, 25*.

Bonk, C. J., Lee, M. M., Reeves, T. C., & Reynolds, T. H. (Eds.). (2015). *MOOCs and open education around the world*. New York: Routledge.

Calonge, D. S., & Shah, M. A. (2016). MOOCs, graduate skills gaps, and employability: A qualitative systematic review of the literature. *The International Review of Research in Open and Distributed Learning, 17*(5), 67–90.

Dobbs, R., Madgvkar, A., Barton, D., Labaye, E., Manyika, J., Roxburgh, C., . . . Madhav, S. (2012). *The world at work: Jobs, pay, and skills for 3.5 billion people*. Washington, DC: McKinsey Global Institute. Retrieved from www.mckinsey.com/~/media/McKinsey/dotcom/Insights%20and%20pubs/MGI/Research/Labor%20Markets/The%20world%20at%20work/MGIGlobal_labor_Full_Report_June_2012.ashx

Durndell, A., & Haag, Z. (2002). Computer self efficacy, computer anxiety, attitudes towards the Internet and reported experience with the Internet, by gender, in an East European sample. *Computers in Human Behavior, 18*(5), 521-535.

Ho, A. D., Reich, J., Nesterko, S., Seaton, D. T., Mullaney, T., Waldo, J., & Chuang, I. (2014). *HarvardX and MITx: The first year of open online courses* (HarvardX and MITx Working Paper No. 1). Cambridge, MA.

Hoxby, C. M. (2014). The economics of online postsecondary education: MOOCs, nonselective education, and highly selective education. *American Economic Review, 104*(5), 528–533.

John, J., Bundi, D., Riungu, N., & Anondo, T. (2016). *Implications of massive open online courses for university education in Kenya*. Proceedings from the 10th Annual Decolonizing the Spirit Conference. Embu University College. Embu, Kenya. Retrieved from http://conference.embuni.ac.ke/wp-content/uploads/2018/05/PROCEEDINGS-FROM-THE-10TH-ANNUAL-DECOLONIZING-THE-SPIRIT-CONFERENCE-April-2018.pdf#page=208

Johnson, L., Becker, S. A., Cummins, M., Estrada, V., Freeman, A., & Hall, C. (2016). *NMC horizon report: 2016 higher education edition*. Austin, TX: The New Media Consortium.

Karaim, R. (2011). Expanding higher education: Should every country have a world-class university? *CQ Global Researcher, 5*(22), 551–572.

Kühn, S., Milasi, S., Yoon, S., Mourelo, E., & Viegelahn, C. (2018). *World employment and social outlook 2018: Trends 2018*. Geneva: International Labor Organization. Retrieved from www.ilo.org/global/research/global-reports/weso/2018/WCMS_615594/lang-en/index.htm

Liyanagunawardena, T. R., Adams, A. A., & Williams, S. A. (2013). MOOCs: A systematic study of the published literature 2008–2012. *The International Review of Research in Open and Distributed Learning, 14*(3), 202–227. Retrieved from www.irrodl.org/index.php/irrodl/article/view/1455/2531

Pappano, L. (2012, November 2). The Year of the MOOC. *The New York Times*, ED26. Retrieved from www.nytimes.com/2012/11/04/education/edlife/massive-open-online-courses-are-multiplying-at-a-rapid-pace.html

Perna, L. W., Ruby, A., Boruch, R. F., Wang, N., Scull, J., Ahmad, S., & Evans, C. (2014). Moving through MOOCs: Understanding the progression of users in massive open online courses. *Educational Researcher, 43*(9), 421–432.

Reeves, T. C. (2006). How do you know they are learning? The importance of alignment in higher education. *International Journal of Learning Technology, 2*(4), 294–309.

Savery, J. R., & Duffy, T. M. (1995). Problem based learning: An instructional model and its constructivist framework. *Educational Technology, 35*(5), 31–38.

World Bank. (2016). *Kenya, country economic memorandum: From economic growth to jobs and shared prosperity*. Washington, DC: World Bank Group.

Younous, A. (2012). Online education for developing contexts. *XRDS: Crossroads, 19*(2), 27–29.

SECTION 7
The Future of MOOCs and Open Education

The previous sections of this book reflected on distance learning history or described what is currently transpiring in the world of MOOCs and open education throughout the Global South. However, there were limited glimpses of the future. If opportunities for MOOCs and open education are better understood, we can more extensively and thoughtfully prepare for their possible applications in the future. No predictions about open forms of education will land with 100 percent accuracy. In fact, Nils Bohr, Nobel laureate in physics, famously stated, "Prediction is very difficult, especially if it's about the future." Despite this warning, we cannot avoid addressing the future of MOOCs and open education at the end of a book of this nature. After all, although the past cannot be changed, the future remains within our grasp.

As detailed in Chapter 27 by Paul Kim from Stanford University and Jieun Lee from SMILE (Stanford Mobile Inquiry-based Learning Environment) Korea, recent advancements in the fields of data analytics and artificial intelligence (AI) have led educational innovators to design and deploy a series of learning technology solutions and assessment models for the entire K–16 education spectrum and beyond. With increasing investments from the private sector, numerous companies have launched solutions that are claimed to help most stakeholders in the education ecosystem. The ultimate implications as well as the scope of these emerging solutions related to online education, and especially MOOCs, remain unclear at this time. In response, Kim and Lee call for scholarly discussions and negotiations at multiple levels.

In an attempt to explore ways to understand and leverage AI and relevant features designed to promote higher-order learning and enable assessment strategies involving new types of future learning activities, Kim and Lee discuss some of the notable innovation examples integrating AI and their future potentials in education. They propose that scaffolded learning and learning assessment will be two key areas where analytics and AI will play increasingly larger roles in education as well as society as a whole. As such, they discuss some of the AI-based scaffolding and assessment tools now in development.

In accord with Kim and Lee's prognostications, the *2019 EDUCAUSE Horizon Report* (Alexander et al., 2019) lists "Analytics Technologies" and "Artificial Intelligence" as two of the six "Important Developments in Educational Technology for Higher Education" in the near term or in the coming five years. The other four developments listed in the EDUCAUSE report relate to "Mobile Learning," "Mixed Reality," "Blockchain," and "Virtual Assistants." One sign that these predictions are becoming reality is the fact that Ashok K. Goel, Professor of Computer Science at Georgia Institute of Technology, has been using an AI-based teaching assistant named Jill Watson in his online course since 2016 (Maderer, 2017). Reportedly, students in this "Knowledge-Based Artificial Intelligence" course cannot distinguish between the feedback that they receive from the AI TA and the human TAs that Professor Goel still employs.

The other future view in this section, Chapter 28, has been co-authored by the four co-editors of this volume in reverse order from the book editorship, namely, Tom Reynolds, Tom Reeves, Curt Bonk, and Ke Zhang. Evident in the closing chapter is that the present examination of the MOOC and OER landscape across the Global South has proved to be filled with innovation, progress, and success, but many future opportunities and challenges are also equally apparent. Directing attention at how big data, AI, and data analytics can contribute to a more comprehensive analysis and accounting of education change and impact, the authors encourage readers to take up the challenge and become innovators, chroniclers, or participants in the burgeoning Global South OER ecology. Guidance for those undertakings is provided by way of positing predictions that will characterize and influence future OER-based endeavors.

The key takeaway for the four book editors, Ke Zhang, Curt Bonk, Tom Reeves, and Tom Reynolds, is that the current edited volume offers hope and optimism for the future of OER across the Global South and beyond. Although warranted, such optimism is dependent upon the continuation and further expansion of the trends and insights established in the stories and analyses of the 68 contributors to this book. While none of us four editors claims to be a futurist, per se, our past experience and present scholarship enables us to suggest how MOOCs and open education will evolve over the next few years. We hope that you find a few of our predictions enticing and at least partially accurate.

References

Alexander, B., Ashford-Rowe, K., Barajas-Murphy, N., Dobbin, G., et al. (2019). *EDUCAUSE horizon report: 2019 Higher education edition*. Louisville, CO: EDUCAUSE. Retrieved from https://library.educause.edu/resources/2019/4/2019-horizon-report)

Maderer, J. (2017, January 9). Jill Watson, round three. *Georgia Tech News Center*. Retrieved from http://www.news.gatech.edu/2017/01/09/jill-watson-round-three

27
EVOLUTION OF ONLINE LEARNING ENVIRONMENTS AND THE EMERGENCE OF INTELLIGENT MOOCs

Paul Kim and Jieun Lee

Introduction

Since it was coined at the 2016 World Economic Forum (Schwab, 2016), the phrase, "4th Industrial Revolution" has been a topic for many debates among educators and those who are concerned about the workforce skill development for upcoming industries. As part of the debates, the importance of understanding and leveraging AI (Artificial Intelligence) or machine intelligence has surfaced and triggered public sector leaders globally to examine possible implications of relevant AI technologies. In parallel, private sector innovation leaders also have been releasing prototypes and working solutions integrating AI or at least certain degrees of deep learning models that are useful for diverse types of predictions and decision-making processes.

As an example of these efforts, the Chinese government wants to bring artificial intelligence to its classrooms to boost its massive education system (Jing, 2017). The sheer volume of big data that can be organized by the Chinese government will most certainly become envied by many other governments; it will likely also become a form of fuel to boost all aspects of research around AI in the near future.

While the US has yet to reveal any national AI strategy, France and the EU have not only released national AI strategies, but they had also pledged billions of dollars on AI research and educating their workforce for an intensively automated future (Delaney, 2018). In other nation states such as the UAE, education institutions claim to have already started to use AI and machine learning to predict students at risk of dropping out, the employability of graduates, and other important patterns institutional administrators would like to carefully monitor (Masudi, 2018). Any inquiry on how to best prepare a massive workforce in the most efficient and effective manner for future industries—that may be already here—is certainly paramount to reflect upon and address on a global scale.

Generally, it is believed that AI and relevant technologies of today can produce quite useful sets of data analytics (Stanley, 2017) and classification services based on the quality of given datasets and modeling algorithms (Sessions & Valtorta, 2006). Education administrators can use such results to build system features that can be plugged into numerous facets of existing systems from student management systems to learning management systems (Rouse, 2016) and from admission tracking systems to placement advisement systems. When one piece of AI technology is considered today, it may not seem so intelligent or useful, but when multiple sets of AI modules are combined, such integration may result in implementing quite powerful automated services (Sze, Chen, Yang, & Emer, 2017).

Some of those services can even tell students what skills they would need to build on to pursue their chosen career path (Clarke, 2018). In California, its community college system has launched a program named "Doing What Matters" with a sophisticated enterprise resource planning system that takes and analyzes regional job market data to help colleges plan local programs and courses (DWM, 2018). This initiative is a proactive and timely approach to best utilize big data to link geolocation-specific job needs with precise job skill training initiatives through tailored degree or just-in-time micro-credential programs. In such a scenario, AI services can also advise instructors as they are figuring out best lesson plans (e.g., especially in math and science courses) for diverse groups of learners with different needs so that students can individually strengthen their skills at their own pace (Ascione, 2017).

In short, the interest in the use of data science and AI in education is rapidly increasing and many attempts are made to design and deploy services that are believed to be highly useful for learners and instructors. At the same time, AI is gradually fulfilling various types of functions and tasks that were handled by humans before. By combining AI services in learning, skill development, assessment, advisement, or placement, future education systems and learning models may become a turn-key academic solution for learners of diverse backgrounds and needs in K–16 education and beyond.

We believe that future learning environments including MOOCs will evolve quite rapidly while they become more integrated to better understand and support learners at all stages of their learning cycles. At the same time, future learning models could be redesigned to move away from a knowledge dissemination system (i.e., instructionism triggering passive learning) and towards a more knowledge co-creation system or environment (i.e., constructionism triggering active learning) (Peters & Besley, 2017) that is intelligent enough to accommodate individual learning needs and goals as they are pursuing higher-order learning opportunities at a massive scale.

Education Technologies Integrating AI

Considering the speed of advancement of technology, it is not surprising to witness an increasing volume of edtech solutions being released to the market as the value of investment in innovative edtech companies is also increasing (McKenzie, 2018; Research and Markets, 2018). Some of those edtech firms are already leveraging AI in their commercial product portfolios. For example, AdmitHub is an edtech startup that is creating conversational artificial intelligence (AI) services to guide students to and through college (Johnson, 2017). Although that particular product is still at its infancy stage, the AdmitHub solution is designed to provide students with counseling services with various topics. For example, it can help students with their student loans. It can also help them determine what courses they should take, in what sequence, and what activities they should engage in through mobile text messages and queries that are answered by an AI chatbot (AdmitHub, 2018).

In order to build a chatbot service such as AdmitHub, school administrators will need to use a development tool such as Dialogflow by Google or the Alexa Skill Development Kit by Amazon (i.e., depending on user interfaces and applications) to define intents, entities, and contexts of a conversation. Recently, a major online education service provider, Udacity, partnered with Passage AI, a chatbot technology provider, to help Udacity students in selecting courses, answering questions, and guiding them as they navigate through contents and learning objects in their platform integrating AI, NLU (Natural Language Understanding), and Deep Learning (Passage AI, 2018). Their goal is to provide their students with a service similar to the real interaction they might expect from interacting with their instructors (Dickson, 2018).

In terms of leveraging big data and innovative learning analytic models, Civitas Learning has been offering services to post-secondary institutions. Their solutions are designed to help reduce time and cost to degree completion, improve college readiness, and minimize achievement gaps of under-resourced students (Civitas Learning, 2018). In the K–12 community, Bright Bytes solutions help to identify children who may be at risk for dropping out of school or experiencing other academic delays (Bright Bytes, 2018). Bright Bytes achieves its goals by analyzing historical data from across a large school district to compare current students' progress with those who have graduated and were considered ready for college. The solution identifies potential issues and explains what has been done in the past to try to mitigate such problems.

A company such as Cerego uses deep learning models at a much higher level than the other companies. Cerego uses AI to help instructors prepare instructional materials, automatically generate assessment items, and track what students know as well as what they need to solidly learn since the retainment of certain critical knowledge or skill sets is required by government regulations or in certain professions with licensures (Cerego, 2018). Cerego also uses the Alexa personalized learning platform to enable near-natural dialogs to answer questions regarding learning contents for students or instruction plans for instructors.

At a specific subject level, there is a solution for students in learning math with artificial intelligence. Thinkster Math helps students solve math problems with ease as the system learns what students are struggling with and coaches them on how to solve problems step by step. Also, the system tailors their learning paths and contents based on the student's progress so that the student is not left behind (Gross, 2018).

In short, education technology systems and solutions are increasingly integrating AI and deep learning models in order to enhance their existing services or create new possibilities linked to better serving students and instructors. While the changes may appear gradual or localized on the surface, the combined impact will soon be deemed transformative in nature. Stated another way, while the difference that AI may present today may still seem miniscule or even undetectable, the potential that it will bring to the global education ecosystem will become much more significant and widespread in an accelerating manner.

Intelligent MOOCs and Questioning

With the use of artificial intelligence in conversational bots, the opportunity to leverage such models in online education and MOOCs is quite promising (Lim & Goh, 2016). In a course at Georgia Tech, Jill Watson, an AI-backed teaching assistant (TA), made a debut by answering student questions and providing discussion topics (Goel & Polepeddi, 2016). The level of sophistication of such AI-based TAs for student question answering is still at an early stage, but with increasing data and the availability of deep learning models, the quality of system-generated responses will only improve over time. However, such improvement will have its own share of challenges and setbacks. Unlike self-driving cars or face recognition features, understanding human inquiries requires highly sophisticated efforts and the ability to tap into complex deep learning models. Earlier approaches with NLP (Natural Language Processing) which leveraged rule-based algorithms are now replaced with statistical model-based algorithms (Polson & Scott, 2018) and this shift has helped advance NLP research and applications to a new level.

Nonetheless, the AI-backed systems of today (i.e., still basic AI) can challenge students mostly with lower-order learning opportunities (e.g., asking simple recall questions as part of an automated assessment process). However, with continuous research and development in this regard, we expect that AIs can eventually offer learning activities that can trigger deep reflection as well as critical and creative thinking. Such a strand of research has substantial implications in online education because AIs can help enhance interactivity between learning stimuli and students. They can also enhance the learning situation by automating assessments of various types that can extend beyond multiple choice questions. For example, a basic AI may automatically generate a lower-order thinking question based on a lesson on photosynthesis and such a question may be, "Which of following process is not part of photosynthesis?" Whereas an advanced AI would be able to assess the learner through an interview and present a higher-order thinking question such as, "Based on your understanding so far, how would you design an artificial photosynthesis mechanism if you were to build a commercial photosynthesis factory?" In this scenario, an advance AI would be able to evaluate student responses and offer feedback for further learning opportunities.

In typical MOOC environments today, instructors deliver lectures by recording videos and generally assess students with questions that are pre-formulated by instructors. Giving grades based on student interactions in online discussion boards or student-generated questions not only requires a significant amount of an instructor's time, but also make it extremely challenging in evaluating student performance objectively. In order to address these issues, AI can be employed to maximize learning effects and teaching efficiencies (Rosen et al., 2018). Coupled with AI, a MOOC can treat every single student comment, question, or action as a data point which can be accumulated to develop a series of deep learning models.

Deep learning models developed based on data from MOOCs are particularly interesting because of the sheer volume of student questions, comments, and actions. With a massive volume of data, educators can make prediction models, intelligent support systems, and interactive assessment solutions which can be continuously trained and improved over time. These resources become extremely valuable when automatically evaluating student work objectively. They can also provide students with various types of interactive assessment objects (e.g., real-world problem-solving simulations). Most of all, the types of reporting, instant feedback (i.e., visuals, speech, or text), and guidance services (e.g., chatbots or animated avatars) are just part of early stage manifestation of AI in education at the current time.

Personalization

The concept of adaptive teaching based on different learning styles has been around us for decades. Pask (1976) described different styles of learners as being holists or serialists. Some 15 years later, Riding and Cheema (1991) used the wholistic-analytic approach to describe how learners acquire knowledge. In contrast, Felder and Silverman (1988) detail learners of different styles with labels such as "global" and "sequential." Generally speaking, holists or globalists are to take bits and pieces of information from various contexts and assemble them into a knowledge schema, whereas sequential and linear learners take incremental steps in an orderly fashion while mastering a certain level of knowledge in a domain. Holists do not seem to mind gaps and leaps in the pursuit of learning, while serialists would find such gaps or missing information uncomfortable. Clarke (1993) asserts that most learners probably have mixed traits with a reasonable degree of preferences.

In short, by understanding different learning preferences and pace, adaptive learning algorithms for personalization have been developed to best accommodate learners for decades. In recent years with the advancement of AI, personalized learning is becoming a new norm in educational technology. AI can help educators better understand individual learners and offer quite sophisticated and personalized learning opportunities (Yu, Miao, Leung, & White, 2017). Such a systematic personalization approach is also applicable in a massive online learning environment (Hill, 2018). Furthermore, in a MOOC environment, AI can be used to find and best match collaborators or communal teaching assistants for students or even provide high-level coaching and tutoring if any of the participants show early signals of falling behind.

Questioning and Answering by AI

With rapid advancement in AI, having systems answer questions or generate critical thinking questions to challenge students is becoming an important R&D topic for educational technology companies and researchers at leading universities (Oh, 2017). In this regard, companies such as Google, Amazon, and Apple have come up with digital assistants that can currently answer simple factoid questions. Getting systems to automatically generate higher-order thinking questions has not been done because of the difficulty of forming questions that are accurate and contextually relevant to a broad array of learning topics.

The main issue with such a challenge is that the dataset containing high-level questions is not sufficiently large enough. Consequently, at least for the foreseeable future, the intelligence required to deal with higher-order thinking questions remains solely with humans (McGivney & Kim, 2016). However, as discussed throughout this chapter, the world currently stands at the precipice of major educational changes due to AI technology. We now turn to a project which the first author has helped design and implement in emerging economies throughout the world during the past decade including Rwanda, Tanzania, Ghana, Colombia, Mexico, India, Argentina, Vietnam, and Thailand.

One education project that may change the landscape of generating and answering higher-order thinking questions is SMILE (Stanford Mobile Inquiry-based Learning Environment). Implemented in over 30 countries, SMILE is collecting various types and levels of questions from learners of all types of education and training scenarios. Factoid questions are used to check students' simple recall ability, but higher-order thinking questions are employed to trigger critical and creative thinking. In the age of search engines and a highly connected world, question generation skills are valuable both now and for the foreseeable future (Berger,-2014).

As shown in Figure 27.1, the SMILE interface is integrated into Stanford's course learning management system. In this learning environment, students are not only engaged in discussing course topics, but also generating challenging questions that trigger higher-order thinking. With millions of questions collected in the SMILE database and the database becoming a training dataset for various types of deep learning models and systems, digital assistants will be able to deal with a much higher level and complexity of questions in the near future.

Having students generate, exchange, analyze, evaluate, and reflect on questions would be considered higher-order learning activities. As shown in Figure 27.1, questions asked and discussed by engineering students in one class can become a part of fruitful deep learning models for future students. The more higher-order thinking questions collected, the more accurate and intelligent services will become possible with digital assistants or AI-backed personalized tutors in future online and MOOC learning environments.

One substantial dilemma at this point is that having students generate higher-order thinking questions—triggering student-centered inquiry-based learning—is not a simple task. Teachers educated and trained in traditional transmission and reception-based learning models find it extremely challenging and difficult to shift to the inquiry-based teaching and learning models (Herman & Pinard, 2015). In order to lead such activities successfully, teachers must be adequately trained to provide advance exercises and extensive scaffolding (Bates, Galloway, Riise, & Homer, 2014), while giving students sufficient guidance and room for self-reflection and modeling (see Nardone & Lee, 2010). Nonetheless, moving teachers toward adopting a new intervention involving a student-centered learning is a multifaceted effort that has a better chance of success when implemented over sufficient time with appropriate levels and types of support and mentoring (Thoonen, Sleegers, Oort, Peetsma, & Geijsel, 2011).

In short, teachers need to be trained to practice using such questioning models effectively. At the same time, students must learn higher-order questioning skills with proper digital literacy (Suwono & Wibowo, 2018).

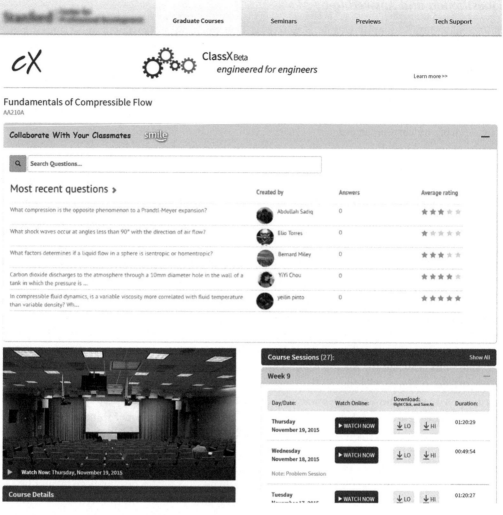

FIGURE 27.1 SMILE (Stanford Mobile Inquiry-based Learning Environment) Integrated in a Learning Management System

Questioning Skill Scaffolding Tools in SMILE

In order to help teachers and students learn and develop questioning skills, SMILE offers a series of tools for integrating machine learning and deep learning algorithms. As shown in Figure 27.2 illustrates a question evaluation tool integrated in Canvas as an LTI (Learning Tools Interoperability) which takes user questions and evaluates them based on the question type and quality. As displayed in the figure, the system believes that the student question on education entrepreneurship can be classified as Level 4 question with a 97% confidence level. The evaluation result is not an absolute value indicator, but a simple reference point for both teachers and students to open up a dialog regarding the very issue the question may be raising and the possible creative answers that may be followed during group reflections.

Figure 27.3 unveils a similar question evaluation tool, but it is used for contextual questions, which means that students are to read an article and generate critical questions. The instructor is to consider the quality of the student question as evidence of learning. In this scenario, students are to ask as many questions and short responses critical to the reading materials. If a student asks obviously simple recall or factoid type of questions, the instructor would be justified in not giving high marks. With this tool, students can practice asking high-quality critical and creative questions while

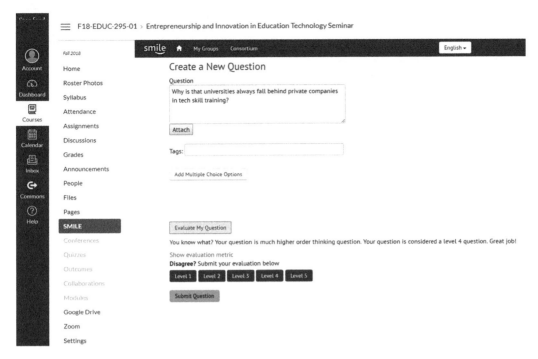

FIGURE 27.2   Question Evaluation Practice Tool

obtaining immediate feedback to reflect upon and perhaps modify their question asking repertoire. In effect, they would be learning life skills central to their success in this digital age.

Oftentimes, students may have difficulty generating their own critical and creative thinking questions (Choi, Land, & Turgeon, 2005). In such a scenario, students can enter a few keywords for the system to automatically generate questions that are linked to recent research studies. Figure 27.4. shows a tool that takes user keywords and looks for the most recent questions asked by academic communities. With keywords such as "lymphoma" and "gene type," the tool is presenting a question such as, "Are we ready to stratify treatment for diffuse large B-Cell Lymphoma using molecular hallmarks?" Students and instructors could use such system-generated questions to enrich class discussions in both offline and online learning environments. Since no one knows what questions may be automatically generated at a given time, these highly relevant, yet randomly generated, questions can trigger higher-order thinking and deep discussions in numerous, unexpected, and divergent directions.

Figure 27.5 demonstrates a method of evaluating student assignments that involve visual artifacts. For example, if students are to submit assignments involving graphs, charts, diagrams, sketches, and screenshots or even videos, the system can automatically evaluate such artifacts and determine how close the submission is to the instructor's sample assignment. In Figure 27.5, the system gives 0.0207 for an image of the hamburger which is far from what the instructor is looking for. Other images show closer distance scores than the hamburger image, but the left-bottom screenshot correctly reflecting the features the instructor is looking for shows the 0 distance score even though the image is much blurrier than other submissions. When the distance score is 0, it means that the student submission matches with the instructor's suggested sample. An automatic evaluation tool such as this can save instructors tremendous time, especially if the instructor is dealing with assignments of various kinds in a class with a massive number of students.

Now imagine if a suite of such question generation and evaluation tools and resources were embedded in every learning management system and were available in every MOOC, now totaling over 11,400 MOOCs globally (see Shah, 2019). How might such tools be used to raise the level of engagement

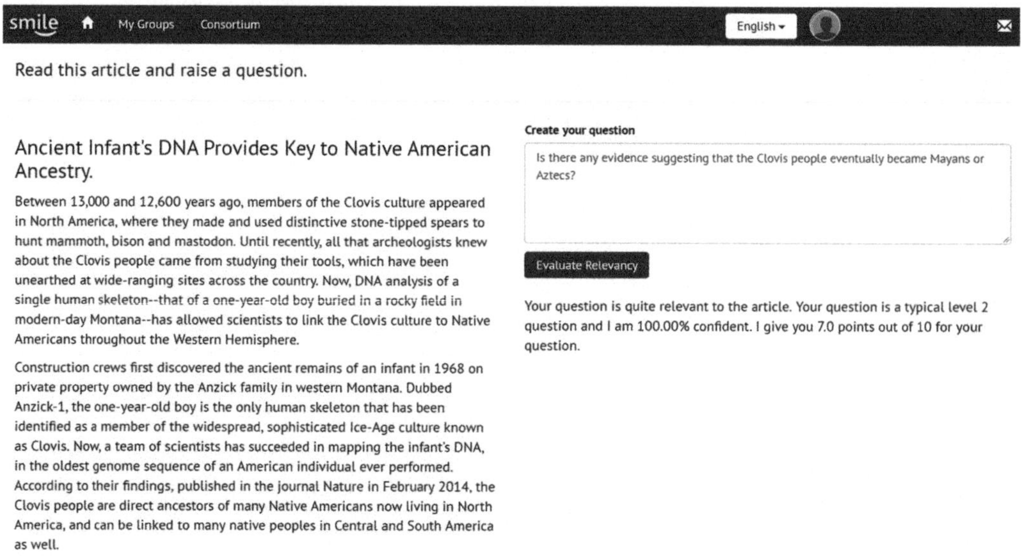
smile
My Groups
Consortium
English
Read this article and raise a question.
Ancient Infant's DNA Provides Key to Native American Ancestry.
Between 13,000 and 12,600 years ago, members of the Clovis culture appeared in North America, where they made and used distinctive stone-tipped spears to hunt mammoth, bison and mastodon. Until recently, all that archeologists knew about the Clovis people came from studying their tools, which have been unearthed at wide-ranging sites across the country. Now, DNA analysis of a single human skeleton--that of a one-year-old boy buried in a rocky field in modern-day Montana--has allowed scientists to link the Clovis culture to Native Americans throughout the Western Hemisphere.
Construction crews first discovered the ancient remains of an infant in 1968 on private property owned by the Anzick family in western Montana. Dubbed Anzick-1, the one-year-old boy is the only human skeleton that has been identified as a member of the widespread, sophisticated Ice-Age culture known as Clovis. Now, a team of scientists has succeeded in mapping the infant's DNA, in the oldest genome sequence of an American individual ever performed. According to their findings, published in the journal Nature in February 2014, the Clovis people are direct ancestors of many Native Americans now living in North America, and can be linked to many native peoples in Central and South America as well.
Create your question
Is there any evidence suggesting that the Clovis people eventually became Mayans or Aztecs?
Evaluate Relevancy
Your question is quite relevant to the article. Your question is a typical level 2 question and I am 100.00% confident. I give you 7.0 points out of 10 for your question.

FIGURE 27.3 Question Evaluation Based on an Article

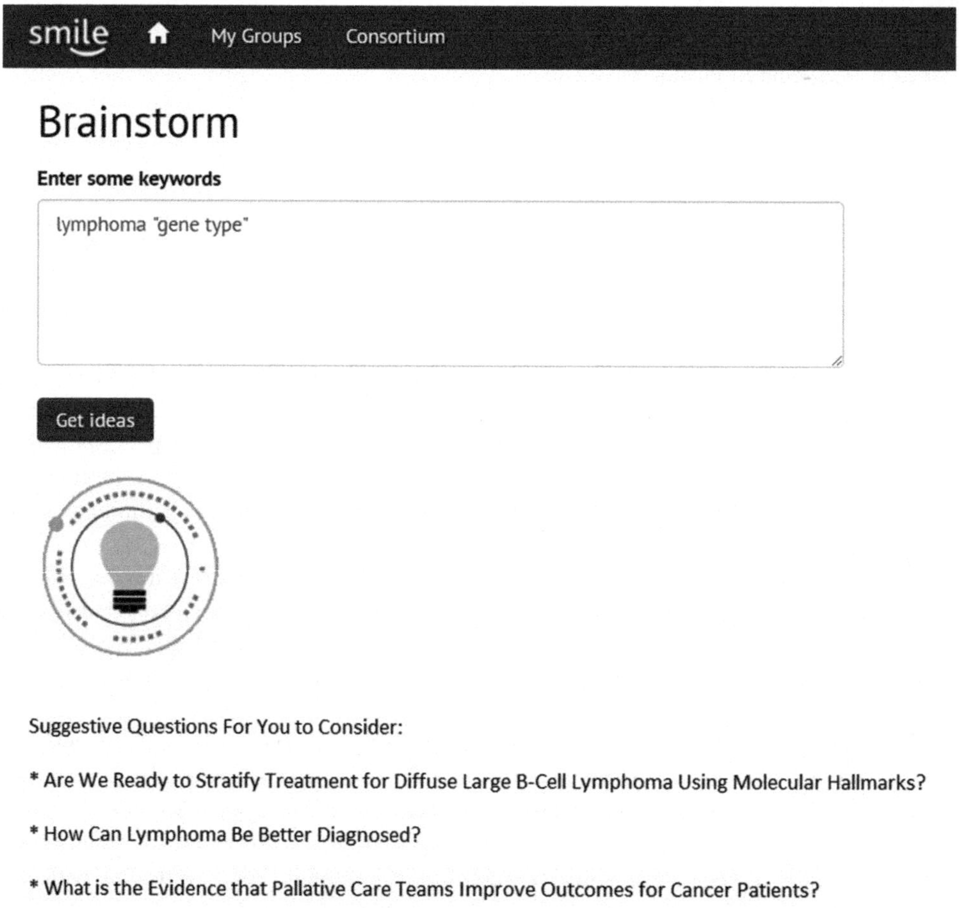
smile
My Groups
Consortium
Brainstorm
Enter some keywords
lymphoma "gene type"
Get ideas
Suggestive Questions For You to Consider:
* Are We Ready to Stratify Treatment for Diffuse Large B-Cell Lymphoma Using Molecular Hallmarks?
* How Can Lymphoma Be Better Diagnosed?
* What is the Evidence that Pallative Care Teams Improve Outcomes for Cancer Patients?

FIGURE 27.4 Question Generation Tool Based on Keywords

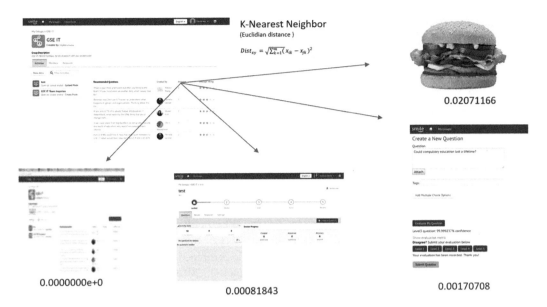

FIGURE 27.5 Visual Artifact Assignment Evaluator

and overall learning results of the more than 100 million participants who at present are enrolling in MOOCs annually (Shah, 2019)? How might these tools be put to use in elevating the digital literacy skills and overall self-confidence of learners in emerging economies from Thailand to Kenya to China to Brazil to Indonesia to Chile to Turkey—all places that are highlighted in different chapters of this book. What if you were to reread those chapters and ponder what those authors might be saying 10 or 20 years from now if such AI types of tools and others yet to be developed were increasingly common in 2030 or 2040? And what would education look like right here today if they were?

This chapter presents just a few examples of educational tools integrating deep learning models, but many more sophisticated tools are being developed and experimented with by educators worldwide. Some of the upcoming projects involve innovative intelligent tutors capable of engaging students in continuous conversations on subject matters and others involve AI modules analyzing students' athletic or musical performance through live videos. In short, "Deep Learning as a Service" (i.e., similar to "Software as a Service" – SaaS) as a new species in the global education ecosystem is about to take the center stage in upcoming years.

Conclusion

Future learning environments including intelligent MOOCs will certainly leverage AI in varying degrees as appropriate (see Anderson, Rainie, & Luchsinger, 2018). From student counseling to student project assessment and from achievement predictions to program planning, the possibilities are infinite in every facet across the entire spectrum of education. When AI-backed systems become widely available to improve student services and make better predictions, educators will increasingly welcome such changes and will likely recommend other areas in need of other intelligent inroads.

However, when educational technology leaders with AI systems start promoting new learning and assessment models, they will certainly face huge challenges (Anderson et al., 2018). First, instructors will have a hard time adapting to new teaching and learning approaches because such changes undoubtedly require extensive training and significant cultural shifts in classrooms. Second, when AI-backed systems begin to show promise in generating and answering questions, instructors may feel vulnerable and even threatened because the sense of intellectual authority (i.e., where traditionally instructors were the sole source of knowledge) may be diminished. Third, due to increasing data privacy concerns globally, it is highly plausible that educational data will become harder to access, thereby limiting processes meant to improve deep learning models and associated learning efficiencies and successes. Without a massive quantity of workable data, AI will not have a bright future. Lastly, the current digital divide will be worsened as AI will be more directly available to those who have access to advanced technology infrastructure and personal devices, while countless others will only dream of such possibilities.

To address such concerns and worries, my team and I are in the midst of an effort to make AI solutions available on portable devices combined with SMILE functions (see www.smile-pi.org) as a last-mile solution. In this project, Google's Tensorflow (i.e., machine learning library) is being loaded and tested on portable computing devices. We hope to be ready for large-scale implementation with prominent global education partners. Overall, AI is certain to make substantial strides in the education ecosystem worldwide but addressing these immediate challenges should be central to the discussions among educators of the 21st century. Whether in Egypt, South Africa, Sri Lanka, Nepal, Brazil, Turkey, or the Philippines, as in the chapters of this particular book, there are now possibilities for huge impacts when such AI technology is combined with opportunities brought by MOOCs and other forms of open education (Anderson et al., 2018).

We will certainly keep pushing the envelope of the possible. The citizens of this tiny planet deserve no less.

Paul Kim is the Chief Technology Officer and Assistant Dean of the Graduate School of Education at Stanford University. He served as an advisory committee member for the National Science Foundation, a member of the Grand Challenges for International Development Committee at the National Academy of Sciences, a member of the board at WestEd, a member of the advisory committee at Edify.org, and an advisory member to Exceed Capital. He taught a MOOC on designing new learning environments in the Stanford Venture Lab (now called NovoEd) which attracted over 20,000 students from around the world. His government-backed international development projects include the design of a new science and technology university for the Sultan of Oman as well as the strategy design for the national online learning initiative of Saudi Arabia. Dr Kim has also been involved in a national education technology assessment initiative for Uruguay. He founded Seeds of Empowerment, a nonprofit global education organization and developed SMILE (Stanford Mobile Inquiry-based Learning Environment), a program recognized as one of the most innovative education models by the United Nations in 2016. He can be contacted at Phkim@stanford.edu.

Jieun Lee is a curriculum developer, trainer, and graduate student. For the past decade, Jieun has been developing ICT-integrated pedagogies and facilitating training programs with topics such as design thinking, entrepreneurship, youth empowerment, and SMILE (Stanford Mobile Inquiry-based Learning Environment). Recently, she taught SMILE Entrepreneurship and SMILE teacher training programs at numerous universities and metropolitan school districts in Korea. Prior to joining Hanyang University as a graduate student in educational technology, she helped develop ICT teacher training programs in Sri Lanka and design thinking programs with SAP. She is currently the Director of Academic Programs for SMILE Global.

References

AdmitHub. (2018, August 6). *Conversational AI for college success*. Retrieved from www.admithub.com/

Anderson, J., Rainie, L., & Luchsinger, A. (2018, December 10). *Artificial intelligence and the future of humans*. Pew Research Center. Retrieved from www.pewinternet.org/2018/12/10/artificial-intelligence-and-the-future-of-humans/

Ascione, L. (2017, October 12). New AI tool helps teachers tackle math. *eSchool News*. Retrieved from www.eschoolnews.com/2017/10/12/ibm-ai-tool-teachers-tackle-math/

Bates, S. P., Galloway, R. K., Riise, J., & Homer, D. (2014). Assessing the quality of a student-generated question repository. *Physical Review Special Topics-Physics Education Research*, *10*(2), 020105.

Berger, W. (2014). *A more beautiful question: The power of inquiry to spark breakthrough ideas*. New York: Bloomsbury Publishing USA.

Bright Bytes. (2018, August 2). *New software aims to track struggling SCS students, identify what helps*. Retrieved from www.brightbytes.net/resources-archive/shelbynews

Cerego. (2018, November 10). *Transforming the learning experience for everyone*. Retrieved from www.cerego.com/whycerego-page

Choi, I., Land, S. M., & Turgeon, A. J. (2005). Scaffolding peer-questioning strategies to facilitate metacognition during online small group discussion. *Instructional Science*, *33*(5–6), 483–511.

Civitas Learning. (2018, August 2). *Built for outcomes*. Retrieved from www.civitaslearning.com/technology/

Clarke, J. A. (1993). Cognitive style and computer assisted learning: Problems and a possible solution. *Association for Learning Technology Journal (ALT-J)*, *1*(1), 47–59.

Clarke, K. (2018, January 21). Student portal AI to help students recognise their skills. *Online Sense.* Retrieved from https://onlinesense.org/ai-student-skills/

Delaney, J. (2018). France, China and the EU all have an AI strategy. Shouldn't the U.S.? *Wired Business.* Retrieved from www.wired.com/story/the-us-needs-an-ai-strategy/

Dickson, B. (2018). How AI could help improve the education enrollment process. *Venture Beat.* Retrieved from https://venturebeat.com/2018/03/08/how-ai-could-help-improve-the-education-enrollment-process/

DWM. (2018). Innovate what matters for jobs and the economy. *Doing What Matters.* Retrieved from http://doingwhatmatters.cccco.edu/Overview/DWMFramework/Innovate.aspx

Felder, R. M., & Silverman, L. K. (1988). Learning and teaching styles in engineering education. *Engineering Education, 78,* 674–681.

Goel, A. K., & Polepeddi, L. (2016). *Jill Watson: A virtual teaching assistant for online education.* Georgia Institute of Technology. Retrieved from https://smartech.gatech.edu/handle/1853/59104

Gross, E. L. (2018). 4 ways artificial intelligence is revolutionizing education. *DELL Technologies.* Retrieved from www.delltechnologies.com/en-us/perspectives/4-ways-artificial-intelligence-is-revolutionizing-education/

Herman, W. E., & Pinard, M. R. (2015). Critically examining inquiry-based learning: John Dewey in theory, history, and practice. *Inquiry-Based Learning for Multidisciplinary Programs: A Conceptual and Practical Resource for Educators, 3,* 43.

Hill, J. (2018). Artificial intelligence can make MOOCs smarter. *Blog on Learning Development.* Retrieved from https://bold.expert/artificial-intelligence-can-make-moocs-smarter/

Jing, M. (2017, October 14). China wants to bring artificial intelligence to its classrooms to boost its education system. *South China Morning Post.* Retrieved from www.scmp.com/tech/science-research/article/2115271/china-wants-bring-artificial-intelligence-its-classrooms-boost

Johnson, S. (2017). College chatbot service AdmitHub raises $2.95M in seed funding to guide students through school. *EdSurge.* Retrieved from www.edsurge.com/news/2017-01-11-college-chatbot-service-admithub-raises-2-95m-in-seed-funding-to-guide-students-through-college

Lim, S. L., & Goh, O. S. (2016). Intelligent conversational bot for massive online open courses (MOOCs). *arXiv* preprint *arXiv:1601.07065.*

Masudi, F. (2018, February 25). Artificial intelligence dawns on UAE education sector. *Gulf News Education.* Retrieved from https://gulfnews.com/news/uae/education/artificial-intelligence-dawns-on-uae-education-sector-1.2178820

McGivney, E., & Kim, P. (2016). Using technology to teach the art of asking questions. *Stanford Social Innovation Review.* Retrieved from https://ssir.org/articles/entry/using_technology_to_teach_the_art_of_asking_questions

McKenzie, L. (2018, September 26). Pushing the boundaries of learning with AI. *Inside Higher Ed.* Retrieved from www.insidehighered.com/digital-learning/article/2018/09/26/academics-push-expand-use-ai-higher-ed-teaching-and-learning

Nardone, C. F., & Lee, R. G. (2010). Critical inquiry across the disciplines: Strategies for student-generated problem posing. *College Teaching, 59*(1), 13–22.

Oh, S. W. (2017, March). What the human beings need in the A.I. era: Questions and inquiries. *Newspaper & Broadcasting, 555,* 6–10.

Pask, G. (1976). Styles and strategies of learning. *British Journal of Educational Psychology, 46,* 128–148.

Passage AI. (2018, August 2). *We listen our customers, so should you.* Retrieved from www.passageai.com/2018

Peters, M., & Besley, T. (2017). *Co-creation in higher education students and educators preparing creatively and collaboratively to the challenge of the future.* Retrieved from www.sensepublishers.com/media/3279-co-creation-in-higher-education.pdf

Polson, N., & Scott, J. (2018). *AIQ: How people and machines are smarter together.* New York: St. Martin's Press.

Research and Markets. (2018). AI in education market—forecast to 2023: Market is expected to grow at a CAGR of 47%. *Business Wire.* Retrieved from www.businesswire.com/news/home/20180510005723/en/AI-Education-Market-Forecast-2023-Market

Riding, R., & Cheema, I. (1991). Cognitive styles: An overview and integration. *Educational Psychology, 11*(3–4), 193–215.

Rosen, Y., Rushkin, I., Rubin, R., Munson, L., Ang, A., Weber, G., & Tingley, D. (2018, June). *Adaptive learning open source initiative for MOOC experimentation.* Proceedings of the International Conference on Artificial Intelligence in Education (pp. 307–311). Springer, Cham.

Rouse, M. (2016). AI (*artificial* intelligence). *TechTarget*. Retrieved from https://searchenterpriseai.techtarget.com/definition/AI-Artificial-Intelligence

Schwab, K. (2016). The 4th industrial revolution. In *World economic forum*. New York: Crown Business.

Sessions, V., & Valtorta, M. (2006). The effects of data quality on machine learning algorithms. *ICIQ, 6*, 485–498.

Shah, D. (2019). Year of MOOC-based degrees: A review of MOOC stats and trends in 2018. *Class Central*. Retrieved from www.class-central.com/report/moocs-stats-and-trends-2018/

Stanley, R. (2017). Smart implementation of machine learning and AI in data analysis: 50 examples, use cases and insights on leveraging AI and ML in data analytics. *Engagement Optimization*. Retrieved from https://callminer.com/blog/smart-implementation-machine-learning-ai-data-analysis-50-examples-use-cases-insights-leveraging-ai-ml-data-analytics/

Suwono, H., & Wibowo, A. (2018, January). *Problem-based learning through field investigation: Boosting questioning skill, biological literacy, and academic achievement*. AIP Conference Proceedings (vol. 1923, no. 1, p. 030049). AIP Publishing.

Sze, V., Chen, Y. H., Yang, T. J., & Emer, J. S. (2017). Efficient processing of deep neural networks: A tutorial and survey. *Proceedings of the IEEE, 105*(12), 2295–2329.

Thoonen, E. E., Sleegers, P. J., Oort, F. J., Peetsma, T. T., & Geijsel, F. P. (2011). How to improve teaching practices: The role of teacher motivation, organizational factors, and leadership practices. *Educational Administration Quarterly, 47*(3), 496–536.

Yu, H., Miao, C., Leung, C., & White, T. J. (2017). Towards AI-powered personalization in MOOC learning. *npj Science of Learning, 2*(1), 15.

28
MOOCs AND OPEN EDUCATION IN THE GLOBAL SOUTH

Future Opportunities

Thomas H. Reynolds, Thomas C. Reeves, Curtis J. Bonk, and Ke Zhang

Visualizing OER Trends and Big Data

The simple observation that progress comes from people solving problems is one of the major themes in Harvard author Stephen Pinker's (2018) latest book, *Enlightenment Now*. Evident in Pinker's analysis is that by looking at trends, we become aware of the progress we have made, and, we would add, where next we will progress. Accordingly, if the present volume is any indication of the present state of MOOCs and OERs, then a celebration of our progress is definitely warranted and perhaps overdue.

Why do we conclude that? Well, the clear takeaway contained herein is that individuals, consortia, programs, and institutions designing, using, and evaluating MOOCs and OER have been solving countless educational access and delivery problems on behalf of learners across the Global South. They are solving serious problems that affect the human condition. And by reasonable extension, these achievements bode well for other metrics of well-being insofar as education is a leading indicator of advances in healthcare, economic viability, and democratic governance, to name a few.

Lacking in the previous assessment is a big data analysis supporting our general conclusion that the sampling of efforts chronicled in the present volume are applicable across the Global South, a designation representing widely diversified people, languages, customs, educational needs, and governmental support structures. Each region and country within each region vary according to key dimensions such as the present state of educational policy, the training of instructors, the pervasiveness of OER development and sharing, the targeted audiences for MOOCs, the criteria for determining success, and the suggested impact. To that end, at the time of this writing in early May 2019, the MOOC and OER landscape offers numerous opportunities for performing other analyses using large data sets to estimate the impact MOOCs and OER are having on learners across the planet in more quantitative ways.

Although not an easy undertaking, we are reminded of Hans Rosling's (2006) TED talk where he employs big data from United Nations and World Bank data sets to produce unique global models and captivating visualizations of health and well-being progress across the countries of this planet. As an OER pioneer, Rosling's efforts to use data analytics to study the relationship between economic development, agriculture, poverty, and health are exemplary in their scope and impact. Using his own Trendalyzer software, Rosling was able to animate global patterns and assess progress as well as freely share the results of his efforts in media and scholarly works.

Sadly, Rosling is yet another OER innovator who has passed during the years between our previous MOOCs and OER publications and this current volume. Fortunately, his various TED talks and other presentations remain available in YouTube and other websites as OER that can educate the world community and help policy makers and government officials make better decisions related to health, poverty, crime, drugs, agriculture, and economic development.

In addition, a compilation of his ideas can be found in his posthumously published book (Rosling, 2018). His exemplary efforts using big data and data analytics to chart and assess global trends provide a blueprint of opportunity for others to do the same for MOOCs and OER. Perhaps one of you, our readers, will take up the challenge and develop tools to track and better visualize global education trends and opportunities.

The Twin Book Companion

As we did in our first book on MOOCs and open education around the world four short years ago (Bonk, Lee, Reeves, & Reynolds, 2015), we want to thank you, our reader, for finding your way to the end of this volume on MOOCs and open education across the Global South. As you have likely discovered from the current volume, much has transpired in the years between that 2015 publication and the present. What seems clear is that the development and delivery of MOOCs and open education has increasingly addressed the needs and desires of those from resource-poor contexts. With significant government and organizational initiatives in countries like Egypt, Indonesia, Brazil, China, the Philippines, South Africa, and Thailand, as described in various chapters of this book, no longer must those in developing parts of the world solely rely on MOOCs developed from English-speaking countries or prominent Ivy league types of schools. Suffice to say, MOOCs are no longer out of reach in terms of the development or evaluation of courses specific to the needs of the local citizenry.

A key difference between the present book and our earlier volume is that many goals and visions and ideas related to MOOCs are now operationalized and institutionalized. As detailed in this book, MOOCs are now impacting collegiate and career aspirations of secondary students in Nepal as well as the environmental awareness of youth in the Caribbean, Zimbabwe, South Africa, Columbia, and Mexico. MOOCs are now the go-to place for the professional development of teachers in Turkey, Thailand, South Africa, and many other parts of the Global South. Also evident is that in addition to MOOCs, various forms of open educational resources (OER) are also improving teacher training and ongoing professional development across the African continent including Kenya, Tanzania, Uganda, Somalia, Zambia, and Zimbabwe. Of course, such positive results are not just experienced by teachers; those in computer science, data science, healthcare, business management, and a wide array of other disciplines now receive their professional development and career reskilling opportunities via MOOCs and other forms of open courseware.

As with our earlier MOOCs and Open Education volume with Routledge (Bonk et al., 2015), we editors are grateful for the abundance of support from the 68 contributors who have shared many wonderful examples of progress in the preceding chapters. It is important to note that a few of these writers have been with us for several previous book and special journal issue efforts; however, the majority of them are welcome fresh faces with amazing passion and energy to add to the open learning world with their insights and initiatives.

You might look at these two "MOOCs and Open Education" books published by Routledge as a two-volume set wherein the first one, with chapters on different models, quality standards, research results, and instructional experimentations, in effect, sets the stage for the present one. In fact, we editors found the chapters on countries of the Global South in the previous book so fascinating and illuminating that we decided to edit an entire book devoted to that part of the world.

The resulting product is just one emerging picture of the state of MOOCs and open education in such regions. Given the newness of the topic and the potential for impact, there is much room for additional scholarship in this vein.

As mentioned in both the foreword from Mimi Lee and the preface from us editors, a magnificent assembly of talent and ideas was apparent in October 2017 when we gathered in Vancouver for the International E-Learn 2017 conference. The one-day preconference symposium that we enthusiastically organized on "*MOOCs and Open Education in the Developing World*" became the cornerstone for this book. Notably, there was a "virtual preconference" in Zoom the evening before the physical preconference with participants from Thailand, Kenya, the Philippines, Fiji, China, Malaysia, Canada, the United States, and several other countries. The immediate excitement felt among us during that virtual meeting confirmed not only the need for this book, but the fact that it was possible. Fortunately, those intuitions proved correct.

Attempts to design, deliver, and better understand MOOCs and OERs has definitely been a journey worth taking. Keep in mind, too, that while the various chapters in this edited book come from scholars and educators in more than two dozen countries, we could only skim the surface of possible chapters here; there are likely hundreds, if not thousands, of interesting projects occurring right now in dozens of other countries in the Global South that are not included herein but are, nonetheless, contributing to the march of progress. If you are from such a country and have a memorable or life-changing story to tell, we encourage you to contact us and describe it; the four of us would love to hear from you.

We ended our last volume with a nod to the fact that, by 2015, the world of MOOCs and open education had already been subjected to many unique proclamations and predictions. And, as we closed that book, we also noted that today's world is brimming with educational *challenges, opportunities*, and *success* stories. Those of you reading all 28 chapters of this particular book as well as the foreword and the preface will have had your fill by now of what those challenges and opportunities are today. We hope you have also been delighted by the present contributions as well as encouraged by future expectations for MOOCs and open education.

Challenges, Successes, and Opportunities

You may, in fact, have noticed that the subtitle of this book is indeed "*challenges, successes, and opportunities*." To be honest, that was not intentional. On the contrary, it is sheer coincidence that the ending of our previous book meshes so well with the focus of the present one. As per the book dedication engraved at the start of the previous book, we once again firmly hope that the respective chapters in this book not only detail what is presently occurring around the planet in the area of MOOCs and open education, but that they inspire new ideas toward educational futures that are increasingly open and filled with options for learners of all types, be they informal, nontraditional, underprivileged, at-risk, or educationally disadvantaged as well as those studying in formal educational settings or living in the more economically affluent parts of the world with abundant and well-known learning options.

With that, this foray into the world of open education detailed throughout this edited volume, including MOOCs and MOOC-like derivatives, comes to a terminating point due only to word count limits. As should be clear by now, this is only the end of this volume, not the end of the MOOC and OER journey. There is no end point in sight at the present time—nor do we wish one to emerge. MOOCs offerings and associated enrollments will continue to expand, degree and specialization programs will proliferate, and research approaches will multiply.

Already, there are hundreds of nano-degrees, micro-credentials, specializations, and certificates as well as dozens of master's degrees (McKenzie, 2018; Pickard, 2019) which did not exist in 2015 when our first MOOCs and open education book came out (Bonk et al., 2015). Some players in this space will attempt to monetize every open education idea, resource, and initiative. Others will be focused on novel means to expand educational access and opportunities that are genuinely open. Just what might the intriguing world of MOOCs and Open Education look like a little over four years hence in 2024 is quite difficult to forecast. We, nevertheless, offer some perspectives and potential insights into the future of MOOCs and open education in the section below.

Some Predictions

Speaking of unique specializations, as we write this chapter near the end of April 2019, an email arrives from Coursera. It announced that the University of Illinois has designed two 8-week instructional design MOOCs leading to a certificate in instructional design as well as significant credits toward a master's degree. Perhaps not earth-shattering, but what is interesting is that one of the lead designers and instructors of these particular MOOCs is a former student of two of us editors. While sometimes this open world seems enormous and far beyond any single person's grasp, at other times, it appears relatively compact and knowable. If the latter is the case, it is easier to map out possible routes and journeys within it. Though, as was discussed at the start of the preface with Antonio Machado's poem, we may just need to keep wandering for a bit more in this new age of MOOCs and increasingly open forms of education.

Are these momentous, perhaps even disruptive, times? When our colleagues, friends, and former students are offering MOOCs to learners spanning the globe, the power that resides in their hands to improve the state of humanity and help change the world, or a small piece of it, is worthwhile and impactful. No longer are we minting young scholars with hopes that they will enhance, extend, and transform the world when teaching class sizes of 10, 20, or 30 students. Instead, they need to be prepared to be teachers of the world with thousands of potential students in each class.

Clearly, MOOCs and other forms of open education might soon become the norm and not the exception. And teaching learners across countries and regions of the world may be more common than teaching those in your own district, state, or province. That technological innovations have reduced the transactional distance between the field and the classroom such that virtual observations, advice, and assistance can be carried out on every activity from practicing teachers offering learner feedback to doctors performing delicate medical procedures further attest to the reach and impact that innovative instruction can have on learning when the time–space challenge has been conquered—anytime, anywhere, anyone learning is now close at hand.

We predict the following related to MOOCs and open education:

1. MOOCs and open education will be an expected part of the learning journey of many, and perhaps most, people around the globe within the next few years.
2. As part of this transformation in legitimacy and acceptance of open forms of learning and training, MOOC experiences will be increasingly reflected and expected on one's resume.
3. Global South participants will be the majority of MOOC participants by 2040.
4. The primary focus areas of MOOCs in 2040 will target adult learners in the workforce with opportunities for professional development and job reskilling and upskilling. They will also play a role in late adulthood hobbies, entertainment interests, and career change.
5. MOOCs will also offer free and credentialed educational experiences for all secondary school academic requirements as well as the first year or two of higher education by 2025.
6. More than 25 percent of secondary students will enroll exclusively in MOOCs and other forms of online learning by 2035.
7. AI technology, especially machine learning, will be designed that can update MOOC and OER content with limited human intervention other than quality review.

8. Many countries will be able to document clearer connections between MOOC involvement of their citizenry and levels of educational attainment as well as economic growth.
9. MOOC design will evolve from primarily didactic pedagogy to much more authentic, interactive, and learner-driven learning-based models.
10. Assessment will shift from traditional high-stress test modalities to opportunities to demonstrate and validate competencies through authentic tasks and online simulations.

These are just a few such predictions. The coming decade will offer greater insight as to the possibilities and potential for MOOCs and open education in the Global South and elsewhere around the world.

Further evident in this collection is that MOOCs and OERs have extended their presence and are becoming useful tools across a wide range of labor and life. We think that this advance is vitally important. When farmers in India or laborers in Guatemala can upskill or better manage their work while tapping into current knowledge, skills, and advice from educators and innovators on the other side of the world, a more comprehensive ecological educational system is clearly upon us.

We're Off to the Future

Knowing that there are currently some 11,400 MOOCs serving over 100,000,000 learners (Shah, 2019) begins the process of understanding the potential of OER to effect human progress. However, pressing questions remain. For instance, is the 100 million MOOC participants a watershed event? What role can big data analytics and artificial intelligence play in the empowerment of women or the response to climate change? What can an OER ecology or mandate do to raise the last 10% of us out of abject poverty? And how might such an OER ecology contribute to the democratization on behalf of the half of the world's population who, as yet, do not live under those laws and principles?

Rosling (2018) argues that things are not as bad as we think. Accordingly, we believe that the chapters in this book present a similarly optimistic perspective on the future. Of course, there are other views. Harari (2018) challenges educators to move away from preparing learners for jobs and careers that will likely cease to exist because of rapid developments in robotics and machine learning. As part of this preparation, he sees a need to emphasize emotional intelligence and psychological resilience as the major outcomes that will prepare people for the unpredictable future.

Harari is not the only one raising such concerns and suggestions (Anderson, Rainie, & Luchsinger, 2018; Robbins, 2016). Several years ago, a key report from the Obama administration was released to help the United States prepare for the growing role of artificial intelligence (AI) in society (National Science and Technology Council, 2016). While many experts say the rise of artificial intelligence will make most people better off over the next decade, many have concerns about how advances in AI will affect what it means to be human, to be productive, and to exercise free will.

In a recent report for the Pew Foundations, Anderson, Rainie, and Luchsinger (2018) highlight dozens of forecasts of this future world as seen by nearly 1,000 technology innovators, business and industry leaders, researchers, policy leaders, and others. Their predictions about AI, automation, speech recognition and language translation, sophisticated analytics and pattern recognition, and many other topics on the horizon are eye-opening. There are many exciting and enticing ideas to contemplate in this report.

For instance, in this report, NYU professor and founder of the Future Today Institute Amy Webb suggests that as AI becomes more entrenched across industry sectors over the next 50 years, a new breed of "hybrid-skilled workers" will be necessary. As Webb notes, such individuals will find employment in jobs that never previously existed including "farmers who know how to work with big data sets. Oncologists trained as roboticists. Biologists trained as electrical engineers." She further argues that dramatic curriculum changes will be required to help support a workforce that will need to learn a wide array of new procedures, processes, tools, and systems on an ongoing basis. Higher education will be continually needed, not just a singular four-year stop early in one's life path. Accordingly, this is exactly where MOOCs and other forms of open education will likely play a crucial role; they will fill in the gaps available as needed to enhance one's career and future employment opportunities.

Given such a changing economic landscape, many questions need to be raised. Can MOOCs and other open forms of education prepare people for an unpredictable future? If so, how? And how soon, if ever, will MOOC-based training be legitimized and more broadly accepted and expected so that greater numbers of individuals are willing to take part in such courses as well as disclose their involvement and completion of them on their resumes and in their job interviews?

Of course, we cannot just keep asking questions. Eventually, we must offer answers and solutions to such pressing and highly difficult questions. Ultimately, can a massively open and universally distributed education ecology of MOOCs and OERs be the high tide that lifts all vessels for human well-being and flourishing? We hope so, but time will tell.

Thomas H. Reynolds is Professor of Teacher Education at National University in La Jolla, California, where he researches design of online learning, standards-based online assessment, and innovations in e-learning. Among his awards and honors are two Fulbright Scholar awards (2010 in Colombia where he researched open educational resources, and 1998 in Peru where he lectured on Web-based learning and technology-enhanced instruction), a Texas A&M University honored faculty recognition, director and co-principal investigator of a multimillion-dollar center for professional development and technology, and, in 2016, the First Place Book Award from the AECT Division of Distance Education (DDL) for *MOOCs and Open Education Around the World* that was co-edited with Mimi Lee, Curt Bonk, and Tom Reeves and published by Routledge. Present activities and responsibilities include research on the status of e-learning in Latin America and academic program direction of an e-teaching master's degree at National University. He can be contacted at treynold@nu.edu.

Thomas C. Reeves is Professor Emeritus of Learning, Design, and Technology at the University of Georgia. Professor Reeves has designed and evaluated numerous interactive learning programs and projects. In recognition of these efforts, in 2003 he received the AACE Fellowship Award, in 2010 he was made an ASCILITE Fellow, and in 2013 he received the AECT David H. Jonassen Excellence in Research Award. His books include *Interactive Learning Systems Evaluation* (with John Hedberg), *Guide to Authentic E-Learning* (with Jan Herrington and Ron Oliver), and *Conducting Educational Design Research* (with Susan McKenney). His research interests include evaluation, authentic tasks for learning, educational design research, and educational technology in developing countries. He can be reached at treeves@uga.edu and his homepage can be found at www.evaluateitnow.com/.

Curtis J. Bonk is Professor at Indiana University teaching psychology and technology courses. He is a passionate and energetic speaker, writer, educational psychologist, instructional technologist, and entrepreneur as well as a former certified public accountant and corporate controller. He has published more than 340 manuscripts and spoken in dozens of countries around the world. Among his numerous research and teaching awards are the Cyberstar Award, the Charles Wedemeyer Award for Outstanding Practitioner in Distance Education, the AACE Fellowship Award, and the Online Learning Journal Outstanding Research Achievement Award in Online Education. Bonk has been annually named among the top 100 contributors to the public debate about education from more than 20,000 university-based academics. He has authored a dozen books, including *The World Is Open*, *Empowering Online Learning*, *The Handbook of Blended Learning*, *Electronic Collaborators*, *Adding Some TEC-VARIETY*, which is free (http://tec-variety.com/), and *MOOCs and Open Education Around the World* (www.moocsbook.com/). He can be contacted at cjbonk@indiana.edu and his homepage is at http://curtbonk.com/.

Ke Zhang is Professor in Learning Design and Technology at Wayne State University in Detroit, Michigan, USA. As a multilingual, international educator and researcher, her work focuses on e-learning, innovative technologies, and emerging methods for research and development. Her collaborative research is supported by the federal government and agencies, like the US Department of Health and Human Services and National Institute of Health, as well as private foundations, with multimillion-dollar grants to design, develop, and research on emerging technologies for education, professional development, and health information management. Dr. Zhang is also a popular speaker and consultant in Asia, Eurasia, the Middle East, Latin America, and North America. She has consulted for large-scaled projects and initiatives by international organizations, national governments and agencies, corporations, educational institutions, and healthcare systems in the USA and overseas. Inquiries are welcome by email to: ke.zhang@wayne.edu.

References

Anderson, J., Rainie, L., & Luchsinger, A. (2018, December 10). *Artificial intelligence and the future of humans*. Washington, DC: Pew Research Center. Retrieved from www.pewinternet.org/2018/12/10/artificial-intelligence-and-the-future-of-humans

Bonk, C. J., Lee, M. M., Reeves, T. C., & Reynolds, T. H. (Eds.). (2015). *MOOCs and open education around the world*. New York: Routledge.

Harari, Y. N. (2018). *21 lessons for the 21st century*. New York: Spiegel & Grau.

McKenzie, L. (2018, October 12). EdX: From micromasters to online master's degrees. *Inside Higher Ed*. Retrieved from www.insidehighered.com/news/2018/10/12/edx-launches-nine-low-cost-online-degrees

National Science and Technology Council. (2016). *Preparing for the future of artificial intelligence, technical report, United States*. Washington, DC: Executive Office of the President.

Pickard, L. (2019, March 4). 35+ legit master's degrees you can now earn completely online. *Class Central*. Retrieved from www.classcentral.com/report/mooc-based-masters-degree/

Pinker, S. (2018). *Enlightenment now: The case for reason, science, humanism, and progress*. New York: Viking.

Robbins, G. (2016, December 15). How robots will change the American workforce, Gary Robbins. *The San Diego Union-Tribune*. Retrieved from www.sandiegouniontribune.com/news/science/sd-me-robots-jobs-20161213-story.html

Rosling, H. (2006). The best stats you've ever seen. *TED2006*. Retrieved from www.ted.com/talks/hans_rosling_shows_the_best_stats_you_ve_ever_seen?language=en

Rosling, H. (2018). *Factfulness: Ten reasons we're wrong about the world—and why things are better than you think*. New York: Flatiron Books.

Shah, D. (2019). Year of MOOC-based degrees: A review of MOOC stats and trends in 2018. *Class Central*. Retrieved from www.class-central.com/report/moocs-stats-and-trends-2018/

ACKNOWLEDGMENTS

Gosh, this was a huge undertaking. We could not have done it without the timely, consistent, and kind support of Daniel Schwartz and his production team at Routledge and Taylor and Francis. They insightfully helped us to plan the drafting of this book many months in advance in order for all the pieces to come into place at just the right time.

We thank each of the 68 wonderful contributors to this book. They represent more than two dozen countries and a plethora of exploratory and extraordinary initiatives that have made the world a better place. We are extremely fortunate to have met and worked with many of these MOOCs and open education thought leaders in the past and feel equally lucky to have now met dozens more such leaders as we communicated with the contributors to this book for more than a year. Each author is making a unique contribution to the Global South and the world community as a whole. Good fortunes have come our way to be able to work with each of you. We will cherish your friendships for the rest of our lives. At the same time, we wish to reach out to those who have not authored a chapter in this book but who are also investing significant time and effort designing MOOCs and other open forms of education in your communities. Perhaps we too will meet someday.

Of the contributors, we specifically want to extend our gratitude to Professor Jianli Jiao and Yibo (Jeremy) Fan, authors of Chapter 3, who successfully led a team at South China Normal University to translate our previous MOOCs and open education book to Chinese. Perhaps they will find the time and energy to do the same with this volume.

There are countless others whom we need to thank for helping to open the world of education, but space is limited. Among them are Grace Lin, Okhwa Lee, Sir John Daniel, Paul Kim, David Wiley, John Hilton, George Veletsianos, Charlie Miller, Susie Gronseth, Theo Bastiaens, Xun Ge, David Porter, Stacy Morrone, Brad Wheeler, Lucifer Chu, Ana-Paula Correia, Asha Kanwar, Zoraini Wati Abas, Meina Zhu, Annisa Sari, Wali Cunningham, Johannes Cronje, Richard Baraniuk, Susie Gronseth, Gerry Hanley, Ron Owston, Charlotte "Lani" Gunawardena, Linda Harasim, Terry Anderson, Ron Oliver, Lin Lin, Jan Herrington, Stephen Downes, George Siemens, Stefanie Panke, Chris Devers, Mark Curcher, Yayoi Anzai, Helene Fournier, Rita Kop, Bernard Robin, Sara McNeil, Ali Carr-Chellman, Kyle Peck, Tim Spannaus, Ray Schroeder, Minkyoung Kim, Shuya Xu, and Cassandra Brooks. Sadly, since the publication of our last book on MOOCs and open education in 2015, many e-learning and open education pioneers and innovators are no longer with us, including Erik Duval, Colin Latchem, Sangkom (Sam) Pumipuntu, Glenn R. Jones, Jay Cross, and Fred Mulder. The world community misses you all.

We need to step back and thank Sarah Duke Benson, Director of Conferences of AACE, and Dr. Gary Marks, Founder and Executive Director of AACE, who encouraged the four of us to submit a preconference symposium proposal for the International E-Learn 2017 Conference in Vancouver. Many of the contributors to this book were physical or virtual contributors to that event.

Finally, we need to also make a special shout-out thank you to Professor Mimi Miyoung Lee from the University of Houston who wrote the foreword to this book. Mimi extensively collaborated with us on several other previous book projects and special journal issues related to e-learning in Asia as well as MOOCs and open education. Her enthusiastic commitment to pen the thoughtful and integrative introductory piece to this book was greatly appreciated. We are most fortunate to have Mimi's insights in this book.

INDEX

Note: Page numbers in *italic* indicate a figure and page numbers in **bold** indicate a table on the corresponding page.

Aboulmagd, Nadine 53
Abuhamdeih, Sumayyah 267
academic gatekeeping: and Virtually Connecting 50–51
academic life: and IDBx 218
accessibility 58; access to connectivity 296; in Kenya 311; at a relatively lower bandwidth 301–302
Adala, A. Atieno 298
adaptation 45–52, 56–58, 276, 291, 301, 332
administrators 116
adults: distance education for North Korean adults 24–25
affordability 302
affordances, technological 319
Africa: OER-integrated teacher education elearning program in 286–297; *see also specific countries*
African Virtual University (AVU) 271, 286–297, **288**
age: and IDBx 214–215
AgMOOCs: in India 300–307
AI *see* artificial intelligence (AI)
Amiel, Tel 233
AMOOCs 264, **265**
anxiety 315
APEC *see* Asia-Pacific Economic Cooperation
Arabic content: and Edraak 49–50
Arab world: MOOCs in 259–263
artificial intelligence (AI): education technologies integrating AI 330–331
Asia-Pacific Economic Cooperation (APEC): MOOCs in 199–207
aspiration 171
assessment 320
attitudes 315, **316**
awareness, lack of 296–297

bachelor's programs: and skills accelerator 310–321, **314**
Bahamas, the: and courses for a cause 188–189
Bali, Maha 53

Bandalaria, Melinda dela Peña 253
bandwidth: access at relatively lower bandwidth 301–302
barriers: lowering barriers to entry 305; technology-related barriers to OEP 296
Belawati, Tian 69
"Better Place for All" 181–196
Bhartu, Deepak 87
big data: visualizing 342
Bilgeİş Project 130–137; pdMOOC portal 131–132
Blockchains: public blockchain 302
Bonk, Curtis J. xxix, 11, 348
Bosman, J.P. 176
Brazil: open education policy in 229–234, *232*
Brimhall, Craig 323
broadcasting 24
building at scale 304–305
business models: for sustainable development of MOOCs 241, *242*

Cagiltay, Kursat 137
capacity building: faculty capacity development 305; and SDGs 276–278, *277*, 281–283; of teachers 156–165
Caribbean, the: impact of MOOCS from IDB 212–223
case studies: of AgMOOCs in India 300–307; of a skills accelerator 310–321, **313**; of TEL MOOC 156–165
celebrity status 306
Celik, Berkan 138
certification 306
China: and courses for a cause 189–190; current state of practice and research on MOOCs in 28–36
Cleveland-Innes, Martha 166
Climate Change and Pacific Islands MOOC 83–84
Coleman, Brittney López Hampton 193; and courses for a cause 185–186

collaboration 322; and doctoral students 117; and K-MOOCs 17–19; multi-country 179–180; and repurposing 291; sharing as collaborative practice 294; team-based 313–314
collections: multi-country 179–180
Colombia: and courses for a cause 186–187
communication 313, 322
Community of Inquiry (CoI) 165; for TEL MOOC *159*
compatibility 302
completion: IDBx 214; and MOOC usage among young learners in Nepal 92–95; and pdMOOC 134–135; and TEL MOOC 163
complexity 172–174
connectivity: and OEP 296
content: for employer-engaged project-based learning 312–314, 317; quality and relevance of 306
content, inadequate: and low use 295–296
content areas 204–205
contextual conditions 291
cost 289; affordability 302
course designers 116, *117*
course liaison 118
courses for a cause 181–196
CPD MOOCs 73, 76–78
creation 45–46, 56–58, 172–173, 287–297, 298; impact of OER on the practice of 292–293
creativity 322
critical thinking 322
cultural influence 203
curriculum: impact of sharing on updating curriculum 294–297

data privacy 58–59
de Klerk, Miné 177
demographics: and APEC 203; of pdMOOC users 132–133
design 318; current 41–43; instruction design of TEL MOOC 159–160; perspectives and practices about 72–78; poor course design 204; research-based design approach 140–154; *see also* course designers
development: responsive innovations in MOOCs for development 300–307; and the World Bank 273–283
digital learning platform: condition of management via 143–144
digital literacy 204
digital redlining 57–58
disruption: of AMOOC **265**
disruptive innovation 261–263
disruptive learning: and the Middle East 256–265
distance education 143–145, **144**, 293–295; and North Korea 23–25
diversity: emotional benefits of 113–123, **120**
doctoral students 117
Doxey, Graham 324
Doxey, Scott 324

Edraak 49–50
educational resources *see* open educational resources
educational technology: and Nepal 92

education gap: and UOOC Alliance 36
education practices: and educational resources 8–9
Egypt: open education in 45–52
e-learning 24, 201, 204, 236–238, 251–252, 256–262; teacher education program 286–297
emerging economies: dawning of MOOCs in 90–91; MOOC architecture for 81–87, **85–86**, *86*
emotional benefits: and diversity 113–123, **120**
employer-engaged project-based learning 312–314
engagement: in TEL MOOC 161–162, *162*
enrollment **314**
Esfer, Sezin 138
evaluation: of accelerator onboarding program 315
experimentation *see* instructional experimentation

faculty: and barriers to entry 305; capacity development 305; celebrity status of 306; and easy-to-use interfaces 302; *see also* teachers
faculty development 151–152
Fajardo, Jennifer Christine 208
Fan, Yibo 38
feedback: student feedback after completing an accelerator 316–317
Figueroa, Roberto B., Jr. 209
fluency 313, 315, **317**
freedom to use: OER 297

gap analysis: of open education operations 144
García, Antonio 224
gatekeeping *see* academic gatekeeping
Gautam, Bishwa Raj 96
gender: and IDBx 215
generalizability 320–321
Ghimire, Baman Kumar 95
global knowledge 278–279
global learners: and diversity 113–123, **114–115**, **120**; merits and challenges of engaging global learners 118–119
Global South xv; challenges facing 6; countries discussed in this book **3–7**; MOOC hype and open education realities in 45–46; MOOCs and open education in 342–347; successes in 6–8; successes and challenges 1–9; *see also specific countries*
global trends: and sustainable development of MOOCs in Malaysia 236–242
Golshani, Zahra 193; and courses for a cause 184–185
González, Edgar 223
governmental support 205
government policies and strategies 227–228; *see also* policy

HarvardX 259
higher education: Brazilian 229–234, *232*
higher education regional network hubs: in Thailand *142*
high school students: Nepali 90–95
historical perspectives 15–16; historical journey into K-MOOCs 17–25
human development index (HDI): and IDBx 214

ICT *see* information and communication technology
immersive learning: and disruption to MOOCs 263–264
incubation: and South Africa 169–175
India: AgMOOCs in 300–307
Indonesia: about 63–65, **65**; MOOC development and implementation 200; MOOCs in 63, 65–68, **67**
information and communication technology (ICT) 25, 64–66, 81, 92, 237; ICT Development Index (IDI) 219, *219*; ICT personnel 143; ICT resources 294–297; and professional development 127–129, 132, 140; and teacher education eLearning 286–288, 292
innovations: responsive innovations in MOOCs for development 300–307
institutional learning: MOOCs as incubation space for 170–171
instructional experimentation 36
instructor roles 319
integration: with a public Blockchain 302; and reusing open content 47–48
intelligent MOOCs: emergence of 329–338
Inter-American Development Bank (IDB) 212–223; enrolled learners 214–217, *214–217*; IDBx learners 213–217; IDBx Program 212–213, *213*; impact on learners in Latin America and the Caribbean 218–221
interfaces: easy-to-use 302
internet: in Nepal 91–92
Iran: and courses for a cause 184–185

Jagannathan, Sheila 284
Jhangiani, Rajiv S. 60
Jiao, Jianli 38
Jung, Insung 207

Karunanayaka, Shironica P. 79
Khlaisang, Jintavee 154
Kenya: and skills accelerator 310–321, **313**
Kim, Ock Tae 26
Kim, Paul 338
Kim, Yong 26
K-MOOCs: courses classified by academic field **20**; distance education for North Korean adults 24–25; historical journey into 17–19, 25; introduction to 17–19; layout of K-MOOC operational system *18*; medium-term strategy of **19**; outcomes of 20–21; top priority projects of **19**
knowledge 297; and repurposing 292
Krasny, Marianne E. 192

lack of awareness 296–297
lack of motivation 297
languages 204–205
Latin America: impact of MOOCS from IDB 212–223; MOOC authors in 104–105, **104–105**; MOOCs in 99–109
leadership 322
learner experiences: TEL MOOC 163–164, **163–164**

learner perception and acceptance 203
learner profiles: TEL MOOC **161**
"learning engine" 74
learning environment: SMILE (Stanford Mobile Inquiry-based Learning Environment) *334*
learning management system (LMS) 143
learning organisation: capabilities of 171
learning tasks 318
Lee, Jieun 339
Lee, Mimi Miyoung xv
level of education: and IDBx 215
limitations: in access to MOOCs 305; in building at scale 304–305; generalizability limitations 320–321; and innovations 301–302
local experts: and APEC findings 202–206
local practices: and courses for a cause 190–191
local solutions 278–279
low use 295–296

Macher, Carlos 224
Malaysia: MOOC development and implementation 200–201; sustainable development of MOOCs in 236–242
management: and a digital learning platform 143–144; and easy-to-use interfaces 302; MOOCs as strategic managers of sustainability practice 191
massive open online courses *see* MOOCs
Mayath, Michael C. 323
MBA programs: skills accelerator 310–321, **314**
Mendoza, Gibran A. Garcia 208
mentoring 305
Mesa, Juan Felipe Restrepo 186–187, 194
Mexico: and courses for a cause 185–186; MOOC development and implementation 202
micro-credential 117
Middle East: advancement of MOOCs in 256–265, **257–258, 260**
Mishra, Sanjaya 166
MITx 46, 51, 259; integration of 47–48
mobile communications paradigm: and compatibility 302
MOOCs: authors in Latin America 104–105, **104–105**; case study on Thai MOOC 147–154, *149–150*, **150**; Climate Change and Pacific Islands 83–84; contributions to a "Better Place for All" 181–196; current situation in Turkey 130–137, **131**; current state of practice and research in mainland China 28–36, **31**, *32–34*, **35**; design of 72–78; development cycle *84*; in emerging APEC member economies 199–207; and emerging economies 84–85, 90–95; emotional benefits of diversity in 113–123; future of 327–328; future MOOC development and research 206–207; global MOOC providers 206; and impact xxiv–xxvi; as incubation space 170–171, *173*; and instructional experimentation 36; from Inter-American Development Bank (IDB) 212–223; in Latin America 99–109; learner profile 30; learners and learning experiences 202–203, 205–206; in

Malaysia 236–242; in the Middle East 256–265; MOOC architecture **4**, 42, 81–87; MOOC hype in the Global South 45–46; MOOC-related conferences, reviews, and books 105–106; MOOC sponsorship 106; Nepali high school students in 90; and open education xvi–xxviii; and open education in the Global South 342–347; platforms and courses 29–30, **30**; and professional development 127–129; research literature 99–104, 107–109; roles of MOOC instructors 116–118, *117*; and skills accelerator 310–321; and South Africa 169–175, *173*; the state of practice in Indonesia 63–68, **67**; as strategic managers of sustainability practice 191; successes and challenges 1–9; and sustainability practices 182–183; Teaching for Change (TFC) 169–170; TEL case study 156–165; in Thailand 140–154; trends in development and implementation 199–207; usage among young learners in Nepal 92–95; *see also* AgMOOCs; AMOOCs; K-MOOCs; CPD MOOCS; intelligent MOOCs; MOOC architecture; pdMOOC portal; xMOOC

motivation: lack of 297; and MOOC usage among young learners in Nepal 92–95

multi-sector influence *278*

Naidu, Som 79, 88

Nepal: educational technology in 92; high school students in MOOCs 90–95; internet in 91–92; MOOC usage among young learners in 92–95

North Korea: contributions of K-MOOC to Korean learners 21–22; and distance education for adults 24–25; and distance higher education 23–25; educational collaboration with 22–23; and K-MOOCs 17–25

objectives: skills accelerator 317, 322

Oceania: MOOC architecture for 81–87

OCW *see* OpenCourseWare

OEP *see* open educational practices

OER *see* open educational resources

OERs for development (OERs4D) framework 228; in the Philippines 245–253

offline redundancy plan 314

onboarding 315

online courseware for self-learning 143

online education: and diversity 113–123, **120**

online learning environments: evolution of 329–338

online-only programs 310–321

open content: reusing 47–48

OpenCourseWare (OCW) 246; emergence of xix–xxii; KOCW 17–18, 25; in Turkey 130–137

open education xvi–xix; contextualizing 46; current operation conditions relating to 144; in Egypt 45–52; emergence of open educational resources xix; future of 327–328; in the Global South 342–347; open educational resources to open education practices 8–9; open education operations 144; and parity of participation 50; policy in Brazil 229–234, *232*; and professional development 127–129; realities in the Global South 45–46; successes and challenges 1–9; in Thailand 140–154; in the World Bank 273–283; *see also* open educational resources

open educational practices (OEP): design of CPD MOOCs on 73; and OER-integrated teacher education elearning program in Africa 286–297; technology-related barriers to 296

open educational resources (OER): design of CPD MOOCs on 73; and education practices 8–9; module development process 287, **288**; OER-integrated teacher education elearning program in Africa 286–297; the Philippines OER journey 247, *249*; pitfalls and strategies 56–59; and skills accelerator 310–321; visualizing OER trends 342; *see also* OERs for development (OERs4D) framework

open learning 278–279; in action 281–282

Open Learning Campus (OLC) 271, 273, 279–281, *280–281*

open license: process for adoption of 287

open resources 289; permissions to 293

Open University of Brazil (UAB) 227, 229–234

open washing 57, 59

operation conditions 144

organizational innovations 271–272

Ostashewski, Nathaniel 167

outcomes: and IDBx 221

Pacific, the: MOOC architecture for 81–87; *see also* University of the South Pacific

parity of participation: in open educational experiences 50

pdMOOCs 130–137; Bilgeİş Project 131–137; completion rates 134–135, **135**; most and least preferred 134–135, **134**, *135*; registration trends 133, *133*

pedagogical approaches: for sustainability of MOOCs 240–241

pedagogical appropriateness: for sustainability of MOOCs 240–241

permissions: to open resources 293

personalization 332

Phan, Trang 125

Philippines: MOOC development and implementation 200; OERs4D in 245–253

policy: open education policy in Brazil 229–234, *232*; and SDGs 276–278; and sustainable development of MOOCs in Malaysia 236–242

Prabhakar, Tadinada V. 308

practice of creation: impact of OER on 292–293

practice of repurposing: impact of OER on 291–292

practice of sharing 293

practice of use: impact of OER on 290–291

practices: current 41–43; current state in mainland China 28–36; and design of MOOCs 72–78; and inadequate content 295–296; low use 295–296

presentation skills 313–314

problem solving 313, 322

professional development 127–120, *151*; see also faculty development
professional learning: MOOCs as incubation space for 170–171
professional/work life: and IDBx 219
project-based learning 312–314
promotion of courses 306

quality of content 306
quality management: K-MOOC 21
questioning: and intelligent MOOCs 331–332; questioning and answering by AI 333; questioning skill scaffolding tools in SMILE 334–337

Raghunathan, Shriram 267
Ravichandran, Purushothaman 242
redlining *see* digital redlining
redundancy: offline redundancy plan 314
Reeves, Thomas C. xxx, 11, 348
registration: pdMOOC trends 133, *133*
relevance of content 306
repurposing: impact of OER on practice of 291–292
research 104, 321; and APEC 202–207; current state in mainland China 28–36; research-based design approach 140–154; research literature 99–102; research methodology 102–104, **103**
reusing: open content from the Global North 47–48
Reyes-Rojas, José 110
Reynolds, Thomas H. xxx, 12, 347
roles *see* instructor roles; student roles

Sánchez, Jaime 109
scalability 301
Schrenk, Michael 187–188, 194
SDGs *see* Sustainable Development Goals (SDGs)
self-efficacy 315
self-identification 94–95
self-learning: online courseware for 143
sharing 182–183, 190–191, 201, 203, 287–289, 293; and updating curriculum 294–297
sharing age xxii–xxiii
Shon, Jin Gon 27
Singh, Abtar Darshan 266
skills 297; presentation skills 313–314; and repurposing 292; skill scaffolding tools in SMILE 334–337, *335–337*; see also skills accelerator
skills accelerator 310–321, **313**; learning dimensions applied to 317–320, **319**
SMILE (Stanford Mobile Inquiry-based Learning Environment) *334*; questioning skill scaffolding tools in 334–337, *335–337*
Soares, Tiago C. 234
social life 220
social network graph *86*
South Africa: and courses for a cause 187–188; MOOCs as incubation space for professional and institutional learning in 170–171, *173*
Southeast Asia 205; collaboration for MOOCs in 201–202; *see also specific countries*

South Korea 7, 15–16, 22–25, 199; and North Korea 22–23
specialization 117–118
stakeholder involvement 291
Stellenbosch University (SU) 169–175; Teaching for Change (TFC) 169–171
strategic business models: for sustainability of MOOCs 241, *242*
Stroup, Joshua 325
student roles 318
sustainability: of pdMOOC portal 132
sustainability practices: MOOCs and 182–183, 191
sustainable business models 205
sustainable development: in Malaysia 236–242
Sustainable Development Goals (SDGs) 273–283, *274*; and a framework for capacity building 282–283, *282*
SWOT (Strength, Weakness, Opportunity, and Threat) analysis 132, 145; of open education operations 144, **144**

Tan, Siaw Eng (Janice) 209
teacher education: OER-integrated 286–297
teachers 116; capacity building of 156–165; *see also* teacher education
Teaching for Change (TFC) 169–171
technological infrastructure 204
technology *see* affordances, technological; artificial intelligence (AI); educational technology; technological infrastructure; technology-enabled learning (TEL); technology fluency
technology-enabled learning (TEL): case study of 156–165; challenges 164–165; community of inquiry model for *159*; completion 163; delivery of 160–161, *160*; instruction design of 159–160; learner experiences 163–164, **163–164**; lessons learned 164; overview 157–158, **157–158**; participant engagements 161–162, **161**; successful strategies 165
technology fluency 313, 315, **317**
testimonials: and IDBx 221
textbooks: unaffordable 56–57
Thailand: case study on Thai MOOC 147–154; higher education regional network hubs in *142*; MOOC development and implementation 201; open education and MOOCs in 140–154
Thailand Cyber University Project (TCU) 127–128, 140–143, 151–152; organizational structure *141*; phases of institutional research project *142*; strategic plan on open education 144–147, *146–149*; SWOT analysis of 144, **144**
Thammetar, Thapanee 153
Turkey: current situation of MOOCs and OCW portals in 130–137, **131**; and pdMOOC portal 130–137

unbundling: and SDGs 276–278, *277*
University of the Philippines Open University (UPOU) 200, 205, 247–251, *249–252*
University of the South Pacific (USP) 81–87, *82*

UOOC Alliance 29; and the education gap 36
updating: impact of sharing on updating curriculum 294–297

van der Merwe, Antoinette 176
Venkataraman, Balaji 307
Vietnam 117, 121, 179, 199, 204; MOOC development and implementation 201
Virtually Connecting 41, 52; and academic gatekeeping 50–51
voluntary academic labor 58

Warakula, Masango Roderick 188, 195
Western models: and Edraak 49–50

Woon, Gail 188–189, 195
work life: and IDBx 219
workplace: and IDBx 219–220
World Bank 342; open education in 273–283; Open Learning Campus (OLC) 279–281

xMOOC 45–46, 49, 52, 81–82, *82*, 130, 164–165

Yu, Yueyang 189–190, 196

Zhang, Dou 225
Zhang, Ke xxix, 10, 349
Zimbabwe 288–290, 292–295, 297; and courses for a cause 188